PENGUIN BOOKS

The Pengu...

THE TW...

Martin Dodsworth is Professor of English at Royal Holloway,
University of London. He is author of *Hamlet Closely Observed* (1985)
and has edited *The Survival of Poetry* (1970), a book of essays on
poetry since 1950. He has also written the introduction to *North and
South* by Elizabeth Gaskell for the Penguin Classics.

Titles in this series:

THE TWENTIETH CENTURY

EDITED BY

MARTIN DODSWORTH

VOLUME 7 OF THE
Penguin History of Literature

PENGUIN BOOKS

PENGUIN BOOKS

Published by the Penguin Group
Penguin Books Ltd, 27 Wrights Lane, London W8 5TZ, England
Penguin Books USA Inc., 375 Hudson Street, New York, New York, 10014, USA
Penguin Books Australia Ltd, Ringwood, Victoria, Australia
Penguin Books Canada Ltd, 10 Alcorn Avenue, Toronto, Ontario, Canada M4V 3B2
Penguin Books (NZ) Ltd, 182–190 Wairau Road, Auckland 10, New Zealand

Penguin Books Ltd, Registered Offices: Harmondsworth, Middlesex, England

First published 1994
3 5 7 9 10 8 6 4

Set in 10/11 pt Monophoto Ehrhardt by
Datix International Limited, Bungay, Suffolk
Printed in England by Clays Ltd, St Ives plc

CONTENTS

INTRODUCTION

This volume replaces an earlier one in the same series, edited by Professor Bernard Bergonzi and published in 1970. Since that time many more books have been written, both about and of literature; a new volume has therefore been designed, more or less the same in size as Professor Bergonzi's, but attempting to cover as much of what has been done in the last twenty years as possible, together with what was covered in the earlier book. This naturally entailed giving the whole volume a different structure. Professor Bergonzi offered entire chapters on W. B. Yeats, James Joyce, D. H. Lawrence and T. S. Eliot. In the new volume these major authors, who certainly deserve the close attention previously paid to them, are merely dominant figures within chapters devoted to a specific genre and a certain space of time. W. B. Yeats even suffers the indignity, or honour, of having his poetry discussed in two distinct chapters. I hope that, in recompense for the loss of close attention to individual authors, a fuller sense of the development of English literature as a whole in the twentieth century will emerge.

The literature of our own century presents the historian with special problems. Increased population, a higher standard of general education and an improved technology have been instrumental in allowing many more published authors to be considered than in earlier generations, and, because we are closer to them, it is more difficult to be sure that we have any great understanding of their relationship to each other. One of the aims of this volume is certainly to suggest which authors might be best worth the time of a reader, but it would be wrong to think that there is any absolute value in the list of authors discussed. Considerations of space and emphasis meant making difficult choices and exclusions, and any reader should bear this in mind. In particular, Professor Bergonzi was able to include in his volume chapters on literary criticism and the popular novel, areas barely touched on here, not because they do not have intrinsic value, but because their inclusion would have meant the sacrifice of material of potentially greater interest. Those who want to know more about the development of English criticism in the period and the significant achievement of I. A. Richards, F. R. Leavis and Sir William Empson will therefore have to turn, for example, to the relevant volume of René Wellek's *History of Modern Criticism*. They are luckier than those who are interested in British popular fiction for whom no satisfactory general account exists. The arrangement of chapters dealing with either drama, poetry or the novel should prove convenient to most readers, but does entail some loss, notably of prose writers whose concern is not fiction. Memoirs, travel books and biographies figure here only incidentally, if at all; their existence should not be forgotten. Bibliographies for this period could, of course, be all-embracing, but we have, instead, tried to be concise in the suggestions for further reading, believing that our choices will of themselves lead the interested student to the many changing and complex bibliographical aids available today.

This book is intended to give a sense of the way literature has developed in the twentieth century. The chronological limits of its chapters are therefore designedly ill-defined and wide-ranging. T. S. Eliot and Yeats in his later years are primarily dealt with in Chapter 6, 'Poetry in the 1920s', but the discussion is by no means confined to what they wrote or published in that decade. The intention has been to discuss writers under the chronological heading which seemed most appropriate to them, and to avoid an excessive dispersal of information and comment. Anthony Powell published his first novels in the 1930s, but his reputation depends largely on the sequence which started to appear in the 1950s; he is, therefore, discussed in Chapter 9, 'The Novel since 1950'. Samuel Beckett's novels are discussed in Chapter 7, 'The Novel in the 1930s and 1940s', even though they did not receive much critical attention until much later, for numerous reasons which appear in Richard Jacobs's stimulating essay.

This volume considers English literature of the British Isles including Ireland, though the coverage of Scottish and Welsh literature is minimal. It does not cover writers in English in other cultural traditions, therefore American authors are not discussed here; two volumes are devoted to them in the *Penguin History of Literature*. Caribbean authors such as Derek Walcott and V. S. Naipaul are excluded on similar grounds to those which lead to the absence of Australians like Les Murray and Patrick White. The hardest decision was not to discuss the work of Doris Lessing, but it was felt that, despite her many novels conceived in Britain and written for a British audience, her most distinguished work placed her with writers like Nadine Gordimer and Dan Jacobson. Compactness is won at a price, but I hope it will be felt that the price of this volume was worth paying.

It tells an engrossing story, in which the First World War plays a central part, creating a vacuum in British culture that enabled the virtual triumph of self-consciously modernizing writers like Joyce and Eliot. It is a perplexing question why this modernizing impetus should so largely have petered out in the new generation of 1930s' writers. One answer might be that the pressure of historical circumstance – the events in Russia, Germany and Spain, in particular – faced writers anew with the problems of representation which seemed of secondary importance to their immediate predecessors. Another would suggest that because the modernizers depended on an absence in the culture in which they triumphed, their triumph could only last as long as there was no attempt within the native culture to re-establish a traditional conservatism. Here I have in mind the sense in which the ex-American Eliot, the Irishmen Yeats and Joyce, and the working-class exile Lawrence, like the Bloomsbury intellectual Virginia Woolf, were all at a distance from, for example, the trauma of grief which ensued on the First World War. The British concern with representing an only occasionally philosophical reality for the most part distinguishes English literature since the thirties from that of the rest of Europe and has something to do with the attempt to face up to the consequences of the First World War. In one sense, the history of English literature since then is the story of a struggle to anchor writing more securely in actuality; in another sense, it is about a series of attempts to return to the broader perspectives and more philosophical procedures of the modernizing generation. It is the conflict between these two versions of literary development that gives the more recent English literature its special interest.

1

DRAMA TO 1950

Ian Clarke

Dates which conveniently mark off periods in the history of the theatre and dramatic writing are, as a matter of course, notional and arbitrary. Consequently 14 March 1891 is as appropriate as other contending dates for the start of a discussion of twentieth-century drama. On this day the leading article in the *Daily Telegraph* described Ibsen's *Ghosts*, which had been staged by the Independent Theatre Society at the Royalty Theatre the previous evening, as 'an open drain; a loathsome sore unbandaged; a dirty act done publicly; a lazar-house with all its doors and windows open'. Now justly notorious, the temper of the attack indicates the extent of the shock which Ibsen's play administered. The reverberations were out of all proportion to the number of people who actually saw Ibsen's work and must have been felt even by those with little interest in the theatre; the *Daily Telegraph*, for instance, chose to draw attention to *Ghosts* in its leading article as well as in its theatre column. Ibsen's plays, with their open discussion of subjects taboo in the theatre and their questioning of the traditional (and therefore supposedly natural) role of women, pricked deep-rooted late nineteenth-century anxieties of a general social and political disintegration.

While Ibsen could not be accommodated to or by the commercial theatre of the 1890s, that theatre necessarily felt the reverberations of Ibsen's intrusion. Shaw noted that a theatre manager 'must be very careful not to produce a play which will seem insipid and old-fashioned to playgoers who have seen The Wild Duck, even though they may have hissed it' (George Bernard Shaw, *Our Theatres in the Nineties*, Constable, 1932, vol 1, p 165). Arthur Wing Pinero (1855–1934), a dramatist who had already achieved some commercial success with a series of farces, produced a serious problem play, *The Second Mrs Tanqueray*. The chronology of the appearance of this play in 1893, following so closely on Ibsen's turbulent appearance on the English stage, is, like Shaw's remark, misleading as well as instructive. *The Second Mrs Tanqueray*, in its examination of the double standard of morality and the unfairness with which a woman with a past like Paula Tanqueray is treated by society, superficially seems to offer a compassionate treatment of serious moral and social issues.

The debt to Ibsen is, however, more apparent than real. The play shows not a direct Ibsenite influence (Pinero and his fellow commercial dramatist Henry Arthur Jones (1851–1929) were emphatic in disclaimers of such influence), but a reflection of an extension of tone and subject matter to which Ibsen's presence contributed. More than this, though, from the start of the 1890s both the Ibsenite enterprise and the work of dramatists such as Jones and Pinero were a function of the desire of theatre managers, actors and playwrights in the late nineteenth century to be taken and to take themselves more seriously. Developments which had started roughly in the 1860s were consolidated in the last decade of the nineteenth century and were to determine the nature of twentieth-century theatre and drama. First, there was the consolidation of the social respectability of the theatre and the upper echelons of the acting profession; this alone determined not just the fabric of the theatres but theatre-going as a class-defined social activity. Second, dramatists, coincidentally with copyright legislation, could see their profession as both serious and lucrative and, consequently, part of a cultural as well as a social establishment. If playwrights were to be persons of letters, then the product had to be both serious and worthy to stand alongside other literary forms (a reiterated point in Jones's collected essays *The Renascence of the English Drama* (1895) and *The Foundations of a National Drama* (1913)). The drama thus acquired an intellectual respectability which was validated by the seriousness with which it was taken by theatrical commentators. This late Victorian theatrical settlement, albeit with some variation according to the style and conditions of the day, lasted in essence to at least 1950 and arguably is little changed at the time of writing.

However, the ways in which social respectability and intellectual respectability can come into conflict are fully manifest in *The Second Mrs Tanqueray*. Pinero's play, like many others of the period, is a compromise between the outspokenness of Ibsen, which audiences found objectionable, and the conventional realistic play to which they were accustomed. The play examines the misalliance between Aubrey Tanqueray, upper middle-class and stolidly respectable, and Paula, who has previously had numerous liaisons in the *demi-monde* of Europe. The marriage inevitably ends in disaster. Yet the inevitability arises not from the psychological mismatch of husband and wife, nor from society's hostility to the misalliance, but from a coincidence in the plot introduced by Pinero in the last act. Tanqueray's daughter returns from abroad intending to be married to a man who turns out to be a former lover of Paula. Paula's suicide ends the play and resolves the problem. Pinero's technique derives in part from French models of the well-made play, but the experience it mediates is not of a mysterious intersection of character and fate but of a universe dedicated to the preservation of dominant social and moral codes and the punishment of women who have transgressed them. The aesthetic of the well-made play is in essence a function of this ideological imperative. Similarly, the attempt of the eponymous woman with a past in Jones's *Mrs Dane's Defence* (1900)[1] to re-enter society is foiled by an apparently chance discovery in a topographical dictionary which exposes her true identity and past indiscretion. What such plays offer is a passing flirtation with the daring and the mildly risqué, but one which is safely contained by an action that provides resolutions endorsing the validity of the orthodoxies supposedly under serious discussion. Thus Tanqueray's indictment of the double standard of morality is subsumed by the conventionality of the conclusion; indeed, the society drama of Jones and Pinero needs the double standard as a kingpin in its endorsement of what is a more extensive conservative ideology and sexual politics.

Other plays raise different problems to be resolved. Pinero's *The Notorious Mrs Ebbsmith* (1895) asks whether a woman of socialist and feminist beliefs can put them into practice by openly keeping house with Lucas Cleeve, a man of some public prominence; while Jones's *The Case of Rebellious Susan* (1894) asks whether a woman can openly repay her husband's adultery in kind and remain in society. Mrs Ebbsmith's beliefs are rendered invalid when what is represented as her 'natural' femininity reasserts itself and she becomes a theatrically more familiar figure – a fallen woman. Her transformation in the last act to penitent fallen woman intending to retire to a life of prayer and contemplation in the north of England is not just a sign that she now recognizes the error of her ways but allows Cleeve to return to his promising political career. In *The Case of Rebellious Susan* Susan Harabin abandons her rebellion and returns to a patently less than perfect marriage. Jones may have claimed in the dedicatory epistle to the published text that 'My comedy isn't a comedy at all. It's a tragedy dressed up as comedy', but any

1 Dates of plays indicate the first United Kingdom performance unless otherwise stated.

apparent cynicism in the thought that her rebellion can be bought off by what the Bond Street jewellers offer and her wealthy husband can afford is subsumed by the sense of relief that not just social mores but the very fabric of society have been preserved. Similarly, in Jones's *The Liars* (1897) Jessica Nepean, who is on the point of breaking from an unsatisfactory marriage, returns in the final act to the safety of home and husband. Despite the way in which the plays seem to place women centrally in the drama, the notion that Jones and Pinero, apparently emulating the Ibsen of *A Doll's House* and *Hedda Gabler*, offered a serious critique of women in society is a sham. The plays depend upon and endorse social, economic and moral formations which oppress women and, further, promote traditionalist gender constructs as an essential part of their judgemental systems. For instance, Nina Jesson in Pinero's *His House in Order* (1906) finally wins approval when she conquers her desire to be assertive and dons the mantle of self-sacrifice and wifely duty.

While as a whole the drama of both Jones and Pinero is essentially reactionary, the experience mediated by individual plays is seemingly far more liberal. This is in part due to the skill with which the plotting and ideological strategies are implemented, and is partly due to a tone created by the presence of *raisonneur* figures in the plays. The *raisonneur*, by authoritatively commenting on events, providing sound advice and occasionally directly intervening in the action, is able to ensure appropriate resolutions. In many respects he carries the ideological burden of the plays. Such figures include Cayley Drummle in *The Second Mrs Tanqueray*, Sir Daniel Carteret in *Mrs Dane's Defence*, Hilary Jesson in *His House in Order*, Sir Richard Kato in *The Case of Rebellious Susan*, and Sir Christopher Deering in *The Liars*. Here is Deering's advice to Edward Falkner and Jessica Nepean who are considering decamping together:

Now! I've nothing to say in the abstract against running away with another man's wife! There may be planets where it is not only the highest ideal morality, but where it has the further advantage of being a practical way of carrying on society. But it has one fatal defect in our country today – it won't work! You know what we English are, Ned. We're not a bit better than our neighbours, but, thank God! we do pretend we are, and we do make it hot for anybody who disturbs that holy pretence. And take my word for it, my dear Lady Jessica, my dear Ned, it won't work. You know it's not an original experiment you're making. It has been tried before. Have you ever known it to be successful?

(Act 4)

His pronouncements are unruffled, detached, controlled. His slightly cynical pragmatism allows him to endorse conventional codes of behaviour without appearing idealistic or moralistic. His style is part of that sophistication which administered a sense of the daring but no serious undermining of orthodox assumptions.

In the last decade of the nineteenth century the society drama of Jones and Pinero implicitly proposed that subjects worthy or interesting enough for dramatic treatment were only to be found among members of the upper classes, and that the most appropriate way of mediating their experience would be through the conventions of realist staging. It also proposed that what would be most interesting about people from the upper classes would be their peccadilloes, usually their sexual peccadilloes. In this they established a pattern for drama which would persist for at least the next fifty years.

The plays of Oscar Wilde (1854–1900), particularly *Lady Windermere's Fan* (1892), *A Woman of No Importance* (1893), and *An Ideal Husband* (1895), show a clear affinity with the conventions of the social problem dramas of Jones and Pinero. Their class settings, their thematic concerns and their plot structures which contrive to preserve the façade of social structures are often taken as unfortunately slavish imitations of the late nineteenth-century English adaptation of the French boulevard drama. Where Wilde's plays are universally acknowledged to differ is in the epigrammatic wit of their dialogue. This results in a common critical unease which perceives a disjunction between the wit, validated by its linguistic skill and intellectual paradox, and the use of discredited theatrical formulas. The melodramatic intonation of, for instance, the third-act curtain line of *A Woman of No Importance* where Gerald, ignorant of his parentage, is checked from attacking Lord Illingworth by his mother's declaration of 'Stop, Gerald, stop! He is your own father!' is seen to fit uneasily with the rather more elegant style of the Wildean epigram. The critical unease is exacerbated because Wilde is scarcely interested in concealing the improbabilities and coincidences of the plot mechanics which create the melodramatic structures of the plays.

The relationship between the wit and the conventional theatricality of the plays is not so much one of disjunction as challenging juxtaposition. Thus Wilde's epigrams, in their paradoxical style, tone and subject matter, undermine and subvert the assumed social hierarchies and the ethical orthodoxies which are constructed in the setting and conventions of late Victorian society drama. And the obviousness of his plotting in effect serves a similar function. Though the plotting arrives at roughly similar resolutions to those of Jones and Pinero, Wilde draws attention to the mechanism of its own operation in ways that the others were far more adept at assimilating into the supposed plausibility of the action. Wilde's plays thereby expose the conservative ideologies supported by the plotting strategies of society drama which, in the case of Jones and Pinero, are partially obscured by the very sophistication of those strategies' implementation. The achievement of Wilde's three society dramas in subverting the assumptions of their own genre is, I think, largely underestimated; however, there is in *The Importance of Being Earnest* (1895) a more effective matching of wit and genre and, moreover, the genre itself subverts the conventionally endorsed social hierarchy.

Although Wilde is often acknowledged as a satirist of social mores and a moral critic, his plays contain a radical political critique of the upper classes. Hester's attack in *A Woman of No Importance* illustrates firstly the moral critique and then a critique of the economic and power structures by which the upper classes maintain their privileged position:

You rich people in England, you don't know how you are living. How could you? You shut out from your society the gentle and the good. You laugh at the simple and the pure. Living, as you all do, on others and by them, you sneer at self-sacrifice, and if you throw bread to the poor, it is merely to keep them quiet for a season.

(Act 2)

Hester is perhaps too sententiously earnest in her condemnation; Lady Bracknell's earnestness is of a very different order, yet she embodies Wilde's sternest critique. The famous scene where she interviews Jack to test his eligibility as a suitor is primarily richly comic, yet what can supposedly be passed off as the extravagant logic of an English eccentric or a comedic parody of theatrical conventions in fact exposes the heart of the power base of the class she represents. The thematic centre of society drama, the threat of misalliance, is revealed through Lady Bracknell as a political as well as a social and moral issue:

To be born, or at any rate bred, in a hand-bag, whether it has handles or not, seems to me to display a contempt for the ordinary decencies of family life that reminds one of the worst excesses of the French Revolution. And I presume you know what that unfortunate movement led to?

(Act 1)

The political implications which remain unstated in the work of

Jones and Pinero are here made explicit. The underlying anxiety is not of an undefined disintegration of social and moral values but is one specifically of class conflict and insurrection, of anything that might 'prove a serious danger to the upper classes and . . . lead to acts of violence in Grosvenor Square'.

The ending of *The Importance of Being Earnest*, in keeping with the play's genre, re-establishes the previously disrupted social order, that Jack really is Ernest and is of acceptable social position – his mother a Lady, his father a general. Yet the play equally suggests that the social settlement is as arbitrary and as absurd as when he was the foundling Jack Worthing and descended from hand luggage.

Wilde lays in the political critique by a sleight of hand; consequently he gets away with it. His plays, despite some contemporary unease, could be accommodated by the commercial stage because of their class setting and wit. Other dramatists, John Galsworthy (1867–1933), Harley Granville-Barker (1877–1946) and George Bernard Shaw (1856–1950), were more overt in their opposition to the class setting, the conservative ideologies and the patriarchal agenda of the typical society drama. Their work, initially at least, was accommodated by short-run and repertory theatre ventures which stood aside from the long-run commercial theatre system. The most notable of these were the New Century Theatre (1898), the Stage Society (1899), the repertory seasons of Granville-Barker and J. E. Vedrenne at the Court (1904–7) and the Savoy (1907–8), and Charles Frohman's season at the Duke of York's in 1910.

Using superficially similar material Galsworthy questioned central assumptions of society drama; thus *Joy* (1907) depicts country-house society in decline, *The Fugitive* (1913) uncompromisingly condemns economic and social formations which render middle-class women fit only to be rich men's wives, and *The Eldest Son* (1912) makes a jaundiced examination of the misalliance theme. But Galsworthy seemed to his contemporaries particularly to offer a challenge to the predominating social setting of the drama: 'Mr. Galsworthy has reaffirmed the existence of the common man; an individual long ignored upon the English stage' (Ashley Dukes, *Modern Dramatists*, Palmer, 1911, p 141). *The Silver Box* (1906) established a pattern that would become characteristic. Two virtually identical petty thefts are committed, one by an unemployed workman, the other by a wealthy man. The parallelism, once established, proves by the very different fates of the two men at the end of the play the social thesis that there is one law for the rich and another for the poor; the inequity promotes the emotional force of the play – sympathy and pity, not so much for this specific working man who is represented as brutish, but for his family and for the poor in the abstract.

Galsworthy sought by the presentation of parallel plots to attain an impartiality. Thus the two sides in the industrial dispute in *Strife* (1909) are both shown as neither right nor wrong. By intercutting between analogous scenes showing the two sides, parallel developments, apparently without authorial comment, are established until the identical fate – betrayal by their followers – befalls the two leaders. Galsworthy may not overtly take sides, but the juxtaposition of luxury and plenty in the manager's house as opposed to the starvation in the strike leader's is not emotionally neutral. The material advantages of the owners mean that the fight is unfair; consequently Galsworthy establishes a structure of emotional response whereby pity is generated for the workers and their families. In *Justice* (1910) a similar emotional structure centres around Falder, a junior clerk apprehended for forging a cheque. But Galsworthy is careful, as he is in his drama as a whole, not to create villains out of those characters who are granted little or no sympathy. As a result social formations and institutions are castigated, rarely individuals. Thus, in *Justice*, the episodic structure of the rest of the play provides a series of settings which allow Galsworthy to demonstrate how aspects of the judicial and penal system wear down and eventually destroy Falder. As individuals in the play merely administer a system which is relentless and inexorable, Galsworthy thereby absolves those individuals of direct responsibility. Nothing could have been done, the play proposes, which could have altered the outcome.

In these plays the existence of the working-class characters is subordinated to Galsworthy's tendentious purpose. In order to illustrate his overriding sense of the inequities of Edwardian society, the working-class characters have to be oppressed and powerless; similarly, his middle-class characters are most often sympathetic and powerless. There is an essential pessimism to Galsworthy's plays; individuals are ultimately unable to ameliorate their own lives, still less to intervene in the workings of institutional or social forces which are consequently represented as unassailable. Galsworthy's drama at times seems ponderous, yet it is testimony to the high seriousness and sombre treatment of the 'new' Edwardian problem drama.

Granville-Barker's handling of the problem play mode seems superficially much closer to the world of Jones and Pinero. Although *The Marrying of Ann Leete* (1902) has a late eighteenth-century setting, Ann Leete is metaphorically as much a New Woman of the 1890s as she is a literal woman of the 1790s. She rejects a politically expedient and socially acceptable marriage, which her father has arranged, by proposing to and marrying the family gardener, significantly named John Abud. In so doing she overturns social and gender expectations and confounds patriarchal oppression. In terms of the symbolic system imported into the play, the marrying represents a force for regeneration in the sterile Leete social and political circles.

Granville-Barker's later plays, by virtue of their contemporary settings as much as their social settings and thematic concerns, are those which take issue with the endorsed ideologies of society drama. *The Voysey Inheritance* (1905) depicts an apparently typical and respectable upper-middle-class Edwardian family. Its wealth and comfort derive from the activities of the head of the house who is a fashionable solicitor. Voysey, though, is dishonest and fraudulently uses his client's capital for his own benefit. When Pinero depicted a fraudulent solicitor in *Iris* (1901), he characteristically suggested that the crime was an isolated case and its cause the dishonesty of one individual rogue; the argument of Granville-Barker's play inverts the ethical assumptions which lie behind Pinero's. Voysey's rejection of conventional codes is represented as a sort of heroism; he is, as one character puts it, 'a great financier . . . a man of imagination'. By the extent to which he makes money work Voysey is the most effective capitalist in the play; his amorality implies an amorality fundamental to capitalism itself. Granville-Barker inverts the logic of capitalist enterprise and thus inculpates the economic base of the class promoted by the society drama. The outline of his next play *Waste* (1907) similarly sounds as if it should be an entirely typical society drama. Henry Trebell, a politician of some importance, is involved in a sexual scandal as a result of which he commits suicide at the end of the play. Granville-Barker differs in the mediation of such themes from Jones and Pinero because he is ultimately little exercised about the social repercussions of Trebell's moral lapse. Further, the relationship between Trebell and Amy O'Connell is stripped of the aura of romance which made acceptable inappropriate sexual relationships in the society drama. Lacking even this laundering, the fact that Amy dies as a result of an abortion (then an illegal operation) was sufficient to incite the official wrath of the Lord Chamberlain's office and the play was banned.

The seemingly conventional plotting of *Waste* which ends in the suicide of the recreant is undermined by the body of the play; a mystery rather than a resolution is reached. Similarly, at the end of *The Voysey Inheritance* there is no certainty that the dishonesty of the Voysey firm will be publicly exposed. *The Madras House* (1910) goes further and dispenses almost entirely with the highly structured plotting of the well-made play and consists of a series of loosely connected vignettes which provide a genuine critique of aspects of the oppression of women. In terms of the context of Edwardian commercial drama it is a remarkable, if flawed, achievement. Both its form and its ideological position deny the validity of the assumptions upon which society is constructed in the commercial drama of the period.

Granville-Barker is one of the most complex and intriguing of Edwardian dramatists, while one of his other major achievements in the Edwardian theatre was his role in bringing the works of Shaw to public attention. The Vedrenne–Granville-Barker seasons at the Court devoted 711 performances to Shaw and staged eleven of his plays.

One of Shaw's first interventions in the theatre of the 1890s was his promotion of Ibsen in *The Quintessence of Ibsenism* (1891); the inclusion of plays provocatively categorized as 'unpleasant' in his first published drama announced Shaw's sense of their allegiance to the independent theatre movement and common perceptions of Ibsen's subject matter. This was confirmed by the subject matter of *Widowers' Houses* (1892), slum landlordism, and of *Mrs Warren's Profession* (1902), prostitution. In these plays Shaw denies the validity of conventional ethical judgements; further he argues that both rackrenting and prostitution are inevitable correlatives of capitalist society as currently constituted and, as economic activity, they are fully integrated into its supposedly more respectable aspects. Thus within the plays not only are the individual rackrenter and brothel owner absolved from personal culpability, but the aristocracy, Members of Parliament, the Ecclesiastical Commissioners and Cambridge University, are also fully implicated, and by implication so is every member of the audience. Shaw, with Ibsen, could indeed be taken to be unbandaging society's open sores. But *Widowers' Houses* derives less from Ibsen than from a remodelling of the conventions of domestic melodrama and romantic comedy, and *Mrs Warren's Profession* from a reworking of the theatrically commonplace representation of the woman with a past.

Here lies a pointer to Shaw's most characteristic method and also his departure from that of most of his fellow progressive dramatists. While they usually aimed to eschew the theatrical conventions of the past which they believed falsified experience, Shaw was flamboyantly open in his declaration of indebtedness to old stage traditions: 'My stories are the old stories; my characters are the familiar harlequin and columbine, clown and pantaloon . . . my stage tricks and suspenses and thrills and jests are the ones in vogue when I was a boy' ('Preface' to *Three Plays for Puritans*, in *The Bodley Head Bernard Shaw: Collected Plays with Their Prefaces*, Bodley Head, 1970–74, vol II, pp 46–7). Many of Shaw's plays are identifiable in terms of conventions and genres which had been the bread and butter of the nineteenth-century commercial theatre: *The Devil's Disciple* (1899), melodrama as practised at the Adelphi; *Caesar and Cleopatra* (1907), large-scale historical drama; *Candida* (1900), domestic drama; *Arms and the Man* (1894), military melodrama; *Man and Superman* (1905), romantic comedy; *You Never Can Tell* (1899), farcical comedy. Shaw's engagement with the traditions of nineteenth-century theatre is to expose its conventions as arrant romantic and sentimental nonsense. More than just a parody of theatrical conventions, Shaw offers a critique of the ethical and ideological assumptions which are inscribed in those conventions. Although vastly differing in style, the strategy of Shaw's plays is similar to Wilde's.

Of the dramatists who set out to oppose the prevailing standards of the late nineteenth-century and Edwardian commercial stage, it was Shaw's work alone which came to be staged with any regularity by commercial managements. No matter how iconoclastic the treatment, the fact that Shaw was still dealing in styles and genres thoroughly familiar to the commercial stage eventually wooed audiences and managers. By the second decade of the twentieth century revivals of plays originally staged under the auspices of the minority theatre and new plays, such as *Fanny's First Play* (1911), *Androcles and the Lion* (1913), *Pygmalion* (1914) and *Saint Joan* (1924), were becoming the property of the commercial theatre and achieving runs comparable with those of popular contemporary dramatists. Ideological discomfort could be outweighed by a sense of delight in the paradoxes of Shaw's ideational pyrotechnics and his genuine comedic skill. Above all Shaw has, particularly in his earlier work, a sure sense of what works in the theatre. This is even true of the discursive disquisitory plays *Misalliance* (1910) and *Getting Married* (1908) which superficially seem to be conversation and nothing else, but are in fact driven along by the interplay of ideas and Shavian wit. In *Heartbreak House* (1921) the apparently aimless discussion and the overall sense of stasis become the perfect theatrical image for Shaw's depiction of a society helplessly awaiting catastrophe. Even the theatrical intractability of the five-part 'metabiological penta-teuch' *Back to Methuselah* (1923) stands almost as an act of pure Shavian provocation, a challenge to the notion of what a play can or should be.

Although Shaw's last play to be staged, *Far-Fetched Fables*, ap-peared in the year of his death and memorable plays continued to appear when he was in his seventies – *The Apple Cart* (1929), *Too True to be Good* (1932), *In Good King Charles's Golden Days* (1939) – the bulk of his significant work had been written by the end of the second decade of the twentieth century, by which time he had established himself as a dramatist capable of achieving commercial success. Perhaps the mere fact of Shaw's acceptance began to take the urgency, or at least the barefaced cheek, from his provocative challenges to the theatrical establishment. When *Widowers' Houses* was performed by the Independent Theatre Club in 1892, it was received with almost the same level of hysterical vituperation which greeted *Ghosts*; in 1949 his puppet play for the Malvern Festival, *Shakes Versus Shav*, was one of his last, but completely characteristic, acts of irreverent self-promotion. Yet the greater truth is that by his death Shaw had become not just part of the theatrical establishment but, like Shakespeare, part of establishment culture.

The repertory ventures which promoted the work of dramatists like Galsworthy, Granville-Barker and Shaw were not confined to London. Equally important for the future development of theatre in Britain was the establishment in the Edwardian period of regional repertory theatres: in Glasgow in 1909, Liverpool in 1911 and Birmingham in 1913. These ventures had been preceded by the opening in 1908 of a repertory theatre at the Gaiety, Manchester under the direction and financial patronage of Miss A. E. F. Horni-man. While these theatres brought to the public similar repertories to those of the London repertory enterprises, a further significant contribution was their encouragement of a specifically regional iden-tity in dramatic writing. The Gaiety in particular gathered around it a group of dramatists which came to be known as the 'Manchester School'.

The regional drama entailed not only a shift in the geographical setting of the drama but also in its class settings and in its wider cul-tural contexts; instead of country houses and Mayfair drawing-rooms the regional drama, a near-contemporary noted, more frequently offered 'the tradesman's parlour or the unlovely but sumptuous dining-room of the rich manufacturer. The older drama had an atmosphere of anglican respectability: the drama of the younger school breathed close dissent' (A. E. Morgan, *Tendencies of Modern English Drama*, Constable, 1924, p 174). At the same time the drama, like much of the drama already discussed, offered a challenge to the gender assumptions of the dominant society drama. Harold Brighouse's (1882–1958) farcical comedy *Hobson's Choice* (1916) links the reversal of gender expectations with a self-conscious regionalism evident in Maggie Hobson's defence of her aggressive wooing and bullying into marriage of the man she wants: 'a Salford life's too near the bone to lose things through fear of speaking out.' Stanley Houghton's (1881–1913) comedy *Hindle Wakes* (1912) reverses a century-old tradition of seduction melodrama when Fanny, a mill hand, refuses to marry the son of the mill owner after she has been away with him for an illicit weekend in Llandudno. At the end of the play Fanny is presented as a sort of latterday Lancashire Nora Helmer in Ibsen when she asserts a sexual and economic independence which is inextricable from the regional setting and work opportunities provided by local industry: 'I'm a Lancashire lass, and so long as there's weaving sheds in Lancashire I shall earn enough to keep me going.'

Githa Sowerby's (1876–1970) much grimmer drama *Rutherford and Son* (1912) shows a woman who renounces conventional constructs of maternity and comes to a financial arrangement by which she sacrifices her son to the tyrant Rutherford's need for a male child to train up for the continuance of the family business. Where *Rutherford and Son*, *Hobson's Choice* and *Hindle Wakes* differ from, for example, Galsworthy's *The Eldest Son* and *Strife*, which also aimed to explore relationships between different social classes, is in the contextualizing specificity of the industrial settings. What is mediated, particularly in *Hindle Wakes* and *Rutherford and Son*, is a cultural and industrial history which predetermines the sets of relations in the plays. Unlike Galsworthy, who was ultimately mainly interested in the ways of living and ideologies of the upper middle classes, the regional drama more effectively explored the values and attitudes of the lower middle-class and working-class characters it depicted.

Elizabeth Baker (1879–1962) was not so much concerned with depicting inter-class relationships as exploring the hinterland between upper working-class and lower-lower middle-class experience. In her one-acter *Miss Tassey* (1910) it is the conditions of women's shop work which are implicitly indicted. In *Chains* (1909) her achievement was to dispense with any sense of a strong plot, and yet to create a drama from what is presented as the unexceptional mediocrity of the typical experience of a junior clerk and his family. With the exception of the plays of D. H. Lawrence, it is difficult to envisage an English play which so comprehensively challenged the theatrical experience inherent in the social setting and plotting strategies of the society drama.

In the context of Edwardian regional drama and its treatment of working-class experience, it is necessary to remark on Lawrence's three colliery plays, *A Collier's Friday Night*, *The Daughter-in-Law* and *The Widowing of Mrs Holroyd*. Although they were all written before the First World War, they had to wait until the 1960s before they received successful stage productions under the direction of Peter Gill at the Royal Court.[1] Although one item on the agenda for a significant section of Edwardian drama was to present on stage characters from the lower social classes, that presence was most frequently validated largely by its relation to higher social classes. It is only now that Lawrence's plays have rightly gained their place on the stage that they can be recognized as the plays which most effectively create their drama of their period purely from the representation of working-class ways of living.

The English regional drama had in one respect been prefigured in Ireland. Before her involvement with the Gaiety in Manchester, Horniman had been the financial benefactor who in 1904 provided the Irish National Theatre Society with a permanent venue at the Abbey Theatre, Dublin. But it is probably only in this juncture that any real link between the Irish and the Manchester theatres can be made. There is occasionally a note of Lancashire chauvinism in the work of Houghton and Brighouse, but their plays promote only a regional identity. In contrast the aim of W. B. Yeats (1865–1939) and his fellow directors of the Abbey was to create a national theatre and drama, and this at a crucial point in the politics of Irish nationalism and British colonial rule.

Yeats's early work, in keeping with the Irish literary revival of the 1890s, was to establish Irish folklore and legend as appropriate material for the national drama. This was in marked contrast to those contemporary English movements which showed their opposition to the dominance of London's commercial theatre by drawing their inspiration from a contemporary conception of the sociological Ibsen of *Ghosts* and *A Doll's House*. The Irish theatre was to take a

---

1 *The Widowing of Mrs Holroyd* had been staged twice before the Royal Court productions: by the Altrincham Garrick Society in 1920, and by the Stage Society and Three Hundred Club in 1926.

radically different line and, consequently, predominantly realist play-wrights like George Moore (1852–1933) and Edward Martyn (1859–1923), who had been participants in the earlier Irish Literary Theatre (1899), were not to join Yeats at the Abbey.

Yeats's earliest plays, *The Countess Cathleen* (1899) and *The Land of Heart's Desire* (1894), both show conflicts between Christianity and pagan tradition in Irish folklore. In the first, during a time of famine the countess sells her soul to the demon merchants to prevent them buying the souls of her starving peasants; in the second, the conflict lies between respectability, husband and marriage on the one hand and the attraction of the fairy child and the sidhe on the other. Both plays suffer from a reliance on clichéd images and manners of late nineteenth-century poetry; similarly the dreamlike mood of the Celtic Twilight is probably overdone. Nevertheless, even here Yeats avoids the danger of using folktale sources merely for the purposes of nostalgia.

On Baile's Strand (1904) marks a considerable advance. The heroic legendary action (in verse), which relates Cuchulain's unwitting killing of his own son, is framed by the bickering and deceit of the Blind Man and the Fool (in prose). The juxtapositions create an internal system of ironic commentary and correspondence. Past and present seem to merge, the visionary poetic and the folk peasant styles offer competing sets of values and perceptions of reality which combine into a single dramatic experience. *On Baile's Strand* was Yeats's first treatment in play form of the Cuchulain legend; he was to return to it in several subsequent plays: *The Golden Helmet* (1908) (to be rewritten in verse as *The Green Helmet* (1910)), *At the Hawk's Well* (1916), *The Only Jealousy of Emer* (1929), *Fighting the Waves* (1929) and *The Death of Cuchulain*, the last, which was published in 1939, the year of his death, and first performed in 1945. The plays vary in style and tone, and thematically they reflect the personal preoccupations which are refracted in Yeats's poetry.

Yeats's rejection of the representational realism which dominated English staging conventions, while always evident in his work, intensified with the plays published in *Four Plays for Dancers*. These include two of the Cuchulain plays, *At the Hawk's Well* and *The Only Jealousy of Emer*, and *The Dreaming of the Bones* (1931), and *Calvary* (published 1921). Inspired by the non-representationalism of the Japanese theatre, the plays emphasized a sense of dramatic ritual through the use of music and dance and the highly stylized gestures of masked performers. Thus Yeats writes in a prefatory note to *At the Hawk's Well*: 'My theatre must be the ancient theatre that can be made by unrolling a carpet or marking out a place with a stick, or setting a screen against the wall.' (The preface accompanied the first publication of the play in *Harper's Bazaar* in March 1917, quoted in A. Norman Jeffares and A. S. Knowland, *A Commentary on the Collected Plays of W. B. Yeats*, Macmillan, 1975, p 84.) The 'plays for dancers' demonstrate an internationalist interest which is almost totally lacking in early twentieth-century English dramatic writing. Yet in denying so emphatically the theatrical expectations of the day they presupposed a coterie audience and performance in non-theatrical contexts. Yeats recalled of *At the Hawk's Well*: '[It] was performed for the first time in April 1916, in a friend's drawing-room, and only those who cared for poetry were invited . . . A few days later it was revived in Lady Islington's big drawing-room at Chesterfield Gardens' (Preface to *A Commentary on the Collected Plays of W. B. Yeats*, Macmillan, 1975, pp 85–6). Yeats had achieved his aim of 'an unpopular theatre and an audience like a secret society where admission is by favour and never to many'. Yeats's élitism must, however, be seen in the context of a popular theatre which could hardly begin to accommodate the visionary poetic cast in this particular dramatic form.

Along with Yeats the most significant dramatist of the early Irish theatre was John Millington Synge (1871–1909). His last unrevised play, *Deirdre of the Sorrows* (1910), took for its subject the sort of legendary material Yeats was using. Employing a frequently collo-quial prose the play is a non-naturalistic tragedy. Synge's most characteristic mode is, however, a drama of Irish peasant life, the sort of drama which was undistinguished in the hands of the co-founder of the Abbey, Lady Gregory (1852–1932), and had been brought off more successfully in Yeats's *Cathleen ni Houlihan* (1902) and *The Pot of Broth* (1902). While this material might seem to lend itself more to dominant realist conventions than subjects drawn from heroic legend, even here Synge signals his distance from late nineteenth-century naturalist drama:

In the modern literature of towns . . . richness is found only in sonnets, or prose poems, or in one or two elaborate books that are far away from the profound and common interests of life. One has on the one side, Mallarmé and Huysmans producing this literature; and on the other, Ibsen and Zola dealing with the reality of life in joyless and pallid words. On the stage one must have reality, and one must have joy; and that is why the intellectual modern drama has failed.

(John Millington Synge, 'Preface to *The Playboy of the Western World*' in
Plays, Poems and Prose, Dent, 1941, pp 107–8)

Synge's first play, *In the Shadow of the Glen* (1903), is a comedy in which an ageing husband feigns death in order to catch his younger wife with her lover. The situation of the supposed or feigned death is a dramatic commonplace, whether treated as comedy as in Stanley Houghton's *The Dear Departed* (1908) or as *grand guignol* in *The Mask* (1915) by F. T. Jesse and H. M. Harwood. What distinguishes Synge's play is the quality of the language evident at the end of the play when Nora elopes not with her lover but a passing tramp:

I'm thinking it's myself will be wheezing that time with lying down under the heavens when the night is cold; but you've a fine bit of talk, stranger, and it's with yourself I'll go. [*She goes towards the door, then turns to Dan.*] You think it's a grand thing you're after doing with your letting on to be dead, but what is it at all? What way would a woman live in a lonesome place the like of this place, and she not making a talk with the men passing? And what way will yourself live from this day, with none to care for you? What is it you'll have now but a black life, Daniel Burke; and it's not long, I'm telling you, till you'll be lying again under that sheet, and you dead surely.

Synge's achievement lies not in the documentation of real speech, but in the creation of an effective stage convention of a certain sort of Irish rural speech which derives its impetus from rhythm, syntax and intonation more than from dialect.

  Like *In the Shadow of the Glen*, *The Tinker's Wedding* (1909) and *The Well of the Saints* (1905) both employ a similar language and mediate a comic and ironic experience. *Riders to the Sea* (1904), however, uses the language to express the tragedy of those who work the sea. At the play's centre lies a representation of the relentless conflict between humankind and the sea which is offered as an emblem of the inevitability of defeat. The pessimism is palliated by the stoicism and resignation with which the catastrophe is met and a sense of the particularity of individuals as the mother iterates the names of the sons she has lost.

  In the preface to *The Tinker's Wedding* Synge wrote, 'The drama is made serious – in the French sense of the word – not by the degree in which it is taken up with problems that are serious in themselves, but by the degree in which it gives the nourishment, not very easy to define, on which our imaginations live' (Synge, in *Plays, Poems and Prose*, Dent, 1941, p 33). The action of *The Playboy of the Western World* (1907) celebrates this process. Christy, the playboy of the title, becomes a heroic figure neither solely from his own relating of the story of how he murdered his father nor solely from the encouragement and embellishment of the telling of the tale by the peasant community he enters, but from a creative collaboration of the two. It is only when his father appears alive that the created fiction is seen as a lie, and only when Christy again apparently kills his father that the realization comes that 'there's a great gap between a gallous story and a dirty deed'. It is the imaginative creation, the telling of the story that is important, not the deed itself. But the fiction has turned into its own reality; Christy wins the games and in actuality becomes the champion playboy of the western world and, transformed utterly, he leaves the community that created him to go 'romancing through a romping lifetime from this hour to the dawning of the Judgment Day'. Synge's most successful and enduring play is a celebratory enactment of his view of the function of drama and his craft as playwright.

The plays of Sean O'Casey (1880–1964) first appeared on the Abbey stage shortly after the signing of the 1921 treaty which established the Irish Free State. While some of the plays of Yeats and Synge could be read (or misread) as political allegories, O'Casey's most famous early plays were set at critical points in and dealt directly with the events of the recent political history: *The Shadow of a Gunman* (1923) with the Anglo-Irish war in 1920, *Juno and the Paycock* (1924) with the civil war which followed the 1921 treaty, and *The Plough and the Stars* (1926) culminating in the Easter rebellion of 1916. The political action is set against the lives of the inhabitants of the Dublin tenements.

Like Synge, O'Casey established a stage convention of a sort of Irish speech, in his case that of the urban working class. As an expression of the characters' extravagant flights of fancy, O'Casey's language is more clearly manipulating a comic literary model than Synge as can be seen in the following exchange from *Juno and the Paycock*:

JOXER: God be with the young days when you were steppin' the deck of a manly ship, with the win' blowin' a hurricane through the masts, an' the only sound you'd hear was, 'Port your helm!' an' the only answer, 'Port it is, sir!'

BOYLE: Them was days, Joxer, them was days. Nothin' was too hot or too heavy for me then. Sailin' from the Gulf o' Mexico to the Antanartic Ocean. I seen things, I seen things, Joxer, that no mortal man should speak about that knows his Catechism. Ofen, an' ofen, when I was fixed to the wheel with a marlin-spike, an' the win's blowin' fierce an' the waves lashin' an' lashin', till you'd think every minute was goin' to be your last, an' it blowed, an' blowed – blew is the right word, Joxer, but blowed is what the sailors use . . .

JOXER: Aw, it's a darlin' word, a daarlin' word.

(Act 1)

Here the language does not, as it did in *The Playboy of the Western World*, create a new reality but only a sense of personality, engaging but deceiving. The deception is signalled at one level by the verbal solecisms of what is a conventionally patronizing representation of the speech of working-class characters. The language, the talk creates a fantasy in order to evade other realities; in *Juno and the Paycock* Boyle evades his traditional responsibility as provider for his family, and in all three plays the characters aim to evade the actualities of the political action.

O'Casey's characters attempt to maintain a distance between sets of oppositions: public and private, political and personal, the safe interiors of the tenements and the political violence outside on the streets. The oppositions meet and merge. The political violence literally invades the interiors – the British army, the Black and Tans, the Republican Diehard execution squad. In *The Shadow of a Gunman* and *The Plough and the Stars* what is represented as the anarchic comic spirit of the tenements, although under threat throughout the play, is shattered by the final tragic results of the political action. The ending of *Juno and the Paycock* mediates a more complex experience and demands a more complex response from the audience. When the son of the house is taken away for execution, his punishment for betraying the cause, the play does not, like the others, end with the tragedy of the political action. The stage is reinhabited by the comic double act of the fantasists Boyle and Joxer. The savage irony of the play's final moments is that Boyle's new self-deceiving, self-promoting fantasy is of his own supposed heroic involvement in the Republican cause during the events of Easter 1916.

The three Dublin plays constitute O'Casey's major achievement. His next play *The Silver Tassie* (1929) was rejected by Yeats for production at the Abbey; O'Casey not only severed his links with the Abbey and Irish theatre but went into self-imposed exile in England. While he continued to experiment with dramatic forms, it is probably *The Silver Tassie* which is his most important play after the Abbey period. The first and last acts, in a similar realist mode to the Dublin plays, relate a football hero's departure for war and return as a cripple. But it was to techniques of German expressionist drama (stylized, symbolic set instead of realistic domestic interiors, orchestrated chanting and singing instead of conventional Irish garrulousness) that O'Casey turned to express a sense of the horror and futility of the war and the dislocated alienation of those forced to undergo it.

Certain sorts of English drama in the first quarter of the twentieth century showed, like the Irish drama, departures from the dominant realist mode discussed in the earlier part of this chapter. The plays of J. M. Barrie (1860–1937) often worked a vein of whimsical fantasy overlaid with suggestions of the supernatural. While they have a predisposition to excessive sentimentality, this is tempered by social satire and a dark, menacing edge to the fantasy. There was also a poetic drama which, although now counted of little worth, was granted serious consideration throughout much of the first half of the twentieth century. The pseudo-Elizabethan verse plays of Stephen Phillips (1864–1915) – *Paolo and Francesca* (1902), *Herod* (1900) and *Ulysses* (1902) – in many ways were legitimized as serious drama by the mere fact that they were in verse. In this they represented the tail-end of a persistent nineteenth-century tradition of verse drama which supposedly drew strength from looking back to the glories of Shakespeare. The success of the plays on the early twentieth-century stage partly derived from their staging in the pictorial tradition of Beerbohm Tree and Henry Irving in which the exoticism of the settings was lavishly and literally reproduced on stage. The use of verse was seen as an appropriate verbal medium to match the exoticism of the setting, whether it was the Italianate Renaissance of *Paolo and Francesca* or the orientalism of James Elroy Flecker's (1884–1915) *Hassan* (1922). The voguish success of this latter play is often taken as the final flowering of this sort of pseudo-Elizabethan drama. The play is, in fact, in prose, but its periphrasis and habit of syntactical inversion were taken for the poetic by contemporaries. Also in prose but best viewed as an example of early twentieth-century poetic drama is John Masefield's (1878–1967) *The Tragedy of Nan* (1908). In a more grimly realistic mode than Phillips or Flecker, it is one of the very few plays of its sort which retains some critical esteem. The rest have little more than a curiosity value.

English verse drama took a radically different turn in the 1930s. It was centred around Rupert Doone's Group Theatre (1932) and Ashley Dukes's Mercury Theatre (1931), and its most enduring achievements were the plays of T. S. Eliot (1888–1965) and the collaborations of W. H. Auden (1907–73) and Christopher Isherwood (1904–86).

Auden's plays demonstrate a conscious rejection of the dominant tradition of realist drama, and in their staging by the Group Theatre, which relied on only minimal scenery and properties, they achieved a practical dismissal of contemporary production values. Further,

Auden dismissed completely the tradition of English verse drama which preceded him; thus in 1934 he begins his review of Priscilla Thouless's study *Modern Poetic Drama*: 'This book is like an exhibition of perpetual motion models. Here they all are, labelled Phillips, Davidson, Yeats, some on the largest scale, some on the tiniest, some ingenious in design, some beautifully made, all suffering from only one defect – they won't go' (Quoted in W. H. Auden and Christopher Isherwood, *Plays and Other Dramatic Writings by W. H. Auden, 1928–1938*, ed. Edward Mendelson, Princeton University Press, 1988, p xiii). He goes on to argue that as drama is essentially a social art the earlier poetic drama fails precisely because it bears no valid relation to society. Unlike the esoteric nature of Yeats's adaptation of Japanese theatre, Auden, influenced to some extent by the techniques of German cabaret, turned to English comic traditions and popular forms. Some of these derive from medieval drama and mummers' plays, but the most striking elements employ aspects of contemporary popular entertainment and commercial culture – pantomime, musical comedy, the variety show and the revue. At the end of *The Dance of Death* (1934) Karl Marx is heralded on stage in pantomime style:

> CHORUS: [*singing to Mendelssohn's 'Wedding March'*]
>   O Mr Marx, you've gathered
>   All the material facts
>   You know the economic
>   Reasons for our acts.

And at the end of the published version of *The Dog Beneath the Skin* (1936) the chorus sung by the assembled cast is from the world of comic operetta:

> O Day of Joy in happiness abounding
> Streams through the hills with laughter are resounding
> For Pressan is delighted
> To see you thus united.
> Handsome he.
>   Lovely she.
> Riches, children, every blessing
> Be to you for your possessing
> Love be round you everywhere
> Happy, Happy, Happy pair.

(Act 3, Scene 5)

The forms of commercial entertainment are employed in the service of political commentary, a strategy not uncommon among radical theatre groups throughout the 1930s; both the Workers' Theatre Movement's *Malice in Plunderland* (1929) and Unity Theatre's long-running *Babes in the Wood* (1938) were pastiche pantomimes which satirized real contemporary political figures and British political policy. Neville Chamberlain's appeasement of Hitler, for instance, is a target of the latter. Auden and Isherwood's *The Dog Beneath the Skin* (1936) reflects on recent European history, but the play as a whole is generally less specific. The quest to find Sir Francis Crewe, the missing head of the village, is also the search to remedy society's political ills. Yet the thematic concern of the Quest can also be extrapolated as a purely literary archetype. This on the one hand gives the play a currency beyond its relation to immediate events, but on the other makes its engagement with contemporary politics problematic.

The difficulties of these relationships become more acute in *The Ascent of F6* (1937). The play is more conventional than its predecessors in its sustained study of the personal psychology of the central figure and his obsession with conquering a mountain peak. The various elements – the political commentary and the fairy-tale archetype, the quest for personal salvation and the salvation of society – do not fuse and become mutually illuminating but compete uneasily for centrality in the play.

Auden and Isherwood's last play *On the Frontier* (1938) drops the extensive use of popular forms. As a result it loses the comic vitality of the earlier work and is simply dull. Its failure is on one level the failure of Auden and Isherwood to find a form which could encapsulate what turned out to be two conflicting agendas – personal concerns and engagement with contemporary politics. As a whole their *œuvre* is peculiar to the 1930s and that moment of theatrical and political history.

Eliot's sense of the function of verse in drama was somewhat different. 'The tendency of prose drama', he wrote, 'is to emphasise the ephemeral and superficial; if we want to get at the permanent and universal we tend to express ourselves in verse' ('A Dialogue on Dramatic Poetry', in T. S. Eliot, *Selected Essays*, 3rd edn, Faber, 1951, p 46). He would not have, as Auden and Isherwood had of the Group Theatre, a vision of the role of the 1930s theatre in the fight against fascism. Nor would his drama engage with the specific political context. Like Auden and Isherwood, though, the fragments which make up Eliot's unfinished 'Aristophanic melodrama' *Sweeney Agonistes* are in a contemporary idiom drawing its rhythms from popular music and, in particular, American jazz.

This was not a line Eliot was to follow. In *Murder in the Cathedral* (1935) he turned to the sort of historical subject matter, in this case the familiar story of the death of Thomas à Becket, which had been deemed suitable for verse drama throughout the nineteenth and early twentieth centuries. While Eliot's serious (as opposed to popular) modern verse forms are far from the pseudo-Elizabethanism which embellished Phillips's historicism, they are a consummate means of mediating the play's subject not in its historical detail but in its religious significance. The martyrdom and sacrifice of the archbishop are of course thematically central to Christian belief. But Eliot's real achievement is to re-present that action through the liturgical resonances of the verse so that the experience of the play in performance modulates from narrative to an enactment of Christian ritual in which the audience are potentially included as participants. The unifying conjunction of the form and the subject is such that Eliot can afford, without damage to the play, radically to fracture both the convention and the level of the experience when the four knights break abruptly into prose in their specious self-justification and cynical invocation of political pragmatism.

Critical regard for *Murder in the Cathedral* has endured better than it has for other similar plays, but this should not obscure the fact that Eliot's achievement can only be truly measured in relation to a vogue for the dramatization of religious and biblical material throughout the 1920s, 1930s and 1940s; for example, Masefield's (1878–1967) *The Trial of Jesus* (1926) and *The Coming of Christ* (1928), Charles Williams's (1886–1945) *Thomas Cranmer of Canterbury* (1936), Christopher Fry's (b. 1907) *The Boy with a Cart* (1938), and *Noah* by the French playwright André Obey (1892–1975), which was a success in 1935 with John Gielgud in the title role. One could also point to James Bridie's (1888–1951) very different retellings of biblical narratives in *Tobias and the Angel* (1930), *Jonah and the Whale* (1930) and *Susannah and the Elders* (1937). A late successor to *Murder in the Cathedral* is Ronald Duncan's (1914–82) ironically inverted hagiography *This Way to the Tomb* (1945).

Eliot achieved a match between form and material in *Murder in the Cathedral*, but his next play, *The Family Reunion* (1939), demonstrates the difficulties of marrying verse to a contemporary setting precisely located by the conventions of realist staging. The disjunction between some of the verse forms and the costuming of the characters and the dressing of the stage is heightened by the play's resemblance to the conventional weekend country-house murder mystery, that mainstay of twentieth-century commercial drama.

Some of the verse, especially that which mediates the prosaic surface of social ritual and everyday concerns, differs little from familiar conventions of stage prose and easily made characterization:

IVY: I shall have to stay till after the funeral: will my ticket to London still be valid?
GERALD: I do not look forward with pleasure to dealing with Arthur and John in the morning.

(Part 2, Scene 3)

The chauffeur and the policeman could come from any realist play which relied on the conventionally comic speech patterns which place working-class characters. Other similar passages, however, come across as nothing more than awkward, stilted prose:

> Nevertheless, Harry, best tell us as you can:
> Talk in your own language, without stopping to debate
> Whether it may be too far beyond our understanding.

(Part 1, Scene 1)

The confident jazz rhythms of what might have been Sweeney's reply seem in many ways a more effective medium precisely because they make no claim to be other than they are:

> I gotta use words when I talk to you,
> But if you understand or if you don't,
> That's nothing to me and nothing to you.
> We all gotta do what we gotta do.

('Sweeney Agonistes')

The formal problem facing Eliot is the relationship of the prosaic to the visionary verse which is also a problem of the relationship of different levels of experience in the play. The prosaic dialogue of Ivy and Gerald quoted above counterpoints another level of experience (supposedly deriving from Eliot's adaptation of Aeschylus' *Oresteia*) which is apprehended in the choric passage preceding it:

> We understand the ordinary business of living, . . .
> We are insured against fire, . . .
> But not against the act of God.

(Part 2, Scene 3)

At other points, the moment of transition to a more complex level of experience comes across as dislocation rather than juxtaposition:

> GERALD: That reminds me, Amy,
> When are the boys all due to arrive?

AMY: I do not want the clock to stop in the dark.
If you want to know why I never leave Wishwood
That is the reason. I keep Wishwood alive
To keep the family alive, to keep them together.

(Part 1, Scene 1)

This would not perhaps matter so much if Eliot had been able to find formal conventions which could contain and illuminate the dislocations. The change in function from the realistically represented grouping of aunts and uncles to a unison choric commentary is difficult to bring off precisely because the play's dominant realist mode makes it difficult to accept them as the latter. Similarly, the Eumenides may be sensed as a sort of brooding presence throughout the play, but Eliot himself subsequently admitted the failure of the various attempts to make their presence on stage work specifically as an effective stage image. Ultimately, Aeschylus merges uneasily with Edgar Wallace. Over and above Eliot's formal difficulties, the two modes present irreconcilable experiences: the murder mystery demands answers to very specific questions (Did Harry really kill his wife? If so, what was the motive?), whereas the play's essential action deals with a non-specific compulsion and guilt. Eliot overcomes some of these formal problems in his later plays – *The Cocktail Party* (1949), *The Confidential Clerk* (1953) and *The Elder Statesman* (1958) – by abandoning those elements which disturb the realist conventions of *The Family Reunion* – 'no chorus, and no ghosts' as Eliot said of *The Cocktail Party* ('Poetry and Drama', in T. S. Eliot, *On Poetry and Poets*, Faber, 1957, p 85). The effect is a disappointing accommodation of the plays to the conventional realist modes of theatre and playwriting to which they most closely approximate.

During the first half of the twentieth century, the throughline of the dominant forms of drama in English was to bypass the achievements of the Irish stage and of the revival of English verse drama in Auden and Isherwood, Eliot and their successor Christopher Fry. Ironically, the form Eliot took for his plays from *The Cocktail Party* onwards indicates that the real throughline would predominantly lie in a tradition of domestic realism, taking as its subject middle-class life. The tradition had of course been firmly established as a dominant mode by Edwardian dramatists before the First World War.

The tradition was of necessity subject to development, which superficially appears as an increasing sophistication and daring. But the actual process of the development is indicated at the very start of the period by the relationship of *The Second Mrs Tanqueray* to *Ghosts* and, as a process, it would continue beyond its close. The mainstream theatre was able to assimilate potential challenges to the social and moral orthodoxies it traditionally dealt in and re-present them in an acceptable form. Before the First World War the overt challenges of Shaw, Granville-Barker and Galsworthy were incorporated in spirit if not in substance, and the drama of the 1920s was prefigured by the plays of St John Hankin (1869–1909). His *The Return of the Prodigal* (1905) and *The Cassilis Engagement* (1907) left the surface of society intact, but flayed it with a cutting cynicism which neither Jones nor Pinero cared to muster.

In the 1920s itself, the process is apparent in the common treatment of the theme that was central to the society drama of Jones and Pinero – sexual misbehaviour. The following is from Somerset Maugham's (1874–1965) *The Circle* (1921):

TEDDIE: But I wasn't offering you happiness. I don't think my sort of life tends to happiness. I'm jealous. I'm not a very easy man to get on with. I'm often out of temper and irritable. I should be fed to the teeth with you sometimes, and so would you be with me. I daresay we'd fight like cat and dog – [*she turns to face him*] and sometimes we'd hate each other. Often you'd be wretched and bored stiff and lonely, and often you'd be frightfully homesick, and then you'd regret all you'd lost. Stupid women would be rude to you because we'd run away together. And some of them would cut you. I don't offer you peace and quietness. I offer you unrest and anxiety. I don't offer you happiness; I offer you love.

ELIZABETH [*stretching out her arms*]: You hateful creature, I absolutely adore you.

(Act 3)

The first half of Teddie's speech comes across as an anti-romantic realism, an inversion of a convention perhaps rather than the creation of a new one. But the second half shows how comprehensively a convention has been inverted. In Jones's *The Liars*, for instance, Sir Christopher Deering's account of the disadvantages of eloping is structurally central to that play's strategy of preserving conventional moral and social formations; here it specifically elicits Elizabeth's acceptance of Teddie's irregular proposal. Also in *The Liars* the mere fact that a man plans to have dinner with a married woman is sufficient to bring about a real threat of scandal and divorce. Frederick Lonsdale's (1881–1954) comedy *Spring Cleaning* (1925) opens with an illicit embrace interrupted by the butler, Walters. What in the society drama before the First World War had to be taken as serious because from it sprang the whole machinery of the plotting is here passed off as a matter of total inconsequence: 'Walters has had too much experience in the service of respectable families to even notice anything so trivial.' What the drama, like its pre-war predecessors, continued to offer was the thrill of the acceptably risqué; there is merely some alteration to the levels of what is acceptable. This change necessarily had an effect on certain sorts of plot expectation. The stage male, as Somerset Maugham ironically remarked,

can now have a girl to tea in his rooms without hopelessly compromising her, he can even kiss a pretty woman in a public place with the certainty that no one will come by and discover him, and he can leave indiscreet letters anywhere he likes without danger of their being found.

(W. Somerset Maugham, 'Preface' to *Plays: Volume V*,
Heinemann, 1934, p xii)

Such developments are, though, more cosmetic than structural.

What has altered in the mainstream drama is a question of its tone and a more nebulous sense of its style. Perhaps the style of the theatre and drama between the two world wars is embodied in the dressing gown and cigarette holder of Noel Coward's (1899–1973) public persona. It is inconceivable, I think, that Henry Arthur Jones could have written this exchange from *Private Lives* (1930) or, indeed, any exchange which dealt with sexual impropriety with Coward's lightness of touch and emotional detachment:

AMANDA: When we were together, did you really think I was unfaithful to you?

ELYOT: Yes, practically everyday.

AMANDA: I thought you were too; often I used to torture myself with visions of your bouncing about on divans with awful widows.

(Act 2)

The clipped prose of Coward's often inconsequential dialogue looks forward, in form if not in effect, to Pinter rather than back to the Edwardian settlement. In comparison the *raisonneurs*' set speeches in Jones and Pinero come across as ponderous verbosity, and the sober earnestness of the style Galsworthy continued into the 1920s in such plays as *The Skin Game* (1920) and *Loyalties* (1922) seems worthy but leaden.

Given the cataclysm of the First World War and political and economic events in Britain and abroad in the 1920s and 1930s, very few plays engaged with what might be thought of as these more serious issues. R. C. Sherriff (1896–1975) had a considerable success with a war drama, *Journey's End*, in 1928. The play, which centres on a group of officers during the build-up to a German attack, shows a fundamental ambivalence towards public school codes of behaviour, which are presented as irrelevant to the experience of trench warfare and at the same time necessary both to make it bearable and to continue its conduct. In comparison to *The Silver Tassie* it has not worn well. While there was a considerable body of documentary and fictional accounts of the effects of the depression and mass unemployment, the theatre showed little interest. Walter Greenwood's (1903–74) *Love on the Dole* (1934) was a noteworthy exception. Its enormous success was perhaps due to its representation of the working class as largely apolitical and comprised of conventionally colourful characters. Further, the play demonstrates that no answer can lie in political militancy (represented as futile and destructive); the resolution for the heroine does not lie there, but in her theatrically more familiar acceptance of the position of kept mistress, in this case to the wealthy but unappealing local bookmaker. Less compromising plays such as Joe Corrie's (1894–1968) *In Time o' Strife* (1929), which depicted the effects of the General Strike on Scottish mining communities, and Montagu Slater's (1902–56) *Stay Down Miner* (1936), which was about the 1935 pit-bottom sit-ins in South Wales, were characteristically ignored by mainstream theatre.

Indirectly, a sense of the needs arising from the national crises of the 1930s and 1940s found expression in Coward's patriotic pageant plays of twentieth-century British history, *Cavalcade* (1931) and *This Happy Breed* (written 1939, first staged 1942). The message of *Cavalcade* coincided with that of Ramsay MacDonald's National Government, that only through collective sacrifice and national unity could Britain pull through difficult times. Thus was constructed an image of a unified class structure which asserted the importance of the lower-middle and working class so long as its members kept to their own station and did their bit. Social class was quite clearly demarcated and represented by immediately obvious semiotic devices. In the 1940s this was to be a hallmark of the way in which official wartime propaganda constructed a notion of England and is clearly apparent in Coward's film *In Which We Serve* (1942). The central image is that of Captain Kinross (played by Coward) and a group of other ranks afloat on a raft in hostile waters and the action, intercut with flashbacks to the characters' domestic lives, sums up the values and virtues necessary for survival. J. B. Priestley's (1894–1984) *Desert Highway* (1943) transferred the action to the Syrian Desert and substituted a broken-down tank for the life raft. The play offers a highly conventional representation of working-class regional variety (the cockney, the Yorkshireman, the Welshman, etc.); initially a cause of conflict, the regional variety becomes a strength as the group bonds into what is a national rather than a class unity in the face of possible enemy attack.

The dominant mode of dramatic writing during the 1930s and 1940s continued to be the realist play presenting middle-class experience. However, in the plays of Priestley and Terence Rattigan (1911–1977) there is a significant shift downwards from the upper-middle classes of Jones and Pinero to a sort of professional middle-middle class: the schoolteacher in Rattigan's *The Browning Version* (1948), the professor in Priestley's *The Linden Tree* (1947). The family in Rattigan's *The Winslow Boy* (1946) represents, in contrast to the aristocracy of Jones and Wilde, a suburban, moderately wealthy, middle-class existence; further, the action of the play shows the family in conflict with establishment power rather than embodying it as Winslow fights to clear the name of his son who is wrongly accused of theft and consequently dismissed from the Navy. There is also, in *The Browning Version* and *The Linden Tree*, a sense of a middle class growing old, of becoming an irrelevance, and in Rattigan's *Separate Tables* (1954) the middle class are presented in decay, living out their days in a faded hotel in straitened economic and social circumstances. In this there is a sort of nostalgia, an implicit looking back to a previous age which predates the characters' present situations. The nostalgia is also implicit in the pre-1914 setting of plays like *The Winslow Boy* and Priestley's almost Chekhovian *Eden End* (1934).

What is more significant is the way in which the drama looks back in terms of its adherence to familiar realist forms. Notwithstanding the non-realist allegories of Priestley's *Johnson Over Jordan* (1939) and *They Came to a City* (1943), at the very end of the period under discussion Allardyce Nicoll could write with some considerable justification that 'the roots of the modern drama are set in Edwardian, even Victorian, soil . . . The styles dominant in 1949 ultimately may be traced back to those of 1900–10' ('Foreword' to Ernest Reynolds, *Modern English Drama: A Survey of the Theatre from 1900*, Harrap, 1949, p 5). Thus the second act of *The Winslow Boy* where a lawyer's gruelling interrogation is followed by the climactic statement that 'The boy is plainly innocent. I accept the brief' would have been familiar to any playgoer who had witnessed, forty-six years earlier, the third-act interrogation of Jones's *Mrs Dane's Defence* which climaxed with Sir Daniel Carteret's words, 'Woman, you're lying!' The realist form doesn't just offer a familiar experience but in many ways a comforting one, so that the potential disturbance of

Priestley's exploration of *outré* theories of parallel and serial time in *Dangerous Corner* (1932), *Time and the Conways* (1937) and *I Have Been Here Before* (1937) is contained and made familiar by the homely realism of those plays' settings. Ernest Reynolds was just one commentator who at the very mid-point of the century felt unable to detect any real innovation in the drama: 'At the time of writing [1949] not very much new ground is being broken by English playwrights, and there seems to be a serious shortage of dramatists of the younger generation with both fresh ideas and an ability to write for the theatre' (*Modern English Drama: A Survey of the Theatre from 1900*, Harrap, 1949, p 159). Formal experiment on the English stage in the mid- to late 1940s appeared to contemporaries to come from American dramatists toying with expressionist techniques: Thornton Wilder, Tennessee Williams, Arthur Miller.

When Kenneth Tynan gave an overview of the state of early 1950s drama, he wrote, 'To become eligible for detailed dramatic treatment, it was usually necessary either to have an annual income of more than three thousand pounds net or to be murdered in the house of someone who did' ('Summing Up: 1959', in *Curtains: Selections from the Drama Criticism and Related Writings*, Longmans, 1961, p 231). The remark is not so much valuable for its literal accuracy (which is open to question) as for its indication of a widespread feeling as to what was wrong with the theatre. The objection could just as easily have been made by those who wanted to expand the drama beyond the offerings of Jones and Pinero during the heyday of the Edwardian society drama. One might be forgiven for thinking nothing much had changed. What is surely under scrutiny is not just the class-determined subject matter of a drama, but a drama and theatre that are part of a class-determined cultural establishment. And into that establishment those who had once been perceived as threats – Ibsen, Shaw, Galsworthy, even Noel Coward who wrote the disconcertingly and unpleasantly shocking *The Vortex* (1924) – had been taken over and assimilated. None of the dramatists writing in 1950 seemed to offer any sort of real challenge. The challenge (or what was seen at the time as the challenge) to the class determinants of a conservative cultural establishment came in 1956 with John Osborne's *Look Back in Anger*. In retrospect Tynan's enthusiasm for *Look Back in Anger* – 'It is the best young play of its decade' (*Curtains: Selections from the Drama Criticism and Related Writings*, Longmans, 1961, p 132) – was not only predictable but as extravagant as the *Daily Telegraph*'s excoriation of *Ghosts* with which we began. Both are occasioned by precise moments of cultural and theatrical history which, while being part of a continuum, can be seen to mark the beginning and end of a significant period of modern English drama.

2

POETRY TO 1914

Catherine Koralek

'War Poetry', 'Thirties Poetry', 'Forties Poetry' are recognized literary historical terms. But what of the decade and a half before the First World War? It is nor 'Victorian', although a few eminent Victorians lingered; nor is it 'Modern', despite the presence of Yeats and Pound. The difficulty present-day critics have in giving these problematic years a label was anticipated by the poets themselves. Their persistent toying with group names – Imagist, Vorticist, Georgian – is some indication of their sense of historical uncertainty and individual inadequacy. The new generation of poets in the years 1900–14 seems unduly anxious to place itself in literary history, and to identify itself with a unifying literary cause.

Their self-doubt has infected the later criticism. For a start, there is the assumption that the period extending from 1900 to 1914 is richer in fiction than in poetry. The poets writing in these years are reputed to be 'minor' or 'slight'; they are either precursors of the 'real achievement' of this century, Modernism, or relics of the enfeebled Victorian age. Bernard Bergonzi, for example, summing up the poets of the period in the previous edition of the *Sphere History of English Literature*, writes:

They were inclined to the small-scale, unpretentious treatment of familiar subjects, and a poetic diction that was unelevated and which might, on occasion, even be vigorously colloquial.

(vol 7, p 37)

The present chapter aims to show that the widely applied label 'Georgian' means very little, and that the poets who did not really fall into the category deserve greater critical attention than they often seem to have been granted by previous surveys. Ezra Pound's appreciation of W. B. Yeats's *Responsibilities* should not be overlooked; nor should T. S. Eliot's fascination with Rudyard Kipling as a craftsman.

The ambitions of Edward Marsh's prefatory note to the first volume of *Georgian Poetry* in 1912 can hardly be described as 'small-scale':

This collection may, if it is fortunate, help the lovers of poetry to realise that we are at the beginning of another 'Georgian Period' which may take rank in due time with the several great poetic ages of the past.[1]

This bold optimism is, with hindsight, easy to mock. Even more absurdly excited is Lascelles Abercrombie's belief in the dawning of a new age:

What with modern science, modern philosophy, modern religion, modern politics and modern business, the present is a time fermenting with tremendous change ... the present resembles more the time of the pre-Socratic Greek philosophers ... than any other time.
    ('John Drinkwater: An Appreciation', *Poetry Review*, I, 1912, p 169, cited
                in Robert H. Ross, *The Georgian Revolt*, 1965, p 39)

The assumption of a Georgian identity, while it does seem to have exerted an attraction, does not stand up to scrutiny. There is certainly (as with most anthologies) a randomness about who is, or is not, included. A. E. Housman refused to participate, insisting that he was not part of a 'new era'; Pound was rejected, ironically, for not being 'modern' enough; Thomas Hardy was excluded; Edward Thomas's poetry was not yet quite under way; John Masefield only joined in after much persuasion; and the presence of D. H. Lawrence too confounds the notion of group solidarity. Reading through *Georgian Poetry 1911–1912*, one is struck more by its motley diversity than by any coherent, programmatic gathering of poems: subject matter and style are astonishingly various. Most familiar is Rupert Brooke's (1887–1915) self-satisfied chauvinism in 'The Old Vicarage, Grantchester':

> God! I will pack, and take a train,
> And get me to England once again!
> For England's the one land, I know,
> Where men with Splendid Hearts may go;
> And Cambridgeshire, of all England,
> The shire for Men who Understand.

While this is, in some ways, akin to Masefield's (1878–1967) rugged

---

1 *Georgian Poetry 1911–1912*. Poems included in the anthology are quoted from this edition.

adventurism in his Boys' Own 'Biography', it is certainly at odds with W. W. Gibson's (1878–1962) albeit unconvincing efforts at social realism in 'Geraniums':

> Stuck in a bottle on the window-sill,
> In the cold gaslight burning gaily red
> Against the luminous blue of London night.
> These flowers are mine: while somewhere out of sight
> In some black-throated alley's stench and heat,
> Oblivious of the racket of the street,
> A poor old weary woman lies in bed.

Here is ordinariness, although not as delicately evoked as it is in Walter de la Mare's (1873–1956) 'Miss Loo', which recalls unassumingly the sad and lonely leftovers from Victorian England, where ladies had 'satin bosoms'. The flashes of social detail he observes – 'large hands folded on the tray' and 'She made some small remark to me' – conjure up, through their very inconsequentiality, a distinct sense of time and place which Gibson's generalized squalor misses completely.

If de la Mare fits the definition, small-scale and unpretentious, T. Sturge Moore (1870–1944) and Gordon Bottomley (1874–1948) certainly do not. Both these poets indeed deserve to be remembered for contributing extraordinary literary oddities. Moore's 'A Sicilian Idyll' is a lengthy pastoral dialogue, whose awkward combination of the affected antique and attempted naturalism recalls the work of eighteenth-century hack translators:

> There rolls thy ball of worsted! Sit thee down;
> Come sit thee down, Cydilla,
> And let me fetch thy ball.

This certainly does not signal a new age. Bottomley's 'Babel: The Gate of God' cannot be described as small-scale, although it remains half-formed. The diction is idiosyncratic and the conception pretentiously epic; the disintegration of language it documents oddly anticipates *The Waste Land*:

> Birds molten, touchly talc veins bronze buds crumble
> Ablid ublai ghan isz rad eighar ghaurl . . .
> Words said too often seemed such ancient sounds
> That men forget them or were lost in them;
> The guttural glottis-chasms of language reached,
> A rhythm, a gasp, were curves of immortal thought.

In his 1962 anthology of *Georgian Poetry* James Reeves concentrates on the easy, deliberately limited scope of the Georgians and ignores these wilder extremes. Defending the poets against accusations of pedestrian sentimentality, Reeves maintains that their essential qualities are 'natural simplicity, emotional warmth, and moral innocence' (p xx). Yet his selection from their work is marked by images of death and decay, and pervaded by frequently macabre or disillusioned tones. If anything does indeed unite the 'Georgians', it is not the easy 'celebration of England', with its cottages and cricket: what recurs most noticeably in the poems of William Henry Davies, de la Mare, Ralph Hodgson, Andrew Young and Brooke is a preoccupation with the pleasures and sins of the flesh. Tones of disillusionment are mingled with the rhymes of the nursery: the short stanzas and tripping octosyllabic lines favoured by Davies (1871–1940), for example, give the poetry a veneer of gaiety that belies its subject matter. This conflict between manner and matter has been seen as one of the strengths of Housman (1859–1936) (Christopher Ricks, 'A. E. Housman: The Nature of His Poetry', *The Force of Poetry*, 1984, pp 163–78); in Davies's poetry the disagreement usually results in an unsatisfying uncertainty of tone.

Davies's 'A Dream' and Housman's 'Tell me not here' are both about a favourite figure, the enchantress, 'La Belle Dame Sans Merci'. Both poems see warmth disappearing from emotional experience and are confessions of moral guilt: there is little here of the fresh-faced zest welcomed by Reeves. Davies's poem is at once more overtly erotic and less haunting than either Keats's or Housman's. Housman is master of the grim understatement:

> For she and I were long acquainted
> And I knew all her ways.

Here 'acquainted' at once deceptively veils the lovers' intimacy and ominously foreshadows its brevity; 'all her ways' flickers ambivalently between admiration for, and even tenderness towards, the beloved's idiosyncrasies and mocking contempt for the betrayer's wiles. There is, by contrast, a trace of absurdity in Davies's close-up vision of attractive danger:

> I met her in the leafy woods,
>   Early a Summer night;
> I saw her white teeth in the dark,
>   There was no better light.

What would be a warning of a predatory nature is let down by glib rhymes and unconvincing exclamation:

> And what is this, how strange, how sweet!
>   Her teeth are made to bite
> The man she gives her passion to,
>   And not to boast their white.

Erotic experience is suggested with neither the languor of Housman's setting 'In aftermaths of soft September' or Keats's mystified fascination. Davies attempts to be frank, but succeeds only in evoking an elbow-nudging coarseness:

> When we lay down, she held me fast,
>   She held me like a leech;
> Ho, ho! I know what her red tongue
>   Is made for, if not speech.

Rupert Brooke's presentation of physical passion is cloyingly mismanaged for different reasons: hailed as a great intellectual and the new John Donne, Brooke struggles to philosophize about sexuality. 'Thoughts on the Shape of the Human Body' endeavours to explore the rift between soul and body, but leaves the reader only with an overwhelming impression of physical contortion:

> No perfection grows
> 'Twixt leg, and arm, elbow, and ear, and nose,
> And joint, and socket; but unsatisfied
> Sprawling desires, shapeless, perverse, denied.
> Finger with finger wreathes; we love, and gape,
> Fantastic shape to mazed fantastic shape,
> Straggling, irregular, perplexed, embossed,
> Grotesquely twined, extravagantly lost
> By crescive paths and strange protuberant ways
> From sanity and from wholeness and from grace.

Writhing limbs, clinging or sucking lips and blood are favourite images; sensual excess is indulged in with none of the verbal exactness of Keats. We do not have to be familiar with Brooke's biography to detect a lack of moral innocence. The loss of innocence is, in fact, the subject of Ralph Hodgson's (1871–1962) 'Eve' who is curiously presented as a nursery rhyme character, the victim of a childish game:

> Oh had our simple Eve
> Seen through the make-believe!

and Milton meets Mother Goose when it actually comes to the Fall:

> Oh what a clatter when
> Titmouse and Jenny Wren
> Saw him successful and
> Taking his leave!

This warping of an innocent childish world with sinister adult knowledge anticipates Auden's early poetry, but lacks his assurance and control: where Auden cunningly brings out latent horror in unexpected places, Hodgson – like Davies – awkwardly throws the childlike and the solemn together.

De la Mare frequently juxtaposes childhood and adult visions. He has indeed often been accused of being childish, concerned less with 'the real world' than with nursery teas, dreams and ghosts. His early volumes are indeed full of slumber, moonlight visions and flitting phantoms; the idiom is often archaic, and the picture of childhood sentimental. But Randall Jarrell comes to his defence:

It is easy to complain that de la Mare writes about unreality; but how *can* anyone write about unreality? From his children and ghosts one learns little about children and nothing about ghosts, but one learns a great deal of the reality of which both his ghosts and his children are projections, of the wishes and lacks and loves that have produced them.

(Randall Jarrell, *Poetry and the Age*, 1955, p 141)

Childhood experience in de la Mare's poems is often captured with disturbing exactness: the child's fascination with death is a recurrent theme. In the mock-heroic 'The Massacre', the child is presented in a ruthless act of senseless destruction as it mows down flowers:

> Lightly and dull fell each proud head,
>   Spikes keen without avail,
> Till swam my uncontented blade
>   With ichor green and pale.
>
> And silence fell: the rushing sun
>   Stood still in paths of heat,
> Gazing in waves of horror on
>   The dead about my feet.

The fantasy world which slaughters epic deities is met by heated nausea and self-disgust. 'Dry August Burned' too conveys the child's half-comprehension of death, and its morbid fascination with dead things: the child can be both grieved and almost callously dismissive. The poem opens with the alarming tranquillity of a still life which thinly conceals amid its ripe abundance the mouldy and the rank:

> Dry August burned. A harvest hare
> Limp on the kitchen table lay,
> Its fur blood-blubbered, eyes astare

The child's grief is pushed aside by her absorption in the violent energy of the soldiers. Her innocent enjoyment of the spectacle of destruction is transformed into a lust for blood:

> . . .   'Mother', she said,
> Her tear-stained cheek now flushed with red,
> 'Please, may I go and see it skinned?'

And yet the respectful politeness of request leaves a lingering uneasiness: the child, in all naivety, can ask for what the squeamish adult finds horrible as though she were asking for sweets.

Questioning and loss are recurrent features of de la Mare's poetry; he will often evoke the vividness and elusiveness of imaginary worlds. Many of the poems in *The Listeners* (1912) and *Peacock Pie* (1913) share the qualities of Edward Lear's or Lewis Carroll's nonsense verse; indeed, de la Mare's monograph on Carroll (1932) reveals his interest in the genre, which he defines as essentially English. These poems – like nursery rhymes – appeal to our enjoyment of the sinister or horrific; they are often mournfully comic, like 'Jim Jay':

> Do diddle di do,
> Poor Jim Jay
> Got stuck fast
> In Yesterday.

Here the comedy of the fat boy mingles with our fear about time passing. The image of being helplessly stuck, like the little Jellyby with his head between the railing, is inevitably funny:

> And stuck was Jim
> Like a rusty pin.

But the victim's plight is evoked with pathos:

> We pulled and we pulled
> From seven till twelve,
> Jim, too frightened
> To help himself.

The end of the poem glimpses his disappearance; the simple expression of pity merges with matter-of-fact reported statement:

> Come to-morrow,
>   The neighbours say,
> He'll be past crying for:
>   Poor Jim Jay.

The poem refuses to settle either to the world of fantasy invoked by the gibberish in line 1, or in the real world of neighbours and handkerchiefs; it avoids letting Jim Jay be an ordinary child by giving him an alliterative bird's name. De la Mare tells a good story and leaves the reader with a powerful sense of the unsatisfactory way in which we try to explain death. An example of the more overtly sombre side of his imagination is 'Never-to-be'. The King of Never-to-be is a kind of underworld 'Pobble who has no toes', an inhabitant of the vaguely Gothic adventure landscape of 'The Listeners':

> Grey-capped and muttering, mad is he –
> The childless King of Never-to-be;
> For all his people in the deep
> Keep, everlasting, fast asleep;
> And all his realm is foam and rain,
> Whispering of what comes not again.

The phantasmagoria, as in 'The Listeners', breathes loss. The intangible kingdom of 'foam and rain', the barely audible 'whispering', the certainty of it all slipping between the fingers reveal and touch anxieties about sleep and dreams, about the precariousness of our grasp of reality.

Whereas Hodgson seems to be falling back on nursery rhyme without a clear purpose, de la Mare reworks the idiom with coherence and force. 'The Song of the Mad Prince' adopts the rhythms and syntax of 'Who Killed Cock Robin?' with chilling keenness. The nonsensical juxtapositions have an ominous logic to them:

> Who said, 'Peacock Pie'?
>   The old King to the sparrow:
> Who said, 'Crops are ripe'?
>   Rust to the harrow.

Submerged suggestions of age, corruption, death and disintegration accumulate and come to a climax in the poised metrical disruption of the penultimate line:

> Who said, 'All Time's delight
>   Hath she for narrow bed;
>   Life's troubled bubble broken'? –
>   That's what I said.

The seemingly childlike framework of the poem contains elements of fantasy and reality. The exotic, romantic images of 'Green dusk for dreams,/Moss for a pillow' jar with the perhaps querulous, perhaps reassuring ordinariness of the stanzas' endings, 'That's what I said'. As Jarrell observed, the poem is about our very real preoccupation with unrealities.

De la Mare's claim for the Englishness of nonsense literature is not an original one, but it is none the less an example of what has been plausibly seen as a characteristic urge of the period 1880–1914: the desire to identify England and Englishness. John Lucas asserts that writers of the period are particularly anxious to define and capture national character, 'to stabilise an image' (John Lucas, *Modern English Poetry: From Hardy to Hughes*, 1986, p 10. Compare also Chapter 3, pp 50–69). Brooke's 'The Old Vicarage, Grantchester', with its predictable whimsy, reflects the search for comfort and stability at its most complacent. But Lucas goes on to accuse Kipling, Housman and Thomas of being 'weekend ruralists': what they write about, he argues, 'isn't really England at all, but a mythic land'. This assumption – that the 'real' and the 'mythic' Englands are readily separable – is perhaps unjustly simplistic.

Kipling's (1869–1936) England is a strongly realized physical presence, as a comparison between his poem 'Sussex' (1902) and Brooke's 'The Chilterns' makes clear. Brooke's landscape is unspecific:

> The autumn road, the mellow wind
>   That soothes the darkening shires,
>   And laughter, and inn-fires.
>
> White mist about the black hedgerows,
>   The slumbering Midland plain,
> The silence where the clover grows,
>   And the dead leaves in the lane,
>   Certainly these remain.

There is nothing recognizably 'Midland' about this soft-focus view. The image here is for advertising or for tourists who do not know the place, as the easy vocabulary indicates: 'mellow', 'mist', 'shires' and 'inns'. Kipling's picture of the Downs, though, is rhythmically energetic and verbally precise:

No tender-hearted garden crowns,
  No bosomed woods adorn
Our blunt, bow-headed, whale-backed Downs,
  But gnarled and writhen thorn –
Bare slopes where chasing shadows skim,
  And, through the gaps revealed,
Belt upon belt, the wooded, dim,
  Blue goodness of the Weald.

The carefully sustained stubbornness of Kipling's adjectives reflect the enduring nature of what they describe, and their Anglo-Saxon etymology enforces a reminder of the land's past. Kipling is not so naive as to pretend that a country is merely its landscape, but tacitly insists that it is inseparable from – indeed, is – its history, its mythic identity. (More recently, Geoffrey Hill's concern with what Coleridge terms 'the spiritual, Platonic Old England' makes an illuminating comparison. The contemporary reality he presents reveals time past to be unmistakably present: 'Weightless magnificence upholds the past' ('An Apology for The Revival of Christian Architecture', *Tenebrae*, 1978).) 'Sussex', like Housman's 'On Wenlock Edge', at once recalls earlier occupiers of England and asserts the literal embodiment of past national experience in the land. The 'chasing shadows' of the downland are partly caused by the mounds and hollows of old forts and camps, ghosts of Roman and Saxon Britain:

> The barrow and the camp abide
> The sunlight and the sward.

The rhyming pun 'sward/sword' reminds that the green grass has been suffered for and fought for.

Kipling has suffered more than most at the hands of crassly ideological criticism. He remains in the popular mind, as Randall Jarrell puts it, 'someone people used to think was wonderful, but we know better than that now' ('On Preparing to Read Kipling: The Best Short Stories of Kipling', 1961, *Kipling, Auden and Co.*, 1980, p 332); he is *the* imperialist poet – repressive, narrow-minded and arrogant. Actually reading the poems, one is struck neither by the unthinking patriotism voiced in 'The Old Vicarage, Grantchester', nor by a celebration of English power abroad: what emerges instead is a lament for failed ideals and a vision of human frailty. Take 'A Song of the English' (1893), for example. The start of the poem is a rousing, complacent public school exhortation to imperial power, war and duty:

> *Fair is our lot – O goodly is our heritage!*
> *(Humble ye, my people, and be fearful in your mirth!)*
> > *For the Lord our God Most High*
> > *He hath made the deep as dry,*
> *He hath smote for us a pathway to the ends of all the Earth!*

But this is stated in italics and detached from the rest of the poem. A quieter, more worldly voice tells the reader:

> *Hear now a song – a song of broken interludes –*
> *A song of little cunning; of a singer nothing worth.*
> > *Through the naked words and mean*
> > *May ye see the truth between,*
> *As the singer knew and touched it in the ends of all the Earth!*

The singer's experience, for all its range and zest, results only in worthlessness, brokenness and meanness. The truth between 'the naked words' which the poem points to, is that men yearn for more than they can have, and are destroyed by their foolish, tragic, heroic ventures. The desire for empire is a delusive one; they are dreamers who seek it; faith in it is hollow; and yet it continues to lure with siren-like power:

We were dreamers, dreaming greatly, in the man-stifled town;
We yearned beyond the sky-line where the strange roads go down.
Came the Whisper, came the Vision, came the Power with the Need,
. . . Then the wood failed – then the food failed – then the last water dried –
In the faith of little children we lay down and died.
On the sand-drift – on the veldt-side – in the fern-scrub we lay,
That our sons might follow after by the bones on the way.

This section of 'A Song of the English', 'The Song of the Dead', conveys both the irresistible urge to explore and conquer and the dream's inevitable end in disaster. The rhythmic pressure, the internal rhymes and repetitions, suggest at once the compulsive strength of the 'Vision', and the certainty of defeat: 'Then the wood failed – then the food failed – then the last water dried'. The regular drum beat itself collapses in the final phrase: the initial confidence has disintegrated. 'The Song of the Dead' concludes not with encouragement, but with a grim warning: 'By the bones about the wayside ye shall come to your own!'

The 'Vision' referred to above is not simply a vision of English glory and power abroad: it is a vision of the Golden Age. Kipling yearns for a world linked by common understanding, prosperity and peace, as does Pope in *Windsor Forest*, where 'seas but join the regions they divide', or Dryden in *Annus Mirabilis*:

> The Ebbs of Tydes, and, their mysterious flow,
>   We, as Arts Elements shall understand.
> And as by Line upon the Ocean go,
>   Whose paths shall be familiar as the land.
>
> Instructed ships shall sail to quick Commerce;
>   By which remotest Regions are alli'd:
> Which makes one City of the Universe
>   Where some may gain, and all may be suppli'd.

'The Song of the Banjo' presents the creation of this 'one City of the Universe' as the Mission of the bard:

> So I draw the world together link by link:
>   Yea, from Delos up to Limerick and back!

And yet this too is revealed as an unattainable goal: the banjo has power to move, to promote enjoyment and wisdom, to praise and blame,

> But the Song of Lost Endeavour that I make,
>   Is it hidden in the twanging of the strings?

The dreamer who 'yearned beyond the sky-line' is not simply a Victorian empire-builder: he is a recurrent feature of our imagination and can be traced back to the Anglo-Saxon 'Seafarer' and Marvell's 'Bermudas'. None the less, the seafarer is particularly in evidence in the nineteenth and early twentieth centuries, whether it be in the guise of Tennyson's 'Ulysses' or Masefield's bluff, melancholic navigator, 'I must down to the seas again, to the lonely sea and the sky', or Kipling's restless Vikings in 'Harp Song of the Dane Women'. Part of the poets' fascination lies in the appeal of the mysterious kingdom under water. Partly inspired, perhaps, by Tennyson's 'The Kraken', Kipling's 'The Deep-Sea Cables' (in 'A Song of the English') reflects the stimulus of a primeval, unconquerable world which washes over and erodes human endeavour:

> The wrecks dissolve above us; their dust drops down from afar –
> Down to the dark, to the utter dark, where the blind white sea-snakes are.
> There is no sound, no echo of sound, in the deserts of the deep,
> Or the great grey level plains of ooze where the shell-burred cables creep.
>
> Here in the womb of the world – here on the tie-ribs of earth
>   Words, and the words of men, flicker and flutter and beat –
> Warning, sorrow, and gain, salutation and mirth –
>   For a Power troubles the Still that has neither voice nor feet.

They have wakened the timeless Things; they have killed their father Time;
   Joining hands in the gloom, a league from the last of the sun.
Hush! Men talk to-day o'er the waste of the ultimate slime,
   And a new Word runs between: whispering, 'Let us be one!'

One of Kipling's earliest critics, Dowden, noted in 1901 the romanticism inherent in the urge to explore: 'The passion for adventure, which drove Defoe's forlorn hero away from the hearth and home still lives in English hearts' (Edward Dowden, 'The Poetry of Mr Kipling', *New Liberal Review* XXXVIII, February 1901, in Roger Lancelyn Green, ed., *Kipling: The Critical Heritage*, 1971, p 268). The lure of abroad, of 'strange roads' has a long history in English literature. Pope (anticipating the wealth of Masefield's 'Cargoes') relishes the exotic beauty and warmth of the Indies in *Windsor Forest*:

> For me the Balm shall bleed, and Amber flow,
> The Coral redden, and the Ruby glow,
> The pearly shell its lucid Globe infold,
> And Phoebus warm the ripening Ore to Gold.

Warm climates, as Byron reminds us, offer liberation to withdrawn Northern souls, but whereas the Romantic poets hanker after the Mediterranean, this later generation was able to seek release in the East. The speaker in Tennyson's 'Locksley Hall', with his idealized view of the the far-away, anticipates Kipling in 'Mandalay':

>   Ah, for some retreat
> Deep in yonder shining Orient, where my life began to beat;
> . . .
> Or to burst all links of habit – there to wander far away,
> On from island unto island at the gateways of the day.
> . . .
> There the passions cramp'd no longer shall have scope and breathing space.

'Mandalay' uses the experience of the Londoner abroad as a vehicle for similarly romantic desires for the perfect existence, for an escape from 'the weariness, the fever and the fret'.

> I am sick o' wastin' leather on these gritty pavin'-stones,
> An' the blasted English drizzle wakes the fever in my bones;
> Tho' I walks with fifty 'ousemaids outer Chelsea to the Strand,
> An' they talks a lot o' lovin', but wot do they understand?
>   Beefy face an' grubby 'and –
>   Law! wot do they understand?
>   I've a neater, sweeter maiden in a cleaner, greener land!
>   On the road to Mandalay . . .

It would be misguided to read the poem as a celebration of empire; the poem's poignancy lies rather in its expression of the simple human misconception that elsewhere the grass is greener. Conversely, the speaker in 'The Roman Centurion's Song' is happy where he is: he has become used to a life of exile and welcomes the 'changeful Northern Skies'. These two poems reflect two opposing impulses of a poet who never really had a native land: on the one hand is the irrepressible desire to travel, to explore the unknown, and on the other the need for comforting familiarity. The Roman centurion rejects abstract nationalism in favour of experience. It is nothing as arbitrary as birth which creates one's native land, but rather custom:

> Here where men say my name was made, here where my work was done;
> Here where my dearest dead are laid – my wife – my wife and son;
> Here where time, custom, grief and toil, age, memory, service, love,
> Have rooted me in British soil. Ah, how can I remove?

The tree metaphor suggests our permanent relationship with the Roman: we are his heirs. Housman makes the same point more deliberately in 'On Wenlock Edge', where Roman occupier is physically related to modern Briton.

> The blood that warms an English yeoman,
> The thoughts that hurt him, they were there.

Housman also uses the image of the tree to convey the process of heredity:

> The tree of man was never quiet:
> Then 'twas the Roman, now 'tis I.

Like the family tree, the woods link past and present: man and nature share a common history of turbulence.[1]

Kipling's preoccupation with roaming and distant lands is comparable to de la Mare's constant explorations of the realms of dreams and romance, fantasy and nonsense. (Both, of course, wrote a great deal for children.) These poets respond to what is remote and inaccessible, whether it be their own youth and infancy, imperial greatness, mastery of the sea, or imaginary places. Kipling's 'The Way Through the Woods' laments the passing of something valued and nearly magical: the 'road' has a fairy-tale quality to it, it takes us 'through' the woods, and not to any known destination; its mythical nature is tempered with the actuality suggested by natural detail:

1 Masefield's poem, 'On Malvern Hill', relates a similar episode from the Roman occupation of Britain, but fails to link the past with our present.

> It is underneath the coppice and heath
> And the thin anemones.

(Like the 'road to Mandalay', this road exists primarily in the imagination: 'there ain't no 'buses runnin' from the Bank to Mandalay'.) Compared to de la Mare's 'The Listeners', however, where the setting is vividly realized but distinctly part of an incantatory dream-world, the setting of 'The Way Through the Woods' is more or less mundane. The conversational matter-of-factness of the opening, the ambiguous metre and unobtrusive rhyme give the poem an inconsequential air; there is nothing obviously awe-inspiring or unreal:

> They shut the road through the woods
> Seventy years ago.
> Weather and rain have undone it again,
> And now you would never know
> There was once a road through the woods
> Before they planted the trees.

Kipling creates a definite sense of familiarity in the first two lines, but allows a nostalgic vagueness to impinge in line 6, with the unspecified 'Before'. The animal world is introduced casually carrying out its natural functions, 'the otter whistles his mate', and 'the ring-dove broods,/And the badgers roll at ease'. But these details also build an idyll of tranquillity and freedom, which is acknowledged in the second stanza, 'Yet, if you enter the woods'. The sober, restrained dactyls of lines 3–7 in stanza 1, 'Weather and rain have undone it again', are transformed into excited anapaests in stanza 2, 'When the night-air cools on the trout-ringed pools'. The internal rhymes force the reader to acknowledge 'the beat of a horse's feet'; to hear the existence of the road. The metre slows down and gradually returns to the rhythms of speech, although the romantic images momentarily linger:

> Steadily cantering through
> The misty solitudes.

The last line – almost, as it were, an appendix to the poem – returns to normality: childlike vexation and disappointment mingle with the adult's reluctant resignation or brusque acceptance. The fact that the last line is extraneous to the body of the poem, however, leaves the imagination room to entertain the possibility of the road's existence; and the ellipsis makes a space for it:

> The old lost road through the woods . . .
> But there is no road through the woods.

The tension between romantic vision and reality is particularly striking in Yeats's (1865–1939) poetry at this period. Leavis's astonishment at the contrast between *The Wind Among the Reeds* (1899) and *The Green Helmet* (1910) reflects this change in literary direction:

It is hard to believe that the characteristic verse of the later volume comes from the same hand as that of the earlier. The new verse has no incantation, no dreamy hypnotic rhythm; it belongs to the actual waking world, and is in the idiom and movement of modern speech . . . It is like an awakening out of drugs, a disintoxication; the daylight seems thin and cruel.

(F. R. Leavis, *New Bearings in English Poetry*, 1950, p 42)

Pound, reviewing *Responsibilities* in 1914, similarly welcomes the poetry for its new quality of light: 'We have had so many other pseudo-glamours and glamourlets and mists and fogs since the nineties that one is about ready for hard light' (Ezra Pound, 'Poetry', May 1914, in A. Norman Jeffares, ed., *Yeats: The Critical Heritage*, 1977, pp 186–9). One need only glance at the contents pages of Yeats's 1890s collections ('A Faery Song', 'The Man who Dreamed of Faeryland', 'Into the Twilight', 'He tells of perfect beauty') and set them against the titles in *The Green Helmet* or *Responsibilities* ('The Fascination of What's Difficult', 'At the Abbey Theatre', 'A Friend's Illness', 'On Those that Hated "The Playboy of the Western World" 1907') to hear the new tone. With this shift in tone comes new subject matter: Yeats moves away from the legendary past of Ireland, from heroes of fairy tale, and writes instead about his world of politics and letters. The fictitious wandering Aengus and his crew no longer dominate, but are joined by a cast of real people – Maud Gonne, Major Robert Gregory, the Markewiecz sisters.

Edward Thomas (1878–1917) admired Yeats's prose for its 'fine voice, at once mobile, capable of magnificent monotone' ('As the Wings of a Dove', *The Week's Survey*, 13 August 1904, in A. Norman Jeffares, ed., *Yeats: The Critical Heritage*, 1977, pp 146–9). Yeats and Thomas (like Kipling in his dramatic monologues) are both preoccupied with the sounds of the spoken word. Yeats's development away from a lulling 'poetic' sound towards a grumpier, recognizably *speaking* voice reflects this, as does Thomas's individual tone that captures the tentative movement of thought and remembrance.

Thomas's poems often open with a line that could easily be part of a prose description:

> The green elm with the one great bough of gold
>> ('October')
>
> The long small room that showed willows in the west
>> ('The Long Small Room')
>
> Half of the grove stood dead.
>> ('Ash Grove')

Thomas characteristically begins a poem *in medias res*, as though the poet has already been in conversation with you, or thinking unuttered thoughts. The subtle force of his first lines relies partly on a strong sense of what takes place before the poem, as though his utterances are pushed out by the silent pressure of thought:

> There they stand, on their ends, the fifty faggots
>> ('Fifty Faggots')
>
> And you, Helen, what should I give you?
>> ('Helen')
>
> Women he liked, did shovel-bearded Bob
>> ('Bob's Lane')
>
> Thinking of her had saddened me at first
>> ('Celandine')
>
> Yes, I remember Adlestrop.
>> ('Adlestrop')

Leavis's discussion of Thomas concentrates on this imitation of speech:

A characteristic poem of his has the air of being a random jotting down of chance impressions and sensations, the record of a moment of relaxed and undirected consciousness. The diction and movement are those of quiet, ruminative speech.

> (*New Bearings in English Poetry*, 1950, p 69)

The poems indeed have the air of randomness, but Thomas's careful revisions show this not to be the case. How is this illusion created and sustained?

'Bob's Lane' opens as though the poet is in the middle of a conversation about a recently dead farmer:

> Women he liked, did shovel-bearded Bob,
> Old Farmer Hayward on the Heath, but he
> Loved horses. He himself was like a cob,
> And leather-coloured. Also he loved a tree.

The conversational, fragmentary syntax presses delicately against the quatrain; the final sentence, 'Also he loved a tree', emerges as an unstudied afterthought; just another contribution to the collective memory of Bob; yet it quietly, almost secretively completes the stanza. Thus Thomas suggests that Bob's love of trees sums him up; it is his *raison d'être*. The imitation of 'ruminative speech' is also sustained by Thomas's combination of simple and complex syntax: the straightforward brevity of 'Also he loved a tree' or 'No one was to blame' simply and directly acknowledges truth. By contrast, the inverted word order in stanza 3 – 'To name a thing beloved man sometimes fails' – through its halting and reluctant movement towards the main verb, 'fails', enacts the difficulty of fulfilling the desire to name. The line begins in hope and unfolds unwillingly to admit the inevitable disappointment. The failure is made to matter more than it would have had Thomas dismissed it with the genuine casualness that would result from the more natural word order: 'Man sometimes fails to name a beloved thing.' The pattern of this line is representative in miniature of the poem's structure: the truth of the matter is not reached until the end. The poet's circumstances are revealed in the final stanza: he is not in conversation, but alone; Bob is long dead, and probably forgotten by most. Only through word order does the poet's isolation become clear.

The track, we are told, is abandoned, and yet the poet's knowledge of it betrays his own solitary passing there:

> Many years since, Bob Hayward died, and now
> None passes there because the mist and the rain
> Out of the elms have turned the lane to slough
> And gloom, the name alone survives, Bob's Lane.

The final naming of the track is a tiny triumph. While it partly counteracts the failure remarked on in the preceding stanza – the name, after all, survives (like Larkin's half-heartening, half-disappointed assertion, 'What will survive of us is love') – it also records inadequacy: the name is all that is left; the thing itself has gone. Nothing concrete or substantial endures; the life that Bob loved in 'living things' disappears.

'And yet I like the names': Thomas's poetry is obsessed with names, with simply listing them, with remembering them, with discovering why things are named in the way they are. His comments on Hardy, for example, reflect this interest:

I prefer Mr Hardy's poems to his novels, and there the place-names offer many pleasures and provoke several kinds of curiosity. Sometimes the place is given, it appears, out of pure fidelity to the fact. He writes no poetry that could suffer by names and dates.

> (Edna Longley, ed., *A Language Not to be Betrayed: Selected Prose of*
> *Edward Thomas*, 1981, p 74)

In Clare, by contrast, Thomas feels that the fascination threatens the poetry: 'He often wrote long formless pieces full of place-names'. Like 'Bob's Lane', 'Old Man' presents the importance of names while suggesting their inadequacy: names are delighted in, but are not substitutes for the things themselves. The poem's opening apparently asserts the irrelevance of names, only to undermine the assertion:

> Old Man, or Lad's-love, – in the name there's nothing
> To one that knows not Lad's-love, or Old Man.

The teasing insistence on the names, together with the odd, half-contradictory relationship between the alternatives, alerts us to their elusive importance. They 'Half *decorate*, half *perplex*, the thing it is' [emphasis added]; they seem partly optional extras – ornaments – and partly things obstructing the poet from understanding the plant itself. The failure of perfect recall recorded in the poem is a failure to name – or understand – experience. The obliterating string of negatives in the last line culminates in the frightening chasm of the permanently unknown: 'Only an avenue, dark, nameless, without end.' An earlier draft of this final line interestingly reads, 'Only an avenue dark without end or name.' Ending the poem with an assertion of engulfing endlessness dizzies the reader: a heightened consciousness of the poem's finite nature intensifies our inability to imagine infinity. Naming the avenue (like Bob's Lane), would give it comforting limits, would put it within the frame of human under-standing, within the poet's grasp. Thomas often seems to be following Shakespeare's definition of the poet's task in *A Midsummer Night's Dream*:

> And as imagination bodies forth
> The forms of things unknown, the poet's pen
> Turns them to shapes, and gives to airy nothing
> A local habitation and a name.

The failure to name the avenue leaves it a taunting 'airy nothing' and reveals the limits of the imagination.

Habitation and name are closely linked in Thomas's imagination. Names are the way in which poets reach places or things and Thomas, like Clare, delights in listing the names of local habitations:

> I'll buy Codham, Cockridden and Childerditch,
> Roses, Pyrgo and Lapwater

('Bronwen')

> Margaretting or Wingle Tye
> Or it might be Skreens, Gooshays, or Cockerells,
> Shellow, Rochetts, Bandish, or Pickerells,
> Martins, Lambkins, or Lillyputs.

('Merfyn')

But they are only substitutes: 'What I saw/Was Adlestrop – only the name.'

In 'Lob', Thomas brings together ideal habitation and namer. Lob, like the poet, is the namer of parts and an essential part of the place. Like 'Old Man', 'Lob' begins with a quest for an unnamed, nearly unlocated 'something':

> At hawthorn-time in Wiltshire travelling
> In search of something chance would never bring,
> An old man's face, by life and weather cut
> And coloured, – rough, brown, sweet as any nut, –
> A land face, sea-blue-eyed, – hung in my mind
> When I had left him many a mile behind.

Thomas seeks a corporeal identity for the elusive image, but local ordinary attempts to name the face are inappropriate.

> ''Tis old Bottlesford
> He means, Bill.' But another said: 'Of course,
> It was Jack Button up at the White Horse.'

The identity of Lob defies naming or placing, temporal or spatial. He belongs to an unspecified age and place – 'the spiritual Platonic Old England' – and refuses to be pinned down to any one person, but lives instead in the popular imagination:

> He sounds like one I saw when I was a child
> I could almost swear to him. The man was wild
> And wandered. His home was where he was free.
> Everybody has met one such man as he.

His abundant names are the names of the child's nursery tales, of legendary and historical figures, of anonymous characters and of plants. He is a kind of irrepressible Everyman, the source and protagonist of folk tale, the inventor of proverbs and common lore. He provides a bridge between the natural world and literary creation, giving poets the names they use:

> And when at eight years old Lob-lie-by-the-fire
> Came in my books, this was the man I saw.
> He has been in England as long as dove and daw,
> Calling the wild cherry tree the merry tree,
> The rose campion Bridget-in-her-bravery;
> And in a tender mood he, as I guess,
> Christened one flower Live-in-idleness,
> And while he walked from Exeter to Leeds
> One April called all cuckoo-flowers Milkmaids.
> . . .
> The man you saw, – Lob-lie-by-the-fire, Jack Cade,
> Jack Smith, Jack Moon, poor Jack of every trade,
> Young Jack, or old Jack, or Jack What-d'ye-call,
> Jack-in-the-hedge, or Robin-run-by-the-wall,
> Robin Hood, Ragged Robin, lazy Bob,
> One of the lords of No Man's Land, good Lob, –
> Although he was seen dying at Waterloo,
> Hastings, Agincourt, and Sedgemoor, too, –
> Lives yet. He never will admit he's dead
> Till millers cease to grind men's bones for bread.

Lob's spirit, though elusive, is given some solidity. He is part of the landscape, 'English as this gate, these flowers, this mire'. Like Lob, his historian, the speaker in the central part of the poem, is a curiously indefinable mixture of humanity and vegetation: 'With this he disappeared/In hazel and thorn tangled with old-man's beard.'

Lob is both a part of the historical and mythical pasts, and a contemporary, 'now a Wiltshireman': he is a kind of embalmed essence of people and places English. Thomas is frequently concerned to preserve the apparently ephemeral: particular moments, seasons, weathers, 'the dust on the nettles'. He turns to the most fragile and unenduring things, and finds in them images of permanence. In 'Bright Clouds' the delicate, transient clouds of may-blossom are both precariously short-lived and powerfully unchanging: 'Still the may falls.' In 'Haymaking', a poem about the most fleeting of rural labours, to be done only on the rare occasions when the sun shines, the moment is captured and given permanence. The scene seems eternal and unchanging, like a painting:

> The tosser lay forsook
> Out in the sun; and the long waggon stood
> Without its team; it seemed it never would
> Move from the shadow of that single yew.

The poem's ending anticipates a future where the scene will seem antiquated and where its characters will have 'gone out of the reach of change', yet the image remains immortal. Thomas also reaches back into the nation's past: his poem is able to preserve something because it describes something which in itself is a preserve, an actual moment and an archetypal moment:

> All was old,
> This morning time, with a great age untold,
> Older than Clare and Cowper, Morland and Crome,
> Than, at the field's far edge, the farmer's home,
> A white house crouched at the foot of a great tree;
> Under the heavens that know not what years be
> The men, the beasts, the trees, the implements
> Uttered even what they will in times far hence –
> All of us gone out of the reach of change –
> Immortal in the picture of an old grange.

The quirks and details of English weather and seasonal change are central to the accuracy and reality of Thomas's vision of an archetypal or mythical England. 'The Manor Farm', like 'Haymaking', begins with a pictorial exactness which conveys rural tranquillity and un-laboured harmony:

> I came down to the old Manor Farm,
> And church and yew-tree opposite, in age
> Its equals and in size. Small church, great yew,
> And farmhouse slept in Sunday silentness
> The air raised not a straw.

Thomas creates an almost idealized image of decorum, peace and stability. But his eye for detail ruffles it slightly. Winter refuses to be wintry; the horses seem to have stepped out of summer:

> There was no sound but one.
> Three cart horses were looking over a gate
> Drowsily through their forelocks, awishing their tails
> Against a fly, a solitary fly.

The reality of the observation leads Thomas to transcend the seasonal cycle; the term 'season' is no longer purely temporal:

> But it was not winter –
> Rather a season of bliss unchangeable
> Awakened from farm and church where it had lain
> Safe under tile and thatch for ages since
> This England, Old already, was called Merry.

The tentative, backwards movement through the cliché indicates Thomas's mixture of reassurance and uncertainty: does the Manor Farm momentarily reveal a world irrecoverably lost or return it to us?

It is Thomas's observation of a vivid present, combined with his consciousness of the past's importance, which gives his poetry its individual air of physical reality tinged with imaginative speculation. The assurance with which Adlestrop is realized, for example, is transferred into the poem's last line: nobody doubts, briefly at least, that Thomas heard *all* the birds of Oxfordshire and Gloucestershire. If he successfully creates an image of 'Old England', it is through sensitivity to its particularities and his appreciation of the way legendary ideals have grown out of real things.

'How is it possible for a writer to be at the same time so poetic and so casual?' (Unsigned review in *The Athenaeum*, 1910, in R. G. Cox, ed., *Hardy: The Critical Heritage*, 1970). That the question could have been asked of Thomas, or Yeats, or, as it was, in fact, of Hardy (1840–1928), perhaps alerts us to the dominant tone of our period's poetry: a tone of artful informality. Part of an answer can be found in the title of Hardy's 1914 collection, *Satires of Circumstance*. Circumstance and all its seemingly insignificant attendant detail provide a constant source of imaginative stimulation for Hardy. His poems are full of casual, circumstantial stuff: place, time, clothes, furniture, what was said, what was done, eaten or played on the piano. They share in many of the qualities of the novel, and are often little compressed pieces of human experience, stories in miniature.

'Beyond the Last Lamp (Near Tooting Common)' was first published under the title 'Night in a Suburb'. Thomas particularly admired Hardy's use of place-names, and his comments are helpful:

[*The names*] if anything, emphasise the littleness, yet save it from abstraction ... The general effect of using local names with no significance for the stranger, and no special private value of sound or association for the poet, ... the general effect is to aid reality by suggestion of gross and humble simplicity.

(in R. G. Cox, ed., *Hardy: The Critical Heritage*, 1970, p 75)

The casual precision of the second title brings added poignancy to
the vision of middle-aged lovers. As Thomas suggests, the slightness
of the poem's content is emphasized. Hardy is almost asking, 'How
could Tooting Common, of all places, be significant or poetic?' But
conversely, while the universality of the subject matter is diminished
– the action did not happen in any suburb, but in Tooting – the
poet's powers of observation and depth of feeling are intensified: his
range extends even to Tooting Common. A couple of people in a
little-known place on the periphery of human affairs have been
remarked by the poet's keen eye. Tooting Common may be unimportant to the indifferent eyes of the President of the Immortals, but
Hardy is 'a man who noticed such things'. The name also makes the
reader believe in the experience's documentary actuality: the location
of the pair firmly in 'time and place', even though they themselves
are 'blinded' to it, gives us a sense of historical accuracy, and
reminds us that time and place are irrelevant to suffering – like
Larkin's 'nothing', it happens anywhere. The suburban setting is
important in another way: it sets the action beyond civilization, in a
kind of No Man's Land, 'Beyond the Last Lamp'. The loiterers are
outside where it is comfortable to live, beyond the reach of modern
comforts in a place of night and rain and 'wild woe'; almost, indeed,
an urban Egdon Heath.

Like place, weather plays a characteristically central role in the
poem. While heightening the couple's emotional bleakness, it creates
the impression that their unknown sorrow could almost be an optical
illusion, a trick of the weather. Their faces are inevitably wet,
blinded by tears or rain; they are 'wan, downcast' both because of
their suffering and because their faces are lit only by the distant
'lamplight's yellow glance'. The lovers' grief becomes part of Hardy
the poet-observer's own tragic experience. The syntactical ambiguity
of the first stanza:

> Beyond the last lone lamp I passed
>   Walking slowly, whispering sadly,
>   Two linked loiterers, wan, downcast;

allows the speaker to share the slowness and the sadness; like the
rain, it seeps into both spectator and protagonist. The very act of
remembering is itself presented as a rain-drenched one:

> Though thirty years of blur and blot
> Have slid since I beheld that spot.

For Hardy, like Feste, 'the rain it raineth every day'. Time is represented as a constant obliterator and obscurer, moving unstoppably and almost imperceptibly, like rain on glass. Hardy's suffering as a writer is also evoked: the almost vindictive rhyme 'blot/spot' suggests the difficulties and frustrations of writing, and the alliteration 'bl/bl/sl' effects an aural equivalent of ink spreading through wet paper while conjuring up an image of tears smudging ink.

The determination with which rain – and with it suffering and time – pushes its way through all human affairs is powerfully displayed in 'During Wind and Rain'. The casual, fragmentary structure of the poem perhaps takes its keynote of unsentimental melancholy from Feste's painfully shoulder-shrugging refrain, 'With hey, ho, the wind and the rain'. Reading the poem is not unlike looking through an old photograph album where nothing is fully annotated and some of the pictures are torn at the edges, giving only 'a glimpse of the bay'. The characters' actions and moods are vividly – and yet, it seems, accidentally – captured:

> They sing their dearest songs – . . .
> With the candles mooning each face . . .
> They clear the creeping moss – . . .
> They are blithely breakfasting all – . . .

Who they are, 'He, she, all of them', remains obscure. We gain a haphazard intimacy with them; the quirks and 'insides' of their lives are exposed 'While pet fowl come to the knee' and with

> Clocks and carpets and chairs
> On the lawn all day.

The dominant perspective, though, is one of distance; we are reminded of our separateness from these 'men and maidens' and of their anonymity. The poem's final image is of unnamed names on unidentified graves: 'Down their carved names the rain-drop ploughs'. The ellipsis at the end of each stanza's fifth line, followed by the sighing 'Ah, no;' sounds dramatically unintentional the first time, as though the poet has momentarily forgotten his business. As the poem proceeds, it acquires a sombre regularity which suggests the gap between past and present that refuses to be bridged. The movements which end each stanza ('the sick leaves reel down . . .', 'storm-birds wing across!' 'the rotten rose is ript from the wall', 'the rain-drop ploughs') all create a sense of turbulence, windy upheaval and finality. Autumnal decay and migration frame each vignette of human gaiety and life. The movements are at once wild and unpredictable and purposefully determined. As with Thomas, the casualness is a cunningly constructed artifice.

Rain on graves haunts Hardy's writing. The deluging gargoyle in *Far from the Madding Crowd* reappears modified in 'Rain on a Grave'. The different extremes of the weather reflect Hardy's violent grief and the precision of his recollections. The unsentient corpse is victim to the weather's ravages:

> Clouds spout upon her
> Their waters amain
> In ruthless disdain.

Alive, her sensitive delicacy is remembered through her response to rain:

> One who to shelter
> Her delicate head
> Would quicken and quicken
> Each tentative tread
> If drops chanced to pelt her.

The weather's vicissitudes, seem – like Hardy's style – to be both cruelly intentional and ironically random.

Rain is not invariably an image of desolation. 'A Thunderstorm in Town' (also significantly revised in favour of circumstantial fidelity to 'A Thunderstorm in Town (*A Reminiscence: 1893*)') recalls with whimsical amusement a moment of frustrated desire. A deliberately quaint 'old-fashionedness' is created through the social detail stressing the lady's novel refinement: 'She wore a new "terra-cotta" dress.' The rather staid country-town decorum – 'the hansom's dry recess', the snug safety – are gently teased by the rapid excited movements in the second stanza which confesses the speaker's urge to break propriety:

> Then the downpour ceased, to my sharp sad pain,
> And the glass that had screened our forms before
> Flew up, and out she sprang to her door:
> I should have kissed her if the rain
> Had lasted a minute more.

The feeling of vacancy and pointlessness with which the poem ends perfectly mirrors the incident's inconclusive brevity.

Hardy uses details of weather, clothes, furniture, with tremendous sureness of touch. The clarity with which a face, a colour, a pair of gloves are visualized gives to 'The Voice' a photographic accuracy which poignantly intensifies our sense that these things or people are out of reach.

> Can it be you that I hear? Let me view you, then,
> Standing as when I drew near to the town
> Where you would wait for me: yes, as I knew you then,
> Even to the original air-blue gown!

The sartorial exactness with which Hardy recalls his dead wife is delicately confounded by the hollow unreality which she now is. The 'air-blue gown', for all its worldly concreteness, dissolves into the landscape and the weather, and becomes as intangible as the sky it mimics: 'Or is it only the breeze, in its listlessness . . .?' Hardy is a poet conscious of social manners and mores. The predominance of material objects in 'Lament', for example, gives them historical and social authenticity:

> How she would have loved
> A party to-day! –
> Bright-hatted and gloved,
> With table and tray
> And chairs on the lawn.

The humorous nostalgia of 'In the Days of Crinoline' teases our assumptions about wholesome rustic old-fashionedness. The wife's puritanical exterior masks betrayal and the vicar's naive complacency about the surface is faintly derided:

> A plain tilt-bonnet on her head
> She took the path across the leaze.
> – Her spouse the vicar, gardening, said,
> 'Too dowdy that, for coquetries,
>   So I can hoe at ease.'
>
> But when she passed into the heath,
> And gained the wood beyond the flat,
> She raised her skirts, and from beneath
> Unpinned and drew as from a sheath
>   An ostrich-feathered hat.

Like clothes, houses reveal and conceal social truths. 'Architectural Masks' ridicules the snobbish assumption that tasteful old houses are synonymous with virtue and study, while modern 'desirable' villas go hand in hand with materialism. The 'gaudy box' houses the life of the mind as effectively as 'ivied walls' or 'mullioned windows' do in the popular imagination. Hardy is particularly sensitive to buildings and rooms. It is no coincidence that the final uprooting of human stability in 'During Wind and Rain' describes moving house. Losing or changing a dwelling-place is a powerful imaginative stimulus for

Hardy, linked with the experience of losing his wife. Revisiting their old house in 'His Visitor' enforces a recognition of the unrecoverable nature of the past, of the way time changes all things, and of the separateness of human lives:

> The rooms new painted, and the pictures altered,
> And other cups and saucers, . . .

are horribly real signs of Hardy's alienation and loss. The unfamiliarity of the teacups reflects the disruption novelty and change bring. The search for newness, though, is a persistent feature of human society; 'Starlings on the Roof' is the monologue of those left behind. The birds observe the human ritual of moving house with world-weary detachment; men are viewed as restless nomads in search of newness and determined to escape from the ghosts of the past:

> They look for a new life, rich and strange;
> They do not know that, let them range
> Wherever they may they will get no change.

The poem's final stanza conveys the temporariness of existence: a house, however much it seems to represent stability and comfort, is 'but the scene of a bivouac'. The stuff we surround ourselves with, 'house-gear', is a burden to be dragged around until the final 'move'. The starlings' lamenting cry becomes a parody of social squawking:

> They will find that as they were they are,
> That every hearth has a ghost, alack,
> And can be but the scene of a bivouac
> Till they more their last – no care to pack!

The rattling rhymes, which notate the starlings' chatter, comically suggest human nature's hollow preoccupation with useless things.

And yet things in Hardy's poetry frequently acquire importance through their private histories: haunted houses and haunted furniture are common. Objects provide homes for ghosts, like 'The Garden Seat' to which 'Those who once sat thereon come back'. In 'Old Furniture', again, Hardy presents himself surrounded by Victorian clutter 'amid relics of householdry', and in the faded, often nameless objects that furnish lives there are comforting links with the past:

> I see the hands of the generations
>   That owned each shining familiar thing
> In play on its knobs and indentations,
>   And with its ancient fashioning

The interiors are distinctly 'shabby-genteel', darkened and muffled, and they almost defy the progress of time:

> On the clock's dull dial a foggy finger,
>   Moving to set the minutes right.

They are often dominated by outsize items, like 'The Cheval-Glass':

> Why do you harbour that great cheval-glass
>   Filling up your narrow room?

The reason for the object's brooding presence is that it is haunted by its former owner, the parson's daughter. In the glass are multiple histories – the speaker's youthful love in 'ancient England'; the unhappy marriage of the daughter; the ruin of her father, accompanied by the inconvenience of a house sale:

> and next was the auction –
> Everything to be sold:
> Mid things new and old
> Stood this glass in her former chamber.

Like the 'house-gear' in 'Starlings on the Roof', the mirror is a permanent weight to be borne, 'I bought it oversea,/And drag it about with me.'

The speaker in 'The Re-Enactment' has arranged a meeting with her lover in a hired dwelling, and instead is confronted by a Hardy-like figure, a ghost looking for his former love, who is pathetically disconcerted by the rearranged furniture:

> And the house-things are much shifted.
>   Put them where
> They stood on this night's fellow;
>   Shift the chair:
> Here was the couch: and the piano should be there.

The engulfing re-emergence of the past – 'the parlour's hidden tale' – quenches the passions of the present. So full is the house of 'the intenser drama' that there is literally 'no room for later passion'. In 'The Ghost of the Past', the past is personified as a wife or house-keeper, 'It was a spectral housekeeping'; and the relationship is comforting and loverlike: 'There was in that companionship/Something of ecstasy.' Accordingly, with age, the past fades from comrade into skeleton; the older the speaker becomes the more remote and ghostly is the past.

Hardy's relationship with the past is an obsessive one: time and again he attempts to recapture it, or to escape from its hold. 'The Photograph' reflects both impulses: it is about destroying a preserved piece of the past. There is an unusual degree of violence and sensuality in Hardy's description of burning the portrait:

> The flame crept up the portrait line by line
> As it lay on the coals in the silence of night's profound.
>   And over the arm's incline,
> And along the marge of the silkwork superfine,
> And gnawed at the delicate bosom's defenceless round.

The violation of this figure from the past is paradoxically more painful to the destroyer than it is to his victim. The past is seen, not as a separable entity, but as a living part of the speaker. Its desecration is almost physically wounding: 'I vented a cry of hurt'. The destruction is only half-effective; the picture, 'unsheathed from the past' like a dangerous weapon, leaves behind it a tormenting phantom: 'The ashen ghost of the card it had figured on.' In the final stanzas, the power of that ghost is unleashed. Attempting to obliterate the past reawakens it in the form of unsettling questions about the woman's unknown present existence. Burning her image is like disinterring a corpse: 'She was a woman long hid among packs of years'. The years are imagined stacked up like packs of cards or picture postcards. The speaker is in their midst, sorting out the paraphernalia that constitutes an individual's history: 'in a casual clearance of life's arrears'. Again, the 'casualness' is at odds with the relentless determination with which the flame eats into the picture and the past rears up. 'Life's arrears' catch up with the speaker and the murder of the past brings it back to life.

Davie's characterization of Hardy not as the honest countryman but as 'the upwardly mobile *déraciné*' is a useful one (Donald Davie, *Thomas Hardy and British Poetry*, 1973, p 17). Not feeling at home in one's old house; moving; being plagued by memory, by things from a previous era – all are recurrent themes. Indeed, the poets who emerge as the major figures of the early years of the twentieth century – Kipling, de la Mare, Hardy and Thomas – all share something of the character of the *déraciné*. Kipling's lack of a native land heightens the feelings of loss and the quests for home in his poetry; de la Mare seems deliberately to uproot himself from ordinary experience and to put himself in the world of fantasy and nonsense; Hardy's obsession with things past reveals his sense of being unhappily cut off from it; Thomas, too, tries to steel himself against 'the reach of change'. If the period 1900–1914 has any definable poetic character, it is perhaps a consciousness of being 'in between'. The best poetry of these years reveals a certainty that the days of sunshades and crinolines are gone but an uncertainty about what what will take their place. Their present is characterized by the remnants of the past – 'Ah – it's the skeleton of a lady's sunshade', Hardy lights upon – and it is such skeletons that fill the poetry and, in Larkin's words also on an old photograph, 'lacerate/simply by being over'.

3

THE NOVEL TO 1914

Philip Horne

H. G. Wells (1866–1946), writing on 'The Contemporary Novel' in 1914, claimed that there was

a definable difference between the novel of the past and what I may call the modern novel. It lies in the fact that formerly there was a feeling of certitude about moral values and standards of conduct that is altogether absent to-day. It wasn't so much that men were agreed upon these things – about these things there have always been enormous differences of opinion – as that men were emphatic, cocksure, and unteachable about whatever they did happen to believe to a degree that no longer obtains.

Some things here can be queried or qualified. This is a sweeping statement, and if what is said here is Wells's belief he seems to be able to call up some 'emphasis' and quite a 'feeling of certitude' about it (*'altogether* absent'?). In 1914 Wells, a Socialist of sorts and a technologist, is by vocation the prophet of instability and of the collapse of tradition, his attention fixed rather on the future and the changes it is to bring than on the past; so we could suspect that it is in his interest to play down continuities and play up the self-conscious loss of consensus.

Even so, the claim has a clear application, and we can identify some fair pretexts for unsettlement. The passage from the Victorian age into a new century with a new monarch (Edward VII) not notable for high 'standards of conduct'; the filtering through society of Darwinist and Socialist ideas, and the weakening of organized religion; the rethinkings of Empire prompted by the Boer War, by the American involvement in the Philippines, and by the atrocities of the Belgians in the Congo; the continuing processes of social change brought about by the Industrial Revolution, which created new affluent classes (including that of writers like Wells and Arnold Bennett) and further urban expansion into what E. M. Forster

(1879–1970) felt as 'the raw over-built country' (*Where Angels Fear to Tread*); the attempts to extend the democratization registered in the Reform Acts of 1867 and 1884 which granted universal male suffrage, both by the strengthening of trade unions and, in a different direction, by the ardent and increasingly violent struggle of the suffragettes to obtain 'Votes for Women': all these contributed to a general sense of the times as, according to inclination and mood, something between a catastrophic fall away from civilized values and a momentous opportunity for the establishment of a newer, truer world.

In Wells's *Ann Veronica* (1909), a materialist conversion narrative, the suburban heroine absconds from an oppressive home to study science in London, and becomes

more and more alive, not so much to a system of ideas as to a big diffused impulse towards change, to a great discontent with and criticism of life as it is lived, to a clamorous confusion of ideas for reconstruction.

To Wells this is exciting, and the fact that 'diffusion' leads to 'confusion' is a minor drawback; he has qualms about some advanced thoughts, but pushes cheerfully on with others. There were other perspectives. Looking back from 1918, a young American who had settled in London to attach his individual talent to the European tradition (something he had first to reinvent) saw this period as disastrously woolly.

England . . . if it is not the Home of Ideas, has at least become infested with them in about the time within which Australia has been overrun by rabbits. In England ideas run wild and pasture on the emotions; instead of thinking with our feelings (a very different thing) we corrupt our feelings with ideas; we produce the political, the emotional idea, evading sensation and thought.

For T. S. Eliot too it is 'not so much . . . a system of ideas'; but its diffuseness signals its evasion of philosophical rigour and its diffusion is an epidemic, a damaging infestation which corrupts perception. The context from which Eliot's view is taken refers us to a friend and critical adversary of Wells, 'In Memory' of whom Eliot is writing: Henry James, whose 'mastery over' and 'baffling escape' from 'Ideas' is being praised. Together with Joseph Conrad and Ford Madox Ford, James was one of the precursors of Modernism, if not the first Modernist; and the cultural success of Eliot, Pound and Joyce was to give a retrospective pre-eminence to these Edwardian novelists which can be misleading for readers of a later period. However influential for the *cognoscenti*, they were not at the centre of public attention, and were scarcely bestsellers: that standing belonged rather to figures since comparatively unadmired (though not all unread), such as Kipling, Bennett, Wells, Galsworthy, and Conan Doyle, and a large number of even more popular writers such as Elinor Glyn.

This historical shift of emphasis, then, bears some pondering in an era such as ours which is dubious about canons: it is often alleged that Modernism produced a cult of difficulty, and we may now reasonably ask why the hard work of reading through the complexities of James and Conrad should be treated as more valuable than the easier going we can find in the spaciousness of many of the other Edwardians – who are indisputably far from negligible, and not only because they also have had a profound influence. David Trotter's survey of *The English Novel in History 1895–1920* richly hints at this hinterland and his *Companion to Edwardian Fiction* will help us to chart our way among the William De Morgans and Horace Annesley Vachells – figures this necessarily selective essay cannot include within its scope.

II

According to *The English Novel from the Earliest Days to the Death of Joseph Conrad* (1930) by Ford Madox Ford (1873–1939), 'the novel has become indispensable to the understanding of life' – by which he means that it is 'the only source to which you can turn in order to ascertain how your fellows spend their entire lives'. This does not seem far from Wells's claims in his essay on 'The Contemporary Novel' (quoted above), where he announces on behalf of all novelists that 'we are going to write, subject only to our limitations, about the whole of human life'. But Wells's 'whole of human life' is not the same thing as Ford's 'entire life'; and neither is quite the same as the concept invoked by E. M. Forster in his *Aspects of the Novel* (1927) where he tells us 'that most of human life has to disappear before [Henry James] can do us a novel'. We can attempt to gloss these utterances by the writers' respective practices.

What Ford, a follower of Henry James (1843–1916) and Joseph Conrad (1857–1924), probably means is that fiction tells us how our fellow spends his 'entire life' by a full 'rendering' of it, by devising some technical means of exactly presenting the way in which this fellow perceives the world. In what is generally regarded as his greatest novel, *The Good Soldier* (1915), Ford's cracked narrator Dowell, an oddly jerky fellow adulterously betrayed by his nearest and dearest, tells us about the whole grisly affair in a fractured first-person account whose self-confessed unreliability teasingly divides our attention between the tricky factual details of the goings-on 'out there' in the secretly promiscuous society of 'good people' at Bad Nauheim and the even more mystifying complexities of Dowell's own mental processes.

This confusing procedure marks a peculiar kind of realism – a fidelity to the perplexing way in which life strikes us with things that become stories only when they are told, and also to the perplexity of someone trying to tell of being so struck. Dowell (whose name may be Ford's injunction to himself to 'do well', to manage a full Jamesian 'doing' of the subject) begins Part Four of the novel with a justification of his method, which he admits may have made it 'difficult for anyone to find his path through what may be a sort of maze . . . I console myself with thinking that this is a real story and that, after all, real stories are probably told best in the way a person telling a story would tell them. They will then seem most real.' The notion of 'entirety' here seems to mean that the novelist, though analysing experience, will avoid tidying it up and packaging it for the reader, thus conforming to James's dictum in 'The Art of Fiction' (1884) that 'In proportion as in what [fiction] offers us we see life *without* rearrangement do we feel that we are touching the truth'.

Wells's 'whole of human life' is less directed towards the psychology of perception, with novelistic technique as its register (though he flirts with the approach), than towards the panoramic survey of up-to-date tendencies and concerns. In his *Experiment in Autobiography* (1934), by which time his views had hardened, Wells describes an opposition between his notion of the novel as an 'ethical enquiry' and the Jamesian one (also that of Ford and Conrad) as 'the rendering of a system of impressions'. If this were a complete account of the matter, the works of the Jamesians would indeed be sterile formalism; but, on the contrary, James argues in much of his criticism that a strict adherence to 'impressions', the maintenance of an 'air of reality', is a necessary condition for the moral validity of a work of fiction, something which evidently concerns him. We can suggest that the burden of Wells's distinction lies in his impatience with the technical laboriousness of 'rendering' as a medium for 'ethical enquiry'; and the tendency of his novels from *Kipps* (1905) – which deals with a single 'affair' (to use Ford's term) and was highly praised by James – to the more kaleidoscopic later works – which were (to use another Wellsian distinction) 'extensive' rather than 'intensive' – is towards a sense of the techniques of fiction as comparatively negligible means to some generally propagandist end (such as the breaking-down of class attitudes or the rethinking of sexual mores). Wells's ethical purpose is not always explicitly set out, and is often not certainly directed towards one side of the question; but his priorities as a writer are no less didactic for that. Fiction becomes a way of inciting speculation.

Forster's 'most of human life', which James has to conjure away before he can write a novel, reflects a view of the novel differing from both these others, a view striving to be simultaneously poetic and prosaic and thus in danger of differing with itself. Forster wants his novels to have a Wellsian variety and inclusiveness of material, but also a psychological intricacy and obliqueness which Wells's techniques after *Kipps* do not attempt. 'Most of human life' registers the frequent objection to James's late fictions (*The Wings of the Dove* (1902), *The Ambassadors* (1903) and *The Golden Bowl* (1904)) that they lack, as Forster puts it, 'fun', 'rapid motion', 'carnality' and 'nine-tenths of heroism'. These are not accurate allegations, one might counter, if 'fun' and 'rapid motion' can be displayed mentally rather than muscularly, if 'carnality' can be potently evoked without explicit gropings, and if more than a tenth of 'heroism' is to be found in the courage required of James's late protagonists for facing betrayal and loss in the most intimate relations of life. The restrictive injustice of Forster's literal-minded cavils about James reflects what is a critical weakness but also to some extent an exciting creative impulse in him: a desire to encompass in fiction the whole spectrum of experience in the lives he chooses to represent, not excluding either the grubbily material or the nebulously ideal. I shall try later, however, to indicate some shortcomings in Forster's unJamesian practice.

III

There was consensus, then, among the most thoughtful Edwardian novelists as to the importance of the novel, but much less as to the direction it was to take and the version of 'human life' it was to represent. Given the decline observed by Wells in the 'feeling of certitude about moral values and standards of conduct', it is not surprising that the age especially demanded, or at least gratefully accepted, such certitude, or at least an appearance of it, from the novelists of the time. Wells is a confident diagnostician in his very declaration that certitude is 'altogether absent'; the vim of the proposition is in itself some consolation for the content; and of course a good deal of the constant appeal of fiction (in which Wells and his narrators take a similarly vigorous line) is lodged in its artificially constructed framework of epistemological certainties, of things the author can know because he or she is their godlike creator. Where in real life we are beset with perplexing difficulties in understanding and dealing with the world and other people, about which and whom our knowledge is incomplete, in novels we are better informed; the unwritten contract between author and reader usually guarantees that our curiosity will be satisfied. We are in Eliot's words 'assured of certain certainties'.

One serious drawback for fiction's attempts to remedy these real-life problems, by simply providing the information about its made-up world that the actual world denies us, is exactly that the difference can be too striking, can remind us too insistently that life keeps *its* secrets. Joseph Conrad, born in Poland as Teodor Josef Konrad Korzeniowski, and a professional mariner for twenty years before he became a full-time writer, was a figure who had accumulated authentic experience all over the world and who might therefore seem likely to speak, as a novelist, with the confidence of that hoard. Yet it could be argued that his artistic distinction springs from a refusal to live off this stockpile as if it were something he uncomplicatedly possessed. Rather, keeping his distance from it as it had kept *him* at a distance from its meaning, he drew on it as a source of mystery and bafflement, of insoluble problems only more acutely defined, not cleared up, for their basis in witnessed fact. His curious alien grasp of English (shadowed both by Polish and French) produces a vivid oddity in his closely-worked and closely-observed descriptions of character and scene – 'Above the mass of sleepers a faint and patient sigh at times floated', for instance – but that vividness ends by giving relief, a substantial frame of circumstance, to the 'darkness' he had come to perceive in the hearts of men.

It was while engaged on *Lord Jim* (1900) that Conrad wrote the even more celebrated *Heart of Darkness* (published 1902), and the two works are alike in more than being narrated by Charlie Marlow, the reflective English sea-captain. Ford's use of his realistically unreliable narrator Dowell in *The Good Soldier* draws in numerous ways on the handling of the narrative scheme used in these works by his mentor and ex-collaborator. In all three stories the narrator is antagonistically but intimately paired with a figure who obsesses him by embodying human weakness, deep inner unreliability, in a way which affects his entire view of the world; and in all three the relation of events is made with a glancing obliquity and frequent confessions of inadequacy to the task of making the matter clear. *Heart of Darkness*, a novella, observes a more-or-less straightforward chronological order in its account of Marlow's voyage up-river through the Belgian Congo to meet the notorious Kurtz; but the story of Lord Jim, a young Englishman who yearns for heroic adventure, is rendered not just through Marlow's eye-witness encounters but also through the latter's interviews with participants in crucial scenes from which he was absent. The tale of Jim's unlucky and revealing jump at his first crisis from the *Patna* (which promises to sink and then humiliatingly doesn't) is given to us in a series of hops back and forth, with the sequence of events as seen by the relevant parties gradually pieced together. Marlow has to be very curious about Jim to make this effort of reconstruction plausible; but in a manner which illustrates Conrad's debt to James (in tribute to whom he wrote an essay in 1905) the subjective impulse which makes him a psychological and philosophical detective – the sense of Jim's defection as showing that 'nobody, nobody is good enough' – becomes as much the focus of the book as Jim's objective lapse (or rather, leap). The mode of narration is, to use a Jamesian term, artfully 're-economised' as part of the argument.

Conrad is evidently a writer with a modern sensibility and sophisticated technique, but it is worth remarking in particular a couple of differences between these two works of his and *The Good Soldier*, differences which point up Ford's comparative Modernist leanings. One is that Marlow's first-person narrations are both framed (like that of a possible model, James's *The Turn of the Screw* (1898)) by the social gathering to which they are spoken, 'after dinner, on a verandah . . . in the deep dusk speckled by fiery cigar-ends' or at the mouth of the Thames on board 'the *Nellie*, a cruising yawl'; whereas Dowell's loopy account of 'the breaking up of our little four-square coterie' is *written*, with only the rather uncannily abstract 'idea of being in a country cottage with a silent listener'. The threat of solipsism is much more intensely felt when there is no reassuring community of like minds (even one, like Marlow's, abused as unreceptive) to receive and approve the uttered perplexity – only a 'you' which seems disconcertingly to mean *us*; and this threat is underlined by the second difference I have in mind.

At the end of the book Dowell finds himself the helpless keeper of the girl Nancy, who has adored the 'good soldier' Edward Ashburnham and been driven mad with guilt through the machinations of Edward's ferociously perverse wife Leonora. Dowell now loves Nancy, we are told, and has done so since the suicide of his own wife

Florence, who has been having an affair with the poor overstretched Edward. Only since then has Dowell even begun to suspect the sexual horror beneath the respectable surface of their communal life, and he tries to piece the fragments together with the help of talking to Edward and Leonora. So far as we know, however, he has no such talk with Nancy before she lapses into mad taciturnity, and we have no evidence either that Nancy has given Leonora (her rival for Edward) a blow-by-blow relation of her intimate feelings in the period leading up to the crisis; and yet we find Dowell giving us *as a matter of fact* Nancy's most interior mental processes ('Nancy had, in fact, been thinking . . .'), and her drunken fantasy that Edward 'was kissing her on her face, that burned; on her shoulders, that burned, and on her neck, that was on fire'. How does Dowell know? Since no provenance is offered for these so passionately described facts, the reader is in an interpretative quandary to which the openly avowed speculations of Marlow produce no equivalent; we are put in a position to question the sanity of Dowell, and to wonder whether his obsession with Nancy has not led him to *invent* the intimate account of her thoughts. Dowell does not insist on the validity of his interpretation of *part* of Nancy's attitude: 'I don't attach any particular importance to these generalizations of mine. They may be right, they may be wrong.' But it can be said that when the particulars to which the 'generalizations' refer lose their epistemological moorings, we are thoroughly put out, and at sea; as in much of Joyce's *Ulysses*, there is no firm line between the event and its treatment.[1]

The same reservations don't exactly apply to Ford's extraordinary tetralogy *Parade's End* (1924–8), consisting of the oddly-titled *Some Do Not . . .*, *No More Parades*, *A Man Could Stand Up* and *The Last Post*, and telling of the fate of the Edwardian ruling classes in the

---

1 There is, of course, another possibility: that Ford does not intend us to recognize, even does not recognize himself, that Dowell has no specified source for his impassioned private view of Nancy's mental life. If this were a slip on his part, a failure to supply a plausible realistic derivation for Dowell's knowledge of what has to be told, then it would reproduce the disturbing and inexplicable movement in 'Amos Barton', the first of George Eliot's *Scenes of Clerical Life* (1859), from a circumstantially characterized eye-witness first-person narrator, who seems to be just another figure on the scene, to a narrator who somehow omnisciently knows the secret details of the protagonists' lives. (We receive no hint from George Eliot that her narrator is mad.) If it is *not* a slip on Ford's part, or a mystical indication of the telepathic powers of the imagination, it may ironically acknowledge the pressure on Dowell to arrive at a certain certainty about these events which he has no legitimate means of securing; and from a self-conscious craftsman like Ford this irony may be associated with a doubt about the impulses which are satisfied and the gaps plugged by the confident omniscient narrations of most 'popular' novels.

Great War. The work is like a Modernist *Gone With the Wind*, an epic of noble values embodied in family and unsettled by war. The four novels describe England's plunge into a modern and probably fallen world through the pre-War, Wartime and post-War experience of the self-denying feudal civil servant Christopher Tietjens (the name is Dutch), whose sufferings by the tongue of his evil Catholic wife Sylvia help him to be an 'Anglican saint' and martyr (amid the bloody chaos at the front line he thinks of George Herbert and tries to remember as a talisman the name of Bemerton, Herbert's parish). Tietjens falls in love at the start with Valentine Wannop, a young suffragette, and she with him; but unlike the adulterous Sylvia they refrain for years from sexual consummation ('We're the sort that . . . *do not*!'), until the Armistice, when the Last Post is played in the street and they go into a penitential pastoral retreat together. If *The Good Soldier* seems to ask us to understand Dowell's distortions of reality without providing adequate cross-reference, *Parade's End*, though full of the melodramatic Fordian trademarks of 'madness', 'screams', 'gurgling' and characters whose 'eyes stuck out like those of a suffocating fish', is narrated in the third person and can thus be taken as crankily creating its own self-sufficiently grotesque and nightmarish world – one where high moral aspirations come under siege from appallingly widespread corruption and malignity. Tietjens loves a woman not his wife but represents a stand against Edwardian sexual hypocrisy, against 'an, of course, enlightened promiscuity'; this perverse resistance is typical of a work creatively tortured by tensions and contradictions about sex, class, money, politics and religion. The reader is pretty sure in *Parade's End* that the narrator is showing the European social order as having gone mad; there is no evasiveness in the presentation of point of view, just a bleak vision of a shattered civilization which makes no more 'parade' of its values.

In Conrad too the exploration of areas of uncertainty is more clearly defined than in the intriguingly flawed experiment with Dowell. We are aware of Marlow as an interpreter and self-conscious speculator, so that we know him as a troubled and involved individual honourably attempting to make sense of contradictory data, rather than as a shifty or mad possible inventor of them. It must be admitted that there is a telling move from question to statement in his famous exclamation as Kurtz approaches death – 'Did he live his life again in every detail of desire, temptation, and surrender during that supreme moment of complete knowlege?' – since the firm deictic of '*that* supreme moment . . .' dictates our not questioning its supremeness or completeness, and thus steers us towards accepting that he *did* 'live his life again' et cetera. Yet the strong-arm persuasiveness of this rhetorical question about another's mind serves to mark the climax of Marlow's horrified identification with Kurtz as an exemplary casualty of European civilization over-extended and losing its grip in the outposts of progress; and the hypothesis is based on first-hand observation, so that we can place, and maintain reserve about, what is being said.

The focus of Conrad's doubt is ethical; he speaks in the James essay of 'this world of relative values', an insight fostered by his participation in three cultures and the fact that he had actually been to so much of 'this world' and seen its 'relative values' in their local varieties. Other major writers of the period who were extensive travellers – Henry James, Rudyard Kipling and E. M. Forster – also wrote an 'International' fiction dealing with the interrelation between Anglo-Saxon and other ethical codes. That values are only relative, that the codes of conduct which regulate and propel empires have no intrinsic superiority over others when put to the test, is pointedly shown in the case of Kurtz, an enlightened ideologue full of Western promise who discovers himself to be hollow when he gets godlike power among the natives as a procurer of ivory for a Brussels company in the Belgian Congo (a region Conrad had visited in 1890 – 'Getting jolly well sick of this fun', as he confided to his diary). As Marlow puts it, 'His soul was mad. Being alone in the wilderness, it had looked within itself, and, by heavens!, I tell you, it had gone mad.' The 'wilderness' is a place where civilization is tried through its ambassadors, a place of benign or malign fantasy. In *Lord Jim* Marlow asks his hearers:

Do you notice how, three hundred miles beyond the end of telegraph cables and mail-boat lines, the haggard utilitarian lies of our civilization wither and die, to be replaced by pure exercises of imagination, that have the futility, often the charm, and sometimes the deep hidden truthfulness, of works of art?

Jim's 'romantic' efforts to redeem his abandonment of the *Patna* by saving Patusan (in Borneo) are a 'pure exercise of the imagination', one which attaches Marlow to him by its elevated intensity; but the values he acts out become finally 'a shadowy ideal of conduct' for the sake of which he 'goes away from a living woman', and are further called an 'exalted egoism'. 'Egoism' connects him with Kurtz, who is full of himself but whose self then turns out to be empty. The testing of Jim in Patusan is not so severe as to destroy his ethical credibility, which is left equivocal in his self-sacrifice at the end;

whereas what Kurtz faces in the Congo is the 'wild and passionate uproar' of 'prehistoric man', which Marlow sees as a terrible challenge to the value-system with which a modern European holds himself together because it is a truth about human nature:

He must meet that truth with his own true stuff – with his own inborn strength. Principles won't do. Acquisitions, clothes, pretty rags – rags that would fly off at the first good shake. No; you want a deliberate belief.

Such integrity, though, as Marlow finds in the absolute isolation of the fog he encounters on the way up-river to see Jim at Patusan, is hard to sustain when social security is absolutely removed: 'All I had lately seen, all I had heard, and the very human speech itself, seemed to have passed away out of existence.' Jim's original dereliction of duty was preceded by just such a blinding insulation from reality.

This withering experience of sensory deprivation, which strips away and shakes off mere social 'acquisitions' such as 'principles', recurs at the heart of *Nostromo* (1904), Conrad's next large-scale work after *Lord Jim*, in the blackness which descends on Nostromo and Martin Decoud out on the Golfo Placido as they attempt to save a lighterful of silver from the latest band of revolutionaries to make a bid for power in the futile South American republic of Costaguana. ('Guano' – birdshit used as fertilizer – appears in *Lord Jim* as the sort of treasure which dirties those who seek it, and the country here is a ghastly sullying mockery of a European state.) The cynical Parisianized Decoud, who has been pretending to espouse political ideals for the sake of the patriotic Antonia Avellanos, is reduced to unaccustomed powerlessness when Nostromo puts out the light:

It was to Decoud as if his companion had destroyed, by a single touch, the world of affairs, of loves, of revolution, where his complacent superiority analysed fearlessly all motives and all passions, including his own.

Eventually stranded with the silver, but without Nostromo, on the Great Isabel, a barren island on the vacant gulf, Decoud suffers from his lack of 'a deliberate belief' ('He believed in nothing') and starts to doubt 'his own individuality'. A comparable incapacity to feel engagement with life paralyses the equally isolated Axel Heyst, the 'man of universal scorn and unbelief' whose father's injunction to 'look on and never make a sound' spoils him for the kinds of action (loving and violent) which events call for in the fine and ambiguously-titled *Victory* (1915). The unbelieving but decent Heyst profits by the ardent self-sacrifice of a woman (Conrad's women are creatures with inexplicable belief in ideals) and incinerates himself with her corpse in a gesture which can be read as triumphant *liebestod* or despairing acknowledgement of hollowness. Decoud likewise kills himself, prompting the following sardonic epitaph:

A victim of the disillusioned weariness which is the retribution meted out to intellectual audacity, the brilliant Don Martin Decoud, weighted by the bars of San Tomé silver, disappeared without a trace, swallowed up in the immense indifference of things.

What is notable here is that there is no witness except Conrad and the readers to Decoud's suicide, which takes place in the utmost solitude. If this collapse of public brilliance, comparable to Kurtz's, were being narrated even by a Marlow at his most speculative, we would have reason to think him exceeding his brief. But this is a third-person narration by an omniscient author-figure[1], a kind of Marlow empowered to know what it is not humanly possible to know. Thus no one but Nostromo knows Decoud got to the island, so no one doubts that he died earlier in the sinking of the lighter: 'Had the truth of the facts been known, there would always have remained the question, Why?' People who lack 'the truth of the facts' can have no questions. 'But the truth was that he died from solitude.' That is, if people only knew, there would be a mystery; and the solution of that mystery would be that solitude killed Decoud. The narrator answers a question no one but Nostromo knows to ask, brandishes his possession of 'the truth of the facts' whereas Marlow dwells on the 'facts' in the hope of realizing the 'truth' of them.

Such emphatically displayed ironic omniscience, which extends also to Conrad's following novel *The Secret Agent* (1907), a story about a futile anarchist outrage narrated for ironic point through grimly reductive physiological observations, corresponds to an increasingly extensive interest in history, politics and commerce as gauges of the state of modern civilization. *Under Western Eyes* (1910), as its title suggests, reverts to a doubt-filled first-person narrative structure (that of an old English teacher of languages) to tell a gloomy Russian tale of political betrayal, exile, confession and fanaticism. *Heart of Darkness* starts with Marlow looking back to the Roman imperial occupiers of Britain (the subject of part of Kipling's *Puck of Pook's*

---

1 Even so, the narrator has a shadily characterized past as a visitor to the capital of Costaguana, which makes the book's narrative set-up another case of the novelistic sleight of hand practised in 'Amos Barton' (see Note 1 on p 72).

Hill in 1906), and expressing the grim view that 'they were no colonists; their administration was merely a squeeze, and nothing more, I suspect.' Conquering an empire for yourself, he goes on, 'is not a pretty thing when you look into it too much. What redeems it is the idea only. An idea at the back of it; not a sentimental pretence but an idea; and an unselfish belief in the idea.' The Belgians, from a Brussels which reminds Marlow of 'a whited sepulchre', don't have this unselfish belief, only a pious fraud of one, and come to the Congo as 'a lot of faithless pilgrims' whose Company was 'going to run an over-sea empire, and make no end of coin by trade'. This hideous parody of the British Empire (as it seemed to many) aroused deep indignation, and Conrad was later involved in the Congo Reform Association with Anthony Hope (author of *The Prisoner of Zenda*) and Sir Arthur Conan Doyle, who wrote of the Belgian regime: 'Never before has there been such a mixture of wholesale expropriation and wholesale massacre, all done under an odious guise of philanthropy, and with the lowest commercial motives as a reason' (quoted in Pierre Nordon, *Conan Doyle*, 1966, p 74). The 'lowest commercial motives' draws a traditional aristocratic association of trade with unworthiness to the support of humanitarian indignation (Conan Doyle's socially and racially conventional imagination rarely stretched itself beyond 'My good man' or the 'honest black face' of 'Zambo, our devoted negro' in *The Lost World* (1912)).

Another case which stimulated reflection on imperial power was that of the Philippines, ceded to the USA by Spain after the Spanish–American War of 1898 over Cuba, but then independently resisting American control in a guerrilla war lasting till 1902. The notion of America as the youngest imperial nation stimulated Kipling to issue in 1899 the grim punning caveat of 'The White Man's Burden' as from the British experience (it is a refrain – 'Take up the White Man's burden' – but also, the poem argues, a tremendous cost, a burden of responsibility on the imperial country). For Kipling a proper empire (and implicitly the British one) is almost all sacrifice for the sake of the 'captives' and not at all 'squeeze'; it is an exorbitantly altruistic undertaking, 'To seek another's profit, / And work another's gain'.

Conrad in *Nostromo*, no friend of Teddy Roosevelt, applies a bitter scepticism to American intervention abroad, in his cheerless sketch of the relations between the Englishman Charles Gould, proprietor of the silver mine of the Gould Concession, his wise and beautiful wife Emilia, and the American capitalists who fund their operations in Costaguana (to the extent of paying massive bribes to prop up the puppet dictatorship of Don Vincente Ribiera, whose revolution they have indeed partly funded). The activity of mining destroys the original wild beauty of its jungle site, the 'paradise of snakes', but Mrs Gould, inspired by her husband's original idealistic belief in the improving effects of 'material interests', redeemingly construes as a spiritual achievement what the more bloody-minded narration calls 'the flow of silver he had started single-handed from the re-opened scar in the flank of the mountain':

By her imaginative estimate of its power she endowed that lump of metal with a justificative conception, as though it were not a mere fact, but something far-reaching and impalpable, like the true expression of an emotion or the emergence of a principle.

This is 'an unselfish belief in the idea', as desiderated by Marlow; the trouble is that Charles Gould, dependent on the ruthlessly puritanical American mogul Holroyd with his 'insatiable imagination of conquest' (a reflection perhaps of Roosevelt's 'doctrine of the strenuous life'), and humiliatingly forced to make constant compromises with the grotesque shiftlessness of Costaguanan politics, loses his initial faith in the redeeming idea. As Mrs Gould sees, 'There was something in the necessities of successful action which carried with it the moral degradation of the idea.' This paralysing insight could be one of two epigraphs for the book; it has an unsettling counterpart, produced when Decoud's enforced idleness leads to a final collapse of his identity: 'In our activity alone do we find the sustaining illusion of an independent existence as against the whole scheme of things of which we form a helpless part.' As is visible from the cruel twistedness of these twin prongs of the human dilemma, Conrad is not a writer with a Wellsian utopia to offer, nor does he have, like Bennett, a comforting shock-absorber of a style. His narrative omniscience in *Nostromo* and *The Secret Agent*, used to detail a parallelism of capitalists and bandits in the former and of policemen and anarchists in the latter, is a self-conscious and necessary means to convey a vision of people trapped in bleakly dismaying worlds. The knowledge assumed is one the author would obviously be happier without – were it not for the artist's irrepressible pleasure in his own mastery.

IV

Rudyard Kipling (1865–1936), the other great writer of Empire, was privately almost as troubled and depressive as Conrad; and despite his reputation as a jingoist and 'children's writer', he creates in his work a world of darker shadows and more complex relations than the common image of him would allow. He was vigorously appreciated by Henry James as a literary artist of enormous talent – though with reservations about his excursions into public affairs – and it is in this light that his achievement seems most permanent to critical modern readers.

Born in India and educated in England, then a journalist in India, a wandering writer in many places and finally at the turn of the century a settler in Sussex (like James, Conrad, Wells, Ford and Stephen Crane), Kipling was a voracious seeker of initiations and learner of codes. We can certainly take his two best-known works of the twentieth century, *Kim* (1901) and *Puck of Pook's Hill* (1906), as stories of initiation into coded worlds. *Kim*, written in Sussex, is a farewell to India which takes thrilling authority from the command it demonstrates over the swarmingly populated and various subcontinent through which its picaresque but imaginatively unified action threads its way. The boy of the title (his full name Kimball O'Hara) is the orphan child – now neglected in Lahore by an opium-smoking half-caste woman – of a young colour-sergeant in an Irish regiment. He starts the novel a polyglot dodger, already straddling English and Indian cultures, already divided enough to make problematic the question he repeatedly asks himself, 'Who is Kim?':

Though he was burned black as any native; though he spoke the vernacular by preference, and his mother-tongue in a clipped uncertain sing-song; though he consorted on terms of perfect equality with the small boys of the bazaar; Kim was white – a poor white of the very poorest.

And like Conrad's Jim, though not through reading novels and therefore with less high-mindedness, Kim starts life with a thirst for adventure, a thirst which the action of the book both slakes and controls. The form characteristically taken by Kim's sought adventure, though, is less a matter of an egocentric display of personal valour at a moment of crisis (not that either egotism or courageous exploit is excluded) than of a strangely impersonal desire to get into a continuing streetwise relation with the world, a promiscuous information-gathering and acquisition of performable identities (a saturation parallel to that required of Kipling to enable him to *tell* the story).

If there were no check on Kim's expansionism except the bounds of possibility, the book's packed evocation of an India thronging with learnable differences and paradoxical characters would still give it a unique lyrical charge; Kipling's wonderful control of rhythm produces epic descriptions of things seen and people encountered which bear the special significance of Kim's recognizing their signs, of a white boy's passing for – nearly passing into – a native. James wrote to Kipling of *Kim* that

The way you make the general picture live and sound and shine, all by a myriad touches that are like the thing itself pricking through with a little snap – that makes me want to say to you: 'Come, all else is folly – sell all you have and give to the poor!' By which I mean chuck public affairs, which are an ignoble scene, and stick to your canvas and your paint-box.

(*Henry James: Letters*, edited by Leon Edel, Harvard, 1974–84, IV, pp 210–11)

Kim's travels are part of his introduction into the Great Game – the activities of the imperial Secret Service. It infiltrates and thwarts insurrectionary movements and Russian expansionist schemes, which the visible agencies of the law cannot police and apprehend, by means of a network of spies and a cultural omniscience linked with the actual ethnology of the Royal Society.[1] In this noviciate Kim has two pseudo-fathers, Mahbub the ferocious Afghan horse-trader (who is keen for him to kill his first man) and his less bloodthirsty Sahib mentor Creighton. From the beginning of the novel, however, he has also another master, a Tibetan lama on a pilgrimage, following the 'Way' in search of the 'River' where the soul will be freed from illusion. Kim's double commitment, to worldly and unworldly wisdom, matches the urge towards action with a mystical sense of the value of stillness (the lama has outgrown the 'illusion' of doctrine, and his religion is non-denominational). The dialectic of Game and Way, action and calm, has not the tragic resonance it is given in *Nostromo*, not least because of the undaunted stylistic exhilaration – catching Kim's boyish gusto – of the 'myriad touches that are like the thing itself pricking through with a little snap'; Kipling's writing, a magnificently flexible instrument for sensitively registering the value of both modes of experience, seems to offer a middle path, a relativist but undespairing way of being in the world.

Empire is a value for Kipling, but he has fierce contempt for arrogant Anglocentrism and Christian intolerance, as when the complacent Anglican priest Bennett (whom Kim and the lama meet early on their travels) provokes one of the narration's few explicit

1 The Game gives an inter-ethnic communication like that which Kipling describes himself as getting when he joins the Freemasons in India: 'Here I met Muslims, Hindus, Sikhs, members of the Arya and Brahmo Samaj, and a Jew tyler, who was priest and butcher to his little community in the city. So yet another world opened up to me which I needed' (*Something of Myself*, 1937, Chapter 3).

condemnations: 'Bennett looked at [the lama] with the triple-ringed uninterest of the creed that lumps nine-tenths of the world under the title of "heathen".' What the intercultural cross-fertilization of the Empire enables is the establishment of a valuable mutual knowledge and mutual respect: the address of *Kim* is set by the categorically imperative epigraph to the first chapter:

> Oh ye who tread the Narrow Way
> By Tophet-flare to Judgment Day,
> Be gentle when the heathen pray
>   To Buddha at Kamakura!

Empire is obliquely and powerfully defended in *Kim*. The lama points out that 'the Sahibs have not all this world's wisdom', and there is a skill in 'what Europeans, who know nothing about it, call massage', yet the criticism is corrective, not radical, an incitement to maintain, as in the poem 'Recessional', 'an humble and a contrite heart'. The comically excitable but admirably reliable Hurree Babu, player in the Game and admirer of Herbert Spencer, resembles the Sikh narrator of 'A Sahibs' War' (1901; a Boer War story) in expressing frustration at the English complacency which ignores threats to its power: 'It is all your beastly English pride. You think no one dare conspire! That is all tommy-rott.' Complaints about Empire are given voice by Babu, but only in order to deceive threatening Russian agents. It may be that 'he babbled tales of oppression and wrong till the tears ran down his cheeks for the miseries of his land', but he is acting *for* the British 'oppressors' by acting this part. The book's ideal imperial agent is the District Superintendent of Police, who turns out to be 'not less than the greatest' in the Secret Service,[1] and who can trade faultlessly insulting banter with the foul-mouthed old Kulu woman. Her praise of him, glancing as it is, epitomizes Kipling's sense that 'The White Man's Burden' requires the binding of a nation's sons to exile:

These be the sort to oversee justice. They know the land and the customs of the land. The others, all new from Europe, suckled by white women and learning our tongues from books, are worse than the pestilence.

In *Puck of Pook's Hill* (1906), the scene has changed to England and the saturation is with English history rather than Indian culture.

---

1 Kim later discovers him, that is, to be 'one of Us' – the phrase Marlow uses about Jim (without the Kiplingesque emphatic capitalization) in order to express the common humanity of human weakness. In *Kim* it carries rather the glamour of secret solidarity in a narrower élite.

None the less, many of the same patterns – of initiation and of multi-ethnic consensus – apply in this sequence of tales from the distant national past narrated to the manorial children Dan and Una as part of their heritage. The stories are told them by long-dead figures whom the accidentally conjured fairy Puck magically calls up. They hear of the expulsion of the other fairies, of the Norman conquest and the invaders' subsequent racial blending with Saxondom, of a journey to Africa for gold with a Danish adventurer, of a British-born centurion on Hadrian's Wall, of Sussex smugglers in Tudor England, and finally of the machinations by the visionary Jew Kadmiel (involving the gold from the earlier episode) which lead to the inclusion of equal civic rights in Magna Charta. The stories' concerns are with the mutual respect and blending of these racial groups (with reference to a supervening idea of a unified England); and with the establishment or strengthening of continuities with England's historical past (through such connective myths as that whereby the African gold of a proto-imperial expedition (stopping just geographically short of Kurtz's Congo) becomes the means – in an extraordinary turn – of founding English freedom). Dan and Una are implicitly trained by these narratives – as Kim is by his experiences – for their responsibilities as the British Empire's inheritors – in order, as 'The Children's Song' at the end makes explicit, 'That they may build from age to age/An undefilèd heritage'. With the First World War, an invasive threat to English manorial life was added to the threats to Empire, and Kipling brought the exotic violence of far-flung wars home to roost in stories like 'Mary Postgate' (1915), where the stolid housekeeper is moved to cruel revenge on a crashed German airman, who represents for her the 'bloody pagans' responsible for the deaths of young people she knows. Kipling seems to take a sardonic relish in the necessary ruthlessness against would-be defilers here and in 'Sea Constables' of the same year, where a City businessman commanding a naval patrol uncompromisingly harries to death a 'neutral' profiteer ('This is war, sir!').

The sense that England was in danger of being 'defiled', or at any rate of declining, that certain continuities of value were at stake, was common to many writers of the Edwardian period and played a major part in the loss of certitude about standards identified by Wells. A frequent symbolic site in fiction for discussion of questions about who was to own Britain was the country house. James had approached the subject of disputed inheritance in *The Spoils of Poynton* (1896) – a novel which he thought of calling *The Old Things* after the antiques it deals with. 'The Old Things' is what Kipling, familiarizing them *via* the chummy address of 'old thing', calls the ancient gods and fairies in *Puck of Pook's Hill*, driven out of England by the Reformation. And one of Kipling's most potent stories of the 1900s, 'They' of 1904, takes the manor-house and its ties with the past as its leading preoccupation, and refers to it by James's other rejected name for his novel, 'The House Beautiful'.

The story has a motorist-narrator in Sussex come on 'an ancient house' inhabited by a beautiful blind woman and a lot of mysterious ghostly children, heard but not seen (it is a source for Eliot's rose-garden in *Burnt Norton*). The young presences are uncanny but not unfriendly to the narrator (who has lost a child of his own), and the climax of the story arrives when a child, still unseen, steals a kiss of his hand.

The little brushing kiss fell in the centre of my palm – as a gift on which the fingers were, once, expected to close: as the all-faithful half-reproachful signal of a waiting child not used to neglect even when grown-ups were busiest – a fragment of the mute code devised long ago.

Then I knew.

It is his own child, in other words, and 'my soul was torn open within me'. We may compare Kipling's daring touch of a vanished hand here, the electrifying contact he makes between ghost *genre* and a profound personal reality, with the frightening but impersonal and *genre*-bound hauntings of his contemporary Montague Rhodes James (1862–1936), in whose *Ghost Stories of an Antiquary* (1904) the thrill is often touched into life by a supernatural hand, clawlike or resembling 'the tentacle of a devil-fish'. In M. R. James too the apparition is related to a place or object with strong connections to the past – but as a rule its victim stumbles on it accidentally and is comparatively uncharacterized (except for a few donnish quirks – James was a long-standing Fellow of King's College, Cambridge). In 'The Rose-Garden' (1911), where the Anstruthers (he golfs – a bad sign for M. R. James) buy an Essex country house and find their horticultural improvements stir up terrific possessing visions of past gruesomeness, we can see a general warning about the need to respect tradition (indeed, to fear disturbing it) addressed to the new proprietors of English houses. These scholarly stories mostly involve an out-of-the-way world of churches, ruins, and ancient homes where the past is preserved as in a museum, but the exhibits are not quite ready to lie still; they express an ambivalence towards the past, an attachment to it which may become a horrific possession by it.

Kipling's 'An Habitation Enforced' (1905) is not a ghost story, but again has its protagonists (an American millionaire couple, the Chapins) encounter in a Sussex manor house a past which applies to them personally – or rather, only to her: she is a Lashmar by birth, come unknowingly (and by a startling coincidence) to the place of her ancestors. They arrive for a holiday, but the tentacles of the country's still feudal life involve them and they end the story stuck in for good, he still reluctant but she having witnessed a death and given birth and thus become decisively engaged in the life-cycle of Friars Pardon, radiantly in place. The story interestingly fuses, in husband and wife respectively, the claims of new money with its energy and of old blood with its nobility and its rights, and thus takes its place in an Anglo-American tradition including Hawthorne's unfinished American claimant manuscripts, James's 'A Passionate Pilgrim' (1871) and Twain's *The American Claimant* (1892). Whereas those American authors portray what Hawthorne calls 'this diseased American appetite for English soil' only in order to diagnose and purge the disease, Kipling (whose own wife was American) seems to think of the Chapins' American success as the mark of a completed process of overseas regeneration for Anglo-Saxons fitting them for their inheritance. (He saw an analogous frontier-seasoning of British manhood in the Boer War, according to 'The Captive' (1902).) We can see the same idea in cruder form in the representation of Sir Henry, inheritor of Baskerville Hall in *The Hound of the Baskervilles* (1902) by Sir Arthur Conan Doyle: he has been farming in Canada till his uncle's death, and when he returns to 'the home of my own people' Watson, the narrator, approvingly notes his value: 'He . . . had the weather-beaten appearance of one who has spent most of his time in the open air, and yet there was something in his steady eye and the quiet assurance of his bearing which indicated the gentleman.'

'An Habitation Enforced' reverses the usual formula by having the returning Anglo-Saxons claim the land less than the land claims them. Sophie Chapin challenges her husband's sense of possessing their estates: 'It's *not* our land. We've only paid for it. We belong to it, and it belongs to the people – our people, they call 'em.' The irony here in the possessive 'our' when 'We belong to it' emphasizes the passivity of the Chapins' part in their own proprietorial installation – which Kipling makes the sign of a naturalness that removes the sting of their *nouvelle richesse*. In contrast the 'dago' Sangres, a neighbouring millionaire, shows off and will never be accepted.

Short stories with a different twist on the rural sense of place, this time in Ireland, make up the two good-humoured collections (1899

and 1908) of *Experiences of an Irish R. M.* by Somerville and Ross
(the pseudonyms of Edith Somerville (1858–1949) and Violet Martin
(1862–1915)). The same Anglo-Irish authors had, however, consider-
ably exceeded in seriousness these comic tales of drunkenness, fox-
hunting and the trials of a resident magistrate (like the Chapins
helplessly enveloped by rustic traditions and schemes). Their ironic
novel of social observation, detailing the unspinsterly machinations
of *The Real Charlotte* (1894), is still to be found recommended as
'summer reading' in the Sunday papers.

V

One of the other major novelists of the time, Arnold Bennett (1867–
1931), responded with some bitterness to what he saw as the
implications of 'An Habitation Enforced' in 1909. He wrote in his
New Age column of Kipling as regrettably 'against progress', as 'the
shrill champion of things that are rightly doomed', including the
'clayey ideals' of the bourgeoisie, even while conceding his worth as
'an honest and painstaking artist'; and he attacked the story for what
he claimed were *unconscious* failures of realism.

To read this story one could never guess that the English land system is not
absolutely ideal, that tenants and hereditary owners do not live always in a
delightful patriarchal relation, content . . . And the worst is that for Kipling
the English land system probably *is* perfect . . . His sentimentalization of it
is gross – there is no other word – and at bottom the story is as wildly
untrue to life as the most arrant Sunday-school prize ever published by the
Religious Tract Society.

The concern with the injustices, actualities and grimnesses of the
English structure of class and property is characteristic of Bennett,
for whom 'truth to life' involves a rejection of the pieties of 'Sunday-
school prize' fiction and of the truths taught in Sunday schools.

Bennett's third novel, *Anna of the Five Towns* (1902), set in his
native Potteries far from Kipling's Sussex pastoral, opens with its
heroine, Anna Tellwright, emerging from the Sunday school where
she teaches. The name 'Tellwright' punningly suggests Bennett's
care about finding an honest storytelling technique, and the book
does its best to avoid 'sentimentalization'. Like Joyce's *A Portrait of
the Artist as a Young Man* (1916), it is an escapee's novel about the
emotional and intellectual restrictions of provincial life, about an
individual's struggle for freedom within a socially enforced religious
system (here not Catholic but Methodist). A vital difference is that

Joyce deals with an artist and escapee (Stephen Dedalus, who may even be the autobiographical author of the novel), whereas Bennett follows affectionately but at a distance here and in his later *The Old Wives' Tale* (1908) conformist lives of almost uninterrupted emotional incarceration, scarcely touched by aesthetic interests or ideas (Anna responds only to the most straightforward 'realism' in art; and in the later novel Sophia Baines, despite her long sojourn in Paris, never ceases to be a philistine and dislikes Zola without reading him). Bennett's impulse to commemorate such ordinary lives, like George Eliot's at the beginning of her career, can be seen as deriving from the Wordsworthian desire 'to make the incidents of common life interesting by tracing in them, truly though not ostentatiously, the primary laws of our nature' (William Wordsworth, 'Preface' to *Lyrical Ballads*, 1800, edited by W. J. B. Owen, Oxford, 1969, p 156).[1] Again, as in Jane Austen's *Northanger Abbey* (published 1818), a truthful account of 'human nature, at least in the midland counties of England, was to be looked for' not in novels of romantic incident – for Jane Austen Mrs Radcliffe's Gothic; for Bennett perhaps Rider Haggard's imperialistic or Elinor Glyn's erotic fantasy – but in a steadfast adherence to the solid details of mundane existence among members of a class neither remotely aristocratic nor exotically impoverished.

It was exactly Bennett's patient ironic attention to the embedding of his characters in the social and economic fabric of their place of confinement ('*of* the Five Towns') that infuriated or failed to satisfy two of the main novelists of the next generation, for whom the individual had come to be conceived more psychologically and poetically, more in relief against the prosaic world of daily living.[2] D. H. Lawrence, another Midlander, who had already begun as a novelist with *The White Peacock* (1911) and *The Trespasser* (1912), read the story of Anna in Italy ten years after its publication and reacted violently to its solidity, which seemed to him stolidity.

To-day, to be in Hanley, and to read almost my own dialect, makes me feel quite ill. I hate England and its hopelessness. I hate Bennett's resignation.

1 The *Staffordshire Sentinel* in 1902 greeted *Anna of the Five Towns* as fulfilling a long-felt hope for a Potteries novel 'of the "Mill on the Floss" type' (*Arnold Bennett: The Critical Heritage*, edited by James Hepburn, 1981, p 156).
2 According to Alan Friedman, 'the energy of the novel shifted from a polar distribution between its two centres – the individual self and the social world – to an unbalanced concentration in the self' ('The Novel', in *The Twentieth-Century Mind: History, Ideas and Literature in Britain*, edited by C. B. Cox and A. B. Dyson, 3 vols, Oxford, 1972, I (1900–1918), p 414).

Tragedy ought really to be a great kick at misery. But *Anna of the Five Towns* seems like an acceptance – so does all the modern stuff since Flaubert. I hate it. I want to wash again quickly, wash off England, the oldness and grubbiness and despair.

(*The Letters of D. H. Lawrence*, edited and with an Introduction by
Aldous Huxley, London, 1932, pp 64–5)

The basis on which Bennett has rejected Kipling's England is in turn rejected by Lawrence. In *Sons and Lovers*, to be published in 1913, Lawrence would start from the misery of Paul Morel's mother, for whom 'the prospect of her life made her feel as if she were buried alive', and progress to Paul's final desolate emancipation – not unlike Stephen's at the end of *A Portrait of the Artist*. The 'great kick at misery' in Lawrence and Joyce, though, is administered in the first instance by a rebellious male foot; Bennett's Anna, like his Constance and Sophia later in *The Old Wives' Tale*, has her roots in a culture of feminine submission, and never comes into contact with the 'clamorous confusion of ideas for reconstruction' which motivates the Ann Veronica of H. G. Wells in her rebellion against *her* tyrannical parent. (In *Clayhanger* (1910) Bennett took on his first serious male protagonist of a Potteries novel.) Revolt against the burden of a father's restrictive expectations gave a creative 'kick' to Samuel Butler's influential *The Way of All Flesh* (posthumously published in 1903) and Edmund Gosse's masterpiece *Father and Son* (a memoir anonymously published in 1907), both stories of sons refusing to buckle under to paternally enforced Christian beliefs; but Bennett's insight, while he was sympathetic to these revolts, lay in his realization that a huge mass of the population was unliberated by intellectual 'progress', by advanced ideas.

An even better-known repudiation by a succeeding writer of the Edwardian novel with Bennett as its chief exemplar is Virginia Woolf's essay 'Mr Bennett and Mrs Brown' of 1924, in which she contrasts her own sense of individual character as a unique 'phantom' to be rendered by sensitive impressions with Bennett's exhaustively classificatory detail about the social and economic circumstances of the houses his characters inhabit. 'Mrs Brown' is a real, mysteriously inspiring person seen by Virginia Woolf on a train; and the advice of 'the Edwardians', whom she lumps together, on how to deal with her is imagined ('an enormous stress on the fabric of things') and crushingly rejected: 'if you hold that novels are in the first place about people, and only in the second about the houses they live in, that is the wrong way to set about it.' She fails in this, however, to give due attention to Bennett's use of such detail as a means of making intelligible the less unique aspects of an individual's existence – not the subtlest experiences of the soul but the tangle of environmentally determined strains which the art of writers from more socially elevated origins than Bennett's has often too hastily sketched. Although an uneven book, 'a history / Homely and rude' as its epigraph admits, with occasional striking crudities of presentation, *Anna of the Five Towns* achieves its peculiar acuteness of effect not through the social crossover romance of Wells's fine *Kipps* (1905), where an inheritance bumps the naïve hero from working class to idle riches, or of Bennett's own *Buried Alive* (1908), where an abnormally reclusive great painter takes over on impulse the identity and class of his dead valet and comes down to appreciate the 'bounce' of the middling sort in suburban Putney, but through persistently observing the tragically repressive conditions of Anna's life, the muted passions scarcely guessable by the world which only an omniscient narrator can reveal.

Anna no doubt provokes Lawrence's queasiness by showing on her first appearance what the narrator calls (with a characteristic deictic gesture) 'that resigned and spiritual melancholy peculiar to women who through the error of destiny have been born into a wrong environment'. In fact, however, this description is misleading, for in the course of the novel she both discovers that she has no capacity for profound religious feeling (there is a vividly evoked Methodist conversion drive comparable to the Jesuit retreat in Joyce's *Portrait*), and rebels against the patriarchal tyranny of her excessively rich and miserly father Ephraim Tellwright, when he tries to make her conform to his ruthless business methods, by destroying a document that he will otherwise use to disgrace his victims, the Price family. The rebellion, the 'kick at misery' Lawrence misses, does take place, then – but as part of what Bennett sees with quasi-anthropological detachment and lucidity as a short-lived adolescent resistance to the (for her) finally inevitable course of Bursley affairs. The novel's narrator takes on his role of omniscient interpreter, full of proleptic remarks for the reader's guidance, as soon as Anna appears; she realizes that the handsome and highly respectable Henry Mynors loves her, and 'this was one of the three great tumultuous moments of her life'. The holiday she spends in the Isle of Man with some amiable neighbours, away from the oppressive home rule of her father, and on which she gets engaged to the ambitious industrialist Mynors, is announced when she leaves Bursley as 'the brief and unique joy of Anna's life'. It is ill-preparedly revealed to us and her, however, in 'an intense and painful gaze' on the next-to-last page, that she loves not Mynors (who is too much a businessman to share her agonized compunction about tough commercial practices) but the helpless and disgraced Willie Price. But Price despairingly jumps into an abandoned pitshaft, 'a simple and meek soul stung to revolt only in its last hour'; and Anna (thinking him in Australia) reverts to being one who 'submitted and bowed the head', marrying Mynors. Not much Lawrentian 'kick' there, certainly on the part of the characters.

The novel's triumph lies less in the handling of the love interest, which is intermittent and frequently falters, than in the unwavering representation of a society ruled apparently by religious ideals (Methodism) but really by financial stringencies and money. Willie Price's father, who hangs himself when his landlord Ephraim Tellwright presses him for the repayment of debts, provokes by his suicide – 'an abject yet heroic surrender of all those pretences by which society contrives to tolerate itself' – an apostrophe on the real hollowness of Bursley pretences: he was a man 'whose whole career was made up of dissimulations: religious, moral, and social'. In killing himself he abandons 'the decent sham' and lets down 'the general self-esteem', crying (as the narrator imagines), 'Behold me; this is real human nature. This is the truth; the rest was lies. I lied; you lied. I confess it, and you shall confess it.' For Bennett, socially speaking, self-interest *is* 'human nature, at least in the midland counties of England'. Money rules at all levels: the bank manager is 'probably the most influential man in Bursley', with 'the impassive and frosty gaze of a criminal judge'; a manufactory of pots is called (Bennett's footnote explains) a 'bank'; and the leader of the Methodist crusade is named Banks, an eloquent preacher who calls himself 'God's mountebank'. Tellwright himself, the arch-capitalist, has no humane imagination of how his investments come to pay, through the painful labour of others; at this point Bennett is close to the working-class socialist writer Robert Tressell (1870–1911), whose *The Ragged Trousered Philanthropists* (posthumously published in a truncated version in 1914) attacks money as the source of social injustice and distortion.

Bennett's double-plotted masterpiece, *The Old Wives' Tale*, begins with an illustration of Virginia Woolf's dictum (meant sarcastically) that 'House property was the common ground on which the Edwardians found it easy to proceed to intimacy'. Constance and Sophia Baines begin the novel, like Anna, on the threshold of life – looking out on St Luke's Square from the awkwardly designed family house and shop – and they end it many years later dying in the same place.

They are both full members of the obstinate and thrifty house of Baines, and there is an elegiac sense of the degeneration of their race in their sole direct descendant at the end, the worthlessly metropolitanized artist Cyril: Bennett has a quasi-Darwinian sense of racial strength and weakness, which finds, for instance, Sophia, a 'fragile slip of Baines stock, unconsciously drawing upon the accumulated strength of generations of honest living'.

Anna gets no further than the Isle of Man; we might seem in the later novel to be in the presence of a Lawrentian or Joycean emancipation, for one of the Baines sisters, Sophia, elopes from Bursley to Paris at a crisis with an adventurer, Gerald Scales. This might seem to epitomize romantic exploit, but in fact Bennett uses it to show the depth of family programming – to virtue, or to repression – which even a Baines in revolt can't help manifesting. Sophia's Paris, in failing to alter her, is far from the glamorous shining city of James's *The Ambassadors* (1903), though we could note that the hero Strether's young American protégé there only *seems* to be improved by his social and aesthetic contacts, and ends by abandoning his mistress for deeply ingrained commercial motives to return to an American career of advertisement. Even when Scales has fecklessly fallen from her, and she is in love with a French admirer, Sophia is unable to act in accord with her feelings towards Chirac:

She scowled. She would not abate one crease in her forehead to the appeal of his surprised glance. Yet she did not want to repulse him. The instinct which repulsed him was not within her own control.

Her life is baffled by 'this obstinate instinct', and cunningly contrived parallels between her Parisian life and that of her sister Constance, back in Bursley, enforce the reader's sense of predetermined character, of the impossibility for these women of adaptation to other circumstances than those of the life they were born to ('Sophia's life, in its way, had been as narrow as Constance's'). Even in their revolt against their mother they show themselves to be Baineses.

In 1911, prompted by reading *Clayhanger*, Henry James wrote to his friend, the American novelist W. D. Howells, to express his doubts about Bennett's artistic purposes, as distinct from his copious journalism:

I would at any rate give it all (what he does – so commonly! – say) for ten words from him on the question of what, for himself, such things as the old wives and Clayhangers represents and *signify* – what idea, to his own imagination, they express.[1]

James goes on to doubt if Bennett's fictions meet *his* criteria – of 'having a determined subject and ... the subject's having a determined centre'. He finds him 'interesting and "conscious"' in spite of these lacks, he says. We should wonder here whether the rigorous James, with his high valuation of formal experiment, is not failing to recognize some defensible strategy in Bennett which simply eludes his categories. It would be arguable that the 'idea' of *The Old Wives' Tale* is not a special idea just because it is deliberately a general one: that the tragedy and comedy, the value of human life is to be found in the most ordinary cases. Not to make a special case of one's subject may be a means of achieving emphatic representativeness for a writer with a levelling muse; while James's sense of the necessity of a 'centre', meaning a figure from whose point of view the action is to be reflected, tends to assume (as in his own works) a high intelligence in the characters selected.

We find in *The Old Wives' Tale* that Bennett's own narration, the account of events rendered as by an omnipresent observer and mind-reader, constitutes the 'centre' in this Jamesian sense. It's a tale *about*, not by, the old wives. Thus sensations are rendered which no one actually feels, as when the youthful Sophia has her hand taken by her narrow-minded invalid father:

She was so young and fresh, such an incarnation of the spirit of health, and he was so far gone in decay and corruption, that there seemed in this contact of body with body something unnatural and repulsive. But Sophia did not so feel it.

If Sophia doesn't feel it so, her father is scarce likely to; and we have to take the statement as a fact – repulsiveness taking place – even though no one present is repelled. Bennett's narration is there throughout ironically mediating all that happens – with an irony whose main perspective is the long view (the action covers forty years) in which the moment's crisis gets diminished by distance, and in which the laws of nature themselves are treated as ironical (which happens also in Galsworthy). One of the most powerful moments in the book takes its force from this epic span. After Sophia's elopement we follow Constance in her Bursley marriage, motherhood, bereavement and finally abandonment by her son Cyril, which leaves her

1 Unpublished letter, Harvard, 20 April 1911. I should like to thank Alexander R. James for permission to quote this passage.

'a lonely old woman'; then 'Book Three: Sophia' starts and we are carried back almost thirty years to the hopeful youth of the younger sister. The daring shift – which seems at first cruel to Constance, marooned in middle age – poignantly brings home the mere fact of ageing and mortality in a way a purely sequential narrative hardly could, anticipating the emotion of the later scene where the old Sophia sees the old corpse of her estranged husband Scales:

Sophia . . . experienced a pure and primitive emotion, uncoloured by any moral or religious quality. She was not sorry that Gerald had wasted his life, not that he was a shame to his years and to her. The manner of his life was of no importance. What affected her was that he had once been young, and that he had grown old, and was now dead. That was all. Youth and vigour had come to that. Youth and vigour always came to that. Everything came to that.

Constance, who has suffered much but never pitied herself, ends by thinking 'with a sort of tart but not sour cheerfulness: "*Well, that is what life is!*"' For Bennett life is a fact, subdivided into copious minor facts, all deserving of attention; and the material solidity of experience is primary, deserves artistic respect.

What remains with the reader of *The Old Wives' Tale* is the combination of irony and respect in the book's impersonal narration, which observes the evolutionary workings of 'the everlasting purpose' and recognizes the heroic sufferings of ordinary lives. I have said the narration is 'impersonal', but nearly half-way through there is a striking occasion where Bennett's narrator, moved by the death of Sam Povey, Constance's mildly ridiculous but good-hearted husband, appears in the first person for the only time in a novel of over 600 pages – in order to pay tribute to the dead man, who had tried to save the life of his relative, the murderer Daniel Povey. The stoical attitudes behind the irony elsewhere emerge here with an admirable candour:

He lacked individuality. He was little. I have often laughed at Samuel Povey. But I liked and respected him. He was a very honest man. I have always been glad to think that, at the end of his life, destiny took hold of him and displayed, to the observant, the vein of greatness which runs through every soul without exception.

Povey is 'liked and respected' as a representative real human being, and for the levelling Bennett, as he declares in a review of Wells's *Tono-Bungay*, 'human nature is good enough' (for Conrad's Marlow, we remember, 'nobody, nobody is good enough'). It is to this plenitude of 'packed actuality' that James refers in his essay on 'The New Novel' where he suggests that in Bennett 'the state of inordinate possession on the chronicler's part . . . *was* the sense and the meaning and the picture and the drama, all so sufficiently constituting them that it scarce mattered what they were in themselves'.

VI

If Bennett takes a position of omniscience within his fictional world, the bounds of comment he allows himself are comparatively restricted. In a 1910 article he found a feature contrary to his own practice and to what he called 'the ethics of creative art' in the work of John Galsworthy (1867–1933) – an 'extraordinary passionate cruelty towards the oppressors as distinguished from the oppressed'. He did admit, though – even if the concession may only manifest his benign critical persona – that 'the result in Mr Galsworthy's work is sometimes very pleasing'.

Galsworthy's 'oppressors' are the Forsyte family, upper middle-class embodiments of the principle of property. If the miserly Ephraim Tellwright in *Anna of the Five Towns* 'belonged to the great and powerful class of house-tyrants, the backbone of the British nation, whose views on income-tax cause ministries to tremble', then the stolid Forsytes, first realistically described as a single family, expand metaphorically during *The Man of Property* (1906) to symbolize England's dominant class. 'They are . . . half England, and the better half, too, the safe half, the three per cent half, the half that counts. It's their wealth and security that makes everything possible; makes your art possible, makes literature, science, even religion, possible.' These words are spoken by young Jolyon Forsyte, who has left the clan years before by acting out of sexual passion (something Forsytes deplore) and becoming an artist; he is warning the gentlemanly but impoverished architect Bosinney, who is building a country house for the 'man of property' of the title, Soames Forsyte, and embarking on an affair with Soames's wife Irene, that 'It's dangerous to let anything carry you away – a house, a picture, a – woman!' According to young Jolyon, moreover, 'seven-eighths of our novelists' are Forsytes.

As D. H. Lawrence was to comment in a characteristically insistent but challenging and perceptive essay of 1928, *The Man of Property* has 'elements of a very great novel, a very great satire . . . But the author has not the courage to carry it through' ('John Galsworthy', in *Phoenix: The Posthumous Papers of D. H. Lawrence*, London, 1936, p 542). The strength of its conception is to be found in the relentlessly comprehensive sarcastic commentary Galsworthy's narration (rather like his friend Conrad's on the materialist characters in *The Secret Agent*) applies to the property-minded Forsytes, for whom death is unimaginable because they can't take it with them, and some of whom 'come at last to think purely in terms of money'. As in *The Old Wives' Tale* the irony applied comes from the perspective of the very long run, a reductive technique for putting human pretensions and concerns in their natural and evolutionary place which brings with it both comedy and pathos. Galsworthy's 'extraordinary passionate cruelty', as Bennett calls it, is apparent in his obsessively detailed persecution of the Forsyte mentality (as with old Swithin's mind, 'where very little took place from morning till night') and the torture of his noticings into ironic sharpness: he will break parenthetically into the very text of a quoted letter to point out that '(they called their mother Emily – it was so *chic*)'.

This systematic reading of a tribal way of life in terms of the property instinct (linked to emotional repression, 'the power of never being able to give yourself up to anything soul and body') attains its most interesting, indeed startling intensity in the treatment of Soames Forsyte's jealously possessive marriage to Irene, who doesn't love him back. The novel is set in 1886, four years after the end of what is for Forsytes 'the golden age before the Married Women's Property Act'; but Soames anachronistically goes so far as to feel the beautiful and unhappy Irene 'his property' – even though Galsworthy has creakily contrived for Soames to have promised Irene her freedom if the marriage doesn't work, which it patently hasn't (a plot measure intended to guarantee Irene our sympathy in spite of her adultery): 'Soames only experienced a sense of exasperation amounting to pain, that he did not own her as it was his right to own her, that he could not, as by stretching out his hand to that rose, pluck her and sniff the very secrets of her heart.' Already baffled by her human autonomy and aloofness, Soames is driven mad with frustration by her affair with his employee Bosinney; divorce is unthinkable as a 'jettisoning of his property with his own hand', and in desperation he commits what the book arrestingly calls 'the greatest – the supreme act of property' – he rapes his wife. In so doing he loses her, of course – and it is this appalling violation rather than his simultaneous driving of Bosinney to bankruptcy that pushes Irene's lover to suicide.

Bosinney's suicide shocks the Forsytes as 'that final renunciation of property'. However, the book's readers know that financial disaster was not decisive for him (as it is for Bennett's Mr Price), but rather the suffering of his beloved Irene. It is with the poetic handling of

Irene and Bosinney as the opposition to Forsyte values that Lawrence in his essay takes convincing issue; Galsworthy arbitrarily decides not to carry the 'satire' through and exempts from its scope their gushily realized passion, which would be equally vulnerable to irony. The adulterous affair is justified for Galsworthy by a sentimentalizing appeal to Nature, like the adolescent sex on the tropical island of H. De Vere Stacpoole's *The Blue Lagoon* (1908), where Dick and Emmeline's coition is 'an affair absolutely natural, absolutely blameless, and without sin ... a marriage according to Nature'. The hackneyed language of irresistible passion is bluntly deployed ('that magnetic force which no consideration of honour, no principle, no interest could withstand');[1] and they are associated with the sexually loaded abundance of purple prose, as for instance in 'the copse where the spring was running riot with the scent of sap and bursting buds, the song of birds innumerable, a carpet of bluebells and sweet growing things, and the sun caught like gold in the tops of the trees'. We can recognize here the vocabulary of a 'love "beyond all words or sense"' mentioned without comic intention in Elinor Glyn's notorious *Three Weeks* (1907), where passionate excess is at centre stage. It is an authorial *donnée* that Irene is 'one of those women ... born to be loved and to love'; but her consciousness is never rendered (it would impair the idealizing projection on to her of rose-tinted images). For Lawrence this bad writing and psychological vacancy are a sign of Galsworthy's 'utter failure to see what you were when you *weren't* a Forsyte'; Irene and Bosinney should be seen as a mere reflection of those they depend on, 'absolutely living off their money and trying to do them dirt' in an anti-Forsyteism which is repellently parasitic. And missing 'the real meaning of sex, which involves the whole of a human being', Galsworthy doesn't succeed in making sex 'important', 'he only makes it repulsive' – 'like dogs copulating in the street', as Lawrence disgustedly puts it.

Galsworthy's difficulty – how to present convincing values to counter those of the established system he is deploring – arises from his partiality of approach, his wish for a clearly identifiable right to triumph (even if only in Irene's assertion that 'love triumphs over everything!' and in minor equivocation about a return of Bosinney's ghost). The opening up of Irene and Bosinney to the kind of corrosive insight into corruption and compromise which his friend

---

1 Lawrence writes scornfully of a Galsworthy lover feeling 'a "hunger"' for her, as if she were a beefsteak'.

Conrad applies in *Lord Jim* and *Nostromo* – rather than their presentation through the indulgently forgiving partisanship of young Jolyon, whose values seem to coincide with those of the narrator – would transform *The Man of Property* into a much darker and more cogently organized novel (like those, later, of Evelyn Waugh); but one with no answers, one whose omniscient narrator would keep a studied silence on questions arising.

H. G. Wells (1866–1946) was a novelist who eventually came to give more answers – not all palatable – than many readers have questions. He started in the 1890s with immensely imaginative 'scientific romances', works like *The Time Machine* (1895), *The Island of Doctor Moreau* (1896) and *The Invisible Man* (1897), where pressing social and moral and scientific preoccupations were worked out with precise symbolic suggestiveness (in *The Time Machine*, for instance, the future proletarians live below ground, and only the middle class inhabits the earth's idyllic surface). With *Love and Mr Lewisham* (1900) and *Kipps* (1905), he turned to a middle phase of social observation, what Bennett called 'daily verifiable actualism'. *Kipps*, a sardonic variation on Dickens's *Great Expectations*, itself none too blithe, was praised by James as 'the first closely and intimately, the first intelligently and consistently ironic or satiric novel', free of 'the sentimental or conventional interference' – a success, we might say, where *The Man of Property* fails. Wells was a writer of genius with a real gift for conveying the experience of a class – the 'lower middle' – through language creatively modelled on their own, for telling 'jest what a Rum Go everything is' and how 'they were all caught', in a manner James called 'vivid and sharp and raw' (quoted in *Henry James and H. G. Wells: A Record of Their Friendship, Their Debate on the Art of Fiction, and Their Quarrel*, edited with an Introduction by Leon Edel and Gordon N. Ray, London, 1958, p 105). *The History of Mr Polly* (1910), probably his best-loved novel, inventively dismayed at the 'bookish illiteracy' of its forlorn hero, was his final real attempt to sustain the praise of his friend Conrad (a Sussex neighbour) for achieving an art that would 'contain [his] convictions' as much as his polemical works of theory – an art 'where they would be seen in a more perfect light' (letter from Conrad to Wells, 25 September 1908, quoted in Frederick R. Karl, *Joseph Conrad: The Three Lives: A Biography*, New York 1979, p 656). *Tono-Bungay* (1908), an extremely ambitious 'Condition of England' novel of panoramic social analysis and generalization, puts these 'convictions' and preoccupations more squarely and crudely than the others, mainly because of its sprawling and explosive first-person narration by George Ponderevo (*Kipps* and *Mr Polly* have third-person narrators). In a 1925 Preface, even so, Wells claimed it as 'the finest and most finished novel upon the accepted lines that he has written or is ever likely to write'.

The title refers to a worthless patent medicine manufactured, advertised and successfully sold by George's pharmacist uncle Teddy Ponderevo (this was the age of Teddy Roosevelt and Edward VII), and the main arc of the story follows the Napoleonic or meteoric rise and fall of this hollow capitalistic venture, motivated at bottom by nothing nobler than an invidious desire for money and rank to 'show' his old enemies. Teddy Ponderevo's *nouveaux* millions buy him the ancient seat of Lady Grove (he is inspired, he tells George, by Kipling's allegorical story of 1902, 'Below the Mill Dam', to 'join up with the old order' – an ironic cut at the 'clayey ideals' of which Bennett saw Kipling as the champion). George helps with his uncle's scheme, thus becoming an involved witness who can testify against capitalism from experience; it is possible, indeed, that Wells modelled George's relation to Uncle Teddy on Marlow's to Kurtz; but the formal structure of the novel stretches – one might judge splits open – to include also George's boarding-school education, his childhood experience of the English nobility at Bladesover (where his mother is housekeeper), his contact with Dissent, his time as an engineering student at the University of London, his marriage to the ideologically-stultified Marion, his vigorous adulteries, his aeronautical experiments, and his final fortnight of 'passionate delights and solemn joys' with his aristocratic childhood *inamorata* Beatrice (a sexed-up echo of Pip and Estella in *Great Expectations*). Ponderevo oddly starts by confessing that the text he is writing is 'something in the nature of a novel'; oddly, since for him (a fictitious character) it is presumably an autobiography. It is as if Wells is speaking to us directly, then (and maybe to the critical Conrad and James in particular), when George declares that 'I want to get in all sorts of things. My ideas of a novel all through are comprehensive rather than austere'. For Wells, it seems, the first-person account by an intellectually adequate figure (unlike Kipps and Mr Polly) offers an opening for the kind of generalized social discussion otherwise restricted to works of social theory like *Mankind in the Making* (1903), *A Modern Utopia* (1905) or *Socialism and the Family* (1906). The heady combination of this level of analysis with the quasi-confessional account of George's marriage and adulteries (based on

Wells's own)[1] and the Conradian pastiche in the desperate expedition to 'the west coast of Africa' in search of 'quap' (a valuable but 'cancerous' radioactive compound) and the unsatisfied visits to the Fabian Society gives the book undoubted vigour; it is difficult, however, to claim a unity for it even in the loose terms it seems to propose for itself. Perhaps the greatest difficulty is the discrepancy between George Ponderevo's role as narrator and as character; he has to be deeply involved in capitalist exploitations (he actually murders a native on the 'quap' island, for example), and it is extremely unclear how far this presumable taint of corruption is supposed to disqualify him as a disinterested observer, *characterize* him or give rise to ironic doubts about his reliability. The impulse to inclusiveness seems to sabotage the possibility of artistic coherence. By 1912 James was writing to Gosse that Wells 'has cut loose from literature clearly – practically altogether' (*Selected Letters of Henry James to Edmund Gosse 1882–1915: A Literary Friendship*, edited by Rayburn S. Moore, Baton Rouge, 1988, p 265).

VII

E. M. Forster (1879–1970) is perhaps the major Edwardian novelist who most directly requires us to come to terms with his style of narration. We can properly question whether the omniscient figure who mediates the action for us is not too much interfering with the reality to be conveyed, is not indeed a know-it-all exceeding the contractually permitted power of an author. If as James suggested 'the state of inordinate possession on the chronicler's part' distinguishes Bennett's fiction, so that his novels become partly displays of the narrator's personality, the subdued and scrupulously even-handed conduct of the narration towards the characters commands our respect and trust. With Forster the case is different. F. R. Leavis, an admirer with reservations, put the point well:

Mr. Forster's style is personal in the sense that it keeps us very much aware of the personality of the writer, so that even where actions, events and the experiences of characters are supposed to be speaking for themselves the turn of phrase and tone of voice bring the presenter and commentator into

---

1 His long-suppressed autobiographical *H. G. Wells in Love: Postscript to an Experiment in Autobiography*, edited by G. P. Wells, 1984, gives an intriguingly detailed and self-righteous account of the many affairs and 'cheerful encounters' he was driven to by his 'restless craving for the clasp of an appreciative body' and his need for 'at least a transitory ecstatic physical realization of my *persona*'.

the foreground. Mr. Forster's felicities and his charm, then, involve
limitations.

('E. M. Forster', *The Common Pursuit*, Penguin, 1962, p 275)

Virginia Woolf, also sympathetic but doubtful, had equally complained of the intrusiveness of the author in Forster's works: 'Just as
we are yielding ourselves to the pleasures of the imagination, a little
jerk rouses us' ('The Novels of E. M. Forster', *Collected Essays*,
edited by Leonard Woolf, London, 1966, III, p 349). Such 'a little
jerk' disturbs us in *Howards End*, for example, when Forster tells us
on one page that a subsidiary character, Aunt Juley, 'developed
acute pneumonia' and 'slipped out of life' in a certain manner, only
to inform us on the next that 'Mrs Munt did not die'. Whatever the
shock effect of this proffering then retraction of fact, the chief
impression it makes is of a facetiously edgy quarrel with the conventions of fiction, the rules by which relations between readers and
authors are normally governed and expectations guided (the chapter
has begun: 'It was not unexpected entirely. Aunt Juley's health had
been bad all the winter').

To what, we must ask, does such a surprise correspond? It seems
excessive as a way of rendering the serious possibility that Aunt
Juley *might* die; and there can be no point of view it is matching,
since no one (except the misled reader) actually thinks she *has* died.
The purpose here seems to be to 'bring the presenter and commentator into the foreground', to issue a forcible reminder of his cleverness,
liveliness and unconventionality.

These reminders, seldom so arresting, occur throughout Forster's
first novel, *Where Angels Fear to Tread* (1905). The work operates,
as Virginia Woolf notes, on the simple axis between 'the disease,
convention, and the remedy, nature'; between the grey English
suburb Sawston and the colourful Italian hill-town Monteriano. The
vulgar and flirtatious widow Lilia Herriton travels to Italy with, as
chaperone, a Sawston friend, the respectable Caroline Abbott, to get
away from her repressively respectable family-in-law, and marries on
impulse a penurious and non-aristocratic native, Gino. Her brother-
in-law, the sapless ironist and Italophile Philip Herriton, is des-
patched to Monteriano as an ambassador from his domineering and
insincerely high-minded mother (James's *The Ambassadors* of 1903
often comes to mind) with the mission of bringing Lilia back
unmarried, but he is too late and anyway ineffectual. Relations are
broken off until Lilia, whose marriage has been a disaster (Gino has
routinely philandered; she has failed to adapt), dies in childbirth,

leaving a son. Caroline Abbott feels guilt at her past dereliction of duty to Sawston values and insists on going out to retrieve the child from Gino's presumed barbarous neglect; Mrs Herriton's family pride forces her to send Philip and his grotesquely puritanical sister Harriet (till now on principle only ever a tourist in Protestant Switzerland) on this second mission, which exposes the English travellers to the sensuous freedoms and generosities, as well as brutalities, of Italy. Philip Herriton and Caroline Abbott, like James's Lambert Strether, find themselves embarrassingly 'open to contradictory impressions', and hesitate, struck by Gino's authentic paternal passion. But the project – thanks to Harriet's stupid persistence – ends in cruel tears and results in a new, wise, tragic, relativistic, humbler consciousness for Philip Herriton, who returns having been tortured (literally) and had a revelation of 'greatness in the world' and thus being, as Forster informs us, 'saved'. Foreign experience, that is, exotic and spontaneous, can redeem the suburban conformist from the shackles of English middle-class life, show him what life is and give him ideals.

The book's value-system is presented with a battery of devices which, as Forster's friend R. C. Trevelyan commented, are directed to 'expressiveness' without restraint. Trevelyan appealed to traditional conventions of narration:

For the purely narrative part of a story, where the author himself speaks, should surely keep throughout a certain sameness of quality, and also a certain dignity, and if possible, beauty, even in a slight or comic narrative, at least it does in all the books I really care about.

(Quoted in Appendix, *Where Angels Fear to Tread*, edited by Oliver Stallybrass, Penguin, 1975, p 163)

Forster's narrative voice unevenly breaks in: sometimes with the colloquial abruptness of one passing a spontaneous bitchy remark, a malicious *bon mot* too good to miss (about Mrs Herriton – 'the map left a good deal to imagination, and she had not got any'; or about Lilia – 'she forgot her nature and began to reflect'); sometimes with more apparent seriousness, as in a sententious glorification of Gino's noble savagery ('The man was majestic; he was a part of Nature . . .') or a sentimental and offensively snobbish mention of his superstitious piety ('he prayed the crude uncouth demands of the simple'); and most notably with generalizations about 'us' and judgments of the characters which refocus the book's thematic argument when it risks being forgotten, as when 'Romance only dies with life. No pair of pincers will ever pull it out of us' or when Philip Herriton despairs of remodelling Sawston by championing aesthetic values, 'not knowing that human love and love of truth sometimes conquer where love of beauty fails'. What gives this narration its peculiar flavour is the 'entertaining' doubleness of its transitions between personal sniping, the tone of a narrator who seems to be on the same level of reality as the characters, and the grander formulaic laying down of provisional laws of life and of the 'nature' of individuals, exercises of the authority to pontificate with an epigrammatic absolutism.

Once married to Gino, Lilia combs her hair in the living-room, 'for she had something of the slattern in her nature, and there was no need to keep up appearances'; but the unhappiness of her marriage ends by conferring a new rank on her: 'Lilia had achieved pathos despite herself, for there are some situations in which vulgarity counts no longer. Not Cordelia nor Imogen more deserve our tears.' 'Pathos', it should be noted, becomes a fixed category to be 'achieved' by a character – as if it were something consciously aspired to; in Forster's decision to leap to a general *critical* term (one which refers to his relation with the reader) rather than to abide in the real particular circumstances of Lilia's misery, we could see what Frank Kermode has called his 'protective facetiousness' (*The Art of Telling*, Harvard, 1983, p 23). Forster awards his own creation this 'pathos', moreover, naming it rather than demonstrating it, and then bullies the reader with the assertively democratic appeal (its syntax flourishingly inverted) to Shakespeare's noble and innocent heroines – who suffer for their virtue rather than their vulgar egotism, and might be thought *more* to deserve our tears on that account. There is irony in the overstatement, perhaps, but its main function is not to qualify Forster's claim, rather to suggest a wise knowingness behind his intervention. And we could register the subtly tyrannical power-relation of narrator to character here: Lilia is attacked in one place and then backhandedly praised later (in a way which reflects more credit on us for our generous sympathy than on her – she's still vulgar). The alternation of praise and blame enforces our sense of the narrator's power to judge; but while such an explicit process of summary judgement is going on the reader cannot feel that the characters are being given enough rope to hang *themselves*, as Henry James for instance insists in 'The Lesson of Balzac' (1905) that they must be.[1] The disconcerting tricks of narration, the omissions of fact

1 Forster would not satisfy James's requirement in the essay of 'that respect for the liberty of the subject which I should be willing to name as *the* great sign of the painter of the first order' (*Literary Criticism*, edited by Leon Edel and Mark Wilson, Cambridge, 1984, II, p 133).

and deliberate non-preparation of effects so that we can be startled when they come out of the blue – these ensure the reader is not in a position to participate in the adjudication of values Forster so clearly signals as in progress.

Howards End (1910), following *The Longest Journey* (1907) and *A Room with a View* (1908), is a 'Condition of England' novel of much ambition and uncertain greatness, his last (except the homosexual novel *Maurice* written by 1914 and unpublished till 1971) before *A Passage to India* in 1924. It deals with the middle class, material which Bennett in his *New Age* column the previous year had said challenged the artist because it 'lacks interest, lacks essential vitality, lacks both moral and spectacular beauty'. Even more than in *Where Angels Fear to Tread* the personality of the narrator is brought into the foreground, and there are indeed passages and propositions that might as plausibly come from an essay as from a novel ('To speak against London is no longer fashionable', and so on). Whereas in Robert Tressell's indignantly socialist report on working-class poverty in Hastings ('Mugsborough') *The Ragged Trousered Philanthropists*, which he wrote between 1907 and 1910, such expository outbursts seem to arise irresistibly from the misery described, Forster's interventions here can be read as more insinuatingly manipulative attempts on the reader's sympathies. The book uses a set of formulae and generalized oppositions of terms which directly or indirectly look back to Matthew Arnold's in *Culture and Anarchy* (1869) and elsewhere: Margaret Schlegel, the heroine, has a motto which is also the work's – 'Only connect! That was the whole of her sermon'; and we find recurrent references to prose and passion, beast and monk, telegrams and anger, panic and emptiness, personal relations, hands on the ropes, or seeing life steadily and seeing it whole.

Like *The Spoils of Poynton*, 'An Habitation Enforced' or *Tono-Bungay*, *Howards End* investigates the disputed inheritance of England symbolically, through a plot dealing with the country house of the title. Arnold's cultural dialectic between Hellenism and Hebraism is reproduced in the two central families – the intellectual, aesthetic and half-foreign Schlegel sisters, Helen and Margaret (much flightier than Bennett's Constance and Sophia), and the unreflective, stolidly Mammonist bourgeois Wilcoxes (not unlike Galsworthy's Forsytes, but approached at first with more apparent sympathy). Margaret (after her sister's abortive crush on a Wilcox son) establishes such a rapport with the enigmatically wise Mrs Wilcox (an older woman rather like *Nostromo*'s Mrs Gould) that when she unexpectedly dies Mrs Wilcox turns out to have attempted to bequeath her ancestral property of Howards End to *her* (a feminine, spiritual heir) rather than to her own family, who are wanting in the necessary sensibility. The Wilcoxes ignobly suppress this informal will. Margaret then, in the spirit of social and psychological 'connection', sees in the practical, male, vigorous Wilcoxes a necessary complementary principle to the theoretical, feminine, hesitant Schlegels and on this theory marries Henry Wilcox, the widower of her friend (a marriage of convenience for Forster's discussion, permitting inside testimony on the bourgeoisie). But the Schlegels have befriended a feeble and ill-educated clerk, Leonard Bast, who has hopeless intellectual aspirations and who represents for them a chance to show a social conscience; and his wife, by a grotesque coincidence, once had an affair with Henry Wilcox (who is thus shown up as a hypocrite and blusterer). Leonard gets Margaret's sister pregnant and is killed by the brutal Wilcox son Charles. The Wilcoxes collapse and the novel ends with a humbled Henry Wilcox at Howards End looked after by Margaret and Helen, with the bastard child to inherit; a mutedly mystical ending in which Mrs Wilcox's will comes to pass, so that Forster's heroine wins a moral and literal 'triumph' because 'the inner life had paid'. Her success as an introspective individual has already been startlingly endorsed by the author: 'It is suggested that Margaret has succeeded – so far as success is yet possible. She does understand herself, she has some rudimentary control over her own growth.'

The explicit approval here reflects a partisanship in Forster's organization of the debate and a circularity in the formulaic terms which have the combined effect of foreclosing on the possibility of viewing the Wilcoxes dispassionately, let alone sympathetically. Margaret's apparent openness to their values is only a pretext for her eventual denunciation of them ('I've had enough of your unweeded kindness'), like George Ponderevo's involvement with capitalist expansionism in *Tono-Bungay*, only with less inventive gusto and even less convincing inwardness. Forster is unable to restrain himself from sniping at non-Schlegels, particularly at the Wilcoxes; his friend H. O. Meredith's remark about *Where Angels Fear to Tread* was still true, that 'you have an immense amount to learn yet especially in . . . your treatment of the characters which you dislike' (p 12). Thus we are told with vindictive authority that Henry 'was really paving the way for a lie', or, even more crushingly, 'as is Man to the Universe, so was the mind of Mr Wilcox to the minds of some men – a concentrated light upon a tiny spot'. Most cruelly, of Henry's daughter-in-law Polly, we learn that 'she was a rubbishy little creature, and she knew it'. It is worth recalling the sarcastic epilogue to Ford's interesting novel: *A Call*, published in the same year, where he reveals only afterwards which characters he dislikes *and* that 'I omitted to add these comments, because I think that for a writer to intrude himself between his characters and his reader is to destroy to that extent all the illusion of his work' (*A Call: The Tale of Two Passions*, with an afterword by C. H. Sisson, Carcanet, 1984, p 162).

As cultural analysis *Howards End* is perhaps stimulating, but Leavis commands assent when he remarks that Forster 'has not seen his problem rightly: his view of it is far too external and unsubtle' (*The Common Pursuit*, Penguin, 1962, p 270). Many of the faults of the novel correspond to Galsworthy's arbitrary exemption of Irene and Bosinney from the ironic scrutiny he never fails to exercise at the expense of Forsyteism; Margaret in particular gets too indulgent a press, too regular top marks, while the Wilcoxes are unsparingly bullied as bullies, for us to feel that Forster's novel, in spite of its parade of spontaneity, has sufficiently respected the liberty of his subject.

A Passage to India (1924) has limiting analogies with Forster's Edwardian novels, but its relative gravity of approach, its meditation on the gulf in 'personal relations' between British and Indian, and its quasi-mystical interest in Hinduism, Buddhism and Islam, set bounds to the narrator's sententiousness and facetiousness. Race plays the same part as class in *Howards End*, and the upholders of Empire receive some of the same ironic sniping as the Wilcoxes for their 'Public School attitude' (they can 'titter brutally', for example). The phrase which carries difficult value for Kipling in *Kim* and Conrad in *Lord Jim* is put in a facile imperial mouth: 'The long and the short of it is Heaslop's a sahib; he's the type we want, he's one of us.' English club-feeling is hounded by ventriloquial ironies: 'We must exclude someone from our gathering, or we shall be left with nothing.' And Forster again asserts the prevalence in life of 'confusion' and 'boredom', claiming with a possibly affected paradoxical extremism that 'most of life is so dull that there is nothing to be said about it, and the books and talk that would describe it as interesting are obliged to exaggerate, in the hope of justifying their own existence.' The proper reply to this would be that interest depends on the quality of one's attention. But the novel, fortunately, does not entirely bear out this claim; it contains epiphanic moments of inter-racial contact, personal intuition and ritual transcendence; and despite its sarcasms it builds a larger community of mutual respect than the earlier novels, so that it feels more ample and more satisfying. Whether it deserves its 'classic' status, though, remains an open question.

The line of ostentatious wit we have examined in Forster – which possibly derives in part from the delight in paradox taken by Oscar Wilde – has other exemplars in the period whose work deserves mention. Wilde's friend Ada Leverson (1862–1933) shared Forster's grasp of fiction's opportunity for the exercise of authorial power, for the epigrammatic putting-down of her own characters – an end achieved in her case through the manipulation of dialogue – and in her trilogy *The Little Ottleys*, whose volumes appeared in 1908, 1912 and 1916, she put her weighting on the side of her heroine in the portrayal of her grindingly unhappy marriage to an insufferable twerp, and her eventual escape from it. The liberty of the subjects is not much respected in her authorial overloading of the die, and the works are deprived of dramatic depth by a sitcom repetitiveness, accurate enough, of course, as an autobiographically based mimesis of marital tedium. As in Ford's tetralogy *Parade's End*, the miserable misalliance shown at the beginning takes long years and several volumes to give place to a happier connection – the protracted deferral of emotional gratification testifying to a more demanding view of the marriage-tie than Wells or Elinor Glyn would have had patience for.

Max Beerbohm (1872–1956) wrote only one novel – the extravagantly sardonic story of Oxford's youth killing itself in the manner of lemmings for love of *Zuleika Dobson* (1911) – but his satirical sharpness and poise also satisfyingly give an edge to the whimsy both in his literary sketches and parodies and in his wonderfully funny cartoons of contemporary writers. There is a different kind of ironic base, less one of high worldliness than of elusive Christian polemic, to the enormous *oeuvre* of G. K. Chesterton (1874–1936), who is most remembered for his creation of the pretty reasonable but very devout little priest–detective Father Brown, a Catholic alternative to Sherlock Holmes, in collections of stories from 1911. In an essay of 1908 called 'The Paradoxes of Christianity' Chesterton presents the world as 'nearly reasonable, but not quite', in a way which calls for the saving twists of theology; and this emphatically skewed logic, which led Henry James to declare that he had 'reduced to a science the art of putting everything *à rebours*' (*Henry James: Letters*, edited by Leon Edel, Harvard 1974–84, IV, p 425), is highly visible in his best-known novel, *The Man who was Thursday: a nightmare* (1908), which responds to Conrad's anarchist-novel of the previous year, *The Secret Agent*, by imagining a philosophical police force that combats intellectual heresies in the hope of preventing terrorist outrages. It is a dazzlingly self-conscious work, unexpected and appealing.

VIII

It is impossible in a short survey of this kind even to mention the full range of novelists whose works deserve or at least reward attention in so productively unstable a period for fiction. Frequently we find the preoccupations of major writers present in less complex form among novels scarcely considered 'literature'. George Ponderevo's sense in *Tono-Bungay* that by spending an adulterous dirty week away from his frigid wife with the secretary Effie he has 'vindicated some right that was in question' has its correspondence with Madame Zalenska's speeches on behalf of adulterous passion as the embodiment of spontaneous emotion against 'the puny conventions of the world' in *Three Weeks* (1907) by Elinor Glyn. In Ford's *Some Do Not . . .* (1924), which begins in pre-1914 peacetime, the lucidly feudalist hero Tietjens bursts out indignantly: 'What's the sense of all these attempts to justify fornication? England's mad about it.' And certainly the twenty-one days of Mrs Glyn's novel are filled with exotic fornications between this Ruritanian queen and a not-very-brainy young English gentleman-stud named Paul, with 'no worries where his banking account was concerned'. His function is to give her an heir for the Ruritanian throne, and also to 'stem the tide of [his] nation's decadence' by becoming 'a strong man' – for which purpose she teaches him 'how – to – LIVE', but not quite in the sense the fastidious Strether intends in James's *The Ambassadors*. Presumably few of the book's two million readers would have been able to respond with a yes to Mrs Glyn's direct question to us – 'Do you know the Belvedere at the Rigi Kaltbad?' – but then social as much as sexual ecstasy was the basis of appeal.

Another bestseller of the period blended erotic fantasy with the dream of a return to the primitive which Darwinian thought inspired: H. de Vere Stacpoole's curiously potent *The Blue Lagoon* (1908), in which two children (fortunately not brother and sister) get marooned and grow up to become lovers on a South Sea island in what is presented as Nature's experiment ('Let me put these buds of civilization back into my nursery and see what they will become . . .'). The primitive for H. de Vere Stacpoole is a lost paradisal state: 'Who is happier than a naked savage in a warm climate?' *Heart of Darkness* is not the only novel of the period to question such a romanticization: Conan Doyle's prehistoric fantasy *The Lost World* (1912) has a scientific expedition to an inaccessible South American plateau; the expedition discovers a place caught in the dinosaur-ridden past, a place of exotic adventure but one where the hirsute Professor

Challenger confronts an apeman king who resembles him – 'an absurd parody' – in every feature except his 'magnificent cranium' and high brow. There is a battle between apemen and a more advanced (more human) tribe which brings the plateau into line with evolutionary progress: 'At last man was to be supreme and the man-beast to find forever his allotted place.'

Conan Doyle's advocacy of the scientific spirit (which he managed to combine with an enthusiastic interest in spiritualism) emerges most famously in the Sherlock Holmes cycle of stories and novels, where the detective is 'the scientific expert'. *The Hound of the Baskervilles* (1902) contrasts helpfully with the ghost stories of M. R. James in this respect. Both deal in ancient documents, curses, monstrous creatures and the horror of being followed by some non-human malignity; but where M. R. James presents such cases swathed in an unearthly indeterminacy which keeps intact their supernatural centres, thus staying faithful to what his biographer calls 'an ineradicable perplexity in the mind of their creator' (Michael Cox, 'Introduction', *Casting the Runes and Other Ghost Stories*, Oxford, 1987, p xxviii), Conan Doyle firmly brings the light of science to bear on the frightening fogs of Dartmoor (which is covered in prehistoric sites) and confirms Holmes's sense that 'the devil's agents may be of flesh and blood, may they not?' M. R. James's spare narratives of superstition and the unknowable frequently achieve their chill through verbal obliquities and evasions at the climatic moment, coming out with no more than 'or – one thing and another', 'some metallic object', 'a rather indistinct personage' or 'I'm not at all sure that he was alive'. Conan Doyle's detective story, on the other hand, rationalist and epistemologically confident, eschews such dimness and fragmentation: Holmes boasts of putting the Baskerville mystery into 'a single connected narrative', and at the end of his work of illumination 'the case has been so entirely cleared up that I am not aware that there is anything which has remained a secret to us.'

A work which retains its literary as well as adventurous power to excite, *The Riddle of the Sands* (1903), the only novel by the remarkable Erskine Childers (1870–1922), belongs to various genres: sea-story, spy-story and, most specifically, invasion-threat narrative (like H. G. Wells's *The War in the Air* (1908)). It was seriously meant to alert the authorities at home to a real threat. The first-person narrator is a Foreign Office clerk, Carruthers, who gets summoned by his old friend Davies to join him on a sturdy old yacht in the grim waters of the North Sea in October, starts as 'an utter duffer at sailing' and has a bad time but is 'finally cured of funk' and learns, like Kim in the Secret Service, to 'play the game'. He joins Davies, that is, in his surreptitious attempts to discover the Germans' invasion plans. Admirable lucidity about nautical details, and a lyrical precision in description, make clear that the vividly under-stated upper-class idiom is a concealment of real thought and feeling – as in *Parade's End* – rather than a betrayal of its absence. The modestly heroic Davies speaks the language of a hearty schoolboy: 'that chap was a spy', 'By Jove, we want a man like this Kaiser', and – which is the point of the book – 'They're apt to be a bit slack at home . . . Those Admiralty chaps want waking up.' But he has a passion for adventure, analogous to that of Conrad's Jim, to which Carruthers, a Marlow without ultimate reservations, learns to pay tribute: 'a fire of pent-up patriotism struggling incessantly for an outlet in strenuous physical expression'; and like Jim with his relish of his 'magnificent chance' in Patusan, he looks forward to the 'magnificent opportunities' that war with Germany would bring for the patriot. With all its limitations of concern (it has complexities, but not of a Conradian order), *The Riddle of the Sands* is an honourable and stimulating book of considerable formal perfection and permanent value.

4

POETRY OF THE FIRST WORLD WAR

Desmond Graham

I had been walking in Westmorland, rather happy, with water-lilies twisted round my hat – big, heavy, white and gold water-lilies that we found in a pool high up – and girls who had come out on a spree and who were having tea in the upper room of an inn, shrieked with laughter.

... Then we came down to Barrow-in-Furness, and saw that war was declared. And we all went mad. I can remember soldiers kissing on Barrow station, and a woman shouting defiantly to her sweetheart – 'When you get at'em, Clem, let'em have it,' as the train drew off – and in all the tramcars, 'War' ... and the electric suspense everywhere – and the amazing, vivid, visionary beauty of everything, heightened by the immense pain everywhere.

(30 January 1915)

In this letter D. H. Lawrence (1885–1930) is writing to Lady Cynthia Asquith six months after Britain's declaration of war on 4 August 1914. His reaction is powerfully personal. None the less, his imagination can conjure up for us the mix of passions, the absurd relief and the heightened effect of the news, at once absolute and, for the moment, meaningless.

Charles Sorley (1895–1915), on a year abroad between public school and Oxford, witnessed the scene in Germany:

The song and guitar were busy in Neumagen all that night. 'When you get back to England,' said the fatherly policeman to me, 'you tell them that Germany doesn't sleep.' But what the lights of the street had hid, the light of day next morning showed us ... The children, who seemed to scent disaster, were crying – all of those I saw. The women were mostly snuffling and gulping, which is worse. And the men, the singers of the night before, with drawn faces and forced smiles, were trying to seek comfort from their long drooping pipes and envying those who need not rejoin their barracks till Tuesday. It was Sunday, and the wailing notes of an intercession service on a bad organ were exuded from the church in the background. I have never seen a sight more miserable.

(From article in *The Cambridge Chronicle*, 14 August 1914, quoted in *The Letters of Charles Sorley*, 1919, pp 214–15)

In the nearby town of Trier, Sorley found things were rather different: he was arrested as a potential spy. On 6 August he arrived back in Cambridge:

I am full of mute and burning rage and annoyance and sulkiness about it [the war]. I could wager that out of twelve million eventual combatants there aren't twelve who really want it. And 'serving one's country' is so unpicturesque and unheroic when it comes to the point.

(Letter to A. E. Hutchinson, 10 [?] August 1914)

The myth that the outbreak of war was greeted joyfully throughout the nation is hard to counter. The war, once it was on, however, brought about a propaganda effort of the most extreme kind. As Britain had no conscription and had, by continental European scales, a small standing army, the public media were taken over in the cause of recruitment. Censorship, as is made clear in *The First Casualty* by Philip Knightley, was to be ruthless throughout the war.

From the very first days poetry was brought to the service of the propaganda machine; for in 1914 poetry was associated with a public – if degenerate – function. It was recited on great occasions and used as a quarry for high-sounding words. It was seen as the expression of grand, national, sublime sentiments. It was also seen as the expression of dreams, personal, sentimental feelings: poetry in the service of the public cause or poetry as escape.

The bulk of the poems jotted on envelopes or in diaries and letters throughout the war were of the latter kind, but placed their dreams of home, of loved ones and of known localities within the context of the public cause. So, oddly, although most poems are on unwarlike subjects, they are public.

It was possible to comprehend something of the war from Britain in 1914 and 1915, and many people did so:

I saw a soldier on the pier, with only one leg. He was young and handsome: and strangely self-conscious, and slightly ostentatious: but confused. As yet, he does not realize anything, he is still in the shock . . . I cannot tell you why, but I am afraid of the ghosts of the dead. They seem to come marching home in legions over the white, silent sea, breaking in on us with a roar and a white iciness.

From this scene described in a letter to Lady Ottoline Morrell in May 1915, D. H. Lawrence also wrote the poem 'We have gone too far'. A set of poems depicting war and his opposition to it, 'Bits', remained uncollected until after his death.

Edward Thomas's (1878–1917) poetry is made from an imaginative understanding of what was happening elsewhere, across the Channel, remote but still most intimately connected with daily lives in Britain. Yet many commentators convey the impression that the war was somehow tolerable until the Somme slaughter in July 1916 revealed the full horror of mechanized war.

In October 1915 Robert Graves (1895–1985) wrote from the Front to Eddie Marsh:

I don't know how I came through the last show unhurt; when our losses in combatant officers are considered, the odds worked out at three-to-one against my being the lucky survivor. Oh Eddie, there were some awful scenes that morning!

At the end of August 1914, Sorley joined a regular army unit. After ending what he called 'that hideous heap of straight-laced conventionality called drill' in a letter to A. E. Hutchinson, by early 1915 he is presenting a convincing picture of military life before embarkation:

Somehow one never lives in the future now, only in the past, which is apt to be morbid and begins to make one like an old man. The war is a chasm in time. I do wish that all journalists etc., who say that war is an ennobling purge etc., etc., could be muzzled. It simply makes people unhappy and uncomfortable, if that is a good thing. All illusions about the splendour of war will, I hope, be gone after the war.

(To R. W. Sorley)

By June Sorley was in France and for three months in a 'quiet sector' of the line:

... out in front at night in that no-man's land and long graveyard there is a freedom and a spur. Rustling of the grasses and grave tap-tapping of distant workers ... Then death and the horrible thankfulness when one sees that the next man is dead: 'We won't have to *carry* him in under fire, thank God; dragging will do': hauling in of the great resistless body in the dark, the smashed head rattling: the relief, the relief that the thing has ceased to groan: that the bullet or bomb that made the man an animal has now made the animal a corpse. One is hardened by now: purged of all false pity: perhaps more selfish than before.

(To Arthur Watts, 26 August 1915)

In his first major action, on 13 October, Sorley was killed. His death received little public attention. With a Cambridge professor for father, and a good school record at Marlborough, however, his poems and letters were gathered and published. He was not forgotten. None the less, it is not to his name that the casual historians and narrators have turned, but to that of Rupert Brooke (1887–1915).

The glamorous myth of Brooke existed even before his death from blood poisoning on the way to Gallipoli in April 1915. Having published five sonnets in 1914, which were not at first especially noticed, one of them was quoted a week before his death, by Dean Inge in St Paul's. Then Brooke's acquaintance Winston Churchill wrote a *Times* obituary on him, and words from Brooke's sonnets were appropriated as those of a generation. People ever since have been told that they were so.

The sonnets, in fact, were an aberration; in a letter Sorley defined their fault:

I think Brooke's earlier poems – especially notably 'The Fish' and 'Grantchester', which you can find in *Georgian Poetry* – are his best. That last sonnet-sequence of his . . . which has been so praised, I find . . . overpraised. He is far too obsessed with his own sacrifice, regarding the going to war of himself (and others) as a highly intense, remarkable and sacrificial exploit, whereas it is merely the conduct demanded of him (and others) by the turn of circumstances, where non-compliance with this demand would have made life intolerable . . . He has clothed his attitude in fine words: but he has taken the sentimental attitude.

The kind of bold parodic bad taste present in Brooke's 'A Channel Passage' and 'Wagner' suggests that he would have found little difficulty in writing satirically and realistically if he had seen action in war. These talents are absent from the sonnets which, like a piece of inspired copy-writing, blend the various propaganda clichés of the period and, most importantly, manage to employ both of the expected roles of poetry. They sound like the heartfelt, intimate feelings of a young man facing the loss of a life he loves and like a public statement of national dedication and significance. 'If I should die, think only this of me:/That there's some corner of a foreign field/ That is for ever England' ('The Dead').

These sonnets achieved a poetry which reads like a set of quotations from a variety of hallowed sources and resonates with the weight of half-remembered phrases. Brooke's young words took in that 'immortal' and above all 'universal' quality looked for in great art at that time and, in one step, he was over the heads of his contemporaries and sounding like a classic. Sorley answered in verse as he had answered in prose:

> When you see millions of the mouthless dead
> Across your dreams in pale battalions go,
> Say not soft things as other men have said . . .
> Say only this, 'They are dead.'

The grand scale of the war is truly envisioned, its denial of sentiment and individuality unflinchingly perceived.

By January 1916 the scale of losses could not be kept up with by voluntary service so, that month, conscription was enforced. On the first day of their offensive on the Somme in July, the British suffered 57,000 casualties: in the next four months, for an advance of seven miles the number had risen to 420,000.

By 1917 Siegfried Sassoon (1886–1967) was attempting publicly to protest against the conduct and continuance of the war. Several mutinies occurred within the French army and mutiny was suppressed within the British forces abroad. Yet in 1917 the horrors of the Somme had been undergone again in the 'Third Ypres' offensive of Passchendaele, where the land was no more than mud. When the war ended in 1918, Edmund Blunden (1896–1974), Graves, Ivor Gurney (1890–1937), David Jones (1895–1974) and Sassoon had all survived, thanks to mental breakdowns which rendered them unfit for further service. Wilfred Owen (1893–1918), Isaac Rosenberg (1890–1918) and Edward Thomas, along with Brooke and Sorley, were dead.

Every one of Edward Thomas's poems was written during the war, although he had been a prolific and hard-pressed prose writer and reviewer long before he met Robert Frost in October 1913. Through Frost's encouragement he turned, a year later, to poetry.

The war first appears innocently as part of what Thomas perceives as Englishness, in 'Tears'. It is absorbed within the occasion of 'Man and Dog'; it takes over and closes 'The Owl': Thomas's sympathy reaching from personal knowledge of hardship and comfort to 'all who lay under the stars/Soldiers and poor, unable to rejoice'. There are references to Germany and the beauty of England in 'Wind and Mist'; 'Lob', as the spirit of England, is seen as 'One of the lords of No Man's Land' who has reached there from Hastings, via Waterloo; and thoughts of war's duration directly occur in 'Fifty Faggots'.

From 'This is no case . . .', written over the Christmas period after his enlistment in July 1915, however, the war's presence is rarely in doubt. 'Rain' and 'Roads', 'February Afternoon' and 'The Cherry Trees' all connect with the war directly. From shortly before Thomas's decision to take a commission, through to his departure from England in December 1916, there is a pervasive sense of elegy. Poem after poem is a kind of preliminary farewell to what he believes he must leave: partings now sound absolute and changes irreversible. A new calm has come with a new but well-buried terror.

'[There was a Time]' offers a complex elegy for himself in which his fear is that he lacks 'strength and youth' to die 'For what can neither ask nor need his death'. Years of uncertainty have focused on a sense of personal fate. Hope, in 'When First', has 'gone forever'. It is a move into the darkness which 'does not disappoint' which concludes the night thoughts of 'Lights Out'.

Here then is a poetry of England in wartime; a poetry of waiting and absorbing into oneself the presence of a war which calls for participation. The poetry's achievement grows from its indirection, its ability to attempt nothing it cannot fulfil. It is a poetry of intimations, half-hints, ignorances and a knowledge of limitations: for the poet the war exists only in the mind, as something ahead of him or something which happens to others. He is in no doubt though of its historical reality for them and perceives this with a sympathetic imagination, a perfectly judged tact.

> The flowers left thick at nightfall in the wood
> This Eastertide call into mind the men,
> Now far from home, who, with their sweethearts, should
> Have gathered them and will do never again.

> ('In Memoriam')

The stumble in the rhythm of the final elegiac line insists that we take notice of the thought: awkwardly, we must read 'and will do never again' and not 'and will never do again'. The poetry will not soothe. Similarly, 'should' is perched at the end of a line and draws our emphasis towards it: the slight oddity of 'left thick' is explained as we find it images the dead, and the sense of volition in 'left' turns to a sense of their being abandoned. At the same time the openly conventional title, the classical parallel between flowers and the dead, the folk-song talk of 'sweethearts', the religious and customary setting of 'Eastertide' all draw the poem into traditions. So briefly, Thomas has overlaid historical and communal versions of order with the present war's disorder: its ending of patterns thought to be timeless.

In writing of how the flowers 'call into mind' the men, Thomas pitches his voice perfectly between the personal admission and the communal address. In his poems the war is a private grief or apprehension or feared future which is also communal. It is a meeting place of individuals as in 'As the Team's Head-Brass', a shared knowledge, but at the heart of that knowledge is aware-ness that it breaks an ancient rural pattern, and brings the individual inconsolable grief. The losses are communal but that is no help.

It is not surprising, then, that when Thomas considers the public presentation of the war, he does so to express his fury. The journalist, the 'fat patriot' and the propagandist abuse the privacy of those who suffer, abuse their suffering – as the title of one poem asserts: 'This is no case of petty right or wrong.' They also take over what is to him most precious: the local, the identified, the specifically communal which, in his case, is synonymous with England. Responding to the public attitude, however, Thomas, by the end of this poem, still leaves it unclear whether he is making a public statement or a private apologia, whether his tone is defiant or celebratory.

For two months an artillery officer in France, Thomas wrote no poems there. He did keep a diary and it has survived. In April 1917 he was killed.

From a poorish and, it seems, unhappy family background, Ivor Gurney (1890–1937) reached enlistment through two great commitments: the one to the landscape and people of Gloucester and the Cotswolds; the other to music – he was to be the great composer of England. He also carried with him, it appears, a hereditary tendency to schizophrenia, an illness which first afflicted him in 1912. Gurney set poems to music, beautifully, and had written poems himself. But his letters suggest that it was going to France and the trenches that turned him to poetry. He wrote then, to make a book. He was, consciously, a war poet: a task which he saw as doubling the demand for courage which soldiering already entailed.

> Now, youth, the hour of thy dread passion comes;
>   . . . When mere noise numbs
> The sense of being, the fear-sick soul doth sway,
> Remember thy great craft's honour, that they may say
> Nothing in shame of poets.
>
>   ('To the Poet before Battle')

When, in July 1917, he gave his frank opinion of his first collection *Severn and Somme* he found it 'true'; possessing some 'melody' but not enough; 'sincere' but 'not very original', with 'scraps of pure beauty'. Then he made an extraordinary apology:

Where it will fail to attract is that there is none, or hardly any of the devotion of self-sacrifice, the splendid readiness for death that one finds in Grenfell, Brooke, Nichols, etc. That is partly because I am still sick of mind and body; partly for physical, partly for mental reasons . . .

Such a defence and such an accusation were to torment him for the rest of his life.

Here, in his letter of July, he moves from it splendidly, into a statement of his greater use to Britain as artist than as cannon-fodder; into an observation on Brooke's good luck in dying early in the war and still therefore 'sincere'; and into the most telling statement of all: 'So often poets write of what they wish to believe, wish to become, as one prays for strength and virtue not yet obtained.' His own first collection, *Severn and Somme* (1917), taken by Brooke's publisher, bears this out, although there are many darker hints in it. In February 1917 he had portrayed the trench soldiers' existence in four sonnets he wrote 'for admirers of Rupert Brooke' 'intended to be a sort of counterblast against "Sonnetts [*sic*] 1914" which were written by an officer.' The blackest of them is 'Pain':

> Pain, pain continual; pain unending;
> Hard even to the roughest, but to those
> Hungry for beauty . . . Not the wisest knows,
> Nor most pitiful-hearted, what the wending
> Of one hour's way meant . . .

Gurney is fully aware of what he is doing, defining just what was wrong with Brooke's poems and the essence of what was to be the poetry of the trenches. His own sonnets are 'the protest of the physical against the exalted spiritual; of the cumulative weight of small facts against the one large. Of informed opinion against uninformed (to put it coarsely and unfairly) and fill a place. Old ladies won't like them, but soldiers may . . .'

Gurney's second collection, *War's Embers* (1919), written mostly in hospital in England, convalescing and on light duties, moves further towards showing what the 'dreadful' service entailed.

> He's gone, and all our plans
>   Are useless indeed.
> We'll walk no more on Cotswold
>   Where the sheep feed
>   Quietly and take no heed.
>
> His body that was so quick
>   Is not as you
> Knew it, on Severn river
>   Under the blue
>   Driving our small boat through.

You would not know him now . . .
  But still he died
Nobly, so cover him over
  With violets of pride
  Purple from Severn side.

Cover him, cover him soon!
  And with thick-set
Masses of memoried flowers –
  Hide that red wet
  Thing I must somehow forget.

('To His Love')

The conventional, period, lyric sentiments – 'We'll walk no more on Cotswold'; the simple, conclusive rhyme at the close of the third stanza, with which the poem should end; the pastoral repose – all these are broken, as parts of speech lose definition and ambiguities threaten at every turn. What is the meaning of 'quick' and 'still' and 'thick-set' and 'memoried'? Rhythms lead to the precipice of the line's ending: meanings and narrative movement are continually adjusted: 'Is not as you/Knew it', 'But still he died/Nobly'.

Nowhere else in *War's Embers* are feelings so expressed; his descriptions of moments out of battle – 'Annie Laurie', 'The Battalion is Now at Rest', 'Le Coq Français', 'Photographs' – do allow the reader, however, to measure through the scale of the relief, what the soldier has left behind him in the line. Gurney also established his main themes: relief from war; the physical pains and exhaustion of the soldier, through cold, work and labour; fear constantly felt, suffered and conquered; fear that terror will prove too great. By late 1917 Gurney had also developed, out of Whitman and Hopkins, an extraordinary and purposeful syntax. Still he could write songs and lyrics, although these gained from his new-found syntactical movement. For the most part, however, his dozens of poems of war are blocked out, freely rhyming, though most commonly with couplets, and moving through an accumulation, layering of remembered and described experience.

O, but the racked clear tired strained frames we had!
Tumbling in the new billet on to straw bed,
Dead asleep in eye shutting. Waking as sudden
To a golden and azure roof, a golden ratcheted
Lovely web of blue seen and blue shut, and cobwebs and tiles,
And grey wood dusty with time. June's girlish kindest smiles.
Rest at last and no danger for another week, a seven-day week.

('Billet')

Detail is the means of progression, 'the cumulative weight of small facts' as he had foretold in his letter of February 1917.

Gurney's poems from 1918 to 1926 build, through this cumulative weight of detail, an all-encompassing view of the war from the ordinary soldier's perspective. From 'First March' and 'First Time In', back to 'Blighty' and on to the 'Strange Hells' of the mind, those who died on the wires ('The Silent One'), 'Laventie' and 'On Somme', he gives an authoritative, wholly convincing picture. The soldier retains pacific virtues which are abused by war and by the military system. He learns a wise humour, a resisting self-interest, and an awareness that he is out of his depth. The inequality of the struggle, against military injustice and against war, one way or another, will defeat him.

As Gurney maps out a variety of scenes from the trench world, increasingly his own state of mind, his sense of grievance, his Lear-like emphasis upon ingratitude becomes his theme. Gurney was confined to a mental asylum in 1922 and his remaining poems read like no others of their period or later. They are too painful to read at length. Yet right through to the long and largely unpublished 'appeals' which he wrote as his health deteriorated, they tell the same story: a cry for the torture to stop; a plea of innocence; hints at the admission of guilt; a dismay that he cannot deserve such punishment, and a terror that if he is so punished then he must have some guilt which he does not recognize. Innocent, wholehearted, Gurney obeyed the call and, faced with its injustice, he blamed himself and struggled against that blame. From being the spokesman for the would-be war poet, denied by his honesty and knowledge the role of 'lucky' Brooke, the one who would hold true to beauty against war, he becomes the spokesman for the destruction from which war's end did not release its victims: for the fact that there could be no peace after what had been borne and done.

> These I should be playing with dearest friends in rooms
> Lit with glooms, dark with firelight's gold power.
> Taking pay for Laventie, or Vermand's hour.
> Or of Ypres, Tilleloy the complete terror.
> Who, first war poet, am under three Hells and lie
> (Sinned against desperately by all English high-sworn to Duty)
> Out of music, out of firelight – or any joy.
> A tale of heroic courage, made pains' mark.

> ('Watching Music')

Isaac Rosenberg (1890–1918), out of heroic and demeaning struggles against poverty, reached 1915 jobless and desperate for his penniless family's survival. He had, however, as a result of benefactions offered by (or begged from) the Jewish community in London, spent some time at the Slade School of Art, and had built up for himself a more informed education – through public library services and personal friends – than most of his more privileged contemporaries. Alongside his art, he was a poet of individuality and distinct imagination. Drawing on Milton, Donne and Blake rather than the decayed romanticism on offer in schools of his time, he had written and had printed at his own expense two pamphlets of poetry by May 1916:

> Her eyes are hidden pools
> Where my soul lies
> Glimmering in their waters
> Like faint and troubled skies.

('Apparition')

The strong visual image may take a moment to discover, for Rosenberg packs his sensuously lyrical verse quite densely. He is describing a 'soul' glimmering in someone else's eyes, like sky reflected in a pool. But his subject is an 'Apparition'. The physical and the metaphorical interact to take us beyond the natural world, to convey sensations, states of feeling, patterns of relationship. From the start, poetry for Rosenberg is a means of entry into areas of experience not graspable within naturalism. It is a mode of discourse which is valuable because it can create its own imaginary worlds which enlarge our understanding.

The war was a catastrophe to him. He joined up with no sense of patriotism, knowing that his endurance of military life would take his time and energies away from the creative work to which his whole life was dedicated. Yet for two and a half years he served in the worst of conditions, living a life which, as a 'Pioneer', amounted virtually to forced labour: lifting, digging, carrying, gathering salvage and so on. He had one leave, of ten days, in late 1917, and was once relieved of trench duty through sickness. He was back in France in September 1917, in hospital with influenza that October, and then back in the trenches where the heavy labour which had broken his health set about breaking him.

How Rosenberg endured this, even his fine letters do not reveal, but it appears that, until that last winter, his total commitment to his art, intellect and writing, to his creative self, helped him through. In autumn 1916, after bitter experience of the trenches, he had written:

I am determined that this war, with all its powers for devastation, shall not master my poeting; that is, if I am lucky enough to come through all right. I will not leave a corner of my consciousness covered up, but saturate myself with the strange and extraordinary new conditions of this life, and it will all refine itself into poetry later on.

Rosenberg retained a detached curiosity, an independence of mind through which he kept himself from war's contamination. It was not *his* war. He was its victim. It was something to be got through, to reach the far side of and then return to the work that mattered. Yet from this detachment Rosenberg, who never refers to comrades in his letters, wrote in his poetry as spokesman for the common soldier. When he uses the first person plural pronoun it is with unreserved identification. He writes, even literally, from within the ranks:

> My eyes catch ruddy necks
> Sturdily pressed back –
> All a red brick moving glint.
> Like flaming pendulums, hands
> Swing across the khaki –
> Mustard-coloured khaki –
> To the automatic feet.
>
> We husband the ancient glory
> In these bared necks and hands . . .
>
> ('Marching (As Seen from the Left File)')

Perhaps because physically, temperamentally and politically he found army life uncongenial, Rosenberg is especially aware of the physical, bodily presence of the soldiery. He writes of their search for sleep, cramped on a troopship ('Troopship'); the impassioned hunting, naked and with candle-light, for lice ('Louse Hunting' and 'The Immortals'); the weary trudge towards rest, surprised by larksong ('Returning, We Hear the Larks'). Their bodies he generally sees as the focal point for their livingness, their vitality, but also for their vulnerability. Beside the 'Strong eyes, fine limbs, haughty athletes' 'Sprawled in the bowels of the earth' at 'Break of Day in the Trenches' the rat can 'inwardly grin', knowing it is safer than the soldiers, who are 'Bonds to the whims of murder'. The war, seeming to have made the men so vigorous, has made them pathetically vulnerable and powerless against the forces that they have unleashed.

So Rosenberg explores in his finest and most sustained poem of war, 'Dead Man's Dump', the relation between the battlefield's living soldiery and its dead. An absolute divide has come between them, yet they are the same species. Where have their energies gone in becoming dead? Can you be terrified to death, sensation climaxing in death? What is the point at which the wounded man slips from life to death, 'sunk too deep/For human tenderness'? The dead draw Rosenberg's gaze, as in 1943 they were to draw that of his successor Keith Douglas. By the end of 'Dead Man's Dump', however, Rosenberg finds only that dead and living are held by war in an impotent, dehumanized intimacy:

> Here is one not long dead;
> His dark hearing caught our far wheels,
> And the choked soul stretched weak hands
> To reach the living word the far wheels said . . .
>
> So we crashed round the bend,
> We heard his weak scream,
> We heard his very last sound,
> And our wheels grazed his dead face.

In all his poems of war Rosenberg still seeks to understand a wider vision of what his eyes see and his feelings register. The soldier is metamorphosed, a 'great new Titan' on whose back 'Napoleon and Caesar', martial emperors, climb. Yet he is awakened: he has outgrown 'the pallid days' and they should fear his revolutionary potential ('Soldier: Twentieth Century'). In his transformation the soldier has also outgrown the reach of a lover's feeling and, in 'Girl to Soldier on Leave', must be abandoned to his heartless world; or, in 'Home-Thoughts from France', must suffer the pull on his deadened feelings by memories of 'Dear faces startled and shaken/ Out of wild dust and sound'. He is the chosen mate, doomed to be the lover for Walkyre-like women in 'Daughters of War'. In his last months 'in the trenches which are terrible now' – 'We spend most of our time pulling each other out of the mud. I am not fit at all now and am more in the way than any use' – Rosenberg tried to gather his knowledge together in a single work. On 8 March 1918 he wrote: 'If I am lucky, and come off undamaged, I mean to put all my innermost experiences into the "Unicorn". I want it to symbolise the war and all the devastating forces let loose by an ambitious and unscrupulous will.'

Rosenberg had written pieces for it the previous summer, and they survive. He had 'the whole of it planned out' but since then, he writes in his March letter, 'I've had no chance of working on it and it may have gone quite out of my mind.' Still his powers of recovery had proved amazing. Three weeks before this letter he had written of being 'appalled at the devastation this life seems to have made in my nature. It seems to have blunted me. I seem to be powerless to compel my will to any direction, and all I do is without energy and interest.'

Rosenberg's poems of war had done much to expose war's 'devastating forces'. His art as a poet, untouched from the first by the literary cant or trivialities of custom which filled the anthologies, had been strengthened by the literal truths of the battlefield, had become more focused and made more accessible. Glimpses of a wider vision had been set down. His poetry's potential even further to absorb the experience of war into a wider political and philosophical vision was denied time. On 1 April 1918 he was killed.

Robert Graves (1895–1985) became an officer in the Royal Welch Fusiliers, just turned nineteen, one month after he had left school. He had met Edward Marsh while still at school, and recalled advice from him which we can see as crucial not only to himself but to a whole group of poets: 'When he had read [my poems] he frowned and told me gently that I was using "an outworn vocabulary" and must reform it. This criticism I took deeply to heart and have never used a *thee*, *thou*, or *where'er* since that day; or hardly ever.' In October 1915 Graves writes, after having experienced heavy fighting: 'In the last month or so an inspiration seems to have come to me of what the New Poetry is to be and I feel that given a good rest and congenial society to settle my shaken mind I could write something really good. But here thought is quite impossible.' This notion, above all of a new poetry made by clearing away archaic and literary habits, Graves was to share with Sassoon who, in turn, shared it with Owen. Graves's version of all this is spelt out in his autobiographical narrative *Goodbye to All That*.

It was Sorley, however, whose work most strongly impressed Graves: 'I've just discovered a brilliant young poet called Sorley . . . It seems ridiculous to fall in love with a dead man as I have found myself doing but he seems to have been one so entirely after my own heart in his loves and hates . . .' This was in March 1916 and in May that year he wrote at length to Sassoon about Sorley. By this time Graves had already delivered the manuscript of his first collection, to be published in May 1916 as *Over the Brazier*, in which he observed a 'tremendous change in tone and method and standpoint . . . between the first and last parts of the verse-cycle, a hardening and coarsening and loss of music'. Graves published a further pamphlet with poems relating to the war in another collection, *Fairies and Fusiliers* (1917). In collections reissued through his lifetime, however, Graves gradually suppressed his poems of war, and it is only in the posthumously edited *Poems about War* (1988) that they are mostly gathered and once more available.

Graves's poems of war have a strange, disconcerting remoteness. Written in the voice of a class, several of the poems are addressed to friends, presented as verse letters or dedicated to intimate acquaintances, most commonly Robert Nichols and Siegfried Sassoon. It is therefore a class within a class, a little élite whose 'sole topics of conversation' are *not* 'wine, women, racing, hunting and musical comedy' – those of Graves's fellow officers in 1915. In this situation Graves can write at once with the confidence of a known and, presumably, understanding audience and with the exclusiveness which the tiny scale of the audience entails. Graves carries out private conversations, protected against 'them' – the philistines and those without the 'exclusive' knowledge of front-line soldiers. There is a strong sense of pride in his regiment – especially after being away from them seriously wounded (July 1916) – together with a cynicism towards the stupidities of military life and military people. From the outset there are no heroics: 'War's hell', it is 'this silly/ Mad war' ('Over the Brazier'); if the grimness of his poems is unpleasing, he writes, 'Blame my dazed head,/Blame bloody war' ('The Patchwork Quilt'). War is a world of human blunders, senseless ironies and atrocities. It is a bitter, incompetent joke against man.

Behind the impersonal, ironically toned verse-forms, the throw-away wit and bravura displays of calculated bad taste, however, there is a pervasive sense of shock in Graves's poems. They declare themselves to be written on the surface so as to leave no mistake about what is underneath. When they approach horror, they protect themselves as 'nursery' memories or as dreams. The swollen corpse in 'The First Funeral' is that of a dog, described with a characteristic emphasis on smell. The poem's true subject, however, is indicated in a note after the title: '(The first corpse I saw was one on the German wires, and couldn't be buried).' The means of indirection which Graves has employed, knowingly makes matters worse. Similarly, poems set as hallucinations, dreams or nightmares – 'The Assault Heroic', 'Corporal Stare', 'A Child's Nightmare' – soon prove to carry no real protection through their specifically conditional, 'unreal' frame. War is literally as well as metaphorically a matter of nightmare, and the hauntings and strange happenings which Graves portrays are evidence of the mind's derangement. A tone of jaunty friendship, the shared jokes, the 'insider' talk are all holds on sanity.

The extremity of Graves's position can be glimpsed through his fine 'Goliath and David'. The poem gives a coolly bitter account of the 'true' story. Brave and puny David pathetically throws stones which the giant effortlessly parries with his shield. David reacts like a schoolboy in a temper: 'Curse your shield!/And curse my sling . . .', and sets about the giant with his staff. Then 'Steel crosses wood, a flash, and oh!/Shame for beauty's overthrow!' In that 'oh!' Graves combines formal lamenting and comically absurd surprise. The story is one of folly, with the giant at first scornful then astonished into laughter. It is anti-heroic at the same time as it sympathetically portrays that common nightmare of impotent fighting. At its close, however, the poem adds another dimension plainly setting its fable in the contemporary battlefield:

> One cruel backhand sabre-cut –
> 'I'm hit! I'm killed!' young David cries,
> Throws blindly forward, chokes . . . and dies.
> Steel-helmeted and grey and grim
> Goliath straddles over him.

Goliath is a Prussian, in field-grey. Thus, in under fifty, seemingly easy lines, Graves has reversed a whole series of myths: the Christian notion of victory to the weak; the idea of divine providence; the fantasy of virtue gaining strength to outfight superior weaponry; the convenient recruiting-lie that intention and skill make up for inadequate equipment. Graves has done this, however, with a distinct and current myth in mind: that of David as brave little England which, through superior dedication and virtue, will defeat the stupid, bellicose Prussia.

Like most of Graves's poems of war, 'Goliath and David' is uncomfortable to read. In it, feeling is pitched towards melodrama in a way which gives us no secure emotional access; cynical ironies threaten any arousal of our own sentiments: if we concur in their hardness we may only be falling into a trap. Graves displays unfeeling as the logic of war. Yet what is most extraordinary about this particular poem is the fact that it is actually presented as an elegy, dedicated 'For David Thomas, 1st Batt. Royal Welch Fusiliers, killed at Fricourt, March 1916'. Here, at least, we need be in no doubt that the 'coarseness', the 'loss of music', derive from abused feeling.

Siegfried Sassoon (1886–1967), twenty-nine and on his fourth day at the front, wrote in his diary for 28 November 1915: 'Walked into Bethune for tea with Robert Graves, a young poet, captain in Third Battalion and very much disliked. An interesting creature, overstrung and self-conscious, a defier of convention.' Four days later he had read some manuscript poems Graves had lent him to read: 'some very bad, violent and repulsive. A few full of promise and real beauty. He oughtn't to publish yet.' Graves, writing to Eddie Marsh a week later, was a little more generous, or more guarded: 'Sassoon was a very nice chap but his verses, except occasionally, don't please me very much.' As Sassoon's *Diaries 1915–1918* reveal, poetry for him at this time was a product of a safe, enclosed dream life. On 3 December 1915 he writes: 'My inner life is far more real than the hideous realism of this land of the war zone. I never thought to find such peace.' Around Christmas he writes 'Brothers' – 'Give me your hand, my brother; search my face;/Look in these eyes lest I should think of shame;/For we have made an end of all things base . . .' This is copied into his diary at the end of a poignant indulgence in nostalgia: 'my dreams are mine, more lonely than ever . . . Anything but a "cushy wound"! That would be a disaster. I must endure, or else die . . . Lovely now seem the summer dawns in Weirleigh garden; lovely the slow music of the dusk . . .' Like Brooke before him, Sassoon is thinking in quotation marks, his mood seeming actually to live the posed lyricism of his rhetorical inversions.

By 15 March, however, Graves is writing to Marsh: 'I think S.S.'s verses are getting infinitely better than the first crop I saw, much freer and more Georgian. What a pity he didn't start earlier!' Graves is correct and must have taken a major role in the change. In February Sassoon had written the satirical 'In the Pink'; in March 'Golgotha', which emphasized the rats rather than redemption, and 'The Working Party', his first sustained trench scene. The trench scene was one of the two main approaches used in his war poems. The other, a satirical style, derived from Graves and Hardy, is the one most associated with him:

> The Bishop tells us: 'When the boys come back
> They will not be the same; for they'll have fought
> In a just cause; they lead the last attack
> On Anti-Christ . . .
>
> 'We're none of us the same!' the boys reply.
> 'For George lost both his legs; and Bill's stone blind; . . .'
>
> (' "They" ')

The manner is simpler, and perhaps for that reason, more directed than that of Graves. Sassoon is prepared to ventriloquize, to ape the men's talk to good purpose, to satirize that of the bishop. Through such mimicry and the sureness of his anger Sassoon's satires are public poems where Graves's are private.

Sassoon's first collection of war poems – balanced by about as many 'Lyrical' poems – came out as *The Old Huntsman* in May 1917. Half a dozen or so of the trench poems were satirical sketches. The hardest-hitting, perhaps, tells the delight of a man at escaping war by having a leg amputated ('The One-Legged Man'). Not in the collection, however, are two poems on more 'sensitive' subjects. 'A Ballad' tells of a captain instructor who got away from the front by shooting himself in the foot. 'Decorated' writes of the soldier as common murderer.

Most of the war poems in *The Old Huntsman* take up a broadly religious theme – moving between the recruiting notion that fighting in war was somehow an 'Absolution' for one's peacetime sins, through the questioning search for God in 'A Mystic as Soldier' to the implications of the one-legged man's exclamation 'Thank God they had to amputate!' and the direct attack on the church leaders in '"They"'. Paul Fussell in an excellent book writes of Christianity as one of the many motifs recurring in the war's literature (*The Great War and Modern Memory*, 1975). One topic he discusses, the cliché of the soldier as Christ, is tested and revised by Sassoon to become an image of the soldier's suffering. Still a poet of sentiment, in 'The Redeemer' Sassoon perceives the fatigued soldier momentarily il-luminated by a flare as transfigured into Christ. It is no more than a trick of the eye and the whole sustained scene is deflated with the man's blasphemy – 'O Christ Almighty, now I'm stuck!' – but the Christian analogy remains a way of drawing sympathy to the ordinary soldier.

In June 1916 Sassoon had been awarded the Military Cross for gallantry in action – his semi-fictional autobiography will be found in *Memoirs of an Infantry Officer* (1930) – but in the spring of 1917, returning to hospital with a shoulder wound, he decided on public protest against the conduct and continuance of the war. Graves intervened and from July to November 1917 Sassoon was treated at the Craiglockhart War Hospital near Edinburgh. There he met the then unknown Wilfred Owen, whose development he was to influence as Graves had influenced his own.

In June 1918 Sassoon's second collection, *Counter-Attack*, ap-peared. Two of the poems show him near breaking-point – 'To Any Dead Officer' and 'Repression of War Experience' – and in a sequence of satires which had appeared in the *Cambridge Magazine* from June to December 1917 his attack had become increasingly distraught. His targets are mainly those who, he felt, supported the continuance of the war from the safety of home – journalists, jingoistic women, fathers and God. A similar briefly presented ferocity, however, may simply portray the trench soldier's life, showing the meaninglessness of military tasks, the facts of mutilation and madness, the terror of battle and the broken 'Survivors': 'Men who went out to battle, grim and glad;/Children with eyes that hate you, broken and mad.' Many of these poems show a desperation: 'In bitter safety I awake, unfriended' ('Sick Leave'); a sense of disloyalty: 'I am banished from the patient men who fight' ('Banishment'), which he can overcome only by living with the men in his mind – 'Love drove me to rebel./Love drives me back to grope with them through hell;/And in their tortured eyes I stand forgiven.'

What was implicit in Graves is explicit here: a mix of personal breakdown, bitterness and a hold maintained on sanity by speaking out. The Graves mix of melodrama and useless pity is extraordinarily blended in 'To Any Dead Officer', which sometimes reads as something posed, too-much designed, and sometimes comes straight through as heartbreak. It is made from officer cliché: a parody of inarticulacy in the face of momentous experience, a bred inarticulacy embarrassingly gauche in the face of death. Language, taken to breaking-point here, breaks down again in the honestly clumsy 'Repression of War Experience'. Again, it is the very awfulness of the writing, its edgy self-dramatization and blatant clichés which give the poem its authenticity. It seems as impossible as it is irrelevant to determine how far Sassoon as artist is in control of his dramatizations: banality and obviousness are too bound up in the poem's effectiveness. Sassoon, as he shows in his attacks on good taste and politeness in 'Does It Matter?', has found a serviceable hotchpotch of a style to portray the extremities of war's impact. And in these later satires, it is consistently the misrepresentation of war through linguistic formulae, the absorption of it into the comforting definitions of set phrases and speech patterns which draw out this fury. The poet who had quickly found articulacy and who had offered convincing trench scenes and biting satires is now declaring his inarticulacy in the face of war.

Two trench scenes – one which gives his volume its title, the other, 'Prelude: The Troops' – show how this threat to the security of his own powers of expression strengthened his work. 'Prelude' almost makes a worthy elegy to 'my brave brown companions', picking its way between old literary props, bits of melodrama, sentiment and sonority. 'Counter-Attack', having outreached itself in a first stanza which tries to encompass war's hideousness through description, focuses on one soldier's consciousness to increasing effect. Then, at its close, it combines the poetry of sensibility which had been Sassoon's desired manner, and the poetry of attack which he wrote so well:

> . . . he choked
> And fought the flapping veils of smothering gloom,
> Lost in a blurred confusion of yells and groans . . .
> Down, and down, and down, he sank and drowned,
> Bleeding to death. The counter-attack had failed.

When Wilfred Owen (1893–1918) met Sassoon at Craiglockhart in August 1917, he showed Sassoon the poem 'Happiness' of which he was proud, a recent piece, composed after a month of appalling trench experience:

> The sun may cleanse,
> And time and starlight. Life will sing great songs,
> And gods will show us pleasures more than men's . . .
>
> The former happiness is unreturning:
> Boys' griefs are not so grievous as youth's yearning,
> Boys have no sadness sadder than our hope.

Sassoon was himself less than two years away from far inferior attempts of lyricism, and these last two lines, of which Owen was rightly proud, were beyond anything Sassoon had managed before he met Graves. But to hear the true resonance of their hopelessness, one would have to have shared the experience of war. For Owen has drawn what is broadly an experience of war back into poetry, just as Sassoon himself had at first done. The cleansing sun, the transcendent qualities of starlight, boys, men and with them gods are categories from books, memories of happy moments' reading.

Yet Owen had only taken the war back into literature when it came to writing poetry. He had very well understood it immediately and had found words for his understanding and what it witnessed:

I can see no excuse for deceiving you about these last 4 days. I have suffered seventh hell.
I have not been at the front.
I have been in front of it.
I held an advanced post, that is, a 'dug-out' in the middle of No Man's Land . . .

Three quarters dead, I mean each of us 3//4 dead, we reached the dug-out, and relieved the wretches therein. I then had to go forth and find another dug-out for a still more advanced post where I left 18 bombers. I was responsible for other posts on the left but there was a junior officer in charge.

My dug-out held 25 men tight packed. Water filled it to a depth of 1 or 2 feet, leaving say 4 feet of air.

One entrance had been blown in and blocked.

So far, the other remained.

The Germans knew we were staying there and decided we shouldn't.

Those fifty hours were the agony of my happy life.

Every ten minutes on Sunday afternoon seemed an hour.

I nearly broke down and let myself drown in the water that was now slowly rising over my knees.

(To Susan Owen, 16 January 1917)

It took Owen's meeting with Sassoon, and the example of Sassoon's poetry, to show him how to write poems of war: to show him that war could be directly portrayed in verse; and to show him that you need not leave your main experiences behind and make poetry a rarefied world. Within hours of his second visit to Sassoon, Owen had written a satirical portrait in direct imitation and tribute, 'The Dead Beat'. Several more slangy, ironic pieces followed, but already, even in them, there was a difference. Owen's attack was on the officer, the participating first person of the poems as much as on others. He wrote satirically, exposing the cruelty of army life and rank, the ironic cruelty of war, but he did so with his own place as officer in mind, as part of the system, as one who gave orders and had lives in his hands: those of the enemy and those of his own men.

Sassoon's 'The Death Bed' had most impressed him and, with 'The Redeemer', provided a seed for much Owen wrote in the year of remarkable creativity which started that August in Craiglockhart. Trench scenes focused on individuals; states of consciousness; paternal sympathy for the suffering soldiers; dramatic reversal in the soldier's situation; the voice of the ordinary volunteer; the delirium of the sick and dying; the insensitivity of the onlookers, even of nurses and, above all, of those claiming to be sympathetic; the gap between jargon, slang, common talk and the extremity of war's experience – all these he could have taken from Sassoon. Of course, it is impossible to say, where experiences between officers could be so closely parallel, whether the link is shared experience or the poems. Owen met Graves too, briefly, but did not take to him or to his poems. Graves, for his part, was prompt to offer him, jocosely, to Marsh as another discovery and candidate for the Georgian's new poetry. Owen was pleased and honoured to be so termed.

Owen brought to his work a dedication which was perhaps even

greater than Sassoon's. His earlier Keatsian and Shelleyan work shows him mastering cadence and sound patterning, shows his theme of poet-prophet and, in its occasional blasphemy and occasional social concern, shows both his readiness to break with convention and his sense of social responsibility. These elements are combined in his war poems.

> Bent double, like old beggars under sacks,
> Knock-kneed, coughing like hags, we cursed through sludge,
> Till on the haunting flares we turned our backs
> And towards our distant rest began to trudge.
> Men marched asleep. Many had lost their boots
> But limped on, blood-shod. All went lame; all blind; . . .
>
> ('Dulce et Decorum Est')

The strong, purposeful, directed consonants and stresses readily turn from evocation to rhetorical force:

> If in some smothering dream, you too could pace
> Behind the wagon that we flung him in,
> And watch the white eyes writhing in his face,
> His hanging face, like a devil's sick of sin; . . .

Authoritative witness is what Owen brings: his poem is shaped as evidence and conclusion. When he attacks, it is as much a measure of the stress of feeling, the degree of the horror and of the lie as it is an indication of aggression.

Owen's style is a mixed one, measuring and contrasting, shifting and defining, as the safety of literature is exposed to the reductive brutality of war; as the spiritual values of literature measure the defeats inflicted by war; and, all the time, as the men's voices, their jargon, slang and language, offer a counter-truth, a living world. 'The Sentry' – derived both from that early experience of January 1917, and from Sassoon's poems of abandoned individuals, 'The Working Party' and 'Counter-Attack' – perfectly blends purposeful narration with just enough poetic heightening:

> We'd found an old Boche dug out, and he knew,
> And gave us hell; for shell on frantic shell
> Lit full on top, but never quite burst through.
> Rain, guttering down in waterfalls of slime,
> Kept slush waist-high and rising hour by hour . . .

Another late poem, 'Spring Offensive', works from the opposite direction, just tilting the scale towards elevation so the gravity of the soldiers' predicament is revealed:

Halted against the shade of a last hill
They fed, and eased of pack-loads, were at ease;
And leaning on the nearest chest or knees
Carelessly slept.
                    But many there stood still
To face the stark blank sky beyond the ridge,
Knowing their feet had come to the end of the world.

Owen's religious awareness rapidly focuses on damnation and hell as the consequence of war. Those driven mad in 'Mental Cases' have been wickedly transformed into Dantesque sufferers, their hell the mental hospital to which the sane consigned them. Those who survive the 'Spring Offensive' battle come back damned from hell. To find his dead counterpart, the enemy, the soldier he killed, the poet descends to hell ('Strange Meeting'). Forgiveness is replaced here by the suffering of having to hear out the destructive loss of life's potential which you caused, of having to be told the feelings of the man who 'parried' when 'through him you jabbed and killed' and who died then because his 'hands were loathe and cold'. Forgiveness is replaced, finally, by resignation, a request to be left in peace, a suggestion that your inquiries take away rest from the dead.

'Strange Meeting' is nightmare, as is 'The Show', where the dream-landscape reveals the horror of war and the witness is shown his severed head. 'The Sentry' is an attempt to purge officerly guilt and to honour the victims by telling their story in order that the survivor may find relief and rest. 'Dulce' draws its attack through personal nightmare; and the mad of 'Mental Cases' are cursed to relive murders they committed. Sassoon's recurrent haunting in his poems had been the sound of the guns: Owen's is far more morally terrible. Beside these nightmare poems are the poems of a reality which would better have been nightmare. Above all there is 'Exposure', where nothing happens, no one dies, the soldiers dream of home; but their cold, their exposure leads to nervous, frightened impotence, suppressed frustration at inaction and a knowledge, through daydream, of being accursed: this is the world of those, like mariners in Coleridge's ship, cursed to a death-in-life, the only action that of a shaking burying-party who pause over half-known faces with eyes of ice.

Owen projected a preface for his book of poems and focused on 'the pity of war' as the only source of 'poetry' to be found in his work. Certainly it is a source of 'poetry' as it was popularly understood at that time – something transcending, something with beauty in it, something positive and heartening. Pity as love for others and sorrow at what is done to them, for the young who are killed (in 'Futility'); pity as the human emotion which should combat war, 'the eternal reciprocity of tears' in 'Insensibility': such pity, such evidence of emotion which war would destroy – and which the soldier himself must censor for survival ('Insensibility') – such pity is ever present in Owen's poetry. But in other senses of 'poetry' – as what he makes, the message of his poems, the experience they portray, the stories, scenes and feelings they create – in any such sense, 'pity' is hardly the word for what his poems carry. Owen is a poet of nightmare and guilt; a poet of war's destruction of Christian values and those of a more pantheistic view. He is a poet of nature disordered and abused by war. He is a poet of war's cruelty and ugliness, its pervasive power which denies even those who survive, relief from its pain.

Owen saw himself as bringing evidence against which the justifications given to war must be measured. He saw that in his time, for that evidence to have the chance of a hearing, it needed the backing of personal proof through one's own actions. To work actively as an officer for men under his command; to be back at the front which nightmare and neurosis had denied him the possibility of mentally leaving; to prove, tragically, that his exposures were not fuelled by personal cowardice – he went back to France in August 1918. On 4 November he was killed.

Edmund Blunden (1896–1974) survived two years in and out of the trenches, from spring 1916 to spring 1918, and devoted much of his subsequent life as teacher and scholar to writings connected with the war. A few months out of Christ's Hospital when he enlisted at nineteen, he had already had poems published. It was only in 1920, however, that his first collection containing war poems, *The Waggoner*, appeared. *The Shepherd*, two years later, contained more of them. The rustic, pastoral titles of the volumes are characteristic, Blunden writing of himself on the last page of his fine 1929 narrative *Undertones of War*: 'I ought to have known the war by this time, but I was still too young to know its depth of ironic cruelty ... No destined anguish lifted its snaky head to poison a harmless young shepherd in a soldier's coat.' The implication of his words which describe his final departure from the trenches is that he had remained innocent: it was the subsequent poisoning anguish which was to bring his fall.

In the poems Blunden wrote during his trench service, his own themes are established: the welcome of relief in which to forget nearby war and the inability long to forget it ('Mont de Cassel'); the uneasy quiet out of the line ('January Full Moon, Ypres'); war memories in scarred buildings ('Les Halles d'Ypres'); hauntings, from ghosts and guilt:

> Now every thing that shadowy thought
>   Lets peer with bedlam eyes at me
> From alleyways and thoroughfares
>   Of cynic and ill memory
> Lifts a gaunt head, sullenly stares . . .

('In Festubert')

This poem ends with Blunden writing that 'the old delight is cursed'; but while his poems describe this curse, they generally retain a calm tone. They are not drawn back into the hell they recall or hear reverberating in distant gunfire. A narrative which Blunden sketched in 1918 and published is more thoroughly innocent, and he was soon to reject it.

By 1922 Blunden was working his passage (as assistant purser) on a freighter to South America, as therapy for a breakdown. By this time he had befriended Sassoon and seen the poems of Wilfred Owen which Sassoon was entrusted with editing. Throughout the 1920s he wrote of war, in part preparing poems to go alongside a second prose narrative, *Undertones of War*, which appeared in the decade's final year. The appendix of poems he placed there includes his finest work: literary in quality, seemingly archaic and not easy to approach but repaying the second and third look.

> O how comely it was and how reviving
> When with clay and with death no longer striving
>   Down firm roads we came to houses
>   With women chattering and green grass thriving.

('At Senlis Once')

The interplay between archaic and modern is deft: the roads, thriving grass and sight of houses place the soldier in a progress like that of the Pilgrim, striving through tribulation towards what will be reviving. The perception of them, however, is through specifically modern, soldierly eyes: the soldier and especially the one withdrawn from the trenches would find the firmness of roads remarkable, the greenness of grass worth noting, the chatter of women a sight of blessed normality. The biblical 'clay', the mortal clay with which they strove, was also quite literally the boot-clogging clay of the line.

Repeatedly in these poems, Blunden shows language transformed by the soldier's experience and view: 'Let me go on', he says in 'The

Prophet', 'and note you here and there/Words with a difference to the likes of us'. He uses the soldiers' language, as with the phrase 'There's something in the air' in 'Two Voices', 'Plain words, which in his hearers bred/A tumult!' In the same poem 'death-news' is given while skylarks sing, carried in the words, 'We're going South, man'; in other poems we find the soldier's naming of his territory, '*Jacob's Ladder*', '*Brock's Benefit*' and '*The Great Wall of China*' – 'a four-foot breastwork, fronting guns'.

Such transformations of the familiar, coming here as a kind of humour, are part of a whole process of metamorphosis accomplished by war. A staff car can send a peaceful sentry 'scampering for his gun', prove an omen of a slaughterous offensive and the mild, shepherd-like soldier can be termed 'the terror of the Hun' ('The Guard's Mistake'). Red lights before dawn in the sky can be artillery fire, and the 'rosy dawn at last appearing' may touch those who had 'ceased to care what hand/Lit earth and heaven', the dead ('Trench Raid near Hooge'). A country-house, embodying homely, comforting values, can be a skull-like image of war, a place of sleeplessness, its evergreens serving as concealment for guns. The battlefield is a deceitful place, ready always to defeat expectations, catch you out, defy appearances. To this the soldier responds with ironic humour, marking the changes, the difference from recalled normality. His is an honourable response, retaining dignity, showing intelligence, but generally it is doomed. Summer will betray the seemingly well-aware lives in the 'House in Festubert', with its season of mass killing. Those amused for a while at the 'Concert Party: Busseboom' leave to find again the gunfire, the knowledge that 'Men in tunnels below Larch Wood/Were kicking men to death'.

The biggest single cheat of war, its full malevolence, is shown in Blunden's sustained dramatic narrative 'Third Ypres'. The poem describes a descent from what at each moment had seemed the worst. When, at the end, with a pillbox hit and his companions dead, the poem's speaker finds he has survived, he is met by his sergeant, desperate for help, forty or more men blown into pieces by a nine-inch shell. Even this is not the poem's end. Blunden surveys 'how for miles our anguish groans and bleeds/A whole sweet countryside amuck with murder': the panoramic view is measure of the scale of death beyond the individual, his friends, his regiment and sector. The killing is of nature as well as man. But there is to be no relief. In his final lines Blunden switches from past to present:

> All to the drabness of uncreation sunk,
> And all thought dwindled to a moan, Relieve!
> But who with what command can now relieve
> The dead men from that chaos, or my soul?

In those last two lines is the folly of the human pretension that men have command; the impotence of military command's power and its vanity; the absoluteness of death; the incapacity to forget and find relief; and the impossibility of conquering guilt.

Blunden's poems are written in retrospect. The poignant wit of 'At Senlis Once' moves from first person plural: 'We could glow, with our tribulation ended', through to third person: 'How they crowded the barn with lusty laughter,/Sang as though nothing but joy came after!' Blunden carries the burden of memory, of the losses and the men's resistance to the inhumanity of their world.

Increasingly, through the poems appended to *Undertones* and afterwards, he saw his task as honouring the memory, preserving them against time for they, as he knew, had sacrificed their lives. However, in the first twenty or so of the poems, mostly written in the mid-1920s, his own attempts to recall and, in part at least, to honour are overtaken by the pain of the waste. Memories are too sharp to be consoled. His own sense of the continuing pain haunting him is too strong, for he is helpless, impotent to restore or intervene. He can convey moments of terror, feelings of betrayal and, occasionally, images of violent brutality; but most of all there is, lingering around the edges of his poems, an unconsolable heartbreak. We hear the level voice, the slightly edgy humour, the consciously literary effects and wordplays, the tracing over and ordering of it all. If we once hear the give in that voice, what we meet is the depth of our own ignorance, the awareness that what Blunden is showing us is beyond our imaginings.

During three years' service on the western front David Jones (1895–1974) made drawings – most of which were destroyed – but he did not write. He had gone to Camberwell School of Art for five years before the war, starting there at fourteen. The account of his autobiography through letters in *Dai Great Coat* (1980) only really starts at 1927. Jones's later life, however, was continually inhabited by powerful memories of the war, although whether or not these were involved in his several breakdowns is disputed. His later poems, from *The Kensington Mass* (draft 1939), are pieces towards an overarching masterwork merging Catholic theology, Romano-Celtic Britain and national history. None the less the soldier, his language, and hardships and spirit remain a presence. In 1937, however, Jones published his first major written work, *In Parenthesis*, an uncategorizable mix of poetry and prose, epic and narrative and personal memoir, a seven-act narrative drama taking the soldier from embarkation through to the wound which brings his survival and release from the battlefield.

Visually powerful as a work by an artist, *In Parenthesis* is a packed storeroom of sensory memory of every sort. The recall is extraordinarily alert to nuance, shift of mood and emphasis. For this reason it is difficult to quote from briefly: even in the most descriptive sections the change of perspective, emphasis and texture is essential, the multifariousness of the experience, the flux of mood:

So they came outside the camp. The liturgy of a regiment departing has been sung. Empty wet parade ground. A camp-warden, some unfit men and other details loiter, dribble away, shuffle off like men whose ship has sailed.

The long hutment lines stand. Not a soul. It rains harder: torn felt lifts to the wind above Hut 10, Headquarter Company; urinal concrete echoes for a solitary whistler. Corrugated iron empty – no one. Chill gust slams the vacant canteen door.

Miss Veronica Best who runs the hut for the bun-wallahs stretches on her palliasse, she's sleepy, she can hear the band: We've got too many buns – and all those wads – you knew they were going – why did you order them – they won't be in after rouse-parade even – they've gone.

Know they've gone – shut up – Jocks from Bardown move in Monday. Violet turns to sleep again.

(Part I)

The recollecting and narrating mind shifts from large things to small, to momentary thought, contrast or detail of observation: each described moment is part of a continuity. Thus, the course of events, the onward momentum is crucial to the work's meaning. Even here, at the outset, the melancholy, unlived-in yet soon to be reinhabited camp which they leave behind, marks an absolute step on the men's way from the ominous, commonplace, homely, known world towards war. Everything in the book tends towards its ending: however sharp the moment, that moment is given to us as moving on somewhere.

For these reasons the allusions and references and quotations and echoes of which *In Parenthesis* is full are part of the mind's capacity to make connections, passing and recurring relationships. His mentor, as is most striking in the paragraphs just quoted, is T. S. Eliot: above all the Eliot of *The Waste Land*. But Jones's use of allusion and echo, the historical and literary past is there for an effect opposite to that in Eliot. The details of the abandoned parade ground are shaped and written down with sensuous relish by Jones:

it is not the vacancy of the scene which most matters to us as we read but its vividness, its familiar, substantial reality, its humanly recognizable mood. The mundane thoughts of Miss Best are far from being a critique of her. They show her participation, her living within a scene of human action. Her stretching, her feeling sleepy anticipate Dylan Thomas rather than look back to Eliot. Her body, so briefly noticed by Jones, has its place in the moment, ordinary, animal and human. Above all, everything connects: unity is recorded, not fragmentation; order is glimpsed, not breakdown; the quiddity of things is held and honoured by the artist, not exposed to distaste. Jones so accurately and lightly holds together all those conflicts of register and association which Eliot's sensibility hears in discord. 'The liturgy of a regiment departing has been sung' is a joke, an accessible humour, for what we have just heard was the ritual of marching: 'Left left lef' – lef' righ' lef' – you Private Ball it's you I've got me glad-eye on.' Long before we ever realize that this amused observation is deeply meant, we are guided by Jones, his shifts of diction, to take its seriousness: 'So they came outside the camp.' There is something ominous in that 'So', something echoing half-heard, half-remembered biblical phrases of purpose: 'So they came unto the place . . .' The style, as with all the successful poetry of the war, consists of a directing and judging pluralism.

Three areas are repeatedly alluded to in *In Parenthesis*. First, there is the epic and dramatic recording of the soldier's life in war – the *Mabinogion*, Malory, Shakespeare's Henry plays. Second, there are Catholic theology and liturgy, especially the Crucifixion story, the liturgy for Good Friday and the Sacraments – Jones became a Catholic in 1921. To help us reach these two areas Jones appends, and directs us to, most helpful notes (another reversal of *The Waste Land*'s methods). We move in and out of the text as the poem moves in and out of its historical present – the war. It is a complex business because the past wars, though drawn from history, are all alive – as Jones refers to them – only in literature: Pistol, Bardolph and Nym are his Tudor soldiers, men who never struck a blow but with a stage sword; even his Roland died in a poem.

The religious allusions are of more sustained importance, suggesting another order of experience which would impose a different set of meanings on what is narrated. The Catholic view would make sense of all that takes place, place it within God's plan; but such a theology has a loophole which Jones exploits. The plan is there, is God's plan, even if we cannot see it: Jones can therefore allow for what does not fit. In fact, he must record such things because they are part of whatever order is God's. For truth's sake, he must not shape or distort the events to prove God's ways, for that would be pride and would deny the chance truly for those ways to reveal themselves. So we are presented with an act of faith and a testing of it, and as a result the reader is free to assent or not.

The third area of allusion wholly conditions the way in which we receive the other two: the soldier's trench-lore, language and military world. For this, too, Jones provides notes; notes which sometimes show his own fascinating tracing of meanings and memories. The poem is full of the heard and half-heard voices of the soldiers themselves: as individuals, differentiated by regional background, rank and class; as representatives of levels in the military hierarchy; as sound itself, varying in meaning from association to association:

> Keep these sections of four.
> Pick those knees up.
> Throw those chests out.
> Hold those heads up . . .

Some like tight belts and some like loose belts – trussed-up pockets – cigarettes in ammunition pouches – rifle-bolts, webbing, buckles and rain – gotta light mate – give us a match chum. How cold the morning is and blue, and how mysterious in cupped hands glow the match-lights of a concourse of men . . .

In the Preface to the first edition of *In Parenthesis*, Jones left no doubt of the limited area of his work, defining it immediately, in terms which raise as many questions as they put to rest:

This writing has to do with some things I saw, felt, and was part of. The period covered begins early in December 1915 and ends early in July 1916. The first date corresponds to my going to France. The latter roughly marks a change in the character of our lives in the Infantry on the West Front. From then onward things hardened into a more relentless, mechanical affair, took on a more sinister aspect. The wholesale slaughter of the later years, the conscripted levies . . . In the earlier months there was a certain attractive amateurishness . . . Anyway, it is exclusively with the earlier period that this writing deals.

Is his cutting short of the soldier's experience of 1914–16 a distortion, the writer stopping at just that point before what is taken to be most characteristic of the period occurred – the mass slaughter on the Somme? In this way does he present an uncharacteristic time within the war, one in which individuality and humanity were retained, where the historical fact which Jones himself acknowledges is that, with a few exceptions, after June 1916 they were not retained? Is it a way of excluding the part of experience which would most threaten the sense of order, of a divine, an unknowable plan, which Jones seeks to affirm? Is it a valid selectivity, the honesty of which is defined in the Preface's start? Or is it a means of sustaining an anachronistic illusion? Is it a means of defining what he believes to have been a better, more human world, for all that it was experienced on the battlefield? Is Jones therefore, as so often in epic, trying to present a turning-point in history, not so much 1914 as 1916: his soldiers in touch with past values; the future, beyond expression?

The end of the work may resolve this, although the extent of disagreement among readers over fifty years makes me aware that this is only one view. By the end, Jones has shown each of his protagonists as a victim of war. The officers, humorously preserved as another caste, are defeated by war's brutality in their attempt to carry polite behaviour into death: the men are variously denied their hopes of survival and are killed. Jones grants them, through the Queen of the Woods, the honoured burial the war denies them, as she strews each with flowers. His one survivor is simply out of it, his rifle cast away as too cumbersome, his identification with the role of soldier and subservience to command ended by a wound. He is carried out of battle. But this, the end of the narrative of Private Ball and his comrades, is not the end. In a series of allusions the continuity of the war, beyond the short compass Jones chose and presented, is revealed:

The feet of the reserves going up tread level with your forehead; and no word for you; they whisper one with another;

> pass on, inward;
> these latest succours:
> green Kimmerii to bear up the war.
>
> Oeth and Annoeth's hosts they were
> who in that night grew
> younger men
> younger striplings.

The punning remains, they are the latest 'succours/suckers', green-horns; they are also the younger men, 'Oeth and Annoeth's hosts'. The notes tell us these are 'a mysterious body of troops that seem to have some affinity with the legions'; but the repeated 'younger' is not an emphasis on new blood, the continued reserves of the army, it is an emphasis on sorrow, the youthfulness of the recruits now, conscripts, whose fate we know.

After his Preface Jones started his work with a dedication, printed like a memorial, and followed this with an epigraph, a passage from the Mabinogi:

Evil betide me if I do not open the door to know if that is true which is said concerning it. So he opened the door . . . and when they had looked, they were conscious of all the evils they had ever sustained, and of all the friends and companions they had lost and of all the misery that had befallen them, as if all had happened in that very spot; . . . and because of their perturbation they could not rest.

The door which for Jones, and through his art, opened in memory, in our minds cannot be closed. The truth is simpler than the weight of allusion may propose. Jones's memory, once aroused, has brought us a war which no pattern of religion, history or legend can assuage. The experience, so physically recalled in the imagination, and so physically conjured in ours, speaks its own unanswered pain. The living fineness and humanity of the men he portrays and their attempts to make sense of their inhuman world cannot define a notion of former character or way of life without having the effect of measuring, not social change but war's destruction of these men. Already, before July 1916, *In Parenthesis* shows us that the means of death, the relations between ranks, the efficiency of the war's con- duct, the ways of dying took forms which retained little room for heroic gesture.

After his lines on the 'younger men/younger striplings', Jones gives another and final allusion. It does not concern shape or meaning but claims the authenticity of the participant's account. It echoes the *Chanson de Roland*, and in doing so the lines remind us of a history of waste and death rather than arousing a sense of heroic purpose. Their emphasis, the final one in *In Parenthesis*, is a demand on us rather than a statement of knowledge:

The geste says this and the man who was on the field . . . and who wrote the book . . . the man who does not know this has not understood anything.

The published war poems of Arthur Graeme West (1891–1917) and Frederic Manning (1882–1935) are few. Manning, an Australian, is best known for his fine fictionalized narrative, *Her Privates We*: his handful of war poems, however, possess a loving and clean-cut lucidity. West's posthumously published *Diary of a Dead Officer* is one of the strongest and most convincing accounts of trench war and its immediate effect on the beliefs of an intelligent man. Like Sorley, West writes with an unfussy directness and this comes through into the half-dozen or so poems appended to the *Diary*:

Only the dead were always present – present
As a vile sickly smell of rottenness;
. . . They lay, all clothed,
Each in some new and piteous attitude
That we well marked to guide us back: as he,
Outside our wire, that lay on his back and crossed
His legs Crusader-wise . . .
Next was a bunch of half a dozen men
All blown to bits, an archipelago
Of corrupt fragments, vexing to us three,
Who had no light to see by, save the flares.

('The Night Patrol: France, March 1916')

West has been neglected. Richard Aldington (1892–1962), also a writer of prose, has been well noticed for his *Death of a Hero*: his imagist poems giving glimpses of trench life, however, deserve to be more widely read. They, too, work best through directness, being uncluttered by rhetoric: their art consisting of precise visual observation, timed to convey a significant image. On occasion, however, the timing becomes a little too posed, too precious.

Both Edgell Rickword (1898–1982) and Herbert Read (1893–1968) survived trench experience to make long and important literary careers: Read especially as a writer on art; Rickword especially as an editor and a writer with political commitment. Rickword's half-dozen or so poems of war are well made, pointedly ironic and forceful. Read's work in both poetry and prose is extensive. His answer to the stereotype from Wordsworth's 'Character of the Happy Warrior' powerfully puts the myth in place:

His wild heart beats with painful sobs
his strain'd hands clench an ice-cold rifle . . .

Bloody saliva
dribbles down his shapeless jacket.

I saw him stab
and stab again
a well-killed Boche.

This is the happy warrior,
this is he . . .

Read also attempted a larger scale and context for understanding war in his 'The End of a War' which is sympathetically discussed by Jon Silkin in his *Out of Battle: The Poetry of the First World War*, 1972.

The work of Dominic Hibberd and J. Onions (*Poetry of the Great War: An Anthology*, 1986) is the best of more recent attempts to broaden the area of war poetry taken as historical evidence. One of the most interesting new points to emerge is the rediscovery of W. W. Gibson (1878–1962), a friend of Brooke's and Marsh's. In *Battle* (1915) Gibson offers an anti-war poetry written with no experience of the front. Using a blend of Housman-like irony and realistic sketch, Gibson creditably portrays the soldier's lot as unheroic and seemingly meaningless. It is another anthology, however, which opens out into entirely new perspectives our understanding and our descriptions of the poetry of the First World War.

Scars Upon My Heart, drawn from the valuable bibliographical work of its editor Catherine W. Reilly (*Scars Upon My Heart: Women's Poetry and Verse of the First World War*, 1981), gives an invaluable new direction to our awareness, drawing together poems by seventy-nine women poets, almost all of whom have been omitted from the post-war anthologies and critical commentaries on the period's verse. Inevitably such a large gathering results in mixed quality, but the attempt is to put before the reader a representative sample. Much of the verse, like the amateur efforts of the more frequently reprinted male poets, comes within Gurney's comment: 'So often poets write of what they wish to believe, wish to become...', but the anthology enables us to see the variety of attitudes from which women wrote poems. It also brings before us themes distinct to them: an emphasis upon the destruction of lives of non-combatants and the pain inflicted on them through the deaths of lovers, sons, husbands and friends; the perception of war as a male phenomenon, connected with indoctrination through boys' toys and boys' education, a consequence of a patriarchal society; the resistance to the demand actively to support the war effort through gratitude to the men for their protection and sacrifice. These themes – part of the whole, submerged women's experience of war now being brought back to light through work on narratives, journals and diaries as well as poems – come across especially well in Vera Brittain, May Wedderburn Cannan, Margaret Postgate Cole, Diana Gurney, Teresa Hooley, Charlotte New and May Sinclair. The republication of collections by these and other women poets will provide the evidence through which our perspectives on the poetry of war will alter. Already, the feminist insights provided in works such as *Behind The Lines: Gender and The Two World Wars*, are altering our perspectives on the work of the male poets through exciting new approaches to such things as 'shell-shock', 'courage' and notions of maleness. From the start, and of its nature, directly involved with every aspect of politics, the poetry of the First World War retains an especial immediacy of importance to readers.

5

THE NOVEL IN THE 1920s

Graham Bradshaw

I

For Henry James and Joseph Conrad, Flaubert was *le maître*, the master revered for his exemplary, infinitely exacting concern with method and with what James called the 'effort really to see and really to represent ... in face of the *constant* force that makes for muddlement'. For Nietzsche, Flaubert was exemplary in a quite different way, as a characteristic outburst in *Twilight of the Idols* suggests: 'Here I have got you, you nihilist!' When seen through the spectacles of Nietzschean vitalism Flaubert's very devotion to his 'art' appears to involve a denial of 'life', and one remarkable passage in *The Case of Wagner* establishes the grounds for that vitalist critique in which Flaubert appears as the exemplary negative portent:

Every art and every philosophy may be regarded either as a cure or as a stimulant to ascending or declining life ... In regard to all artists of what kind soever, I shall now avail myself of this radical distinction: does the creative power in this case arise from a loathing of life, or from an excessive *plenitude* of life? In Goethe, for instance, an overflow of vitality was creative, in Flaubert – hate.

The accents of this Nietzschean vitalism were eventually heard in England – when Orage declared, in the *New Age*, that 'the test of literature is whether it gives and intensifies life or takes away and diminishes life', or when D. H. Lawrence (1885–1930) explained in a 1913 review of Thomas Mann's *Death in Venice* that Mann was 'sick, body and soul' because he belonged to 'the school of Flaubert', and was the 'last too-sick disciple' of that novelist who had 'stood away from life as from a leprosy'. But if we ask how Lawrence knows or thinks he knows that 'the Thomas Mann of fifty-three' had 'never given himself to anything but his art' the answer is clear: Lawrence makes no distinction between Gustav von Aschenbach, the fifty-three-year-old protagonist of *Death in Venice*, and the author Thomas Mann, who was then only thirty-eight. Lawrence's vitalist diagnosis rests on a basic confusion which short-circuits Mann's complex narrative. Since F. R. Leavis was the first critic to present, more than twenty years after Lawrence's death, a compellingly serious argument for thinking him a major novelist, we should notice that Leavis also takes over the Nietzschean-vitalist diagnosis of Flaubert's significance, excludes James Joyce from his 'great tradition', and does to Conrad's *Heart of Darkness* (another key 'modernist' text) what Lawrence did to *Death in Venice*: the confident appraisal of the author's inadequacies shows no awareness of the need to distinguish between Conrad and Marlow, and indeed to distinguish Marlow the narrator from Marlow the protagonist.

Lawrence's impatiently uncomprehending hostility or indifference to the narrative complications which characterize so much modernist writing is worth remarking, not in an adversarial way, but because it suggests where it is misleading to think of Lawrence as a modernist. In James and Conrad, and in Joyce (1892–1941) – another admirer of Flaubert – narrative complications and formal experimentation are not (usually) imposed from without, but issue from, and answer to, an urgently pressing sense of what is problematic both in experience and also, as *Ulysses* sets out to show with such unprecedentedly passionate thoroughness, in all attempts to represent experience. In *Ulysses* (1922) the Flaubertian concern with method combines with the more radical Nietzschean insistence that we interpret the world as we interpret the text. But then neither Lawrence nor Leavis – who were respectively this century's greatest *English* novelist and critic – was concerned in that way with the problematics of representation. Perhaps this helps to explain why, of the three great modernist exiles, Lawrence travels least well outside English-speaking countries: Mann regarded Conrad as the greatest twentieth-century novelist and others have claimed no less for Joyce, but I do not know of one European writer who makes that kind of claim for Lawrence. Lawrence's comments on Joyce (a 'clumsy *olla putrida*'), Proust ('water-jelly', 'masturbation self-enclosure'), Conrad ('snivel in a wet hanky', 'giving in before you start') and other modernists ('Writers among the Ruins') are no less impatiently diagnostic than his reading of Mann: far from being incidental, such impatience characterizes the vitalist concern to establish whatever is not quick but dead, so as to move on, quickly. In 'Surgery for the Novel – Or a Bomb' Joyce, Proust and Dorothy Richardson are mocked for listening to their own death-rattle 'with acute interest, trying to discover whether the intervals are minor thirds or major fourths': 'Which is rather infantile, really.' The adult, vitalist alternative is that set out in a letter to Huxley where Lawrence associates Proust with all the other 'grand perverts' who try 'to kick off, or to intellectualise and so utterly falsify the phallic consciousness, which is the basic consciousness, and the thing we mean, in the best sense, by common sense'. To which one might oppose, as a kind of *tu quoque*, Joyce's scorn for '*Lady Chatterbox's Lover*' – 'the usual sloppy English' and 'propaganda in favour of something which, outside of D. H. L.'s country at any rate, makes all the propaganda for itself'. But I take it that Ezra Pound was simply and impressively right to observe, in a 1914 letter to Amy Lowell, that Lawrence and Joyce were 'the two strongest prose writers among *les jeunes*': we need to resist any idea of having to choose between Lawrence and Joyce, as in a prize-fight. At the same time we need to try to understand and weigh, if we are not to ignore and trivialize, the significance of their very real differences. Here, I want to suggest, it is particularly helpful to consider what is innovatory, or problematic, in their respective modes of narration.

II

Writing to Edward Garnett in 1914, D. H. Lawrence declared:

I don't so much care about what the woman *feels* – in the ordinary usage of the word. That presumes an ego to feel with. I only care about what the woman *is* – what she IS – inhumanly, physiologically, materially.

But then how to convey what somebody *is*, or IS, as distinct from what she or he actually thinks and feels? Lawrence's letter, with its famous and striking protest against 'the old-fashioned human element' and the 'old stable ego', itself 'presumes' that this problem can be overcome and that the novelist can reveal what the character wouldn't know or recognize. And so he can. In *The Rainbow*, immediately before Tom Brangwen suddenly sets off to propose to Lydia, he 'knew almost without thinking that he was going this evening'. Tilly, his cross-eyed housekeeper, trembles at what the 'deep stillness there was in the house' portends and, when the 'still and absorbed' Tom rises to wash himself, 'Queer little breaks of consciousness seemed to rise and burst like bubbles out of the depths of his stillness'. Donning his best coat, Tom sets off across the orchard to gather the daffodils: 'The wind was roaring in the apple trees, the yellow flowers swayed violently up and down, he heard even the fine whisper of their spears as he stooped to break the flattened, brittle stems of the flowers.' In a remarkably assured way, the finely nervous exuberance of the writing sets Tom's inner commotion against his apparent 'stillness' and against his occasional, characteristic comments to himself when some thought does surface: 'The woman's not speechless dumb. She's not clutterin' at the nipple. She's got the right to please herself, and displease whosoever she likes.' And when the friend he encounters by the gate asks, 'What's to do?', Tom's reply is as matter-of-fact: 'Bit of courtin', like.' Part of what is wonderfully managed here has to do with our own sudden, wondering sense that the relatively inarticulate Tom couldn't (and doesn't) represent his inner tumult to himself: like Bottom, Tom has been translated.

At least, 'translation' is one way of characterizing this mode of narration, which conceives of consciousness as something stratified, vertiginous, like a mine-shaft with different levels. Moreover, the relation between author and character issues in a kind of commentary which is, curiously, both privileged or omniscient and tentatively provisional and heuristic – as in this earlier passage, which traces Tom's confused responses to the experience of lying 'with a prostitute woman in a common public house':

But now? He did not know what to feel. There was a slight wonder, a pang of anger, of disappointment, a first taste of ash and of cold fear lest this was all that would happen, lest his relations with woman were going to be no more than this nothingness; there was a slight sense of shame before the prostitute, fear that she would despise him for his inefficiency; there was a cold distaste for her, and a fear of her; there was a moment of paralysed horror when he felt he might have taken a disease from her; and upon all this startled tumult of emotion, was laid the steadying hand of common sense, which said it did not matter very much, so long as he had no disease. He soon recovered balance, and really it did not matter so very much.

But it had shocked him, and put a mistrust into his heart, and emphasised his fear of what was within himself. He was, however, in a few days going about again in his own careless, happy-go-lucky fashion, his blue eyes just as clear and honest as ever, his face just as fresh, his appetite just as keen.

Or apparently so. He had, in fact, lost some of his buoyant confidence, and doubt hindered his outgoing.

For some time after this, he was quieter, more conscious when he drank, more backward from companionship. The disillusion of his first carnal contact with woman, strengthened by his innate desire to find in a woman the embodiment of all his inarticulate, powerful religious impulses, put a bit in his mouth. He had something to lose which he was afraid of losing, which he was not sure even of possessing. This first affair did not matter much:

THE NOVEL IN THE 1920s 149

but the business of love was, at the bottom of his soul, the most serious and terrifying of all to him.

Other novelists in this period would have wanted to *show* that first encounter with a prostitute in a suitably graphic fashion – being 'daring' in the manner of Compton Mackenzie's *Sinister Street* (1913–14). But this isn't what matters to Lawrence – which is better seen in noticing how that phrase 'it did not matter very much' is repeated and revised.

At first, when Tom's various startled responses are summarily collected into 'all this startled tumult of emotion', 'common sense' suggests what 'did not matter very much'; and the next sentence appears to endorse this commonsensical view with an authoritative 'really'. But the next paragraph brings a sudden adjustment. 'But' butts against 'really', and introduces a complicating view of what, after all, did matter – until the paragraph suddenly swivels on 'however', and sets the intimations of some deeper disturbance against the reassuring recovery. This in turn is immediately modified, corrected, readjusted in the paragraph that begins, 'Or apparently so'; and now the earlier, misleadingly authoritative 'really' is set against that authoritative 'in fact', which issues in a different, more ominous summation of Tom's inner state: 'doubt hindered his outgoing.' The unsettled, unsettling nervous energy of these adjustments is something very new in the English novel; nor does the final summation of what did and didn't 'matter much' come until the very end of the next paragraph, after Tom's 'outgoing' has again been reviewed, this time with more attention to the ways in which he is 'quieter, more conscious when he drank, more backward from companionship' – and after the suddenly stabilizing, conspicuously authorial view of what is ultimately at issue, namely Tom's 'innate desire to find in a woman the embodiment of all his inarticulate, powerful religious impulses'. This succinct statement of the *Rainbow* theme does, in one sense, emerge from the whole passage, as the final, ultimately authoritative comment on the relation between Tom's 'startled tumult of emotion' and what 'common sense' suggests; and, although the comment suggests that the author/teller has some kind of privileged or omniscient access to the character's inner life, it is also emerging from this long, unstable process of commentary and revision, as though the author/teller has had to work towards his own view of what is 'really' or 'in fact' at issue. But then this final statement of what *is* at issue is also the most removed from any kind of understanding which we could imagine Tom himself achieving:

that is, we couldn't imagine the character realizing that the desire which took him to a prostitute was an 'innate' desire to embody his 'inarticulate, powerful religious impulses'.

This passage shows where Lawrence's creative preoccupation with what a character '*is*', or 'IS' overlaps with the modernist concern to question the stability and unity of the 'self'. In their very different ways *Under Western Eyes*, *Ulysses* and *To the Lighthouse* are no less concerned with the disintegration of the 'old stable ego': they show how the 'I' is, as Hélène Cixous puts it, 'always more than one, diverse, capable of being all those it will at one time be, a group acting together'. But then a danger appears when we isolate that gap between what Lawrence finally *tells* us about Tom's 'innate' desire and anything we could imagine Tom consciously wanting, or articulating to himself as a need: the danger is that of imposing the writer's own ways of seeing, feeling and understanding on the character's otherness, in a coercive form of wishful or wilful thinking. Here Lawrence is very unlike those modernist writers who, like James, Conrad and Joyce, show their allegiance to the 'school of Flaubert' in determining to avoid this kind of imposition. James's concern with 'point of view' answered to his sense that authorial intrusions involve moral, not merely technical, 'muddlement'. As for Joyce, when he is presenting the workings of his characters' consciousness he is scrupulous in avoiding any words, images or perceptions which would be alien to the characters; here, it's worth noticing, Virginia Woolf's practice is closer to Lawrence than to Joyce.

Although Lawrence certainly isn't scrupulous in that way it would be a mistake, I take it, to enter rigidly Jamesian objections to what is so distinctive and original in his narrative tracing of Tom Brangwen's inner dynamics. The corrective hesitations and adjustments are choric in a peculiar way: it is as though the author were himself perched somewhere above the character, as if in a ship's crow's-nest, watching and interpreting and reinterpreting. So, before *telling* us what Tom's 'innate' desire is, the passage intimates in an imaginatively convincing way how much more there is to understand than the character could understand. On the other hand this isn't happening in 'Shame' (Chapter XII) when we are asked to believe that thoughts like these prompt (and somehow justify) Ursula's curiously malignant exercise in matchmaking:

She knew her Uncle Tom ... still wanted the great machine ... Then, and then only, when the machine caught him up, was he free from the hatred of himself, could he act wholly, without cynicism and unreality ...

She too, Winifred, worshipped the impure abstraction, the mechanisms of matter ... There, in the monstrous mechanism that held all matter, living or dead, in its service, did she achieve her consummation and her perfect unison, her immortality.

Hatred sprang up in Ursula's heart ... If she could destroy the colliery, and make all the men of Wiggiston out of work, she would do it.

The language betrays the insistent presence of an author who is imposing these ideas on his character as well as the reader. Yet this is consistent with Lawrence's vitalism, at those very points where it is problematically at odds with the modernist concern – in James, and in Joyce – to place narrative constraints on authorial intrusion. Moreover, the new, obsessively unreal idea that the miners themselves are hateful because they want, and worship, the machine is ugly and unconvincing in itself, as well as in relation to what we can imagine Ursula thinking and (especially) feeling: the idea resurfaces in *Women in Love* (1920) and much later in *Lady Chatterley's Lover* (1928) – as though the 1926 General Strike had never taken place. Lawrence needed to be a long way from the collieries before he could think such things; in *Sons and Lovers* (1913) he was closer, and wiser.

Indeed, *Sons and Lovers* is probably still Lawrence's most 'popular' novel, and his more apostolic admirers tend to underestimate its achievement. In part this is because the critics are loyally echoing Lawrence himself, whose pleas for intelligent recognition of what the later novels attempt frequently involve some disparagement of his first great novel – for example, when he insists that he is going 'a stratum deeper than I think anybody else has ever gone' in writing that is now 'all analytical – quite unlike *Sons and Lovers*, not a bit visualised', or when he announced that he was writing 'another language almost': 'I shan't write in the same manner as *Sons and Lovers* again, I think: in that hard, violent style full of sensation and presentation.' It is indeed fascinating to see (with the help of Keith Cushman's excellent study) how the extensive revisions of the *Prussian Officer* stories show the author of *Sons and Lovers* turning into the author of *The Rainbow*; or how the *Study of Thomas Hardy* marks out various changes in Lawrence's thinking about 'character', 'tragedy' and 'morality', after his marriage to Frieda. But then, although this development was indeed momentous, the assumptive basis for the 'analytical' language and for the sometimes hectoring contrasts between 'the vast, unexplored morality of life itself' and 'the little human morality play' was also more problematic, more likely to perplex or repel many readers who had warmly admired the earlier novel. But then another reason for being wary of the critical tendency to slight *Sons and Lovers* is that it so often involves consideration of biographical matters, and of the teller not the tale. Lawrence himself worried that the presentation of Walter Morel in the novel involved an injustice to his own father, while the very moving memoir by Jessie Chambers ('E. T.') persuaded most of its readers that Lawrence's presentation of Miriam Lievers involved a cruel misrepresentation of Lawrence's own relationship with Jessie. Here it is relevant to recall Proust's warnings about biographical criticism in *Contre Sainte-Beuve*, and his insistence that the greatest writing issues from 'le moi profond'. Most readers of *Sons and Lovers* know nothing of these biographical issues; far from being disadvantaged, they are less likely to be distracted from the novel itself – and more likely to see how those problems which do occur emerge *within* the fictional narration. For example, when we are told of Paul and Miriam that

If he were really with her, he had to put himself aside and his desire. If he would have her, he had to put her aside . . .

we are being encouraged to suppose that the disabling difficulties lie with Miriam rather than Paul; but the question is not whether this is (auto)biographically true but whether it is fictionally credible, when it is so much at odds with the novel's very full presentation of the ways in which Paul's relationship with his mother has queered his relationships with all other women. Similarly, when we are told, and very much told, that

From his mother he drew the life-warmth, the strength to produce; Miriam urged this warmth into intensity, like a white light . . .

the narrational point of view is once again uncritically merged with Paul's, and is at odds with what the novel shows. 'Life-warmth' is more obviously associated with Walter than with Gertrude Morel, and what the passage unwittingly conveys is a rather poignant authorial determination not to believe that the mother had also queered Paul's development as an artist. If this has biographical implications they also depend on a prior, independent critical appraisal of the novel itself.

The finely nervous, to-and-fro oscillations which give Lawrence's presentation of Tom Brangwen its weirdly tenacious, exploratory energy have a structural counterpart in *The Rainbow*'s magnificent irreducibility. If it is a psychological novel, not least in its very subtle sense of the ways in which parents transmit their unresolved problems to their children, it is also a historical novel much concerned with those social changes which also impinge on familial and sexual relations. Living in what is already a divided, industrial society, transformed by the new canals and railways, Tom and Lydia remain 'entirely indifferent to the general values of the world' (which may be as well, given Lydia's views on peasants); but for Will and Anna the journey to Lincoln Cathedral is a major event, and in attacking Will's response to the cathedral Anna is expressing her dissatisfactions with the marriage; for Ursula and Gudrun a trip to Europe is not remarkable and potential lovers are appraised partly through their views on world events, as when Ursula and Skrebensky argue about the Mahdi and Khartoum. But then, even as such accumulating details suggest that evolution is not progress and may make sexual and communal relations ever more difficult, so that Marvin Mudrick is right to emphasize Lawrence's 'revolutionary awareness' of the 'dying away, in the age of technology, of genuine communal relations', *The Rainbow* also chronicles and celebrates a progressive increase of opportunity, above all for women, that is entirely in keeping with Lawrence's remark that his subject was 'woman becoming individual, self-responsible, taking her own initiative'. If Tom Brangwen's achievement is in some sense an ideal or norm, as Leavis emphasized, we also see Tom drifting back into drink and dying 'unsatisfied'. If we agree to *some* extent with Keith Aldritt that Lawrence is inviting us to think of the Brangwens in class terms, as representing 'England's last opportunity to evolve' some vital alternative to the decadent 'aristocracy and middle class', then we had better also notice how the Brangwens' wealth makes them unusual and unrepresentative: true, it matters a great deal that as a schoolteacher Ursula can earn fifty pounds a year ('which was enough for her to live on independently'), but then her parents have 'four hundred a year' without drawing on any of their capital, and to think of the Brangwens as working class is ludicrous, at least on this side of the Atlantic. And yet in all these cases the effect is not one of confusion, but rather of a fidelity to the different elements which constitute individual and social experience: this sense of flux carries the sense that the processes of life itself are too mysterious and irreducibly complex to be fathomable in conventional moral terms.

Indeed, one episode which has distressed moralistic critics provides a very striking instance of this kind of salutary, complicating truthfulness. After Will Brangwen's seedy encounter with the young girl in the cinema his sexual relations with his wife suddenly and dramatically revive, and now include 'shameful natural and unnatural acts' and 'heavy, fundamental gratifications' – which in turn leads to a less problematically positive transformation in Will's relations with the outside world, and leads to his renewed interest in his woodcarving. Although Lawrence would have hated the suggestion, one might compare the way in which the effect of Bloom's masturbation as he watches Gerty MacDowell is beneficial and (in 'Circe') fortifying. The sense that conventional moral judgements have no real purchase might also recall Hardy's protest, in the 1912 Postscript to *Jude the Obscure*, against the 'forced adaptation of human instincts to rusty and irksome moulds that do not fit them'; but, unlike Hardy, Lawrence has found a narrative mode and structure that breaks free of the rusty moulds. And, without in any way slighting the astonishing and courageous originality of *Jude* and its own pioneering presentation of the New Woman, it is worth noticing how often Lawrence's presentation of Will, Anna and young Ursula recalls Hardy's novel while seeming more assured, and more adequate to the social and intellectual complexities in question. Both novels deal with individuals whose lives are transformed by the social changes accompanying industrialization; both explore the ways in which new conditions of life require new social and intellectual forms. In Will's case as in Jude's, an arrested relationship with the world he inhabits also produces tensions with his chosen mate. Although Jude has read Arnold, his idea of education is largely one of learning by rote (so that the image of him reciting the Nicene Creed in Latin in an Oxford pub is sadly apt); he clings, regressively, to old forms, and it is always Sue whose thinking is more radical and advanced, to a self-wounding degree (as in the ironic contrast between her anti-Christian exaltation of the Greeks and her tormented sexual frigidity). Will's attitude to Christianity is also regressive and rooted in the same historical moment, when medievalism, ritual and crafts offered a specious kind of sanctuary or imaginative escape from the machine's increasing power in society; even Ursula's name pays homage to the Carpaccio painting which Ruskin so admired. The powerful architectural dynamics in Lincoln Cathedral draw one forwards towards the altar, as well as upwards; but the 'Cathedral' chapter shows how the impulse that draws Will to the Church is predominantly aesthetic, and empties religion of any more demandingly ethical content. In seeing how Will wants only the 'swooning', undemanding ecstasy of uplift, without the grounding effect of the gargoyles, Anna is protesting against her husband's inability to live forwards outside the marriage. 'Why must he sink if he were detached from her? Why must he cleave to her?' Anna's inward protest also recalls the dangerous period when Tom Brangwen had 'felt like a broken arch thrust sickeningly out from support', since he 'must find other things than her, other centres of living'; moreover, her impatient sense that Will is 'inarticulate and stupid in thought' looks forward to Ursula's rejection of Skrebensky, and makes Anna herself too disposed to cling, 'almost against herself', to 'the worship of the human knowledge'. On the one hand the historical grounding, on the other the recurrent conflicts and tensions within each generation: it is this interplay which gives *The Rainbow* what Leavis calls its 'depth of recession'.

In the earlier and central sections of *The Rainbow* the narrative moves on from one generation to the next, like nature, when characters have gone as far as they can in their 'struggle into being'. Only in the final chapters, when the novel arrives at the present generation, is this strong forward movement dissipated by the proliferation of minor characters and events; this suggests not only that *The Rainbow* needs a sequel, but that any exploration of the modern malaise must develop in very different ways. If *The Rainbow* is so impressive for its sense of process, for a 'depth of recession' which is, as it were, stratigraphic or vertical, *Women in Love* spreads horizontally, like the ripples on the pool in 'Moony': its thirty-two chapters are much more brief and episodic, and repeatedly make use of some single, poetic or symbolically conceived motif – an African statuette, a mare, the moon, the Alps. This has less in common with *The Rainbow* than with the way in which many of Lawrence's tales, and especially his short novels, employ a unifying symbol whose significance is not something given or asserted by the author but rather something which emerges in, and above all *as*, the subtly revealing difference between the responses of different characters. In 'The Odour of Chrysanthemums', for example, the significance of the chrysanthemums is apprehended in the discrepancy between what Elizabeth Bates so disparagingly says ('it was chrysanthemums when I married him and chrysanthemums when you were born, and the first time they ever brought him home drunk') and what we see, when an unconscious impulse of tenderness makes her pick up the wan sprigs and push them in her apron-band. The history of a marriage is concentrated in that discrepancy: the martyred, self-pitying repudiation of those feelings which originally attracted her to her husband, and the emasculating effect of that denial on him, and also on her, and now on her whinging children. Similarly, *St Mawr*'s significance depends not on the obtrusive authorial cheerleading, which is potentially ruinous (for example, when Lawrence gloats over a chinless wonder's smashed face), but on those passages where the stallion is simply a fine stallion that means plausibly different things to Lou, Mrs Witt, Rico and other *characters*. So too with the captain's doll in that wonderfully witty short novel, or the fox in *The Fox*, or even with the escaped cock in 'The Man Who Died' (where the enlivening local debt to Melville's 'Cock-a-Doodle-Doo' points to a far larger indebtedness to Hawthorne and Melville) – and so too, in *Women in Love*, in the contrast between Gudrun's and Ursula's responses to Gerald's treatment of his mare, or to the lakeside in 'Sketch-Book', where Gudrun is so plausibly and ominously the 'knowing' artist, while Ursula drifts about, 'unconscious like the butterflies'; in Ursula's plausibly paranoid response to Birkin stoning the moon's reflection, or in the way she and Birkin suddenly feel constrained and self-conscious after 'lapsing out' as they watch the poignant, drifting daisies in 'An Island'. Any reference to a 'symbol' invites the rudely monosyllabic question, '*of*?', but in all these cases it is much more fruitful to ask, 'to whom?' – since attention is concentrated on the revealingly different ways in which the so-called 'symbol' is apprehended by characters within the fiction. Lawrence is a great master of the *nouvelle* or *novella* and, since his mature short novels – *The Fox* (1923), *The Captain's Doll* (1923), *The Virgin and the Gypsy* (1930), and (with reservations) *St Mawr* (1925) – are more impressively controlled than any of the novels he wrote after *Women in Love*, it is worth emphasizing their relation to a development which makes this problematic novel unlike its great predecessor – and, we might add, very unlike *Sons and Lovers*, where, as Graham Holderness observes, family quarrels are also always social conflicts.

For a major character to emerge, like Birkin, from nowhere, with no family or past that seems to matter, would have been inconceivable in *The Rainbow*. This makes it all the more poignant and disappointing, if we are recalling the earlier novel, when Birkin finally confronts Will Brangwen in 'Moony' and can see the older man only in summarily vitalist terms, as 'uncreated'. Another related disappointment is that in *Women in Love* Ursula becomes a diminished, far less formidable figure than her namesake in *The Rainbow*. After all her earlier, testing trials the powerfully articulate New Woman suddenly falls victim to a peculiar kind of descriptive Calvinism, in which what is 'unconscious' matters far more: we are constantly told what the damned look like, because characters who are, like Hermione or Gudrun, too 'dead' or 'finished' or 'knowing' are described in 'traditional', visualized terms – whereas the elect are presented in predominantly metaphorical terms, so that the signs of grace in Ursula depend on a repetitive rhetorical strategy which sees her as 'an essential flame that is caught, meshed, contravened', or as a 'strange unconscious bud of powerful womanhood'. That the censorship of *The Rainbow* and the horrors of the wartime persecution prompted the apocalyptic revulsions from 'putrescent mankind' is understandable: as the 'Nightmare' chapter in *Kangaroo* (1923) shows, Lawrence was treated very badly and responded badly. Lawrence's more apostolic critics often flinch away from considering the consequences of this distortion, and also, perhaps, from allowing that wives matter, not least in the literary history of so-called modernism: there is a rather nerveless willingness to suppose that Lawrence's elopement with the stridently aristocratic, confidently opinionated but shallow Frieda was altogether a Very Good Thing. It's hard to imagine the *Rainbow* Ursula, who has more in common with Lawrence's one-time fiancée Louie Burrows, being so submissive to Birkin – while some of Lawrence's more curious revisions, like the startling comment that 'It was an instinct in [Ursula], to deceive herself', suggest that another kind of compensatory response to Frieda's wilfulness is creeping into the novel. Be that as it may, no biographical considerations can or should relieve our disappointment over those resignations in 'Excurse' – when we see Ursula, now a sadly diminished and even docile New Woman, agreeing to live on the discreetly small income which Lawrence has settled on Birkin, as though this were better and braver in moral or vitalist terms than earning their livings as a schoolteacher and school inspector.

If the concluding rainbow-image in *The Rainbow* is taken not merely as a sign of the convalescent Ursula's recovery of a will to live, and live forwards, but as the novel's, or Lawrence's, vitalist and visionary affirmation of the possibility of social regeneration, that vision is awkwardly at odds with the apocalyptic bitterness of *Women in Love*. Yet the last chapter of the later novel also produces its own vitalist affirmation; and whether we think that something that is imposed from without very much depends on whether we think that the slipperiness of Lawrence's narrative mode actually encourages wishful or wilful thinking. At the beginning of the chapter a hotel employee brings Gudrun the news of Gerald's death:

> Gudrun did not know what to say. What should she say? What should she feel? What should she do? What did they expect of her? She was coldly at a loss.
>
> 'Thank you,' she said, and she shut the door of her room. The woman

went away mortified. Not a word, not a tear – ha, Gudrun was cold, a cold woman.

The questions that follow the direct statement that Gudrun 'did not know what to say' seem to relate to Gudrun's own agitated, self-conscious and self-justifying sense of being compromised; but then where is the word 'coldly' coming from? In the last sentence of the next paragraph, we might similarly pause over 'ha, Gudrun was cold, a cold woman': does this register the response of the 'mortified' woman, or Gudrun's irritated imagination of what it might be, or authorial comment? The question isn't as piffling as it might seem, once we notice how the word 'cold' and its variants dominate the rest of this brief chapter. In his classic *Mimesis* Erich Auerbach noticed how, if we ask who is speaking in a paragraph from *To the Lighthouse* where the ideas and images seem only partially attached to any character, the answer appears to be, the author, but an author who is not speaking objectively or with any certainty; some critics think this justifies references to an 'impersonal voice', yet the notion of impersonality can be sharply at odds with our sense of the author's intense and urgently personal investment in what is at issue. If we put Auerbach's question here, it is no less clear that Lawrence's narrative is associating and, as it were, orchestrating the dozens of crushingly reiterated references to the 'cold', 'icy', 'mute' and 'material'. Not only this chapter, but the whole novel, has been moving towards Birkin's crisis on the mountain where Gerald died:

> Was it any good going south, to Italy? Down the old, old Imperial road?
> He turned away. Either the heart would break, or cease to care. Best cease to care. Whatever the mystery which has brought forth man and the universe, it is a non-human mystery, it has its own great ends, man is not the criterion.

Here, we might easily fail to notice how Birkin's crushing sense of defeat leads him to abandon his own belief that he and Ursula might return to Italy and the south: they return to England instead, since there is 'no way out'. More immediately, Birkin goes 'home again to Gerald' (a particularly chilling way of putting it), and to that 'cold, mute, material face', with its 'last terrible look of cold, mute Matter' that 'left the heart cold, frozen, hardly able to beat'. The sense of defeat is wholly crushing: 'To rant, to rave, to be tragic, to make situations – it was all too late.' But then, suddenly, something else is invoked, that allows and even compels the 'new, deep life-trust' and a correspondingly vitalist repudiation of Gerald the 'denier':

Birkin looked at the pale fingers, the inert mass. He remembered a dead stallion he had seen: a dead mass of maleness, repugnant. He remembered also the beautiful face of one whom he had loved, and who had died still having the faith to yield to the mystery. That dead face was beautiful, no one could call it cold, mute, material. No one could remember it without gaining faith in the mystery, without the soul's warming with new, deep life-trust.

   And Gerald! The denier! He left the heart cold, frozen, hardly able to beat . . .

But where does *this* come from? Although its effect is to be momentously restorative, it doesn't refer us back to any character or episode in the novel we have been reading. I see no alternative to the view that the passage is coming from Lawrence's own determination that there must be some vitalist upbeat, affirming 'the mystery' and 'life-trust' – which is then smuggled into one of the many interior monologues where we hear not the character but His Master's Voice. This might indeed be compared with the slipperiness at the end of *The Rainbow*, where the satisfying illusion of affirmative closure depends on a reappropriation of thoughts which are only convincing as Ursula's thoughts: we move from the character's thinking into the author's wishful or wilful thinking.

   Another recurring difficulty might be brought out by contrasting two passages near the end of the 'Rabbit' chapter of *Women in Love*:

And then quite suddenly it settled down, hobbling among the grass, and sat considering, its nose twitching like a bit of fluff in the wind. After having considered for a few minutes, a soft bunch with a black, open eye, which perhaps was looking at them, perhaps was not, it hobbled calmly forward and began to nibble the grass with that mean motion of a rabbit's quick eating.

'It's mad', says Gudrun, whereupon Gerald insists, 'No. That's what it is to be a rabbit' – and this very different passage follows:

There was a queer, faint, obscene smile over his face. She looked at him and saw him, and knew that he was initiate as she was initiate. This thwarted her, and contravened her, for the moment.

The writing in the first passage is continuous with that in *Sons and Lovers*, and unmistakably 'Lawrentian' in its nervous, limber rhythms and its wonderfully keen, exact registering of 'that mean motion of a rabbit's quick eating'. The language in the second passage is indeed very different, and represents that new development away from the 'visualized' towards the 'analytical' and 'allotropic'. The 'queer, faint, obscene smile' can't be visualized, like the rabbit's 'mean motion'; rather, the adjectives are characterizing the effect of the smile on Gudrun, as she is both momentarily repelled and aroused. In one earlier draft (not quoted in the Cambridge edition's apparatus) a more loquacious Gerald explained to Gudrun that the rabbit 'only isn't human' and that she must 'get over the anthropomorphic habit'; but the final, published version might well irritate any reader who wants to know in what more precise sense Gudrun and Gerald are 'initiate'. 'Initiate' has a primarily gestural sense, which beats us back from conceptual understanding. The passage tells us not that Gerald *is* 'initiate' but that this is what Gudrun 'saw' and 'knew' in the smile, before her own face 'relaxed into a smile of obscene recognition'; moreover, what is in question isn't even her *thought* (for, despite that word 'knew', this appears to be yet another instance of something 'Gudrun knew in her subconsciousness, not in her mind') but her excited *sense* of complicity, which overcomes what had momentarily 'thwarted' or 'contravened' her. The sense of words like 'initiate', 'recognition', 'knew' and 'contravened' seems conceptually uncertain because these words answer to the 'allotropic' attempt to register what is preconceptual or subconceptual.

Leavis tended to be markedly unhappy with this more gestural use of language, as his comments on the 'Excurse' chapter show; and many readers will still share his misgivings. What we cannot do is to follow Leavis in regarding such passages as local, isolable blemishes that don't impinge on our general sense of the novel's greatness. If we don't feel, after reading the offending passages in 'Excurse', that Birkin and Ursula have arrived at some new stage in their relationship, answering to Birkin's own preoccupation with breaking through the barriers of language and purely mental consciousness, something more than a local blemish is in question. Similarly, in 'Moony', Birkin's meditations (which often seem authorial) on the apocalyptic contrast between Nordic and Pacific/African 'processes' may seem both strained and schematic. Yet this symbolic opposition is as important to *Women in Love* as Shakespeare's comparable presentation of 'Egypt' and 'Rome' in *Antony and Cleopatra*; in Lawrence's terms, as set out in works like *Fantasia of the Unconscious* (1922), the polarized extremes correspond with imbalances within the individual psyche, when the 'lower' consciousness ('phallic knowledge') is dominated by the 'higher' (mentality and will), as with Gerald's treatment of his mare, or the higher by the lower, as in that ugly African totem which fascinates Birkin. Part of our difficulty follows from the way in which psychic alternatives are being extended into historical and geographical claims. But again, if we reject this altogether, we lose the significance of Birkin's final repudiation of the totem in 'Moony'. The 'African' process of 'knowledge arrested in the senses, mystic knowledge in disintegration and dissolution' is set against the 'ice-destructive knowledge' of the 'Nordic' process, and Birkin finally rejects both in favour of 'the other, the remaining way' which answers to 'the holiness, the desire for creation and productive happiness': marrying Ursula. He rushes off to propose, leaving the reader with a curious problem. On the one hand these symbolic oppositions are important, even clarifying: for example, they suggest why the passages in 'Excurse' which troubled Leavis are invoking 'Greece' and 'Egypt' – as psychic/historical/geographical compromises between the extremes of the 'Nordic' and 'African' processes. But then if we try to think in these symbolic terms, the very idea that connubial contracts are the other 'way' through the Scylla and Charybdis of the looming symbolic apparatus seems comic, even absurd. A stranger argument for marriage can never have been advanced in a major work of fiction; but it corresponds with this novel's elimination of the traditional concerns with children, with familial and social continuities. What if Birkin later feels, like Aaron in *Aaron's Rod* (1922), that his wife no longer satisfies his 'Holy Ghost' of passion? What if accident or disease put Ursula in the situation of Connie with her crippled husband, or even of Frieda with a sexually impotent, dying husband? Such mundane, and mundanely moral, questions seem out of place only because the novel's metaphysic deflects them.

Leavis's account of 'Lawrence' already seems remote and implausible, in its convictions and in its omissions. I myself suspect that the 'Lawrence' of the 1990s will be seen to repay something more like Bakhtin's approach to Dostoevsky – in terms of those 'dialogical' conflicts which correspond with Lawrence's own conception of the novel as a 'thought-adventure'. If this is so, *Women in Love* will seem more central to his achievement than *The Rainbow*, precisely for that 'dialogical' (and deconstructive) impulse which makes Loerke a blackly parodic *schwarz*-Birkin (as Wagner's Wotan is a '*licht*-Alberich'), and for the ways in which the novel explores, without ever resolving, concepts like 'lapsing out' or Birkin's preoccupation with male bonding. Such things look forward to the problematic novels which followed, and to the eruptive way in which characters arise to challenge even the 'Lawrentian' views of a Somers or Rawdon Lilly. But it is hard to believe that Lawrence is in control of these 'thought-adventures', and of course one part of his own vitalist aesthetic insists that he must not be, since the ego, will and idea are to be resisted as a malevolently anti-life triad. Here the comparison between the first and final versions of *Lady Chatterley's Lover* is both instructive and depressing. *The First Lady Chatterley* is a tragicomic 'thought-adventure' which is impressively determined not to fudge Constance Chatterley's dilemma, which involves more than having to choose between real and fancied needs. Her life with her paraplegic husband can provide social and cultural amenities: the need for a 'bit of Mozart' is real, not trivial, and (despite some sketchiness) isn't trivialized. Parkin, a wonderfully conceived and, by the end, deeply moving figure, satisfies Connie sexually but cannot understand or satisfy those other needs; in one richly comic but sadly telling passage the daunted Connie imagines him eating bloaters for breakfast. By the time the novel had gone through its successive revisions some episodes had become unforgettably intense, like the scene at the chicken-coop or that in which the bereaved, confused Connie gazes at her body in the mirror; and the descriptions of the ruined English landscape ache with an exile's double sense of loss. The development of figures like Michaelis or Connie's (implausible) father or the horribly impressive Mrs Bolton forwards the 'dialogical' thought-adventure; but none of this can compensate for the increasingly rancid presentation of Clifford, and the replacement of Parkin with Mellors. Mellors is cultivated, reads foreign novels in the original and, as an ex-officer, is all but a gentleman. Unlike Parkin who can only speak in dialect, Mellors uses dialect as he uses (or instrumentalizes) sex, to bully and change Connie. The original dilemma is defused: once Connie has Mellors, she can have her cake and eat it too. But this also corresponds with that worrying way in which Lawrence's narrative modes so frequently encourage wishful or wilful thinking. In a famous passage in the final version Lawrence discusses 'the vast importance of the novel, properly handled': 'It can inform and lead into new places the flow of our sympathetic consciousness, and it can lead our sympathy away in recoil from things gone dead.' But it is characteristic of Lawrence not to consider whether that concern or determination to 'lead' might be peculiar and disabling; and here the contrast with Joyce could hardly be more marked.

III

Like Lawrence, Joyce had to struggle with his publishers and the censors, and the publication of his first book, *Dubliners*, was delayed by several years, until 1914. In that painful interim Joyce had written 'The Dead' – one of the greatest stories in the language –

and decided to make that the final story in *Dubliners*. As Hugh Kenner observes in *Joyce's Voices*, 'The Dead' begins with a perfect illustration of what Kenner calls the 'Uncle Charles principle'. When Joyce writes, 'Lily, the caretaker's daughter, was literally run off her feet', he is not himself using the word 'literally' in that subliterate sense: rather, there is a 'stylistic contagion' (to borrow Leo Spitzer's term) which, by keeping so close to the vocabulary, idiom and intellectual limitation of the character, gives the third-person narrative some of the features of first-person narration. This is not in itself new: earlier, local instances appear in Jane Austen's *Emma* and James's *The Portrait of a Lady*, for example. There are also precedents for Joyce's later development of this 'free indirect style' in *Ulysses*, where the narration repeatedly slides from a framing third-person narrative into internal monologue. Dickens sometimes used this mode of narrative, and Melville's *Benito Cereno* includes some strikingly 'Joycean' passages:

Ha! glancing towards the boat; there's Rover; good dog; a white bone in her mouth. A pretty big bone though, seems to me. – What? Yes, she has fallen foul of the bubbling tide-rip there. It sets her the other way, too, for the time. Patience.

What was new and radical, and exacting for the reader as well as the writer, was Joyce's extremely rigorous adherence to a narrative mode which, because it scrupulously excludes any direct authorial comment or explicit judgement, often provokes uncertainty about whatever distance exists between the narrator and the character: hence the continuing critical arguments about what judgement is implied of Gabriel Conroy, whose own bitter self-disgust at the end of 'The Dead' needs to be weighed against our sense of those positive qualities which were revealed earlier in the story. On the other hand the implied judgement that emerges from this kind of immersion in a character's language, way of seeing and mode of being, can be devastating (as in the final sentence of 'Clay'). Here it can be misleading to speak of an 'absent' or 'invisible' author, unless we also allow for that directing Joycean intelligence which is constantly at work within the work, organizing its significances and preparing its 'epiphanies'. The famous letter in which Joyce characterized his 'intention' and 'style' in *Dubliners* also shows the intensely purposeful way in which his original design, before he added 'The Dead' and two slighter stories, was to carry a diagnostic judgement of a remarkably comprehensive kind:

My intention was to write a chapter of the moral history of my country and I chose Dublin for the scene because that city seemed to me the centre of paralysis. I have tried to present it to the indifferent public under four of its aspects: childhood, adolescence, maturity and public life. The stories are arranged in this order. I have written it for the most part in a style of scrupulous meanness . . .

The community itself is to be represented in phases, like the evolution of an individual life, and Joyce's decision to examine each of the four 'aspects' in three stories is strikingly systematic, even scholastic. Moreover, as each group of stories diagnoses the different ways in which 'Dublin' threatens or smothers its inhabitants' human potentialities, this thematic progression is paralleled by a subtle but consistent narrational progress which, as it moves from first-person through increasingly distanced forms of third-person narrative, re-enacts the process of critical withdrawal.

So, the three stories concerned with childhood – 'The Sisters', 'An Encounter' and 'Araby' – are all initiatory and written in the first person. Because the boy protagonist is a little older in each story readers often assume that it is the same boy, although there is no real evidence for this; it is more important to notice how, although the narration occasionally reveals an older, more experienced conscious-ness (for example, when words like 'inefficacious' are used), the teller never intrudes his own analysis and judgement. Instead, the three stories show the growth of an increasingly harsh self-conscious-ness which culminates in the savage, self-arraigning moment at the end of 'Araby', when the boy sees himself as 'a creature driven and derided by vanity'. In this way the narration itself moves towards, or grows into, the third-person narration used in those stories concerned with 'adolescence' (cases of immaturity and arrested development) and then with 'mature life' (where the instances of prevarication and 'moral paralysis' have become established, carapaced routines). In the presentation of, say, Eveline, the intimate inner dynamics of her adolescent life are set before us, but the teller remains distanced from the character. 'Clay', in the next group, turns on the loss of a piece of plumcake; yet the superficially trivial incident produces a fissure in Maria's elaborately edited, precariously self-protecting view of the world. And in the next story, 'A Painful Case', the 'mature' Mr Duffy's case is all the more painful because Mr Duffy himself is critically aware of many of those aspects of Dublin life which have crippled, stunted, or paralysed earlier characters; his carefully evolved routines and habits represent his own effort to preserve his intellectual integrity – but then the story also shows how they inhibit and arrest his emotional development, in a kind of double bind. These same, self-guarding habits make Mr Duffy recoil from the only possibility of some liberating emotional relationship and commitment to another person; and later, when he learns that the desperate Mrs Sinico has taken to drink and committed suicide, they shut off that suddenly inundating sense of remorse and responsibility ('he had sentenced her', and was himself 'an outcast from life's feast') which might also, in its far more painful way, have represented a point of growth. In the devastating conclusion everything shuts down: having 'gnawed the rectitude of his life' for a few punishing but promising moments, Mr Duffy recovers by beginning 'to doubt the reality of what memory had told him'. Such a recovery is an inner death. In his fascinating memoir, *My Brother's Keeper*, Stanislaus Joyce wryly observes that much of the material for this story had been taken from his own diary, since Mr Duffy was 'intended to be a portrait of what my brother imagined I should become in middle age'. But then, in a characteristically perceptive way, Stanislaus also sees how this story takes its position within the sequence, so that 'Mr Duffy is the type of the male celibate, as Maria in "Clay" is of the female celibate'. Joyce also gives Mr Duffy some of his own characteristics, like the interest in Hauptmann and Nietzsche, not just 'in order to raise his intellectual standard' (as Stanislaus bleakly surmised), but to make Mr Duffy's inner death a still more chillingly climatic example of what Dublin's 'paralysis' can do even to those Dubliners who think they can rise above it. This further dissociation leads into what would have been the final group of stories presenting Dublin's 'public life', where the narrative distance is absolute. 'Public life' is broken down into politics ('Ivy Day'), art ('A Mother'), and religion ('Grace'). There is no interiority, no access to characters' inner lives beyond that suggested by what they do and say – which conveys not only their own inner vacuity, but that of a city where politics, art and religion are all debilitated by the lack of inward passion and commitment, and by the paralysing effects of being ruled from without, by England and the Church of Rome.

These thematic and narrative progressions make *Dubliners* much more than a miscellaneous collection of stories: we might rather call it a 'fragmentary novel', borrowing the phrase Lawrence used to describe another work which shows the influence of *Dubliners* – Hemingway's *In Our Time* (1925). But then, precisely because the original design of *Dubliners* is so intensely purposeful and, for a young writer, so astonishingly assured in its execution, it can also prompt the same kind of worry as Eliot's early poetry, up to and including *The Waste Land*: a worry about what might seem overdetermined, or deterministic. Are characters like Eveline or Mr Duffy – or Eliot's various personae from Prufrock on – so paralysed *because* they inhabit their modern metropolises, or is Dublin a 'centre of moral paralysis' because it includes so many inhabitants like these? The drafts for *The Waste Land* include one revealingly didactic and deterministic passage in which the city is said to stifle the lives of its inhabitants, who are compared to Nibelungs; Eliot later excised these lines, preferring to imply what he would not state. That is consonant with Eliot's admiration for *Ulysses* as an Eliotic panorama of contemporary futility, and his corresponding disregard for the profoundly unEliotic celebration of the 'ordinary' life in Joyce's great humane comedy. Joyce's later decision to incorporate 'The Dead' and two slighter stories, 'Two Gallants' and 'A Little Cloud', into *Dubliners* certainly affected, and in one sense dissipated, the original, tightly oppressive design. Having four stories within each of the second and third groups introduced new relationships which are lateral rather than progressive, while 'The Dead' becomes an extraordinary summation which now also involves a more sympathetic redirection, not least in narrational terms: instead of concluding with 'Grace' and the most extreme kind of narrative disengagement, 'The Dead' internalizes its third-person narrative in a way that looks forward to *A Portrait of the Artist as a Young Man* (1916). Although critics all agree that 'The Dead' is the greatest story in *Dubliners*, some have argued that its inclusion destroys the original powerful design. Certainly it becomes harder to see the published version of *Dubliners* as Joyce's Waste Land, but we might welcome that complication of an all too purposeful design: the combination of imaginative inwardness and diagnostic irony in Joyce's representation of Gabriel, and the irrepressibly humane relishing of some aspects of Dublin life ('dear dirty Dublin') in the supper party, all keep faith with what makes Joyce so unlike Eliot. 'The Dead' shows 'Stephen Daedalus' growing into 'James Joyce'.

'Stephen Daedalus' was the pseudonym Joyce had used in publishing some early stories, just as he signed some of his letters 'S. D.' – as though to acknowledge, in a half-prescient, half-baffled fashion that he was still writing from an only partially discovered self: to use the metaphor which underlies so much of *Ulysses*, he had not yet been able to create or *father* 'James Joyce'. *Stephen Hero* belongs to the same period as *Dubliners*, and traces the internal development of an artist who also arrives at a 'vivisectionist' view of his own country. Joyce was dissatisfied with this 'schoolboy's production' and abandoned it in 1906, the year before he wrote 'The Dead'. After completing the extensive revision which was to become *A Portrait of the Artist as a Young Man*, Joyce destroyed much of the manuscript of *Stephen Hero*; what survived of it was published posthumously in 1944, and the comparison between *Stephen Hero* and the *Portrait* is as fascinating and instructive as that between Proust's posthumously published *Jean Santeuil* and the great work that preceded. In *Stephen Hero* various passages and, for Joyce, uncharacteristic interventions show very clearly that the authorial or narratorial view of Stephen Dedalus does not coincide with Stephen's view of himself; but *Portrait*, like *Dubliners* and *Ulysses*, rigorously excludes this kind of direct comment. Instead, through a particularly radical development of the 'Uncle Charles principle', the changing style of each of the five chapters keeps pace with Stephen's own growth. Since 1922, when *Ulysses* appeared and made it clear that Joyce was critical of Stephen, it has become difficult to see how critics or readers failed to register some of the distancing ironies in *Portrait*, for example in Chapter IV, when Stephen (who had earlier 'opened a loan bank for his family') 'seemed to feel his soul in devotion pressing like fingers the keyboard of a great cash register and to see the amount of his purchase start forth immediately in heaven, not as a number but as a frail column of incense or as a slender flower', or when we are told that Stephen's 'soul had loved to muse in secret' on the priest's 'awful power', and that in 'that dim life' Stephen would imagine himself as 'a young and silentmannered priest', 'accomplishing the vague acts of the priesthood which pleased him by reason of their semblance of reality and their distance from it'. Here our difficulty is like that of imagining how the narrative in James's *The Turn of the Screw* could ever have seemed straightforward; but, although these and similar passages can and doubtless should be assimilated to a more ironically diagnostic view of Stephen, they are never firmly and clearly dissociated from Stephen's thoughts and feelings. Even the cash register image, which recalls Nietzsche's remark that 'Christians expect to be very well paid', is still something we can imagine occurring to Stephen, with no more conscious irony than is evident in Gerard Manley Hopkins's 'The Starlight Night', when the *paysage sacralisée* pivots on 'all is a purchase, all is a prize ... Buy then! Bid then!' In other words, any distancing is, to an extraordinarily challenging degree, always enmeshed with the internalized representation: it is not direct and external, as it often is in *Stephen Hero*, or structural, as it is in *Ulysses*.

The famous opening of *Portrait* shows why, although Joyce's narrative concerns are often continuous with those of Henry James in his later novels, the Jamesian concept of 'point of view' isn't really adequate:

> Once upon a time and a very good time it was there was a moocow coming down along the road and this moocow that was down along the road met a nicens little boy named baby tuckoo . . .
>
> His father told him that story: his father looked at him through a glass: he had a hairy face.

The opening conveys and centres on the child's consciousness but not in the child's language, while the narrator himself is clearly not – or perhaps we should just say, not clearly – an older Stephen. Here the French narrative theorist Gérard Genette's concept of 'focalization' is helpful, since it addresses those cases where the two questions one needs to ask in characterizing any narrative – 'Who sees?' and 'Who speaks?' – require different answers. Even in the last chapter, Joyce will not go beyond the bounds of Stephen's vision; in isolating, the better to understand, that aspect of himself he calls 'Stephen Dedalus', he provides a portrait of *an* artist which, as Stanislaus's memoir takes pains to emphasize, is not in any full or adequate sense a self-portrait. Rather, Joyce is recycling his own experiences to show what makes, and makes for, Stephen's particular way of apprehending his world – and what it means to *be* like *that*. In this respect Joyce belongs with those novelists who, like Henry James or George Eliot, tend to keep postponing and complicating any judgement of the fictional character, rather than with those novelists who press towards some summary or dismissive judgement. The final judgement on, say, Jane Austen's Mrs Norris or Lawrence's Hermione Roddice or Patrick White's Sarsaparillans tends to be made early and then repeated with minor variations; but the moment when we might finally pronounce on a Maggie Verver or Dorothea Brooke or Stephen Dedalus never arrives, not because the novels in question are evasive or morally pococurantist, but because the novelists have so strong a sense of the various competing potentialities within a 'self', and of the contingency of even a seemingly decisive or determining development. Some readers may protest, like Wilde's Miss Prism, that this is not what Fiction means; but others are more worried by fiction which, like Mrs Mooney in *Dubliners*, deals 'with moral problems as a cleaver deals with meat'. Stanislaus's memoir has much to say of the young Joyce's distaste for the 'lies' and 'sumptuous exaggerations' through which 'literature provided men and women with false consciences, literary consciences'; similarly, and prophetically, Joyce's early essay on Ibsen praises him for dispossessing the 'legitimate hero' and choosing 'average lives in their uncompromising truth'.

Stephen's is no average life, to be sure, but in showing what shapes and limits it – how it is historically and culturally bounded – Joyce is also showing how, as the young Joyce noted of Ibsen, 'action or incident' matters only in relation to 'some great ideal conflict of which we become aware as the play proceeds, and which rivets our attention'. Joyce's play, *Exiles* (1918), shows how he was responding intuitively to this idea of an 'ideal conflict' long before he was ready and able to tease out, and explore, its most profound implications. If *Exiles* testifies to Joyce's admiration for Ibsen, it also shows how all influence involves misrepresentation: his married artist's concern with 'freedom' remains, too tenuously, an idea, like Stephen's idea of expressing his 'spirit' in 'unfettered freedom', while the splitting off of different aspects of the authorial self into 'Robert' and 'Richard' has none of the vitality of the Stephen/Bloom opposition in *Ulysses*. Joyce's poems also show how Joyce or 'S. D.' has not yet *fathered* 'Joyce': we can be glad that Stanislaus persuaded Joyce not to withdraw *Chamber Music* (1907), while still agreeing with Pound's sleek but steely remark that Joyce's poems 'belong in the Bible or in the family album with the portraits'.

In *Portrait*, Stephen's aesthetic issues in aestheticism, in the idea of the artist as a 'God' who 'remains within or behind or beyond or above his handiwork, invisible, refined out of existence, indifferent, paring his fingernails'. It is characteristic of Stephen that he should try to evolve an aesthetic before writing anything of consequence (if he ever does). Having rejected religion, Stephen makes a religion of art in which the emphasis on nailparing betrays the dandyish aesthete. Here *Portrait* offers a fascinating contrast with *Sons and Lovers*: Lawrence, whose presentation of artists and writers is invariably satirical or hostile, is so far from making a religion of Art that he cannot even allow Paul to be, in any full sense, an 'artist'. But in *Ulysses*, when Stephen has returned from Paris with a dawning sense that he has 'much to learn', he has repudiated his earlier aesthetic, replacing it with another in which Shakespeare and the artist's experience are central. This draws John Eglinton's protest:

– You are a delusion, said roundly John Eglinton to Stephen. You have brought us all this way to show us a French triangle. Do you believe your own theory?

Stephen promptly says that he doesn't, while thinking, a moment later, 'I believe, O Lord, help my unbelief'; but whether Stephen believes his theory or not actually isn't the issue so far as *Ulysses* itself is concerned. *Ulysses* shows us its own 'French triangle' in representing Stephen, Bloom and Molly as aspects of their creator's self-understanding. As a woman, and as a male representation of the feminine, or anima, or the Other, Molly is a special case: her singularly unmale stream of consciousness is heard only in the final, eighteenth chapter – which is preceded by a large black dot since the (male) narrative concludes with 'Ithaca'. Joyce himself spoke of the novel's ending with 'Ithaca', and throughout seventeen chapters or episodes the crucial opposition is that between Stephen and Bloom – both as independent fictional characters who engage our sense of sharply contrasted capacities and limitations, and as polarizations of different aspects of the mature 'James Joyce', for whom 'Stephen' and 'Bloom' represent opposed or complementary potentialities within that creative intelligence which creates or fathers itself in bringing them together, and in viewing each in the light of the other within the novel's 'All in all'.

The first three episodes of *Ulysses* – the so-called 'Telemachiad', in terms of the novel's Homeric analogy – pick up from *Portrait* in showing Stephen after his return from Paris to attend his mother's funeral, and take us ever further into Stephen's ways of seeing and experiencing his world during the early hours of 'Bloomsday', or 16 June 1904. When we finally meet Leopold Bloom, starting his day in 'Calypso', we double back to the temporal starting point, as the most pregnant contrast in modern British literature begins to unfold – in a celebration of 'inner organs', 'thick giblet soup', and those grilled kidneys which give Bloom's responsive palate 'a fine tang of faintly scented urine'. A similar contrast underlies their respective attitudes to 'fathering'. Bloom thinks about fatherhood in ways which are directly, but then fragmentarily, experiential, and involve the son he has lost even more than the living Molly: 'My son. Me in his eyes. Strange feeling it would be. From me . . . Life.' The inexperienced, priestly Stephen thinks of fatherhood in intellectually abstract terms which are both scholastic and, as they recall the *Sonnets*, paradoxically Shakespearean: 'a mystical estate, an apostolic succession, from only begetter to only begotten.' A son can't have an only begetter. Stephen is impressively but limitingly abstract, intellectually systematic and unlovable, like the English stereotype of the French theorist; whereas Bloom, who is so passionately and, in a different way, limitingly concerned with his own experience, is more like the French stereotype of the English psychological empiricist. In

Portrait, Stephen's future as an artist – the possibility of his having any future as an artist – did indeed depend on his emancipating withdrawal from Ireland, from the Roman Church, and even from the family that would 'drown' him: but, just as he was constantly defining himself *against* his Dublin environment and what Bloom calls 'warm, breathing life', his mawkishly 'kinetic' poetry was ironically at odds with his aesthetic insistence on 'stasis' and the artist's godlike, nailparing 'indifference'. In *Ulysses* Stephen himself is beginning to realize that his growth as artist depends on his growth as man: that is the real significance of the new, 'Shakespearean' aesthetic, and such growth depends not on withdrawals ('I will not serve') but on engaging with the world he inhabits. He must develop something more like Bloom's vital, passionately curious interest in his environment, as well as that imaginatively compassionate concern with other people that sends Bloom traipsing through Dublin on behalf of Dignam's widow and then makes him no less concerned to help a young man who makes him grieve again for his own dead son. And for Joyce, to bring these two together is to father *Ulysses* and himself: to achieve what Joyce calls, in another crucial metaphor, 'two-eyed' vision. So, in *Circe*, when Stephen and Bloom gaze together into the brothel mirror it shows (but they don't see) the 'face of William Shakespeare, beardless'. Both are, in a sense that matters very much, independent fictional characters, and yet their meeting is also a riddling equation: Stephen + Bloom = *Ulysses* = two-eyed, 'Shakespearean' vision = 'Joyce'. Stephen and Bloom couldn't both see that face, of course, but this is one of several moments in 'Circe' where the hallucinatory psychodrama cannot be related to anything that could be taking place in the 'unconscious' of the fictional characters. We might rather speak of what the novel is recognizing – or, in the old, exact sense, scrying – in that brothel mirror: the process of its own creation and representation of 'Stephen' and 'Bloom' fathers 'Joyce'.

This also suggests why we should not be disturbed when 'Ithaca' refuses to tell us how, or even whether, Stephen's relationship with Bloom will develop. The coming together of Stephen and Bloom as independent fictional characters only matters so much, in 'plotty' terms, because its significance has already been realized in, or as, the coming together of 'Stephen' and 'Bloom' within *Ulysses*. Our sense of Bloom's heroism, of all that justifies the Homeric analogy with Ulysses' return to his wife Penelope, his discovery of his son Telemachus, and his triumph over the rival suitors (which 'Penelope' confirms) is something established by the whole novel. It cannot depend on a contingent, merely plotty outcome, involving the independent fictional characters; it cannot be diminished if Stephen and Bloom never meet again, or if Stephen and Molly never meet, or if Stephen never becomes a great writer and Bloom never fathers another son. This, I take it, is how we should understand Joyce's remark (in a letter to Frank Budgen) that 'Ithaca' had 'resolved' events 'into their cosmic physical psychical etc. equivalents', giving Bloom his 'passport to eternity' and showing Bloom and Stephen as 'heavenly bodies, wanderers like the stars at which they gaze'. A Joycean 'Shakespeare' could have made the same point about Hal and Falstaff.

Ulysses occupied Joyce for eight years; in his final, very extensive revisions and additions, which transformed even the earlier, relatively uncomplicated chapters, Joyce worked to achieve that kind of encyclopaedic completeness which the 'schema' he sent to Carlo Linati forbiddingly charts. One consequence is that important critical disagreement which Michael Groden deftly characterizes by contrasting the accounts of Stuart Gilbert and S. L. Goldberg: 'For Gilbert, Joyce only began to write *Ulysses* in 1919, but for Goldberg he should have stopped (with a few exceptions) after 1918.' The crucial issue is whether, as Groden suggests, 'technique seems to dominate over content' after the first nine episodes, so that our interest in the characters is frustrated and the story 'proceeds through a series of semi-transparent envelopes'. And here *Ulysses* reads its readers, in establishing how much of Bloom or Stephen is in their composition. To talk of envelopes or screens implies that there is something *behind* a fictional narrative; the contrary claim – that there can be no presentation, only representation, since there is no such thing as transparent, unmediated narration – would absorb a critical Stephen Dedalus and bore a Leopold Bloom. Two examples may suggest how the increasing complexity of the later episodes doesn't necessarily entail that their human interest diminishes.

'Cyclops' shows just how little Joyce resembles Stephen's earlier conception of the artist as a fastidiously disengaged nailparing divinity: the satire on nationalism and bigotry is furiously committed. And sane: Joyce's passionate and compassionate humanism is all the more striking if we recall the more or less anti-democratic, and sometimes overtly fascistic and anti-semitic, utterances of other 'modernists', like Eliot, Pound, Lewis and Lawrence. The chapter opens with the first of many variations on the Homeric blinding, as the primary narrator whinges about the sweep who 'near drove his gear into my eye'; but Joyce is above all concerned with the blinding effect of politics and nationalism, one-eyed *vision* in a metaphorical and moral sense. Bloom is in such danger in this episode not only because he is a Jew among bigots, but because he is the despised, reluctantly heroic champion of *two*-eyed vision, as 'old sloppy eyes', 'old plum eyes', 'Bloom with his *but don't you see*? and *but on the other hand*'. The other attribute of the Homeric cyclops – who is not only one-eyed, but also a giant – is also developed metaphorically, through the literary 'gigantism' of the other narrative voices which keep erupting into this episode, with hilariously inflated lists and parodies of nationalist mythologizing, the cult of Celtic saga and Yeatsian spiritualism. Nothing, it might seem, could be more unlike the unmistakable idiom of the primary narrator, a meanminded foulmouthed Dublin barfly ('So anyhow Terry brought the three pints Joe was standing and begob the sight nearly left my eyes when I saw him land out a quid') or the bigotry of the Citizen who finally assaults Bloom ('I'll brain that bloody jewman for using the holy name. By Jesus, I'll crucify him so I will'). Yet the deepest provocation comes in the suggestion that there *is* a connexion between the most inflated and the grubbiest versions of one-eyed vision, and when the Citizen finally hurls the biscuit tin at the 'bloody jewman' the narrative voices merge: 'And they beheld Him even Him, ben Bloom Elijah, amid clouds of angels ascend to the glory of the brightness at an angle of fortyfive degrees over Donohoe's in Little Green street like a shot [i.e. turd] off a shovel.'

Bloom could not be more exposed. Not only are the voices we hear in Barney Kiernan's pub dangerously hostile: the other voices we hear – in this episode's *narrational* setting or environment – are indifferent or hostile to Bloom's courageous, awkward affirmation of 'Love' as 'the opposite of hatred':

But it's no use, says he. Force, hatred, history, all that. That's not life for men and women, insult and hatred. And everybody knows that it's the very opposite of that that is really life.

'And off he pops like greased lightning', sneers the barfly, before yet another narrative voice takes over, erupting into its own prolonged and contemptuous parody: 'Love loves to love love. Nurse loves the new chemist. Constable 14A loves Mary Kelly. Gerty MacDowell loves the boy that has the bicycle. M. B. loves a fair gentleman. Li Chan Han lovey up kissy Cha Pu Chow . . .' If we admire the courage and humanity in Bloom's two-eyed affirmation, we will resent and reject this sneering implication that Bloom is being vapidly sentimental. Yet that reference to 'M. B.' might remind us that, as the hour of Molly's adultery approaches, the dangers Bloom faces are also internal: since 'Sirens' he has been in danger of yielding to self-pity, although his future with the woman he loves depends on what 'Bluwhoo' can confront (not repress) and accept. Moreover, as that mention of 'Gerty MacDowell' suggests, this has its bearing on the next episode, 'Nausicaa' – where strikingly different narrational complications challenge the reader's sense of what to 'make of' Bloom and Gerty in moral and human terms. Most critics (including feminist critics) applaud Bloom's affirmation of 'Love' and then go on to take a strikingly unloving, one-eyed and contemptuous view of the adolescent Gerty. Here, as in 'Eumaeus', the narrational strategies discover to what extent the academic critic is a critical Stephen – is incapacitatingly ready to suppose that feelings which are imperfectly or conventionally expressed must actually be inferior, and that the life and life-responses of a Stephen are in some way superior to, and more real, than those of a Bloom.

In the first part of 'Nausicaa' Gerty is represented through that novelettish language and adolescent sentiment which is her only form of imaginative and intellectual life. Here the language swivels, in a richly ironic fashion, between Gerty's preferred way of seeing and reshaping her world and her more inadvertent registering of those recalcitrant, painful actualities she wants to distance:

Her figure was slight and graceful, inclining even to fragility but those iron jelloids she had been taking of late had done her a world of good much better than the Widow Welch's female pills and she was much better of those discharges she used to get and that tired feeling.

The contrast between these two voices constitutes 'Gerty': the Gerty who is being formed by the world she inhabits, and the Gerty who attempts to refashion herself and her world through fantasies that are both meretricious and touchingly resilient, eager and free from self-pity. Her view of Bloom is correspondingly sentimental and novelettish ('He was in deep mourning, she could see that, and the story of a haunting sorrow was written on his face'), and an indirect warning to us not to sentimentalize; but it is also more perceptively human and generous than that of the vile begobbing bigots in 'Cyclops', so that her own capacity to find Bloom attractive and see something of his 'sorrow' is also a measure of her own attractive potentialities – which are likely to remain undeveloped. The glimpses of her home life are indeed diagnostic in registering what is second-hand in her clichés and banal moralism – when we see her wishing that her father 'had only avoided the clutches of the demon drink', or reflecting that 'if there was one thing of all things that Gerty knew it was that the man who lifts his hand to a woman save in the way of kindness, deserves to be branded as the lowest of the low'. And her consolations and imaginative compensations are no less pathetic – her pride in her 'griddlecakes done to a goldenbrown hue and queen Ann's pudding of delightful creaminess', or in the 'undies' which she displays to Bloom and which 'were Gerty's chief care and who that knows the fluttering hopes and fears of sweet seventeen (though Gerty would never see seventeen again) can find it in his heart to blame her?' Who indeed? Well, for a start, academic Stephens of either sex, who are not unsettled by the wrenching to and fro clash between the narration's diagnostic and compassionate energies, and who are more inclined to notice the undeniable meagreness of Gerty's intellectual resources than what these passages also reveal about her pitifully unpropitious, stultifying home life. Like Stephen's sisters, Gerty is already drowning; like Maria in *Dubliners* and unlike Eveline, she is determinedly swimming. Of course she reads the wrong books, but to take a wholly untender, diagnostic view of Gerty is to deflect Joyce's complex humanity and misread his great book of life. It is to fail in the way we hope Stephen will not fail when he does meet Bloom – and when his difficulty in seeing and appraising Bloom's humanity is so pointedly paralleled by our own difficulties in seeing through, and as it were behind, the narration in 'Eumaeus'.

'Nausicaa' is no less profoundly concerned with reading, and what we bring to our reading of people as well as texts: here, the readerly odyssey involves navigating those contrary narrational currents that pull us between diagnostic astringency and compassionate insight, and make this episode's formal climax both satirically devastating and morally challenging. While Bloom is peering at Gerty's exposed, Virginally blue undies ('drinking in her every contour, literally worshipping at her shrine') and busily proving himself 'a man of inflexible honour to his fingertips', Canon O'Hanlan is 'looking up at the Blessed Sacrament' in a ritual to the Blessed Virgin Mary which also culminates in 'benediction' – where the 'holy vessel' is merely exposed without an act of 'communion'. The 'Roman candle bursts', the canon puts 'the Sacrament back into the tabernacle', and Bloom attends to his wet shirtfront while guessing correctly that Gerty is menstruating. Narrative tumescence is followed by detumescence (as the Linati 'schema' tersely suggests) as the narration itself pivots away from Gerty's anaemic idom into Bloom's unmistakably *terre-à-terre* tones and viewpoint:

She walked with a certain quiet dignity characteristic of her but with care and very slowly because – because Gerty MacDowell was . . .

Tight boots? No. She's lame! O!

Mr Bloom watched her as she limped away. Poor girl! That's why she's left on the shelf and the others did a sprint . . .

It is an extraordinarily upsetting moment, and too charged to allow any single response. The conventionally 'obscene' act – Gerty impulsively exposing herself for Bloom's furtive satisfaction – is also a benediction, and the first kindness shown to Bloom for a long time. (It is amusing, but in no way surprising, to learn that the one American judge who had opposed his colleagues' enlightened, conspicuously unBritish verdict by declaring *Ulysses* 'obscene' had to be removed from office shortly afterwards, for corruption: for the real scoundrels in public office, censorship and the loudly expressed concern for public morals are a wonderfully cheap diversion.) The effect on Bloom is to make him feel more, rather than less, close to his unfaithful wife – and now, at last, his tragicomic struggle not to think about what she is doing suddenly issues in an articulation of what is done, and must be confronted before it can be accepted:

Funny my watch stopped at half past four. Dust. Shark liver oil they use to clean. Could do it myself. Save. Was that just when he, she?

O, he did. Into her. She did. Done.

Ah!

The 'O!' for the lame Gerty was characteristically compassionate, but also disconcertingly bound up with the more detached observations of the detumescent, eased male. The 'Ah!' for Molly and what cannot be undone is momentous: it is what must be taken in, if Bloom and Molly are to have any future. Before dozing off, the exhausted Bloom starts to scratch a message in the sand for Gerty – 'I. AM. A.' – and then flings his stick away. 'The stick fell in silted sand, stuck': if we remember Molly's words here, it is at a moment when we have seen how her Poldy is far more than 'a stick in the mud'. Before he falls asleep, Bloom's mind drifts from Gerty, 'that woman', to Molly, *the* woman: 'return next in her next her next.' That drift is so inevitable and natural to the loving Bloom as to make 'drift' seem the wrong word; it is more like a gravitational pull, and we see it again in 'Penelope' as Molly's drowsing consciousness keeps taking her from Blazes and other men to Bloom, her man. But acknowledging that gravity isn't inevitable either: keeping faith with it, in the navigational odyssey of daily living, is often both difficult and painful, and has threatened to be too much for the Blooms in their own marriage. They have not made 'love, in any 'normal' or conventional sense, since their son's death. In showing how Bloom's return is as heroic as that of Odysseus, Joyce is entering his own protest, like his beloved Ibsen and like Milton, against literary heroism and epic misrepresentations that diminish the ordinary life.

In one sense *Ulysses* explodes 'realism', not least when it catches us responding referentially: its encyclopaedic use of different modes of narration keeps reminding us that any narrative representation is always more, and less, than transparent presentation. In another no less important sense *Ulysses* is the culmination of novelistic realism: not only do we know Bloom better than any other character in fiction, Joyce himself assumes – no less than Tolstoy or George Eliot – that our thinking about fictional characters and issues is and should be continuous with our thinking about people and issues in the world we all inhabit. The first point will always seem more fascinating and important to critical Stephens, and the second to critical Blooms; but I have tried to argue that we can keep faith with both truths in seeing how Joyce's representations carry the Nietzschean insight that we interpret the world as we interpret a text. Seeing how and why *Ulysses* is no less concerned with 'Stephen' and 'Bloom' than with Stephen and Bloom also suggests why far too much has been made of the facile paradox that, although *Ulysses* is the great modern celebration of the ordinary life, 'ordinary' readers can't read it; or of the similarly damaging view that *Ulysses* cannot be read, only studied. Like Wagner's *Ring* or Shakespeare's tragedies, *Ulysses* may be inexhaustible but is not impenetrable. One might think *Finnegans Wake* (1939) the classic example of a book which, although parts of it repay repeated rereadings, nobody should have to read through for the first time; but, whoever or whatever the 'ordinary' reader may be, anybody who reads Shakespeare or Milton can find a first reading of *Ulysses* immensely pleasurable. If such readers don't (rather than can't) read *Ulysses*, it seems likely that this is often because the book's reputation for difficulty has overtaken its more enticing reputation for obscenity, or (in the case of 'Eng. Lit.' students) because the proliferating commentaries seem to surround the work like a barbed-wire fence. Here the contrasts with the *Wake* seem more important than any resemblances, and one crucial contrast is suggested by Joyce's aggressive–defensive avowal, in 1936, that 'since 1922 my book has been a greater reality for me than reality': opposing one kind of reality to another in that way wouldn't be very helpful in approaching *Ulysses*, although it may have helped Joyce in his difficult, sometimes tormenting, final years. In all, *Finnegans*

Wake occupied Joyce for seventeen years, twice as long as *Ulysses*. His brother Stanislaus regarded it as thoroughly misconceived, and it continues to divide critics – for example, in appealing more to Marxists or Jungians or linguists than to feminists or Freudians or moralists. S. L. Goldberg (no critical Stephen) went so far as to declare 'at the outset that I do not believe *Finnegans Wake* is worth detailed exegesis'; since that magnificently unacademic and courageously candid declaration in 1962, the various guides and academic-industrial explications have proliferated, culminating in John Bishop's impressive study. A whole school of 'post-modernist' critics and theorists have taken the *Wake* as 'the supreme example of self-conscious "*écriture*"': their chief regret – as expressed by Christopher Butler (no critical Bloom) – is over the persistence of Joyce's faith 'in the transcribability of things'.

In *Ulysses* our strongly active concern with Bloom, Stephen and Molly as independent fictional characters is consonant with, and even a condition of, our concurrent sense that they are all constructed and refracted aspects of their creator's self-understanding. In the *Wake* this impressive but precarious balance shifts, since there is no corresponding concern with 'characters': instead, what drama there is is located in the mind itself, as it creates and shapes its experience. And there is a corresponding shift in the *Wake*'s linguistic experimentation. *Ulysses* can be very gamesome in its ways of reminding us that the workings of Bloom's mind can never be presented, only represented, and that narrative can never be transparent. At the end of 'Sirens', for example, when Bloom is struggling with his wind and we read 'Prrprr. Must be the bur', introspection quickly confirms that you can't think part of a word like 'burgundy' without thinking the word; similarly with 'dub' for 'Dublin', and so on. Yet this works well as inventive *re*presentation since, in filling out the word, the reader is also establishing his or her sense of Bloom's increasingly incapacitating physical discomfort and inability to think things through. The joke is very good, since recognizing that such representations can only be analogically 'true' carries the witty, thoroughly Joycean rebuke to more naive efforts at psychological realism. In the *Wake*, however, we find ourselves continually trying to make sense of a word by searching for a primary sense and then considering that in the light of a secondary (or tertiary, etc.) senses; this is both tiring, over long stretches, and at odds with Joyce's apparent wish to weld the different senses together.

This isn't to deny that the *Wake* abounds in wonderful jokes, like that about being 'jung and easily freudened', or that the 'Anna Livia

Plurabelle' episode is both an extraordinary *tour de force* and deeply moving in its conclusion – so that it is often suggested as the ideal introduction to the *Wake*. But then its claim to be that also rests, more disconcertingly, on its having been so thoroughly worked and reworked as the prize specimen through which Joyce set out to confute his critics; for that very reason it isn't at all representative, for example of the quite different and more tedious second and third sections. Moreover, that famous or notorious way in which it includes or reworks the names of over a thousand rivers is all too representative of that encyclopaedic impulse which at times threatened *Ulysses* (notably in 'The Oxen of the Sun') and here goes into overdrive: I take it that the proper, sane and humane response to such stockpiling is, 'So what?' Admirers draw the parallel with comparably bloated, encyclopaedic inserts in Rabelais; but then that comparison might remind us that Shakespeare – the master spirit of *Ulysses* – had more on his mind.

IV

One very significant change in this period is reflected in the difference between Joyce's various Dublins. Listening to the dean in the *Portrait*, young Stephen broods that the dean's language, 'so familiar and so foreign, will always be for me an acquired speech'; and the dean, on learning that a funnel is 'called a tundish in Ireland', politely resolves to 'look up' that 'most interesting word'. Joyce's quiet, busily critical ironies challenge us to distinguish the real from the factitious issues. For, as Stephen realizes later and records in his diary, he was quite mistaken about 'tundish', which is also 'good old blunt English'; that the dean doesn't even know the word alerts us to the unreal, abstract nature of Stephen's sense that the language is 'his before it is mine'. The language Stephen uses and masters is his own, first language, and the real force of his bitter complaint that the 'words' are 'made and accepted' elsewhere is not linguistic but historical and political – part of that 'nightmare' of history he wants to 'escape'. If the Dublin of *Dubliners* and *Portrait* is felt to be a centre of paralysis and of little else, that is because it is the capital of an occupied country; the colonial experience of being ruled from without produces this self-punishing sense of being marginalized, removed from a 'centre' which is always somewhere else. Yet by 1922 the 'dear dirty Dublin' of *Ulysses* doesn't seem so desperately marginalized, partly because *Ulysses* is confidently aware of its own centrality, but also because it is Bloom's city, and because we see how Stephen's own growth as an artist depends less on his withdrawals from Ireland, the family and the Church than on achieving something more like Bloom's richly curious and vital engagement with his environment and a human community. Since there is no elsewhere which matters more, where Stephen is matters less – and by the time of *Finnegans Wake* (1939) Dublin itself has become, like the 'English' the *Wake* internationalizes, a global village. The evolution of these different Dublins keeps pace with another familiar aspect of post-colonial experience, the erosion and displacement of the 'centre'. Before the First World War and that strange death of liberal England which *Women in Love* charts with such apocalyptic intensity, London could still seem to be the 'centre', even if 'English literature' was dominated by expatriate Americans, Irish writers and an expatriate Pole. James's 'international' novels and Conrad's ironically probing, Geertzian concern with what being 'one of us' might mean had provided richly duplicitous commentaries, neither native nor alien, on cultural identity, even as it became ever harder to suppose that English cultural values were, somehow, ontologically right. In the 1920s and 1930s – what Wyndham Lewis (1884–1957) called the 'insanitary trough' between the two world wars – the very notion of a 'centre' is finally played out. In 1921 Pound departed from an England which, as he complained to Carlos Williams, no longer offered 'intellectual *life*', and Lawrence's death in 1930 left the 'English novel' seeming more regional, and even – although Virginia Woolf (1882–1941) and Wyndham Lewis were still writing – more marginal than the 'novel in English'. Indeed the good is not the enemy of the best, and the best novels of writers like Ivy Compton-Burnett (1892–1969) or T. F. Powys (1875–1953) are good; but it is important, in considering these idiosyncratic writers, to remember the world elsewhere.

All the more important because, although many of the greatest 'modernist' works appeared in the 1920s, while the *Wake* and *Four Quartets* appeared many years later, a number of novelists writing in the decade were either reacting against, or remained relatively untouched by, modernist experimentation. Indeed, it is misleading to think of the 'reaction against modernism' as something which characterizes the 1930s, and seeing literary history as a succession of -isms and anti-isms is always distortingly lumpish (to recall the historian Jack Hexter's nice distinction between 'lumpers' and 'splitters'). None the less, we might notice, in a broad but wary fashion, how various novelists in the 1920s as well as the 1930s were more inclined to treat the world as 'given', without that intense concern with the problematics of representation which underlies the major modernist innovations. If 1910 was for Virginia Woolf the year when human nature changed (presumably because this was the year of Roger Fry's post-impressionist exhibition), it was also the year which Ivy Compton-Burnett once offered as her cut-off, saying that she didn't pretend to understand the 'world' after '1910'. The First World War is a more obvious watershed, and here the novels of Aldous Huxley (1894–1963) have a representative significance. Although he was Lawrence's friend and rather courageous champion, his attempt in *Point Counter Point* (1928) to make Mark Rampion a mouthpiece for Lawrentian ideas (exempting Rampion from the satire and scepticism other characters attract) was none the less, as the exasperated Lawrence protested, an unwitting travesty – since it is clear that Huxley cannot *believe* in the ideas, even when he seems to want to. Insofar as this reflects the traumatic effect of the war's negative revelations, it also looks forward to that later reaction which, after the next world war, would make writers like Larkin and the so-called 'Movement' poets of the 1950s look suspiciously at the Eliotic 'myth kitty' or Lawrentian appeals to what is 'known in the blood'. As Ted Hughes once remarked in a *London Magazine* interview, these writers were recoiling to 'essential English strengths' because one of the things they had in common was 'the post-war mood of having had enough . . . enough rhetoric, enough overweening push of any kind, enough of the dark gods, enough of the id, enough of the Angelic powers and the heroic efforts to make new worlds'. For Larkin, Hardy was the great early modern poet; and Larkin's own poetry has played its part in making readers more responsive to the 'essential English strengths' of poets like Hardy or Edward Thomas, and to a native alternative to 'modernism'. For the younger Hughes, who 'came a bit later' and was 'all for opening negotiations with whatever happened to be out there', Eliot and Lawrence were still the more important modern masters; and Hughes's own poetry shows many of those 'modernist' characteristics which Larkin rejected – in its internationalism, and its creative preoccupation with myth and primitivism. Although it can be exaggerated, the divergence between Larkin and Hughes shows how our sense of the past constantly involves our sense of the present. So, in this complex dialogue or process of cultural negotiations, where what we make out is part of what makes us, whatever we make of Hughes and Larkin as the major English poets in our own time will affect and be affected by our sense of the achievement of the so-called modernists, and of those other novelists of the 1920s who recoiled to, or were never shaken from, what Hughes calls 'essential English strengths' – and what we make of those 'strengths' will also depend on our sense of the world elsewhere.

Although Huxley's knowingly civilized, undriven novels of the 1920s – *Crome Yellow* (1921), *Antic Hay* (1923), *Those Barren Leaves* (1925) and *Point Counter Point* (1928) – have nothing else in common with the novels of Percy Wyndham Lewis (1882–1957), they are also much concerned with the conflict between intellect and animalism. The more sensitive characters try and fail to resolve it, while yielding wearily to 'disillusion after disillusion'. Denis, in *Crome Yellow*, is the first of several Huxleyan surrogates to sound this representative note when, after explaining what he tries to accomplish in art ('the process by which one constructs the divine reality out of chaos') and life ('the ecstasies of drinking, dancing, lovemaking'), he adds: 'And to think I'm only just beginning to see through the silliness of the whole thing!' More interestingly, characters like Denis, Theodore Gumbril, Francis Chellifer and Philip Quarles convey Huxley's keenly troubled sense of complicity, of being a brilliant and witty representative of that privileged, fashionable intelligentsia which he is satirizing. The most assured and impressive writing in *Crome Yellow* is in the interpolated 'History of Crome', where the failure to integrate culture and nature is traced through four centuries; this calls into play the ranging, lively intelligence that distinguishes Huxley's best essays, like 'Wordsworth in the Tropics' (*Do What You Will*, 1929) and 'Variations on a Philosopher' (*Themes and Variations*, 1950). One can see why Lawrence both complained that the novels projected the 'slow suicide of inertia and sterility' and felt that there was 'much more of a man in the actual Aldous'. *Brave New World* (1932) is probably the novel which has worn best, despite some obvious weaknesses – like the too predictable comedy of embarrassments involving Bernard and his affairs, or the tiresomely emblematic use of Shakespeare. But Huxley's futurist setting is a means of exploring what is already tolerated or taken for granted in the present, above all in the preoccupation with 'happiness' and material well-being. Here the satire is both sharp and wittily inventive – in the opening tour of the Central London Hatchery and Neo-Pavlovian Conditioning Rooms, the exuberant catalogue of palliatives administered to the Savage's dying mother, or in the picture of Lenina obediently chanting 'Was and will make me ill, I take a gramme and only am' as she sedates herself with *soma*: 'Five minutes later roots and fruits were abolished; the flower of the present rosily blossomed.' The Socratic argument that it is better to be an unhappy man than a contented pig has always found more favour with privileged intellectuals than it would with the truly wretched and destitute; something like a reply on their behalf is given in Chapter 16, when the Savage finally confronts Mustapha Mond – Huxley's alarmingly benign, compassionate Big Brother. In readily allowing that 'Actual happiness always looks pretty squalid in comparison with the over-compensations for misery', Mond stands much of the earlier satire on its head: of course 'the Super-Vox-Wurlitzeriana rendering of "Hug me till you drug me, honey"' isn't high art, but, as Mond smoothly argues, if high art is the compensation for misery, violence and horror, might it not be better to eliminate the latter, even if the former also disappears?

This kind of concern with the sufferings of others testifies to Huxley's decency. Yet it also remains notional, an idea rather than a pressing imaginative reality, as a comparison with Dr Johnson's devastating review of Soame Jenyns quickly confirms: what Huxley knows *about*, Johnson knows. This bears on the question of what is involved in speaking of a brilliant novel of ideas. Huxley is brilliant, but one wouldn't use that term of Johnson because he is too profound; and to describe *Crime and Punishment, Ulysses*, or *Women in Love* as novels of ideas would seem odd because they are much more than that. In the preface to his trilogy *The Near and the Far* (1929–35) L. H. Myers (1881–1944) recognizes these difficulties and their bearing on his own achievement: 'The suspicion may come into the reader's mind that what he has before him is a philosophical novel, one in which the characters are abstractions personified. And if that is the case, he will say, the book can hardly be worth reading either as a novel or as philosophy.' *The Near and the Far* is worth reading, and the satire on Bloomsbury in its second part, *Prince Jali* (1931) is more serious and compelling than Huxley's in *Crome Yellow*. Huxley's is wittily, brightly personal: not surprisingly it made Dora Carrington feel 'very, very ill', and Lady Ottoline Morrell can't have felt well. But Myers's assault on Bloomsbury values is more searchingly analytical. In tracing the 'small self-conscious immoralities' of the aesthetes of the Pleasance of the Arts, he shows how they 'depended basically upon a solid, shockable world of decorum and common sense' and to this extent represent an 'inverted orthodoxy'. Myers is above all concerned to expose their 'triviality', a term which for Myers has more serious, inward implications than Forster's comparable but predominantly social (and snobbish) concern with 'vulgarity'; the triviality of the Pleasance finally issues in a casual atrocity – Prince Daniyal's crushing of a cat's head –

which registers in context as a sudden and horrifying revelation of evil as inner vacuity. Myers's other novels are less successful, although *The Orissers* (1922) compares very interestingly with *Howards End*, while *The 'Clio'* (1925), in which a group of people travelling on the most expensive steam-yacht in the world are trapped on the Amazon, provides a no less interesting, and seemingly deliberate, comparison with Woolf's first novel, *The Voyage Out* (1915).

The novelistic output of John Cowper Powys (1872–1963) is all the more extraordinarily large since he was nearing sixty when he wrote his first novel, after decades of supporting himself on the American lecture circuits, like a popular evangelist. Correspondingly large critical claims have been entered by Wilson Knight and George Steiner – critics who would not necessarily notice, let alone object to, any tendency to be windily vatic and portentous. John Cowper Powys also has a chauvinistic appeal, for example in *Obstinate Cymric* (1947) when he asserts of the Welsh that 'no race in the world, except the Jews, have felt the iron enter so deeply into their souls, the *literal iron*, of being dominated by the more cruel weapons of races that mentally, emotionally, and spiritually they felt to be inferior to themselves'. T. F. Powys could never have written that: if (a huge 'if') he had ever wanted to assert that the Romans and the English were 'mentally, emotionally, and spiritually' inferior to the Welsh, he would have placed those words at a grammatically correct point within the sentence, just as he would never have written of what no race 'have felt', or inserted (and italicized) that reference to '*literal iron*'. Literal iron can't enter something that isn't literal, but John Cowper Powys's language is all too often slack, flatulent and unresistant to cliché. This presumably doesn't worry those who think *Wolf Solent* (1929) and *A Glastonbury Romance* (1932) great neglected masterpieces. Another kind of touchstone is provided in *Morwyn* (1937) by that speech which Rabelais delivers, and of which Glen Cavaliero observes, in the most notable full-length study, that 'Powys nowhere expressed his message and beliefs more simply or movingly than here'. Readers who think, as I do, that the 'message' in question is better expressed by Blake or Lawrence or (in our own time) Peter Redgrove, or who think that delivering messages is the business of the postman not the novelist, will find the speech more 'simple' than 'moving'; but then this writer's devotees tend to be apostolic.

That John Cowper's stock seems to be rising as T. F. Powys's falls is saddening, since *Mr Weston's Good Wine* (1927) is a neglected masterpiece, while the best of the *Fables* and short stories are no less impressive. The neglect seems inevitable, since contemporary readers tend to be ill at ease with allegory, and Powys is aggressively and idiosyncratically unmodern. Bunyan is the most obvious and important literary influence, but to call attention to that, as Leavis did in his generous tribute, is quite likely to have a deterrent effect, unless one also thinks of Hawthorne; but Powys, like Bunyan and Hawthorne, is a complicated, rather than simple, writer. His command of prose rhythms is superb, and at its best – when it doesn't slide into whimsy or a complicated sexual sadism – his writing has a wholly distinctive, surprising and disturbing energy:

Thus it was that a beetle that, by its destiny, happened to crawl over Mr Kiddle's great hand, provoked mirth and laughter, and even, what was more strange, a wise remark from Mr Meek, as the dealer shook the beetle off his hand into the burning coals, that the 'insect was given a nice warm bed for which it hadn't paid a farthing'.

Charles Rosen's remark, in *The Classical Style*, that Brahms made music out of his regret at being born too late, might be reapplied to Powys or to the novels of Ivy Compton-Burnett; perhaps the sadistic impulse in both these writers is associated with their distaste for the modern. Compton-Burnett's novels are almost all set in the same period as those of Henry James, although she was born half a century later and, although there is no reason to doubt her denial of any direct Jamesian influence, their 'scenic' method is that of James's *The Awkward Age*. Dialogue dominates, to an extraordinary degree, and her characters – notably her children, like those in James – speak with a fluency and precision which is more faithful to their intellectual and emotional impulses than to anything people would plausibly say; there is a passionately Jamesian horror at the ways in which people impose on each other, while the plotting centres, in a provocatively cool and deliberate fashion, on the family and such familiar familial events as incest, infanticide and matricide. The first novel, *Dolores* (1911), gave virtually no hint of what was to follow, after a silence of fourteen years. The distinction of *Pastors and Masters* (1925) is above all stylistic, and the self-imposed narrowness of range is a condition of the wholly distinctive moral intensity. A first reading of this novel, or (since the achievement is remarkably consistent) any of the seventeen novels which followed, at roughly biennial intervals, is likely to be memorably shocking. Part of the shock is rather like that of meeting an astonishingly and unnervingly formidable aunt – since there is so much tension between the crisp, even starchily old-fashioned exactness of manner and the violent unpredictability of what is said. *The Present and the Past* provides a typical example, when Elton Scrope reflects on 'life':

It is not short and will not soon be gone. It is longer than anyone can realize. And it is very brave to end it. To say it is cowardly is absurd. It is only said by people who would not dare to do it.

Which brings us to Virginia Woolf.

V

Jacob's Room appeared in 1922, with *Ulysses* and *The Waste Land*. In writing it Woolf had resolved, 'the approach will be entirely different this time: no scaffolding, scarcely a brick to be seen; all crepuscular ... a light stepping of my sweet will.' It is sometimes claimed that this was Woolf's first 'stream-of-consciousness' novel, yet the term isn't altogether helpful. Woolf deliberately provides only very limited access to Jacob's own thoughts and inner life, so that we never know him in the sense that we know Mrs Dalloway – or Leopold Bloom. Moreover, although the new 'approach' certainly is 'entirely different', above all in the richly associative fluidity of the sentences, *Jacob's Room* is very much a novel of sensibility in which the sensibility on display is that of the author. As in Joyce's *Portrait* the protagonist's life is traced from childhood, but the narrative presence isn't chameleonic, like Joyce's: rather, it saturates the whole novel, making it step to Woolf's 'sweet will'. Joyce's narrative refuses to look beyond each stage of Stephen's present; Woolf's is constantly foreshadowing Jacob's death ('the people are ghosts', Leonard Woolf perceptively remarked) so that even his name – Jacob *Flanders* ('In Flanders fields, the poppies blow ...') – or the moving description of his college room carry the author's sense of life as 'a procession of shadows' which 'we' see 'depart with such anguish, being shadows': 'Listless is the air in the empty room ... One fibre in the wicker armchair creaks, though no one sits here.' The narrational loops and time shifts constantly recall those destructive forces of which young Jacob and his friends are oblivious ('And now Jimmy feeds crows in Flanders and Helen visits hospitals'), while the elaboration of poetic or symbolic associations achieves a similar effect: so, the unexpected way in which the first chapter applies the word 'weakly' to both Jacob and the trapped crab in his bucket is merely the first of many instances where Jacob is associated with objects which, like the sheep's jaw he preserves, evoke the futility of struggling against a hostile or indifferent universe. Distance and pathos combine in a curiously intense and distinctive way which can also be related to Woolf's feminism. Jacob himself regrets that women are allowed to attend service at King's College Chapel; the idea that they should be in the college itself would have seemed 'rot' to him, although not to the author of *A Room of One's Own* (1929). As a well-connected young *man* Jacob takes for granted that his world is all before him; he never realizes that what Woolf elsewhere calls the 'patriarchal machinery' is also training him for an equally complaisant exit from this world, in one of the 'blocks of tin soldiers' which cover a French cornfield.

Recent criticism has quite properly emphasized the extent to which Woolf's novels do engage with the 'real world', but that engagement embodies the many internal contradictions and tensions in her own privileged social situation. For example, the contradiction between her determination to 'criticise the social system' in *Mrs Dalloway* (1925), making Septimus a shell-shocked survivor who sees that 'this is not worth having', and Woolf's imperious treatment of her own servants, Lottie and Nelly, for daring to demand rooms of their own; or between making Peggy Pargiter speak of feeling 'a sense of guilt always' on thinking of other 'people toiling, grinding', and her own wariness of working-class feminism – or her self-betraying sneer that *Ulysses* was 'underbred'. And yet, although so strongly committed to, and protective of, her own group of 'Bloomsberries', she could see, and say, that her brother-in-law Clive Bell's odious book on *Civilization* reduced civilization to 'a lunch at no. 50, Gordon Square'. Such tensions could hardly be resolved, yet one of the great strengths of *To the Lighthouse* (1927) is its way of transforming them into a remarkably subtle and intelligent appraisal of what Woolf (following writers like Samuel Butler and Bernard Shaw) called the 'family system'.

One danger was that the novel might be overwhelmed by its own fidelity to the nuances of experience, and to the indecisiveness and ambivalence in its characters' sense of each other – as in this typical sentence where Mrs Ramsay is trying, and failing, to make up her mind about Charles Tansley: 'Yet he looked so desolate; yet she would feel relieved when he went; yet she would see that he was better treated tomorrow; yet he was admirable with her husband; yet his manners certainly wanted improving; yet she liked his laugh.' But this danger is avoided, or rather contained, by the strength and suggestiveness of the novel's tripartite structure. Part I is much concerned with the effect of the 'patriarchal machinery' in the domestic politics of the Ramsay household: the strain between them, and their respective self-doubts, engage our sense of much larger social and sexual conflicts. The pivotal Part II, 'Time Passes', is an astonishing *tour de force*, and may well be Woolf's most original achievement, something without any precedent in Joyce, Proust, Lawrence or Dorothy Richardson: the larger, national crisis, the wartime fatalities, and even Mrs Ramsay's death, are all reported in parenthesis as ten years pass. After the war all is changed, changed utterly; but what Part III presents is not the Yeatsian 'terrible beauty' but a complex and moving exploration of relative gains and losses which, insofar as Lily Briscoe is its focus, recalls Lawrence's comparably ambivalent exploration of the inherited difficulties and new opportunities confronting his 'New Woman' in *The Rainbow*. Once that 'patriarchal machinery' which had shaped the Ramsays' life and made even Mrs Ramsay eager to lead 'new victims' to the 'altar' is clearly relegated to the past, the novel can accommodate its and Lily's sense of other values which that lost world had sustained. The view in question isn't Mrs Mcnab's: 'Things were better then than now'. Woolf's sympathies are always with those who find it difficult to arrive at a judgement; but the novel moves towards a more ambivalent appraisal.

Whether the novel connives with the Lily of Part III in idealizing Mrs Ramsay is, and will continue to be, a matter for critical debate – not least among feminists, some of whom have accused Woolf of offering a revamped version of Coventry Patmore's *The Angel in the House* (1854–63). Certainly we see Lily going beyond her earlier Dedalus-like opposition to Mrs Ramsay's beliefs and values, to recognize and reaffirm her love for a woman who could make domestic familial moments stay 'in the mind almost like a work of art'. Not only does Lily think of Mrs Ramsay as another artist, struggling to make 'of the moment something permanent (as in another sphere Lily herself tried to make of the moment something permanent) – this was of the nature of a revelation'. That parenthesis – a late addition to Woolf's manuscript – has a complicated, poign-antly moving effect: even as it supports Lily's 'revelation', it is allowing that the novel itself is attempting something similar, and similarly precarious. The novel's resolution – with Mr Ramsay arriving at the lighthouse and Lily completing her picture ('I have had my vision') – is itself a conjured 'moment' of 'bringing together', like Lily's mature sense of the dead Mrs Ramsay's achievement. It is hard to imagine that Lily will become less troubled, or Mr Ramsay and James more intimate; rather, this 'resolution' or 'vision' is seen as an imaginatively constructive and temporarily healing attempt to wrest meaning and value from chaos. But the chaos presses in from without and, characteristically, the novel's third part also acknowledges the kind of inescapable, routine horror which nothing can redeem or transfigure, in the parenthetical section 6:

[Macalister's boy took one of the fish and cut a square out of its side to bait his hook with. The mutilated body (it was alive still) was thrown back into the sea.]

As in Lawrence, the slipperiness of the narrative relation to characters can produce difficulty or resistance: so, if we examine the various metaphors which are used to present Mr Ramsay in the sixth section of Part I – including the metaphor of the lizard's leathern eye, and of the leader of a doomed expedition – it is difficult to tell whether they correspond with a character's perceptions or are being provided, and then fancifully developed, by the narrator. This can be irritating for those who find it hard to believe that any serious philosopher would characterize his thought as an alphabetical progression from Q to R, or think that this playful, impressionistic slipperiness in the telling (where the author is her own Penelope, weaving all together) carries some more portentous invitation to regard the Ramsays as representative of sexual difference – as the Male and Female, or Testy and Nesty. Any such invitation would inevitably seem tendentious, or imposed, to a reader who, like Iris Murdoch, questions the very 'idea of feminine experience': 'I think there's human experience; and I don't think that a woman's mind differs essentially from a man's, except in the sense that women are often less well educated.' Woolf's own feeling that she was staking out specifically feminine territory appears not only in her famous but rather silly claim that 'each sex describes itself', so that the 'first words in which either a man or a woman is described are generally enough to determine the sex of a writer', but also in her frankly jealous sense of Dorothy Richardson (1873–1957) and Katherine Mansfield (1888–1923) as rivals. In reading Richardson, Woolf admitted in her diary, 'I felt myself looking for faults; hoping to find them . . . If she's good then I'm not'; she similarly recorded her first response to Mansfield's early death: 'one feels – what? A shock of relief? – a rival the less? . . . I was jealous of her writing – the only writing I have ever been jealous of.'

Such territorial anxiety seems unnecessary, in retrospect. True, Richardson's immense, thirteen-volume *Pilgrimage* was already half-complete by the time *Jacob's Room* appeared, and the first volume, *Pointed Roofs* (1915), was contemporary with the serial publication of Joyce's *Portrait* (1914–15) – so that Richardson's literary-historical claim to importance as a founder of the so-called 'stream-of-consciousness' novel is secure enough. But then Richardson's method of wholly identifying the point of view with that of her autobiographical surrogate, Miriam Henderson, while eschewing traditional elements of plot and structure, was wholly unlike Woolf's artful method of sliding from one consciousness to another; and Richardson herself detested the term 'stream of consciousness', which probably owed its appeal to the curious English reluctance to follow the French and Germans in distinguishing more carefully between different kinds of internal or narrated monologue and *erlebte Rede* narration. What the writers do have in common is of doubtful value: just as Woolf's tendency to associate 'male' sentences with eighteenth-century authors like Johnson seems arbitrary, and historically interesting rather than psychologically true, Richardson's own aggressively stereotypical characterizations of 'male' thinking – for example, when she asserts that male thoughts are all 'false to life; everything neatly described in single phrases that are not true' – are curiously at odds with her frank acknowledgement that the authors who helped her most in her search for the 'female sentence' were Henry James and Joyce. None the less, Richardson's contrast between woman as 'the synthetic principle of human life' and man as 'a being whose mental tendency is to departmentalize, to analyse, to separate single things from their flowing environment' corresponds with numerous critical discussions of the Ramsays. Getting through the *Pilgrimage* is not easy, but its 'technical' and 'formal' interest (which becomes stronger in the fourth volume) seems less likely to sustain that effort than its interest as an impressive record of what life was like for an intelligent, lower-middle-class woman in this period – which is a way of confessing that I suspect class differences matter more than gender in Richardson as in Woolf.

I take it that Lawrence and Joyce tower above their novelist contemporaries, and that to place Woolf alongside them as a comparable 'Modern Master' is to surrender critical judgement. More tentatively, I suggest that one reason for Woolf's appeal is that she gave the idea of the 'centre' – London, and in London, Bloomsbury – a beguiling afterlife by marrying modernist method to the concern with what Hughes calls 'essential English strengths'; in her last novel, *Between the Acts* (1941), that concern is both beleaguered and movingly elegiac. Here it seems instructive to compare her with the writer whom T. S. Eliot described in 1954 as 'the most distinguished modern novelist of our times'. Percy Wyndham Lewis's champions not infrequently refer to a 'Lewis boycott' (Roy Campbell) or to the 'tactical errors' which 'damaged his literary career' (Jeffrey Meyers), as though the judicious will not be distracted by Lewis's 'regrettable ideological lapses' (Fredric Jameson); but Lewis's notorious book in praise of Hitler and his later association with Mosley's British Union of Fascists, his filthy abuse of homosexuals and Jews, or for that matter the culpable silliness of his views on music, do not distract us from recognizing Lewis's intelligence, they reveal it. Yet this is not to agree with Leavis that Lewis was merely and always 'brutal and boring'. He was an exceptionally vigorous polemicist who, like his friend T. E. Hulme, detested Romanticism as a defeat of reason, and insisted that he was a 'Tory Bolshevik' rather than a fascist. 'I would rather have an ounce of human consciousness than a universe full of "abdominal" afflatus and hot, unconscious, "soulless" mystical throbbing', he declared in *Paleface* (1929). As that suggests, Lewis can be regarded as Lawrence's strident antithesis, while Bernard Lafourcade has observed that Lewis's fiction offers an inverted mirror image of Joyce's: *Tarr* (1918) provides the portrait of the aggressively external Lewisian artist, *The Childermass* (1928) a lexical fantasy of life-in-death as a dream-wake, and *The Apes of God* (1930) the huge examination of metropolitan civilization. This has its interest, like Donald Davie's essay 'Eliot and Pound: A Distinction' (*The Poet in the Imaginary Museum*), in charting significant oppositions between the 'men of 1914'; the trouble is, such ideological chartings smuggle in the notion that Lewis the novelist is somehow 'up there' with the writers whose 'interiority' he opposes. For all the ferocity of its attack on Bloomsbury *The Apes of God* contains nothing as memorable as Edgell Rickword's wry comment that 'one is reminded of a powerful man tormented by gnats'; and finishing *The Childermass* calls for Lewisian reserves of energy and will. Whether we think Lewis an important and underrated novelist depends, above all, on what we make of *Tarr* and the late novel *Self Condemned* (1954).

Certainly, what happens to Tarr and his 'high standard Aryan bitch' involves us less than the fate of the Hardings in *Self Condemned*, partly because the later novel is semi-autobiographical in a thoroughly traditional, involvingly realistic way. The presentation of the Hardings' desperately impoverished wartime existence in a grubby Canadian hotel is extraordinarily harrowing. Their ordeal parallels that of the Lewises in Toronto's Tudor Hotel and, although fictionalized, the protagonist's disintegration into a 'glacial shell' (like that of the burnt-out, frozen hotel) is also a devastating self-arraignment. Fredric Jameson has praised this novel for its 'uncomfortable honesty' and 'self-knowledge', and when a subtle Marxist critic uses such terms it is all the more pleasant to agree. But then, precisely because *Self Condemned* is so bitterly self-critical and also far less iconoclastic than *Tarr*, to think it Lewis's finest work (as I do) can encourage an overhasty disparagement of Lewis's earlier, more representative work. His early style has an original, determinedly uningratiating and rebarbative energy, in the Marston-like descriptions of Bestre in *The Wild Body* ('with a flexibile imbrication of a shutter-lipped ape, a bud of tongue still showing'), or in the coldly exuberant, carefully paced demolition of that family with which the dancing Kreisler suddenly collides in *Tarr* ('one of those large featureless human groups built up by a frigid and melancholy pair, unhappily fecund, during an interminable intercourse'). Indeed, the accumulation of eruptive local effects tends to dissipate any sense of forward movement; but this is consonant with the remarkable way in which the novel repeatedly subverts (or deconstructs) its own premises. *Tarr* is structured around the contrast between Tarr and Kreisler: just as *The Wild Body* (1929) opposes the 'laughing observer' to the 'wild body', Tarr expresses familiar Lewisian ideas ('Good art must have no inside') while Kreisler recalls Lewis's claim that men are 'things, or physical bodies, behaving like persons'. But then Tarr is an even less productive artist than Stephen Dedalus; and, instead of persuading us that this is because Tarr can't live up to his Lewisian ideas, the novel suggests that the ideas are self-deluding distortions of Tarr's emotional needs. And Kreisler is more interesting than Tarr: if his vitalism is often grotesquely mechanical, there is also (as in Lewis's best portraits, like that of T. S. Eliot) some sense of the human subject's resistance to this harshly reductive externality. Although the novel's presentation of Bertha would be quite enough to justify its author's reputation for misogyny, neither the intellectualizing Tarr nor the vitalist Kreisler begins to be a match for the formidable Anastasya. The tension between Lewis as polemicist and Lewis as interrogative novelist remains unresolved; but if *Tarr* is a less assured novel than *Self Condemned*, it is also more interesting.

Which brings me back to the suggestion that, if Lewis has received rather less than his critical due while Woolf's current reputation is somewhat inflated, this may be because Lewis reviled or betrayed those 'essential English strengths' which Woolf rather too confidently identified with Bloomsbury. None the less, Lewis can't resolve the problems *Tarr* projects because, in this powerful novel as in his fascistic ravings, his formidable cleverness isn't grounded in anything we could call fully human. He is, very commandingly, the *intellectual*, and far more impressive in this respect than Woolf; but then he is also an alarming reminder that the intellectual is not necessarily *intelligent*. The corollary claim – that the intelligence of a Leopold Bloom or a Tom Brangwen has nothing to do with their being intellectual – is something which, in their very different and often troublingly different ways, both Lawrence and Joyce passionately affirm. Much contemporary criticism would find that affirmation as quaint as Milton's idea that a good book is the precious life blood of a master spirit; but that is our problem, and here 'post-modernism' may be (as Karl Kraus said of psychology) the disease of which it pretends to be the cure.

6

POETRY IN THE 1920s

Martin Dodsworth

I

In April 1919 *The Athenaeum*, a weekly paper of high standing, published an essay on the state of Europe after the war by the eminent French poet and intellectual, Paul Valéry:

Elam, Nineveh, Babylon were vague and lovely names, and the total ruin of these worlds meant as little to us as their very existence. But France, England, Russia . . . these would also be lovely names. Lusitania also is a lovely name. And now we see that the abyss of history is large enough for every one. We feel that a civilisation is as fragile as a life. Circumstances which would send the works of Keats and Baudelaire to rejoin those of Menander are no longer in the least inconceivable; they are in all the newspapers.

This dark view of the world is the context for the success of T. S. Eliot's poem, *The Waste Land*, first published in 1922; it is a cry from a world which its author (1888–1965) feels to be slipping into the abyss. 'Falling towers/Jerusalem Athens Alexandria/Vienna London/Unreal' – the listing of names suggests those in the passage quoted, and others in Valéry's essay: 'From an immense terrace of Elsinore which extends from Basle to Cologne, and touches the sands of Nieuport, the marshes of the Somme, the chalk of Champagne, and the granite of Alsace, – the Hamlet of Europe now looks upon millions of ghosts.' *The Waste Land* is a haunted poem for a haunted world. It came to be viewed as the epitome of post-war desolation, so that, for example, Scott Fitzgerald, describing the broken Paradise of *The Great Gatsby*, constantly echoes it.

The war itself is present only allusively in Eliot's great poem. 'I think we are in rats' alley/Where the dead men lost their bones': rats recur in the poem ('A rat crept softly through the vegetation/Dragging its slimy belly on the bank', 'And bones cast in a little low dry garret/Rattled by the rat's foot only, year to year'), as do the bones ('at my back in a cold blast I hear/The rattle of the bones, Dry bones can harm no one') and the dead ('Stetson!/You who were with me in the ships at Mylae!/That corpse you planted last year in your garden,/Has it begun to sprout?'). The rats, the corpses and the dead all suggest the landscape of the battle-front, especially in the third section where there is a vision on the river's bank of 'White bodies naked on the low damp ground'. Yet this *is* only suggestion; the poet depends on its being so, for the poem is also concerned with a deep reluctance to remember. 'Winter kept us warm, covering/Earth in forgetful snow'; memory is painful because associated with fear. What is remembered has to be dug up, like the corpse in Stetson's garden; his friend prays that the body will not be disturbed. 'I had not thought death had undone so many' – the line translates Dante's awed reaction to his first sight of the dead in Limbo, so that it now refers to the crowd of city workers streaming to work in winter over London Bridge. The death that has undone them may be the living death of their work; it may be the living death of the war they survived in order to be delivered to the misery of peace. The poem thrives on its suggestiveness which is itself expressive of uncertainty, loss of nerve, Valéry's 'spiritual crisis'.

The line from Dante illustrates another sense in which the poem is haunted; it is shot through with reminiscence of the literature of the past, as it is with memories of the past. The third section of the poem, 'The Fire Sermon', incorporates allusions to Spenser, Shakespeare, Marvell and Goldsmith, as well as to Sappho and Verlaine; it alludes to the Parsifal story and to the myth of Tiresias, it touches on Wagner's dramatization of the fall of the gods and it conjures up a picture of Queen Elizabeth I and the Earl of Leicester being rowed down the Thames:

> Carried down stream
> The peal of bells
> White towers.

The upshot is to catch something of what Valéry means when he says, 'We feel that a civilization is as fragile as a life'; Elizabeth and Leicester and the unhappy lovers of the present time are on the same level. The eloquence of literature exists only insofar as a fragile civilization permits it to. Eliot follows a quotation from Verlaine's French, which he does not translate, by a series of words imitating sounds:

> Twit twit twit
> Jug jug jug jug jug jug
> So rudely forc'd
> Tereu.

The French line means 'And O those children's voices singing in the dome'; their music, which can only truly be heard by someone sophisticated enough to be able to read Verlaine's language and to hear *his* music, amounts to, or degenerates into, childish, pathetically stylized bird noises associated with mockery, with unelaborated sex and with rape. Civilization is fragile indeed, haunted, merely haunted, by what have seemed its great achievements of art.

The Waste Land is, however, a supremely ambiguous poem. It is instinct with cultural pessimism, but it does not frankly or simply endorse such pessimism. Its poetry is based on a juxtaposition of fragments without comment; the interpretation of the bird-calls which I have just offered is not inevitable – it is merely in tune with certain elements of the poem. Others are more hopeful, notably the poem's conclusion, 'What the Thunder Said'. The thunder in the Indian legend to which this alludes says 'DA', and the single syllable is interpreted variously by those who hear it. Eliot reproduces these interpretations in his poem (in an approximate form: *give, sympathize, control*). But he does not establish their relation to the single utterance of the thunder, whose 'DA' may be far more menacing. Furthermore, all the giving, sympathizing and controlling that the thunder's single syllable evokes is in the past; it is not clear whether they have any practicability in the present or future. The poem closes like this, with a final citation of the three meanings of the thunder (in Sanskrit):

> Shall I at least set my lands in order?
> London Bridge is falling down falling down falling down
> *Poi s'ascose nel foco che gli affina*
> *Quando fiam uti chelidon* – O swallow swallow
> *Le Prince d'Aquitaine à la tour abolie*
> These fragments I have shored against my ruins
> Why then Ile fit you. Hieronymo's mad againe.
> Datta. Dayadhvam. Damyata.
>   Shantih shantih shantih

The lines raise the question whether any order has been achieved; the languages quoted – Italian, Latin, English, French, as well as the Sanskrit – most readily suggest the disorder of Babel. 'Fragments' are not much to shore against 'ruins', and in any case the purpose of doing so is not evident. Hieronymo's madness, in Kyd's play *The Spanish Tragedy*, is assumed but also genuine, and that may be the state of mind of the speaker so desperately shoring fragments here. In which case, it may be the commands *give, sympathize, control* that have put him in that state. Eliot says that 'shantih', with which he concludes, is equivalent to 'The Peace that passes understanding', but can there be an equivalent in Sanskrit for something so specifically Christian ('the peace of God, which passeth all understanding, shall keep your hearts and minds through Christ Jesus')? The poem ends in doubt and pain, notwithstanding the gestures towards order and humane feeling that accompany it.

In any case, one might ask who it is that has shored the fragments of *The Waste Land* against his or her ruins. The 'speaker' of the poem is not clearly defined; Eliot says that 'just as the one-eyed merchant, seller of currants, melts into the Phoenician Sailor . . . so all the women are one woman, and the two sexes meet in Tiresias'. The words of the poem are spoken in several voices, then, or in one – but the one voice would be that of a character in myth, Tiresias, who experienced life both as man and woman, and whose appearance in Eliot's poem is fleeting. Eliot described Joyce's use of myth in *Ulysses*, a book whose presence is felt in *The Waste Land*, as 'a way of controlling, of ordering, of giving a shape and a significance to the immense panorama of futility and anarchy which is contemporary history'; his own use of the same device is far more ambiguous.

Joyce's novel has a story; Eliot's poem has a structure, which is quite a different sort of thing. *The Waste Land*'s juxtaposed fragments are arranged in sections whose titles hint at meaning, and the actions glimpsed in each episode generally refer to themes elaborated in Sir James Frazer's great work of syncretic anthropology, *The Golden Bough* (1890–1915), and Jessie L. Weston's Frazerian account of the Grail legend, *From Ritual to Romance*. However, such an allusive structure must be also elusive, especially in its significance. Leopold Bloom is at the heart of the 'Circe' episode in *Ulysses*, but it is hard to say who or what is at the heart of *The Waste Land*.

In this it is like Eliot's first mature work, 'The Love Song of J. Alfred Prufrock', where the reader is never in doubt that Prufrock is the speaker of his own poem, but Prufrock speaks doubt. He cannot believe in the significance of his own existence: 'No! I am not Prince Hamlet, nor was meant to be;/Am an attendant lord, one that will do/To swell a progress, start a scene or two . . .' Prufrock puts himself in the margins of life and, since the poem centres on him, it has, as it were, no centre, just margins. The author scrupulously abstains from intervening in Prufrock's monologue. As *The Waste Land* floats its voice or voices into the void of post-war Europe, so Prufrock's floats off into a fog that symbolizes his void, an insinuating barrier between him and the 'real' world he fears and hesitates to enter:

> The yellow fog that rubs its back upon the window-panes,
> The yellow smoke that rubs its muzzle on the window-panes . . .

At the end of the poem he revises this metaphor; instead of living in the yellow fog, he now pictures himself as lingering in 'the chambers of the sea' where the 'sea-girls' live, a romance that will end when 'human voices wake us, and we drown'. The cultural pessimism of *The Waste Land* springs out of the life-denial of J. Alfred Prufrock, whose love-song never quite sings itself:

> And should I then presume?
> And how should I begin?

From the uncertain voice of Prufrock to the merging, indeterminate voices of *The Waste Land* to the choric lines with which *The Hollow Men* (1925) begins is not far:

> We are the hollow men
> We are the stuffed men . . .

But these lines introduce another element in Eliot's work. Although *The Waste Land* is tragic (because the positive values which emerge at its conclusion find no confirmation), it is also exhilarating because in it the worst has been faced. Its elaborately allusive structure does at least let us know that it is not ambiguous by accident. The poem's mysteries reflect something that is mysterious in the worst itself, and are presented with all the distinction a great writer can give them:

> April is the cruellest month, breeding
> Lilacs out of the dead land, mixing
> Memory and desire, stirring
> Dull roots with spring rain.

Each participle, *breeding, mixing, stirring*, drives the sense into the next line, enacting the compulsion into life of a spring reluctantly endured, the unexpectedly precise 'lilacs' are also startling because they are *bred* like animals, the abstractions of memory and desire are startling too because their mixing is as far removed from breeding as possible, yet the parallelism leads us to expect the opposite; this is persuasively powerful writing. In 1914 Ezra Pound recognized Eliot's genius immediately; by 1925 he was established as Britain's leading poet of the avant-garde.

He was an American of distinguished family and preternatural intelligence, gifted in languages, and a doctoral student in philosophy at Harvard. In 1911 he visited Paris and heard Henri Bergson lecture at the Sorbonne; he also improved his already good knowledge of French poetry of the day. His early poems reflect the influence especially of Laforgue and Corbière; the irony for which his early poems are notable, whether in the blatant form of 'Conversation Galante' or in the more subtle tones of 'The Boston Evening Transcript', is unlike anything in English of the time. It is far more poised, for example, than anything in Pound, and it is capable of a pathos quite beyond Pound's reach, as for example in the final lines of 'La Figlia Che Piange':

> Sometimes these cogitations still amaze
> The troubled midnight and the noon's repose.

The noon's repose is rendered suspect by the troubled midnight, and the neatness of the antithesis contrasts with the half-rhyme, that is, the imperfect rhyme, of 'amaze' and 'repose' (the two words in fact both make complete rhymes with earlier lines in the poem); the lines are alive with an unease which the odd word 'cogitations' does not conceal, although its first effect is to establish ironic distance. The result is that the irony, which is designed to deny feeling, is instead instinct with the feeling it seeks to deny.

Eliot settled in England as the result of a hasty and imprudent marriage in 1915. The early married years were ones of poverty, hard work as a schoolteacher and then in a bank, and anxiety arising from the physical and mental poor health of his wife, from whom he separated in 1932. (She died in 1947, having spent the last years of her life as a mental patient.) He was reticent and sensitive, despite, and perhaps because of, his intelligence; in a letter of 1914 he speaks of 'those nervous sexual attacks which I suffer from when alone in a city', and his disastrous first marriage seems to be the product of a hunger for experience compensating for the shy man's fear of it. The extraordinary nature of his poetry, at once deeply emotional and contained, reflects the personality. It is not surprising that his critical writings early on elaborated a theory of the impersonality of poetry, given the marked but inexplicit link between the tensions contained in his own poetry and the tensions of his life. He wrote that 'only those who have personality and emotions know what it means to escape from these things'.

Since Eliot was American, one might ask what he is doing in a history of English literature. The answer does not lie simply in the position he acquired in English society as a highly respected man of letters, churchman and conservative thinker, or in the fact of his naturalization, but to a large extent in his identification with European, and especially English, culture rather than American. The critical essays with which he made his early reputation, most notably those in *The Sacred Wood* (1920), are revaluations of English literature – Blake, Swinburne, Shakespeare and his contemporaries – of Dante and of critical and poetic practice in general; they say nothing of significance about American writers, though Eliot admired both Henry James and Mark Twain, for example. The English poets predominate in the notes which he supplied to *The Waste Land*, and even the disagreeably witty quatrain poems of *Poems* (1920), which derive from the French poet Théophile Gautier, are suffused with English literature: 'Webster was much possessed by death' and

> I shall not want Honour in Heaven
> For I shall meet Sir Philip Sidney
> And have talk with Coriolanus
> And other heroes of that kidney.

In 1927 Eliot became a member of the Church of England; this was something of a shock to those who, like the Cambridge critic I. A. Richards, believed that in *The Waste Land* he had effected 'a complete severance between his own poetry and all beliefs'. Eliot's refusal to speak clearly in his own voice in his poems is some justification for Richards; nevertheless, religious concerns are evident in Eliot's poetry from the start. It is unnecessary to cite the early poem, 'The Death of St Narcissus', which was not published until 1950; 'Prufrock' itself imagines an 'overwhelming question' which provokes the response: 'I am Lazarus, come from the dead,/Come back to tell you all . . .' 'Gerontion', which was at one time to have served as the opening of *The Waste Land*, is about an old man whose desolation is summed up in the phrase 'I have no ghosts' and in the image of a suppressed religious truth: 'The word within a word, unable to speak a word,/Swaddled with darkness.'

Eliot's grandfather had been a Unitarian minister. Nineteenth-century Unitarianism was marked by its high ethical principles, rationalism and lack of dogma, revering Christ as an exceptional man rather than as the Son of God. Eliot himself reacted against this. He reacted first against a high-mindedness that was too readily confused with an ineffectual genteel propriety, like that in the poem 'Aunt Helen': 'when she died there was silence in heaven.' This reaction was then reinforced at Harvard by his study of Indian philosophy and the idealism of the English philosopher F. H. Bradley; Eliot developed a scepticism that turned against the basis for comfortable Unitarian rationalism. And yet he hungered for something other than the 'futility and anarchy which is contemporary history'. He had had a glimpse of it as a young man, when 'walking one day in Boston, he saw the streets suddenly shrink and divide. His every day preoccupations, his past, all the claims of the future fell away and he was enfolded in a great silence' (Lyndall Gordon, *Eliot's Early Years*, 1977, p 15). Eliot's Anglicanism was the fruit of this quasi-mystical experience.

It would be wrong to suggest that Eliot found in Christianity a spiritual resting-place. His poetry after 1927 is markedly religious in its concerns, but it is in harmony with the 'Note on Poetry and Belief' that he published in the year he entered the Church of England:

For those of us who are higher than the mob and lower than the man of inspiration, there is always *doubt*; and in doubt we are living parasitically (which is better than not living at all) on the minds of the men of genius of the past who have believed something.

The major achievements of Eliot as a devotional poet are *Ash-Wednesday* (1930) and *Four Quartets* (first collected 1943). The former is a sequence of six poems of contrition; 'I pray that I may forget/These matters that with myself I too much discuss.' The tone is simpler than before, the allusions less frequent and less obvious. Yet the speaker of the poem is no more knowable than in the earlier work. There is no disclosure of the 'matters' that he wants to forget, although the poem's original dedication 'To my wife' is suggestive in the light of biography. Utterance in *Ash-Wednesday* is hesitant, indifferent to any location in time, and formalized by repetition, but all the more forceful for that:

> Because these wings are no longer wings to fly
> But merely vans to beat the air
> The air which is now thoroughly small and dry
> Smaller and dryer than the will
> Teach us to care and not to care
> Teach us to sit still.

'Now' is a moment in the spiritual history of the anonymous speaker, whose identity is merged with that of 'us', the mass of all human beings in the past, present and future who might also experience such a moment. We may exclude ourselves from that 'us', decline to endorse the affirmation of a supernatural order, and yet understand and be moved by the human force of 'Suffer me not to be separated//And let my cry come unto Thee'. 'Separated': the word is used absolutely, without reference to one thing rather than another. It implies, therefore, no attachment to anything in particular, just an absolute fear of being left with oneself and nothing else. Like *The Waste Land*, this poem is a 'cry' of desperation. The sense of crisis, though, is much more personal; no easy parallel with Valéry's account of post-war Europe is possible.

Valéry may nevertheless be relevant. Dante is a notable presence in *Ash-Wednesday*, as elsewhere in Eliot's verse (*The Hollow Men* and *Four Quartets*, for example). His example informs Eliot's use here of visionary motifs; the lines

> Who walked between the violet and the violet
> Who walked between
> The various ranks of varied green

suggest, if they do not recall, the appearance of Matilda in Canto 27 of the *Purgatorio*. Dante is 'one of the men of genius of the past who have believed something', and his shadowy presence behind lines like these points not only to the spiritual malaise from which the speaker seeks release but also to the extent of Europe's decline from its highest standards of integrity. 'The unread vision in the higher dream' is no merely personal concern.

Nevertheless it is given the nearest thing to personal expression in the whole of Eliot's work; it is personal in the way Beckett's work is personal, so taken up with the painful consciousness of self as barely to be able to acknowledge the particular circumstances, let alone the historical or political allegiances, that give that self a reality for the world. *Four Quartets* is, in this way, different; the titles of its four constituent poems allude to places with a personal significance for Eliot, and the poems incorporate fragments of the history he was living, the air raid in 'Little Gidding', for example, or the underground train in 'East Coker'.

Yet these passages contrast oddly with the representation of everyday life in the early poems. The 'sawdust-trampled street/With all its muddy feet that press/To early coffee-stands' (from 'Preludes') has a good deal more of observed reality about it than the fighter plane in 'Little Gidding', 'the dark dove with the flickering tongue', hardly recognizable for the significance with which it is metaphorically loaded. The underground train is also lacking in concrete detail, although, more characteristically of the *Quartets*, it is subject to little elaboration by metaphor:

> Or as, when an underground train, in the tube, stops too long between
>   stations
> And the conversation rises and slowly fades into silence
> And you see behind every face the mental emptiness deepen
> Leaving only the growing terror of nothing to think about . . .

More than anything else in Eliot's poetical work, *Four Quartets* is
concerned with *mental* experience, and especially with the problem
of what it might be to know something. It has its roots in Eliot's
earliest philosophical interests as well as in his Christian conviction
and his reading in mysticism.

The achievement of *Four Quartets* is a puzzling one, like much in
Eliot. Its lack of concrete particulars has led some critics to reject it
altogether; they might object to the passage about the underground,
for example, that it gives a spurious emphasis to everyday occurrence
by its accumulation of clauses and weighty rhythm, an emphasis that
commonplace phrases like 'mental emptiness' and 'growing terror'
do nothing to justify. Certainly this sort of writing makes little
apparent effort to grip. Yet it is accommodated in the careful
structure of the *Quartets*, each of which imitates the five-part form
of *The Waste Land*. If these words lack force in themselves, they
may derive force from what surrounds them. They may, for example,
take on meaning and power from an earlier reference to 'the intolerable wrestle/With words and meaning', just as the faintly sketched
terror of 'nothing to think about' may explain itself from the earlier
inadvertent dip into personal unknowing:

> Out at sea the dawn wind
> Wrinkles and slides. I am here
> Or there, or elsewhere.

As in *The Waste Land*, the sense of an intention to shape what is
uttered, to give it a character and meaning, is as important as the
tendency to lapse into despair and disorder manifest in the utterance
that is shaped. There are indeed linguistically numb passages in the
Quartets, but their inclusion in a form whose intent must be expressive (of the movement of positive statement attempted, if not
achieved, in *The Waste Land*, for example) makes their numbness
dramatic. It validates the doubt from which the *Quartets* spring.

Eliot said that he wanted to write a poetry 'so transparent that in
reading it we are intent on what the poem points at, and not on the
poetry . . . To get *beyond poetry*, as Beethoven, in his later works,
strove to get *beyond music*.' He said this in endorsement of Lawrence's
ambition to attain 'stark, bare, rocky directness of statement'; *Four*

Quartets is bare enough, and rocky, but hardly direct. One reason for this lies in Eliot's own nature; he wanted to commit himself to ideas, but found commitment difficult. His description of himself in 1928 as 'classicist in literature, royalist in politics, and anglo-catholic in religion' strikes one as the product of his yearning for commitment, definition, a life with hard edges (like the quatrain poems written before 1920), but it is not a convincing description. Eliot's efforts at commitment (in prose, the hectic 'primer of modern heresy', *After Strange Gods* (1934), and the hesitant yet constricted *Idea of a Christian Society* (1939); in verse, the choruses for the Church of England pageant, *The Rock* (1934)) produce his weakest work. 'To get *beyond poetry*' to 'what the poem points at' entailed taking the *via negativa* of doubt: 'I said to my soul, be still, and let the dark come upon you/Which shall be the darkness of God.' In *Four Quartets* the darkness, which is an incapacity of language as much as an obscurity of thought and feeling, is such that the hopeful assertion with which the sequence ends, that 'all shall be well', figures as just that – hopeful – not dogmatic or doctrinal.

II

Eliot's ascendancy as a poet in the 1920s needs explaining. How was it that a young American was able so speedily to dominate the English literary scene? He was, certainly, a brilliant young man, but brilliance does not inevitably achieve recognition, particularly when, as in Eliot's case, it is combined with radical innovation. Eliot had the advantage of being well connected. His friendship with Bertrand Russell, who was a Visiting Professor at Harvard in the months before he left for England in 1914, gave him entry to the influential literary circles of Bloomsbury, while thanks to the enthusiasm of Ezra Pound (1885–1972) he was in touch with London's artistic avant-garde. Furthermore, Eliot arrived on the English literary scene (which was, of course, male-dominated) at a time when there were few men of his age who were not in the army; he was himself conscious of the advantage this gave him. When the war was over, there were many of his generation who had not survived, and those who had found it difficult to adjust to the aftermath. All these social factors contributed to Eliot's conquest of London.

There is, however, another element which should not be overlooked, and that is that in 1914 there were many people who were *waiting* for the arrival of a poet whose modernism would rival that of sculptors like Jacob Epstein and Henri Gaudier-Brzeska and painters like Wyndham Lewis and Edward Wadsworth. Indeed, several poets were already working towards a style which it was Eliot's distinction to define by example. 'It is such a comfort', wrote Pound after reading 'Prufrock', 'to meet a man and not have to tell him to wash his face, wipe his feet, and remember the date (1914) on the calendar.'

Eliot's originality and excellence make it easy to forget those who were his forerunners. It is not clear to what extent Eliot himself felt that they should be remembered. As a poet who wrote little it was in his interests to emphasize quality at the expense of quantity, and it was not in his temperament to praise anyone readily ('I cannot endure George Eliot', he wrote to his mother). He wrote contemptuously of the contributors to Edward Marsh's *Georgian Anthology*:

A literature without any critical sense; a poetry which takes not the faintest notice of the development of French verse from Baudelaire to the present day, and which has perused English literature with only a wandering antiquarian passion, a taste for which everything is either too hot or too cold; there is no culture here. Culture is traditional, and loves novelty; the General Reading Public knows no tradition, and loves staleness.

Elsewhere he castigated 'the lack of any moral integrity, which I think is behind all the superficial imbecilities of contemporary English verse', extending the taint of staleness to English poets generally, not just the Georgians. Statements like this made his own originality and severity of judgement stand out, but obscured the small achievements of his predecessors.

He was always ready to acknowledge his debts to Pound, but these were largely for services rendered (including the shaping of *The Waste Land*). Pound himself had gained from knowledge of the work of T. E. Hulme (1883–1917), whom Eliot also admired ('. . . a really great poet . . . I can't think of anything as good as two of his poems since Blake'), and it is with Hulme that one must begin in sketching the literary context for Eliot's English success.

Hulme was a rebellious intellectual, although his radicalism was of a conservative kind; he believed in God and original sin, and abhorred the excess of feeling which he identified with Romanticism ('spilt religion' in his view). Alienated from his father after being sent down from Cambridge, he settled in London, living on a small allowance from a sympathetic aunt, which he supplemented by journalism, writing on artists like Wyndham Lewis and Epstein. He had a considerable interest in philosophy and attended Henri Bergson's lectures in Paris, where he won the French philosopher's admiration. (Bergson bowled Eliot over in 1912.) Hulme's essays were collected posthumously as *Speculations* (1924) after his death in the war.

The essay on 'Romanticism and Classicism' calls for a new poetry, 'cheerful, dry and sophisticated', a poetry to be distinguished by 'accurate, precise and definite description' and having 'nothing to do with infinity, with mystery or with emotions'. Amounting to a rejection of all that Victorian poetry had been, the essay anticipates on its negative side the criticism of Swinburne and Tennyson in Eliot's early critical essays. In its positive aspect it describes perfectly some aspects of the poetry of imagism – which is hardly surprising, since the essay is generally taken to postdate the start of that movement, in which Hulme was closely involved.

In 1908 Hulme had become the secretary of a small circle of writers, The Poets' Club, some of whose meetings were attended by the young Ezra Pound, newly arrived in London from the United States and hell-bent on the construction of a brilliant poetic career. The Poets' Club did not long satisfy Hulme's desire for radical and vigorous argument, and he soon formed a splinter group, whose meetings in 1909 Pound also attended. Perhaps it was in the nature of things that this group should not have lasted long, but in 1912 Pound, returning to England from a lengthy visit to America, formed another group, of which the principal members beside himself were the Englishman Richard Aldington (1892–1962) and the American he was to marry, once Pound's own fiancée, Hilda Doolittle (1886–1961), known as 'H. D.'. Out of this group came the movement called 'Imagism', whose characteristics are implicit in the anthology *Des Imagistes* which Pound published in 1914.

Pound's essay 'A Few Don'ts by an Imagiste', published in *Poetry*, March 1913, shows imagist verse as conforming to Hulme's idea of 'accurate, precise and definite' poetry. Pound laid down three imagist principles as follows:

1 Direct treatment of the 'thing' whether subjective or objective.
2 To use absolutely no word that does not contribute directly to the presentation.
3 As regarding rhythm: to compose in the sequence of the musical phrase, not in sequence of a metronome.

Precision, concision, free verse: Hulme's essay does not elaborate on the last of these, but otherwise agrees with Pound's prescription. Hulme's '*Complete Poetical Works*' (five short poems – a few more have in fact survived) were used by Pound as a kind of benchmark

for poetic quality; he published them as an appendix to his *Ripostes* (1912) and elsewhere.

Hulme's poems do not look so very different from the best poetry in English of his time. 'Above the Dock' is not uncheerful, and is dry and sophisticated – perhaps to an un-Edwardian degree, though much depends on what sophistication is supposed to mean:

> Above the quiet dock in midnight,
> Tangled in the tall mast's corded height,
> Hangs the moon. What seemed so far away
> Is but a child's balloon, forgotten after play.

Implicitly the poem is anti-Romantic. The moon's power, which provokes Hardy to agonized resistance in 'Shut Out That Moon', is disallowed in the comparison with a balloon. Hulme's patteringly extended last line makes the final monosyllable, 'play', the repository of the poem's values, opposing the grown-up world of the dock and all the commerce it implies to the childishness of poetic mooning-about and the child's-play of rhyming. Three lines of nine syllables lead to a final alexandrine, allowing a sustained quarrel between two competing rhythms, iambic and trochaic, to form the musical basis for Hulme's rejection of the past. This is not free verse, nor is it 'sequence of a metronome', but it is intelligent. On the other hand, the poem would hardly look out of place alongside something less demonstratively new like Edward Thomas's 'Cock-Crow' (written a few years later) which also opposes romance and realism in a short, rhymed and daringly cadenced piece.

Pound's own imagist verse is more audacious than Hulme's. Its paradigm, 'In a Station of the Metro' (published 1913) is briefer, more aggressive and more enigmatic:

> The apparition of these faces in the crowd:
> Petals on a wet, black bough.

But Pound's style evolved rapidly from 1912 on, and he soon left imagism behind and, in 1920, England. He certainly exerted consider-able influence on Eliot's development, but his own difficult career, despite the brilliance of his poem on English themes, *Hugh Selwyn Mauberley* (1920), took a course apart from that of English poetry. His anthology, *Des Imagistes*, gave prominence to the work of Aldington, who now seems weakly derivative of the others, and also contained some of his own work along with that of H. D. and F. S. Flint (1885–1960), as well as a few poems by James Joyce and two Americans, William Carlos Williams and the imperious Amy Lowell.

This wealthy woman of letters commandeered the imagist label and produced three further anthologies of *Some Imagist Poets* between 1915 and 1917, by which time Pound had passed on to Vorticism and beyond.

Pound claimed to have invented imagism as a means of identifying the special talents of H. D., five of whose poems he sent to the magazine *Poetry*, where they appeared in January 1913, attributed to 'H. D. Imagiste'. 'Objectivity and again objectivity, and no expression, no hindside beforeness, no Tennysonianness of speech', he wrote to *Poetry*'s editor, but H. D.'s poems, unTennysonian though they may be, are hardly 'objective':

> Hermes, Hermes,
> the great sea foamed,
> gnashed its teeth about me;
> but you have waited,
> where sea-grass tangles with
> shore-grass.

> ('Hermes of the Ways')

The lines are typical of H. D.'s fascination with margins, which in turn relates to her own bisexuality and the marginalization to which she was subjected by her husband. The line between sea-grass and shore-grass is fine, and is felt to be so in the least stressed of possible line-breaks as 'sea-grass tangled with/shore-grass'. H. D.'s poems build themselves slowly with a combination of effortful repetitions and a subdued humility of diction. The setting is very often the Grecian classical of her earliest poems, embodying her aspiration to high art, and by its simplicity and remoteness enabling her to contemplate her own convoluted emotions.

She early objected to the imagist label, and rightly so, for economy and instantaneity are alien to her, even in her first book, *Sea Garden* (1916). Her later poetry develops occult and mystical themes in long sequences like the *Trilogy* (1944–6) and the posthumous *Hermetic Definition* (1972), in which she figures as a poet-priestess with a privileged relation to the supernatural. These sequences compare with Eliot's *Quartets*, but their tone is less varied, more assertive (though not of self), and unorthodoxly liturgical where Eliot is dramatic.

Like much imagist verse, H. D.'s suffers from insipidity. Her diction is spare, but lacks force – this is especially true of her choice of adjectives – and her syntax is uninventive and monotonous.

Similar objections might be made to the poetry of F. S. Flint. He strove hard to develop the new form of free verse which is part of the imagist programme, but was hampered further by a lack of any vital idea. 'Hats', for example, is a call to the bourgeois to repent of his deadly conventionality:

> Become dangerous; let the metaphysical beast
> Whose breath poisons us all fear your understanding,
> And recoil from our bodies, his prey, and fall back before you,
> And shiver and quake and thirst and starve and die.

The multiplication of verbs in the last line, none of them striking, shows the poet striving for an entirely predictable effect of which he is nevertheless incapable. The contrast with one of Eliot's minor satirical pieces, like 'The Hippopotamus', shows just how much assurance and intelligence Flint wanted.

The imagists as a group promised far more than they achieved. Elsewhere two English poets created new styles of poetry of their own without significantly redirecting the attention of their contemporaries as, for a while, it seemed that Eliot did; they were Charlotte Mew (1869–1928) and Harold Monro (1879–1932). Mew, whose prose had appeared in *The Yellow Book*, published only two books, both poetry, *The Farmer's Bride* (1916) and *The Rambling Sailor* (1929), which is greatly inferior. She visited Brittany in 1901, several of her poems are set in France, and at her best she is reminiscent of Corbière. Like him, she relishes the life of the people; like him, she is tough; her poetry incorporates the language of the people and the sounds of everyday life, like his, and the irregular form of her rhyming verse also reflects his practice. Her poems may not be instantaneous, in the fashion of Hulme or Pound, but they do conform to all Pound's rules for the imagist:

> Tonight again the moon's white mat
> Stretches across the dormitory floor
> While outside, like an evil cat
> The *pion* prowls down the dark corridor . . .

This is not far from the Eliot of 'Preludes'. Mew writes a poetry of uncomfortably challenging dramatic monologue; 'Madeleine in Church', for example, lies halfway between Browning and Eliot's 'Gerontion'. Her thinking is, like his, unorthodox, and capable of powerful irony, incorporating, as little imagist verse does, the rhythms of the spoken language with conviction:

> Sometimes in the over-heated house, but not for long,
>> Smirking and speaking rather loud,
>> I see myself among the crowd,
> Where no one fits the singer to his song,
> Or sifts the unpainted from the painted faces
> Of the people who are always on my stair . . .

Charlotte Mew was admired by Hardy and Pound among many others, but her personal life was difficult, reclusive and unhappy, and this seems to be why she was unable to build on the success of her late first volume.

Her publisher was Harold Monro, who founded the Poetry Book-shop in London in 1913. It was a centre for a great range of poetic activity; Monro published, among other things, Edward Marsh's *Georgian Anthology* (1912) and Pound's *Des Imagistes* (1914), but paid for this catholicity by never defining his own poetic objects with certainty. His poetry is nevertheless quietly distinguished; the *Collected Poems* (1933) were introduced by Eliot, who had reviewed Monro's *Strange Meetings* (1917) when it came out.

The essence of Monro's work is in the lines 'I can't learn how to know men, or conceal/How strange they are to me'. They illustrate, on the one hand, his admirable directness and, on the other, his inability to escape the sphere of his own consciousness. Monro's poetry is a haunted poetry, full of ghosts and a sense of the ghostly: 'The vixen woman,/Long gone away,/Came to haunt me/Yesterday.' Its directness is had at a price: 'I can't see you plainly. Are you/The friend that I seem to remember? Are we/The people I think we must be?' The insecurity which in Eliot generalizes itself, thanks to the dramatic method and width of reference of the poetry, remains a merely personal insecurity in Monro.

The fact that Monro and Mew were loners (he was alcoholic, she was possibly lesbian), together with their lack of resolute literary objectives, reduced the possibilities of recognition for them in a literary Britain which, nevertheless, was on the lookout for a new poetry. The imagists had the advantage of a master publicist, in Ezra Pound, but lacked the talent or the inclination to build on the foundations he had provided. Eliot came and conquered.

Pound's original idea for imagism is nevertheless important for what it tells us about aspirations he shared with Yeats and H. D., aspirations which have a bearing also on what Eliot achieved. In an interview with Flint, Pound spoke of 'a "Doctrine of the Image", which we have not committed to writing. It does not concern the public, and would only cause useless discussion.' This smacks of an occultism which Pound could have shared with H. D., who in later years was to see visions about which she consulted Freud. Her imagist poems focus on emblems – 'Sea Rose', 'Sea Lily', 'Sea Poppy', for example – which evoke a complex of emotion like the symbols of a mage. The idea of the 'objective correlative' developed by Eliot in his 'Hamlet' essay ('a set of objects, a situation . . . which shall be the formula of [a] *particular* emotion') is latent in these poems, but it is linked to the secret 'Doctrine'. One can only speculate on the nature of the doctrine; at the time of the interview Pound was close to Yeats who was familiar with magical images, like the 'symbol of the order of salamanders' which was once shown him and produced 'mental images I could not control'. Yeats commended the creative search for an image by whose help a man might bring into being his opposite, his anti-self, the self by which he might act upon the world. It is possible that when he spoke of getting 'beyond poetry' Eliot was also developing an idea of the poem's esoteric and transcendent meaning related to that of the image, though doubtless within his own more orthodox religious framework. Getting 'beyond poetry' cannot, after all, mean simply attending to its prose sense. Imagism is important for its link with the idea of the poem as a magical object, as the entrance to another order of being, not merely for its emphasis on objectivity and concrete detail. In a period when traditional religious belief was on the wane, it may be that such a notion of poetry made possible the scope of reference that we find in Eliot, Yeats and even Pound, but not in the poetry of a Monro, imprisoned in his single consciousness.

III

'Is Mr Yeats an Imagiste?' asked Ezra Pound, writing about *Responsibilities* in the year of its publication, and answering his own question: 'No, Mr Yeats is a symbolist, but he has written *des Images* as have many good poets before him.' This is not very clear, but it must have been good publicity for Pound's little group, and it helped Pound make the point more forcefully that Yeats had in the latest volume struck 'a manifestly new note', something which, as he makes clear, other readers might not be very willing to believe: 'How *can* the chap go on writing this sort of thing?'

Pound felt that Yeats's work was 'becoming gaunter, seeking greater hardness of outline', and he was right. The change in style has been traced well before *Responsibilities* – as Katherine Koralek notes in her chapter of this book. Yet readers continued not to wish to notice any change. In 1919 *The Times Literary Supplement* found that Yeats in *The Wild Swans at Coole* was 'like a fiddler taking down his old dust-covered violin and lazily playing an old tune on it'. To say that the tune was then 'made new' did not remove the impression that this was a poet who had outlived his time. John Middleton Murry (1889–1957), at this time one of England's best critics, recorded of the same volume that 'there has been disaster. He is empty now.' Nine years later, *The Tower* (1928) reversed this way of thinking about Yeats. 'It gets closer to reality' than his earlier work, wrote the reviewer in *The New Republic*, pronouncing a view which was to become commonplace over the years.

The story of Yeats in the 1910s and 1920s is, then, the story of a poet remaking himself. He published the first volume of his autobiographical writings in 1915 and the second in 1922, signifying by this his sense that a part of his life, at least, was over. His marriage in 1917 could be seen as the sign that he believed that a new life was possible. The main effort of that new life, insofar as it was the life of a writer, had a certain implausibility about it. His wife had begun to produce automatic writing; through her he interrogated the spirit world, and in 1925 produced his first account of what the spirits had taught him. It was called *A Vision*, a complex account of human types and their four 'faculties' related to the phases of the moon and a grand theory of world history, the flavour of which may be had from three consecutive section-headings: 'The Gyres of the Great Mythologies', 'The Three Fountains and the Cycles of Embodiment', 'Cones of Nations and Movements of Thought'. Such speculation might serve to illustrate Valéry's thesis about the 'spiritual crisis' of post-war European civilization; it could hardly add to it. The book, after all, presents itself in systematic guise, though within a framework of teasingly ambiguous fictions. At least one sentence in the dedication suggests that, after all, Yeats cared for something else above the possible truthfulness of his *Vision*:

I wished for a system of thought that would leave my imagination free to create as it chose and yet make all that it created, or could create, part of the one history, and that the soul's.

Even the spirits who communicated with him through his wife's writing had apparently said: 'We have come to give you metaphors for poetry.' *A Vision* should be looked upon as something that was important to Yeats for *enabling* his continuance as a poet, and as a poet whose subject was history, history of the world and of the individual. It performed this function by giving him a vantage-point from which to consider these things, one that was his own, and intimately linked with his past, in particular with his long-standing interest in the occult, a reaction against late nineteenth-century rationalism rather like Eliot's against the Unitarian ethos. In 1937 Yeats published *A Vision* in substantially revised form; it is important not to exaggerate its completeness, despite appearances. The poems which it enabled are in dialogue with the author's self about his system; they do not merely illustrate it, nor do they necessarily harmonize with it.

For example, 'Leda and the Swan' is a poem of remarkable power, a power which comes in the first place from Yeats's deliberated mastery of language:

> A sudden blow: the great wings beating still
> Above the staggering girl, her thighs caressed
> By the dark webs, her nape caught in his bill,
> He holds her helpless breast upon his breast.

The verbless immediacy of the first three words is calculated in a characteristic way, and successful too, as is, in the following lines, the use of accumulating phrases which might govern a verb but turn out not to, putting the reader in some of the confused state of Leda herself, the victim of a rape made particularly nasty by careful use of 'caressed', which gains emphasis by its role as a rhyme-word. The poem is a poem about power, and it exhibits power, a heartless and, for example, un-Shakespearean power; it is a disquieting poem, the writing of which Yeats could legitimize for himself by recalling Leda's position in the mythology of *A Vision* as originator of Greek culture and the general doctrine that every civilization is born of destruction.

This does not, however, legitimize the poem for the reader who cannot, as most readers cannot, endorse Yeats's system. What *could* legitimize this imagining of a rape? The last of the lines quoted gives a clue: 'He holds her helpless breast upon his breast' emphasizes by the word it repeats that the swan/god and the woman, the rapist and the victim, have something in common, a breast with all its connotations of emotion, sustenance and solace, so that when the next line comes – 'How can those terrified vague fingers push . . .' – it is not immediately clear, if ever, to whom the fingers belong, Leda or the god within the bird. The poem, that is, extends the confusion of the victim to the reader and then even to the god ('vague' fingers are ill-defined within the swan's body, or their movements are unclear, or they are felt to be remote from control or consciousness, or they are all these). The poem is, then, not merely about the exercise of power in the rape, but also about the lack of power of the one who exercises power. The paradox is driven home by the allusion to the destruction of Troy which will follow on the birth of Helen from this union – 'The broken wall, the burning roof and tower/And Agamemnon dead.' The poem ends with a question:

> So mastered by the brute blood of the air,
> Did she put on his knowledge with his power
> Before the indifferent beak could let her drop?

Since the god's power has been questioned within the poem, his knowledge may be also. The beak is described as 'indifferent'; ignorance could be the cause of that indifference – the god himself may not have foreseen the consequences of his act. To be sure, it may also mean that he knows and does not care that this single act has sealed the fate of all Troy. The additional fact that Yeats's question is an unanswered question makes this doubt about the significance of the word all the more pressing. 'Leda and the Swan' is a stunning poem by virtue of its steady contemplation of the possibility that there is no meaning to be attributed to life. The god may know nothing, his power may be without base, Leda may know nothing of the civilization she will bring to birth, the splendour and the misery of generations may be the product of a rape without meaning. 'A sudden blow'; the poem is an act of aggression itself, turning on the very mythology it uses, and not just the Greek story of Leda but also the elaborate story of *A Vision*, in which it appears, for if the truth of the matter is that life is a kind of rape of consciousness the system of that book is without point.

'Leda and the Swan' is an imagist poem in all but its conventional form. It demonstrates also the 'hardness of outline' that Pound found in *Responsibilities*. It offers a point of entry into the occult mysteries of *A Vision*. It is a modern poem in its shocking concentration on what is potentially meaningless and in its implication that all objects of contemplation may lack meaning. Yet it is also a poem of doubt; the significance of the image is called in question even as it is enforced by all the art at the poet's disposal. The poem takes into itself some of the same kinds of anxiety as we find in 'The Love Song of J. Alfred Prufrock', although it may seem to be without that poem's humanity.

For all his deliberated grandeur Yeats is nevertheless, like Eliot, a poet of personal drama. In one of his greatest poems, for example, 'Among School Children', Yeats refers once again to Leda:

> I dream of a Ledaean body, bent
> Above a sinking fire, a tale that she
> Told of a harsh reproof, or trivial event
> That changed some childish day to tragedy –
> Told, and it seemed that our two natures blent
> Into a sphere from youthful sympathy . . .

But what is a 'Ledaean body'? The humanizing touch lies in the private quality of the phrase. Commentators may tell us that Yeats has here in mind his great love, Maud Gonne, whom he associated with Helen of Troy, who was Leda's daughter; it may be that he has in mind a body capable of bringing into being a whole new civilization, as he suggested that Leda had done in *A Vision*. But the phrase comes to the reader without that commentary, which in any case distracts attention from the fact that what is being dreamt of is a *body*, presumably as beautiful as that of Leda who brought a god down from the heavens. It is a *body*, and not a *figure*, a *person*, a *woman*, or a *form* that bent, although all these wordings would fit the merely formal requirements of the poem at this point. Is this body clothed or naked, as Leda's body is naked in most representations of her? 'Bent/Above a sinking fire' suggests a clothed body, and possibly an ageing one; the body is only visible, only naked, as it were, in the poet's dreaming of it, not in his memory of the moment he is dreaming of. Within this most deliberate of poems a moment of personal desire, of private feeling, flashes out and humanizes the formal language ('youthful sympathy', 'two natures blent') of what is a very public poem.

It builds to a magnificent close, premeditated praise feigning spontaneity, in the way of most poetry, praise of an ideal beauty which is unpremeditated, entire and in ceaseless movement:

> O chestnut-tree, great-rooted blossomer,
> Are you the leaf, the blossom or the bole?
> O body swayed to music, O brightening glance,
> How can we know the dancer from the dance?

The 'body swayed to music' is both clothed and unclothed; since leaf and bole cannot be distinguished in relation to the same identity, it makes no difference whether both are present or not, whether the tree/dancer is clothed by the leaf or not; what was a trace of intrusive personal desire in the earlier part of the poem, superimposing the naked body on the clothed, is now entirely harmonized to its subject matter. The poem exists as a personal drama in which a speaker copes with a desire that threatens his composure, as it threatens that of the poem, and as the sort of grand impersonal statement to be expected of the 'sixty-year-old smiling public man' that other people see.

Yeats's poetry is a poetry of paradox that is given emotional force by touches of this kind. 'In Memory of Major Robert Gregory' (in *The Wild Swans at Coole*, 1919) turns on such a touch in its concluding lines, where the poet says that he had intended 'to have brought to mind/All those that manhood tried, or childhood loved/ Or boyish intellect approved':

> but a thought
> Of that late death took all my heart for speech.

The line suggests two things at once – that all his heart has gone into speaking of the dead man in the poem, or that thinking of the man's death has taken away all the heart he might have had for poetry. The lines affirm and deny the value of what has been said at the same time; one might compare the simultaneous affirmation and denial at the end of *The Waste Land*. The conclusion of 'Sailing to Byzantium' has something of this quality too; the poet says that

> Once out of nature I shall never take
> My bodily form from any natural thing,

but that he will become a work of artifice, a bird of gold

> set upon a golden bough to sing
> To lords and ladies of Byzantium
> Of what is past, or passing, or to come.

The last line tends to cancel out the solemn final wish by dwelling on the natural world the bird is supposed to be escaping. Sturge Moore saw this inconsistency in the poem and objected, but it is what makes the poem, whose violent desire to be out of the body is matched by as violent an attachment to it. These examples have a bearing on 'Leda and the Swan', which is described earlier on as a 'heartless' poem – yet that poem has a heart at its heart, in its central two lines:

> And how can body, laid in that white rush,
> But feel the strange heart beating where it lies?

Yeats's poetry characteristically binds together contradictory ideas and feelings by the force of its rhetoric, and this is so despite his associating himself with Verlaine's ambition to wring the neck of rhetoric. It is the rhetoric, indeed, that is Yeatsian; the contradictions, as the analogies with Eliot suggest, belong to a more general quality of mind in the first half of the twentieth century.

Self-evidently, this is not a developmental account of Yeats. Such an account would be possible; to a remarkable extent Yeats used the same symbols (rose, bird, tower, Helen of Troy) and ideas (beauty, wisdom, vision, the conflict of body and soul) throughout his life, his development being a matter of revised emphases and new points of view. His commitment to the course of Irish nationalism and his desperate need to imagine life as something finer than he actually found it both lend power to his work. That work is far more uneven than most accounts suggest; the very closeness of the texture, the richness of the cross-references in his work, and the never-failing assurance of his style obscure the difference between poems that are simply good and those that achieve excellence. The difference lies in the relative degree of urgency with which a poem negotiates its contradictions.

Yeats is the poet of *but*, a word which he constantly uses, sometimes to mean 'merely', sometimes to mean 'except':

> And maybe the great-grandson of that house,
> For all its bronze and marble, 's but a mouse.

> O what if levelled lawns and gravelled ways . . .
> But take our greatness with our violence?

> What if those things . . .
> But take our greatness with our bitterness?

> Life scarce can cast a fragrance on the wind . . .
> But the torn petals strew the garden plot;

>   . . . their minds are but a pool
> Where even longing drowns under its own excess;
> Nothing but stillness can remain . . .

>   . . . had such a proof drawn forth
> A company of friends, a conscience set at ease,
> It had but made us pine the more.

These examples come from a single sequence, 'Meditations in Time of Civil War' (which is 'good' Yeats compared with the excellence of 'Nineteen Hundred and Nineteen'). *But* is an undistinguished mono-syllable, its short vowel conflicting with the emphasis it receives in Yeats's favourite ways of using it. Its sense is generally to diminish what is said, a habitual belittling element within the grandeur of sound and speculation that are the poems' surface. Yeats's *but* stands, in the forceful musicality of his later verse, for all those qualities that make him pre-eminently a poet of the early twentieth rather than the late nineteenth century.

IV

Eliot and the regenerated Yeats are the great writers of English poetry to come to maturity in the 1920s. The combination in them of a new directness and economy of language (Pound's 'direct treatment of the "thing"') with some belief in poetry as a transcendent power (roughly answering, perhaps, to Pound's 'secret doctrine') gave them a purchase on the multiform character of post-war Europe which more timid poets could not manage. Eliot and Yeats share their formal audacity (juxtaposition of fragments, allusiveness and obliquity) with Joyce, Lawrence and Woolf among the novelists; one may, if one chooses, think of this as 'modernism', although the term is not very helpful, suggesting a conscious striving to keep up with the times rather than the gift to do so while thinking of other things. It allows confusion with those artists of inferior status who were unable to get far beyond the business of meeting the demand for new styles in a new age.

These lesser artists are typified by the Sitwells, a brothers-and-sister threesome of upper-class sensitives. Edith (1887–1964) edited an anthology called *Wheels* (1916), designed as a counterblast to Marsh's *Georgian Anthology* and remarkable for the inclusion of some of Wilfred Owen's war poems. Her own poetry began to appear in 1915, and in its first phase emphasizes surprise and quality of sound; it eschews meaning, or at least meaning very much:

> The hard and braying light
> Is zebra'd black and white
> It will take away the slight
> And free,
> Tinge of the mouth-organ sound,
> (Oyster-stall notes) oozing round
> Her flounces as they sweep the ground.

This is superficially like the dandyism of early Wallace Stevens, but it has no philosophical basis; in this respect it also differs from similar poetries of sound at this time in French and Russian. It is left to be charming and remarkable and insubstantial. The Second World War brought a complete change of style to the solemn-prophetic, of which an example is 'And Still Falls the Rain', which Benjamin Britten set to music. This late poetry has not worn well, and its inflated rhetoric and religiosity ('the Field of Blood where the small hopes breed and the human brain/Nurtures its greed, that worm with the brow of Cain') illustrate precisely what it is that distinguishes Eliot and Yeats as creative artists – their tact and concentration on the task in hand. Edith's brother Osbert (1892–1969) had some slight success with the snobbish satires of *England Reclaimed* (1927), but Eliot was probably right to think that the real talent of the family lay with Sacheverell (1897–1988). That talent was essentially a decorative one.

Other modernizing writers have more to offer – David Jones, for example (1895–1974), whose first, and best, book, *In Parenthesis* (1937), was published by Eliot's firm. *In Parenthesis* is based on the author's experiences as a private soldier in France in 1915–16. Using a version of the 'mythological method' proclaimed by Eliot, Jones superimposes visions from Shakespeare, Malory and the *Chanson de Roland* to write a modern epic in praise of modern heroes. Its successor, *The Anathemata* (1952), is a more ambitious meditation on the artist's work, the Mass and millennia of western European history, contains more that is overtly poetry than its predecessor, and is accurately described in its subtitle as 'fragments of an attempted writing'. Jones's work is learned, at home with ideas, weaving its way happily among etymologies and great civilizations. It has a certain innocence and remoteness about it, as in these lines describing the battlefield in France, from *In Parenthesis*:

> The gentle slopes are green to remind you
> of South English places, only far wider and flatter
> spread and grooved and harrowed criss-cross whitely
> and the disturbed subsoil heaped up albescent

This reflects the artist's eye (and Jones, who was a disciple of Eric Gill, was a considerable artist, particularly noted for his lettering); it is remarkable, and yet 'albescent', a word from some very refined register indeed, pushes the whole scene too far into abstraction, an abstraction confirmed in the poetic diction of the next line: 'Across upon this undulated board of verdure chequered bright'. It is difficult for archetypal meanings to release themselves with great force in a medium handled at such distance from the idiomatic.

Eliot was not greatly imitated (unlike Yeats, whose voice echoes through much American poetry of the 1940s and 1950s), although he was greatly admired. This was doubtless the product of his never settling to a style (except in the three last plays). Herbert Read

(1893–1968), art critic, man of letters and poet, was a loyal follower, whose verse occasionally recalls Eliot in its phrasing or its subject matter. He is a relatively insipid writer, however, except in his earliest imagist pieces, too private to let the passion into his work, and here again the contrast with Eliot and Yeats is instructive. Pound's English disciple is much more interesting – Basil Bunting (1900–85), whose major poem, *Briggflatts* (1966), owes a debt to Pound's American follower, Louis Zukofsky, as well as to Pound himself. It is subtitled 'an autobiography' and offers an effortful music unparalleled in modern English poetry:

> Pens are too light.
> Take a chisel to write.
> Every birth a crime,
> every sentence life.

Like Jones, Bunting suffers from a distracting obtrusiveness in his artistry and from some of the coarseness that accompanies Pound's refinement; the pun on 'life sentence' drives home the point that the poem is grimly serious with a disconcertingly easy gesture, calling in question the integrity of the enterprise it is supposed to endorse. Nevertheless, *Briggflatts* is impressive work, uncharacteristic in its force; Bunting more often aims at elegance and clarity, as in the entirely successful 'Chomei at Toyama'.

He cannot compare in originality with a poet whose work is far less known. Laura Riding Jackson (1901–91) was born an American, came to England in 1926, published her books almost exclusively within the English sphere of influence, and stopped writing poetry in 1940, one year after her return to the United States. Her work began to be reprinted in England after a thirty-year interval. This résumé of her career is necessary to explain her absence from most histories of modern literature; she allowed herself to disappear from view. Since most literary histories emphasize nationality, her uncertain Anglo-American status has contributed also to her invisible status. It is, too, the case that more English writers have been pleased to gossip about her association with the accomplished and disciplined love-poet, Robert Graves (1895–1985), than to discuss the merit of her own work.

Introducing her *Collected Poems* in 1938, Laura Riding sought to defend herself against the charge of 'difficulty' by claiming that no one who read them 'for the reasons of poetry' would find them difficult. She writes out of an idea of poetry as severe and elevated as Eliot's:

A poem is an uncovering of truth of so fundamental and general a kind that no other name besides poetry is adequate except truth ... Truth is the result when reality as a whole is uncovered by those faculties which apprehend in terms of entirety, rather than in terms merely of parts.

This sounds very philosophical, although the central idea of the integrity of truth, which, since poetry is truth, is also the integrity of the poem, harks back to Romantic ideas of organic form, much in the fashion of Eliot in his evocation of the 'unified sensibility' (in the essay on 'The Metaphysical Poets') and of Yeats in his recurrent concern with 'unity of being'. There is no occult implication in Riding's notion of poetry, but there is a transcendent implication.

As it seeks to be truth in the demanding way suggested, Riding's poetry is noted for its sinewy resolve and concern for purity of expression. The contrast with Bunting is to the point:

> To conceive death as death
> Is difficulty come by easily,
> A blankness fallen among
> Images of understanding,
> Death like a quick cold hand
> On the hot slow head of suicide.
> So is it come by easily
> For one instant.

('Death as Death')

For this too is effortful verse, but the effort concentrates on the matter in hand. Death is a 'blankness fallen among images'; seriously to think about it is to admit the defeat of a discomforting, disrupting, unseizable presence in the midst of one's understanding, which may be only an image, or a collection of images, of understanding, not the real thing at all. Trying to conceive of death takes one to the heart of trying to understand understanding itself. The lines reflect and comment on that difficulty, and they do so in a style that has the integrity which I regard as the condition of success as a poet. It is a far more flexible and surprising style than at first appears:

> How well, you, you resemble!
> Yes, you resemble well enough yourself
> For me to swear the likeness
> Is no other and remarkable
> And matchless and so that
> I love you therefore.

('You or You')

Laura Riding and Robert Graves were the original exponents of ambiguity in Shakespeare's sonnets, and suggested to William Empson the basis for his classic work of criticism, *Seven Types of Ambiguity* (1930); this poem shows Riding writing in that Shakespearean mode and sacrificing nothing of her own identity.

It is an impressive achievement, and it derives from the search for a new conception of poetry that, having its roots in the pre-war years, came to fruition in the 1920s, a search for which the current term of 'modernism' hardly seems adequate. 'Experiment' is no better; all good poetry, since it ventures to be new in some way, is involved with 'experiment'. The poetry of Hugh MacDiarmid (real name C. M. Grieve, 1892–1978) was 'experimental' in its revival of literary Scots ('Lallans') and steeped in the poetry of the whole of early twentieth-century Europe, but *A Drunk Man Looks at the Thistle* (1926) and its fellows had more to do with Burns (Burns brought up to date, Burns with a touch of post-world-war intensity of spirit and irritability of temperament) than the kind of writer dealt with in the rest of this chapter. It was Eliot's belief in the local basis of culture rather than any kinship of artistry that led him to admire the Scots poet.

On the other hand, the poetry of D. H. Lawrence, uneven though it may be, does have a vital relation to the poetries of Yeats and Eliot and, indeed, Laura Riding, different as they may be. Lawrence's poetry reflects a strong influence from Walt Whitman; it is self-concerned and triumphalist in *Look! We Have Come Through!* (1917); this is an unpromising start. The fact that Lawrence contributed both to Amy Lowell's imagist collections and Marsh's *Georgian Anthology* indicates talent of some kind. *Birds, Beasts and Flowers* (1923) releases that talent into significant achievement. The style is free verse with much repetition, so that the poems suggest invocation; we are back on the borders of the magical:

> Dusky are the avenues of wine,
> And we must cross the frontiers, though we will not,
> Of the lost, fern-scented world:
> Take the fern-seed on our lips,
> Close the eyes, and go
> Down the tendrilled avenues of wine and the otherworld.

> ('Grapes')

The long sentence, sleepily repeating itself, takes us down the avenue we 'will not' take. Yet this relaxation is itself an affair of will, the sign of which lies in the ambiguous status of the verbs 'take', 'close' and 'go' in these lines – are they imperative or indicative?

The lines compel by not making the fact of compulsion too evident. The basis of Lawrence's best poems is imagist observation – 'Mountains blanket-wrapped/Round a white hearth of desert' – accommodated to all the variations of a speaking voice, as, for example, in 'The Mosquito':

> It is your trump.
> It is your hateful little trump,
> You pointed fiend,
> Which shakes my sudden blood to hatred of you:
> It is your small, high, hateful bugle in my ear.
> Why do you do it?
> Surely it is bad policy.
> They say you can't help it.

In order to perform their invocations of a metaphysical reality, Yeats and Eliot have to wear masks, be unknowable; it is Lawrence's distinction to present himself without a mask. The speaker in *Birds, Beasts and Flowers* is continuous with the speaker in his essays and novels; he is the essential Lawrentian figure, alive, alert, unfixed, doubtless in some sense a fiction, but not a fiction of a mask. That makes a large difference.

Birds, Beasts and Flowers is a book dedicated to personal renewal by identification with the creatures of earth. Lawrence's poetry elsewhere is more ragged at the edges; *Pansies* (1929) is a large collection of repetitious epigrams, and much of *Last Poems* (1931), including the well-known 'Ship of Death', sails dangerously close to Whitman. Yet Lawrence has a carelessness that is always refreshing after the more deliberate works of the period:

> And in the bruised body, the frightened soul
> finds itself shrinking, wincing from the cold
> that blows upon it from the orifices.

The sentence moves with assurance towards that last, cold word, but at the same time it sounds like spontaneous utterance, thanks to the rethinking implicit in 'shrinking, wincing', rethinking which suggests an identification with the utterance not to be found in the more perfect poets, Yeats and Eliot. Lawrence was, then, an important ally and corrective for them in the creation of a poetry adequate to the experience of English culture in the years after the First World War. With the poetry of Auden and his contemporaries we move back into the traditional world of English poetry taking its metaphysics as inconspicuously as it may. It is a world that looks different when one has lived for a while with their predecessors.

7

THE NOVEL IN THE 1930s AND 1940s

Richard Jacobs

I

At the age of forty, novelists (according to one of them) either become prophetic or acquire a style. That, noted in his diary in 1944, was the view of a writer full of the novel he had been negotiating release from army service to write (it would afford, he told the authorities, 'innocent amusement and relaxation' as a 'legitimate contribution to the war effort'). He wrote it unusually quickly, expressing relief along the way that, in his case, he would seem to have acquired a style and not become prophetic, and it was published to huge and perhaps not altogether unexpected popular success. The War Office, or at least his usual enthusiasts, might have expected this novel to have been a welcome instalment of the brittle, barbed stuff they were used to. It would have been unreasonable for anyone to expect it to devote itself with any fastidiousness to recent or current national or international events, to, say, the pre-war depression ('the last decade' of Englishmen's 'grandeur' in which 'the financial slump ... served to enhance my success') or the General Strike ('a beast long fabled for its ferocity had emerged for an hour, scented danger, and slunk back to its lair'). For the novel in the 1930s and 1940s, no less than generically usual, has indirect and difficult relations with social immediacy. This chapter will be concerned with some of the difficulties of that engagement.

What *Brideshead Revisited* by Evelyn Waugh (1903–66) is engaged to, apart from its acquired style, is apparent enough from its title. *Brideshead* (1945, tenderly revised in 1960, lavishly filmed by English TV for international esteem some three dozen years after Hollywood failed to strike the right note or deal) is Waugh's pained and (as he admitted) glamorized reconstruction of Oxford in the 1920s, that garden of compellingly innocent love and uninterrupted idleness made the more glamorous in retrospect from the 'bleak period of present privation and threatening disaster, the period of soya beans and Basic English' (1943–4, when the book was written). The allure of *Brideshead* is the allure of lost glamour and lost innocence, the two coexisting as a paradox at the heart of all retrospective yearnings. It is the adult's dream of the happy childhood – community without responsibility, attachment without commitment, love without loving – and Charles Ryder, *Brideshead*'s narrator, notices the connection:

Now, that summer term with Sebastian, it seemed as though I was being given a brief spell of what I had never known, a happy childhood, and though its toys were silk shirts and liqueurs and cigars and its naughtiness high in the catalogue of grave sins, there was something of nursery freshness about us that fell little short of the joy of innocence.

The same formula is used in Waugh's trilogy of the Second World War, *Sword of Honour* (1952–61). The diffident Guy Crouchback reflects that in his first few weeks with the hospitable and distinguished Halberdiers Corps 'he had been experiencing something he had missed in boyhood, a happy adolescence'. From 1942 the 1920s seem a happy childhood; from 1952, 1939 seems a happy adolescence. In both cases the experience is of something never known or missed at the time. In the last volume of the trilogy the impulse that led Waugh to write *Brideshead* is reinvoked, but now in an attempt to expiate, by parody, its nostalgic glamour. The ghoulish Ludovic writes a novel – 'very gorgeous, almost gaudy . . . melancholy suffused its pages' – and Waugh comments:

half a dozen other English writers, averting themselves sickly from privations of war and apprehensions of the social consequences of the peace, were even then, severally and secretly, unknown to one another . . . composing or preparing to compose books which would turn from the drab alleys of the thirties into the odorous gardens of a recent past transformed and illuminated by disordered memory and imagination.

The impulse to glamorize, to recover and to be unified with the mirages of memory, is dominant in Waugh and figures pervasively in the period, however indirectly, however deflected or displaced. This impulse offers itself as a significant aspect of writers' responses to the alienations and upheavals of economic depression, burgeoning fascism and war: a deflection of the questions, a displacing of current anxieties on to more distant and more wistful longings. The popular hobbit sagas (*The Hobbit*, 1937, *The Lord of the Rings*, 1954–6) of J. R. R. Tolkien (1892–1973) date originally from 1937, and their depressing morality of uncomplaining suburbia, suggesting that the proper thing to do with power is not to have anything to do with it, is a clear enough response to current anxieties. (The single convincing character in the series, Boromir, is axed as soon as he shows the anxieties of endeavour.) Tolkien's influence on C. S. Lewis (1898–1963) is evident: his Narnia cycle 'for' children, started at the end of the period, provides enchanting and often poignant Christianizing allegories that none the less routinely endorse class divisions (for instance) by naturalizing them in glamorous myth. For example, the Duffers, 'common' dwarves in *The Voyage of the Dawn-Treader* (1952), are incompetently unionized workers, paternalistically – but according to them ruthlessly – presided over by a magician given the island and its work-force by divine authority, for whose enrichment they darkly suppose they work, whereas they 'really' work for their own benefit: they are childish, stupid, gullible, vain and treacherous – yet sweet and lovable and funny despite it all. *Brideshead*'s explanation of why war heroes had to die ('so that things might be made safe for the travelling salesman, with his polygonal pince-nez, his fat wet hand-shake, his grinning dentures') is an equivalently bitter-wistful symptom (and as 'prophetic' a moment as any), its hatred expressive of difficult and displaced longing.

Waugh's novels dramatize such longings with peculiar clarity – and with a curiously appealing blend of wry dispassion and poignant vulnerability. The childishness of his world – the innocent amorality of the monied young, the glamorous adventurism of the childishly pouting Basil Seal (whose relationship with his sister, in the work of any other novelist, would be incestuous), the nannies and nurseries and prep schools, the petulant aristocrats and the regressive boobies of clubland – is evoked with a strange coolness: coolly disengaged and cooled of strong feeling and opinion, but also coolly glistening, as if translucent, precarious, fragile, as if it might (or should) be subject to strong feeling, strong cultural and social pressures, but is not, or not quite. The poignancy derives from this. It is the childhood return, held in suspension, the material world bracketed off but threatening by virtue of the very *élan* with which it has been relegated to the sidelines.

The celebrated style – not quite clipped or colourless as in early Powell, nor quite leisurely as in later Powell, but something between, indebted to Firbank for brio and lightness of touch but quite without his camp, to Wodehouse for timing and bravura invention but quite without his breeziness – appropriately registers the tension between engagement and disengagement that activates Waugh's vision. The poise and gleam of the style is most assured in the early novels. Notable features include the deftly deployed adverbs and adverbial phrases ('"God damn and blast them all to hell," said Paul meekly'; '"That," said Dr Fagan with some disgust, "is my daughter."'), the mock-heroic touches ('the meadow of green glass seemed to burst into flower under her feet as she passed from the lift to the cocktail table'), the sharp ear for comic idiom ('"Chokey thinks religion is just divine"'), and a deadpan pseudo-judiciousness (Adam saw 'the long-sought figure of the drunk Major. He looked sober enough this morning . . . When they had finished their champagne, the Major – now indisputably drunk – rose to go'). The unruffled, understating ironic voice, committed most to its own cool achievement, corresponds to some characteristic features of structure and plot: the numerous casual reversals and madly logical consequences, the circular narratives of *Decline and Fall* (1928) and *Scoop* (1938) that effectively deny the possibility of growth and change, the inconsequentialities and randomness of *Vile Bodies* (1930). The latter is appropriately imaged in Colonel Blount's film-show:

One of its peculiarities was that whenever the story reached a point of dramatic and significant action, the film seemed to get faster and faster. Villagers trotted to church as though galvanized; lovers shot in and out of windows; horses flashed past like motor-cars; riots happened so quickly that they were hardly noticed. On the other hand, any scene of repose or inaction, a conversation in a garden between two clergymen, Mrs Wesley at her prayers, Lady Huntingdon asleep, etc., seemed prolonged almost unendurably. Even Colonel Blount suspected this imperfection.

'I think I might cut a bit there,' he said, after Wesley had sat uninterruptedly composing a pamphlet for four and a half minutes.

Vile Bodies has not received the popular attention of *Decline and Fall* (and its author disparaged it), but it is a more acutely realized (as well as more comic) novel. The ambivalence of Waugh's attitudes is here most pressing, as his role is tensed between social historian, memorial celebrant and critic. The 'bright young things' are correspondingly charmed as well as charming, doomed to replay their ritual inventions, creations of their own fantasy-nightmares, desperate for sensation and difference ('"I'd give anything in the world for something different"') but condemned to pursue them as images reflected in the gossip-columns where they are trapped, as if in adolescent amber. The casual cruelty and casual deaths carry a more bitter charge than in *Decline and Fall*, the charmed circle of irresponsible revelling easily reverting to Miss Runcible's nightmares of 'an enormous audience composed entirely of gossip writers and gate-crashers . . . all shouting to us at once to go faster, and car after car ... crashing ...'. Adam's pursuit of Nina, of the drunk Major, of money, of gossip-column material – the general pursuit of something 'different from everything' – is driven not by appetite but by the perception of being dared 'to go faster', to crash – to self-destruct. A displaced perception of the uneasy demands for social change pervades the novel, and the pressure built up by the energy of that displacement is released in its apocalyptic ending.

The party has broken up in *Black Mischief* (1932) – 'a lady in a dressing jacket sat in an armchair by the gas-fire, eating sardines from the tin with a shoe-horn' – and the narration here, as in the subsequent *A Handful of Dust* (1934), is unenchanted, sparer and flatter, the passages of comic exuberance more grotesque, the cruel consequences of plot more calculated. The grip of the former novel is loosened, its force sapped by the sentimentalized Basil Seal (featured also in *Put Out More Flags*, 1942); the latter is unremittingly controlled and inward driven. This tale of comprehensive betrayal (of Tony Last by his wife, his ambitions, his Victorian values, his correct behaviour) was curiously described by its author as his only venture into humanism; but its technical resources are deployed principally to give pain. Its understating slang functions as a weapon ('it was thought convenient that Brenda should appear as the plaintiff') and its ironic juxtapositions, and the intercutting between London and the Brazilian jungle, are calculated to cause the maximum jar. The cruelly circumscribed plot is given both as grave archetype of squirearchic decline and as a larger version of the game of Animal Snap, which is played out at the novel's grim centre.

The evident in-driven anger of this novel is often viewed as a delayed response to Waugh's abandonment by his first wife (after which he joined the Catholic Church); but it can just as well be seen as a more generalized betrayal, that of a leisured, threatened class by its own worst instincts. It is pertinent that the survivors in both *Black Mischief* and *A Handful of Dust* are the colourless, decent, administrative class, getting by.

The scene for Tony Last's staged infidelity is a grand hotel in Brighton. A crowd is attracted by Tony's attempts to amuse the infant Winnie: ' "There's a man who's eaten two breakfasts and tries to drown his little girl", they informed other spectators ... Tony's conduct confirmed the view of human nature derived from the weekly newspapers which they had all been reading that morning.' In Graham Greene's (1904–91) *Brighton Rock* (1938) – just as *Scoop*'s Uncle Theodore is humming about change and decay in all he sees – a mounted policeman on a 'lovely cared-for chestnut' passes a beggar with half his body missing and the horse turns its head aside 'delicately like a dowager' from the offending item. (The policeman's response is not recorded.) The horse is 'like an expensive toy a millionaire buys for his children . . . it never occurred to you that the toy was for use'. Clashes between mounted police and hunger marchers were a feature of the early half of the 'devil's decade' (years for which the Home Office helpfully estimated that two unemployed men committed suicide every day), but Greene's delicate horse and his beggar suggest the more usual features of social life in the period: extremes of lived experience, mutual incomprehension between the extremes, futility. For the bulk of the populace (at least, for those in work), you got by, like Brighton's daytrippers, extricating 'with immense labour and immense patience . . . from the long day the grain of pleasure'.

Pinkie, *Brighton Rock*'s villain-hero, is in comprehensive and purist revolt: against the poverty of his upbringing (in 'Paradise Piece'), against the complacent indulgences of his peers, against the compromises of human attachment. Inheritor of a gang of incompetents, survivors from an easier world, he is pitched both against the bountiful optimism of the suspicious Ida Arnold and the smooth machine of the super-competent gangster Colleoni whose world (if it would only get its act together as he has) would adequately consist of 'lots of little electric clocks controlled by Greenwich, buttons on a desk, a good suite on the first floor, accounts audited, reports from agents, silver, cutlery, glass'. Pinkie's weapons (apart from the razors bequeathed by the dying Kite) are his 'board-school cunning' and the 'poison' that 'twists' in his veins. The book occasionally veers towards unhelpful melodrama (Pinkie eventually self-ignites with his own vitriol and evaporates), but this bravura novel is remarkable most for its casually maintained multiple operations, as deft thriller, sexual psychodrama and socio-political fable.

It is the story of 'The Woman' and 'The Boy' (as Ida and Pinkie are routinely called). The Boy has a fierce revulsion from sex, derived from primal witnessing of his parents' weekly grinding ('it sickened him like the idea of age . . . like ordure on the hands'), and when he feels the 'prick of sexual desire' it disturbs him 'like a sickness'. A Hamlet isolating himself from change, age, intimacy, the worst terror for him is procreativity ('the rivet of another life'), the primal enemy the mother. The Woman has extravagant and bounteous sexuality, 'great breasts', a weakness for alcohol and boozy kisses (The Boy is 'afraid of the mouth'), and is childless. Her mission to rescue Pinkie's child-victim Rose both displaces her mothering im-

pulses and uses up her frustrated and disappointed appetite. Like
Pinkie she denies the possibility of change and her motivations are
ambiguously charged (she 'hooked on another smile, as you hook on
a wreath'): she is in part a regressive figure, formed by the sentimentalities of Edwardian pub culture and closer to the gangland of Kite
(Pinkie's Old Hamlet) than to the New Man Colleoni.

Here we come to the novel's socio-political level. It has two
components: the first registers the transition of power from Kite,
who dies musing about a woman's 'tits', to Colleoni, from your
friendly neighbourhood (Anglo-Saxon) gangster to the bullying vacui-
ties of new dirty (continental and/or Jewish) money, from the sharp
deal at the racetrack to the lordly vulgarities at the Hotel 'Cosmopoli-
tan'. The other is suggested in the multiple references to waves
'breaking up from France', 'storms coming from the Continent' –
intimations of the tides of war, fascism, communism, against which
Brighton Rock may or may not prove adequate. Pinkie's rebellion, in
this light, is religious and political: against the 'Paradise Piece' of his
class expectations and against the European protestant settlement of
the piece of paradise to come. Pinkie of the not-quite-red, Pinkie the
Blakeian infant-rebel trailing 'the clouds of his own glory . . . hell lay
about him in his infancy', Pinkie the boy (lower-case) in the 'unhappy
cement school playground': however confused, his is a political
response both to the Rose of blushing repentance and to the (Ida)
Arnold of emollient and classical bounty, like (Matthew) Arnold up
the coast at Dover, saving the working class from itself. An attenuated
Coriolanus who rages against being thought a boy and who routinely
tears insects to bits, a Claudius who can't 'repent of something
which made him safe', a Macbeth 'driven further and deeper than
he'd ever meant to go' (and a Hamlet, as noted above), Pinkie is a
revolution in embryo.

Pinkie's austere disinclination to concern himself with others'
experiences and his 'dim desire for annihilation' are, in their extreme
form, prototypical. Pinkie is (dimly) aware of 'the vast superiority of
vacancy'; the lieutenant in The Power and the Glory (1940) knows
'vacancy, a complete certainty in the existence of a dying, cooling
world'. And if Pinkie lives by a process of elimination, so does the
lieutenant ('quite prepared to make a massacre') – and so does
Scobie (The Heart of the Matter, 1948) who lives by a 'process of
reduction', discarding what others accumulate. But as the pattern
repeats itself, it develops a manipulative moral stress. Pinkie's
absolutism has a bleakly absurd impressiveness that emerges with
little moral comment; the struggle between the absolutisms of the

lieutenant and the priest (in *The Power and the Glory*) and the internal struggles of Scobie's conscience are unequally loaded from the outset by the novels' Catholic agenda – and this despite the gestures (like making the priest a secret drinker and a secret parent) that signal the opposite.

The lieutenant (like virtually everyone in Greene, most evidently Greene himself) is exercised by memories of early misery; he appears to be motivated to hunt the last priest in a post-revolutionary Mexican state by the desire to save future children from equivalent horrors, but the novel is skewed to undermine this. Both he and the priest, for example, voice separately the belief that a child is of inestimable worth, but the lieutenant merely, and bluntly, asserts it ('this child is worth more than the Pope in Rome') and his listeners are mute and solidly uncomprehending, while the priest's thinking is mediated through an approving narrative consciousness that is difficult to resist: 'that was the difference, he had always known, between his faith and theirs, the political leaders of the people who care only for things like the state, the republic: this child was more important than a whole continent.' Similarly, in the crucial dialogue between the two, the priest 'commented', 'said' or 'giggled' while the lieutenant 'said furiously', 'harshly', 'grudgingly', 'contemptuously', 'savagely', displays 'physical disgust', has a 'sour face' and sweats. The gross artifice of the shock ending is evidently manipulative; less evident is the persistent blurring of priestly musing and narrative comment, supporting each other in their gnomic utterances. It is impossible to know which of the two is so sure, and why so sure of our agreeing, that 'the more evil you saw and heard about you, the greater glory lay around [Christ's] death'.

It is a frequent rhetorical ploy, also resorted to extensively in *The Heart of the Matter*. Scobie/Greene is routinely certain that 'no human being can really understand another', that it is 'absurd to expect happiness in a world so full of misery'; one or both of them peremptorily orders the reader to 'point me out the happy man and I will point you out either egoism, evil – or else an absolute ignorance'. This slips easily into smugness; Scobie wonders whether he was the only person to recognize responsibility for human misery. In apparent justification, pity is said to smoulder 'like decay' at his heart, his process of reduction merely concentrating it and identifying it more utterly with Catholic faith ('God was lodged in his body and his body was corrupting outwards from that seed').

The logic of the novel's ending, though tendentious, has a certain predictability: having failed to fool his rival about his suicide, and everyone else about his affair, it would appear safe to assume that Scobie will have failed to fool God into withholding his mercy from him. That logic is not as fantastic as the wholly implausible *The End of the Affair* (1951) which awkwardly attempts a semi-comic manner and which characteristically elides anti-theological rationalism with facial disfigurement (the narrator's limp and scar are signs of distinction) and God's mercy with his punishment. More assured is the fully realized comedy of *Our Man in Havana* (1958) in which the little man, Wormold, successfully exploits the idiocies of British Intelligence in pro-Castro Cuba. But the casual death of the obstinately real Raul is sour in an unexamined way – in that 'Raul' has enriched Wormold enough specifically to send his daughter to a Swiss finishing school. The smart cynicism of this is more typical of Waugh's later comedies, of which *The Loved One* (1948) is a peculiarly repellent example. Here the callow English protagonist (with Waugh's all-too-evident approval) enriches himself with novelistic material from the seduction, exploitation, suicide and refrigeration of his American lover, European experience thus expediting its responsibilities to American innocence. The cynicism of that is the manifestation of deep cultural (and political) boredom (those 'apprehensions of the social consequences of the peace').

Greene, like Waugh but more openly, identifies boredom as his prime enemy. It is the ennui of the craftsman whose commitment to his craft is his strongest commitment and whose sense of craftsmanship is itself perceived, increasingly, as threatened, by forces of circumstance, personal but more particularly social, out of his control. This boredom is in part a response to, the flipside of, betrayal. Characteristic of many post-war intellectuals in this respect, Waugh and Greene evince a sense of generalized betrayal, no less edgy for being unspecific, and apparent in the almost routine assumptions, in Greene particularly, that people will always let each other down and that nothing much can be expected from human relationships. (Greene's priest expects nothing else but betrayal of anything human. Is it permissible to ask why? That George Orwell insisted on the same deeply conservative conclusion is correspondingly more shocking.) The recurrent social and political betrayals in later Greene are metaphorical variations on this given presupposition, just as his typical relationships are (initially at least) impelled less by romance than by acquisitive sexual competitiveness. Waugh, less thick-skinned, none the less has a more clearly defined sense of who the post-war enemy is (identifiable, in a usefully economical way, with everything that happened in his lifetime) and in Waugh the responding boredom is the more pathological, as *The Ordeal of Gilbert Pinfold* (1957) makes adequately clear. But it is Greene's Querry in *A Burnt-Out Case* (1961) who is most ambiguously documented.

Querry (the name encodes quarrying, query and *quaere* – presumably as in 'why bother?') has 'no interest in anything', desires nothing but 'empty space' and has reached this position through the devourings of self-expression, which 'eats everything, even the self. At the end you find you haven't even got a self to express.' This austerely concentrated boredom must, it is suggested, correspond to the kind of spiritual aridity that is redeemed and recuperated by the novel's Catholic purposes (Querry comes 'to feel part of the human condition' by suffering with and for 'an egoism as absolute as his own'), but a counterstress is provided by an alternative suggested source for Querry's condition: the wounded pride of a misunderstood craftsman. Like Waugh, and like the novelist Maurice in *The End of the Affair*, but more cripplingly, Querry has a 'disgust of praise', a fastidious dislike for popular success. It 'nauseates' by its 'stupidity'. The success of the craft delivers the craftsman to popular success; he is betrayed by its stupidity and renounces his calling (until called elsewhere). That pattern of betrayal is one variation; Waugh's Guy Crouchback displays another.

Delivered, ready (so he hopes) for 'immediate consumption', from his 'tiny stroke' of spiritual 'paralysis' by the Nazi–Soviet pact (the enemy 'at last . . . in plain view, huge and hateful') and by his glamorizing belief in such men as the stylish Ivor Claire, Guy is promptly betrayed in both respects – by Claire who deserts at Crete and by the awkward reconfigurations after the German invasion of Russia. 'Courage and a just cause were quite irrelevant,' he decides, 'in the old ambiguous world.' All he can hope for is one good act; a 'small service', his 'function in the divine plan', both to 'redeem the times' and to fill his emptiness. The impulse here is weighted towards the expected betrayal: Guy's identification of the Modern Age in Arms and of Claire as the quintessence of Englishness is almost too obviously ripe for disillusion; the 'paralysis', like Querry's 'burnt-out' condition, is so evidently a datum of the character that Guy's sad recognition of himself in the Jewish refugee Mrs Kanyi's bitter analysis of those impelled to war 'in recompense for having been selfish or lazy' is, again, almost automatic. Guy's paralysis is an absent centre; like Querry he claims that he can't, doesn't 'love any more', and his response to the news of his wife's death is cold in a way of which Waugh doesn't seem to expect us to disapprove: 'The news did not affect Guy greatly . . . far less than the departure of his two Jewish protégés.'

The trilogy is skewed towards the inevitability of personal betrayal and providence's 'divine plan', as *Decline and Fall* is not. Guy considers his attempts to help the refugee Jews to be his 'function'; in the event he is betrayed by his own good offices. Earlier in the war he gives whisky to his feverishly weakened friend Apthorpe; it kills him. Here, he sends American magazines to the Kanyis; they are arraigned for fascist–collaborationalist tendencies and killed by the partisans of Yugoslavia. ('Why bother?' is easily enough decoded there.) Guy's 'real' function turns out to be the father of a son, not his, but Catholic (this could also have been the ending of *A Burnt-Out Case*). The retreat from the socio-political arena is thus, and thus violently, justified.

The *Sword of Honour* trilogy is impressive and ambitious: in its account of the débâcle at Crete we have perhaps both the most concentrated manifestation of Waugh's art and the single most powerful contribution to the fiction of the Second World War. *Gilbert Pinfold*, a fictionalized account of breakdown into madness (hallucinations brought on by cocktails of drugs and alcohol), is also impressively executed, but is a far less consciously determined response to betrayal. Apparently quite open in its use of autobiographical material it is actually in retreat from revelation and insight, pitched as it is as comic grotesquerie. (Waugh destroyed the relevant diary entries.) At one point the 'hooligans', Pinfold's supposed tormentors, accuse him of being 'in a funk'. The implicit self-accusation has point; the hallucinations, even inside the safe boundaries of craftily fictionalized form, represent a puzzled and fearful sense of being betrayed, found out and named, at the height of success, as the schoolboy in a funk, acting among adults – and, worst of all, as not only bored but a bore. Pinfold, before his madness, notes that 'at intervals during the day and night he would look at his watch and learn always with disappointment how little of his life was past'; an entry in Waugh's diary (1954) has 'clocks barely moving. Has half an hour past? no, five minutes.' A later entry is more disturbing precisely because – and this is the source of the accidental pathos of *Pinfold* – it reads like fiction. In his club Waugh is asked why he is sitting alone. 'Because no one wants to talk to me.' The other member replies: 'I'll tell you why. It's because you sit there on your arse looking like a stuck pig.'

II

During the war Cyril Connolly (1903–74), who founded and edited *Horizon*, a journal that Waugh mocked on more than one occasion in his novels, notably on the first page of *The Loved One* (first published in its entirety in Connolly's *Horizon*), wrote this, about a Rolls-Royce:

The sooner we accept the Dark Ages the faster they will be over. In the streets round this office . . . an enormous Rolls-Royce often passes. Each time one sees this mammoth of luxury, one wonders to whom it belongs; some fatcat of Bloomsbury? A ground landlord? A member of the Corps Diplomatique? But as it glides past it becomes transparent, and reveals on well-oiled bearings its only passenger, a neat wooden coffin. The limousine belongs to the last people who can afford it: the luxurious dead.

A few years later his schoolmate George Orwell (real name Eric Blair, 1903–50), talking shortly before his death to Stephen Spender, was put out by the excessively visible signs of wealth in the city, particularly by the number of Rolls-Royce cars he saw. 'There shouldn't be visible signs of one class being much better off than another. It is bad for morale.' Neither of these rings quite true. Connolly's rhetoric is too pleased with its own doom and Orwell's stewardship of morale sounds a bit brisk coming from that demoralizing novelist.

His late beast-fable, *Animal Farm* (1945), is, perhaps for many young people, the first book with an unhappy ending they will have read. Nothing remarkable in that, except for how remarkable an ending it is, how remarkably the novel drives towards it, and the remarkable degree to which this profoundly and antagonistically dispiriting book has, alongside *Nineteen Eighty-Four* (1949) with its yet more debilitating ending, been an essential component (in many hands a weapon) in the post-war educational apparatus, here and more or less everywhere else in the 'free' world. The two books are likely to have constituted, and to continue to constitute, for many, the extent to which the canon of acceptably teachable modern English Literature allows itself access to political projection and political allegory.

Not that many young readers decode the politics of either book at the level of content; but that is the point, because they receive it instead as form or structure and what they receive is a set of attitudes that underwrites an ideological position that can prove tenacious. Nor is it surprising that the political content of either of these novels is not instantly accessible; their particular and localized political meanings are in uneasy tension with the generalizing force of the allegorical form and, in any case, those specific meanings have proved disconcertingly open to conflicting interpretation. *Nineteen Eighty-Four* in particular is often read as anti-democratic. Orwell's sympathetic publisher, after all, was stirred to circulate, among his staff, his view that it was a 'deliberate and sadistic attack on socialism and socialistic parties generally'; and William Empson, thanking Orwell for *Animal Farm*, noted wryly that his 'delighted' son 'said it was very strong Tory propaganda'. But at the level of form there is less room for question; and the heavy overdetermination of the endings is decisive. These shocking endings amount to an affirmation that endeavour and effort are futile, and this prognosis is supported by a set of assumptions common to Orwell's work generally, two of which can be stated bluntly: that human beings betray each other and that, among the species generally considered, intellectuals can be relied upon to be not only worse than most but the prime enemy. It is the clever pigs who 'become' human (and Napoleon has a reputation for being especially deep): Empson, again, had a point when he told Orwell that 'the story is far from making one feel that any of the other animals could have turned into men'; it is the professor-type O'Brien, with his donnish mannerisms, who is the crazed torturer. More mundanely, it is young men who examine art books in shops who can be expected to walk 'nancily' and (also in *Keep the Aspidistra Flying*, 1936) it is ineffectually lefty editors like Ravelston whose girlfriends can't see that it matters whether to call people 'the lower classes' or 'the working class' on the grounds that 'they smell just the same'. The wonderfully learned and cultured Porteous (in *Coming Up for Air*, 1939) unsurprisingly sees 'no reason for paying any attention' to Hitler, and the 'rakish' painter Warburton (in *A Clergyman's Daughter*, 1935) talks 'amusingly' about books before 'brutally' assaulting his female guests.

The antagonism towards intellectuals is more than characteristic British ambivalence – fear and derision – as regards thinkers. (Greene and Waugh make routine use of comically hypocritical literary editors.) In Orwell it has a personal force and has to do with the deliberate contrivance of the character of 'George Orwell' – not just a pseudonym. It is as if the creation of 'Orwell' meant forcing himself into a cultural vacuum. Intentionally estranged from his ruling-class background, determined to present things as they 'really' were, Orwell could only retain what he took to be the necessary attitude of transparent observation by a process of self-cancellation, being curiously absent in the thick of his reportage, as if not trusting to his judgement and intellect but to a willed suspension of both. (Isherwood is an equivalently problematic figure of absence in presence – 'I am a camera' – as suggested below.) In Paris and London, at a hanging or shooting an elephant, at prep school in Eastbourne or walking to Wigan, Orwell's impression of solid reliability seems achieved at the expense of his not being there, in frame, a vulnerable or critical presence.

In practice, the celebratedly neutral observations are subject both to a programme of heavy editing – so that, for instance, the northern working-class thinking radicals, whom he met and stayed with, get conveniently left out of *The Road to Wigan Pier* (1937) – and to a sentimentalizing vision of machismo miners and of England as a grandly eccentric family with the wrong uncles and aunts in charge. The effect of transparency is so coercive that the manipulative processes are rarely apparent. Recounting the horrors of a Paris hospital in his essay 'How the Poor Die', it seems perfectly reasonable for Orwell to contrast the situation in England in terms of 'the advantage we enjoy in having large numbers of well-trained and rigidly-disciplined nurses', although 'no doubt English nurses are dumb enough', and almost unreasonable for a reader to wonder who exactly is included in 'we', in 1946 in England, and what exactly 'dumb' nurses were enjoying at the time. Nor is the guise of unjudgemental description, for instance of the tramps in *Down and Out in London and Paris* (1933), usually ruffled, so that it may puzzle a reader learning about Paddy, Orwell's 'mate' for a fortnight, suddenly to be told that his ignorance was 'appalling' and that he had 'a low worm-like envy' of better-off people. Did his mate apprise him of these findings? The decent ordinariness of the colloquial voice is difficult to resist, just as difficult, and for similar reasons, as not surrendering to the defeat and failures of the novels' endings. The effort necessary to resist is equivalent to the unconscious process by which Orwell adopted his manipulative programme in the first place.

One important example, symptomatic of the complex interaction between effortless obviousness and heavy repression, is the silence at the centre of *Nineteen Eighty-Four*, its refusal to answer its most pressing question, the question at which Winston Smith's reading of Goldstein's book conveniently breaks off, not before the reader has begun to want the same question answered: namely, '*why* should human equality be averted' by the ruling party, intentionally and at such elaborate expenditure of effort and lives? What is the 'original motive' that Goldstein identifies but isn't suffered to name? O'Brien, torturing Smith (in a scene that Ian Fleming might have remembered), answers: the Party 'seeks power entirely for its own sake'. The political thinness of this, its tautological banality, is rendered yet more suspect when O'Brien casually reveals that he (and a committee, of course) wrote 'Goldstein's' book in the first place, a trick that makes the whole enterprise of that extended political analysis an elaborate joke at the expense of intellectual inquiry. Orwell has to proceed thus; to do otherwise would be to take the possibility of a massed radical, informed movement seriously – and that would have been in the face of the crucial Orwellian preconception, that working people are incapable of such informed and productive radicalism. The portrayal of working people in Orwell is, as observed, sentimentalized, but not so much out of sentiment or longing (as in Dickens, whom Orwell rather loftily diagnosed in this respect), but out of a kind of repressive wishfulness. The 'proles' in *Nineteen Eighty-Four*, the prostitutes in *Aspidistra* are snapshots from a retrospective, not a current family-album of 'England', and Orwell moves among them as Winston Smith moves (Winston and George, the absent dragon-slayers), as if insubstantial, among the London poor who ignore him not because he is a camera quietly observing them but because he is not even seeing them.

Only, perhaps, in Spain, in revolutionary Barcelona and a civil war, elsewhere, is Orwell substantial. *Homage to Catalonia* (1938) draws productively, and not without poignancy, on a complex response, a kind of uncertainly heroic engagement that charges the reporting voice with urgency. But it was in Spain where Orwell's nerve of betrayal was first and most rawly exposed, and it is plausible to trace to this source the sense of failed and benighted aspiration that attends the novels. For the novels display a willed, grim satisfaction at their ends, a sense of a need to keep proving, by narrative fiat, the inevitability of betrayal. Two minor motifs may be relevant: imagery of baits and traps, and a pattern of guilt for the sacrifices made by one's family on one's behalf. The former (recurrent in *Aspidistra*) suggests that negotiating life may entail failure by not recognizing apparent goals (like marriage or socialism) as the loaded traps that they are; the latter (a key feature of that novel but most telling in Smith's earliest recollections in *Nineteen Eighty-Four*) suggest that sacrifices, far from liberating the beneficiaries, are an imposition and burden on the possibilities of progress. In both cases there is a sense that commitments are most predictably things to be withdrawn from in case they let or weigh one down. (Better alone the dragon-slayer against his enemies.)

The structure of the novels generally may be perceived as a process of entrapment; *Coming Up for Air* works by demonstrating an attempt to break from entrapment (and, of course, its bleakly awful failure). George Bowling's trip back to what he hoped would be unspoilt country and market-town life is brutally mocked by the suburban and commercial blight of progress (his childhood love, in another recurrent Orwell motif, has, equivalently – we are presumably meant to think – lost her figure), and the blight is registered as if in justification for the thoughts of extermination (let the bombs drop) that occur to Bowling (as they do to the altogether exasperating Gordon Comstock in *Aspidistra*). Here is the clearest expression of something never far away in Orwell: the dream of England as the insulated, organic country community. The brutality of Bowling's disappointment is Orwell's self-punishing awareness of the hold that the dream exercises, just as the cityscape of *Nineteen Eighty-Four* could only have been conceived by a massively disappointed pastoral longing. Here also is one reason for the abiding readability of a series of fictions that in other respects has aged badly, for this dream of the vanished organic community is also the determining impulse behind the critical programme of the Leavises and their journal *Scrutiny* (which ran, after all, from 1932 to 1953). Leavis and Orwell had in common an anti-theoretical thrust, a sense of self-imposed embattled exile and this version of pastoral. In Orwell it surfaces unexpectedly. Lovers in the country seem to step into quite different novels when they are out of the city. *Animal Farm* is an anti-idyll, but its impulse is pastoral-idyllic. So it is not altogether surprising to read what Orwell proposes for the problem of the down-and-out tramps: 'make them grow their own food.'

The trajectory of Christopher Isherwood (1904–86) would seem to be that of a paradigmatic retreat from the political to the personal – in his case the turn to Eastern mysticism not being even a particularly startling development, given that one preoccupation from the beginning was the precise status of the personal, as suggested in the title of one late book *My Guru and His Disciple* (1980). There is a continuum between the early 'I am a camera' narration of the Berlin stories, where the observing participant of disguised autobiography operates as if disengaged from the claims of any biography ('Christopher Isherwood' is announced to be a 'ventriloquist's dummy'), and the late autobiography *Christopher and His Kind* (1976) written in the third person.

In other respects, too, Isherwood's work is of a piece. *Mr Norris Changes Trains* (1935) (in the United States, *The Last of Mr Norris*) and *A Single Man* (1964), for instance, have in common an emphasis on sexual transgression as a focus for meaning (Mr Norris's predilections underpin and outlast his more uncertain affiliations) and on those who survive against indifference by treating events and emotions as stimulants to living (single man George's 'hate' is 'a stimulant – nothing more'). The apparent differences are of less interest: for example, between history in the making in the former novel, and history as occasional and bitchily noted reflections on California's decline from raffish colonial bohemianism in the latter ('The cottages which used to reek of bathtub gin and reverberate with the poetry of Hart Crane have fallen to the occupying army of Coke-drinking television-watchers'). As it happens, history is more urgent in *A Single Man* than in *Mr Norris*, surfacing as it does in unassimilated and casual references to bombs and Cuba, while in *Mr Norris* it functions as a garish stage-set.

'I am a camera with its shutter open, quite passive, recording.' This notorious sentence from *Goodbye to Berlin* (1939) needs to be unpacked. The pose is of someone neutral, merely passively mirroring reality, an inversion of the omniscient narrator of classic realist fiction, a more appropriate stance for the machine-age, the age of world-politics staged outside everyone's window. More matter, with less art. But the artistry is apparent enough, even in the analogy's own terms. For someone has to choose to point the camera and work it, and choose which exposures to share (and which to suppress), the selection then 'developed, carefully printed, fixed'. And the artistry with which Isherwood arranges the apparently disparate, unmediated elements of his Berlin fiction, its tricks of superior insight ('hysteria . . . flickers always behind every grave, grey Prussian facade'; 'these people could be made to believe in anybody or anything') are (often crudely) evident on every page.

But the camera analogy is interesting in other ways. Passivity suggests what Isherwood never actually can say: that, far from being the disembodied recorder, he is a participant in Berlin's political troubles and guiltily half-conscious of his moral and ethical passivity, yet physically involved in the city in ways that he feels obliged to choose to be silent or even evasive about. It is this odd combination that makes the pretence of the neutral camera necessary. In *Mr Norris* the narrator is struck, at a communist meeting, by the faces of the Berlin working class. It is tempting to italicize the words 'they', 'their' and 'them' in this:

They had not come here to see each other or to be seen . . . They were attentive, but not passive. They were not spectators. They participated, with a curious, restrained passion, in the speech made by the red-haired man. He spoke for them, he made their thoughts articulate.

The narrator is 'elated' but stands outside it. 'One day, perhaps, I should be with it, but never of it' – an oddly prescriptive remark. The combination also makes for the odd sense of unreality attendant on the cast of 'characters' that Isherwood selectively chose to portray, Sally Bowles, Natalia and Bernhard Landauer, Mr Norris and the rest of them. It is difficult not to get the impression that Isherwood is trying them on, justifying the gaps, suppressions and reticences in his own self-presentation by (as it were) over-exposing their images. The result is that they, no less than he, but for the opposite reason, float curiously free from their circumstances and histories. At the least this has something to do with Isherwood's tendency to 'fix' them in stagey anecdotes and presumably the way *Mr Norris*, 'Sally Bowles', and 'The Landauers' (sections of *Goodbye to Berlin*) are shaped very much towards their closures is contributory. But that it has more to do with this curious process of transference may be seen in one revealing passage in the account of Bernhard Landauer.

He tells us stories. He is sympathetic, charming . . . He is not going to tell me what he is really thinking or feeling, and he despises me because I do not know. He will never tell me anything about himself, or about the things that are most important to him. And because I am not as he is, because I am the opposite of this, and would gladly share my thoughts and sensations with forty million people if they cared to read them, I half admire Bernhard, but also half dislike him.

This is precariously close to self-recognition and identification with the charming, aloof, perplexingly reticent story-teller, half-admired, half-disliked: but most revealing are the unusual over-assertiveness of 'I am the opposite of this' and the astonishing claim to 'gladly share my thoughts and sensations with forty million people if they cared to read them'. These are precisely what Isherwood does not share; and the lurking suggestion is that it is our fault for not caring to read his thoughts. Thus the camera is excused.

The suppressions of the Berlin texts are more than adequately compensated for in the later works, among which *A Single Man* is notable for sexual candour. Beginning with a bowel movement and ending with a genital spasm (in one of the period's semi-conscious gestures towards Joyce's *Ulysses*), it may be candid but, if the novel is embarrassing, it is not for this candour but because of its manifest dislike of people, its governing impulse of a disgust that is projected self-disgust. This is manifested in various ways, from open physical hatred of the woman's body, to routine arousal by young men sensed only as animals, to an arch and self-mocking inverted sexism ('let them write about heterosexuality if they must . . . Just the same, it is a frightful bore and, to be frank, a wee bit distasteful. Why can't these modern writers stick to the old simple wholesome themes – such as, for example, boys?'), to sentimental references to the supposed mores of classical Greece. Characters are stereotypically drawn, the boy Kenny more or less taken (unconsciously, it must be assumed) from Salinger's Holden Caulfield. Regressive in almost every way (apart from its modishly frank homosexuality), the novel has one scene regressive in a particularly interesting way. In it George and Kenny swim late at night, drunk:

Intent upon his own rites of purification, George staggers . . . to receive the stunning baptism of the surf . . . The dry are going dryly to their own beds. But George and Kenny are refugees from dryness; they have escaped across the border into the water-world, leaving their clothes behind them for a customs-fee.

The images of purifying, baptism, refugees and borders significantly belong to pre-war and early wartime texts.

In retrospect a key text about borders is *Journey to the Border* (1938) by Isherwood's friend Edward Upward (1903–89). It presents in the hallucinatory experiences of a private tutor an argument for revolutionary action (the borders are of mental condition and of class consciousness). Upward wrote laboriously and it is dutiful labour to read his trilogy of political life from the 1930s to the 1950s, *The Spiral Ascent* (collected version 1977), but there is a certain grim, dogged obstinacy about his perceptions, a sign of both the perceived importance and the difficulty of registering politics and history in fiction just before or in the early years of the war. Another way of coming at this would be to juxtapose a group of characteristic texts from those years with a couple from the end of the war. There is more than a war between *Mr Johnson*, *The Aerodrome*, *Hangover Square* and *Party Going* on the one hand, and *Brideshead Revisited* and Cyril Connolly's *The Unquiet Grave* (1944) on the other. The latter are canonical as if timeless in their retrospective longings; the former seem 'period', as if their very urgent concerns were available only as coded messages from the front line conveyed across a vast distance. Two moments in Rebecca West (1892–1983) are illustrative. In January 1941, closing up her London home, she sees her familiar

'Empire table' obscurely ruined by the vibrations of local bombs: 'it stood there like something dead and unspeakably mangled. Under the gentlest blow, this honest and beautifully made article of furniture would have fallen to pieces.' She feels a 'sick yet distant anger that was extreme and not quite my own'. This is expressive of difficult, 'distant' feelings about 'Empire' and the survival of old artisanship. After the war, observing William Joyce's treason trials, she notes that 'we were pleased, and pleased to be pleased' by the performance of the new Labour government's Attorney-General: 'For the English were pathetically eager to approve of whatever the new government did; we were tired out by such excitements as had produced this trial, and what we wanted was to hear the machine ticking over.' The Labour government was able to exploit this complaisance in its drift to a watered-down centre. The machine ticking over is symbolic of a longing for order to be managed from elsewhere, by the machine, the experts and planners: for capitalism to be made efficient while art gets on with its own affairs, its own longings and retrospections. The thinning down of history in the novel is the result of this complaisance. In fiction before and at the start of the war, there was an effort to meet, if only in ways muted and displaced, its insistence.

It is not to be met with, however, in the romances of Elizabeth Bowen (1899–1973), ambitious reminders, more so than other mainstream work in the period, of the pre-modernist tradition of the novel: in all its relentlessly ruminative, leisurely and intelligent qualifications. In Bowen, the authorial intrusions, the direct address to the cultured reader, the moral debates and the crises over social minutiae remind one of Henry James. These are romances of behaviour and manners (Jane Austen is rather archly referred to, as if the coinciding details of plot were a surprise, in *The Death of the Heart*, 1938), less momentous than their reflective delivery and the (often disproportionate) anxiety of their emotional tangles suggest. *The Death of the Heart* impresses with its Jamesian perceptions, but the overall effect is closer to that of rather knowing moral essays, themselves dependent on a way of living, and a way of reading, nearly antiquated in the late 1930s and surviving elsewhere only in popular period fiction (which Bowen's *A World of Love* (1955), for instance, remarkably resembles). *The Death of the Heart* and *The House in Paris* (1935) have unwieldy blocks of dialogue that again, for all their sharpness, have (as in Compton-Burnett) the air of costume-drama. The weirdly unsettling children in Bowen talk with the shocking clarity of innocence but also in the stage tones of written-to-order cleverness. (L. P. Hartley's *The Go-Between* (1953) has more credibility, if only in this respect.) These novels are too unillusioned to be melodramatic, but the effect is of melodrama, for there is a stiffness and an awkwardness, not just in the recourse to such formulae as flashbacks and letters but in the recurrence of hearts uncompromisingly broken and dark family secrets rattling down the generations. Sometimes Bowen even sounds like *Cold Comfort Farm* (1932), a debunking by Stella Gibbons (1902–87) of the steamier rural romances of Mary Webb (1881–1927) (debunking, that is, until its own grotesquely Mills-and-Boon ending).

Joyce Cary (1888–1957) is best known for two trilogies: *Herself Surprised* (1941), *To Be a Pilgrim* (1942), *The Horse's Mouth* (1944); and *Prisoner of Grace* (1952), *Except the Lord* (1953), *Not Honour More* (1955). These exercises in carefully apportioned perspective (each volume of each trilogy is narrated by one of the trilogy's three protagonists) have the air of attempting to consolidate by exhaustiveness the classic realist tradition (the interminable qualifications of *Prisoner of Grace* are also exhausting) rather than of enlarging its potentialities. But *Mr Johnson* (1939), the most interesting of his earlier African novels, is altogether less leisurely.

Mr Johnson is the 'Stranger', both to the Nigerian natives who think him 'mad', and to the white colonial class who think him 'quaint' and who employ him as a clerk. His real function turns out to be the surprising one of enabling and realizing the roadbuilding ambitions of his hero, the administrator Rudbeck. This he does by enticing and charming the tribal natives into doing the necessary clearing and construction work, hitherto considered impossible. The building of the road marks the moment when the natives tentatively step into civilization, the tribe becoming 'men', and doubts simultaneously come to the colonialists about civilization's effects: 'roads upset things, brought confusion, revolution. And wasn't there confusion enough?' This paradoxical moment produces a pressure that must be relieved (Rudbeck senses that 'he has been used and driven like a blind instrument. This gives him a very disagreeable sensation'), and it is relieved by the sacrifice of Mr Johnson, 'Mr Wog' as Rudbeck's wife pertinently calls him. In 1939 it 'looks as though the whole show is going phut', civilization 'getting on a bit too fast' or perhaps 'not fast enough' – 'yes, there's that too' – and this bland confusion masks the perception that 'children are starving in Fada, bush villages and the slums of London and New York for exactly the same reasons', which have to do with the order that democracy would upset. Johnson is the sacrificial victim to appease that order.

It is remarkable that the pattern of Johnson's career, crime and death accidentally mirrors that of *Billy Budd* (Herman Melville's late reading of Christian archetypes, written in the 1880s, first published in 1924). Johnson, like Budd, is innocent creative energy, a galvanizer, dancer and poet (Johnson's elaborately inventive lies and fictions have an innocent transparency), a medium for the absorption and reproduction of Africa as 'perpetual experience' in reflections, comments, songs, jokes: but he is also a stranger, an alien, an impossibility. Johnson and Budd enable those around them to function more efficiently and more happily, and this realizes the officer–administrative class ambitions at the same time as it forges the potentially threatening will of the workers. When Johnson kills (as is believed) the bullying and brutal Gollop by responding, for once, to his violence with a knock-out blow, he is replicating Budd's 'murder' of Claggart: but this is a premonitory emblem only, for Gollop is merely stunned. So later, and with a certain predictability, Johnson robs, stabs and kills Gollop – although to the 'judge' Rudbeck at the 'trial' who, like Captain Vere, tries to evade the responsibility he holds over Johnson's fate, the murder may as well be 'accident': Johnson, like Budd accused of mutinous activities, 'lost his head' (to quote the clerk's statement, written for him by Rudbeck). Rudbeck endorses the death sentence, driven like Captain Vere in Melville's story not least by fears of the effect this charismatic figure might have on variously discontented workers (the policemen guarding Johnson at the end are affectionate to him and contemptuous of Rudbeck). At the moments of execution, and with a mesmeric effect on the sailors and on the 'whole population of the barracks and station', Billy Budd cries out, 'God bless you, Starry Vere'; Johnson cries, 'Oh Lawd, I tank you for my frien' Mister Rudbeck – de bigges' heart in the worl'.' In both cases, the cry is the moment of the novels' released tensions, the martyred victims blessing their executioners (and mesmerizing workers back to work) in a rhapsody of pseudo-erotic, pseudo-filial fulfilment by abandonment, releasing political pressure by displacement on to the psycho-religious level. This suggests analogies with the early work of Rex Warner (1905–87).

Warner's *The Aerodrome* (1941) is, like his *The Wild Goose Chase* (1937), a political allegory. It is the more interesting of these two books in so far as it articulates its allegorical account of the take-over of a country village by the neighbouring aerodrome against an extraordinarily tangled story about rival clergymen and uncertain parentage. The two interlock with a bizarre air of ordinariness and the narrative is delivered in a curiously oracular mandarinese (it is not easy to say how much of the bathos is intended): the eerie effect is of Agatha Christie crossed with Kafka. The more easily assimilable *Wild Goose Chase*, with its set-pieces (like the football match between the 'Pros' and 'Cons' in which the goal posts literally recede as the Pro team is threatening to score), has less of a charge than the surreal double articulation of *Aerodrome*, its parallel development of provincial family intrigue and of the training of an elite for political power.

The young narrator, like the villagers generally, is at first repelled by the clinical regime of the aerodrome but circumstances lead him to join and to succeed with the Air Vice-Marshal and his corps, and so renounce the ties of the country, the old feudal arrangements and the demands of women, to acquiesce and participate in the running of the village as a police-state. (The villagers' 'misery and their happiness' both seem 'abject and pointless' to the narrator.) Love and the country eventually reclaim him (he had looked down at the country 'with a kind of contempt'; inefficiency and hypocrisy may have been abolished by the élite, but so is 'the sweet and terrifying sympathy of love') at the expense of a crisis with the air vice-marshal, however, whose visionary rhetoric ('your purpose – to escape the bondage of time, to obtain mastery over yourselves, and thus over your environment') had earlier inspired him – and who turns out (the phrase is appropriate) to be his father.

There would seem to be a complex set of feelings in this. The village life is recognized as drunken and inefficient; the air vice-marshal's vision, despite its destructive impulses ('we shall destroy what we cannot change'), has elements of utopian, even Fabian thinking, quite different from Orwell's bathetic identification of power for its own sake as the driving force in *Nineteen Eighty-Four*; and the narrator's disenchantment with it is managed more schematically ('I began for the first time to wonder what was the point of our tremendous programme') than most things in this admittedly schematic novel.

But the most striking feature of *The Aerodrome* is that the visionary élite's prognosis is overlaid on a feudal system (the word is used and 'capitalism' is not); the real conditions of capitalism are kept out of the novel, merely alluded to by the air vice-marshal as 'worse things' happening darkly in the cities (people acquiring money by 'cunning and hypocrisy' – hardly a comprehensive analysis). This symptomatic silence, this expressive hiatus between the feudal village with its 'Squire' and the rest, and the vision of a transformed world is, one might say, filled with the family crisis of the father, his discovery and rejection. The necessary rejection (for love and home-land) of the visionary father is Oedipally complex and would seem to embody difficult responses to the concept of fatherland, as well as traces of a need for heroes in a retrospectively rural England in which, after all, clergymen (the narrator's two 'fathers') are also scheming and philandering murderers. The moral ambivalence is underlined at the end by a process whereby the old village system and the new visionary order are brought into difficult contact but only at the level of language. Thus we are blandly informed that the two orders each have 'vices and virtues', that 'until recently' no one had thought the air vice-marshal's ambitions 'necessarily inhuman or monstrous', and that 'no corner of the country that had felt the force of his ideas could afterwards relapse wholly into its original content'. (*Relapse, wholly, original, content*: all four words are slippery customers.) And the loading of ideological freight on the book's last two sentences is as symptomatic a problem as could, from the period, be asked for: '"That the world may be clean": I remembered my father's words. Clean indeed it was and most intricate, fiercer than tigers, wonderful and infinitely forgiving.'

Hangover Square (1941) by Patrick Hamilton (1904–62) is set in 1938–9 and charts George Harvey Bone's obsessive, servile devotion to the shallow schemer Netta. George has increasingly prolonged 'dead' periods when something clicks in his head, draining his world of colour and sense, and in these periods he must remember that he has something very important to do: and that is to kill Netta. The book is a comic thriller with an assured and expertly realized seediness, though not without some awkwardness of narrative perspective and a certain sentimentality (particularly about theatrical people, as is also the case with Hamilton's *Slaves of Solitude*, 1947). But more than this needs to be said. For, like *Brighton Rock* (two crucial scenes are in Brighton), *Hangover Square* is seemingly artless in its manifold operations. George's raging devotion to the idealized, halo-emanating woman is, in this period, unmatched in its physical intensity; this debilitating sexual possession is medieval courtly love with a vengeance, literal rather than literary, adolescent in the terrible raw way in which Shakespeare's most painful sonnets are adolescent (Sonnet 57, most painful of all, is quoted in excerpt at the head of one chapter). George knows all the inadequacies of the loved object, but obstinately continues in self-abasement. George is also a Hamlet, under obscurely derived instruction to avenge, to kill the source of threatening sexual power, castigating himself for neglecting his duty in procrastination, proud of his special cleverness that outsmarts them all. As in *Hamlet* the polarities of sane and mad may be reversed. In his dead phases George perceives things with a curiously limpid clarity, as if somnambulistically tuned into the resourcefulness of real purpose and judgement. He judges acutely the fascist sympathies of Netta and her friend Peter. As the novel reaches its calmly murderous conclusion, Poland is invaded and war is announced. Two possible readings here are in fruitful tension, suggestive of the ambivalence in Hamlet's role as scourge *and* minister. In his dead phase George may be making civilization's last gesture, a last attempt to snuff out fascism, or he may be reproducing civilization's drift into mindless violence. The ending of *Slaves of Solitude* (set in 1943) is similarly and richly ambivalent. In allowing Miss Roach to triumph in her boarding-house feud with the German Nazi-sympathizer Vicky, the novel underpins the kind of provincial ethic that expects things eventually to come out 'in the wash' (as one character puts it) and that hands out lucky legacies at the end; but this ethic is threatened by a scene in which Miss Roach, having escaped from her boarding-house, is 'purified' by witnessing a pantomime comic purifying his audience of children, whose excitement in turn purifies him. The children look at the stage with 'ferocious intensity', and in 1943 this can hardly be read innocently – particularly as the comic routine in question involves the ethics of the school-bully (Miss Roach also triumphs over the boarding-house bully), tormenting another comic and then claiming, in 'cruel conspiracy' with the children, that '*I* didn't do it'. It is always the other who is guilty, never one of the select. The ambivalence at the end of both novels suggests unresolved anxieties about the war that otherwise remain unarticulated in either.

The most remarkable aspect of *Hangover Square*, much the most interesting of Hamilton's books, is its concern with language and desire, and with the woman as other. An unobtrusive but important presence is George's absent sister Ellen. He was happy with her once, at Maidenhead, and she died. George's 'instructions' are to return, after killing Netta, to Maidenhead where everything will be all right, at last. As in *Coming Up for Air*, Maidenhead turns out to be 'not of any use', the one source of happiness, once, the maidenhead and Ellen, of no use. Ellen is Netta reversed, with, one might say, the Ts uncrossed, softened. As George drowns Netta, he says, 'It's all right. Don't be frightened' – which is exactly what he 'hears' Ellen say to him as he dies himself, holding her hand in imagination among the 'great coloured whorls of whisky and gas'. Ellen's hand reassures self against the terrors of the woman as other: and it is the novel's master-stroke to recognize and re-present that other in the realm of language. Netta (the cross tease) is torment merely as a word:

Netta. The tangled net of her hair – the dark net – the brunette. The net in which he was caught – netted. Nettles. The wicked poison-nettles from which had been brewed the potion which was in his blood. Stinging nettles. She stung and wounded him with words from her red mouth. Nets. Fishing-nets. Mermaid's nets. Bewitchment. Syrens – the unearthly beauty of the sea. Nets. Nest. To nestle against her. Rest. Breast. In her net. Netta.

Language slides in its agonizing associativeness; the object of desire evades being netted, but also operates as a net, entrapping in its collusiveness all efforts towards definition. George tires of concentrating on a newspaper's list of films ('*Astoria*, Ger. 5528. Racket Busters (A), 1.35, 4.20, 7.10, 10. Rich Man, Poor Girl (U), 12, 2.45, 5.30, 8.20. News, etc.'), of the wearying processes of signification, and just goes to the *Plaza* 'because he usually went there when he was up like this'. A number of chapters are headed with entries from Roget's *Thesaurus* and with literary excerpts; the latter cumulatively threaten rather than reassure with the weight of traditional authority, while the former enact hypnotic dances around blandly crucial words (*excitation*, *drunk*, *provoke*); both are in poignant contrast with George's 'dumb' inarticulacies and silence. Netta is an (unsuccessful) actress who schemes towards fame, and whose friends chatter in a private, glamorously seedy argot. George, painfully direct and simple in speech, is caught in the net of her language, her lies and evasions, the woman as volatility, the illusions and elusion of the artist: the dumb Bone caught in the evanescent Net. So it is with uncanny appropriateness that, having killed Netta (and Peter), George feels impelled to wind thread elaborately round the flat's furniture and fittings, as if preserving the bodies from 'meddling' in a structure that is at once a cat's cradle (his own body cradles a cat in his lodgings, his one physical intimacy), a web-like trap and a maze: a private place with everything in order, 'all threaded together' and all 'gathered up' – their bones in his net.

The novels of Henry Green (real name Henry Yorke, 1905–73), use birds. Peacocks in *Loving* (1945) strut across the lawns of the English-run Irish country-house in wartime, one of them mindlessly throttled by an odious English child, the rest of them sullenly withdrawn by the incomprehensible Irish gardener (neutral, out of the combat). A zoology of birds (trapped and free) crowds the pages of *Living* (1929), not least in ever bolder Homeric extended images; a

dead pigeon (it was confused by fog and went 'flat into a balustrade')
is rather madly tended at the railway station where *Party Going*
(1939) is set. Somewhere in all this, most evidently in the latter case,
is a folk-memory of the Anglo-Saxon bird whose brief passage from
dark to the dark through the lighted convivial hall was taken as
emblematic of living. And the most interesting passages in *Party
Going* take a bird's-eye view of what may be read as the potentially
revolutionary moment in pre-war Europe. Thick fog has paralysed
the station; a set of bright but not very bright young things dispose
themselves in the well-cushioned station hotel and take occasional
glances at the crowd seething below them.

The crowd is like 'corpuscles in blood' and, when a narrow stream
of it moves, it is 'like veins'. Julia, looking down on it, is like a queen
'looking at subjects massed below', although to Alex the same scene
is 'like a view from the gibbet'. The king's or queen's two bodies
survey the body politic, with an uneasy recognition of the people as
royalty's own life-blood: they see the subjects who support them or
the agents of their own doom. The crowd is also a spectacle,
removed from the privileged by glass and steel. Julia 'had not
realized what this crowd was, just seeing it through glass', and the
hotel management, remembering an earlier incident in which a quiet
crowd, through sheer weight of numbers, had 'smashed everything'
in their need for shelter, has 'shut the steel doors down'. The crowd
is individual distress: Julia can hear a woman shrieking somewhere
in it, but realizes there is nothing that she, behind the glass and
steel, can do. 'One must not hear too many cries for help in this
world. If my uncle answered every begging letter he received he
would have nothing left in no time.' Pictures in one hotel room are
inspected. 'One of these was of Nero fiddling while Rome burned
. . . women reclined on mattresses in front while behind was what
was evidently a great conflagration.' In front, behind; above, below:
the crowd is chanting 'WE WANT TRAINS' (Julia 'didn't know
there were so many people in the world'), but its threatening chant
turns (although it is still menacing) to 'boisterous good humour' and
the people become 'like sheep with golden tenor voices', a Welsh
group in the crowd singing 'of the rape of a Druid's silly daughter'.
From being a sea of intimidatingly urban facelessness the crowd is
prettified like one of the other pictures in the hotel (a church in
Scotland, 'snow and sheep'), threatening only obliquely, through the
song, the rape of a 'silly' daughter of privileged, mysterious power-
holders. 'By having money' Julia feels safe ('they were underneath
and kept there'); she is assured that 'these people' aren't violent

'because they never are, they never have been in hundreds of years'. Indeed, as the platforms open, Julia sees that 'they became people again and were no longer menaces as they had been in one mass'. But they aren't really people to Julia, they're still sheep: 'she could even smile at them, they were so like sheep herded to be fold-driven, for they were safe now, they could be shepherded into pens', ready to go home. As the first train goes, Julia swallows, 'she was so afraid she was going to cry. Dear good English people, she thought, who never make trouble no matter how bad it is, come what may no matter.'

It is difficult to assess the tone intended there, in 1938 (the novel took Green many years to complete). The openly sentimental ending of *Loving* suggests that Julia's thought about the good English people is available to be read without irony; the least that can be said is that, from the perspective of *Living*, and in the light of the suggestiveness of the imagery, and the brittle, shallow observations of the young rich, this remark about the English never making 'trouble' may be freighted with bitterness close to despair.

Living (1929) is Henry Green's *tour-de-force*. It is not quite the only serious inter-war novel to register working-class life in unsentimentalized, felt sensation; Grassic Gibbon's astonishing *A Scots Quair* is the masterpiece from the period in which working history is bruisingly delivered. It is argued below that the fictions of Beckett and Jean Rhys work with alienations and disempowerment at the limits of representation; *Living* and *A Scots Quair*, though rich in experiment, lock more directly into the novel's mainstream.

Living starts by interweaving the concerns of the wealthy Dupret family who own an engineering works in Birmingham with those of a group of workers in that factory, and their families. Old men are dying in both; in both young romance is troubled. The ironic connections are telling but, as if conscious that his text is constrained by the double perspective, Green (who, like young Dupret, formatively acquainted himself with his family factory in Birmingham) focuses ever closer, but with a broader and deeper intensity, on the story of Lily Gates and her attempt to escape, with her man Bert Jones, from her narrow horizons to Liverpool where his parents live. The attempt fails. At the novel's opening three men, including her unsympathetic father and her sympathetic grandfather, fail to release a trapped bird from a window; her motherly neighbour Mrs Eames gently and easily frees the bird. Mrs Eames's new baby, at the novel's close, is Lily's comfort and release after the agonizing failure to untrap herself in her bid for a new start, for motherhood, for not being 'like the others'. Lily's perceptions of her constriction in Birmingham are fraught with eloquence:

She saw in feeling. She saw in every house was woman with her child. In all streets, in clumps, were children.

Here factories were and more there, in clumps. She saw in her feeling, she saw men working there, all the men, and girls and the two were divided, men from women.

All was black with smoke, here even, by her, cows went soot-covered and the sheep grey. She saw milk taken out from them, grey the surface of it. Yes, and blackbird fled across that town flying crying and made noise like noise made by ratchet. Yes and in every house was mother with her child and that was grey and that fluttered hands and then that died, in every house died those children to women. Was low wailing low in her ears.

The celebrated mannerist style is utterly functional here; in the later work it seems more willed.

In Liverpool Bert cannot find where his parents have moved to, and the journey through the intimidating city, from poor to poorest addresses, enacts for Lily a nightmare of yet deeper entrapment. Bert's stinging failure shames him into seeing that 'he couldn't ask her to take on any wife's life in this town, the ordinary kind of life anywhere, when she'd come out to get on in the world' and that 'now was nothing but to leave her get home'. What follows is as painful in its quiet immediacy as anything in the period (and the shift into and out of the present tense is particularly deft and poignant):

Here they were in this tall street. He stopped by lamp post where trams stopped. She stopped. Then he sees she is crying quietly. He comes close to her and she leans a little on him. He stood for a bit then he said, 'Lil, here's your bag.' Without thinking, she was all blank, she reached down to pick it up. She looks up to him then. But he was running away down this street. She picked up bag and began to run after him, still not realizing and like obediently, like small children run, in steps, not strides. She put forefinger in her mouth. She could not see distinctly so did not see him turn down alley way. (When he got into dark court at end of this alley he crouches down in a corner beyond cone of light which falls in front of it.) He looks back over his shoulder but she had not seen him turn, she is still trotting.

At one point Lily watches a neighbour digging: 'She wondered at him digging in that unfruitful earth and that he was out of work and most likely would be for most of the rest of his days. There he was digging land which was worn out.' Literally and figuratively worn out, and wearing out its people.

A Scots Quair (1932–4), the masterly trilogy by the Scots Marxist, Lewis Grassic Gibbon (1901–35), operates symphonically, developing the inter-penetrating contexts of a woman's life, in family, class, community, country and nation-state. Here working Scottish people are given their voice for their history. Chris Guthrie is a crofter's daughter in the Grampians, and the novel tells the story of her and of working Scotland for the thirty or so years from before the First World War. This it does in extraordinarily compelling language, proudly regional and exorbitantly resourceful, richly textured and resonant, rhythmic and comic, and from a narrative perspective that is multifarious in its generous and unsentimental sympathies. It is a work of such rich and startling originality that it seems odd to reflect how solid it is (unlike Rhys and Beckett) in its mastery of novelistic tradition. (Hardy and Lawrence may come to mind, but then so may Joyce and Woolf, and so may Dickens, Gaskell and Sterne.) Not least startling is the fact that it is by a man, albeit one writing under the pseudonym of what is in all but a syllable his mother's maiden name, for among other things *A Scots Quair* is (if a male reader can say so) the most forceful psycho-sexual study of a developing woman available in this period. This force derives from the radical perception of Chris's subjectivity (her name's ambiguity is pertinent) as constituted in a network of belongings, bondings and bindings, in a process that registers the provisionality and vulnerabilities of identity, its dependencies and remakings in terms both of sexual psychology and of political history.

This sense of identity's fluidity is underpinned by the novel's extravagant habit of dropping in and out of second- as well as third-person address, not just with Chris and her intimates but, disconcertingly, with those uncomprehending of or hostile to her or hers. The effect is to expose, but in sympathetic comedy, the limitations of that incomprehension. The comedy needs emphasis as Gibbon can sound portentous in summary. In the third volume Chris sees a Hollywood film and (unlike Lily Gates who is hypnotized in an equivalent scene) her response is a bravura demolition-job:

Chris was just thinking it fairly was time, would they never get the job over and done? – when in rushed the hero and a fight began and chairs were smashed and vases and noses, and the lass crouched down with her cami-knicks showing but respectable still, she wouldn't yield a inch to anything short of a marriage licence. And that she got in the end, all fine, with showers of flowers and the man with the face like a mislaid ham cuddling her up with a kiss that looked as though he was eating his supper when the thing came banging to an end at last.

The three volumes signify in their titles a process of hardening and tightening. From the *Sunset Song* of seasonal farm work on the croft, to the darkening *Cloud Howe* in a community of miners and weavers, to the *Grey Granite* of factory work in the city; from the open community of grandly eccentric crofters in their scattered houses, to the Manse in the class-divided town, to the constrictions and necessities of a boarding-house in the city; from the vague threat of land-buyers and developers, to the uncertain motives of English absentee landlords, to the all too obvious stranglehold of armament-making corporations. Chris herself negotiates a sense of herself divided into three (the Scottish child, the English student, the Chris of dawning sexuality), and her perceptions of herself hardening to experience ('light after light went down, hope and fear and hate') are entangled with her son Ewan's hardening of social awareness, from archaeological curiosity towards the past, to a cool contempt for political systems, to commitment to revolutionary activity (a crucial moment finds him, like his mother, deconstructing received art: at a picture gallery a 'flaring savage sickness' makes him read the pictures 'as though suddenly unblinded', seeing what they suppress and depend on, 'the poor folk since history began, bedevilled and murdered, trodden underfoot'). The reflections Chris sees in mirrors at other crucial moments are articulated against a pattern of triangular dependencies, with suggestions of incestuous and homoerotic energies between mother and son, and mother and her son's lover Ellen. A creative tension thus persists between history's hardening processes and the dissolving and reforming of emotional ties. And structurally determinate is the novel's movement from country to city to country (where Chris returns), utter in its refusal to valorize one at the expense of the other; and overreaching that is the intimation of the longest story, the one that starts in primitive communism and ends ('we're all on leading strings out of the past'), somehow, in socialism: this great novel's thirty years being, in that context, both a long and a very short time.

III

A game of chess is played in *Murphy* (1938). The players devote their opening five moves not to developing control of the board's centre but to developing (if that is the word) on the board's margins, and their next four moves to bringing the developed pieces (no doubt suitably refreshed) back to their original positions. This formality over, they play with disconcertingly pointless elaboration, only modified when White adopts a surprising suicidal game-plan, committing his pieces to more and more unmistakable martyrdom. But Black is too austerely preoccupied with his elaborations to take notice, or pieces, and so no capture is effected throughout the game. The marginal meanderings, the mirror-imaged process, the obsessive elaborations, and the gesticulations of presence-in-absence are symptomatic gestures towards the goal of coherent meaning, a goal characteristically receding towards illusion in the novels and fables of Samuel Beckett (1906–89).

One internal mechanism of this fiction is the self's convoluted shadow-boxing with itself, the relationships, and the flight from those relationships, between the speaking voice and the unnameable terrors, or silences, of unitary identity; one external mechanism is the quest or journey. The journeys are inverted or regressive pilgrimages, impelled not to knowledge, insight or spiritual contentment, but (at best) to an evacuation of purpose, a cancellation of quest: Pascal's goal of being able to sit quietly, in a room. Beckett's narrator–narratees yearn for a suspension of process (Molloy hears its voice and it is 'of a world collapsing endlessly'). They do not do so because of the need, common to much 1930s writing, to slough off the burden of identity in order to incorporate it elsewhere, across some border or other (geographical, political, sexual) which must be actively negotiated and crossed; the yearning is at once more absolute and more characterless. It is also more vulnerable, and Watt, Beckett's most oddly touching narratee, most startlingly embodies it.

It is easy to discount (not least because it is not always in print) the radical originality of *Watt* (1954; written 1943), a masterpiece of de-refamiliarizing, a comic-poignant construct that creates its own conventions while seeming unconcerned by their extravagant oddities, and that locks, with an uncanny purposelessness, on to the most urgent of anxieties: the uneasy and tenuous hold of quotidian circumstance, the ambivalent needs to belong and to find authority, the fears of exile, of displacement, of the losses of employment, purpose, reason. Like much of Beckett, it is fable with the compelling authority of allegory, but its manner is neither authoritative nor loftily interpretative, but obliquely, confidingly consonant with the attritions of material lived experience – just making them (very) strange.

Beckett underwent a violently productive half-dozen or so writing years after the Second World War: in them he wrote *Watt*, *Godot*, the great trilogy, as well as important novellas. Beckett's war (he chose to remain in the Resistance in France) was difficult and dangerous; in these texts can be read, in correspondingly violent refraction, the tensed strangenesses of occupied and unoccupied territories, minds, bodies, languages: the figurations of the defamiliarized.

The most defamiliarizing feature of *Watt* is not, for all its permutationary wonders, the succession of heavily charged insignificancies, but Watt himself. He is a figure of bewildering pathos, at an odd narrative angle to the book's repertoire of comic extravagancies. At both outset and end he is represented as an inconvenient object ('a parcel, a carpet for example, or a roll of tarpaulin, wrapped up in dark paper and tied about the middle with a cord'); and the novel's promiscuous narrative perspectives have the effect of colluding in a process that exerts pressure on Watt's diffident grasp of identity in two ways: by the dis-informing and de-forming processes of being in Mr Knott's household, and by a pervasive uncertainty as to the sources of the narrative material. The result is that Watt's pathos seems a casual by-product – something awkward and embarrassing, an uncertain prickly intimacy.

In Mr Knott's service, Watt 'found himself in the midst of things which, if they consented to be named, did so as it were with reluctance'. Of one, and at one, of Mr Knott's pots, for example, 'it was in vain that Watt said, Pot, pot. Well, perhaps not quite in vain, but very nearly'. For the more Watt reflects, the less of a pot it seems. 'It resembled a pot, it was almost a pot, but it was not a pot of which one could say, Pot, pot, and be comforted'. And Watt makes the 'distressing discovery' that the same applies (under Mr Knott's dispensations) to himself. He had 'found it a help, from time to time, to be able to say, with some appearance of reason, Watt is a man, all the same, Watt is a man, or, Watt is in the street, with thousands of fellow-creatures within call'. But no longer. Nor does it help, in his need of 'semantic succour', to 'set to trying names on things' (saying of the pseudopot, for instance, 'after reflection, It is a shield, or, growing bolder, It is a raven, and so on'), for he cannot imagine what to call himself, if not a man. 'So he continued to think of himself as a man, as his mother had taught him, when she said, There's a good little man, or, There's a bonny little man, or, There's a clever little man. But for all the relief that this afforded him, he might just as well have thought of himself as a box, or an urn.'

The waverings here, where we (as Watt) expect to be 'comforted' by solidities, are at once disturbing – threatening dissolution and abandonment – and, oddly, reassuring, as the impossibility of knowing and the struggle to name are presented with an earnestness such that it disallows an appeal (and thus does appeal) to the pathetic. In the same passage, Watt is said to hope, 'of a thing of which he had never known the name, that he would learn the name, some day, and so be tranquillized'. Not enlightened through a grasp of solidities; but put to rest, the mind quietened, or drugged.

Watt journeys to and from stations, his *via dolorosa* (staunching 'inconspicuously, with the little red sudarium that he always carried in his pocket, the flow of blood' after Lady McCann spiritedly throws a stone at him), and into, up and out of Mr Knott's household, his employment prospects always already apparently incorporating randomly timed obsolescence. Watt's eventual finishing point, but only eventual in literal time, is a home for the mentally impaired, where his story (in part) is discovered to be (to be being, or to be having been) retailed to 'Sam', an inmate of an adjoining (mirror-image) home. But the final section of the novel is at a railway station, where Watt is an inconvenient object, again.

After leaving Mr Knott, Watt is, comprehensively, in retreat. In retreat from logic and syntax, his narrative to Sam (conveyed between their retreats) emerges in all varieties of inversion and regression; at its close Sam's poor eyes follow him 'over the deep threshing shadows backwards stumbling, towards his habitation'; in retreat from all expectations, his request for a ticket at the station is for 'the end of the line': the 'nearer end', he first thinks he wants, but then he asks for the 'farther end'. It is a potent and moving emblem.

Far or near, collapsing endlessly; and each movement compromised in its emblem or pattern. Mirror-image, circle – and also spiral and pendulum. *The Unnameable* (last volume of the great trilogy, written in French, 1951–3) imagines the narratee arriving home 'turning, faster and faster, more and more convulsive, like a constipated dog, or one suffering from worms, overturning the furniture, in the midst of my family all trying to embrace me at once, until by virtue of a supreme spasm I am catapulted in the opposite direction and gradually leave backwards, without having said good-evening'; earlier, he suspects that he is located at a still point within a huge circular structure, on which his putative narratee-ancestors ('all these Murphys and Molloys and Malones'), or some or one of them, revolve, periodically homing (not the word) into view. *Molloy* (the first volume) proceeds with cunning:

Having heard, or more probably read somewhere, in the days when I thought I would be well advised to educate myself, or amuse myself, or stupefy myself, or kill time, that when a man in a forest thinks he is going forward in a straight line, in reality he is going in a circle, I did my best to go in a circle, hoping in this way to go in a straight line.

Elsewhere, after a rest, 'I resumed my spirals'. An analogous theatrical puzzle faces directors of *Waiting for Godot* (originally in French, 1953): does Act II see Pozzo and Lucky enter from the same side of the stage as they used in Act I, or the opposite? The former suggests that they are caught on a vast (inwardly spiralling?) structure; the latter that they swing to and fro, as on a pendulum (slowing down?).

Watt ends, in a home, backwards; his novel ends in a waiting-room, preparing for a terminus. The narrative of *Molloy* is his abortive journey home, to his mother, to 'settle the matter between us', the old primal score. Molloy's crippled quest takes him, instead, to a mother-figure, Lousse, whose dog, having been run over by Molloy on his bicycle, he reasonably enough helps bury: this burial, he notes, may as well be his, for Lousse requires him to fill the place of the dog that filled the place of a child. There he spends his time, largely in the garden, which men ceaselessly labour to preserve from 'apparent change', his activities circumscribed to now and then 'making a little bound in the air', and ('less surprisingly') suddenly collapsing 'like a puppet when its strings are dropped'. Thence, and with uncertain eventuality, his quest takes him to a boundary, a ditch, between the forest and the plain, on which further movement is deemed pointless, across which he sees a town which might be his mother's and from which he longs ('though not a real longing') to return to the forest. That is where his narrative ends: but it begins delivered from his mother's room ('it's I who live there now') and he doesn't know how he got there. Moran (whose narrative forms the second half of *Molloy*) has (meanwhile?), accompanied by his son, been sent out, by his employer Youdi, to find Molloy. What he is expected to do with him, once found, is vexingly unclear. The double narratives both invite and repel unitary reading; the variously absent, dominant presences of Youdi and Molloy's mother – the outer and inner rims of its structure – may none the less be said to hold the novel in uneasy, generative tension.

Beckett left Ireland for Paris in 1937, and left behind his mother-tongue and his mother. He made his language double, to shuttle between the proud ancestries, as if in only provisional association with both. And Irishness is mother, the blandishments and bindings of eloquence, the illusions of identifying wholeness. But the father's demands are only binding in a different way. In the late (and surprisingly autobiographical) novella, *Company* (1980), two incidents are, in this respect, very expressive. In one the narratee is made to recall climbing, as a child, a tall tree, overhearing his mother discussing him with a neighbour ('he has been a very naughty boy'), and throwing himself off, the boughs breaking his fall; in the other (later?) incident the boy is being encouraged, by his father bobbing up and down in the swell beneath him, to jump ('be a brave boy') from a high board into the sea. The invitation to manly camaraderie is an ordeal that obscurely involves jumping on to the father; the bid for the mother's attention, to spite her obscurely perceived betrayal, is by self-obliteration. From the tall, upright object; into the swelling liquid.

If Molloy's mother is the narrative goal of *Molloy*, the presiding genius, the father, is Youdi (Yahweh? Urizen?). Youdi, who sends the emissary Gaber (Gabriel? Gabbler?) to Moran with his detecting instructions to find Molloy, is one of a number of Beckett's shadowy, doubtfully benevolent deity-figures, another of whom is Watt's Mr Knott. (Godot is another.) Their authority promises knowledge and enlightenment; in practice (not that they practise) they elude, evade and bemadden. Masters of inactivity and absence, their wills are inflexible and impenetrable. (Moran will explain to Youdi: 'What would I explain to him? I would crave his forgiveness. Forgiveness for what?') Their terrestrial representatives are dimwitted amnesiacs; they are sticklers for order, details, reports. Their word is, in its various inscriptions, the source of darkness in Beckett's enterprise. Godot will not come today but surely tomorrow. Youdi delivers himself of an opinion, relayed to Gaber who travels the wastes of Ballyba to relay it to the ravaged Moran (whose condition has duplicated Molloy's):

He said to me, said Gaber, Gaber, he said, life is a thing of beauty, Gaber, and a joy for ever. He brought his face nearer mine. A joy for ever, he said, a thing of beauty, Moran, and a joy for ever. He smiled. I closed my eyes. Smiles are all very nice in their own way, very heartening, but at a reasonable distance. I said, Do you think he meant human life? I listened. Perhaps he didn't mean human life, I said. I opened my eyes. I was alone.

Watt, who never heard Mr Knott speak, or laugh, or cry, once 'heard him make a strange noise, *PLOPF* PLOPF *Plopf* Plopf *plopf* plopf plop plo pl. This was in the flower garden.' A song of decreation, calling his creatures into (k)not(t)-being.

Moran and Watt unlearn, dis-integrate. Like Bunyan's pilgrim, Moran takes good note, at the outset, of his wicket-gate (Molloy leaves Lousse's changeless garden through its wicket-gate); back from his pilgrimage to dereliction, he smashes it open, hurling himself at it. 'I had come home, as Youdi had commanded me.' He lives in the garden, trying, like Gulliver with his horses, to understand the language of wild birds, 'without having recourse to mine'. His report for Youdi – his father's will – will be done.

Moran's narrative is and is not his report to Youdi: Watt's narrative is and is not his telling it to Sam. Stories in Beckett are typically the process of being impelled to tell stories, to keep out the silence, to tell stories of others to keep out the story of self. The energies of Beckett's fabulists have a source in the desire, recognizable in Shakespeare's most articulate artificers, Hamlet and Iago, to avoid or forget their own formlessness. The voice that comes to the 'one in the dark' in *Company* has a 'trait' of repetitiousness, as if 'willing him by this dint to make it [that is, what is said] his. To confess. Yes I remember ... To have the hearer have a past and acknowledge it.' The voice is intolerable ('at each slow ebb hope slowly dawns that it is dying'), but the 'craving' for its companionship recognizes the worse horror of 'the unthinkable last of all. Unnameable. Last person. I. Quick leave him.' The narrator of *Ill Seen Ill Said* (1981) despairingly wishes that his fictive creation 'could be pure fiction. Unalloyed.'

Malone (in *Malone Dies*, the second volume of the trilogy) is a peculiarly inventive storyteller, his impending demise giving urgency to his invention. Two of his characters call for particular comment. One is Lemuel, the warden of the home where Macmann, Malone's narratee, (nearly) ends. Lemuel (Gulliver's name: but also Le/Samuel, the reified author) embodies the masochistic mutilations of authorship. 'Flayed alive by memory, his mind crawling with cobras, not daring to dream or think and powerless not to, his cries were of two kinds, those having no other cause than moral anguish and those, similar in every respect, by which he hoped to forestall same.' He carries a hammer, the more conveniently to deal himself blows, and 'the part he struck most readily, with his hammer, was the head, and that is understandable, for it too is a bony part, and sensitive, and difficult to miss, and the seat of all the shit and misery, so you rain blows upon it, with more pleasure than on the leg for example, which never did you any harm, it's only human'. The other is Mrs Lambert, the young wasted wife of a pig-slaughterer. The brief account of her alone is surprisingly poignant; its further interest lies in its premonition of a late series of narrator-narratee women in the fiction and the plays, the mother's presence at last. 'Her day of toil over, day dawned on other toils within her, on the crass tenacity of life and its diligent pains.' The weary tribulations find little relief: 'it helped her, when things were bad, to cling with her fingers to the worn table at which her family would soon be united, waiting for her to serve them.' Without comfort or solace 'her mind was a press of formless questions, mingling and crumbling limply away'. The figment-woman of *Ill Seen Ill Said* is one evening followed by a lamb: 'Reared for slaughter like the others it left them to follow her.' The observing voice notices that the woman's puniness 'leaps to the eye. Thanks it would seem to the lowly creature next her.' Together they move towards some (grave?) stones, where she sits. 'Does she see the white body at her feet? Head haught now she gazes into emptiness. That profusion.'

There's no lack of void, in Beckett's fiction. But the word 'void' is less than useful if it suggests mere vacuity; its terrorizing force needs to be activated and is, in the visions and prospects ('inspiring prospects') of Beckett's men and women, getting on with their impoverishments as with their urges to communicate. 'Thanks, I suppose', says the urchin whose dropped marble Molloy restores to him; it's a cherishable enough remark, being remarked at all: a recognition, however etiolated. Otherwise the inviting 'relief of letting go: tumbling comfortably into the abyss' (which 'one day, no doubt, one will grow used to') – into, for instance, starvation which 'has its compensations, but they do not come at once' – is all too obvious and obviously was in this period, not least for Jean Rhys (1890–1979) (one of whose early Paris stories, collected in *The Left Bank* (1927), is quoted above). Her spare, fraught novels beat the bounds of their own trapped intimacies with a delicacy as precise as it is shocking; Rhys's unplanned project seems, in retrospect, like Beckett's, at the other end of the period, to make modernism's unvaunted affiliation to the abandoned and exploited, to the lost ones journeying to and from homes, to women. She herself was routinely abandoned and forgotten and then (the literary sensation) rediscovered in a famous flurry of publishing activity. ('Too late', she said.)

Jean Rhys's place in literary history is hedged about by paradox. Like Emily Dickinson (one of whose poems furnishes the title of her most assured novel), she operated both vulnerably and resiliently, within and quite without the usual literary resources; an *ingénue* abroad, she was formidably well-read (Dickinson in 1939?); she wrote out of her life and 'for' herself, but was obsessively self-critical over minutiae, retrospectively deeming her last novel prematurely published because of two superfluous words; her work seems nakedly autobiographical, and is more fictionalized than it seems; it is artless and highly crafted; it appears to be focused from the exclusive narrative viewpoint of the one vulnerable woman – and yet it is not, the 'she' of the sympathetic narrative consciousness (of *After Leaving Mr Mackenzie* (1930), for instance) sliding, on the one hand, into the 'one' and 'you' of greater intimacy and, on the other, without warning, into the thwarted, frustrated or mechanical intimacies (or worse) of a quite other (female or male) narrative voice. The enabling paradox of vulnerability and resilience makes for a surprising and fluid deployment of interior and exterior narrative consciousnesses. It implies both the self-focused certainty of the child's vision and the disciplined scrutiny of adult self-criticism. Two further features of narrative perspective derive from the same paradox: a poignant recourse to quoted thought, regretfully not uttered (yet vulnerably available for scrutiny); and the disconcerting habit, in dialogue, of following a paragraph ending, for instance, 'he said' with another from the same source, the effect being that we hear and don't hear the hopeless no-reply (what to say? why bother saying it?) pressured silently between the paragraphs.

Rhys's pre-war novels deal with the salient features of a life marked by exile and homelessness ('perpetually moving to another place which was perpetually the same'), by deferred and thwarted longings and by an unrelentingly wearying perception of social process. The penniless young woman, exiled from her richly perplexed, heightened sensations of Dominica and its own social exclusions, estranged from a mother's intimacies ('from being the warm centre of the world her mother had gradually become a dark, austere, rather plump woman'), finds England cold, grim ('my nicest Cambridge memory was of the day an undergraduate on a bicycle knocked me flat') and money-obsessed, Paris more relieving to the spirit (London 'tells you all the time, "Get money, get money, get money, or be for ever damned." Just as Paris tells you to "forget, forget, let yourself go"'). She works disconsolately for and is exploited, adopted and abandoned by men, drifting, surviving, ever raw to experience's touch. It is a story (or, rather, half a dozen books) disquieting because it is both shockingly routine and also compulsively odd in its muted intensities.

At the centre, and yet at a curiously oblique angle to the texts, is the figure of woman as an alienated exile, fissured by the paradoxical needs and resiliences of this one woman, parcelled out among the personae of the novels and stories, suspended somewhere between wars, European capitals and Dominica, at difficult ages, at difficult odds with sexual ethics. A divided consciousness offers at once the frank admission of the 'perpetual hunger to be beautiful . . . and to be loved' and the need to beg the world 'not to notice that they were women or to hold it against them'; inside, there is the 'heart a heavy jagged weight', outside, the 'big advantage' of looking 'just like most other people'; there are unaccountable fears ('the last time you were happy about nothing; the first time you were afraid about nothing. Which came first?') and ungainsayable memories ('she accepted all she was told to accept, tried to remember all she was told to remember. The trouble was she could not always forget all she was told to forget'). Like Beckett, Rhys records failure, in painstaking response to compelling voices within. 'I don't know what I want. And if I did I couldn't say it', and yet 'the trouble is I have plenty to say. Not only that but I am bound to say it.' And if it is not written, 'I will not have earned death. Sometimes, not often, a phrase will sound in my ear clearly, as if spoken aloud by someone else. That was one phrase. You must earn death.'

Wide Sargasso Sea (1966), where the pains were most evidently taken (Rhys only allowed its long delayed publication after dreaming of giving birth to 'a puny weak thing'), is her most celebrated book, but it is less focused and more willed than the pre-war novels, the best of which is *Good Morning, Midnight* (1939). The accounts of abortion (*Voyage in the Dark*, 1934) and of the mother's death (*After Leaving Mr Mackenzie*, 1930) have unforgettable immediacy, but *Midnight*, in which the narrator is back in Paris in her late thirties ('but I've never been young') after the 'bright idea' of drinking to death in London, in conditions that curiously replicate Malone's ('my supper of a glass of milk and bread and cheese on the ledge outside. On this ledge you also put the dirty plates when you had finished eating'), is unremitting in its pressure and, even more than the spectacular last pages of *Sargasso Sea*, its ending has overwhelming power. In 'what they call an impasse' with her past, gingerly, as if in what Emily Dickinson calls the 'Trance' by virtue of which 'Memory can step/Around – across – upon' the painfulness of the past's 'Abyss', Sasha revisits the painfully associative bars and restaurants, dressed in clothes that 'extinguish' her (but in a fur coat that finally betrays her), her nerves shredded by the 'rosy, wooden, innocent cruelty' of human eyes in everyday encounter ('boiled eyes, served cold'), agitatedly determined not to 'grimace and posture before these people' and yet 'indifferent' underneath, as in calm 'stagnant water'.

Two memories haunt with especial horror. One is of Sasha's baby. The room in the 'funny house' where people are 'having babies all over the place' is not ready for Sasha; she has to wait and walk about for seven hours: 'Has anybody ever had to do this before? Of course, lots of people – poor people. Oh, I see, of course, poor people.' When at last in the room, she hears other labouring mothers: '"Jesus, Jesus", says one woman. "Mother, Mother", says another. I do not speak. How long is it before I speak? "Chloroform, chloroform", I say when I speak. Of course I would. What nonsense! There is no doctor to give chloroform here. This is a place for poor people . . . No Jesus, no Mother, and no chloroform either . . .' In her labour she sees that 'I am an instrument, something to be made use of', and after the birth she is no more illusioned: 'I don't know if I love him. But the thought that they will crush him because we have no money – that is torture.' Eventually unbandaged Sasha is, as she was promised, unchanged: 'not one line, not one wrinkle, not one crease. And there he is, lying with a ticket tied round his wrist because he died in a hospital. And there I am looking down at him, without one line, without one wrinkle, without one crease.' The unblinking vision is the more harrowing for its vague but no less certain identification of the 'they' who will (and do) 'crush' the impoverished.

The other memory is of a job in a luxury clothes shop. A mannequin elsewhere in her novels, Rhys's understanding of the precariousness of the woman's self-image is made more acute by its placing in the context of the peculiar commodification of that image in fashion and its marketing. Breaking down, faced with the cold aggression of her English manager in the shop, Sasha rushes and hides – in a 'hardly ever used' fitting room – to cry 'for all the fools and all the defeated'. In the fitting room, with yet more ghastly appropriateness, is a dress, worn so much by the mannequins, that she has been promised it cheap. 'It is my dress. If I had been wearing it I should never have stammered or been stupid.' Now, 'utterly defeated', she knows she will 'never have that dress'. But it is in that defeat that she perceives the brute powers of economic division. She addresses the manager: 'You, who represent Society, have the right to pay me four hundred francs a month . . . to lodge me in a small, dark room, to clothe me shabbily, to harass me with worry and monotony and unsatisfied longings' – and the right is his because 'that's my market value, for I am an inefficient member of Society, slow in the uptake, uncertain, slightly damaged in the fray, there's no denying it'. It would be 'so much less fun' if we were all happy and rich for 'some must cry so that the others may be able to laugh the more heartily. Sacrifices are necessary' – and particularly so as to enable you 'to despise the people you exploit', the right held

8

POETRY IN THE 1930s AND 1940s

Grevel Lindop

I

The 1930s were a self-conscious decade. At the beginning of 1930 journalists and literary editors were asking – sometimes in these very words – 'What will the Thirties bring?' By the end of 1940 Auden had labelled the period 'a low dishonest decade' and David Gascoyne had written a 'Farewell Chorus' to the 'grim Thirties'. To see the 1930s as a period with a particular identity is not unreasonable: history itself seems to bracket the years as a time of painful insecurity and transition from the bad to the worse. Crisis dominated, from the Wall Street Crash of 1929 and the Great Depression which followed, through the bitter violence of the Spanish Civil War to the outbreak of the Second World War in September 1939. In Britain it was a period of mass unemployment, poorly resisted by a trade-union movement weakened by the failed General Strike of 1926. Partly as a result of that defeat, leadership of the political 'left' passed from the unions to a Labour Party theoretically more extreme but, once Ramsay MacDonald had joined a Conservative-dominated coalition government in 1931, actually almost powerless. Since the 'left' came to encompass very many of those who wished to see honest and intelligent responses to the problems of the time, these conditions lent an air of unreality to the period's politics: there was much talking and writing, much argument and propaganda, but surprisingly little was achieved.

Poetry was not especially popular. The most widely read verse-writer of the decade was probably Patience Strong, the first volume of whose uplifting doggerel sold 100,000 copies in its first year. Auden's *Look, Stranger!*, selling 2,350 in three months, was considered a best-seller for 'serious' verse (figures from Valentine Cunningham, *British Writers of the Thirties*, 1989, p 297). The small world of those who wrote and read 'modern' poetry, however, was an energetic and highly articulate one. Many little magazines sprang up and died;

the most successful, like Geoffrey Grigson's *New Verse* and John Lehmann's *New Writing* (the stress on 'newness' is typical of the period), were influential, and the poets they championed were in many cases taken up as 'personalities' by radio and the press, becoming known by name to countless people who never read their poems.

The peculiar nature and predicament of poetry in the 1930s are exemplified in the career of the poet who also dominated the decade, W. H. Auden (1907–73). Wystan Hugh Auden spent a comfortable, middle-class childhood in Birmingham. From an early age he was fascinated by mythology (especially Norse mythology) and by what would now be called industrial archaeology: he loved railways, machinery and even the Solihull gasworks near his home, and dreamed of becoming a mining engineer. At about the age of fifteen, however, he made two important discoveries. One was that he wanted to write poetry; the other was that he was homosexual.

In 1925 he went to Oxford, initially to read biology but soon changing to English. He wrote prolifically and his poetic gifts, impatient energy and dominant personality soon made him the centre of a circle of devotees – a situation that was to persist throughout his life. Among those who came under his spell were Cecil Day-Lewis, Stephen Spender and Christopher Isherwood, who was not at Oxford but whose autobiographical novel *Lions and Shadows* (1938) gives a vivid picture of the young Auden as 'Weston'.

Spender and Isherwood shared Auden's homosexuality and, although Auden avoided intense relationships (pursuing a vigorous but casual sex life), the circle was linked by sexual attitudes as well as literary aspirations. After Auden left Oxford with a third-class degree in 1928, it was Stephen Spender who printed, partly on his own hand-press, Auden's first publication, a thirty-seven-page pamphlet entitled *Poems*. T. S. Eliot at Faber and Faber had already rejected a collection of his poems, but in 1930 Faber published a new book containing thirty short poems and a 'Charade', *Paid on Both Sides*. Once again, the title was simply *Poems*.

By now Auden was working as a schoolteacher, having first spent nearly a year in Berlin, absorbing psychoanalysis (including an interesting if eccentric variety purveyed by followers of Homer Lane, who regarded all illness as psychosomatic and all problems as self-inflicted) and learning about politics: he had seen fighting between police and Communists, and Hitler's Brownshirts roaming the streets.

Auden's 1930 *Poems* were startlingly original. He had learnt from Eliot to use a gaunt, modern diction and from Hopkins to experiment with vigorous wrenchings of syntax and new combinations of words. His interest in science and psychoanalysis gave him a readiness to use technical terms and adopt a dispassionate, objective tone. Above all, he wrote as if the poem were an object in itself, less obliged to yield a clear, accessible 'meaning' than to be alive, intricate and intriguingly well-crafted. Isherwood's claim that he would construct new poems by putting together the best lines salvaged from discarded ones may not be factually true, but it well conveys the poems' strangeness and look of brilliant fragmentation. The concluding lines of VIII (characteristically, Auden left the poems untitled and simply numbered them) are a good example:

> The street music seemed gracious now to one
> For weeks up in the desert. Woken by water
> Running away in the dark, he often had
> Reproached the night for a companion
> Dreamed of already. They would shoot, of course,
> Parting easily who were never joined.

A story seems implied, but we cannot deduce it. Earlier lines have identified the 'he' of the poem as a 'trained spy', but more than that we do not know. Where is he? What is the running water? How real, and of what kind, is the 'companion'? Who are 'they'? Who will be 'part[ed] easily' in the impressively paradoxical last line, with its odd echo of the marriage service ('What God hath joined let no man put asunder')? One can devise any number of answers, but none gives us much purchase on the poem. Certain themes are discernible: leadership, the notion of boundaries and borders, personal insecurity, fear and threat, and these undoubtedly derive from the political situation as well as from Auden's individual experience. But at last the poem remains as teasingly obscure as it was at first. The 1930 *Poems* as a group are perhaps best regarded as fascinating labyrinths without centres: they offer countless interesting and suggestive interconnections but no decisive meanings. This is a limitation but also the source of the curious delight they offer the reader.

The dramatic piece *Paid on Both Sides* is equally strange but easier to interpret. Set in a northern landscape, in a curious a-historical time where manners and turns of speech drawn from the Icelandic sagas mix with factories, guns and football games, it presents the climax of a long-standing feud between two families, the Nowers and the Shaws. The hero, John Nower, is prompted by a bizarre revelatory dream to resolve the feud by marrying his enemy's daughter, Anne Shaw. The bride's mother, however, prefers to perpetuate the feud by bullying her son into murdering Nower after the wedding. A laconic chorus sums up:

> Though he believe it, no man is strong.
> He thinks to be called fortunate,
> To bring home a wife, to live long.
>
> But he is defeated: let the son
> Sell the farm lest the mountain fall:
> His mother and her mother won.

The 'charade' is clearly a fable about the tyranny of the past and the older generation – a theme common in the work of writers who grew up in the shadow of the First World War. Auden, however, gives it a Freudian twist, attributing the violence essentially to a dominant mother-figure and encoding its possible solution in an apparently irrational dream.

With its unabashed mingling of ancient and modern, its psychological diagnosis of evil and its tendency to view adult behaviour as the worrying antics of overgrown children, *Paid on Both Sides* established perspectives which were to be constant throughout Auden's work.

One other quality of the 1930 volume deserves mention. However puzzling the writing at times appears, its style is throughout strikingly free from wordplay, verbal ambiguity or 'denseness' of texture. At all times Auden maintains a precise, specific and lucid use of words. When the poems are cryptic, we feel it is because we are being denied some of the information we need, not because the poet is writing vaguely or constructing his phrases to yield multiple interacting ambiguities. This quality – often referred to as a 'clinical' quality in Auden's writing – sets him sharply apart from most other modern poets (in particular from Yeats and the early Eliot) and seems to have been quite deliberate, although Auden rarely acknowledged it directly. Indeed, his clearest formulations of principle in this area are easily overlooked, though highly illuminating once noticed. In 1929 he wrote in a journal:

While Yeats is right that great poetry in the past has been symbolic, I think we are reaching the point in the development of the mind where symbols are becoming obsolete in poetry. This does invalidate [symbolism] in modern poetry, just as an attempt to write in Chaucerian English would be academic.

(Edward Mendelson, ed., *The English Auden: Poems, Essays and Dramatic Writings 1927–1939*, 1977, p 11)

An aphoristic 'Short' jotted down forty years later points in the same direction:

> Psychological critics, do be more precise in your language:
> Symbols must not be confused with allegorical signs.

Critics like to find symbols, which are evocative and richly indeterminate in meaning. Auden's poetry, however, tends to the use of 'allegorical signs' – images which have a clear central meaning and refer to a region of easily recognized generalities. It is a style capable of great intelligence and playful intricacy; it is also, perhaps, the style of a writer who does not want to see, or reveal, too much of himself.

The 1930 *Poems* were received with a mixture of incomprehension (from most reviewers) and delight (from Auden's fellow-poets); but they established his name as that of a new and exciting poet. In his doggedly confident way, Auden had no intention of moderating the strangeness of his writing and his next book, *The Orators: An English Study* (1932), is perhaps the oddest he ever wrote; looking at it forty-four years later Auden himself admitted that '*The Orators* ... defeats me. My name on the title-page seems a pseudonym for someone else, someone talented but near the border of sanity' (quoted in H. Carpenter, *W. H. Auden: A Biography*, 1981, p 130).

The Orators consists mainly of three 'Books': the first, 'The Initiates', is a series of surreal prose pieces, the first of which, 'Address for a Prize-Day', is certainly one of the funniest and most brilliant things Auden ever wrote. Auden always enjoyed concocting public addresses (later examples include the 1934 prose-poem 'Sermon by an Armament Manufacturer' and, in verse, 'Under Which Lyre?', which he actually delivered from the platform at Harvard in 1946). Like all his exercises in this vein, 'Address for a Prize-Day' divides people into categories and passes judgement on them. In this case the categories are vaguely psychoanalytical: the schoolboy audience is incited to pick out 'excessive lovers' of self or of their neighbours, 'defective lovers' and 'perverted lovers' – each characterized by a rich and bizarre collection of symptoms – and to deal summarily with them:

All these have got to die without issue. Unless my memory fails me there's a stoke hole under the floor of this hall, the Black Hole we called it in my day. New boys were always put in it. Ah, I see I am right. Well look to it. Quick, guard that door. Stop that man. Good. Now boys hustle them, ready, steady – go.

Despite its school setting and Christian–psychoanalytic terminol-ogy, the address probably parodies the Nazi intimidation Auden would have come across in Berlin. The other prose sections of *The Orators* are perhaps best regarded as a kind of scrapbook into which Auden gathered a wild range of jottings, fictional and satirical fragments linked only by a recurrent concern with violence and social breakdown, and speculations on the self-importance and emo-tional instability of leaders – several passages seem to mock the cultish followings of both D. H. and T. E. Lawrence (widely regarded in the period as exemplary figures who might hold a cure for Europe's social ills). Auden probably hoped that the fragments would cohere (as, in an infinitely subtler way, the parts of *The Waste Land* do) into a vision of the contemporary world. But they do not and, as Auden himself recognized later, the book's most accessible theme – its concern with Fascism and leadership – is so mined with unmarked ironies that it can as easily seem a celebration of Fascism as an attack on it.

None the less, Auden's readers – and there were now many – had no doubt that *The Orators*, for all its fascinating obscurity, was somehow a political work, and Auden's writing soon began to show an explicit concern with politics and public events. The poems in his next volume, *Look, Stranger!* (1936), express an awareness that Britain is a haven temporarily sheltered from impending calamity, and that even here economic crisis and loss of political nerve require a new, and probably Communist, solution. 'Now from my window-sill I watch the night' invokes the 'Lords of Limit', emblematic figures of protective har-mony, to fend off violence and anarchy, and several jaunty though less impressive poems – 'Brothers, who when the sirens roar', for example (originally entitled 'A Communist to Others') – suggest that the only hope lies in a political union of worker and intellectual.

Many of Auden's friends had by now joined the Communist Party, and it was inevitable that Auden, the leading poet of his generation and one whose work would at least bear a broadly Communist interpretation, should be under some pressure to become the laureate of the Left. He was in no hurry, however, to turn propagandist, and it was a trip to Iceland with Louis MacNeice to gather material for a travel book which led to his next major poem, 'Letter to Lord Byron', written in Iceland in the summer of 1936. The 'Letter' shows Auden's usual skill with an elaborate verse-form (a seven-line stanza adapted from that of Byron's *Don Juan*), but in place of the self-protective obscurity of the earlier work it sketches a witty self-portrait, moving easily from engaging inconsequence –

> I'm writing this in pencil on my knee,
>> Using my other hand to stop me yawning,
> Upon a primitive, unsheltered quay
>> In the small hours of a Wednesday morning . . .

– to sharp reflection on contemporary culture and society:

> Britannia's lost prestige and cash and power,
>> Her middle classes show some wear and tear,
>> We've learned to bomb each other from the air;
> I can't imagine what the Duke of Wellington
> Would say about the music of Duke Ellington.

This new accessibility was sustained, and with some modification it provides the tone for Auden's most impressive political poem, 'Spain'. Auden had gone to Spain in January 1937 intending to drive an ambulance for the Republican side in the civil war. For some reason this did not happen, nor did he reach, as planned, the front around Madrid, where fighting was fierce. He found himself shocked by the faction-fighting among the Republicans and by their cruelty to the priests. Seeing a Fascist victory as the greatest danger, however, he kept his doubts to himself and immediately on his return in 1937 began 'Spain', which he finished within a month. The poem offers a brilliant bird's-eye view of human history in terms of technological development –

> Yesterday all the past. The language of size
> Spreading to China along the trade-routes; the diffusion
>> Of the counting-frame and the cromlech

– and presenting the Spanish war as both a turning-point in history and a test for the individual conscience:

> 'What's your proposal? To build the Just City? I will.
> I agree. Or is it the suicide pact, the romantic
>> Death? Very well, I accept, for
> I am your choice, your decision: yes, I am Spain.'

In the near-surreal inventiveness of its imagery, its tempering of a didactic tone with tinges of Romanticism and scientific detachment, the poem is a fascinating and delightful work, yet one feels it is not wholly honest. Its presentation of politics is unenthusiastic ('the flat ephemeral pamphlet and the boring meeting') and its vision of future democratic enjoyments almost ludicrous ('the photographing of ravens . . . The bicycle races/Through the suburbs on summer evenings'). Its hard-boiled reference to 'the necessary murder' infuriated Orwell, who, unlike Auden, had experienced battle. It is hard not to see 'Spain' as Auden's strenuous but slightly tongue-in-cheek response to what he felt was expected of him. After the *Collected Shorter Poems* of 1950 he never allowed it to be reprinted (except once, in an anthology of 1930s poetry) and it seems likely that the poem and its origins made him uneasy.

Indeed, the affair typifies the difficult situation in which Auden found himself, relentlessly praised or criticized as a public, semi-political figure who was increasingly expected to conform to a left-wing ideology about which he had serious reservations. A trip to China with Isherwood in 1938 produced the glittering sonnets of *Journey to a War* (1939) but failed to resolve his sense of political and cultural unease, and in January 1939 Auden and Isherwood left England for permanent residence in the United States.

Their emigration probably had little to do with the war which was inexorably approaching in Europe (although once it had broken out they were widely accused, in England, of cowardice) and much to do with a sense that America would provide a less claustrophobic intellectual climate. Auden was also undergoing a change of attitude, reflected in the poems he began writing soon after his arrival in New York. He had always been preoccupied by the idea of a love that transcended sexuality; as early as 1933 he had undergone an experience of mystical ecstasy that seemed to unite him with a group of friends (celebrated obliquely in his poem 'Out on the lawn I lie in bed'). Now he began to turn towards Christianity, and soon became a regular Episcopalian churchgoer.

The 'American' phase of Auden's work shows shifts of attitude and technique. He studied the syllabics of Marianne Moore, and began to use similar forms: an early example is 'In Memory of Sigmund Freud', whose stanza is built from lines with eleven, eleven, nine and ten syllables. He abandoned the cryptic tone of the earlier work; increasingly his poems become statements of a detached, quizzical but friendly observer of fallible humanity, full of sympathetic common sense but mostly without personal passion. Often the tone becomes distinctly classical (the elegy for Freud ends, 'sad is Eros, builder of cities,/And weeping anarchic Aphrodite'). Auden appears to see himself more than ever as a spokesman for his age, and his longer works approximate to 'public' forms: *The Sea and the Mirror* (1944) uses characters from *The Tempest* to explore relations between art, politics and moral values, and poses as an enormous epilogue to the play; *The Age of Anxiety* (1947), articulating the fallen human condition through the conversation and thoughts of a group of lonely New York drinkers, reads at times like an opera libretto (and indeed Auden collaborated with Chester Kallman, his lifelong companion from 1939, on a number of libretti, including that for Stravinsky's *Rake's Progress*, 1951).

It is hard not to feel that a certain energy deserted Auden's poetry after 1939. He can be as precise and wittily surprising as ever:

> . . . Not to lose time, not to get caught,
>   Not to be left behind, not, please! to resemble
> The beasts who repeat themselves, or a thing like water
>   Or stone whose conduct can be predicted, these
> Are our Common Prayer, whose greatest comfort is music
>   Which can be made anywhere, is invisible
> And does not smell.

('In Praise of Limestone')

But the relentless, if lightly worn, determination to express only a Christian-tinged common sense, to say nothing (as it were) that a modest, reflective late-twentieth-century citizen could disagree with, becomes tiresome. Despite the extraordinary individuality of his beginnings, there are resources of language, and of the self, that Auden chose not to explore, and as a result critics generally felt, when he died in 1973, that in some hard-to-define way he had never quite become the great poet his early work had promised.

II

Auden was important, however, not only as a poet but as a catalyst. As we have seen, his early work aroused keen partisanship and during the 1930s he came to be seen as the leader of a group of young poets, and his followers delivered public tributes that could be embarrassingly fulsome. Charles Madge confessed pompously: 'There waited for me in the summer morning,/ Auden, fiercely; I read, shuddered and knew.' C. Day-Lewis succumbed to masochistic hero-worship: 'Look west, Wystan, lone flier, birdman, my bully-boy!' These lines attest to the power of Auden's work, but also to the risk that it might stunt that of less robust talents.

Auden's earliest significant poetic associate was Stephen Spender (b. 1909), who met him at Oxford in 1926. Spender, formerly preoccupied with Romantic notions of the poet, was soon converted to Auden's doctrine that (as Spender later put it) 'a poet was a kind of chemist who mixed his poems out of words, whilst remaining detached from his own feelings' (Stephen Spender, *World Within World*, 1951, p 51). Leaving Oxford in 1930 Spender went to Hamburg for the first of a series of visits. He watched with horror the beginnings of Hitler's rise to power, a period he describes in his fine autobiography, *World Within World* (1951).

Spender had printed small pamphlets of poems on his own press in 1928 and 1930, but it was *Poems* (1933) which established him as a significant poet of the 'Auden generation'. The volume shows a tension between lyric impulses, a conscientious desire to engage with recalcitrant, 'modern' subject matter (typified by poems of industrial technology like 'The Express' and the 'The Pylons') and an interest in analysing the nature of the self. These tendencies run through all Spender's work, and it is the last that has been most fruitful. 'An "I" can never be great man' is an extraordinary poem exploring the delusory nature of the various self-images by which we attempt to grasp our existence:

> Central 'I' is surrounded by 'I eating',
> 'I loving', 'I angry', 'I excreting' . . .
> Quarrelling with 'I tiring' and 'I sleeping'
> And all those other 'I's who long for 'We dying'.

'My parents kept me from children who were rough' uses autobiography to examine the moral and psychological problems produced by class distinctions. Spender joined the Communist Party in 1937 soon after the outbreak of the Spanish Civil War and went to Spain to write propaganda for the Republicans. He soon became dissatisfied with Communism, but remained a prominent sympathizer with left-wing causes. This, and his continuing association with Auden, probably helped to sustain a reputation which his poetry and rather tepid literary criticism alone might not have borne. Spender's writing is often clumsy, his rhythms lame and his imagery lurching between the wildly original and the sadly conventional. 'An Elementary Classroom in a Slum', often cited as his best-known work although very few people know more of it than its title, contains vivid patches – the children, for example, include 'The stunted, unlucky heir/Of twisted bones, reciting a father's gnarled disease,/His lesson from his desk' – but collapses into sentimentality, as in the final stanza's hope that the school windows may

> Break O break open till they break the town
> And show the children to green fields, and make their world
> Run azure on gold sands.

Spender's compassion is obvious and commendable, but there is too little observation and too much rhetoric.

Such poems appealed to an appetite for socially concerned poetry, but their slackness is now evident. One feels that Spender relied too much on ideas from Auden and from his public about what he should write, and failed to discipline his talent patiently enough, producing poems of obvious but short-lived appeal. After 1950 Spender largely abandoned poetry, and probably his autobiography and his *Journals* (1985) will be his most enduring work.

Another close associate of Auden's was Cecil Day-Lewis (1904–72). Like Spender, he met Auden at Oxford (in 1925 or 1926) after an ordinary public-school career and immediately became 'a willing disciple', overwhelmed by Auden's intelligence and self-confidence as well as by his poems. Auden accepted his homage and invited him to help edit *Oxford Poetry 1927* (they wrote alternate paragraphs of the introduction). Day-Lewis, who in 1923 had published a volume of weak pastoral verse, *Beechen Vigil*, at once took to writing (in his own words) 'pastiche Auden': indeed, *Transitional Poem* (published in October 1929) marked the first public appearance of the 'Auden group' and itself helped to project the notion that such a group existed. The poem – in thirty-four untitled sections – is relentlessly bombastic. Its subject, insofar as it has one, is the quest for unity of a mind filled with confusion. Full of rich and romantic imagery, it makes great claims but conveys little:

> In that one moment of evening
> When roses are most red
> I can fold back the firmament,
> I can put time to bed . . .

It is a style that anticipates the 'New Apocalypse' poets of the 1940s. It was dedicated to Rex Warner and contains references to several other literary friends, including Auden:

> The tow-haired poet, never done
> With cutting and planing some new gnomic prop
> To jack his all too stable universe up.

(It is a sign of Day-Lewis's hero-worship that he should have seen Auden's uneasy and shifting mental universe as 'all too stable'.) The critics were not enthusiastic, but – what was perhaps more important – they recognized the poem as representing something 'new'. Its images of 'a forbidding coast/Where ironworks rust' and where 'Earth has/No promise for proprietors', its sense of the poet as one who must 'twist the dials, catch/Electric hints' from the consciousness of the time, introduced an ominous political and scientific awareness which soon became identified as the hallmark of the Auden school.

Day-Lewis's second volume, *From Feathers to Iron* (1931), although loosely focused on celebrating the birth of the poet's first child, is as 'transitional' and chaotic as its predecessor. The poet sees himself as 'waiting here between winter and summer,/Conception and fruition, . . . prepar[ing]/For a new route, a change of constitution'. Further efforts to resolve this sense of an irresolute and divided self are visible in *The Magnetic Mountain* (1931) where the future socialist state is viewed as, above all, a creator of direction, an antidote to drifting:

> Somewhere beyond the railheads
> Of reason, south or north,
> Lies a magnetic mountain
> Riveting sky to earth . . .
> Iron in the soul,
> Spirit steeled in fire,
> Needle trembling on truth –
> These shall draw me there.

The poem contains some violent rhetoric, particularly against the capitalist press:

> Scavenger barons and your jackal vassals,
> Your pimping press-gang, your unclean vessels,
> We'll make you swallow your words at a gulp
> And turn you back to your element, pulp.
> Don't bluster, bimbo, it won't do you any good;
> We can be much ruder and we're learning to shoot . . .

Yet the mixed metaphors and the puerile threats ('We can be much ruder') make it hard to take any of this seriously. Day-Lewis certainly tried to make a wholehearted commitment and joined the Communist Party in 1936; but he resigned after two years, and it is striking that throughout this period he continued to write regular literary columns for those pillars of the Conservative press, the *Daily Telegraph* and *The Spectator*. After 1935 he also produced (as 'Nicholas Blake') a series of ingenious detective novels which are models of their kind and are really a more interesting literary achievement than his poetry.

A Time to Dance (1935) was Day-Lewis's last attempt to link his natural romanticism with a tougher political awareness. Thereafter his work became blander, exploring landscape and memory in styles derived from Hardy and Edward Thomas. He became a prominent lecturer and the respected translator of Virgil; his absorption into the 'establishment' was completed by his becoming Poet Laureate in 1968. A talented minor poet, he seems to have been too swayed by contemporary fashion and by his public career as a literary figure to develop the gifts with which he began.

Sometimes regarded as a follower of Auden, although apart from an early political element he has far more affinities with the neo-Romantic poets of the 1940s, is George Barker (1913–91). The son of a policeman, Barker early devoted himself to the practice of poetry and a bohemian lifestyle (his recipe for poetry was 'a dictionary, alcohol and love', quoted in C. H. Sisson, *English Poetry 1900–1950: An Assessment*, 1981, p 24). His first book was *Calamiterror* (1937), ostensibly a meditation on the Spanish Civil War (Barker's sympathies were broadly left-wing) but largely occupied with more general reflections on the linked wonder and terror of the universe, the mysterious forces at work within life, death and the human body, and so on. These are the abiding themes of Barker's work, which shows little development. Barker is clearly interested in the sounds and rhythms of words, as well as in the idea of poetry and the poet; and whatever the ostensible subject of a poem, it tends to be these concerns that dominate. His work at every period (he published steadily into the 1980s) is characterized by a torrent of colourful imagery, mostly of a 'visionary' or 'archetypal' nature. Trees, rivers, birds, the sun, moon and stars, tears and blood, sand, rocks, the sea and above all the parts of the human body (particularly eye, breast, womb, heart, bones and genitals) recur endlessly in new combinations.

At its best this style creates a pictorial, even cartoon-like vividness, as in 'Kew Gardens,' where the turmoil of wartime Europe is presented through the sufferings of a pair of lovers:

> Struck at them from the sky as the Berlin Eagle
> Explored with lines of fire the environs of Russia,
> Fire and fury. With their hair on fire like fuchsia
> Fled to the Swiss lakes and dipped their faces
> In Peace like water, but were nearly drowned . . .

At last, in Kew Gardens,

> Among the bluebells, the birds, the pagodas, the paths,
> They lay a long while resting from Europe's wrath,
> While their wounds went white and were lost among the daisies.

At its worst – and often – Barker's style degenerates into a display of incoherent rhetoric. In his autobiographical poems (*The True Confession of George Barker*, 1950, and *The View from a Blind I*, 1962) the style becomes simpler but there is still a pervasive sentimentality; one feels that for Barker the notion of 'being a poet' has always taken precedence over the task of actually saying something.

Louis MacNeice (1907–63) is a poet of a very different order, although perhaps his best work arose from a personal development of techniques first made available by Auden. Although he attended a public school, followed by Oxford (where he met Auden, Spender and Isherwood), MacNeice's beginnings were rather different from those of most British poets of the period, for he was the son of an Irish Anglican clergyman. The poems of his first book, *Blind Fireworks* (1929), show a rather desparate resentment of the constricting middle-class values of his childhood:

> Dutifully sitting on chair, lying on sofa.
> Standing on hearth-rug, here we are again,
> John caught the bus, Joshua caught the train,
> And I took a taxi, so we all got somewhere;
> No one deserted, no one was a loafer,
> Nobody disgraced us, luckily for us
> No one put his foot in it or missed the bus.

('Happy Families')

Auden had guyed such family scenes with a tinge of affection: Spender had found in them a certain fascination; MacNeice, however, views them with horror. None the less some of the scepticism and detachment MacNeice displayed throughout his career may have come from his father, a Protestant Irish Nationalist who regarded sentimental Catholic nationalism and Orange Protestantism with equal distaste. When in *Poems* (1935) MacNeice began to find a distinctive voice two features became evident which were to characterize his work to the end: an interest in the hard, ungainly particulars of experience (epitomized by his most famous poem, 'Snow') and a slightly distant compassion for the individuals caught in the network of social injustice.

In 'Belfast' the shops are full of 'celluloid, painted ware, glaring/ Metal patents, parchment lampshades, harsh/Attempts at buyable beauty', while

> In the porch of the chapel before the garish Virgin
> A shawled factory-woman as if shipwrecked there
> Lies a bunch of limbs glimpsed in the cave of gloom
> By us who walk in the street so buoyantly and glib

and

> The sun goes down with a banging of Orange drums
> While the male kind murders each its woman
> To whose prayers for oblivion answers no Madonna.

MacNeice produced many such 'survey' poems – other examples are 'Birmingham', 'Train to Dublin', 'An Eclogue for Christmas' and

'Carrickfergus' – which offer an overview of a community, making their points by the careful juxtaposition of observed detail. The culmination of this tendency is the doggerel-poem (MacNeice was a great experimenter with metre, and enjoyed the careful construction of apparently loose and casual effects) 'Bagpipe Music', where a cacophony of ludicrously 'bad' rhymes and a kaleidoscope of absurd and grotesque images creates a panorama of the cynical, materialistic decadence MacNeice saw in the Britain of 1937. These poems are among the best political poetry of the period: avoiding the abstract rhetoric that has made so many of Spender's and Day-Lewis's poems fade badly, their sharp, metonymic imagery appears fresh and contemporary: to read 'Belfast' or 'Carrickfergus' is to find oneself already in the world of Derek Mahon and Seamus Heaney.

In 1929 MacNeice had edited *Oxford Poetry* with Spender; in 1937 he collaborated with Auden on *Letters from Iceland*. His membership of the 'Auden group' reached its culmination in 1938 with *Modern Poetry*, a critical book seen at the time as a manifesto for the poets of its generation. MacNeice argued for the poet as 'a blend of the entertainer and the critic or informer', and suggested that 'for the production nowadays of major literature . . . a sympathy is required in the writer with those [political] forces which at the moment make for progress'. None the less the book was mildly critical of 'Poets like Auden, Spender, and Day Lewis [who] have adopted a system of belief which they have not yet quite grown into'.

MacNeice's most ambitious poem, *Autumn Journal*, was started in August 1938 as a verse diary and deals with his personal experience of the crisis-ridden period before the outbreak of war. The poem is masterly in conveying the agonizing uncertainty of the time through details of daily life:

> Today they were building in Oxford Street, the mortar
>   Pleasant to smell,
> But now it seems futility, imbecility,
>   To be building shops when nobody can tell
> What will happen next. What will happen
>   We ask and waste the question on the air;
> Nelson is stone and Johnnie Walker moves his
>   Legs like a cretin over Trafalgar Square.
> And in the Corner House the carpet-sweepers
>   Advance between the tables after crumbs
>   Inexorably, like a tank battalion
>   In answer to the drums.

(V. 37–48)

At first reading the poem seems too long, but even its length and occasional diffuseness play a part in conveying the suspense of the period. *Autumn Journal* performs a historical *tour-de-force* in combining clarity, readability and an appearance of direct spontaneity with the transcription of a complex sensibility at a period of peculiar historical tension.

In 1939 MacNeice, who had been lecturing in classics at Reading University, took a job at the BBC, working on propaganda broadcasts to the United States; he worked in broadcasting for the rest of his life. His work for the BBC included numerous verse radio plays, some of which are among his best work. The most notable is *The Dark Tower* (1945), a 'parable' suggested by Browning's poem. A work of mysterious symbolic power, it is yet consistent with Mac-Neice's work as a whole: the dreamlike country through which Roland seeks the tower is an allegory of the modern world, a desert of 'doubts and dried-up hopes' inhabited by, among others, a cynical and corrupt blind man who represents fascism and an alcoholic identified by MacNeice as 'a sort of caricature of the despairing intelligentsia'. Auden's influence is clearly perceptible: the treatment of the quest theme recalls Auden's 'Atlantis', and the way Roland is forced by his mother into a quest on which his male ancestors have already perished owes much to *Paid on Both Sides* and *The Ascent of F6*.

None the less, merely political or psychoanalytical readings of *The Dark Tower* do it a disservice. It is, above all, a play about death and the shadow it casts on life, informed by the sensitivities and anxieties to which MacNeice had opened himself by rejecting his father's religion. Its verse has an excellence typical of MacNeice, using poetry not as decoration but as a means to extreme brevity, clarity and pungency. It grips the hearer's attention and it is very funny. Here, for example, is the Soak falling asleep:

> Unity, Mabel, unity is my motto.
> The end of drink is a whole without any parts –
> A great black sponge of night that fills the world
> And when you squeeze it, Mabel, it drips inwards.
> D'you want me to squeeze it? Right. Piano there.
> Piano – I must sleep. Didn't you hear me?
> Piano, puppets. All right, pianissimo.
>   Nissimo . . . nissimo . . . issimo . . .
>   [*The music ends and his snoring is heard.*]

This is a kind of writing which was possible only because of what Auden, and Eliot before him, had already done, and MacNeice's achievement perhaps was to domesticate their innovations, producing a flexible style which could be used for many purposes without calling attention to itself. In this sense MacNeice's is a second-order talent, but a rich and interesting one. No one could follow the path he had taken any further.

III

Auden and his friends were not, of course, the only poets of the time to have their lives and work moulded by political concerns. At least three English poets of notable promise – Christopher Caudwell, John Cornford and Julian Bell – died as volunteers in Spain. All wrote poetry very different from that of Auden and his imitators. Caudwell (real name Christopher St John Sprigg, 1907–37), had learned from Eliot and Brooke to study the Jacobeans, and his few poems show an astringent wit, neatly compressed into traditional verse forms. Addressing a lover in 'The Hair', he writes:

> This was a part of you until it went
> Which now doctors but rate as excrement;
> And in my vision, blessed because mine,
> This trifle shone too, thin but present line
> For nothing that was you was missed. That gone,
> This hair is all my hopes can fatten on . . .

Caudwell is remembered mainly for his ambitious volume of Marxist literary theory, *Illusion and Reality* (1937). An example of the 'vulgar' Marxism common at the time, viewing culture as straightforwardly determined by the economic structure of society and demanding that literature express a 'progressive' social view, it is none the less a lively and stimulating book, properly sceptical about claims that the Auden group represented a 'Proletarian' poetry of the future: indeed, with a fair degree of accuracy, it accuses them of 'an unconscious dishonesty – as of a man exploiting the revolution for his own ends'.

Julian Bell (1908–37) excelled at 'fiercely naturalist' descriptive poetry rooted in his admiration for eighteenth-century landscape poetry: John Cornford (1915–36) wrote in Spain a handful of poems which come closer than any others in English to a successful merging of Marxist theory and traditional lyric. 'Full Moon at Tierz', written before a battle on the Huesca front, treats the theme of the revolutionary's present responsibility for the course of history far more seriously, though with less glitter, than Auden's 'Spain' (1937):

> Time present is a cataract whose force
> Breaks down the banks even at its source
> And history forming in our hand's
> Not plasticine but roaring sands,
> Yet we must swing it to its final course.

His most famous poem, known variously as 'Poem' or 'To Margot Heinemann', takes its first line – 'Heart of the heartless world' – from Marx's famous pronouncement on religion. His was the most interesting English poetic talent to be lost in the civil war.

It was not only on the Left that writers engaged with the Spanish war. Conservative, and more especially Catholic, writers in substantial numbers supported Franco. The most prominent propagandists were essayists and Catholic apologists such as Hilaire Belloc and G. K. Chesterton; but their ranks were joined by Roy Campbell (1901–57), a poet of substantial achievement whose work has suffered undue neglect. Campbell was born in South Africa and came to England in 1918 to study at Oxford. Probably as a result of his colonial background, Campbell's early work shows no sign of his having read any English poetry written after 1900, and its technique represents a direct, though far more aggressive and vigorous, continuation from the work of Swinburne and the poets of the 1890s, with some fruitful influence from the French Symbolists. *The Flaming Terrapin* (1924), a long visionary poem calling for a renewal of human energies after the devastation wrought by the First World War, is a riot of rich and colourful imagery in neatly built heroic couplets. It was hailed by some critics as heralding a powerful revival of traditional verse. In *Adamastor* (1930) and *Flowering Reeds* (1933) Campbell produced collections of vivid lyrical meditations in traditional forms, praising the colour and energy of nature in a somewhat Lawrentian fashion, but with a metrical control very different from the open unpredictability of Lawrence's free verse. 'The Zebras' is typical:

> Harnessed with level rays in golden reins,
> The zebras draw the dawn across the plains
> Wading knee-deep among the scarlet flowers.
> The sunlight, zithering their flanks with fire,
> Flashes between the shadows as they pass
> Barred with electric tremors through the grass
> Like wind along the gold strings of a lyre.

Preferring an 'outdoor' life close to that of his Natal childhood, Campbell spent much of his time in Southern France and Spain, and became a Catholic in 1935. *Mithraic Emblems* (1936) is a fascinatingly complex Symbolist sonnet-sequence where a Christian view of life blends with images drawn from ancient Roman Mithraic religion and from bullfighting. By Modernist standards the poems are emotional and overwritten; but they possess a striking visual brilliance as well as a teasing, labyrinthine intellectual patterning, and deserve more readers than they have had.

When the civil war broke out in 1937 Campbell, politically naive and appalled by Communist violence against the Church, took Franco's side. He wrote biased war-correspondence for *The Tablet*: visiting Britain, he loved to horrify left-wingers with fictitious tales of his bloodthirsty anti-Communist exploits at the front. (In reality, his only active part in the conflict was humanitarian: at some personal risk, he sheltered fugitive priests and the Carmelite archives in his house.) He also antagonized even the uncommitted by his sprawling, repetitious and crudely pro-Franco satire, *Flowering Rifle* (1939) (although he scored a small but effective point with his contemptuous lumping-together of Auden and his three best-known friends as the composite left-wing poet 'MacSpaunday').

Campbell was pro-Church rather than truly Fascist: in 1939 he joined the British army without hesitation and served throughout the Second World War. Nor was he a racist; an early poem, *The Wayzgoose*, satirizes the brutal philistinism of Boer society; lyrics such as 'The Serf' and 'A Zulu Girl' show respect and sympathy for the Africans. But the Spanish episode tarnished his reputation, and when he died suddenly in a car accident in 1957 he was still under a cloud. The only work of his that has been widely current since his death is his translation of the poems of St John of the Cross, which has become the standard English version.

IV

So far we have been concerned with poets who led fairly conspicuous public lives and who readily accepted the role of political propagandist, having little concern in practice with a 'pure' poetry detached from everyday affairs. The 1930s also saw the emergence, however, of more austere talents, whose orientation was more academic. William Empson (1906–84) and F. T. Prince (b. 1912) exemplify this tendency. Both were university teachers of English; both engaged in scholarly and critical work of the highest standard; both lacked a large public for their poetry, but have been influential on other poets. Perhaps because their work is tinged by the intellectualism of the professional critic, both seem closer in spirit to the 'impersonality' and 'difficulty' demanded by Eliot than to the slightly naive rough-and-tumble of the political poets.

Empson is far better known as critic than as poet: generations of English students have read, or dipped into, *Seven Types of Ambiguity* (1930), *Some Versions of Pastoral* (1935) and *Milton's God* (1961), most of them probably unaware that he had written a line of verse. Yet the poems (which appeared in two slim volumes, *Poems*, 1935, and *The Gathering Storm*, 1940) are very much of a piece with the criticism. Both display an immense range of interests; an intellect fascinated by scientific method and analysis but less than rigorous in its use of them (neither the critical arguments nor the poetic analogies are as convincing as Empson seems to want us to think); strong feelings, even prejudices, masked as detached judgements; and a weird sense of humour. In his personal life Empson enjoyed playing the absent-minded professor, marking a place in a book with a dried kipper-bone or going out wearing odd shoes, and part of the pleasure of all his writing is its faintly surrealist air of eccentricity. Who else, for example, could have constructed an argument for reading *Alice in Wonderland* not just as a pastoral, but as a specifically 'proletarian' form of pastoral? Yet his discussion, in *Some Versions of Pastoral*, remains one of the best things written on *Alice*.

Seven Types of Ambiguity (1930), which made his name, is simply a systematic application of the perception that a word, or a line, or a whole poem, may mean more than one thing. Empson is said to have been inspired by the chapter in Graves and Riding's *Survey of Modernist Poetry* which analyses the multiplicity of meanings to be found in Shakespeare's Sonnet 129. He read the *Survey* as a Cambridge undergraduate and, according to his tutor I. A. Richards, produced the first draft of *Seven Types* in a fortnight. It was published when Empson was twenty-four. Analysing the kinds of multiple meaning generated by a range of texts from Chaucer to Eliot, the book is still regarded as a landmark in literary theory.

Empson's Cambridge education and his contact with I. A. Richards are important. In the 1930s Cambridge literary circles were more 'scientific' and less 'political' than those at Oxford; important research in biology, astronomy and nuclear physics was going on, and there was generous interchange between the arts and sciences.

Empson went to Cambridge initially to read mathematics; Kathleen Raine read biology there; a leading student literary magazine was edited by Jacob Bronowski. Cambridge criticism was serious-minded, self-confident and analytical. Empson's criticism contributed to this tendency and, together with the works of Richards in *Principles of Literary Criticism* (1925) and *Practical Criticism* (1929), provided foundations for the growth, in British universities, of a 'New Criticism' similar to that which was emerging in America, a criticism which drew attention away from the reader's emotional response and the historical context of a work's production, emphasizing instead the value of close, and often ingenious, interpretation of 'the words on the page'.

Empson's own poems lend themselves to this procedure. Cast in strict metrical and rhyming patterns, often using intricate forms such as the sonnet or villanelle, they are highly obscure and full of images taken from the natural sciences used in complex ways as analogies of human emotional or political processes – a technique in which Empson seems to mimic the surprising conceits of the 'Metaphysical' poets. The poems revel in ambiguity – a point made neatly by the two notes Empson wrote at different times for an early poem, 'The Ants'. The first merely states that 'The ants build mud galleries into trees to protect the greenfly they get sugar from, and keep them warm in the nest during winter'; the second states that the poem is 'a love poem with the author afraid of the woman'. The poem can be read as about ants – although this seems banal; or one can venture interpretations having to do with human emotion or society, with the ants as metaphor. Empson's extraordinary intellectual playfulness is exemplified by 'Camping Out', which uses, among other things, ideas from theology, astronomy and the physics of surface-tension to generate a highly erotic image of a girl, but which is best known for its shatteringly anti-Romantic opening line, 'And now she cleans her teeth into the lake'.

At times Empson can produce lines as rhetorically satisfying as any Romantic poet – for example, the sombre repeated lines of his villanelle 'Missing Dates': 'Slowly the poison the whole bloodstream fills . . . The waste remains, the waste remains and kills.' Apart from a few anthology pieces ('Homage to the British Museum', 'Aubade', 'Missing Dates') his poetry is not much read except by scholars and other poets. Its influence, none the less, has been substantial, encouraging intricate, analytical thought in poetry and inspiring poets to explore the potential of strict traditional verse-forms through a period when free (or at any rate loose) verse might have become wholly dominant. Later poets as various as Donald Davie, Thom Gunn and Geoffrey Hill have all learnt from the intellectual demands and formal rigour of his work.

F. T. Prince is another little-read poet who has been influential, though less extensively so than Empson. Prince was born in South Africa and came to study at Oxford in 1931 (an accessible account of some aspects of his life can be found in his long poem *Memoirs in Oxford*, 1970). His name is inextricably linked with his one well-known poem, 'Soldiers Bathing', which gave its title to his second (1954) collection of poems. 'Soldiers Bathing' presents the meditations of an officer in wartime as he watches his men relaxing on a beach. The men become a compassionately viewed symbol of human vulnerability and essential innocence, as the 'poor bare forked animal' of Shakespeare's *King Lear*

> Stands in the soft air, tasting after toil
> The sweetness of his nakedness: letting the sea-waves coil
> Their frothy tongues about his feet, forgets
> His hatred of the war, its terrible pressure that begets
> A machinery of death and slavery,
> Each being a slave and making slaves of others: finds that he
> Remembers his old freedom in a game
> Mocking himself, and comically mimics fear and shame.

From this contrast of violence and innocence, Prince draws religious reflections, though unorthodox ones – the root cause of warfare is our fear of love, including the love of God: 'because to love is frightening we prefer/The freedom of our crimes.'

The poem is a moving one, which conveys a sense of painful integrity not least because of its occasional slight clumsiness. Its diction is by turns eloquent and stilted, its rhymes and metre irregular, and its conclusion ('I . . . kiss the wound in thought, while in the west/I watch a streak of red that might have issued from Christ's breast') languidly Romantic in a manner that recalls the 'Decadent' poets of the 1890s. One senses a highly intelligent consciousness grappling with, and almost embarrassed by, the strength of its own feelings.

'Soldiers Bathing' is not altogether typical of Prince's work, which for the most part is oblique, reticent and, at times, academic in its use of historical detail. *Afterword on Rupert Brooke* (1976), for example, is almost unintelligible unless one has an intimate knowledge of Brooke's biography; 'The Old Age of Michaelangelo' is a dramatic monologue intricately elaborated from material on Michelangelo in Vasari's *Lives of the Artists*.

A striking characteristic of Prince's work is its diversity of forms: each of his longer poems seems to be composed in a completely different manner from all the others. Thus *Memoirs in Oxford* uses a brisk rhyming ballad-stanza; *Drypoints of the Hasidim* – a collection of anecdotes about the Jewish mystics of that sect – is in a typographically spaced-out free verse reminiscent of the Jewish–American 'Objectivists', Charles Reznikoff and Louis Zukovsky. Thus Prince's work lacks the sense of cumulative unity generally expected of a poet. Although all his poems are excellent of their kind, they do not seem to form a greater whole and this has perhaps prevented him from gaining wider recognition. One of his most powerful works remains the first item in his *Collected Poems*, 'An Epistle to a Patron', published in 1935 by Eliot in *The Criterion*. The poem is spoken by an Italian Renaissance architect-engineer – another Leonardo or Brunelleschi – who begs a princely tyrant to employ him and allow him to fulfil his creative talents, no matter what the moral cost. Despite its historical setting the poem is fiercely contemporary, exploring the psychology of Fascism and confronting the temptations that face the artist in a world where the common democratic culture has no interest in his art. The poem uses a superbly ornate and brutal rhetoric, and one suspects that its example has been at work on such later twentieth-century poets as Geoffrey Hill (whose 'To the Supposed Patron' in *King Log* seems to echo its style and attitudes).

V

For convenience we have so far grouped poets who emerged in the 1930s into loose categories. Inevitably there are also recalcitrant individuals who resist any such sorting-process, who are oddly and uncompromisingly themselves. Prominent among these is John Betjeman (1908–84), whose progress from his poetic debut with *Mount Zion* (1931) to the status of household name, popular broadcaster and (from 1972) Poet Laureate, surely constitutes one of the strangest poetic careers in twentieth-century Britain.

Betjeman (the name was German and properly Betjemann, but two world wars and an uncertainty over its spelling encouraged him to think of it as Dutch) came from a dynasty of London furniture-manufacturers: a fact which is not as irrelevant as it seems, for although Betjeman refused to join the family firm his work is permeated by a knowledgeable fascination with design, household furnishing and architecture, which he treats as the intricate manifestations of class relationships. Betjeman is a poet of life-styles, and his preoccupation with material goods and settings is fundamentally a matter not of snobbery but of realizing that in an industrial society most people reveal themselves most naturally through the objects they surround themselves with and the places they frequent. His poems thus encompass many telling ephemera – brand-names, fashions, minor social rituals – which flavour modern life strongly but which are neglected by more obviously ambitious poets.

Betjeman grew up in Highgate, North London, attended boarding schools at Oxford and Marlborough, and returned to Oxford to read English in 1925. He quickly made his name as a student journalist and humorist, writing on art, architecture and student life. He also gained a reputation as a poet, although his verse was mainly humorous and parodic. The coherent concentration of his interests is typified by the one poem from this period to survive into his *Collected Poems*, 'Hymn', a satire on insensitive Victorian church-restoration framed as a parody of a well-known hymn, 'The Church's One Foundation'. The poem's verse-form exactly matches its content, making it a criticism at once of the oddities and constraints of Victorian hymnography and of the materialistic values concealed, or expressed, by its embellishment of churches. In a similar way much of Betjeman's subsequent poetry remained a matter of brilliantly integrating parody, nostalgia, aesthetic criticism and implied moral comment. People and their physical surroundings are evoked in poetic styles which both enhance and criticize them. Nothing is held up to unqualified scorn, nor is anything viewed with simple nostalgia.

An instantly recognizable Betjeman stanza is this, from 'Myfanwy', a poem from *Old Lights for New Chancels* (1940):

> Oh! Fuller's angel-cake, Robertson's marmalade,
> Liberty Lampshade, come, shine on us all,
> My! what a spread for the friends of Myfanwy,
> Some in the alcove and some in the hall . . .

The subject is a children's tea-party; the poetic voice shares the innocence of the children ('My! what a spread . . .'), but also emphasizes its precariousness – it is only for the *friends* of Myfanwy (one senses the risk of jealous childhood exclusions) and depends on the unbroken supply of standardized consumer goods taken for granted by a complacent middle class. The verse-form has, no doubt, several models, but an obvious prototype is Stevenson's 'Keepsake Mill' from *A Child's Garden of Verses*, a nostalgic celebration of childhood which might well have been read to Myfanwy at bedtime.

Betjeman left Oxford at the end of his first year, having failed his exams, and soon took an editorial job at *The Architectural Review*. Thereafter he lived by journalism and criticism, writing and broadcasting on film, architecture and the urban landscape. In the 1960s he became the leading popular advocate for a renewed appreciation of Victorian architecture.

Betjeman's poems show a gradual increase in both warmth and seriousness. *Mount Zion* (1932) looks like a somewhat random collection of occasional pieces: most impressive in the sombre 'Death in Leamington', less brilliant in the rollicking light verse of 'The Varsity Students' Rag' and the malicious private jokes of 'The Wykehamist'. *Old Lights for New Chancels* and *New Bats in Old Belfries* (1945) are, despite their titles, only occasionally concerned with matters of church architecture. Rather they are collections of portraits and social sketches showing less bitterness and more affection than the earlier poems.

A notable development of the 1940s is the emergence of a strongly erotic element in Betjeman's writing, typified by his celebration of alarming tomboy heroines in 'Pot Pourri from a Surrey Garden' and 'A Subaltern's Love-Song'. Like most of Betjeman's poems, these combine a quirkish oddity of conception with extremely acute social observation. However, under their fascination with Surrey's opulent suburbia and their fantasies of 'great big mountainous sports girl[s]', one senses loneliness, vulnerability and social insecurity.

Betjeman's own account of his childhood and youth, given in his long poem *Summoned by Bells* (1960), offers ready explanation for this pervasive melancholy – the religious terrors implanted by a 'hateful nurse who . . . was the first to tell me about Hell/Admitting she was going there herself': his failure at Oxford; and his guilt at refusing to join the family firm, a burden which stayed with him for years:

> 'Well now, my boy, I want your solemn word
> To carry on the firm when I am gone:
> Fourth generation, John – they'll look to you . . .'
>   In later years,
> Now old and ill, he asked me once again
> To carry on the firm, I still refused

Whatever the reasons, the experience of reading Betjeman's poems at length is not a comfortable one. Death, anxiety and quiet unhappiness are everywhere.

Betjeman's elevation to the Laureateship in 1972 was perhaps a tribute to his creation of a popular interest in architecture as well as to the accomplishment and accessibility of his verse (his 1958 *Collected Poems* sold more than 100,000 copies). It may, moreover, have marked a recognition that his poetic practice, which in 1931 must have seemed so absurdly eccentric and limiting, had always been concerned with issues that now engaged many of the most admired British authors – the validity of traditional forms, the significance of popular culture and middle-class values, the search for a valid aesthetic stance in a democratic but class-riven society dominated by commercial interests.

Another poet who must be placed in this class of the unclassifiable is Stevie Smith (1902–71), who mocks the whole business of literary classification in 'Souvenir de Monsieur Poop', where a pompous professor proclaims:

> In the service of literature I believe absolutely in the principle of division;
> I divide into age groups and also into schools.
> This is in keeping with my scholastic mind, and enables me to trounce
> Not only youth
> (Which might be thought intellectually frivolous by pedants) but also
>   periodical tendencies,
> To ventilate, in a word, my own political and moral philosophy.

Stevie (really Florence Margaret) Smith lived an outwardly uneventful life. Her father, a seaman, left during her early childhood, and Stevie lived with her mother, sister and aunt in a house in Palmer's Green, North London. As time went by her mother died, her sister left and Stevie pursued a modest but successful career as a secretary with Newnes, Pearson, the magazine publishers, writing poetry in her spare time. When her aunt fell ill in 1953 she gave up her job to care for her, still in the same house in which neither furniture nor decoration was ever changed.

Her first publication was *Novel on Yellow Paper* (1936), written in response to a request for a novel by Jonathan Cape, the publisher to whom she had submitted her first collection of poems. *Novel* – an account of life in 1930s London seen through the eyes of a seemingly naive (though actually rather shrewd) young girl – was a commercial success and emboldened Cape to publish the poems as *A Good Time Was Had by All* (1937), the first of ten volumes which appeared in her lifetime.

Smith's style is instantly recognizable. It combines simple diction (often tinged with parody) with a biting sense of the absurd. Often there is an element of visionary imagination – animals, trees or the dead speak; angels intervene – and verse-forms tend towards the hymn, the nursery rhyme or doggerel, but with frequent rhythmic surprises and breakdowns. Conveniently, her most famous poem is fully representative – 'Not Waving But Drowning' is spoken, for the most part, by a dead man and his lament sums up a life of quiet desperation:

> Oh, no no no, it was too cold always
> (Still the dead man lay moaning)
> I was much too far out all my life
> And not waving but drowning.

The human tendency to ignore suffering and rebuff attempts at uncomfortable communication is a constant concern in Smith's poems. Another recurrent theme, usually lightly handled, is suicide. Frequently the absurdities of adult social behaviour are thrown into relief by the unsentimental gaze of observant children or animals. Despite its playful tone her work has a wide range and great, though idiosyncratic, power. She is an important and still underrated poet.

VI

To help us make the (necessarily arbitrary) transition to the poetic climate of the 1940s, no poet could be more appropriate than David Gascoyne (b. 1916).

> Let us fill
> One final fiery glass . . . to 'the Pre-War'
> Before we greet 'the Forties', whose unseen sphinx-face
> Is staring fixedly upon us from behind its veil;
> Drink farewell quickly, ere the Future smash the glass.

Gascoyne is appropriate here not only because his 'Farewell Chorus' is an explicit valediction to the decade, but because his career falls into three clearly defined segments: a 1930s period dominated by surrealism: a body of very different wartime work, including his *Journals 1936–1942* (1992) and *Poems 1937–1942* (1943): and a post-war phase of chiefly religious poems, most significantly *Night Thoughts* (1956).

Gascoyne's first book appeared in 1932. Although the poems of *Roman Balcony* were slight, they showed the influence of the imagists and Eliot: Gascoyne was from the beginning a modernist and he quickly turned to French surrealism, whose irrationalism and technical experiment seemed to him a way of renewing 'the ancient and supposedly discredited notion of inspiration'. He became – and has always remained – a frequent visitor to France, and his poetry should perhaps be seen in the light of his claims that he is not really an 'English' poet at all but a European one, working in symbolist traditions that are little-understood in Britain. The poems collected in *Man's Life Is This Meat* (1936) include the purest examples of surrealist writing in English, poems ruled by what André Breton called 'pure psychic automatism':

> Crescendo of flowers, the steps
> Of stone that lead onto the swamp
> Where wanderings begin and the first birds
> The last birds, the sun's bicycle racing,
> Our eyes lose one another, autumn splutters
> On the sidewalks houses eat the afternoon . . .
>
> ('The Cage')

Other poems, though bizarre in their imagery, seem tinged with horror at the European political situation and with an unfocused sense of spiritual need. In 1935 Gascoyne published *A Short Survey of Surrealism*, and in 1936 he helped organize the International Surrealist Exhibition in London. Although for a short time it was fashionable to claim to be a surrealist (Dylan Thomas, for example, welcomed visitors to the exhibition, offering them cups of string), Gascoyne was almost the only English writer to whom surrealism meant more than an excuse for eccentric behaviour or the lavish use of colourful poetic imagery. His notion of surrealism was an austere one, and it led him to the study of European poets of the irrational and visionary, notably of Hölderlin, on whom he published an important essay with translations in *Hölderlin's Madness* (1938).

In a brief Communist phase he visited Spain as a propaganda broadcaster; during the Second World War he worked as an actor, entertaining the troops with ENSA. *Poems 1937–1942* contains much of his best work. Gascoyne's war poems are powerful in their bleakness, confronting 'The hollow and annihilating war/Of final disillusion' with 'a lucid despair'. They treat the war as a symptom of the spiritual void within man, something horrific yet wholly without drama or dignity. 'A Wartime Dawn' is the best example: the speaker, after a sleepless night, gets up to

> Draw . . . with prickling hand the curtains back;
> Unpin the blackout-cloth; let in
> Grim crack-of-dawn's first glimmer through the glass.

Beyond the window over the roofs 'hangs flaccidly a lone barrage-balloon' and 'the newsboy's bike winds near,/Distributing to neighbour's peaceful steps/Reports of last-night's battles.'

After the war Gascoyne's work became more explicitly religious. His radio play *Night Thoughts*, set in a dreamlike version of the 'Megalometropolis' of London, explores the crowded loneliness of the modern world and the possibilities of redemption that lie in recognition of our common fear and isolation. A series of nervous breakdowns, combined with acute self-criticism, have kept Gascoyne's output small, but he is recognized as an important figure who has remained true to a dauntingly austere vision. His poems have little popular appeal, for they lack fluency and suggest a man conscientiously wrestling with language rather than intuitively at home in it; but their honest sensitivity to loneliness and the bleakest aspects of twentieth-century European society makes them valuable.

VII

It was natural that Gascoyne should offer a poetic farewell to the 1930s, just as that Auden, from the uncertain edge of his new life in America, should look back on 'the clever hopes . . . Of a low dishonest decade' in 'September 1, 1939'. For the 1930s were cut off, dramatically, by the outbreak of war. The political battles of the previous ten years began to look somewhat futile: the Left had made little headway in Britain and had failed to deal effectively with Fascism in Europe; on the other hand, everyone in Britain was now officially 'anti-Fascist'. Everyone was also utterly uncertain about the future. In such a situation of continuing crisis, where the war and the blackout increasingly disrupted social life and those in the forces had to spend much time in transit or simply waiting about, far from the usual sources of entertainment, there was a renewed appetite for literature. Paper rationing put limitations on magazine publishing, but books could be passed from hand to hand and poetry needed less paper than fiction. Thus, for both emotional and practical reasons, more poetry was written, published and read during the war than before or after – Eliot's *Little Gidding* (1942) appeared in a first edition of 16,775, a staggering figure for a volume of 'difficult' verse (A. T. Tolley, *Poetry of the Forties*, 1985, p 3). Literary periodicals throve – though not, on the whole, those that had thrived during the 1930s. Most successful was John Lehmann's *Penguin New Writing* – a quarterly volume published in book form after its earlier version, the magazine *New Writing*, was killed by restrictions on magazines; *Penguin New Writing* sold up to 100,000 copies an issue. Far less widely read but important in discovering new talent was *Poetry London*, founded in 1939 by James Tambimuttu, a Tamil whose bohemian lifestyle and generous but chaotic editorial methods are still affectionately remembered. The two magazines typified two main currents in 1940s poetry. *Penguin New Writing* championed poetry and fiction that was intelligent, modest and controlled; there was a certain earnestness about it, and it preserved a high standard of technique and sensitivity. *Poetry London*, by comparison, was unpredictable and messy. Tambimuttu believed that poetry was a matter of 'the universal unconscious' and 'incantatory rhythms'. Not surprisingly, work that appeared in *Poetry London* might be dull, derivative or plain dotty. It might also be great, and the most important thing about *Poetry London* is that it first published W. S. Graham, David Wright, Kathleen Raine and much of Keith Douglas, as well as important work by Dylan Thomas, David Gascoyne, Norman Nicholson, Louis MacNeice and many others. While *Penguin New Writing* continued the intelligent, sensitive scepticism of the best 1930s poetry, *Poetry London* was attuned to something quite different – a revival of 'Romantic' attitudes and values which was to gather strength as the decade went on.

This 'Neo-Romanticism', as it came to be known, is now often thought of as the hallmark of 1940s poetry; but it was far from universal, and one of the finest poets of the decade, Keith Douglas, was largely untouched by it. Douglas (1920–44) would surely have been more than a 1940s poet but for his early death (he was killed by a shell during the Normandy landings). As it is, he is the Second World War's closest counterpart to the soldier-poets of the First World War. A professional soldier, he was an admirer of Wilfred Owen's work and, rather paradoxically, looked keenly forward to the experience of battle, hoping that it would enable him to write like his hero. His gift was precocious: his earliest surviving poem, 'Mummers', written when he was fourteen, is a vivid and resonant piece that needs no apology; two years later he was reading *New Verse* and writing poems influenced by Auden.

Douglas spent two years reading English at Oxford before joining the army as a cavalry trooper in 1940. Cavalry having been replaced in modern warfare by tanks, he soon found himself in the Middle

East, based chiefly in Cairo and Alexandria, and taking part in the battle of El Alamein and the allied advance on Tripoli in late 1942. Early in 1943 he was wounded and while convalescing wrote a series of war poems and a prose narrative of his experiences, *Alamein to Zem Zem* (published posthumously in 1946). His poems, peacetime and wartime alike, are remarkable for their sharp detail, their sense of the grotesque and their compassion. In form, he is something of a traditionalist, often using rhyming stanzas loosened up with slight irregularities of meter and minor distortions of syntax in the manner of Auden, but his vision is highly, often weirdly, individual and shot through with a trenchant wit. In 'The Marvel' the poet watches a sailor prise out the lens from the eye of 'A baron of the sea, the great tropic/swordfish', and use it as a burning-glass to write on a piece of wood 'the name of a harlot in his last port'. The moment focuses a sense of elemental powers: the lens is 'an instrument forged in semi-darkness' and a stimulus to the imagination which will

> take you where . . . forgotten ships lie
> with fishes going over the tall masts –
> all this emerges from the burning eye.
>
> And to engrave that word the sun goes through
> with the power of the sea,
> writing her name and a marvel too.

The fish's eye is a symbol for poetic vision; the poem derives in part from Baudelaire's 'L'Albatros' and, as in that poem, the plight of the great creature 'spreadeagled on the thirsty deck/where sailors killed him' embodies the poet's sense of pride and vulnerability.

The lens is a recurrent image in Douglas's work, as if human individuality were for him embodied in the unique viewpoint and perceptions of each person. In 'Vergissmeinicht' he notes death most vividly in 'the dust upon the paper eye' of a corpse; in 'How to Kill' it becomes the 'dial of glass' of a sniper's telescopic sight. 'How to Kill' is an extraordinary poem, reflecting Douglas's troubled awareness that a soldier is not merely a victim but also, potentially, a killer – a fact rather rarely acknowledged in war poetry. Douglas's sniper, choosing his target and pulling the trigger, recognizes that he is 'damned' – watching his victim die, he is 'amused' at 'how easy it is to make a ghost', yet appalled at the fragility of life and at his moral responsibility for destroying it. On the whole, however, Douglas's poems describing the desert war are not his best (although 'Cairo Jag' presents a world, fractured by the social and physical disruptions of the war, strikingly reminiscent of Eliot's *The Waste Land*, from which Douglas has clearly learnt techniques of disturbing juxtaposition). More effective is *Alamein to Zem Zem* (p 28), which unforgettably conveys the sense of absurd unreality created by mechanized warfare:

The view from a moving tank is like that in a camera obscura or a silent film – in that since the engine drowns all other noises except explosions, the whole world moves silently. Men shout, vehicles move, aeroplanes fly over, and all soundlessly . . . An illimitably strange land, quite unrelated to real life, like the scenes in 'The Cabinet of Doctor Caligari'.

With its balancing of dry humour and irony against personal emotion, Douglas's work continues certain elements of poised intellectualism transmitted by the work of Auden and his associates from early modernism.

Close to Douglas in the wit and occasionally contrived brilliance of his language is Sidney Keyes (1922–43), who was also killed in North Africa. Keyes, however, rejected Douglas's irony and sceptism, viewing the task of poetry (under the influence of Yeats and Rilke) as 'to give . . . some inkling of the continual fusion between finite and infinite, spiritual and physical, which is our world'. In his lifetime he published only one book, *The Iron Laurel* (1942): another, *The Cruel Solstice*, appeared posthumously in 1943. His long poems *The Foreign Gate* and *The Wilderness* have won praise from some critics, but seem rather self-conscious attempts at grandeur, the first inflated by a pastiche of Rilke's abstract rhetoric, the second reading like imitation Eliot – neither at all surprising or discreditable in a poet of less than twenty-one.

Keyes's strength is in poems like 'The Bards', 'The Glass Tower in Galway' and 'Sour Land', which combine vivid physicality with a nightmarish vision of fatigue, frustration and hopeless death. The opening of 'The Glass Tower in Galway' is surely one of the oddest yet most authoritative in modern poetry:

> One was an eye and others
> Snake-headed travesties; one high-legged and mincing
> As a stork. And there were whining small ones
> Like sickly children. O they were a beastly
> Sea-born race, spawned on the rocks of Galway
> Among the dried shark-eggs and the dirty froth . . .

And parts of 'Sour Land' sketch a territory of myth with a resonance many poets of the 1940s aspired to but few achieved:

This is a very ancient land indeed;
Aiaia formerly or Cythera
Or Celidon the hollow forest called;
This is the country Ulysses and Hermod
Entered afraid; by ageing poets sought
Where lives no love nor any kind of flower
Only the running demon, thought.

Keyes is still little known but he has inspired many subsequent poets, among them Ted Hughes and Geoffrey Hill, and his work shows signs of enduring.

Another soldier-poet who died on active service (and whose work has been preferred by some above that of Douglas) is Alun Lewis (1915–44). Lewis came from a South Wales mining village where his father was the local schoolmaster. Strong literary and intellectual interests nearly led him to an academic career as a historian, but his desire to write had already interrupted his research into medieval history when the war broke out. He joined the army in 1940, but – moved from one camp and training-course to another, then on the long voyage by troopship to India – had ample time to write both poetry and prose. Both his short stories and his poems draw directly on his own experience, the stories in particular concentrating on army life and the poems chronicling his experience from the Welsh valleys ('The Rhondda'; 'The Mountain Over Aberdare') to military training ('All Day It Has Rained . . .': 'To Edward Thomas'), then on to departure ('On Embarcation': 'A Troopship in the Tropics') and the impact of India – which was a spiritual and social experience, rather than a military one, and resulted in a final group of impressive poems, notably 'To Rilke', 'Karanje Village' and 'The Mahratta Ghats', which reflect on India's disturbing blend of spiritual wealth and material poverty.

Neither Lewis's fiction nor his poetry ever quite reaches full achievement. He works clearly under the influence of his literary models: his most admired 'English' poem, 'All Day It Has Rained . . .' is explicitly a tribute to Edward Thomas, and mimics his style; 'A Troopship in the Tropics', with its laconic selection of odd, picturesque detail draws on the tone of Auden's *Journey to a War*; and the Indian poems are strongly influenced by Rilke, as represented by the translations then available.

The short stories display a flexible, plain and vivid prose-style and an exceptional ability to suggest, without sentimentality or criticism, the world-views of a wide range of characters. Yet, like the poems, they often fail to achieve a clear focus on the matter in hand, tending to digress or become distracted at crucial points by other, peripheral interests. Lewis was fully aware that he was serving a literary apprenticeship, and his work was steadily gaining strength; but for the most part his poems are wholly satisfactory only when he consciously imitates another writer. He can produce unforgettable images. For instance, this from 'Raider's Dawn':

> Blue necklace left
> On a charred chair
> Tells that Beauty
> Was startled there.

Or, from 'The Mountain Over Aberdare', there is 'the church/ Stretched like a sow beside the stream'. However, he cannot sustain such sharpness for more than a few lines. He lacks the confidence and panache of Keith Douglas; though a more likeable figure, and perhaps one who promised more, he achieved less. He was killed in India in circumstances which remain obscure, apparently accidentally shot during night manoeuvres by one of his fellow-soldiers.

A poet who first became known as a 'war poet' but survived to win solider recognition as a wry observer of social life and personal feeling is Roy Fuller (1912–91). Fuller spent his professional life as a solicitor, with contrasting periods in the Royal Navy (1941–5) and as Oxford Professor of Poetry (1968–73). His first widely noticed book was *The Middle of a War* (1942). Although several of its poems tackle the large issues of warfare directly – 'An ambulance bell rings in the dark among/The rasp of guns, and abstract wrong is brought/ Straight to my riveted thought' ('London Air-Raid, 1940') – it seems significant that Fuller uneasily notes a sensory experience as bringing an abstraction to 'thought', for the most striking poems are also the most muted and personal:

> Sitting at home and reading Julien Benda;
> Evening descending in successive gauzes –
> Pantomime transformation scene reversed;
> A point releasing Haydn from a groove
> In waves alternately severe and tender:
> A curious way to spend a night of war!

The picture of the poet reading and listening to records is a recurrent one in Fuller's poetry, and typifies the modest, wry and domestic tone of much of his work. Although the reference to Benda (author of *La Trahison des clercs*) hints at a serious view of the poet's responsibilities, Fuller's verse deliberately rejects claims to bardic authority and the heightened tone that asserts it. Indeed, most aspects of his verse – apart from the persisting influence of Auden and a liking for syllabics – resemble the values espoused by the 'Movement' poets of the 1950s, a fact which perhaps explains the steady and uncontroversial rise of his reputation in the post-war years. His work is a friendly, compassionate meditation on ordinariness: never of high intensity, but constantly intelligent, and oddly reassuring in its unfussed acceptance of flawed human nature.

VIII

Douglas, Lewis and Fuller are all poets to whom irony and intellectual control are of the first importance. The intellectual assertiveness of the previous decade had, however, been badly shaken by events, and war, with its ubiquitous threat of violent death, had brought something of a religious revival. Perhaps partly for some such reasons, much poetry of the 1940s moved towards what may usefully be called (adopting a term hesitantly used by an assortment of critics during the period) a 'Neo-Romantic' mode. David Wright has written that he and his contemporaries

rejected what seemed to us the over-simplistic political commitments of our immediate predecessors, the poets of the 1930s. Some of the things that did interest us were the symbolism of Yeats, the reaffirmation of orthodox religious themes in the poetry of T. S. Eliot and Charles Williams and some others, and the exploration of poetic myth in the work of Robert Graves.

(David Wright, Collected Poems 1943–1987, 1988, p 2)

The result was a poetry which tended to be non-ironic, even earnest, and to draw on mythical or religious sources, expressing a vision strongly charged with emotion. Few poets of the 1940s show all these qualities together; rather, one finds a spectrum of poetic styles. At one end were witty and urbane poets like John Heath-Stubbs, whose fascination with pagan myth and Dark-Age Britain was tempered by a very 'classical' delight in wit, control and playful ornateness of technique; at the other extreme were the poets of the 'New Apocalypse', such as J. F. Hendry, Nicholas Moore and Henry Treece, who regretted the 'absence of rhodomontade or rhetoric of fine language in poetry' (as their associate Alex Comfort put it) and felt a need to 'inject more eloquence and a more archimagical touch into poetry'. The 'New Apocalypse' group's two anthologies (*The New Apocalypse*, 1939, and *The White Horseman*, 1941) on the whole lived up to this dismayingly crude notion of poetry: although they included work by such notable figures as Dylan Thomas, Norman MacCaig and Vernon Watkins, they showed above all a rejection of intellectualism and a delight in rhetoric for its own sake.

Indeed, the presence of Thomas is especially significant, for without his example and the taste he created the poetry of the 'New Apocalypse' could not have achieved even a temporary prominence. Thomas cannily refused ever to associate his name with a 'group', and despite his many friendships no one has argued for the existence of a 'Thomas gang' on the lines of the 'Auden gang'. None the less, his work remains the most interesting and powerful Neo-Romantic writing of its time, and Thomas was as influential on younger poets between about 1939 and 1956 as Auden had been before the war.

Dylan Marlais Thomas (1914–53) was born in Swansea, the son of a schoolmaster at the local grammar school, where Thomas himself was educated. He began to write seriously during his last year at school and the notebooks he kept then and until 1934, when he gave up his job as a reporter on a local paper and went to London, show an intense effort to develop a poetic style out of a fascination with metaphor and symbol.

In his teens Thomas was already well read, having had access to his father's well-stocked library, which contained much modern literature. The notebooks show traces of Blake and Shakespeare, Hopkins and Eliot, but are most striking in the way they allow full rein to their imagery. Like the early Auden, Thomas had a very high tolerance of obscurity; very many of the poems have no identifiable theme beyond the generalities (sex, birth, death, time, the cosmos) dear to most adolescent poets, but derive energy from an odd intertwining of imagery which seems to develop by a process of free association:

> On these blue lips, the lime remarks,
> The wind of kisses sealed a pact
> That leaping reins threw to the wind
> And brains turned sour;
> The blood got up as red as wax
> And kisses froze the waxing thought,
> The spirit racked its muscles and
> The loins cried murder.
>
> (Ralph Maud, ed., *Poet in the Making:
> The Notebooks of Dylan Thomas*, 1968)

The lines are given a loose unity by imagery drawn from the parts of the body, and accordingly the reader can produce interpretations to make a vague sense out of them. But they lack particularity: in the

last line we could probably delete 'loins' and substitute (say) 'hands'
or even 'ears' without much altering the effect.

The impression that Thomas's style allows an independent life to
imagery is confirmed by Thomas himself, who wrote:

A poem by myself needs a host of images ... I make one image ... let it
breed another, let that image contradict the first, make of the third image
bred out of the other two together, a fourth contradictory image, and let
them all, within my imposed limits, conflict[.]

(Paul Ferris, ed., *Collected Letters*, 1985, p 281)

Thomas's first book, *18 Poems* (1934), was published jointly by
David Archer (bookseller and friend of many poets) and the *Sunday
Referee*, a newspaper whose poetry competition Thomas had won.
He had already published poems in *The Criterion* and *New Verse*,
and quickly integrated himself into London's literary bohemia, gaining a growing reputation as both writer and boon-companion.
Twenty-five Poems appeared in 1936 and *The Map of Love* in 1939.
Of the fifty-nine poems contained in these three books, no fewer
than forty-five had been developed from drafts in the Swansea
notebooks: an indication both of Thomas's precocious gift and of the
difficulty he found in developing – features which may well be
related to the verbally self-generating nature of his art.

Many of these poems are, individually, of impenetrable obscurity,
and attempts to make sense of them have generated a large body of
criticism. Collectively, however, they build up a picture of a world
where life and death interpenetrate, where all activity is cyclical and
where man is viewed as intimately integrated with nature: indeed, if
the poems have a single identifiable theme, it is that man and nature
are identical. The level of accomplishment of the poems varies
widely. The sense, unavoidable for most readers, that the poems are
somehow sentimental, stems chiefly from two factors: first, from the
lack of a clear structure of thought – often one feels that anything
may symbolize anything else, and the result is a sense of flailing but
pointless activity like that created by the weaker poems of George
Barker and Vernon Watkins (both, significantly, friends of Thomas);
and second, from the nostalgia which tinges so many of the poems.
The line 'I see the boys of summer in their ruin', for example, is the
clearest line in the poem it opens and sets its entire emotional tone.
It is hard to believe that the poem could have become as well known
as it is without this striking and melancholy opening, beyond which
the poem never really develops.

The poems from these early volumes which have caught the

public imagination, however, are those which are the least obscure and which sum up the world-view Thomas held at this time. 'The force that through the green fuse drives the flower' and 'And death shall have no dominion' work by insistent, repetitive rhythms, simple, vivid but wholly traditional imagery, and uncomplicated feeling: the first is given relish by a touch of self-pity ('And I am dumb to tell the lover's tomb/How at my sheet goes the same crooked worm'), the second by an assertive optimism that (like much of the poem's diction) derives from the traditions of the evangelical hymn:

> Though they go mad they shall be sane,
> Though they sink through the sea they shall rise again;
> Though lovers be lost love shall not;
> And death shall have no dominion.

They are what Orwell would have called 'good bad poems': strong, lively, memorable and a bit crude, expressing what we would like to feel rather than what we do feel.

By the end of 1939 Thomas's poetry had won adulation, typified by Herbert Read's 'these poems cannot be reviewed: they can only be acclaimed' (review of *The Map of Love*, in *Seven*, No 6, Autumn 1939) but also scepticism (as from Louis MacNeice, who compared Thomas to 'a drunk man speaking wildly but rhythmically, pouring out a series of nonsense images . . .', *Modern Poetry: A Personal Essay*, 1938, p 160). Exempt from military service because of weak lungs, Thomas spent the war working for a company which made propaganda films and in 1941 sold his notebooks, source of so much of his earlier poetry, to an American library.

His poetry of the war years, produced with great difficulty and many 'dry' periods, shows a greater clarity and more real originality than the pre-war work.

Although natural and archetypal imagery are still prominent, there are subtleties of tone new to Thomas. 'A Refusal to Mourn the Death, by Fire, of a Child in London' manages to elevate its subject rather than the poet's ego and (despite the still-elaborate rhetoric) there is at least an awareness of the value of modesty in its declaration that

> I shall not murder
> The mankind of her going with a grave truth
> Nor blaspheme down the stations of the breath
> With any further
> Elegy of innocence and youth.

The poem's famous last line – 'After the first death there is no other' – has an impressive simplicity of diction and, although it is weighted with ambiguities, they are fruitful and important ones that the poem seems to recognize. 'Poem in October' and 'Fern Hill', celebrations of romantic delight in an idealized countryside, though not profound works, are at any rate delightful pastorals, their verbal ornateness a manifestation of joy in the textures of language and the world. Like a Chagall painting they offer a childlike vision which has charm but also the strength of a recaptured innocence expressed through enjoyment of the artist's medium. They deserve to be remembered and undoubtedly will be.

These poems and other wartime work were collected in *Deaths and Entrances* (1946), a substantial volume which was greeted with ecstatic reviews. Thomas, however, was drifting. Drinking heavily and unable to hold on to money, he failed to secure a permanent home or steady work in broadcasting. He moved with his wife and child (he had married Caitlin Macnamara in 1937) from one temporary home to another until in 1949 he settled at The Boat House, Laugharne in South Wales, and early in 1950 undertook the first of his four reading-tours in the United States. On the tour Thomas displayed his remarkable gifts as a reader of poetry (his orotund and rhetorical delivery, though of a kind that has since gone out of fashion, is still impressive in recordings) but also indulged in outrageous and irresponsible behaviour, often egged on by 'admirers' to whom this vulnerable and disorganized poet appeared a novel source of excitement. He returned with almost no money to show for his efforts, but was able to work at new poems (including 'Do Not Go Gentle Into That Good Night') and 'Poem on His Birthday') and his 'Play for Voices', *Under Milk Wood*, whose composition was interrupted by a second American tour in 1952.

Despite several very competent film scripts, *Under Milk Wood* is Thomas's only significant dramatic work. It follows the inhabitants of a small Welsh seaside town – playfully caricatured from Thomas's own Laugharne – through twenty-four hours, tracing their foibles, dreams, fantasies and relationships in a series of interwoven dramatic monologues. The play has been harshly criticized – for lack of form, lack of action, lack of a 'moral centre'; for its shallow vulgarization of techniques borrowed from Joyce's *Ulysses*; for its infantilism, its indifference to economic, social or political problems, and a hundred other supposed failings that seem curiously beside the point when one listens to the play or reads it. For what *Under Milk Wood* transmits above all is a feeling of affection, of delight in the strangeness, vitality and sensitivity of people. The play is not a representation of Wales so much as of human nature, and to call its characters stereotypes is simply a hostile way of recognizing that they are 'humours' of the sort comic drama has always dealt in. Mrs Ogmore Pritchard, obsessed with hygiene; Willy Nilly the postman, who reads the letters before delivering them; Polly Garter, endlessly susceptible to men but always thinking of her dead lover – they are absurd and without psychological depth, but they represent real human tendencies.

Like all his work, *Under Milk Wood* displays Thomas's linguistic exuberance, but gives it a new twist, as if he had at last fully realized the comic potential of his own loquacity:

NARRATOR: The Reverend Eli Jenkins inky in his cool front parlour or poem-room tells only the truth in his life-work – the Population, Main Industries, Shipping, History, Topography, Flora and Fauna of the town he worships in – the White Book of Llaregyb. Portraits of famous bards and preachers, all fur and wool from the squint to the kneecaps, hang over him heavy as sheep, next to faint lady watercolours of pale green Milk Wood like a lettuce salad dying. His mother, propped against a pot in a palm suffers in her stays, with her wedding-ring waist and bust like a black clothed dining-table.

REV ELI JENKINS: Oh angels be careful there with your knives and forks . . .

Interestingly the rhymes and ballads interspersed in the text are in a plain style quite unlike Thomas's typical work – a use of contrast indicating greater stylistic self-awareness than Thomas is usually credited with.

Under Milk Wood has remained popular and, though written for radio, has often been successfully staged. It deserves its popularity as a vivid and well-executed work, although to claim Thomas as a great poetic dramatist – as has been done – would be ridiculous. *Under Milk Wood* is precisely the kind of fine, small work which cannot be repeated.

When he finished the play, hastily, during his third American tour in 1953, Thomas was in no position to make a fresh start. Tired, disorganized and drinking heavily, he returned to England in June and tried ineffectually to work before setting off, desperately, for yet another American tour in October. Early in November he collapsed in New York and died from obscure causes, probably including alcoholic poisoning. His reputation was at its height, but there had always been fiercely dissenting voices and a reaction soon set in. As personal adulation fell away, Thomas could be seen as the author of a few fine poems and of many more failed, eccentric experiments, one who had pursued an idiosyncratic method to a surprising number of successes but who offered no way forward and had indeed been a disastrous model for a number of younger poets.

IX

Apart from Dylan Thomas the poet who undertook most substantially a visionary poetry, free from irony and Modernist fragmentation, rooted in the Romantic tradition by way of Yeats, was Vernon Watkins (1906–67). After a brilliant year of study at Cambridge, Watkins rejected the intellectual approach to literature and returned to Swansea, where he spent his life as a bank clerk, always refusing promotion. Despite great fluency in verse – which he saw as a danger – he was reluctant to publish and spent ten years practising his art before Faber and Faber published *The Ballad of the Mari Lwyd* (1941). The *Ballad* is one of his most powerful works; drawing on Welsh folk-tradition it celebrates a moment on New Year's Eve when the dead and the living communicate and argue – afraid and envious of each other but admitting a fundamental kinship. The poem is eerie and frightening but powered by a strong, springy ballad-rhythm:

> Midnight. Midnight. Midnight. Midnight.
> Hark at the hands of the clock . . .
>
> Go back. We have heard of dead men's bones
> That hunger out in the air.
> Jealous they break through their burial-stones,
> Their white hands joined in a prayer.
> They rip the seams of their proper white clothes
> And with red throats parched for gin,
> With buckled knuckles and bottle-necked oaths
> They hammer the door of an inn.

The 'bottle-necked oaths' perhaps reflect the influence of Watkins's friend Dylan Thomas, but the simplicity and profusion of the imagery, and the sense of a welter of activity which is none the less somehow outside time, are altogether typical of Watkins.

The *Ballad* was followed by six more books in Watkins's lifetime, and by three posthumous collections, now superseded by the 1986

Collected Poems. His work shows no fundamental stylistic development, partly perhaps because his published volumes are thematic
rather than chronological in content: poems published late in life
were in some cases written very early and held back until
companion-pieces existed. In any case his vision, by its nature, was
not one to change much. His weakness is that in his haste to reach
the mythical or timeless he too often neglects to establish the
particularities of a common world from which the visions might
start. The welter of archetypal images, the constantly exalted tone,
create monotony. When he can keep the mundane and the visionary
in balance, as in 'The Collier', 'Yeats in Dublin', 'Thames Forest'
and 'A Man With a Field' or where he adopts a quieter, more
aphoristic tone ('After Summer'), his poems have great emotional
power and convince in their double vision of man as an eternal being
immersed in time.

Not all poets concerned with spiritual matters followed Thomas
and Watkins into an unintellectual poetry dominated by imagery,
strong rhythm and turbulent emotion. A poet much harder to
classify and of at least equal interest is Charles Williams (1886–
1945), who is sometimes treated as a poet of the 1930s but whose
influence made itself felt chiefly during the 1940s. Now principally
remembered as the friend of C. S. Lewis and J. R. R. Tolkien – an
association that flourished during the war, when he lived in Oxford –
he was a prolific writer and of striking originality as a poet and
novelist. A committed Christian, Williams attached great importance
to the part played by the poetic imagination in religious understanding. His early poems, published between 1912 and 1924, are written
in a heavily Victorian style reminiscent of Rossetti and Patmore, and
struggle unhappily to express a vision of the divine and sacred seen
through, and manifested in, the mundane. Love, marriage and
worldly business are represented as embodying, or incarnating,
attributes of God and his relationship to the world. This vision
found adequate expression in the far more original and powerful
work of *Taliessin Through Logres* (1938) and *The Region of the
Summer Stars* (1944), where Williams develops an Arthurian myth:
Arthur, a type of the Christian, established the ideal kingdom of
Logres, largely through the agency of the bard and sage Taliessin
(the creative imagination); it falls again, as man must always fall,
through human selfishness, but not before it has manifested the
spiritual order man must seek to embody in his life. This theme,
hardly new in itself, is developed with great richness, yet with a cool
eloquence and fragmentary perspective that recall Yeats, the later

Eliot and the *Anathemata* of David Jones (Eliot and Jones both knew and admired Williams's work). Williams's style is capable of moving between levels of symbolism with great fluency. Here, for example, is Taliessin at the decisive battle of Mount Badon, turning to Virgil, poet of the Roman national epic, for inspiration:

> Civilized centuries away, the Roman moved.
> Taliessin saw the flash of his style
> dash at the wax; he saw the hexameter spring
> and the king's sword swing; he saw, in the long field,
> the point where the pirate chaos might suddenly yield,
> the place for the law of grace to strike . . .
> The Aeneid's beaked lines swooped on Actium;
> the stooped horse charged . . .
> The household of Taliessin swung on the battle[.]

Here Taliessin is simultaneously military tactician, poet and embodiment of divine grace. Each patiently waits for the right place and moment to strike, to change humanity and history. Williams's poems are often obscure, and their unexpected welding of modernist techniques with attitudes close to those of medieval Christianity make them particularly uncongenial to contemporary tastes; but they show a remarkably strong use of language, and represent a challenge which perhaps modern readers and writers should more often try to meet.

More accessible are Williams's six novels, 'supernatural thrillers' dealing with the occult, whose entertaining treatment of moral and religious issues has earned them a following denied to Williams's poems and his copious theological and critical works.

One poet who has been directly affected by Williams is John Heath-Stubbs (b. 1918), whose poetry shows a persistent fascination with mythology and an eclectic style. Heath-Stubbs's abiding characteristic is the wry, melancholy wit with which he reflects on the repetitious patterns of human existence. A close associate of David Wright and Sidney Keyes, he achieved critical (though not popular) reputation with *Wounded Thammuz* (1942) and *The Divided Ways* (1946), but his most impressive achievement may well be *Artorius* (1973), 'A heroic poem in four books and eight episodes', which lacks the symbolic depth of Williams's Arthurian sequence but exceeds it in readability, linguistic exuberance and sense of comic absurdity. The late Auden is an obvious influence, but Heath-Stubbs adds insights and erudition of his own: the Arthur story is seen as the archetype of every man's life –

> his season's progress
> From spring's heyday to high summer and harvest,
> And lastly to the laggard lagoon of old age
> Where his son supplants him and the cycle returns

– and the poem ends with the five words that began it, so that it reads as a closed circle. Yet it finds room for topical satire, as when the criticism of F. R. Leavis is brilliantly parodied in lectures by Pillidas, a dark-age rhetorician who mercilessly dissects the Roman poets. Heath-Stubbs's poetry is a delightful gallimaufry of styles and subjects, flawed only by a sense that it has been a little too easily written, its materials played with rather than fully explored.

Sharing the cooler, more 'classical' end of the Neo-Romantic spectrum with Heath-Stubbs is Kathleen Raine (b. 1908). Educated at Cambridge, where she read biology and was a friend of Empson, she none the less found Cambridge intellectualism, with its secular materialist assumptions, uncongenial. Her earliest significant work (published in *Stone and Flower*, 1943), was done at Martindale in the Lake District, where she spent the war years, and consists of poems meditating on glimpses of the transcendent perceived through nature:

> There is a fish that quivers in the pool,
> itself a shadow, but its shadow, clear.
> Catch it again and again, it is still there.
>
> Against the flowing stream, its life keeps pace
> With death – the impulse and the flash of grace
> hiding in its stillness, moves, to be motionless.

> ('In the Beck')

Her best work has this limpid, suggestive clarity. Her poetic output has been small but steady, and much of her best work has come late: *The Lost Country* (1971) and *The Oval Portrait* (1977) both contain work where the insights are expressed through vivid imagery that saves it from the abstraction which always threatens such strenuously otherworldly verse. Raine is well known as an interpreter of Blake and Yeats and of other visonary and religious poets such as Edwin Muir, Vernon Watkins and David Jones: equally important, perhaps, is her fine autobiography (four volumes, beginning with *Farewell Happy Fields*, 1973), which gives a vividly personal account of literary and cultural life in Britain spanning most of the twentieth century.

X

In Ireland, the most important poetry of the 1940s is represented by the work of Patrick Kavanagh (1904–67) and, interestingly, embodies a determined reaction against the 'Romantic' and visionary attitudes espoused by Yeats. Born at Mucker in County Monaghan, Kavanagh was the son of a small farmer, and when he left school at the age of twelve to work on the farm he was already an enthusiastic reader and writer of poetry. In 1930 he met the poet George Russell ('AE') in Dublin and began to publish poems and articles in the Dublin press. His first book, *Ploughman and Other Poems* (1936), was acclaimed in both Britain and Ireland for its strong, plain language, vivid imagery and powerful feeling. Kavanagh had found a voice in which the local attachments and personal feelings of the Irish Catholic farming culture gained universal resonance. Inevitably he was patronized in some quarters as a 'peasant poet', but his work has a clarity and vehemence that stand up well beside the poems of Edward Thomas or the later Yeats:

> My black hills have never seen the sun rising,
> Eternally they look north to Armagh . . .
> They are my Alps and I have climbed the Matterhorn
> With a sheaf of hay for three perishing calves
> In the field under the Big Forth of Rocksavage.
>
> The sleety winds fondle the rushy beards of Shancoduff
> While the cattle-drovers sheltering in the Featherna Bush
> Look up and say: 'Who owns them hungry hills
> That the water-hen and snipe must have forsaken?
> A poet? Then by heavens he must be poor.'
> I hear and is my heart not badly shaken?
>
> ('Shancoduff')

Kavanagh loathed the romanticized notion of Ireland cherished by the English and exploited, he felt, by Yeats and the writers of the Protestant ascendancy. He truckled to it a little in his early autobiographical novel *The Green Fool* (1938) – a work he later rejected – but his major poem *The Great Hunger* (1942) is an eloquent and compassionate criticism of the cultural and emotional starvation imposed on rural Ireland by poverty and a timidly mean-spirited religion.

The Great Hunger is the work where Kavanagh comes closest to Modernism. Its irregular verse with occasional rhyme owes a good deal to the early Eliot, and its sharp, selective imagery is close to

Imagism, but its moral outrage, spiritually tinged compassion and intimate acquaintance with the grim details of its subject make it a unique and powerful work. It traces the life of Maguire, a small farmer, whose life is dominated by his aged mother, the poor soil of his farm, and the small authority of the church. Maguire tries to do his duty to all three, and the result is a bitterly lonely, joyless and ultimately almost meaningless life. Kavanagh introduces his protagonist starkly:

> Clay is the word and clay is the flesh
> Where the potato-gatherers like mechanised scarecrows move
> Along the side-fall of the hill – Maguire and his men.
> If we watch them an hour is there anything we can prove
> Of life as it is broken-backed over the Book
> Of death? Here crows gabble over worms and frogs
> And the gulls like old newspapers are blown clear of the hedges, luckily.
> Is there some light of imagination in these wet clods?

Maguire's dominating mother early advises him to make his farm his bride; the demands of work and the warnings of the church turn this into an ironic reality:

> He saw his cattle
> And stroked their flanks in lieu of wife to handle.
> He would have changed the circle if he could,
> The circle that was the grass track where he ran.
> Twenty times a day he ran round the field
> And still there was no winning-post where the winner is cheered home.

Barely literate, shy of the few women he meets, Maguire lives in a tiny world bounded by church and pub, in which sexual frustration is a major torment. In a sad and symbolic moment, he masturbates over the ashes of a dying fire while his mother dozes upstairs (an episode which nearly led to the poem's being prosecuted by the Irish authorities). He remains an innocent, and there are occasional glimpses of beatitude which break the brutal monotony of his life:

> One day he saw a daisy and he thought it
> Reminded him of his childhood –
> He stopped his cart to look at it.
> Was there a fairy hiding behind it?
> . . . And one rare moment he heard the young people playing on the railway
>   stile
> And he wished them happiness and whatever they most desired from life.

But the only final escape from his condition is death. Kavanagh strongly hints that Maguire's plight typifies that of Ireland; the poem's title alludes to the potato famine of the 1840s, and our last glimpse of Maguire points to the country as a whole:

> He stands in the doorway of his house
> A ragged sculpture of the wind,
> October creaks the rotten mattress,
> The bedposts fall. No hope. No lust.
> The hungry fiend
> Screams the apocalypse of clay
> In every corner of this land.

Kavanagh had left his farm in 1939 and moved permanently to Dublin, confronting the problem often faced by writers who find their literary career removing them from the imaginative roots of their work. Kavanagh came to feel that his decision to 'go/Over the field to the City of the Kings/Where art, music, letters, are the real things' had been a disastrous error. Dublin was, inevitably, a disappointment, and he spent much of the 1940s involved in personal and literary feuding, producing unimpressive satirical verse, although there was a return to his earlier, more deeply felt manner in *A Soul for Sale* (1947). The troubles of this period culminated in an ill-judged libel action against a newspaper, followed immediately by major surgery for lung cancer. This crisis unexpectedly led to a renewed tranquillity and a group of important poems that celebrate it in a style of radiant simplicity – 'Canal Bank Walk', 'The Hospital' and 'Come Dance with Kitty Stobling'. The perspective of his work is best summed up in a sonnet (entitled, with typical irony, 'Epic') where he affirms his faith in the 'parochial' as poetic subject matter, recalling a village quarrel over land in 1938:

> That was the year of the Munich bother. Which
> Was more important? I was inclined
> To lose my faith in Ballyrush and Gortin
> Till Homer's ghost came whispering to my mind
> He said: I made the Iliad from such
> A local row. Gods make their own importance.

Like *The Great Hunger*, 'Epic' has greatness. Kavanagh's rural Catholic perspective and continuation of a romantic individualism that none the less rejected the high rhetoric of Yeats made him an inspiring writer for later Irish poets such as Derek Mahon and Seamus Heaney. He is a major poet and still scandalously little-known in England.

In other respects the plain-speaking realism, accessibility and social concern of Kavanagh's work anticipated qualities which would soon become typical of the poetry written in mainland Britain. For with the death of Dylan Thomas the 'Neo-Romantic' wave had broken. There seemed no prospect that the future of English poetry would be an exuberantly rhetorical one, and even poets as restrained and traditional as John Heath-Stubbs and Kathleen Raine would have to wait two decades for substantial recognition. By the time of Thomas's second American tour, Philip Larkin in Belfast was already at work on poems that would form the nucleus of *The Less Deceived* and, rejecting the 'potent music' of Yeats, was turning for stimulus to the example of Hardy. From now on 'the colour of saying' would be a drabber one, but more modest and perhaps truer to the quiet uncertainties of life in post-war Britain.

9

THE NOVEL SINCE 1950

Martin Dodsworth

I

In Britain the Second World War led to disenchantment. The new order which emerged in Europe was not much better than the old; the threat from Germany was replaced by the threat from Russia. At home, austerity lasted longer than anyone expected. The radical reforms of the post-war Labour government ran into difficulty. The dismantling of Empire and the failure at Suez in 1956 spoke of a loss of power and status to which British people found it hard to adjust.

These were depressing circumstances for a novelist, particularly one with a name to be made. The war itself had fostered a romantic extravagance in fiction, exemplified by the Gormenghast trilogy of Mervyn Peake (1911–68): *Titus Groan* (1946), *Gormenghast* (1950), *Titus Alone* (1959). Peake's Gothic fantasies, like the Welsh sentiment of Dylan Thomas (1914–53) in *Portrait of the Artist as a Young Dog* (1940), created imaginative space where the pressures of the everyday could be held at bay. These are works of originality, but of an originality difficult to sustain. Peake was hampered by the onset of Parkinson's disease, Thomas by his alcoholism. The mood of disillusion in 1950s Britain favoured neither. That mood sustained Graham Greene in the late flowering of his art, but not the public-school wit of Evelyn Waugh. It carried Beckett as a writer of prose into the 1960s and 1970s, fostered a revival in the fortunes of Jean Rhys but rendered the passion and sensibility of Elizabeth Bowen archaic. It was not welcoming to new talent.

It is tempting to suggest that the failure of Philip Larkin (1922–85) to mature as a novelist into the 1950s had something to do with that mood, but the case would be hard to sustain. Larkin's interest in the underdog, and the underdog as woman, as well as in the negative aspects of human existence, allies him with both Beckett and Rhys. His anti-romanticism makes him a forerunner of angry writers like John Osborne or his own friend Kingsley Amis

(b. 1922). His second novel was well received and his first was something of a cult. He should have been the novelist of the 1950s, but poetry took him elsewhere. His fiction is nevertheless important in itself and, in its concerns, for much that followed.

Precise, original and, in a chilly way, humane, *Jill* (1946) and *A Girl in Winter* (1947) are both written from the point of view of an outsider. In the former, John Kemp, a grammar-school boy at Oxford, invents Jill, a sister/girlfriend, with whom to impress his unpleasant public-school room-mate; in the latter, Katherine Lind works in a library in wartime Britain, an exile from her own country, remembering happy times which cannot be revived. Both novels show their central character coming to terms with life by a kind of negative transcendence:

Then if there was no difference between love fulfilled and love unfulfilled, how could there be any difference between any other pair of opposites? Was he not freed, for the rest of his life, from choice?

(*Jill*)

Truly she did not care one way or the other, being neither insulted nor flattered. She could easily refuse, yet refusal would be dulling, an assent to all the wilderness that surrounded them. If she did not refuse, he would go back to his camp and boast about it, to cover the humiliation he suffered in making her accept. She did not mind. Her spirits were rising higher. He could not touch her.

(*A Girl in Winter*)

This is in essence the bleak philosophy of Larkin's poetry. Probably not many readers would endorse it; yet to have it spelled out so plainly, so lucidly, bespeaks a kind of courage to which respect is due.

These are novels about innocence; the supreme value is personal not political and not, except in the broadest sense, religious – it is the refusal to hurt others. John imagines Jill: 'he thought he saw exactly what she was and how he should express it: the word was *innocent* . . .', that is, 'not procuring harm'. John's invention of Jill springs from his own aversion to cruelty: it is a longing for the good so intense that it takes the form of imagined possession by the good. He writes letters from Jill, he writes Jill's diary, and at last suffers a secular-mystic experience, like 'looking into the centre of a pure white light'. The imagery anticipates later poems such as 'Water' or 'High Windows'. In *A Girl in Winter* the insensitive, importunate Robin Fennel who sleeps with Katherine is, nevertheless, unable to 'touch' her. She is another innocent. What she has to learn is that the person who loves her is Robin's sister, Jane. The relationship, like that of John with Jill, is not sexual. The novel pointedly leaves Katherine at a distance from Jane: the knowledge of her love seems to be enough to sustain.

Larkin completed his remarkable, elegant and deeply serious novels by the time he was twenty-five. He started other novels, but none was completed. A vision of pure white light can be extended over two hundred pages or more only with difficulty (both the novels are formally very exact), and the more succinct beauties of poetry were truer to it. 'Mr Bleaney', for example, sums up a life in twenty-eight lines. The brevity is reticence, a refusal to love in the wrong way. 'Where's the sense/In saying love, but meaning interference?' ('He Hears that his Beloved has become Engaged'). The novel risked 'interferences', risked discriminating 'love fulfilled' from 'love unfulfilled'.

Larkin's recoil from the harm that he saw in life is balanced by a fellow-feeling for the wounded and disadvantaged. John Kemp is a working-class boy represented with a self-effacing tenderness that is wholly successful, and which surfaces later as an attitude to 'ordinary' life in poems such as 'Show Sunday' or 'To the Sea':

> It may be that through habit these do best,
> Coming to water clumsily undressed
> Yearly; teaching their children by a sort
> Of clowning; helping the old, too, as they ought.

This feeling of human solidarity, however, went with intense moments, in the man, of self-loathing and to an anti-intellectualism that in later writings got out of control. It is something also to be found in the work of his friend and contemporary Kingsley Amis, whose fierce, funny, inventive and very unequal novels are often flawed by blasts of unconvincing populist sentiment. They suggest how difficult a thing the aesthetic refinement of *A Girl in Winter* must have been to achieve. Given the social and political changes in Europe of the ten years from 1945 to 1955, it is easy to see why the uncertainties of Amis, initially marked as comedy, should have had such strong appeal. His populism (which is, one must be clear, associated with predominantly middle-class values) had an important part to play in reassuring his public that the frustrations he expressed were nevertheless within the bounds of a decency which he, along with his readers, could acknowledge. Amis puts his homage to Fielding, humane judge and decent, common-sense novelist, at the heart of his third novel, *I Like it Here* (1958). But this homage reflects an attraction of opposites. Amis is a writer of extremity; his human sympathy is vulnerable, liable to sudden swings of irritation, even fury, or, on the other side, sentimentality.

At the heart of Amis's novels, the view of life is as bleak as anything in Larkin, but there is no vision of transcendence to sweeten it, only a tic of nervous, infantile laughter. As in Larkin, the deep desire of Amis's characters is not to hurt or to be hurt, an emotion corresponding to that of nations in the Cold War period. It follows that the serious moments in Amis are those where characters experience their lives as luck, as existence where the price of not hurting or being hurt is an absence of identity which is itself a kind of pain. In *Take a Girl Like You* (1960), an updated version of Richardson's *Clarissa*, for example, Lord Edgerstone describes the loss of sexual power with age:

It is as if one's right hand suddenly ceased to function. There it is, it is still part of one, of course, it can pick things up, it can open doors, it can hold a pen, it can pour a drink, it can tie a shoelace. Until one tries. Then it can't. Then it's useless. And it isn't going to get better. That's the thing one can't ever quite believe, I suppose. And what would one do if one did manage to believe it? That's the really fascinating question.

The 'comic' uproar of the novels is a reaction to this potential in life not to be 'life' at all, and their sentimentalism an apology, for the hurt that accompanies the uproar. Similarly, the novelist's populism is not just a matter of cultivating his public; it is the obverse of what makes solitary existence hard to take. Passages as direct, as apparently effortless, and as indifferent to rhetoric as the one just quoted are therefore not frequent in Amis, but are essential to an understanding of what he does.

Age and its sequel, death, sex and its sequel, impotence, bring out the best in his writing. *Ending Up* (1974) about five elderly people, invalid or nearly senile, living together in an unharmonious attempt at self-supportive independence, is Amis's best and blackest novel, recalling Larkin's poem 'The Old Fools', and, like that, equivocal in effect. Do its characters command our sympathy or not? The question is like that prompted by *Stanley and the Women* (1984): is it or is it not an 'attack' on women, as some women readers have claimed? *Jake's Thing* (1978), a glumly tendentious comedy about sex therapy, lacks this equivocal quality and fails. *The Old Devils* (1986) is about a group of miserably married old men, but reverses the question in *Stanley and the Women* by suggesting that the women are miserable too, and possibly because of the men. The humour here is stoic, the novelist at his closest to his chosen subject matter.

Amis is prolific in the matter of form. His admiration for the popular spy thrillers of Ian Fleming (1900–64) led him to write *Colonel Sun* (1968), reviving Fleming's hero, James Bond. *The Riverside Villas Murder* (1973) is a 1930s detective story; *The Alteration* (1976) and *Russian Hide and Seek* (1980) are essays in alternative and future history related to Amis's interest in science fiction; and *The Green Man* (1969) is a supernatural thriller deriving from M. R. James (1862–1936), author of *Ghost Stories of an Antiquary* (1904), and Charles Williams (1886–1945). He *uses* popular fiction, that is, and the restlessness in his choice of form is indicative of something unsatisfied, the fear or dread unappeased, to which attention has already been drawn. But it does also signify a radical imperfection in his *oeuvre* as a whole, in which the moments of power rarely combine with the more conventional elements which should cushion them.

Even Amis's first novel, *Lucky Jim* (1954), dedicated to Larkin, which was instantly successful and still maintains a high reputation as comedy, is badly flawed. Jim Dixon, university lecturer in search of tenure, is a good man among pretentious aesthetes (whom Amis dislikes almost as much as 'lefties'). He cannot manage to toe the line drawn by his professor, who loves madrigals and such. Jim is an English *Zazie dans le Métro*, an anarchic child who cannot, although he tries hard, tell a lie. So far, so good, in a limited way. But Jim falls prey to Margaret, 'one of those people – they're usually women – who feed on emotional tension'. The book's panicky farce derives from Margaret's tension and Jim's attempt to escape it. At the level of morality, nothing holds together. Jim's justification for his abandonment of Margaret is not good enough: nor is his acceptance of a virtual sinecure as an escape from the academic rat race. At the level of feeling, Margaret commands more sympathy than the farce allows for. In its failure to cohere, *Lucky Jim* embodies much of the essential Amis.

His novels often allude to, or aim to be, popular fiction. Larkin's novels also allude to the popular novel: *Jill* and *A Girl in Winter* both thrive on not being the romances they resemble. The ground-base in both these authors is a sympathy with middle-class values from which they ostensibly react. The sympathy comes out in their admiration for two novelists in the genteel tradition of women writing about the romantic ambitions of women. Larkin admired Barbara Pym (1913–80) as Amis does Elizabeth Taylor (1912–75). Both these women command an irony which qualifies romance, and both are superb in dialogue (as is also the case with Larkin and

Amis, although it is a rare gift in the period as a whole). Comparisons with Jane Austen seem, however, exaggerated. Pym and Taylor are indeed artists, but it is significant of a failure to adapt talent to form that their best work is in neither case typical: Taylor's *Angel* (1957) is about an old-fashioned romantic novelist in decline, Pym's *Quartet in Autumn* (1977) about four lonely people coming to terms with age and death. Someone who might be deemed one of their successors, Anita Brookner (b. 1928), brings a more refined and dedicated artistry to the tradition. In her early novels she portrays lonely women and weakly coercive men in stories that parallel and parody those of romantic fiction. This is the case in *Hotel du Lac* (1984), but she has moved on to more sombre accounts of a generalized alienation, sensitive, restrained and, by comparison with Larkin, a trifle overextended.

None of these novelists is particularly innovative in form, and they all rely on a fairly conventional view of the novel as more or less realistic. A preference for convention and for the conventionally representational novel is largely typical of the 1950s at least, and persists well after that, as the success of *A Dance to the Music of Time* by Anthony Powell (b. 1905) suggests.

This is a sequence of twelve novels of which the first, *A Question of Upbringing*, appeared in 1951 and the last, *Hearing Secret Harmonies*, in 1975. All the novels are narrated in the detached tones of Nick Jenkins, whose life traces much the same pattern as that of his creator – Eton, a gentlemanly job in publishing, war service, further literary–artistic–journalistic occupations. They give an assured account of changing circumstance in the upper levels of English society from the 1920s on. They are as accessible as the novels of Amis or Pym.

There is, of course, an implicit parallel to Proust's *Remembrance of Things Past*. No other English novelist has sought to chart on this scale the way in which changing historical circumstance alters the ambitions and aspirations of those who live in history, and so changes them themselves. The length of the sequence, which takes some time to catch fire, justifies itself in the revisions and revaluations that it permits. The mode is comic, perhaps because history provokes in Powell some of the fears that sex and death hold for Amis, and this perfectly suited the nervous caution of the years during which the sequence appeared. It is hardly Proust, though. It wants a philosophy, it wants Proust's hard edge, above all it wants Proust's quality as a writer.

It is hard not to read some significance into the fact that Powell had begun his career as a novelist in the 1930s. The best of his early works is *Venusberg* (1932), sharp, elegant, Waugh-like. He is fundamentally a rather old-fashioned novelist, old-fashioned in attitude as well as in technique, and this is what was gratifying about him in the 1950s and 1960s. The *Dance* is in some respects a reworking of Waugh's study in heroic failure, the *Sword of Honour* trilogy. Powell's equivalent for Guy Crouchback is Peter Stringham who, when the war comes, refuses to go along with the expectations of his privileged class and declines to take a commission. As a result he dies unnecessarily and ignominiously on the margin of someone else's egotistical pursuit of success. The event is compelling in itself, but conspires with something backward-looking in the series as a whole, something which the prose is too polite to allow to appear boldly.

Even 'experimental' work in the 1950s turns out on inspection to preserve a fundamental conventionality. Lawrence Durrell (1912–90) was better known as a poet until he published the four novels which make up his *Alexandria Quartet* (*Justine* 1957, *Balthazar* 1958, *Mountolive* 1958, *Clea* 1960). The *Quartet* was designed, Durrell said, as a challenge to the serial form of the conventional novel – 'the time-saturated novel' – but the challenge does not amount to much. The first three novels deal with interrelated events taking place simultaneously and seen from three distinct points of view, while the fourth is a 'true sequel' rounding off the story and explaining it. This hardly needs reference to the theory of relativity to be understood, but Durrell claimed that he had innovated in some way to which Einstein was pertinent. The *Quartet* is a fantasy of life in the devious, exotic East and draws upon the stereotypes of orientalism with zest. There is a desperate will to astonish in these novels, and British readers were the first to succumb. The *Quartet* was subsequently an international success. The Alexandrian setting is not so far removed from the fantastic halls of Peake's *Gormenghast*; both present stories of mythic intent, focusing on the artist and the curse that is also the creative power of imagination. By contrast, the work of Amis, caught up in its complex and contradictory feelings about the condition of human life itself, looks, however imperfect, alive, spasmodically self-aware as well as evasive, while Larkin's novels radiate uncannily the clear pure light of which they speak.

II

As a novelist Kingsley Amis is conventionally associated with 'angry' writers of the 1950s: William Cooper (b. 1910), whose *Scenes from Provincial Life* (1950) is sometimes regarded as seminal; John Wain (b. 1925), whose *Hurry on Down* (1953) has a hero comparable to

Jim Dixon; and John Braine (1922–86), whose *Room at the Top* (1957) is about the rise to success of a working-class anti-hero. But these writers did not form a group, with common aims, and only Amis was able to sustain his creative impulse and produce a series of continuously inventive and arresting novels. It is better to think of the new novelists of the 1950s as splitting into two groups – those who, like Amis or Pym, used the form in an expressive but largely unreflective manner, and those who sought to reintroduce large ideas to English fiction by a reassessment of its forms.

Chief among these is William Golding (1911–93) whose first novel, *Lord of the Flies* (1954), appearing in the same year as *Lucky Jim*, was yet very different from it. It is a novel with an idea, expounded clearly by Golding in his essay 'Fable' (*The Hot Gates*, 1965):

I decided to take the literary convention of boys on an island, only make them real boys instead of paper cutouts with no life in them: and try to show how the shape of the society they evolved would be conditioned by their diseased, their fallen nature.

It is hard to imagine any of Amis's novels emerging from a decision of this kind, and the fact points to something characteristic of Golding's art: he stands at a remove from it. The concern with humanity's fallen nature, a concern with specific religious association, is present in all his work, but it is not associated with the force of such a personality as the contradictions and fancies of Amis's novels suggest. Golding's novels, in John Bayley's words, forgo any intimacy between novelist and reader. Each is a separate creation, distinct from any other of his works and offering no overt hints as to the nature of the author himself. These settings are very varied: prehistory in *The Inheritors* (1955); the English Middle Ages in *The Spire* (1964); a voyage to Australia at the beginning of the nineteenth century in the trilogy made up of *Rites of Passage* (1980), *Close Quarters* (1987) and *Fire Down Below* (1989); English provincial life in the 1920s and 1930s in *The Pyramid* (1967). But the variety does not reflect restlessness and uncertainty, as it does in Amis. Here it betokens the confidence that certainty, of means and ends, can bring.

Golding's words have a crafted feel about them: everything tends to fit or to be made to fit. He is himself deeply interested in other people's craft. He imagines in great detail the building stone by stone of *The Spire* and, although the burden of the tale is the moral cost of that achievement, it depends on the conviction with which the physical cost is given the reader first. Similarly, *Close Quarters* depends on the author's ability to convince the reader that the inner space of Captain Anderson's ship must have both been and felt as it is described by the naive and egotistical Edmund Talbot:

Two yards beyond the light of the gun-room and there might never have been in my world such things as light and direction. By the time I had gone five yards I was more thoroughly lost than I had ever been in a covert! All I knew was sound, much creaking and gritty straining, but there were sounds of water as if I were crouched on a gravel beach!

The detail of sensation here matches the apparent mastery of marine techniques when, later in the same novel, a dragrope is used to clear the hull of weed. In 'Envoy Extraordinary' (1956, collected in *The Scorpion God*, 1971) the premise is that Phanocles has invented the field-gun, the steamship and the pressure-cooker, and has done so at the time of the Roman Empire; the collocation of steamship and pressure-cooker is characteristic, as is the humour of the denouement which develops, like a smoothly operating machine, from the overheating of the steamship's boiler.

The words share a concern with man's fuller nature, a concern which is given conscious religious value in most of them. His engagement with Christianity may seem an archaic touch in an age when few intellectuals will admit to a metaphysic of any kind. Yet the novel since the Second World War has, in England, frequently tackled questions of faith in a religious sense. Kingsley Amis, for example, might seem an unlikely candidate for the title of religious novelist, but both *The Anti-Death League* (1966) and *The Green Man* show an obvious concern with spiritual value and faith – the latter even includes a conversation with the deity, unsettling and serious. Neither of these novels insists on a specific form of Christianity, differing in this way from the work of Graham Greene: Greene's specific loyalties mark him out as fundamentally of the 1930s generation. Golding's contemplation of fallen humanity is characteristically unspecific in its Christian allegiances: he writes with certainty for and within a world of post-war uncertainty.

This means that his craftsmanship and certainty are both complex. The decline into moral disorder of the boys in *Lord of the Flies* parallels the decline into atomic warfare that has precipitated their arrival on the island. But this decline into murderous intent is put in perspective by a change in point of view at the end of the novel, when the young officer who has come from a British cruiser to rescue the children sees 'a semicircle of little boys' where two paragraphs earlier the reader was imagining an ageless human depravity.

The irony here cuts two ways, since it exposes the lieutenant's own lack of self-knowledge but also dares the reader to discount the simple faith in innocence that is nevertheless part of that lack. Golding's fascination with the machinery of fiction can encourage excessively simple interpretation, as though his machines were designed to do only one thing, but the machinery is not the sum of his art and it serves humanely devious ends. His subject is not simply the fallen state of man, but the mysteriousness of it too.

Pincher Martin (1956) is a characteristically original and tightly knit work, the story of a man whose heroic selfishness not only blasts the lives of those around him but leads him to refuse to die, even when he has experienced death. The whole novel relates the fantasy of a dead or dying man, that he has escaped death at sea and has fought his way to a desolate rock in the middle of the ocean, clinging desperately to the idea of himself in a seven-day ordeal that parodies the Creation. At the end of the novel we are told of Pincher Martin's death: 'He didn't even have time to kick off his seaboots.' The novel is built around a most profound game with time: the false time of fiction, the real time of God. Yet the effect of this deliberated story is ambiguous: 'Would you say that there is any – surviving? Or is that all?' asks the man who discovers Martin's body washed up on the shore. The novelist offers no answer and, in the hesitation before the word, suggests that to ask about 'surviving' is to ask a question whose very import is undetermined. This mystery, this ambivalence, reflects back on the novel's polarities and collapses them in an uncertainty that is at once religious and humane.

Golding's prose does, on occasion, have designs too palpable on us, and his attempts to image forth innocence are both more conventional and less successful than Larkin's (see, for example, *Darkness Visible*, 1979). But there is a side to this art less familiar and more relaxed. *The Pyramid*, three linked stories of provincial English life in the years between the two world wars, is wholly successful in its less deliberated pursuit of loss of innocence, and the same may be said with only some qualification of the *Rites of Passage* trilogy, whose priggish hero is humanized and in the process comically dulled as he learns in his world too of the universal fallibility of human nature. This relaxation speaks of a robustness which is part and parcel of Golding's attitude to writing itself, and which springs, perhaps, from his rare ability to detach himself from his work as a novelist.

Muriel Spark (b. 1918), although she shares Golding's religious concern and his interest in the fashioning of novels, is without his genial unselfconsciousness. *The Hothouse by the East River* (1973) drives home both the similarities and unlikeness, for it is, like *Pincher Martin*, a story about someone's willed continuance of his 'life' past the moment of death. As in *Pincher Martin* the reader does not know that this is the case until the end of the book. But whereas Pincher Martin 'survives' on a rock in the Atlantic, Paul 'survives' in 1960s New York, surrounded by old acquaintances, and is gifted with illusory and problematic children. Where *Pincher Martin* comes to rest on mystery – the mystery of creation, of the creation of identity – Spark's novel presents a puzzle: how is life in the Waste Land of wealthy 1960s Manhattan to be distinguished from death? The question is given urgency by the choice of present tense to tell the story. There is no sense of a temporal perspective from which to view what happens, yet what happens creates the desire for such a perspective, one from which such an obtrusive oddity as the shadow that falls *against* the light can be explained. The novel sets out to create a sense of metaphysical *angst* in the reader. If it fails, and it does, the reason is that the story, though brief, does not vary itself enough in tone or substance to hold the attention consistently. It is uncharacteristically intense and unfunny; but it is characteristically aggressive in the way it puts the reader on the spot.

Spark withholds kindness from her characters and from her readers. The former are given an edgy, mechanical vitality, marked out by stereotypical idioms and repetition of phrases from their own or other people's speech. Their vitality argues freedom; their mechanical quality suggests the opposite. In *The Girls of Slender Means* (1963) Jane Wright, 'the woman columnist', is unchanged by the passage of years and unable to understand the story to which she is a witness. In *Memento Mori* (1959) old people receive the same anonymous (and unexplained) telephone call: 'Remember you must die'; they are incapable of doing so. Change is total and entails pain, as it does for Jane Wright's quarry the anarchist Nicholas Farringdon, who sees a vision of evil, becomes a missionary and is martyred in Haiti. In *The Prime of Miss Jean Brodie* (1961) Sandy Stranger becomes a Roman Catholic and enters a convent, and so enters a world of spiritual pain: 'She clutched the bars of the grille as if she wanted to escape from the dim parlour beyond ... the dispensation was forced upon Sandy, and she clutched the bars and received the choice visitors ...' The absurdities of Miss Brodie, self-indulgent and self-dramatizing, imposing her will on her impressionable young pupils, circle around the point of Sandy's pain. Spark is kind to neither Miss Brodie nor Sister Helena, once Sandy.

In her first novel, *The Comforters* (1957), a 'bad' novel, an adventure story about diamond smuggling competes for attention with a discomforting one about Caroline Rose, who has become a Roman Catholic, is writing a book on form in the novel, and 'hears' a novel being written about her – it is the one we read when we read *The Comforters*. The pursuit of this paradox in the context of a silly adventure story amounts to unkindness to the reader. The novel is about freedom: Caroline does not want to be the novelist's pawn and fights back. All the freedom she wins for herself is, however, rather like the dispensation that is 'forced' on Sister Helena. She learns with difficulty to accept her place in the novel *and* her own reality: 'this physical pain convinces me that I'm not wholly a fictional character.' She knows 'that the narrative could never become coherent to her until she was at last outside it, and at the same time consummately inside it'. This sort of thing puts the reader under strain at the same time as it serves to place the carnival of worldly absurdity that circles around it.

Spark's characters are snoopers and blackmailers, assassins (or their victims, as in the memorably unpleasant piece, *The Driver's Seat*, 1970) and egotists. Her stories need to move fast, lest her characters' shallowness and wickedness be too apparent. When they work, they do so because Spark is absolutely clear about what she is doing and her ability to do it. Her novels are intricately patterned, rapid, marked by precise observation and beautiful economy. She is economical even with her expansiveness, which is always accountable. Her Catholicism is certainly a point of reference for the reader, but it is not exactly what the novels are about. They raise the questions of what is really real and what constitutes true freedom with a light certainty of touch, but these questions are not answered dramatically. Her least heartless novel is *The Mandelbaum Gate* (1965): it is generally underrated. There followed a succession of short, dark tales of which *Not to Disturb* (1971) is the best, very palpably concerned with the Calvinist ethos of her Edinburgh childhood from which her Catholicism is, in part, a reaction. *The Takeover* (1976) announces another change of direction, to a fiction of greater restraint in the use of horror and more development of humour. The best of these later novels, which reverts to the subject matter of authorship, freedom and truth, is the very good *Loitering with Intent* (1983).

Iris Murdoch (b. 1919) is probably regarded as a more serious novelist than Muriel Spark, and indeed she tackles large themes, and does so with the authority of someone who taught philosophy at Oxford. Economy, however, is not her style. She has written more novels than Spark, and much longer ones. The comparison is not superficial – while Murdoch shares with Spark a concern with truth and freedom in the novel and with both Golding and Spark a belief in the fallen state of humanity, she derives from these a different conclusion:

We are not isolated free choosers, monarchs of all we survey, but benighted creatures sunk in a reality whose nature we are constantly and overwhelmingly tempted to deform by fantasy. Our current picture of freedom encourages a dream-like facility: whereas what we require is a renewed sense of the difficulty and complexity of the moral life and the opacity of persons.

('Against Dryness')

You could say that Spark gives the 'opacity of persons': her characters are impenetrable beyond the surface. But they also suggest that beneath the surface there is not much: there is good, there is evil or there is nothing. Murdoch's enterprise is summed up in her belief that 'through literature we can re-discover the density of our lives'. The result is long novels, relatively highly populated, stocked with surprising and often symbolic incident. Incest and adultery, high tides, floods, fogs and thunderstorms as appropriate, dark secrets and strong feelings are standard. Since the underlying issues are serious and since the extended plots give these issues complex shadowing, the novels themselves can be, and are, taken seriously. Yet the writing itself is often slack when it needs to be taut. The fiction is Shakespearean in concept but falls short in practice, lacking the intentness that would carry through from improbable situations to the passionate ethical debate they imply:

'We mustn't talk of these things – we're just sort of – plunging about – and it doesn't mean anything now. Look, I must *tell you certain things* only you won't *listen* –' I thought I mustn't go mad with emotion, I must stop questioning her now, though I *will* find out, I *will*. 'Hartley, have some wine.' I poured out a glass of the Spanish wine and she began mechanically to sip it. 'Have an olive.'

(*The Sea, The Sea*, 1978)

The incoherence is appropriate to the description of a contingent world which Murdoch aims at, and the olive is undoubtedly comic by intention, but these long narratives are insufficiently nuanced to carry off passages like this. Murdoch's best work is her earliest, the disciplined, shorter novels whose succinctness keeps them in more vital relation to their philosophical themes. In particular, her first novel, *Under the Net* (1954), wrongly identified as an 'angry' novel when it first appeared, and *A Severed Head* (1961) are to be recommended, both significantly antedating the programmatic essay 'Against Dryness' already quoted.

Murdoch's popular success has something to do with the wild and romantic aspect of her fiction, and more with the fact that it copiously handles ideas. Golding and Spark are by contrast economical, sometimes bafflingly so. The taste for Murdoch is like the taste for Doris Lessing (b. 1919), whose best work is her earliest, dealing with the matter of her own early years in Rhodesia. She settled in London in 1949, and after 1962 much of her work is allied to English interest. As a novelist of any quality, however, she belongs with writers of the Commonwealth and South Africa. More pleasure is to be had from the work of A. S. Byatt (b. 1936), author of an early study of Murdoch, and attuned to her kind of seriousness. Byatt's novels are complexly patterned and intelligent but tend to a stiffness which is much mitigated in her prize-winning novel *Possession* (1990). She would, probably, be surprised to find herself set alongside John Fowles (b. 1926), but they share a taste for the patterned novel with which this section has dealt, and also for the association of large ideas with those patterns. Fowles, however, is something of a bully in his attitude to the reader; he writes always from a position of confident intellectual superiority. This takes away from the pleasure afforded by even his most successful novel, *The French Lieutenant's Woman* (1969), an essay on relative social and historical values and the attempt to be free of them. Ingenious and thoughtful though he is, he makes one grateful for the imagining of human diversity and the relish in human event that distinguish the work of Iris Murdoch.

III

The roots of British fiction in the 1950s lay, it has been suggested, in the middle-class tradition of genteel fiction, in the lingering romanticism of the 1940s, and the social observation of Waugh. Golding's exploration of fable or parable owes something, perhaps, to the last works of George Orwell and the novels of Albert Camus, but if so, the debt is overlaid by the specifically Christian nature of his vision. It is as though novelists either retracted to resolutely un- or anti-intellectual models or felt constrained to invent their own forms with little allusion to the past. It is as though the examples of Lawrence and Woolf and their peers had no force at this moment. It may even be a sign of provinciality that Joyce should have been so formative an influence on Brian Moore (b. 1921), whose first novel, *The Lonely Passion of Judith Hearne* (1955), recalls much of the careful realism and the chill of *Dubliners*. Judith Hearne is a lonely, middle-aged Roman Catholic who tries to keep herself occupied by teaching the piano badly in Moore's native Belfast and who drinks to cushion herself from the pain of her life. *Dubliners* is an apt model for such a story, which is complemented by its successor, *The Feast of Lupercal* (1958; originally *A Moment of Love*), about a schoolmaster bachelor out of touch with life who attempts a disastrous affair with a young Protestant girl. Both these books were successful with the critics; neither seems to be leading anywhere. The second novel ends with the schoolmaster acknowledging his own hopelessness and watching the girl disappear from his life. He is standing by a horse and cart in the street:

Mr Devine, watching as Una turned the corner, absently put out his hand and fondled the horse's neck. The powerful muscles fluttered at his unexpected touch and the horse swung its head up, looking wildly down the avenue in the narrow focus of its blinkers. Horse and man looked down the avenue, and there was no one there. The horse, harnessed, dumb, lowered its head once more. The man went back into the house.

This is good writing. The horse, blinkered, harnessed, dumb, stands for the Belfast life to which Devine has consigned himself, but the gesture by which he reaches out 'absently' for companionship, being psychologically convincing, naturalizes the symbolism as does the verb 'fluttered' applied to the horse's muscles. Yet in the end it is unclear whether the comparison of horse and man is meant to extend to an opposition, prompting the reader to think that men are capable of reason, horses not. It fails of a Joycean hardness.

Moore emigrated to Canada in 1948 and finally settled in California, writing screen plays. Not surprisingly his fiction reflects some indecisiveness about setting. Canada, America, Ireland figure equally in the *oeuvre* as a whole. What keeps him appropriately within the range of this study is his continuing interest in depicting female consciousness and in intimations of a supernatural order, both dealt with in terms of an Irish history registered in complex ways British readers are particularly able to understand.

Three later books especially concern themselves with women's experience. The first of them, *I am Mary Dunne* (1968), is a first-person narrative set in New York and covering just twenty-four hours (so recalling *Ulysses*); Mary Dunne is Canadian, of Irish origin, she is menstruating, she is moving from one man to another.

The novel evokes the flow of life in a peculiarly modern guise; as does *The Doctor's Wife* (1976), in which a married woman lets her Belfast family go hang, takes off to the South of France with a young American, and then gives him up to make her own life in London. The novel plays off grim North against warm South, but does more too; Moore uses the sexual licence won by writers in the 1960s to emphasize the physicality of the lovers' encounters, but its significance derives from the restless haste of telecommunications and air travel and the abstract threat of terrorism: 'In her mind she saw the two Saracen armoured cars barricading the lower end of Clifton Street . . .' Sex is a retreat as well as an affirmation. But *Cold Heaven* (1983) is the most remarkable of these books. The story is again about a woman who leaves one man for another, but this time the husband dies just before she goes: and then miraculously revives and pursues wife and lover across America. Marie, an emancipated convent-school girl, has been made the unwilling victim of what is a miracle indeed and has to beg the Virgin Mary to rescind the gift. The pressure is not merely that of late twentieth-century stress, it is theological: Marie has to fight off the divine in order to maintain the secular humanity in which she believes. This is not a book that was enthusiastically received, but is nevertheless important, serious and moving, summing up, bringing to a head that concern with religion and its absence that is of vital concern to novelists of Moore's generation.

It is something to which Moore returns again and again, for example in *Catholics* (1972), about the enforcement of the vernacular rite in a remote community of Irish monks, and in *The Temptation of Eileen Hughes* (1981), about an Irish businessman's obsession with an ordinary girl who works in one of his stores: he sees in her a saintly innocence she has to deny. Belief is put to the test in his only historical novel, *Black Robe* (1985), about a French Jesuit's solitary journey to convert Canadian Indians in the early seventeenth century.

Moore is a great storyteller, and his fiction has a convincingly wide social range: his Irish origin perhaps released him from the concern with or confinement to middle-class manners that largely characterizes the other novelists so far considered. The trouble is that he evades the most fearful encounters which his fictions suggest. His novels end too soon or too neatly, or there is a failure to develop character commensurate to the underlying theme (as happens in *The Colour of Blood*, 1988). Guilt, associated with sexual release and the abandonment of the old values which include religion, is frequently the very British subject matter: *Fergus* (1971) is particularly good in this respect, but, as with Graham Greene, there is a willingness to gloss over its harsher implications. Moore learned from Joyce, but, in a different time and a different place, could not follow through his Joycean impetus or realize himself with the completest success. Yet he is undeservedly neglected by the scholiasts. This may also be his good fortune.

Ireland is, in any case, the land of British guilt, and writers who understand that, whether or not they are Irish (Henry Green's *Loving* (1945) is English through and through – and very good) are at an advantage in England. The sense of an unpurged past, for example, makes of Jennifer Johnston (b. 1930) a more interesting writer, in novels like *The Gates* (1973), than if her indefinitely sad characters inhabited England. Ireland also fuels the work of William Trevor (b. 1928), although it is far from omnipresent in his work. He has written many novels, but his acknowledged mastery lies in the short story. As with Moore, one notes the range of social types, the amplitude of interest so often lacking in the purely English writer of the period. He is an acute observer of manners; the stories work by implying a future they do not elaborate or by displaying a content which might otherwise be denied. The novels, more restricted in their range, tend to be strong on caricature but weak on plot: they generally turn on the threat of exposure, as in *The Old Boys* (1964) or *The Children of Dynmouth* (1976). Trevor is remarkable for his ability to evoke sympathy for middle-class grotesques. *Fools of Fortune* (1983) is his most audacious and best novel, a strongly plotted novel in the tradition of *The Big House of Inver* (1925) by E. A. O. Somerville (1858–1949) and Martin Ross (1862–1915) and of *The Last September* (1929) by Elizabeth Bowen. This one is about the long-drawn-out consequence of violence, a family broken but surviving, love and forgiveness. Only Irish history now provides the historical perspective for this kind of humanist vision in English, and if Trevor overwrites at times, the effect of the whole is not as greatly diminished as all that:

That moment when I guessed the truth in Mr Lanigan's office; that moment when she opened the secret drawer; that moment when he stood at his mother's bedroom door and saw her dead . . . Truncated lives, creatures of the shadows. Fools of fortune, as his father would have said; ghosts we became.

As his father would have said: the phrase-making is naturalized.

IV

William Trevor and John Fowles (*The Collector*, 1963) are the only novelists discussed so far to have published their first novels in the 1960s, a decade which seems to have been oddly barren of new talent. Although publishing thrived in this decade, much of it was directed towards the export market; a more significant fact for novelists was the closure of Boots' circulating libraries in 1965, a mark of slackening demand for the newest fiction. A degree of social ferment and liberal legislation was paralleled by a mood of experimentalism, best exemplified in the work of B. S. Johnson (1933–73), but he is a writer without much subtlety, and very much in the wake of his masters Joyce and Beckett. *Albert Angelo* (1964) is interesting; a fiction that breaks down halfway through for the 'real' grief of the 'author' to come through.

The 1960s saw the creation of a youth culture in Britain and the breaking of sexual taboos. The commune was a powerful ideal, and writers of the 1970s and later do look back to this decade as a watershed. The novel, too, changes, becoming more aggressive, and more violent, than before; it tends to be more ostentatiously stylish, and it eschews the bourgeois expectations that are still the groundbase for novelists as different as Murdoch and Amis.

The difference may be established by looking at the work of Martin Amis (b. 1949), whose first novel, *The Rachel Papers*, appeared in 1974. His sixth and most ambitious is *London Fields* (1989), which illustrates well the new style initiated by novelists of his generation. It is a complex book in outline. Sam Young, an American writer of fictionalized documentary, has swapped flats with the British man of letters and man about town, Mark Asprey. The book he writes is about a murder which, he foresees, will take place because the victim, Nicola Six, wishes it. The designated murderer is a petty criminal, Keith Talent, whose image of himself as a great darts player is the final giveaway of his failure to realize an identity. As Sam writes his book he fills the reader in on what he is leaving out: a story behind the story, which has to do with Sam's own failures and betrayal, is shadowed forth without quite appearing. The setting is London in the near future, a hateful caricature of the present conveyed in a hateful synthetic style:

Where does a lady go, in a pullulating pub, if she wants to meet a gent, and enjoy a bit of privacy? Nicola knew the answer. Not the Ladies; you can't have a gent in there. The ladies wouldn't like it. Not the Ladies. The Gents, the Gents – the gents being so much more tolerant and fun-loving in this regard.

The style colludes knowingly with its subject matter, but because it *is* knowingly aware, the author is distanced from his repellent creation. Just as the story of Sam's book and the story of Sam's life compete for attention, so do the novel's ostensible pleasure in parodying the already-grotesque and its pleasure in shaping this material. The book is not only about Sam Young's life and art; it is also about Martin Amis. The book is prefaced by a note signed 'MA', alerting the reader to the ambiguous relationship of the fictional Mark Asprey to the actual Martin Amis. Nicola Six's surname is surely significant in Amis's sixth novel, and significantly she is the victim of the novel's novelist. The book's view of the created world is horrific (the setting is redolent of the Last Days), but so is its view of creation. It is a stable model of an unstable world, a disenchanted vision of a place in which all is relative – or may be. In fact Sam discovers the ability to love – to love Keith's infant child Kim; and it even turns out that Keith, however amoral, wants to protect his own child from harm. Within the palace of mirrors that is *London Fields*, then, a moral idea lurks. The force of the book lies in its being impossible to prise it out from its relativistic setting.

The effect is both more deliberate and more ambiguous than in the novels of Amis's father. Martin Amis has been compared to Swift, but Jonson is just as appropriate. Both authors have a puritan streak (Amis is fascinated by pornography as an object of satire), both enjoy catch-phrases and argot (Amis is particularly good on the phony language of sports reporting), and both are similarly interested in form. Amis is as perplexing as these authors and harder to take.

London Fields shares with its predecessors a concern with doubles, mirrors intimating relativity (derived from Nabokov, but used to very different ends), with authorial responsibility and with the 'moronic inferno' we have made of the world – the phrase comes from Saul Bellow, and Amis used it as the title for his essays on America (1986). *Success* (1978) is about upper-class Gregory and his foster-brother Terry who is gross and foul-mouthed; the two change places and personalities in the course of the novel, leaving the truth of their first-person narratives in doubt; the reader learns neither what success is nor whether it has been achieved. *Other People* (1981) is described as a 'mystery story': it is, at any rate, another 'after-life' story, an updated *Pincher Martin* playing with metaphysics in an uncommitted, secular manner. Is Mary Lamb's policeman/ protector also her creator/author? Is Mary Lamb also Amy Hide? This is Amis's most restrained novel, but also the most considerable, because the view of life from the bottom up − baffling, strewn with obstacles − matches the story's view of the metaphysics it flirts with.

Money (1984) is, like its successor, long and almost exclusively peopled by unlikeable characters. The protagonist, John Self, is a chain-smoker, heavy drinker, pornography addict, drug-taker and slob who is also a film director of sorts. He gets taken for a ride by an insane American and possibly also by his creator, the novelist Martin Amis who figures in the novel. The book's idiom is aggressively uncertain: Self describes Manhattan's 'heavy faggot hangouts' as places where 'you get zapped and flogged and dumped on − by almost anybody's standards, you have a really terrible time', and the flat concluding phrase denies the force of the three powerful verbs at the start, implying a question about how it is that we can become used to the things we are used to. Self is trapped in a tawdry modern world.

The trouble with Amis is overstatement. *Money* and *London Fields* are too long, their plotting too weak to hold every detail in place. The novels constantly refer to an idea of what they are (Jonsonian, Swiftian, even, in a morbid way, Dickensian), but an elaboration of immediate sensation diminishes the idea's importance. Furthermore, the idea itself is one deeply committed to paradox and relativism. The look into the abyss becomes a fall into the abyss.

In Amis's novels, overstatement goes with a would-be moralist's satiric intent. The novels of his contemporary, Ian McEwan (b. 1948), are more sensational in content, but their sensationalism is undercut by a deliberately restrained style. The result is a fiction more economical and perplexing than Amis's, yet evidently stemming from the same historical moment.

McEwan started as a writer of short stories, in *First Love, Last Rites* (1975) and *In Between the Sheets* (1975). The subject matter, in McEwan's own words, combines 'lurid physical detail and a sense of cold dissociation' which he derives from the work of writers like 'Burroughs, Céline, Genet and Kafka'. The stories are part of that exposure of the hitherto unacknowledged underlife of modern consciousness over which Freud presides, and they use a graphic and unexcited prose to portray masturbation, child abuse, incest and murder. Adolescents are often at the heart of these stories, as they are in McEwan's first novel, *The Cement Garden* (1978), about a family of children whose mother dies shortly after their father; they bury her in the garden and carry on without reference to the world outside. The girls dress their youngest brother up in girl's clothes: the narrator makes love with his sister. As Blake Morrison has said, the novel might have been another *Lord of the Flies*; but the interest here is psychological rather than theological. The result is disturbing, certainly, but it is especially disturbing because the first-person narrator, by withholding comment, makes it difficult for the reader to construe an intention in the novel.

The Comfort of Strangers (1981), by contrast, supplies everything the reader needs without forcing the issue. Colin and Mary are staying in Venice on holiday. They sleep together, but 'this was no longer a grand passion'. Then they are befriended by Robert and his wife Caroline who live in the city. Robert holds forth on what it means to be male and takes pleasure in hurting his wife. In a characteristically horrific climax Robert, with his wife's collusion, uses a razor to take Colin's life: this is the most restrained of all McEwan's descriptions of violence.

The significance of the story lies in the failure to name Venice as Venice. The city's present as an embodiment of its past has, therefore, no reality in the book. Colin and Mary are indifferent to it. They make love, smoke marijuana, go out to dine or to swim, and lie about their hotel-room reading – they could be anywhere. And they lack the identity they fail to bestow on Venice, too. Vaguely liberal, they are not precisely anything, and this is what makes them easy prey for Robert:

They often said they found it difficult to remember the other was a separate person . . . When they talked of the politics of sex, which they did sometimes, they did not talk of themselves. It was precisely this collusion that made them vulnerable and sensitive to each other, easily hurt by the rediscovery that their needs and interests were distinct.

This recalls the etiolated relationship with which the story 'Psychopolis' begins ('I met her there lunchtime on my second day in Los Angeles. That same evening we were lovers, and not so long after that, friends'). That story ends with a heated discussion of Christianity in a house on the edge of the desert which precipitates the narrator's decision to break out of all he has merely gone along with and to discover himself in terms neither Christian nor West Coast beat, and one might suggest that *The Comfort of Strangers* is yet another post-war novel, like *Other People*, like *Cold Heaven*, about the *angst* of doing without religion.

In a sense this is true, but the talk about the 'politics of sex'

(Mary is a feminist in some ill-defined way) and the marijuana point more directly to this couple as uncertain radicals surviving from the 1960s. McEwan's unpleasant stories exploit the freedoms won in that decade, but do so not in the spirit of libertarian joy but in frustration and bitterness. He has said that he was surprised when early readers of his stories were shocked by them, and has described their writing as often motivated by 'very trivial rhetorical ambitions', but that is hard to believe, given the intense psychological curiosity displayed. 'Pornography', a story which ends in a castration, can be justified as a piece about the ideas of masculinity and femininity promoted by a certain kind of western culture, but the subject matter has more (offensive) force than the idea, an effect the writer does not seem to have calculated. The importance of *The Comfort of Strangers* lies in the control over subject matter and idea which the writer is now able to exercise equally and to effect.

McEwan's following novels, *The Child in Time* (1987) and *The Innocent* (1990), are attempts to move away from the painful cry of the early work to a fiction of responsibility and ethics matching the author's increasing engagement with political issues, exemplified by his support for a British bill of rights and in the films *The Imitation Game* (1980) and *The Ploughman's Lunch* (1983: in *A Move Abroad*, 1989). *The Child in Time* is by far his most ambitious work, the story of a couple whose pre-school-age child disappears in the course of a mundane supermarket visit. The horror here is psychological, not physical as before, and the whole movement of the book is towards consolation and restoration, ending with the birth of another child. Despite some excellent writing, the novel fails to cohere. Its setting is a Britain of the near-future in which right-wing politics has triumphed, beggars are licensed and education is a tool of government policy. The idea of a lost child in a 'lost' state is present, but the scratchy satire takes away from the human pain of the central drama instead of complementing it, and the idea's unifying ambition is thwarted. *The Innocent* is more of a piece. Leonard Marnham is a nondescript young man: but is he innocent? He is working on an Anglo-American spying project in Cold War Berlin, where no one is to be trusted: the background is one of moral simplicities (America supports democracy) and blurred morality (the British seek to spy on their partners who in their turn distrust them). Leonard ends up having to get rid of the body of his fiancée's former husband, first by dismembering it, then by dragging it in two heavy suitcases to a place where they will not be found. This is comic-grotesque, or should be, but the dismemberment is gruesome in excess of what is needed. The colourless nature of Leonard also gives McEwan trouble, since it renders the bulk of the narrative insipid. Nevertheless, the conclusion, in which an interval of more than thirty years has brought a kind of understanding and a kind of forgiveness, makes sense of the book and pushes it in an interesting direction, as though at last he might get beyond the obsessions of the early work.

Martin Amis and Ian McEwan write as members of a generation traumatized. The violence and nastiness of their books are what they see and an expression of what they feel about what they see. For both, moral positions are made difficult by a sense of relative values which chimes with the concerns of advanced thought in this period, as represented by writers like Jacques Derrida or Paul de Man. McEwan's progress is particularly worth watching because it represents an attempt to get out of the dead-end of post-modernism, even if it is as yet an unsuccessful attempt.

V

McEwan was one of the first graduates of the postgraduate course in creative writing at the University of East Anglia started by Malcolm Bradbury (b. 1932), a proficient comic novelist; the lack of geniality in his style means that he is at his best when his satire has a palpably worthy object, as in *The History Man* (1975). The establishment of creative writing as a subject suggests the extent to which recent fiction has made itself more available to ideas, and to ideas, in particular, of what fiction is. The tendency is further exemplified in the work of Graham Swift (b. 1949), whose novel *Waterland* (1983) is one of the most ambitious of the period, a long, ingeniously plotted, philosophical novel about the interactions between personal and public history, covering a hundred years or so with the greatest confidence. (His first novel, *The Sweet-Shop Owner* (1980), is striking for its narrow focus on one man, his wife and daughter.) Although Swift's designs are assured and although his subject matter is full of potential, he is hampered by a vicious style which uses rhetorical question, repetition, verbless and simple sentences to excess, so that no point is made without its being signalled as having been made; it is also a style with little permeability, so that characters tend to sound the same; the idea predominates at the expense of individualization.

For all that, and despite the gratuitous horror of the crucial abortion in this novel, *Waterland* must be reckoned with. Its schoolmaster-protagonist is being pensioned off: 'history' is a redundant subject, according to his opponents, and the book is his attempt to affirm history's meaning, although for him public and personal history alike turn out to depend on lies – the novel is a new variation on the relativist theme, reinforced by the ingenious interweaving of its several strands of story.

However, there is a much better novel about history from this period and this generation. Bruce Chatwin (1940–89) published *On the Black Hill* in 1982; it is the story of twins, unmarried men who inherit their parents' farm in the Welsh Marches and live out their days there, encountering the facts of historical change as they filter through to their remote homestead, but remaining untouched by them. The book is about history, about those encounters, as when the twins, who are conscientious objectors, avoid getting sent to the front in 1918:

... he did remember the vicar leaning forward to ask whether, or not, he believed in the sanctity of the Allied Cause. And he remembered hearing his own voice reply, 'Do you believe in God?'

The vicar's head shot up like a startled hen.

'What gross impertinence! Do you realize I'm a clergyman?'

'Then do you believe in the Sixth Commandment?'

'The Sixth Commandment?'

'"Thou shalt not kill."'

The moment is convincing: Benjamin's reply stems from a tradition of Welsh chapel piety already fully presented in the novel. The moment is also one that offers the book's other subject, which is innocence, a quality of interest to Larkin and McEwan and most of the novelists of this period, whether or not they are also concerned with the shortcomings of their age. The innocence of Chatwin's twins is juxtaposed at the end of the book with that of Theo the Tent, a white South African who has dropped out and become a Buddhist: he wanders, they stay put, but it is the same innocence. The novel's epigraph, from Jeremy Taylor, says that 'we must look somewhere else for an abiding city, a place in another country to fix our house in . . .' and the novel endorses this transcendent view of reality without suggesting that there is anything other than innocent simplicity on which to base it.

Chatwin started off in the 1960s by working for the auction-house Sotheby's, and his prose, modelled, he says, on that of Lawrence and Hemingway, is that of someone who respects the harmonies of art. In 1975 he started a new career as a traveller. He had a particular interest in nomads, which is best seen in the passages from his notebooks in *The Songlines* (1987), the account of a visit to Australia in quest of an understanding of Aboriginal culture. Chatwin's relation to the hippy culture of the 1960s is more relaxed, and less disappointed, than McEwan's, perhaps because he could draw on a more secure sense of artistic achievement and historical perspective. His first book, *In Patagonia* (1977), is also a travel book, and entitles him to be thought of as the best travel-writer of the century after Wilfred Thesiger (b. 1910). But whereas in *Desert Sands* (1959) and *The Marsh Arabs* (1964) Thesiger's objective is scrupulously to *record* what he has seen and what he knows, Chatwin makes a good deal more of his travels. His Patagonian book is as carefully shaped as Graham Swift's, and like *Waterland* it weaves many stories together, the central thread being his desire to find out more about his grandmother's cousin who, years gone, brought back a piece of brontosaurus skin from the ice of a glacier. The journey is a piecing together of that man's story among the other stories of southern Argentina, stories of crime and politics, all told in Chatwin's clear, laconic style which does, indeed, owe something to Lawrence, particularly to the best of the latter's short stories.

Chatwin's last novel, *Utz* (1988), is a brief, elegant, enigmatic account of a collector of Meissen who guards his porcelain from the greedy hands of a philistine state (the setting is communist Prague, and the narrator is a cultivated westerner). Utz is allowed to keep his Meissen only on condition that it should go to the state museum on his death; but when he dies it has disappeared. We are not to learn where or why, for the narrator surmises that at the last Utz's affections were diverted from the works of art to a more true object, his servant-wife Marta, and this surmise is what the book is about – a narrator who can conceive the superiority of human love to aesthetics. This chapter has already suggested how difficult an achievement that must have been. Chatwin's knowledge of the commercial art-world and his rejection of it have something to do with it, implying a choice of values and a refusal to be fascinated by relativist ideas. His first novel, *The Viceroy of Ouidah* (1980), is a horrific account of slaving in the nineteenth century; it sums up the gift of western civilization to Africa in his final image of the African lieutenant-colonel in Dahomey: 'he paced up and down, waving to an imaginary crowd, creaking the floorboards and crushing a cockroach under the heel of his combat boot.' Chatwin's art removes itself from that manner of address to the mass – he sees and writes, for individuals, evoking with enviable economy and apparent ease:

One morning there appeared an elderly and anachronistic gentleman in a black Astrakhan-collared coat, carrying a black silver-tipped cane. His syrupy eyes and brushed-up moustache announced him as a relic of the Ottoman Empire.

('The Bey', *What am I Doing Here*, 1989)

One wants to go on reading, for what lies behind this writing is a sensibility, not an idea.

The hero of Musil's *The Man Without Qualities* has a theory called 'Essayism' which extols the essay for taking a thing from many sides without comprehending it wholly – 'for a thing wholly comprehended instantly loses its bulk and melts down into a concept.' This resembles the method of Julian Barnes (b. 1946) to avoid the tyranny of the idea as exemplified by Amis, McEwan and Swift. Barnes's first two novels (in his own name – he also writes detective stories as 'Dan Kavanagh') are fairly conventional affairs. *Metroland* (1980) starts off with a brilliant account of precocious schoolboys at Westminster in the genteel tradition, and then turns into a story of how the vital radicalism preserved by one is betrayed by the other. *Before She Met Me* (1982) concerns a man's obsession with his wife's former lovers; its defect is the poverty of its characterization which marries badly with the smartness of the writing. *Flaubert's Parrot* (1984) is in the essayistic mode. It brings together a mass of information about Flaubert, presented in a variety of ways – an alphabet of 'accepted ideas' about the author, three chronologies of his life (each from a different point of view), a Flaubert bestiary. There is a narrator, the compiler of all this, a retired doctor whose wife has committed suicide, and his need to explain what he has undergone is shot through the Flaubertian material. At its simplest level the book rewrites B. S. Johnson's *Albert Angelo*, but the presence of Flaubert adds a great deal; there is, to begin with, the inaccessibility of the past in which the author lived, an intimation of the impossibility of the narrator's search for the 'truth' of his circumstances, and there is also Flaubert's dedication to art which the biographer subverts by placing life first, although in this case the biographer's own life supervenes, to doubtful effect. *Flaubert's Parrot*, then, is a more palatable version of the idea-bound relativist novel than anything offered by Amis or McEwan. Its 'essayism' lies partly in the essays on, or assays of, Flaubert's life which do not add up to a single view of that life, partly in the artful reticence with which the narrator's life is done. Nevertheless, it might be felt to 'melt down into a concept', although the concept is of an unstable kind – the concept of an ambiguous dialectic between art and life.

The trouble with essayism is that, although its object is to avoid the stasis of comprehension in a 'concept', it is a concept itself, and it has difficulty in thickening into life. *Staring at the Sun* (1986) is a bold attempt to overcome this difficulty. It begins conventionally with an account of Jean Serjeant's wartime childhood but moves rapidly and unpredictably to her fifties, when she visits her own version of the seven wonders of the world, and into the future, when her son – now aged sixty – contemplates suicide and is comforted by his mother. There is no plot here, any more than there is in its successor, *A History of the World in $10\frac{1}{2}$ Chapters* (1989), but both books are written to suggest a web of ideas (compare the interweaving of *In Patagonia* or *Waterland*). Courage, perseverance, wonder are associated with Jean's unnovelistic (because 'unplotted') experience of her own life: this human link makes *Staring at the Sun* more successful than *A History* whose chapters are each complete in themselves, are sometimes fiction, sometimes not, and are linked by recurrent images more than ideas, notably that of the flood and the ark whose ordering has mythic significance. Both novels have significant religious concern. Jean's son asks her three questions:

'Is death absolute?'
'Yes, dear.' The reply was firm and exact, declining the need for supplementary question.
'Is religion nonsense?'
'Yes, dear.'
'Is suicide permissible?'
'No, dear.'

Barnes allows us to understand that Jean's decisive answers reflect her nature: 'part of that confidence was mere parental habit.' The qualification does not feel like a restriction on the value of that confidence. On the other hand, the last chapter of *A History*, which is about the benign necessity of death's absoluteness, lacks that sort of qualification and is reduced to an over-simple homily, despite the complexity of its setting. Both books are rather too comfortable to make one feel the subject matter has been fully comprehended: but that is, of course, implicit in 'essayism', which is based on the assumption that knowledge, though possible, is dispensable. More recent thinkers would deny the possibility of knowledge, and Barnes's work can seem to harmonize with this view. He is, however, more conservative and backward-looking than first appears, and this may prove to be his strength.

It is certainly the strength of David Lodge (b. 1935), best known as the author of comic university novels – *Small World* (1984) is a witty footnote to the academic politics of English. He is another novelist of ideas, but of ideas firmly seized and held: *How Far Can You Go?* (1980) is a history of English Roman Catholicism since 1960 told in a succession of graphic episodes, while *Nice Work* (1988) rewrites Elizabeth Gaskell's *North and South* to comment on the condition of England in the late twentieth century.

For although the novelists of the 1970s and 1980s show remarkable inventiveness in their attempts to recast fiction and to adapt it to a world seen as even less stable and less fulfilling than in the 1920s or 1930s – and Barnes is no exception where this inventiveness is concerned – a sense of experience as something solid, of art as reflecting that solidity, seems necessary still to make a novel work. *On the Black Hill* and *Staring at the Sun* have that quality, and in both cases it overrides blemishes that are nevertheless regrettable. But much recent fiction has been drawn in another direction, toward fantasy. The remarkable example of Gabriel García Márquez (b. 1928) has attracted writers to imitate his 'magic realism' which combines strong narrative drive, fantastic incident and absence of authorized direction. It is exemplified in the work of Angela Carter (1940–92) who published her first novel *Shadow Dance* in 1966. Her collection of stories *The Bloody Chamber* (1979) retells fairy stories in a way that emphasizes their quality as sexual fantasy – Ian McEwan, not surprisingly, admires her. In 'The Company of Wolves' Little Red Riding Hood happily embraces the handsome werewolf who has just devoured her grandmother:

She will lay his fearful head on her lap and she will pick out the lice from his pelt and perhaps she will put the lice into her mouth and eat them, as he will bid her, as she would do in a savage marriage ceremony.

The style is too mannered to take us far into the dark places of the mind: in this dreamy, cumulative sentence the word *savage* merely gives a delightfully Gothic *frisson*. Those who want a fiction that voices the protest and potential of feminism would do better to turn to the novels of an earlier writer, F. M. Mayor (1872–1932) – *The Third Miss Symons* (1913), *The Rector's Daughter* (1924) and, most pertinent to the present, *The Squire's Daughter* (1929). Mayor exploits the conventional novel-form to devastate its expectations of satisfaction for the reader. Carter's view of the free and sexually active woman owes much to the idealism of the 1960s, as the commune setting of her apocalyptic *Heroes and Villains* (1969) suggests. Her longest book, *Nights at the Circus* (1984), evokes Zamyatin as well as

García Márquez; the author herself has described it as a work of *bricolage*; and this defines its charm and lack of passion well. Needless to say it is a book with an idea, but the idea is subordinate to the pleasure taken by Carter in the adolescent dreams of revolt and gratification at its heart.

Salman Rushdie (b. 1947) is a more serious novelist in the magic realist line. His *Midnight's Children* (1981) is a long, dense, highly patterned and structured account of Indian history since independence, embodied in a series of fantastic, grotesque and farcical incidents whose gravity lies in their absurdity. The models, besides García Márquez, are Laurence Sterne and Günter Grass; the conclusion is a bleak one as far as the prospects for India are concerned. Rushdie's next novel, *Shame* (1983), was in a similar mode, and concerned with the ills of Pakistan. It gave great offence to some readers in Asia, but hardly as much as *The Satanic Verses* (1988), a critical fictional meditation on Islam which led to the author's condemnation to death by the Ayatollah Khomeini of Iran. As Rushdie's work has proceeded it has, however, become less interesting. Its techniques remain fundamentally the same, the same surprises are sprung, the same ambiguous passages are opened up. The ambiguity depends on the relation between truth and fiction, author and narrator, narrative and statement, familiar poles of current scepticism about meaning, and this makes Rushdie a very sophisticated western writer (born in India, he was largely educated in England). But is he an English author? The question is not one about passports and legality, but it is one about the society for whom the author writes. The fact that *Midnight's Children* was a successful novel in Britain suggests that Rushdie is, as a writer and in this peculiar sense, English; yet its political concerns are, however, deplorably remote from those of most British readers. It is questionable whether this novel (or its successors) has extended those concerns very significantly, since the novel's structure is so glitteringly complex, so beguilingly fanciful as to make its political concerns marginal in terms of interest just because they are central to its concept. Yet it cannot be only its exoticism that attracts. Its very nature as a novel based on an idea puts it in the same category as the work of native authors like Martin Amis or McEwan. Rushdie then stands for the novel's increasing immersion in ideas, an immersion that one may regret if one sympathizes with John Bayley's epigram: 'In life, we could say, things only seem to happen, whereas in fiction they really do.' Rushdie's political concern feels like the other side to not believing that things 'really' happen in fiction.

Since the 1960s increasing notice has been taken of the fact that Britain is a multi-racial society. The fact implies a possible regeneration for the English novel. *Sour Sweet* (1982) by Timothy Mo (b. 1953) is about a couple from Hong Kong living in England and running a pretty basic Chinese restaurant; it is full of humour and interest, but suffers, firstly from a melodramatic and journalistic parallel plot about the Tongs (Chinese secret societies), and secondly from a flat, unincisive style. This is also the trouble with Kazuo Ishiguro (b. 1954), although his first two novels are largely about Japan and the flat style heightens the ambiguous presentation of the central figure. Both *A Pale View of the Hills* (1982) and *An Artist of the Floating World* (1986) are first-person narratives in which judgement of the narrator is a complex affair: they are, too, economical and carefully designed. But Ishiguro's third novel, *The Remains of the Day* (1989), shows the limitations of his art. The narrator this time is an English butler, and the subject is British, not Japanese, fascism. The result is disastrous, the butler a music-hall parody of atrophied feeling, self-importance and abasement, and the political rhetoric of the 'good' American unbelievably crude and so ineffectual. This novel suggests Mo's wisdom in avoiding purely English subjects in his work after *Sour Sweet*.

The English novel in the 1950s and 1960s reflects the frustration of a nation in decline and the anxiety of one that is not happy with its own secularism. The 1960s are an important divide, intensifying the feeling of frustration, but also bringing a new experimentalism and an increased social range in characterization. If there are few masterpieces there is a great deal of energy, an inventiveness perhaps ill-served by the general tendency to invoke a relativist theory of knowledge rather than take a stand. The period also marks the beginning of a remaking of Englishness itself. The enterprise is as dangerous as it is necessary.

10

POETRY SINCE 1950

Alastair Fowler

The 1950s saw almost as great an interruption in poetic tradition as that forced by modernism (though a quieter and less obvious one). After the Second World War, many felt the need for renewal, for a complete break with the past. The forward youth had now to let his unused armour rust: shibboleths of heroic idealism aroused only indifference or distrust. Change was also invited by the weakness of recent verse. For, whether or not gaps in the poetic line corresponded to casualties of the First World War, there is no doubt that the current New Apocalypse school produced extremely bad poetry. (Norman MacCaig, George Barker and W. S. Graham all had cause to regret early connections with this group.) To cap all, Dylan Thomas's late work seemed not to have fulfilled his earlier promise of greatness – although his *Collected Poems* (1952) achieved huge sales. Vernon Watkins continued to keep Romanticism alive with lyrics of a more chastened eloquence. But it was time for new initiatives.

Just how new and different the poetry that resulted was, remained for a time concealed. Philip Larkin, Kingsley Amis and the others of 'The Movement' seemed merely to be following Graves, Muir and witty Empson, and reasserting modernist dryness against the incipient Romanticism of the 1940s. True, they rejected all ambitious subjects and large concerns – too closely associated, perhaps, with conflicts such as the war just suffered. But that might be a natural contraction of focus, such as appeared also in the deceptively small poems to which MacCaig now turned. Certainly the Movement's dislike of the New Apocalypse's 'mad' imagery seemed in line with what is now sometimes called 'popular modernism'. Its rejection of obscurity was similarly accessible. For difficulty, rather indiscriminately deployed by earlier modernists, was now as automatically distrusted. Larkin told *Paris Review* that unlike the 'mad lads', he 'us[ed] words and syntax in the normal way'. Poetry was not only to be as well written as prose, but equally intelligible. Finally, Movement poets accepted the modernist paradigm for short poems – epigram, rather than the lyric of late Victorian practice. (By epigram, I mean a poem unrestricted in subject, colloquial in diction and dependent for its effect on witty precision of language rather than development of metaphor.)

Despite these apparent affinities, however, the Movement was fundamentally at variance with modernism. Pound and Eliot, for all their assiduous innovations, were deeply traditional, though not in a Victorian way. Pound may have been a 'barbarian on the loose in a museum' (as Yvor Winters called him); but at least he was a rapt barbarian with an eye for a fine image. It was quite another thing to dispense with museums altogether, or to say, as Amis did, that 'Nobody wants any more poems about philosophers or paintings or novelists or art galleries or mythology or foreign cities or other poems' (in D. J. Enright, ed., *Poets of the 1950s*, 1955). The Movement poems discarded so much (as we can now see) that they contributed to the greatest rupture in cultural tradition since the eighteenth century. They rejected old literature; Romanticism; tradition; ideas; psychoanalysis; the 'common myth-kitty' (Larkin's phrase, in *Poets of the 1950s*); even literary allusions and diction – what Amis calls 'bookish cries' ('Against Romanticism'). Simplifications so radical were easily taken as a charter for philistinism.

Nevertheless, Larkin himself was no philistine. He may have hated Oxonian élitism; but he was not ignorant of English literature: his first volume, *The North Ship* (1945), shows Yeats as an early influence, and subsequently Auden and Hardy are often made use of. True, Larkin was culpably dismissive of literature beyond England's borders; but that may have been the deliberate provinciality of one who consistently rejected international modernism. In his own poetry he characteristically lays aside the masks of more than a century, and speaks as if simply to be understood – uses, that is, a persona of intimate sincerity. This careful immediate intelligibility is a little deceptive, however: like Ben Jonson's clarity, Larkin's is underlined (very effectively in a poem such as 'Going') by confirming resonances that are less obvious. And, on occasion, as in 'Sad Steps' and (increasingly) in late poems like 'Sympathy in White Major', there are references to other texts.

Larkin uses traditional metrical forms with considerable technical accomplishment, and maintains a high standard of economy, clarity and unity of effort. Yet his power (for he sometimes has great power) derives more from the weight of his rigorous honesty. Such a poem as 'Church Going' has touchstone authority in its accurate recognitions of the claims of differently serious truths. There is no obvious coherence in the various attitudes this celebrated poem expresses – now 'I take off/My cycle-clips in awkward reverence', now 'the place was not worth stopping for', now 'though I've no idea/What this accoutred frowsty barn is worth,/It pleases me to stand in silence here'. Yet Larkin's very inarticulacy seems genuine, and has awakened a broad response. By clearing the air of sham, he found 'everyone felt the same'.

Larkin's method of speaking with ruthless honesty (which recalls that of his master, Hardy) meets its greatest challenge in communicating depressive feelings: the fears of death and loneliness that dominate his descriptive meditations. In most of these, even in late poems like 'Aubade', his unusual aim is neither resolution nor resignation, but full exposure of an apathetic terror. Thus, in 'The Old Fools' (*High Windows*, 1974), the calmness of the aged baffles him – 'Why aren't they screaming?' –

> An air of baffled absence, trying to be there
> Yet being here. For the rooms grow farther, leaving
> Incompetent cold, the constant wear and tear
> Of taken breath, and them crouching below
> Extinction's alp, the old fools, never perceiving
> How near it is. This must be what keeps them quiet:
> The peak that stays in view wherever we go
> For them is rising ground. Can they never tell
> What is dragging them back, and how it will end? Not at night?
> Not when the strangers come? Never, throughout
> The whole hideous inverted childhood? Well,
>   We shall find out.

Larkin's more external descriptions have been called one-sided and lacking in beauty. But this is as unfair to him as it would be to Dickens: for each has a compensating vitality – a dogged relishing of contingency – 'An Odeon went past, a cooling tower.'

Larkin's authoritative example has been of mixed value. He had a deleterious influence on many who took his *faux-naïveté* more simply than it was intended; for his method of direct explicit personal address validated a short-circuiting of traditional poetic ambages. And his reassertion of Englishness, salutary though it was at first, went too far, and exacerbated the prevailing insularity. He can be said to have recovered qualities of clarity and precision; but then one might ask why, if these prose objectives were enough, he should ever have written in verse. Nevertheless, Larkin wrote some successful, 'classic' poems of undeniable emotional power. Their number is not great, and all lie within a narrow range, both emotionally and formally – a range no wider than that, say, of Landor's epigrams – seeming positively to shrink from violation by anything like an idea. Yet their beautiful phrasing is not only inventive but able to justify prolonged attention – and this, in spite of his setting a scrupulously high benchmark of perspicuity. It is an unusual achievement for a minor poet, to change the course of the art so decisively. Larkin did much to save poetry from obscurantism, and to restore the circuit of the word linking poets and readers.

Other Movement poets can be reviewed more briefly. Kingsley Amis (b. 1922) and John Wain (b. 1925) are both prose writers, although each has written effective poems. Amis's success rate is higher; but Wain ranges more widely and has had more of a development, growing away from Movement style into other creative engagements. (One of his strongest recent poems, 'The Shipwreck', is even a poem on a picture.) Robert Conquest (b. 1917) now appears a mainly representative figure, characteristic in his dislike of 'great systems of theoretical constructs' and his admiration of Orwell and the 'principle of real, rather than ideological honesty' ('Introduction' to Robert Conquest, ed., New Lines, 1956, pp xiv–xv). Thom Gunn (b. 1929) was early praised, and perhaps over-praised. Yet his poetry from Fighting Terms (1954), The Sense of Movement (1959) and My Sad Captains (1961) to Moly (1971) and The Passages of Joy (1982) displays richer resources than those of most other Movement poets. His sharp eye is sharpened on the axe's edge of past literature, and he has a ferocious determination to look at everything. He is even prepared to explore things he does not fully understand, like 'earth powers' and other Lawrentian matters. But his work can be insensitive, nihilistic, even incoherent; for good and ill he is the least commonsensical of the Movement poets. In any case, his emigration to California in 1954 takes him out of the present survey.

The very different poetry of Donald Davie (b. 1922) – witty, hard-won, unfluent, compactly close-built – added intellectual weight to the Movement (Brides of Reason, 1955; A Winter Talent, 1957; Collected Poems 1950–1970, 1972). And his criticism, particularly Purity of Diction in English Verse (1952) and Articulate Energy (1955), redirected attention to Augustan strengths: exact words, shaped syntax, consecutive rational content and connections. Davie's poems often have an intellectual wit as sharp as Empson's; but they tend to develop more soberly, and at times read like essays in verse. They may not always be perspicuous; yet upon reflection they generally seem lucid. Though not a natural poet, Davie has grown in several directions. *The Forests of Lithuania* (1959), his imitation of Mickiewicz, has fine variety in matching diverse matter with attendant manners.

Even if not altogether a Movement poet, R. S. Thomas (b. 1913) is in some ways closest of all to Larkin, particularly in such a poem as 'The Welsh Hill Country'. Thomas, whose instant intelligibility is clearly not modernist, has been called 'belated Georgian'; but there is little of the Georgian in his bitter sentiments. He might more happily be placed in the perennial line of country poets, the line of Edward Thomas and Andrew Young (that clear-cut Bewick of literature). R. S. Thomas is no less 'anti-Romantic' (or anti-humanist) than Larkin, if for different reasons. Where a Georgian connection shows is in his oblique use of imagery for effects of delayed action or surprise. Indeed, his use of metaphor is stronger than Larkin's, and his intensity greater. But he, too, collapses persona into poet, exposing with scathing reductiveness his own spiritual sterility, or the distance he, as priest, feels from his parishioners. Thomas's poetry can still move the reader, and has continued to speak to the present generation, offering moral touchstones.

Tomlinson, Clarke and MacDiarmid

Not all the new poets of the 1950s belonged to the Movement – nor, perhaps, the best of them. While Larkin was confirming the English tendency to underachieving, unthinking acquiescence in the 'reality' of drab ugliness, others began the complex task of renewing larger poetic traditions. Among these, the most impressive is Charles Tomlinson (b. 1927). Where Movement poets boasted their provinciality, Tomlinson was a spiritual emigrant to Europe and (increasingly) America. Many individual poems, and an entire volume (*American Scenes and Other Poems*, 1966), refer to travel in the United States; and from the first, intertextuality with Wallace Stevens is very evident (*The Necklace*, 1955). Tomlinson found models for his characteristic short lines and sentences in Ezra Pound and (later) in William Carlos Williams. Williams, in spite of his painter's eye, was harder to assimilate, although eventually Tomlinson drew from him a relaxed posture and coolly impersonal distance, poles apart from Larkin's intimate directness. Against Williams's dullness, Tomlinson is protected by his keener intellect.

Tomlinson's characteristic genre is the traditional landscape meditation – but with two vital differences. First, his sensory observations are extraordinarily minute, adding time and again to the sum of transcribed experience. Second, he treats the relations of things with an epistemological awareness that recalls MacDiarmid's, and contrasts (again) with the philosophical illiteracy of the Movement. Tomlinson's visual precision continually impresses one. Himself an accomplished painter, he is able to combine accurate observation, imagist definition, nineteenth-century symbolism and other ingredients in an individual complex that gravitates towards the condition of visual art – as if in answer to Pater's musical *Anderstreben*. Tomlinson's observation, like that of Stevens's snowman, offers a world of facts:

> Facts have no eyes. One must
> Surprise them, as one surprises a tree
> By regarding its (shall I say?)
> Facets of copiousness.
>
> ('Observation of Facts', 1955)

Disciplined to impersonality ('when we have silenced ourselves'), it regards the challenges of nature and history with the persistence of patient indirection. His work explores the laws which experience suggests to the receptive observer – patterns 'mitigating mere aggression'.

In a long course of development, Tomlinson's poetry has enlarged its range in several directions. One such approach to larger reality has lain through translation, about which he has thought deeply. Others are changes of subject and method, such as the political themes and intertextual procedures of *The Shaft* (1978), although Tomlinson (in contrast to a poet like Peter Porter) has remained unimpressed by the new. Nature is ever the object central to Tomlinson's attention:

> One can no longer see
> The high recession stretching beyond each tree,
> But the view, shut round, lets through
> The mind into a palpitation of jostled surfaces.
> Nudging, they overlap, reach out
> Beckoning, bridging the underdeeps that stir
> Unsounded among the foliage of a hundred trees
> That fill an aerial city's every thoroughfare
> With the steady vociferation of unhuman witnesses.
>
> ('The Witnesses', 1974)

Here each image has a metaphysical resonance, which, just because it resists immediate reverbalizing as a coherent proposition, in turn simulates receptive experience for the reader.

Such hymns to life are a rewarding experience. Yet Tomlinson's poetry has proved hard to assess, in part because its American critics, who have received it most warmly, lack appreciation of delicate English rhythms, slow pace and concentrated, 'heavy' style. There are certainly limitations, although these seem less to arise from moral preoccupation than from a method that sometimes becomes routine. Impersonal observation brings its own problems: multiplicitous details can have a confining effect. Sometimes, too, Tomlinson's poetry tries to be more strenuously visual than can be realized verbally. (His aural textures, by contrast, can be perfunctory, or marred by liaisons that commit forbidden mixtures of different *s* and *z* sounds.) Again, there are occasional sentimentalities and flickers of class consciousness. In general, however, Tomlinson's patterned verse has maintained its progressive elevation remarkably. His is one of the main continuations of poetic tradition in our age; enduring work that will be remembered when Movement correctives are long forgotten.

In Ireland, too, a fuller tradition was being affirmed, notably in the neglected volumes of Austin Clarke (1896–1974). It is hard to do justice here to Clarke's many-sided work, ranging as it does from epigram and satire in his earlier volumes (*Ancient Lights*, 1955; *Too Great a Vine*, 1957; *Flight to Africa*, 1963) to narrative in the later (*Mnemosyne Lay in Dust*, 1966 and *Tiresias*, 1972). A fine metrical craftsman, he had important formal ideas that several other poets were to take up. He favoured an unemphatic patterning, whereby endwords related to internal rhyme words in a following line, often by off-accent rhyming. This allowed polysyllabic words at the ends of lines, making possible, as he explained, 'a movement common in Continental languages such as Italian or Spanish':

> O when the forehead is too young,
> Those centuries of mortal anguish,
> Dabbed by a consecrated thumb
> That crumbles into dust, will bring
> Despair with all that we can know;
> And there is nothing left to sing,
> Remembering our innocence.

('Tenebrae')

The subtle structuring is hardly noticed, amid the pungent details that give Clarke's verse much of its force, but to a poet of passion, its value is inestimable.

In the 1950s, the politics of the Movement were incomprehensible, even if its anti-expansionist anti-liberality now seems recognizable enough in hindsight. Certain other stances, however, were only too clearly defined: notably those of Ezra Pound (1885–1972) and Hugh MacDiarmid (1892–1978). Criticism has understandably preferred MacDiarmid's early 'golden lyrics', poems like 'The Water-gaw'; yet in the later volumes – *Three Hymns to Lenin* (1957), *The Battle Continues* (1957), the new poems in *Collected Poems* (1962) – and in the long poem *In Memoriam James Joyce* (1975), the great volcano continued to throw out, among quantities of lax, uneven ashes, diamonds such as would make the reputation of several lesser poets. The problem with MacDiarmid's later poetry in English is not exactly its ideological materialism. It is not so much that shouting drowns out the softer voice of the poet (although that sometimes happens), but that the clenched hand of logic tends to crush the seeds of new form.

Outside Scotland, the other great modernist Pound had more impact. Unfortunately, this influence issued not from the wonderfully lucid *The Classic Anthology Defined by Confucius* (1955), but from the poorer late *Cantos* – *The Pisan Cantos* (1949); *Section: Rock-Drill* (1957); *Thrones* (1959). Some of the political verse-rhetoric of the 1960s, on both political wings, stemmed from Pound's example.

Minimalism and Concrete Poetry

Larkin was content to retain traditional forms, while emptying them of aptness to the content. But several 1960s poets pared their poetry down to essentials, or even eliminated long-standing conventions altogether: it was the decade of Samuel Beckett (1906–89) and minimalism. In one view, minimalism expresses minimal affirmation, disillusioned caution – an interpretation that fits well enough with Larkin's negativity, and with low-profile imagery like the sexual symbols in 'The Whitsun Weddings'. But minimalism was a diverse phenomenon; it can also be related to more positive ideas: to 'less means more', 'small is beautiful', or a (timeless aspiration) *multum in parvo*.

Norman MacCaig's (b. 1910) thirteen volumes, with little formal development except the introduction of free verse, constitute the *oeuvre* of a minor master. His tiny subjects are deceptive: he meditates them with the eager intensity of a Vaughan, until they acquire visionary significance. The Metaphysical wit and chilling penetration of a poem like 'Brother' (*The Sinai Sort*, 1957) would hardly have seemed out of place in the seventeenth century.

In MacCaig's poetic world everything has meaning, although the meaning's status may be undercut by evasive ironies (occasioning charges of whimsy). Unusual slants on life disclose undeniable marvels, which his metaphorical fluency fixes easily:

> A dragonfly of mica whirs
> Off and up; then makes a thin
> Tottering grass its anchor-post,
> Changed to a small blue zeppelin.
>
> ('Laggandoan, Harris', *Riding Lights*, 1955)

Long before the Martians, MacCaig had visual imagery of a crisp precision:

> The dinghy across the bay
> Puts out two hands and swims
> An elegant backstroke over
> A depth full of images.
>
> ('No End, No Beginning', *A Man in My Position*, 1969)

MacCaig is as anti-intertextual as any Movement poet, and almost as dryly anti-Romantic. And he has stoutly defended his privacy against demands for 'openness' and 'depth'. Criticisms of MacCaig recall those of Herrick. What if his epigrams are like miniature Georgian poems? Do they not please?

In others, minimalism took an altogether more conceptual turn. The work of Ian Hamilton Finlay (b. 1925), notably his influential *The Dancers Inherit the Party* (1969), teems with ideas, eclectically derived in the 1960s manner. The sequence of imagery in a poem like 'Orkney Interior' defeats expectation with the nimble grace of an intellectual harlequin. His earlier concrete poems display a sustained linguistic interest; exploring extreme understatement, perhaps through the minimal difference of a single phoneme ('star/steer', *Honey by the Water*, 1972), or even of a silent grapheme ('sea ms'). Compression can go to the extreme of one-word poems like 'sea' (titled 'A PINNATE EVERGREEN' on a botanical name-plate on a fir-tree at Stonypath). Significantly, however, Finlay has also investigated lateral manipulation of media and context, uncoded communication of a sort quite foreign to structuralism:

> ultramarine
>
> Ultima Thule
>
> ultramarine
> ultramarine
>
> (*Honey by the Water*)

Finlay's concern with media extends to contextualization by visual environment – not only in emblem books but in the gallery and (returning to an original meaning of 'emblem') in his miniature garden at Stonypath, the smallest great garden in Europe.

Both Finlay's important avant-garde magazine, *P.O.T.H.* (1962–7), and the earlier imprints of his Wild Hawthorn Press were antipathetic to large concerns. But his more recent work (much of it conceptual art rather than poetry) has addressed larger and larger issues, until now its characteristic form is that of a strategic image from past tradition, iconically singled out and revalued. Such intertextual art – obscurely portentous until its allusion is recognized – is poles apart from that of the Movement. To some extent it belongs, with minimalism like Vasarely's, to the mannerist stage of modernism. But Finlay is not content with mere readjustments of tradition. His ferocious going-over of the past – as in his cyclopean epigraph from the revolutionary Saint-Just, 'THE PRESENT ORDER IS THE DISORDER OF THE FUTURE' – suggests rather a post-modern reaching for a new classicism. And in his returns to classical epigraphy, or to the Renaissance emblem, Finlay is engaged in a heroic effort of principled overgoing: he means to distance the past justly. His output is sparse, but of the very highest calibre.

Concrete poetry is too international (and, with its semantic-constellation aesthetics, too far from ordinary communication) to have many British practitioners. But the sound poems of Bob Cobbing (b. 1920) may be mentioned as part of the 1960s tendency to stress poetry's performance element. And Edwin Morgan (b. 1920) has surely done as much as anyone to popularize conceptual poetry in Britain. His concrete poems are often generated from the substrate by rule, so that in a sense they are linguistically defined – as if the language wrote. Nevertheless, they characteristically issue in unpredictable flashes of wonderfully deranged imagination – as in the sound poem 'Chinese Cat' (*The Second Life*, 1968):

> p m r k g n i a o u
> p m r k g n i a o
> p m r k n i a o
> p m r n i a o
> p m r i a o
> p m i a o
> m i a o
> m a o

Morgan's concrete constructions range from such language games (for which he has been censured by some of his uncomprehending countrymen) to visionary affirmations like 'Message Clear', with its glorious emergence of 'I am the Resurrection' from Saussurean hypograms in reverse.

The Scottish Post-Renaissance

Morgan's concrete work can now be seen as the play of a poet complete in every way except evenness of finish. He is the archetypal 1960s poet, but with an endless versatility, strong experimental drive and metrical resources rare in any age. Among Morgan's multifarious formal inventions and imports are to be counted the matrix poem, the instamatic and the science-fiction poem. And *The Whittrick* (written 1955–61, but not published until 1973) uses Landor as a springboard for much funnier imaginary conversations. From *The Second Life* (1968) onwards, urgency overtakes Morgan's work: the city poems in that volume and in *Glasgow Sonnets* (1972) are, indeed, highly political, though too serious for ideology:

> Hugh MacDiarmid forgot
> in 'Glasgow 1960' that the feast
> of reason and the flow of soul has ceased
> to matter to the long unfinished plot
> of heating frozen hands.

(Glasgow Sonnets, iv)

Morgan's objective description of the urban waste makes Carlos Williams's *Paterson* seem aesthetic trifling. Yet it has its own formal purpose: no less than Eliot, Morgan is purifying the language of the tribe:

> A mean wind wanders through the backcourt trash.
> Hackles on puddles rise, old mattresses
> puff briefly and subside. Play-fortresses
> of brick and bric-a-brac spill out some ash.
> Four storeys have no windows left to smash,
> but in the fifth a chipped sill buttresses
> mother and daughter the last mistresses
> of that black block condemned to stand, not crash.
> Around them the cracks deepen, the rats crawl.
> The kettle whimpers on a crazy hob.
> Roses of mould grow from ceiling to wall.
> The man lies late since he has lost his job,
>   smokes on one elbow, letting his coughs fall
>   thinly into an air too poor to rob.

(Glasgow Sonnets, i)

At this point Whitman seems to become as much of an influence as Williams, and Morgan's textures loosen, until in *Instamatic Poems* (1972) – multi-viewpointed notations of news items – he moves away from style towards total impersonality (*le degré zéro est le peuple*). Yet, even here, Morgan extends literature by assimilating its contemporaneous opposite; just as he does in the visionary science-fiction poems of *Star Gate* (1979).

Not all Morgan's profuse taproots established themselves successfully. His earlier love lyrics, in particular, were weak, possibly because poetic traditions were lacking for the sort of love he meant to write about. Partial success in this direction came only with the close syntax and rich imagery of *The New Divan* (1977), sweet epigrams using Persian models. Another reservation concerns the poems of social conscience. In speaking for the people, or for Glasgow, Morgan avoids the egotistical sublime so rigorously that he begins to run an opposite risk: that his personality will lose its voice, or come to seem an intrusion. Taken at large, however, Morgan's *oeuvre*, with its informing vision of post-ideological improvement, has the consistency and strength to move. Sometimes it achieves the eloquence of a classic popular song. And it has contributed a distinctively contemporary diction that communicates easily yet is capable of literary weight.

Morgan has only gradually emerged as the leader of the Scottish post-Renaissance. After the songs of Soutar and the thoughts of Muir, after the early golden lyrics and late lucubrations of the great MacDiarmid, what was to follow? In the event, it was as if MacDiarmid's strengths were shared out among the next generation – intellectual power and versatility going to Morgan; demonic energy to Sydney Goodsir Smith (1915–75); pungency to Robert Garioch (real name R. G. Sutherland, 1909–81) and Alex Scott (b. 1920); lyricism to Iain Crichton Smith (b. 1928) and George Mackay Brown (b. 1921). Scottish endeavours were also divided (as they had been since the seventeenth century) on the issue of poetic language. After much debate, and expressions of strong views such as Alan Jackson's (in 'The Knitted Claymore', *Lines Review*, 37), it became clear to many that writing in Scots limited poetry's readership fatally – and clear to others that for a peripheral culture to abandon its linguistic substrate was suicidal. Those who wrote mostly or entirely in English, like MacCaig, Morgan, Graham, Crichton Smith and Dunn, had perhaps learned from the sinewy flexible language of the later MacDiarmid; but they were syntactically shorter-breathed, and a good deal more accessible. Crichton Smith, the most naturally gifted of the group, has an enviably effortless fountain of imagery, which flows through almost all his poems; although its energy is seldom fully canalized, because of a constitutional disinclination to revise – at least until *A Life* (1986). The beginner should start with this, his last and most finished volume. The *oeuvres* of Crichton Smith, MacCaig and Morgan, together with those of the expatriate Scots, seem for the time being to have settled the language issue decisively in favour of English.

The opposite choice, however, was made by Robert Garioch and Sydney Goodsir Smith, who wrote in a partly synthesized literary Scots. Goodsir Smith was not a native Scots speaker – which makes the terrifying fluency of his tirades the more remarkable. His best work – notably the irresistible *The Eildon Tree* (rev. edn, 1954) – has something of Dunbar's courtly command of language, although its mac-MacDiarmid swagger portends a Scottish baroque rather than Renaissance:

> Here I ligg, Sydney Slugabed Godless Smith,
> The Smith, the Faber, *Poietes* and Makar,
> And Oblomov has nocht til lear [teach] me,
> Auld Oblomov has nocht on me . . .

('Slugabed')

By comparison Garioch's is a quieter, slyer talent. His brilliant imitations of Giuseppe Belli's satiric sonnets use the double mask of Italian original and demotic persona to sugar subversive purges which go down with the rhythmic precision of a minor master. Garioch is a reminder that peripheral cultures need not be provincial. The bilingual, internationally minded Scots have long had a penchant for translation, which in the eclectic 1960s helped to win their poetry attention. Its internationalism, however, perhaps also helps to explain why it is not generally appreciated in the south. Only in part a matter of Scots vowels and words misconceived as dialectal, this may in greater part be due to suspicion of regrettably uninsular ideas.

Augmenting the Tradition: Translations; Ted Hughes

At this juncture, translation seemed to many poets to offer advantages – eclectic internationalism; a breathing space for personal development; an opportunity to practise poetry as an objective art; and the possibility of rising above personal limitations. Among these, Edwin

Morgan is outstanding: his *Beowulf* (English, 1952), his Sándor Weöres (English from Hungarian, 1970) and his Vladimir Mayakovsky (Scots from Russian, 1972), besides many other volumes, make him Scotland's *grand traducteur*, as C. H. Sisson is England's, with *The Poetic Art* from Horace (1975) and *The Aeneid* (1987); there are also renderings of Lucretius and Dante. Some poets have done much of their best work in translation – notably Christopher Logue (b. 1920) in his vivid Homer imitations (*Patrocleia*, 1962; *Pax*, 1967); the fastidious Elaine Feinstein (b. 1930) (*Marina Tsvetayeva: Selected Poems*, 1971); and Michael Hamburger (b. 1924), whose renderings of Hölderlin (1966), and especially Célan, have a wonderfully economical inevitability:

> Thread suns
> above the grey-black wilderness.
> A tree-
> high thought
> tunes in to light's pitch: there are
> still songs to be sung on the other side
> of mankind.

> ('Thread Suns', 1972)

Ted Hughes's (b. 1930) *Selected Poems: Janos Pilinszky* (from Hungarian, 1976), may well have been important for his own development in a sparer, more gnomic direction. The list could be a long one. However, it may suffice to mention: Christopher Middleton (b. 1926), in *Selected Poems, by Georg Trakl* (1968); Peter Porter (b. 1929), in *Epigrams by Martial* (1971); John Fuller (b. 1937), in *The Art of Love* (1968); Alastair Reid, in his many Neruda translations; Thomas Kinsella, in *The Tain* (1969); Crichton Smith (b. 1928), in *Poems to Eimhir* (1968–71); Tony Harrison (b. 1937), in his Aeschylus and Racine translations; and Geoffrey Hill (b. 1932), in his Ibsen's *Brand* (1978) – all of whom achieve translations or imitations that work in English as poems in their own right, and do much to relate contemporary writing to earlier or foreign literature. For translation, above all, offered a way to circumnavigate the rupture in tradition opened by the Movement's negations.

While these drew on foreign or ancient resources to enlarge British poetry, others (or, in some cases, the same individuals) were more concerned to deepen it by addressing unconscious levels of personality. Ted Hughes had models in Dylan Thomas, in contemporary American poetry and in the Yugoslav Vasko Popa (to whom he turned for 'the surrealism of folklore'). But Hughes perhaps relied more on memories of his Yorkshire childhood. And older memories still became his staple – of a racial past reimaginable through the freedom and violence of animals. Or fish, like 'Pike':

> The jaws' hooked clamp and fangs
> Not to be changed at this date;
> A life subdued to its instrument;
> The gills kneading quietly, and the pectorals.

The underlying impulse is often ultimately fear – fear of 'What might move' in 'the dark pond'. Even if the animal fables of *The Hawk in the Rain* (1957), *Lupercal* (1960) and *Wodwo* (1967) are a little too methodically overstated, they have undeniable power in realizing strangenesses that challenge recognitions. But life is not all spent at the zoo; and in the forum or the library Hughes has turned out to have little to communicate.

Hughes's was a poetry of man's dark side; and in 1970 he invoked darkness to say its worst in the 'supersimple and ... superugly language' of the cosmic trickster and survivor-bird who broods malignantly over *Crow*. It is no objection that the volume implies a gnostic theology. Still less, that its secret narrative remains hidden: this could be said of most visionary poems. At its best, Hughes's sequence offers the moral holiday of acknowledging forbidden aggressions and despairs – and perhaps offers the possibility of an authentic realism. But if 'crow is realist', as Wallace Stevens said in another connection, 'Oriole, also, may be realist.' And, *Crow* represents, less defensibly, a recrudescence of violence and cruelty, without much creative amelioration, or even understanding, to offset the darkness. If Hughes had been a poet without reputation, or had lived in a more stable period, little harm would have been done. But in the unleashed 1960s the freewheeling crudity and formal looseness of *Crow* had a most unfortunate influence.

Hughes's earlier 'narratives' were balanced and held to the substrate by stanza forms, compact syntax and close aural textures. But already ellipses loosened the grammar dangerously – 'Then they grown grey, like men./Mown down, it is a feud.' ('Thistles', 1967) – and when this combined with arbitrary fragmentation, as often in *Crow*, incoherence threatened. Often it was the incoherence of living immediacy. But this looseness of structure in a leading poet – conformable as it was to the 'international' style of Pound – had a pronounced effect on English poetic form. When in addition prosody was abandoned in schools, appreciation of metrical structure declined sharply.

The example of Hughes's crude thrusts in *Crow* also encouraged other short-circuitings of poetic potential. Here was a voice capable of saying other things than the southern articulations of the Movement could utter. And now the Liverpool poets – Adrian Henry (b. 1932), Adrian Mitchell (b. 1932) and Roger McGough (b. 1937) – added theirs, in the more direct challenge of apparently abrasive politics, slogans, prose in verse. The 1960s were a silver age of 'poetry in performance', when the golden silence of poetry on the page was forgotten, when large audiences listened to scripts of small literary interest, and when Robert Louis Stevenson's prophecy was fulfilled, that metrical structure would disappear. The vague shibboleth was now 'open form'; and pop verse had a form so open that poetry was apt to fall out of it. Nevertheless, even if the Liverpool poets' emotions were often stereotypic or sentimental, they had the vitality belonging to the Lawrentian tradition. And the audiences they won for the new art sometimes also became readers of poetry.

The Matter of History

While many poets shared the 1960s' political daydream of escaping the past by ignoring it, others were grappling with history. These attempted to deepen poetic tradition by assimilating the past in a more discriminating way, such as might orientate citizens of the present. The genre for history writing was supposed to be epic; but for English poets the large stance a long poem called for had become very difficult. Pound's *Cantos* rumbled on; and David Jones (1895–1974) continued to publish parts of his Casaubon-like project (*In Parenthesis*, rev. edn, 1961; *The Anathemata*, 1952; *The Tribune's Visitation*, 1969; *The Sleeping Lord and Other Fragments*, 1974) – solemn, impressively marmoreal at times, but uncertain in tone, and unreadably remote, as if belonging only slightly to the modern world. Jones cannot be said to have been in touch. The only successful English epicist (if the term is quite right even for him) was Basil Bunting (1900–85), a poet in whom intellect and wide experience were unusually balanced. Bunting had wielded Poundian material with articulate ease in 'Chomei at Toyama' (1932, based on an Italian version of a medieval Japanese text); and *Briggflatts* (1965), his most ambitious achievement, has been compared for its musical structure to Eliot's. But the northern poet is more heroically direct in stance than either modernist. He is not a symbolist, and where the sequence of his thought seems at first discontinuous, all is at last put together on a personal basis. Bunting achieves a robust integration: emotionally forthright (if not always very sensitive); roundly formed; and fully realized in the richest textures since Swinburne and Hopkins.

Although Bunting's history is potentially realized, it is not commented on; so that his unification can be hard to share. Since the 1960s most poets approaching the matter of history have taken for granted that it must be treated fragmentarily; Morgan even speaks of the sequence (on modernist models like Pound, Williams and Muir) as the contemporary equivalent of epic. Robert Lowell (1917–77) showed the way with a collection of grand though intimate epigrams, connected loosely enough to be repeatedly rearranged, from *Notebook 1967–1968* to *History* (1970). A similar plan is followed in Morgan's *Sonnets from Scotland* (1984). Geoffrey Hill (b. 1932) turned to more continental models for his *Mercian Hymns* (1971), a sequence of prose poems interweaving dark childish memories, dark-age history, local survivals and recrudescences. This brilliant work distantly recalls David Jones's *Anathemata*; but Hill's approach is more psychological than mythic. Or, rather, his Offa belongs to a personal myth, a means of controlling and expressing – a little evasively – modern drives and aggressions (which are further controlled by the closely textured, measured form of syllable-counted paragraphs). Then the drabness of Hill's present-day Mercia ('Gasholders, russet among fields'), only superficially like that of the Movement's England, tends to blacken into a Websterian gloom of horror and disgust at childish evil – 'After school he lured Ceolred, who was sniggering with fright, down to the old quarries, and flayed him.'

Hill's earlier poems, such as 'Requiem for the Plantagenet Kings' in *For the Unfallen* (1959), appear to treat history objectively, but a youthful emotional intensity, especially concerning aggression, makes them also poems of self-discovery. Technically impressive, they nevertheless seem to strain too much for importance. Critics of later volumes, particularly *Tenebrae* (1978), have commented on an elusiveness, whereby the focus of reference shifts from things present to things remembered or historical. Is this writing of presence, or of absence? Clearly Hill is not ignorant of the currently fashionable non-referential mode. But he is no deconstructive sceptic: his treatment of the past gives the impression of being pervasively informed by a vision of history's availability for redemptive recreation. For Hill the past may not, indeed, be present; but it is in the present. This vision of simultaneity leads to a remarkably compressed style, calling for expansions manageable only by those who share (however temporarily) Hill's particular scepticisms. Thus '"A resurgence" as they say' makes sense only if the historians' term 'resurgence' is seen as the unbelievers' way of evading the term 'resurrection'. In his corrections of corrections ('the flawless hubris of heroic guilt') Hill is marvellously scrupulous; only sometimes discipline's pruning-knife pares away too much living tissue. Yet this is not to suggest that he lacks sensuousness. His most accessible sequence, 'An Apology for the Revival of Christian Architecture in England', calls up sensuous particularity at will, realizing opulently Victorian moods with luxuriant, exquisite, impeccable taste:

9 The Laurel Axe

Autumn resumes the land, ruffles the woods
with smoky wings, entangles them. Trees shine
out from their leaves, rocks mildew to moss-green;
the avenues are spread with brittle floods.

Platonic England, house of solitudes,
rests in its laurels and its injured stone,
replete with complex fortunes that are gone,
beset by dynasties of moods and clouds.

It stands, as though at ease with its own world,
the mannerly extortions, languid praise,
all that devotion long since bought and sold,

the rooms of cedar and soft-thudding baize,
tremulous boudoirs where the crystals kissed
in cabinets of amethyst and frost.

If we are 'gleaners of its vestiges', Hill has shown how rich one Esther's gathering from the past may be.

Many of Hill's poems seem to be too narrowly concerned with power. This may be hard for him to avoid, so much of the past is the story of power's mystifications. Yet, how helpless to be is not the only question life poses. To put it another way, one might say that Hill has exchanged an ordinary sense of humour for sardonic wit like that of Milton's God – at his own expense. This has been seen as ambivalence; and there is no doubt that the intertextualities of *Tenebrae* allow half-beliefs, quite as much as Browning's masks. But Hill's uncertainties are readily defended: he is more vulnerable to criticism for excessive certainty about what to doubt. I have in mind the inappropriate impersonality of his Christian meditations. Great poetry should, of course, be impersonal. But impersonality needs the support of community of belief – needs, as it were, to be earned by its readership. Much of Hill's middle-period poetry failed to communicate the baroque cultic conventions it depended on. From this point of view, *The Mystery of the Charity of Charles Péguy* (1983) represents a development, beyond the Victorian doubter, towards belief in what is made authentic by praxis.

Both formally and in substance, Hill's later work represents a decisive validation of literature in the traditional sense. His closed forms, lavish rhetoric, florid style and miraculously eloquent diction challenge impoverished fashions: with luck, they may offer models for serious poets in generations to come.

Hill's grieving, guilty sense of history may be contrasted with some Irish poets' involvement in the past. In *The Rough Field* (1972), John Montague (b. 1929) surveys history landscapes as mythic as Yeats's, sometimes, but usually more personal, more specifically realized, better observed. Yet Montague's is a one-sided history. He too easily yields expression to unintegrated passions – and even, in such a poem as 'Hero's portion', gives countenance to barbaric crudities ('sing the ladies/whose bowels crave//its double edge of birth and grave'). He is more sensitive (though less remarkable) in his elegies, which use oblique, low-profile devices – as when a switch from third to second person suggests access of intimacy.

Seamus Heaney (b. 1939) may be no less moved by nationalist fervour than Montague, but the movement seems to be in sensibilities more finely gifted. Heaney's bleak volume *North* (1975) is informed with the idea of poetry as 'almost a mode of power, certainly a mode of resistance' against colonization. But a poem like 'Punishment', about IRA disciplining of collaborators, torn as it is between complicity with 'civilized outrage' and barbaric justice – 'the exact/and tribal, intimate revenge' – and appearing in the end to confess a primitive stance, does so in such a way as to brand his tribe as no better than the bog people. Heaney is valued on almost all sides for his facing up to such ambivalences with sensitive honesty. Taught by Philip Hobsbaum how to imitate such models as Ted Hughes, Heaney was precociously advanced, both in Britain and the United States; but he has since developed steadily in skill and maturity, and now amply justifies the early praise.

Heaney's poetry characteristically concerns itself with history's involvement in the primitive:

> Earth-pantry, bone-vault,
> sun-bank, embalmer
> of votive goods
> and sabred fugitives

(North)

As he chews 'the cud of memory' ('Funeral Rites'), or in his 'piety towards objects' turns over the finds of his poetic field-work, there rises the fume or 'stink' of a pagan mysticism of antiquity in mud: the Tollund man is 'a saint's kept body'. It is as if Heaney, wishing to hold to the best in ancient religion, were always pressing back to find 'the feud placated' in some bog faith that may have existed, before Christianity and history divided his people.

For this investigation of his past, Heaney's special equipment includes unusual awareness of the body of sensuous experience. That applies even to words (and not least place-names), which he savours to an extent almost unknown among recent English poets – except for Bunting, and sometimes Hill. Words are a means of communication for Heaney in more ways than one:

> Sensings, mountings from the hiding places,
> Words entering almost the sense of touch
> Ferreting themselves out of their dark hutch –
> 'These things are not secrets but mysteries'
>
> ('Glanmore Sonnets', ii)

Here the tentative vagueness of 'mountings', in the non-sexual part of its meaning, seems outraged by the other part – which forces a similar division of 'entering', and multiplies rabbit senses that yet keep 'ferreting themselves'. In such ways the poetic process discovers division in language itself: Heaney's own language is neither Celtic nor a specially colonial English – not even in the promisingly earthy word 'hutch'. Compared with Hill's, Heaney's intellect is relatively sluggish. He is content with a few ideas, such as the tragic inevitability of a small people's assimilation. But these few are worked out so fully, with such thorough realization, in so many sly obliquities, that memorable poems result.

There is no doubt of the stubborn authenticity of Heaney's honesty. At the same time, his poems have some of the weaknesses of their social context. Pursuing total authenticity, they perhaps inevitably render feelings that without sufficient chastening emerge as evasive. In correcting and illuminating emotions, art is a strong ally. But how much art can Heaney allow himself? Where poetry is taken seriously – where fellow countrymen on several sides may hang on the implications of his slightest word – the pressure towards non-literary involvement can be overwhelming. Understandably, Heaney longs to escape the political trammels of the past,

> ... angry that my trust could not repose
> in the clear light, like poetry or freedom
> Leaning in from sea. I ate the day
> Deliberately, that its tang
> Might quicken me all into verb, pure verb.

('Oysters', 1979)

Significantly, his longing still takes the form of a wish to escape compromised things (nouns): recrudescent hankering after the primitive 'true belief' that is itself one of the curses of our time.

The Group, and Other 1970s Poets

While Hill and Heaney were rewriting history and weighing how primitive man may be, others were happy to address merely civilized themes, in short epigrams. John Betjeman continued to delight with apparently trivial, nostalgic memories – and even gained a new degree of reputation, as more came to recognize his important achievement: how many new provinces he had added to the domain of poetry. (His light mantle has now floated on to Gavin Ewart.) Stevie Smith (1902–71) similarly belonged to an earlier age; although only now, belatedly, did her oblique confessions become popular. Donald Davie (*Collected Poems*, 1972; *The Shires*, 1974; *In the Stopping Train*, 1977) and Thom Gunn (*Moly*, 1971; *Jack Straw's Castle*, 1976; *The Passages of Joy*, 1982) gave the Movement epigram new leases of life – the former enriching it, at times, into a kind of compressed verse essay. The Eliotic modernist C. H. Sisson (b. 1914) continued to progress from dryness to bleaker dryness, ever more lucid and spare, always more tellingly sharp, more uncongenial, more salutary: harsher to others, but harsher still to himself. His *In the Trojan Ditch* (1974) is a collection that will surely last. And Christopher Middleton (b. 1926), by now an expatriate in the United States, kept surrealist poetry alive – a method that with the advent of popular absurdism had become more acceptable, at least in his small doses.

At first the potent talent of Peter Redgrove (b. 1932) seems devoted to similar ends: his imagery exhibits what is often called 'hypertrophy', and he uses occult ancient and primitive material, together with knowledgeably subverted science. In such volumes as *From Every Chink of the Ark* (1977), *The Weddings at Nether Powers* (1979), and *The Apple-Broadcast* (1981), he undeniably bypasses the moral reason of 'civilized' poetic tradition, to embrace the unchastened unconscious. Redgrove is also a materialist visionary, however,

a biolater and worshipper of natural power and the Life Force –
though not of specially human life. He tends, indeed, to strip the
human off:

> The naked audience, feeling their power
> Stripped from them, their talking clothes, their
> Eloquent masks and attitudes, shall sit
>
> Attentive, naked as pips, while
> The handless, headless, hollow clothes
> Shall pull themselves through each other's textures,
>
> And pray with hollow sleeves held up, and sacrifice
> By unbuttoning and falling off the air, and fly
> Like moths and lie in heaps like leaves.
>
> The conjurer thinks of his act, holding the winged fruit
> In which the seeds sit watching the moths eat.
>
> ('The Cave')

Since much of the human psyche is in agreement with this
tendency, Redgrove can easily swing from deep symbol to deep
symbol, assured of uptake on at least some level. He is able to pull
every well-known organ stop and start, with an astonishing copiousness of rhetoric. Like many 1970s poets, Redgrove is a storyteller;
but his stories are internal ones, unfolded opportunistically, in dream
mode, and left (perhaps again like dreams) in need of interpretative
mediation. This they do not receive; for Redgrove, a polar opposite
to Hill, is weak on structure, and leaves his symbols to be valorized
(if we like) by a psychoanalytic frame of reference.

During the 1960s, Redgrove attended a workshop called 'The
Group', which included, among others, Edwin Brock (b. 1927),
Peter Porter (b. 1929), Alan Brownjohn (b. 1931) and George
Macbeth (b. 1932). Although the Group had more outward cohesion
than the Movement, it did not imply a recognizable style, and its
members developed in very different directions indeed. In retrospect,
however, one can see that they shared a certain determination to
transcend the limitations of the Movement epigram – whether this
was to be achieved by sinister poems about razors (Macbeth), by
surrealism (Redgrove) or by modulation into fiction (Brownjohn).
Brownjohn's fragmentary yet lucid narratives have qualities usually
associated with the short story – observation, precise focus, suggestion. Indeed, he has said that they approach 'the condition of fiction'
(which is almost to say, prose), when he might have chosen to
compare them to Browning's dramatic lyrics.

John Fuller (b. 1937) is the doyen of another grouping. His Sycamore Press was one of the most influential small presses of the decade, publishing James Fenton (b. 1949), Andrew Motion (b. 1952), John Mole (b. 1941) and Mick Imlah (b. 1960) among others. Fuller's own work, however much modelled on Auden, stands in a more intellectual line of wit, which runs from Clough through Empson to Porter. His finely made but misunderstood volumes, from *Fairground Music* (1961) to *The Beautiful Inventions* (1983), show how many innovations are still possible within the epigram and verse epistle. But much of this is caviare to the general, for his allusions and references are oriented to a small in-group. For the most part, the bagatelle is his forte; but when he ventures outside the little worlds of elegant intellectuality and radical chic, he can achieve memorable poems, such as 'The Cook's Lesson':

> Before our eyes
> The litter spurted into the fire, picked out by tongs,
> Eggs hatched into the soup, embryos bled,
> Seeds sprouted in the spoon. As I said, we ate fast,
> Far back into life, eating fast into life.
> Now I understand that food is never really dead:
> Frilled and forked, towered, dusted, sliced,
> In mimic aspic or dispersed in sauces,
> Food is something that will not willingly lie down.
> The bland liquids slid over our tonges as
> Heartbeats under crusts, mouthfuls of feathers.
> *(The Tree That Walked, 1967)*

Ulster Poets

The 1960s were also the decade when Irish, mainly Ulster, poets came into prominence: a prominence sudden and yet, on the whole, well merited. The constellation of various talents is astonishing: Thomas Kinsella (b. 1928); Michael Longley (b. 1939); Derek Mahon (b. 1941); Paul Durcan (b. 1944); Tom Paulin (b. 1949); and Paul Muldoon (b. 1951). The troubles of Ireland (about which all have written) obviously have something to do with this efflorescence. But the national challenge has probably drowned out something of Longley's quiet voice, and has done little good to Paulin (who is given to undigested politics). Other causes may be traced to the general strengthening of Britain's peripheral cultures that followed post-war changes in education, and to the quality of Irish poetic models, notably the undervalued Louis Macneice (1907–63) and Patrick Kavanagh (1905–67).

Thomas Kinsella makes an immediate impact: although he is a little weak on transitions, his wonderfully concentrated images ('I was swallowed in chambery dusk') have the sudden eloquence of a Goya *capricho*. Derek Mahon, who is in some ways like a more literary and allusive Heaney, has a 'perfect pitch' feeling for an ideally proportioned style. The promise he showed in poems like 'A Disused Shed in Co. Wexford' has been fulfilled in *The Hunt by Night* (1982), where development shows in a new tentativeness that seems, paradoxically, to increase his weight. At the same time 'The Joycentenary Ode' can brilliantly outjoyce Joyce:

> What can I tale you,
> Jerms, where you stretch
> In the Flutherin Symatery?

In a more fictive mode, Paul Durcan writes effective easy narratives of gritty naturalism, often amusing or touching, but with underwritten passages. The most interesting of the group may turn out to be Paul Muldoon. Muldoon ostensibly carries Celtic obliquity to the point of whimsical silliness, but all the time (or some of the time) is using it as a means to a serious end. He wishes to focus the reader's attention: his post-modern method will allow no fantasizing. Technically, Muldoon is a master of quarter-rhyme, sometimes with a semantic component: *cobbles/Bibles*; *horse/harness*; *maggots/guts*. His long funny–unfunny narratives often have a grim point, but this is always firmly situated on the other side of a leap of imagination. Like Ashbery's, Muldoon's rhetoric is sometimes too ordinary to have much interest, but, all the same, his quirky poems will not leave you alone.

Narrative Enlargements

The years from 1977 to 1988 saw two developments, both serving to augment the inheritance of post-Georgian or Movement epigram. The first of these extensions works through a marked vogue for narrative, or implied narrative. This tendency, already noticed in Brownjohn, Redgrove, Durcan and Muldoon, seems in part a strategy to hold the new audiences won by 'live' poetry. Story is notoriously one of the forms that work best in performance, and some have probably calculated that with readers unable to respond to rhetoric the best thing is to try fiction.

Narrative poetry had never, of course, quite ceased. John Heath-Stubbs's (b. 1918) *Artorius* (1973) perpetuated the narrative epic, and avoided the Miltonic tradition by a return to alliterative diction. And Charles Causley (b. 1917) had long been enthralling landlubbers and *cognoscenti* alike with his deceptive maritime art-ballads. The master-balladeer achieved subtle strangenesses in various ways, for example by a kind of contrary motion between rhythm and apparent content. The more obviously sophisticated narratives of W. S. Graham (b. 1917) (*The Night-Fishing*, 1955; *Malcolm Mooney's Land*, 1970; *Implements in their Places*, 1977) are all, in a sense, about his dealings with the Muse. Although he can deploy a magnificent rhetoric reminiscent of Dylan Thomas, Graham is more like a British amalgam of Wallace Stevens and John Ashbery: 'It is best I sit/ Here where I am to speak on the other side/ Of language' ('Johann Joachim Quantz's Five Lessons', 1977). But Graham's survival stories have a more distinct sense of urgency:

> Today, Friday, holds the white
> Paper up too close to see
> Me here in a white-out in this tent of a place.
> And why is it there has to be
> Some place to find, however momentarily
> To speak from, some distance to listen to?
>
> ('Malcolm Mooney's Land')

Graham is, perhaps, too narrowly concerned with the impossibility of communication, although he gives the impression of grappling with reality each time on seriously renegotiated terms.

All these storytellers, however, can be regarded as modernist or late modernist. The new narrative poetry, typified by the influential work of Andrew Motion (b. 1952), is unlike either Causley's or Graham's. Representing only a minimal extension of Movement limits, it derives its diction mainly from Larkin (on whom Motion has written a well-weighted elegy). Characteristically its long narratives, like such American predecessors as *The Donner Party*, are in effect short stories in verse, commonly with costume settings. Motion's tend to address the matter of empire, a subject that he handles easily – perhaps too easily. His laconic style – as in *Independence* (Edinburgh, 1981) – recalls the Clough of *Amours de Voyage*:

> strolling late round the pool.
> A three foot scummy drop
> to the water – its glassy length
> steady and speckled with insects
> performing their tiny pointless dance.

However his diction is less adventurous, and reads almost as transparently as that of prose fiction. Motion has considerable gifts, but seems to hold most of them comfortably in reserve, as if waiting for an occasion when they will be sufficiently in control to use them without risk. Narrative, he confesses, is an evasive means of smuggling emotion in, of 'hiding/in fictions which say what we cannot admit to ourselves'. To some younger poets, however, the vogue for a poetry reduced to fiction has proved cramping.

A more important enlargement of the standard epigram has been in the direction of elegy, with its emotional fullness and processes of illumination. This development is associated with the work of Peter Porter (b. 1929), Anne Stevenson (b. 1933) and Douglas Dunn (b. 1942); but here, again, there were significant anticipations, notably Robert Lowell's *Life Studies* (1959) and Robert Graves's *Collected Poems* (1965) and *Poems About Love* (1969). Ian Hamilton's *The Visit* (1970), which pursued authenticity in confessions muted against the grain of the 1960s, was a frail straw in the wind. A more distinct change of direction came with Anthony Thwaite's *Inscriptions* (1973) and Anne Stevenson's *Correspondences* (1974), where Victorian masks facilitated fresh warmth, range, or gentleness of feeling.

Anne Stevenson has developed impressively through eight volumes, from *Living in America* (1965) to *Enough of Green* (1977), *Minute by Glass Minute* (1982) and especially *The Fiction-Makers* (1985). Through her many university writerships she has mediated to younger poets the benignly American influence of Wallace Stevens's eloquence and Elizabeth Bishop's structure. She herself, however, is now so completely naturalized as to write memorable poems of place in a British manner – and is sometimes better at these than Donald Davie or even Peter Scupham, by the measure of her freer movement. (Scupham's densely worked palimpsest-landscapes, transcribed with a craft recalling de la Mare's, can sometimes be almost overrich with literary, historical and personal suggestions.) Stevenson's range (all of it accessible) is very considerable, since it extends from landscapes of feeling like 'The Mudtower' or 'With My Sons at Boarhills', through essays like 'Covent Garden' and literary pieces like 'Re-reading Jane' and 'A Dream of Stones', to subjectless subjective epigrams like 'Colours'. She has found a way to admit the gap between fiction and reality without letting emotional pressure leak away into it. Sometimes she almost seems to cross it, momentarily, in generous leaps of imagination that have the suddenness, the intensity, of Emily Dickinson:

Even you, with your breakable heart
in your ruined skin,
those poems all written
that have to be you, dear friend,
you guessed you were dying now,
but you were dying then.

('The Fiction-Makers', 1985)

In poetry so vulnerable and open, false notes of whimsy cannot always be avoided, while determination to communicate, even at the expense of a poem's own logic (as in 'Ailanthus with Ghosts'), occasionally proves a limitation. But more often these dangers are avoided by a tough critical intelligence. At her best, Stevenson shows that spells of authority can be spoken in a quiet voice.

The officially Australian Peter Porter (b. 1929) is an altogether more talkative, fast-moving poet, who has gone through several fairly distinct phases, from the epigrams and satires of *Once Bitten, Twice Bitten* (1961) and other early volumes, through the midlife stock-taking of *Living in a Calm Country* (1975) and the elegiac eloquence of *The Cost of Seriousness* (1978) and *English Subtitles* (1981), to the difficult, vatic manner of *Fast Forward* (1984). However, there were early ode-like poems; misfortune's dark 'bite mark' can be seen even in the funny poems of the first period; and the sense of transience appeared in poems like 'Ode to Afternoon' (1975), long before the bereavement of 'An Exequy' (1978). In fact, the historian's instruction 'Avoid simplicity' is not so much a discovery of 'Night Crossing' (1975) as a temperamental necessity. Even the ellipses, learnt from Latin epigram, were there from the start: the new development was only the special form difficulty came to take – 'Perhaps you should say something/A bit more interesting than what you mean.' Having himself contributed, by his corrosive Swiftian mockery, to the climate in which deconstruction flourished, Porter took 'late modernity' in his stride as easily as its passing.

It is a criticism of Porter that he has responded to social changes too automatically – as if the former copywriter were under compulsion to assimilate every new form of thought, every latest jazzle, in order to stay in business. Thus, although slow-changing nature is a bit blurred in Porter ('a cormorant/or some such'), artifacts are always precisely registered ('*Country Life* in a rexine folder'). Some think, indeed, that the urban scene is too much with him, so that he threatens to become a wearier, more satiric Betjeman. Is Porter really metropolitan? Is he fully naturalized, even, as a British poet? Such doubts seem to me beside the point. Porter may in some ways write for the urban nomad, for the rootless sojourner in 'a shadow city' that only now slouches to be built. But think how representative his images already are, and how much of the world has been hesitantly yet profoundly immersed in his compassionate mordant. He may not have a 'voice' of the pre-urban sort, but, as with Hill, the preference for written indirections can prove to be a strength.

Although Porter can make brilliant phrases, and wield at will the strong closure of the epigrammatist, he has seldom achieved the completeness of a self-contained, 'perfect' work. That is hardly possible, indeed, when his poems depend as heavily as they do on intertextualities with predecessors. Moreover, his language is also dependent on the momentary enlivening of shared unconscious dispositions. For his special method is to try to follow mental associations as closely as writing can suggest the quickness of living thought:

> *O mors inevitabilis,*
> Not to be held back by more than function,
> A pot of Stephen's Blue Black Ink, a gale
> All night among the pines and yet no air
> Upon our planet – nothing so well observed
> As pain, apothoesis of things out of place.
>
> ('At Lake Massaciuccoli', 1981)

Leaps of thought alternate with rapid swarming over nets of association. This naturally makes for difficulty, besides militating against fine textures. But in an age of disintegrating culture readers may be drawn to tolerate such drawbacks, and give Porter's omnivorous assimilations the study they deserve. Even so, the poetry of ready ideas calls for perpetual compromise between relevance and speed, between the number of things suggested and the amount suggested about them. The danger – not only for Porter but for the Dunn of *Europa's Lover* – is that by saying everything at once you may end up saying nothing much about anything. Porter's finest poems seem to me those in his simpler, elegiac manner. Sometimes, indeed, they are as simple as 'An Exequy':

> . . . I owe a death to you – one day
> The time will come for me to pay
> When your slim shape from photographs
> Stands at my door and gently asks
> If I have any work to do
> Or will I come to bed with you.

Here, the images have still particularity and copiousness, but their connections are less obtrusively difficult, less problematic, gentler, quieter.

Among more recent elegiac poems there should be mentioned Peter Levi's personal elegies, and the politically charged *A German Requiem* (1980) of James Fenton (b. 1949), a poet of considerable promise and already varied achievement. But the finest poetry of feeling has come, among younger poets, from Douglas Dunn (b. 1942). After early observation of Hull in *Terry Street* (1969) – less passionate than Tony Harrison's similarly class-conscious *The Loiners* (1970) and *The School of Eloquence* (1978) – Dunn moved on to meditative poems such as 'Winter Graveyard' in *Love or Nothing* (1974). At this stage there were still echoes of Larkin, to whom Dunn owed a valuable personal debt. The longish photograph title-poem 'St Kilda's Parliament' (1981) speaks for locality again:

> It is a remote democracy, where men,
> In manacles of place, outstare a sea
> That rattles back its manacles of salt,
> The moody jailer of the wild Atlantic.

But now one is impressed by the longer perspective on history, and the distancing – 'For I was then, and am, and I forget'. The long poem *Europa's Lover* (1982) enlarges again, to a global sweep as large as Porter's, though within a somewhat more referential frame. Dunn's stance is like an individual equivalent of Horatian proportion, deliberate, ironic, sensitive, robust:

> Or he might live in the stews of Tortuga, or
> Deliver to the slave-jetties of San Domingo,
> Composing hymns as the Africans
> Enter the mysteries of economics[.]

Dunn's finest achievement is his *Elegies* (1985), which as with Porter's followed a bereavement. Here mourning elegy repeatedly reverts to love poetry, with poignant effect. Dunn's particulars are all the more moving for their reticence:

> The moon rubs through the blue pallor of high east
> And childlessness has no number in the May
> Shadowed with birchlight on the county's crest.
> This year her death-date fell on Mother's Day.

The images almost throughout *Elegies*, as in the best of his earlier work, are memorably distinct. Sometimes, in fact, they are 'roundly evoked, described warmly but without purpose other than the design of delight or a surrender to imagination' (as he phrased his desiderata in his *Times Literary Supplement* essay of 1983). A significant development in his later volumes – new in Scottish poetry and for some time not often seen in English (least of all from the Movement) – is tentativeness of feeling: a sign, perhaps, of fresh exploration.

It is noteworthy that among younger poets Dunn by no means stands alone in disengaging himself from modernism and (for example) resuming closed forms. One also observes many signs of a return to determinate mimesis. Even John Ash (b. 1948), Britain's nearest equivalent to Ashbery, has moved an informative bit nearer to stability of reference in *Disbelief* (1988). And similar tendencies appear in the political referentiality of Fenton's work and in the Martians' well-defined visual imagery. Indeed, the Martians (Craig Raine, Christopher Reid and others: so called from Raine's poem 'A Martian Sends a Postcard Home') often give the impression of concentrating exclusively on strings of visual conceits. On the surface, at least, these can seem to constitute the entire poetic structure of a Raine poem:

> . . . Tethered by a foot,
> their sole giraffe
>
> manipulates its jib
> like an Anglepoise,
> awkwardly precise.

('Circus', *Rich*, 1983)

But, if 'reality' is back, that does not mean there is agreement on how to think about it poetically. Indeed, the recent period has been rather volatile stylistically, perhaps because a largish number of good minor poets have emerged. There is no obvious Milton or Wordsworth; but Hill and Porter, at least, will probably last as poets of canonical status, while Tomlinson, Morgan, Stevenson, Redgrove and Dunn often write no less well. In talent, if not always in skill, British poetry has become increasingly rich, so that the range of options has broadened. One has an exhilarating sense that in almost any direction literature may break out.

11

DRAMA SINCE 1950

Peter Mudford

THE DEVELOPMENT OF THE THEATRE

The development of the drama since 1950 cannot be separated from what has happened to the theatre. 'Drama,' as Raymond Williams has written, 'often shows more clearly and more quickly than the other arts, the deep patterns and changes in our general ideas of reality' (in Boris Ford, ed., *The Pelican Guide to English Literature*, vol VII, 1961, p 544). Such changes have transformed the theatre as a physical space, and as an institution. They have modified the relationship between writer, director and actor, and diversified the nature of theatre audiences. They have also intensified the debate about drama, and about the purposes for which theatres exist.

Since the seventeenth century, polemics have played their part in the development of drama. In the last thirty years, ideological as well as artistic debates have expanded its forms. George Bernard Shaw's vision of the theatre as a 'temple of the ascent of man' has not been realized, except insofar as the theatre has remained a platform for preaching social reform. Shaw sought to achieve this through the play of words, while many dramatists of the later twentieth century have explored non-verbal language – using the body as a means of expression. Flexibility of form has also helped to free the drama from the bondage of naturalism. Fantasy, film-clips, music-hall turns may all find their place in a play which is, for example, about life in a hospital ward. What is not said may be more important than what is said; and mime has achieved a new vitality as a means of expressing the inarticulate. The period has been characterized by experiment and innovation: but at the same time the tradition of dramatic writing associated in the previous generation with Noel Coward, Terence Rattigan and J. B. Priestley has been extended.

At the start of this period the theatre in Britain was confined to the West End of London, to 'little theatres' and a few regional repertory companies. By the end, a great explosion had taken place in numbers of companies and dramatists, as well as theatrical venues. State subsidy, however uncertain, had taken on a dominant role in the financing of national companies, and of much smaller community theatres and fringe groups – some of whom, ironically, wished to do away with the capitalist state from which they derived their funds. Alternative theatre had become well established, acting as the mouthpiece for political and ethnic groups, as had feminist theatre; and theatre-in-education had also become a recognized field of study and practice. Whatever its quality, the amount of drama being performed had increased massively; and the theatre was being used for a number of ends which had little to do with art or entertainment, as well as remaining at the centre of the debate between them.

Equally radical developments had occurred in the theatre as a place. Thrust-stages, raked stages, open stages; theatre-in-the-round, promenade theatres, studio theatres, warehouse theatres, pub-theatres, lunch-time theatres and street theatres had been added to the traditional nineteenth-century theatres with a proscenium-arch stage. The magic of the footlights had been replaced by banks of visible spots; and lighting design had become a specialized skill. Theatre-arts – costume, set design, make-up, wigs – had become more sophisticated, and the technology of the stage more complicated. In machinery, as in subsidy, there was a rich theatre and a poor theatre; and each in their contrasted ways had often proved the truth of the dictum: *Technik ist nicht alles!*

The last thirty years have also seen the theatre in Britain internationalized. In the ten years from 1964, Peter Daubeny's World Theatre Seasons were responsible for bringing to London forty-three companies from nineteen countries, including companies from Japan, India, South Africa, Israel and Russia. The work of directors like Peppino di Philippo, Karolos Koun, Ingmar Bergman, Nuria Espert and Giorgio Strehler; of designers like Josef Svoboda and Pier Luigi Pizzi; of players like Robert Hirsch, Katina Paxinou, Edwige Feuillère, Jean-Louis Barrault, Madeleine Renaud and Martin Held became more familiar in this country, just as it became more common for their counterparts here to work abroad. The influence on styles of production and acting – again in terms of greater freedom – has been considerable; translations and adaptations have become an increasingly important part of the creative life of many dramatists; and theatre audiences are now quite familiar with the work of foreign dramatists, whose names would have been almost unknown at the start of the period.

Critics have often spoken of a renaissance of British drama in the period; and the origins and outlines of this need to be described before coming to the work of individual dramatists. The 1950s are notable for the first production in Paris (1953) and in London (1955) of Samuel Beckett's *Waiting for Godot*: and in 1956 of John Osborne's *Look Back in Anger*. *Waiting for Godot* was a new kind of drama in which the old principles of play-making – plot, character, development, climax and denouement – appeared to be no longer important. Its action has been wittily described as one in which 'nothing happens, twice'. The English Stage Company's production of *Look Back in Anger* the following year was significant in a quite different way: though conventional in form, *Look Back in Anger* restored passion and vitality to the English stage, and established the Royal Court Theatre as a home for new drama, which it has remained until the present time. In 1954 Kenneth Tynan had written despondently of West End apathy, and the innumerable plays set in the country houses of Loamshire. 'The bare fact is that apart from revivals and imports, there is nothing in the London theatre that one dares discuss with an intelligent man for more than five minutes' (*A View of the English Stage*, 1984, p 147). Osborne's play, which Tynan was to praise as the 'best young play of its decade', provided a voice for a post-war generation, disillusioned with a world that was neither brave nor new, and determined to make itself heard. The dramatists of Osborne's generation, as different from him as they were from each other, none the less initiated drama, socially and politically conscious, which in the course of the next twenty years was to become increasingly radical and prominent as a dramatic movement. Among those associated with the Royal Court in this period are: John Arden, Arnold Wesker, Edward Bond, David Storey, Howard Brenton, David Hare, Heathcote Williams, Christopher Hampton and Caryl Churchill.

Joan Littlewood's Theatre Workshop, established at the Theatre Royal, Stratford-atte-Bowe in 1953, was equally significant at the time. Littlewood was inspired by a vision of a people's theatre in a working-class area. This vision did not materialize; but her view of the play as a collaborative effort and her insistence on the importance of improvisation have proved more durable. As well as being responsible for the production of Brendan Behan's *The Quare Fellow* and *The Hostage*, Littlewood gained wider acclaim for *Oh, What a Lovely War*! (1963). This production integrated styles as different as the pierrot show and the newsflash for the purpose of exposing the mindlessness, waste and incompetence of the First World War. The discontinuities of the action, now so familiar a part of dramatic usage, have seldom been used to greater effect.

In the early 1960s the director Peter Brook encouraged the development of experimental theatre as part of the work of the Royal Shakespeare Company. Brook at the time was deeply influenced by the work of Antonin Artaud, who had died in 1948. Artaud had been convinced of the inexorable forces which act upon individual lives ('the sky can at any time fall upon our heads'), and the need to develop in the theatre a physical language which could express through movement, dance, mime and action what words were impotent to express. He wanted a theatre of 'ritual' and 'shock'. Brook's experiments resulted in 1964 in his production of Peter Weiss's *Marat/Sade*. The mad scenes, and the physical violence of the action (for example, the flagellation of the Marquis de Sade with Charlotte Corday's hair) gave a new authority to non-verbal theatre: a technique Brook was to use for more explicitly political ends in his improvised production about the Vietnam War, *Us*. Both productions were intended to shock, but raised unanswered questions about what the shock was intended to achieve.

Since 1968 much of Brook's work has been done abroad, particularly in France, where he founded the International Centre for Theatre Research. As his day-long production of the *Mahabharata* at Avignon in 1986 proved, Brook's work is still capable of expanding the frontiers of theatre; his loss to this country is considerable, but the legacy of his work in the 1960s continues to be felt, particularly in companies like that of Stephen Berkoff.

The importance of 1956 in the 1960s is paralleled by the importance of 1968 for the development of drama in the 1970s. The censorship of plays by the Lord Chamberlain's office finally came to an end in that year, facilitating a more open approach to what could be done and said on the stage. That same year, the student uprising in Paris was to have as profound an effect on a new generation of writers as the Suez Crisis and the Hungarian Uprising had had a generation before. Described as an 'encounter between a revolutionary movement and a non-revolutionary situation', the student riots in Paris were to be decisive in making theatre in this country more politically conscious (though not necessarily more effective); and in creating a leftist theatre whose aims were later to be described by the dramatist David Edgar like this:

The new theatre must be everything the old Theatre is not. It must be serious in content but accessible in form. It must be popular without being populist . . . It must be orientated towards a working-class audience. It must get out of theatre buildings. It must be ideological and proud of it.

(quoted in Ronald Hayman, *British Theatre since 1955*, 1979, p 107)

In the decade after 1968 this attitude was instrumental in the creation of well over a hundred alternative theatre companies; and two hundred and fifty dramatists were working at least part of the time with them. But 1976 also saw the opening of the National Theatre – an idea first conceived in 1848. The National when it was completed included three auditoria: the Olivier with an arena stage, the Lyttleton with a proscenium arch, and the Cottesloe as a studio theatre. The first new play at the Lyttleton Theatre was Howard Brenton's *Weapons of Happiness*. Brenton had been at the centre of the movement in 1968 to create a new theatre for non-theatre people in non-theatre places. But he had come to feel that the fringe had failed in its dream of setting up an alternative culture; and that there was in the end only one society.

The policy of the National Theatre under Sir Peter Hall was to revive the classics, and to present the work of contemporary dramatists – both those whose work is overtly political, and of the left, and those whose work is not. Its three theatres provide facilities for work of very different kinds and scope which have made the works of European and American dramatists more familiar to larger audiences. The Royal Shakespeare Company has expanded from its one stage in the Memorial Theatre at Stratford-upon-Avon to six stages, and a permanent London home in the Barbican Centre. Outside London, new theatres at Chichester, Guildford and Pitlochry, for example, have also made drama an important part of the life of their communities. These developments are on a scale unimaginable at the start of the period. Equally the Fringe Theatre, associated in the past with the Edinburgh Festival where it still continues to flourish, has spread throughout the country. The theatre has become, in a real sense, a theatre for everyone. Much of the work being done – especially in the subsidized theatre – is of the highest professional standards; but its profuseness, among other things, can almost make it less memorable than the productions of the Old Vic Company in the years just before this period began.

FROM VERSE DRAMA TO THE PLAYS OF
SAMUEL BECKETT AND HAROLD PINTER

In 1950 verse drama was regarded as the form most likely to renew
the tradition of serious theatre. T. S. Eliot (1888–1965) had written
The Cocktail Party (1947), and had still to write *The Confidential
Clerk* (1953) and *The Elder Statesman* (1958). Christopher Fry
(b. 1907) had a growing reputation. The young Richard Burton, John
Gielgud, Claire Bloom and Pamela Brown appeared in *The Lady's
Not For Burning*, designed by Oliver Messel, in 1949. The following
year Laurence Olivier directed and took the leading role in *Venus
Observed*; and in 1954 Peter Brook directed Edith Evans in *The Dark
Is Light Enough*. Fry's characters were aware that they were speaking
poetry, and often played facetiously with it. A studied elegance
of expression created a drama that was mannered and artificial,
though often witty and humorous, and not without speculative
interest:

> COUNTESS ROSMARIN Is it not a quaint freedom, that lets us
>   Make up our minds and not be free to change them?
>   Poor me! I change my mind
>   For pure relaxation, two or three times a day
>   As I get wiser or sillier, whichever it is I do.
>   (*The Dark Is Light Enough*, Act I)

But the rough living edge of language is absent, here as elsewhere,
and with so little except words in his plays, Fry did not succeed in
renewing any of the several forms of language of which drama is
composed. T. S. Eliot in his Sweeney fragments of the 1920s
invented a form of dramatic dialogue in which rhythms of speech
reflected the age of jazz; but instead of developing this – 'under the
bam, under the boo, under the bamboo tree' – he chose in his
dramas from *Murder in the Cathedral* to use verse as a means of
expressing and exploring the moments of highest awareness in his
characters. (Ironically the finest of these is Beckett's Christmas Day
Sermon in *Murder in the Cathedral*, and that is in prose.) Eliot's
command of dramatic structure in his later plays was never strong;
and his characters often lacked even the dead-pan vitality of Doris
and Dusty in the incomplete fragments of *Sweeney Agonistes*. But his
plays continue to be revived because he was preoccupied with a
theme central to the modern imagination: the tension often strained
to breaking-point between private self and public being. In his
verse-drama Eliot explores the relationship between the selves we

instinctively feel we are, and the roles we are called upon to play. Harry's decision in *The Family Reunion* (1939) to leave Wishwood and follow the bright angels provides him with a future, as it will lead Celia in *The Cocktail Party* to crucifixion. The inability to resolve this tension will result in later plays – for example, David Mercer's *A Suitable Case for Treatment* (1962) and Simon Gray's *Melon* (1987) – in different forms of breakdown. Both of these are prose-plays, and the language of poetry in drama was to survive in forms wholly different to those of Eliot or Fry.

Samuel Beckett's (1906–89) *Waiting for Godot*, like the rest of his plays, succeeds in areas where Fry's and Eliot's proved weakest. Beckett renewed the language of drama in a manner comparable to Donne's renewal of the language of the Elizabethan sonneteers; however, he did so through a fresh approach not just to dialogue but also to stage-space, scenery, action (or absence of it) and lighting. Everything that happens on the stage – and often the stage itself – is part of the metaphorical meaning of Beckett's plays. An example is the opening of *Act without Words. 2* (1959), which, if it were not a play-text, could equally well be a prose-poem:

Desert. Dazzling light.
The man is flung backwards on stage from right wing. He falls, gets up immediately, dusts himself, turns aside, reflects.
Whistle from right wing.
He reflects, goes out right.
Immediately flung back on stage he falls . . .

In this mime, the man is physically frustrated in all his attempts to control his fate. Whatever he does, powers unnamed and unknown prove his impotence. We do not know who the man is; all his world is the stage; and as long as he continues to exist (that is, as long as the play continues) the nature of his existence (not to speak of its quality) will be determined by the inscrutable forces acting upon him. Like *Waiting for Godot* this mime exemplifies what John Peter has defined, in *Vladimir's Carrot* (1987), as a 'closed drama', an action which we either accept or reject as an image of man's existence. Insofar as it is interpretable, it is so only within its own terms; here, there are no effects of causes, as in Ibsen's drama, only effects in themselves. This character – like other characters in Beckett's plays – has no imaginable future, except to go through again what he has been through before.

Words in Beckett's plays are used with an economy and precision which enable complexity of feeling, and state, to be expressed because everything extraneous has been removed. Waiting for Godot implies the despondency of waiting for something which never happens, but also the hope which nourishes each succeeding day. Between hope and despondency lies the state of unknowing, out of which the tension of the action rises. What Beckett plays upon in the audience is not essentially different to what Shakespeare plays upon in *Hamlet*.

The concreteness of the language half conceals the improvisation needed to get through the day. As the French title implies, *En attendant Godot* is about all that happens while waiting. *Fin de partie* (*Endgame*, 1957) is about the last apocalyptic game, the end of the party, the game that's over, the final throw, close of play, ending with the tableau from which it began. Here is a form of drama which imposes its meaning or meanings, and yet at the same time reminds us that all meanings are provisional. Happy days are not 'les beaux jours'. *Play* (1964) is very definitely not play, and yet is a play, going round and round, in a hellish circle of interrogative light. Characters only speak when the spot shines on them, when they have been cued as in all plays; the spot is also their inquisitor, and finally the light of their dimming consciousnesses. As trapped as Dante's figures in their particular circle of hell, Beckett's characters live out their half-life, half-death in the glare of a stage that is both stage and world, art, and how it is. But also neither, because each is provisional. The play will be repeated; but it will not be the same. It will also be the same, because it cannot be different.

The problems raised in our minds by Beckett's plays are problems of language: of what the language of theatre (everything that happens on the stage) can do and say; but also of what it cannot say or do. We are confronted with the pain of consciousness, the bafflement of consciousness, and its uniqueness (all Beckett's characters are unique); but we are also confronted with the insubstantiality of being (Beckett's characters often seem more like ghosts than people), and the slightness of the change when sleep or silence or death intervene.

The provisional nature of being, fired by the pain of being and the desire not to be ('will night never come?'), underlies the effect of Beckett's plays. As his plays have become more reductive, their effect has also become more intense, until the pain of them would be intolerable if it were not for the astonishing renewal of language, whether in the wordless *Quad*, or in the duologue between the woman in her chair and her recorded voice in *Rockaby*:

WOMAN: More
[*Pause. Rock and voice together*]
v: till in the end
the day came
close of a long day
when she said . . .

Beckett's drama is like a whole evolutionary epoque, summed up in its fossil-record.

Harold Pinter's (b. 1930) plays share with Beckett's the distinction of a style entirely their own, in which language is used with the precision of poetry (which Pinter began by writing). Pinter's work is none the less more circumscribed than Beckett's, more deeply rooted in the social world, its anxieties, self-doubt and violence. In Pinter's early work, the so-called comedies of menace, the social origin of his drama was often heavily overlaid; the situation of his characters, though defined by a recognizable environment – for example, the seaside boarding-house in *The Birthday Party* – was obscure; and the violence which occurred was the result of dimly realized terrors. In more recent plays – *Betrayal* (1983), *One for the Road* (1984) and *A Kind of Alaska* (1984) – the social ambiance has become clearer, and Pinter's feeling for character in relation to social type as defined by class and profession less opaque.

As Pinter is more concerned with type and class than Beckett, the boundaries of his plays are more tightly drawn. His plays are enacted in rooms – social and personal spaces in which his characters are trapped by circumstances which may or may not be of their own making. As in Beckett's plays, we are confronted with effects, of which the causes may be unknown, but are not unknowable. The notes left in *The Dumb Waiter* (1960), like the appearance of Goldberg and McCann in *The Birthday Party*, do have an explanation; but the play is not concerned with them. The clues exist, and the mystery remains unsolved. This is dangerous dramatic territory, because it can become a sleight of hand as it does in *No Man's Land*, or a subterfuge which permits the dramatist a form of self-concealment as in *The Homecoming*. Pinter's Jewishness, like the violence of his East End childhood, pervades his plays elusively: they create an aura of threat and uncertainty which he offers as a more generalized aspect of the contemporary world. In the early plays, in particular, the balance is often uneasy.

Intensity in the stage-action often derives in Pinter's plays from everyday objects (a drum, a bucket, a bed) which are identified with private territories. His rooms which belong to the private domain and the private self ought to be places of refuge, but they turn out to be threatened territories – threatened by intruders from the outside world, like Goldberg and McCann in *The Birthday Party*, Davies in *The Caretaker*, Ruth and Teddy in *The Homecoming*. The intrusion leads to a struggle over territory and rights; a struggle for domination; and in the end either rejection, as Davies is rejected at the end of *The Caretaker*, or assimilation, as Ruth is assimilated at the end of *The Homecoming* by becoming the family whore. As in Beckett's plays, titles conceal complexities which the play cannot resolve: *The Caretaker* is about the impossibility of taking care of someone else if he threatens a private territory. The more Davies identifies himself with the room and its objects, the more inevitable it becomes that he will be thrown out. As among animals, differences of habit, smell and effect determine who is a member of the tribe, and who is not; but these can also be changed by education and circumstance. When Teddy in *The Homecoming* is asked to explain his work as a philosopher, he replies by asserting his difference. He is neither a threat, nor is he threatened, while Ruth, his wife, is both: 'You wouldn't understand my works. You wouldn't have the faintest idea of what they were about. You'd be lost' (*The Homecoming*, Act II). Teddy will return to his work in New York, while Ruth will remain in an environment where her sexuality is her only offering. The customs of each tribe are sufficient only unto themselves: a situation in which Pinter perceives the potential for violence, and also the humour.

In Pinter's later work, *Landscape* and *Silence* show a progression in dramatic technique, and an ability to deploy his powers as a poet to new effect. In both, Pinter works in a non-realistic mode, allowing the characters to create a dramatic action by their attempts to locate themselves within their experience. In *Landscape*, a man and his wife sit in the kitchen of a country-house; they refer to each other; but neither hears the other's words. Duff's monologue is a broken account of a particular day, Beth's of an experience in her past – an encounter with Duff perhaps, or with Mr Sykes who once employed them in the house where they now live. Perhaps it is a recollection of *tendresse*, which belongs to neither one nor the other. The silences with which the play is punctuated are the silences between them; the pauses the attempt to sift their own experience. We sense the presence of a contact which would be made if it could. The play is gentle and abrasive, violent and erotic, somnambulistic and diurnal. The struggle for domination and the need to preserve one's territory which was so important in *The Caretaker* has been superseded here because, although Beth and Duff share the same space, their territories do not touch.

Betrayal (1983) by contrast is Pinter's most naturalistic play, and the one in which his control of form is most obviously displayed. A triangular relationship is seen from its end to its beginning, like a film run backwards. The action is not concerned with what happened, but with the precarious identities of three characters, for whom deceit, lies, betrayal are also needed forms of self-defence. If, in the end, *Betrayal* seems a little too calculated, *A Kind of Alaska* succeeds in that combination of the actual with the suggestive where Pinter's art is most effective. Deborah has lain asleep for twenty-nine years with *encephalitis lethargica*. With the discovery of L-dopa her doctor awakens her, and she attempts to recross the boundary to the waking world, to a present as much changed as she has aged. She makes a brave, almost a miraculous attempt to rise from her bed, to walk alone, then to dance; but in the end the attempt to readjust to the reality of those about her – of her sister, and her family – is too great. All they have told her, she thinks she has in proportion. But who she is in this hall of reflecting glass, she does not intend to find out. 'I certainly have no intention of looking into a mirror.' This line recalls what Pinter himself once said: 'I had – I have – nothing to say about myself, directly. I wouldn't know where to begin. Particularly since I often look at myself in a mirror and say, "Who the hell's that?"' ('H. Pinter: An Interview', reprinted in Arthur Ganz, ed., *Pinter: A Collection of Critical Essays*, 1972, p 20.)

Pinter has described himself as a very traditional playwright who insists on having a curtain in all his plays, and who writes curtain lines for that reason. The curtains are metaphorical too; what they conceal are the themes to which Pinter has kept returning: the problem of who we are, of how our present relates to our past, how memories relate to desire, and fears to the need for self-assertion. His plays are also becoming in the broadest sense more political, if *One for the Road* is indicative.

Throughout his work Pinter's language has many of the qualities of poetry – he uses the specific to express a range of meanings and feelings, to which his audience will respond at different levels, and in different ways: 'Is it my birthday soon? Will I have a birthday party? Will everyone be there? Will they all come? All our friends? How old will I be?' (*A Kind of Alaska*).

FORMS OF NATURALISM

This section will be concerned with a number of dramatists who in one way or another have explored the boundaries of stage-naturalism, allowing flexibility of form to permit innovation in dramatic effect. They have exploited the theatre's self-awareness that it is a theatre, while at the same time using for their own ends the naturalistic tradition which pretended that it was not. The dramatic forms which they have used range from epic to farce; and if their drama is not original to the degree which Beckett's or Pinter's is, it excels in its ability to entertain. Their work is successful at the box office, and regularly performed in the commercial theatre. The political dramatists who will be discussed in the next and final section, and who desire to profit and reform their audiences, have by no means all shared this popularity.

The period under review has produced considerable talent; playwriting has flourished in the theatre, and for television. If space allowed, I should also have written about Robert Bolt (in particular his fine play about the individual's conscience, *A Man for All Seasons* (1960)), David Storey, David Mercer, Michael Frayn and Alan Bennett. In restricting the number considered, I have left room for at least some detailed comment on individual plays.

Peter Shaffer's (b. 1926) first major success in the theatre, *Five Finger Exercise* (1958), established, among other things, his skill in exploiting different areas and levels of stage-space, to dramatize the simultaneous complexities of family life – a skill equally apparent in the work of the last dramatist in this section, Alan Ayckbourn. Different stage-levels were to be used as effectively by Shaffer for other ends in *The Royal Hunt of the Sun* (1964), *Black Comedy* (1965) and *The Battle of Shrivings* (1970). Shaffer handles stage-time with equal precision. In *The Private Ear* (1962) he speeds the action through a meal by transferring the dialogue to tape, which then accelerates to a mad chatter. In the same play too, he used the love duet from *Madam Butterfly* as an ironic comment upon a six-minute wordless sequence in which Bob fails to seduce Doreen. Shaffer here, as in *Amadeus* (1979), enjoys conjuring with and contrasting different kinds of theatricality.

Shaffer has also always been aware that a play only comes into existence when performed. In a note to *The Royal Hunt of the Sun*, he writes:

My hope was always to realize a kind of 'total' theatre, involving not only words, but rites, mimes, masks and magic. The text cries for illustration. It is a director's piece, a pantomimist's piece, a musician's piece, a designer's piece, and of course an actor's piece, almost as much as it is an author's.

('Author's Notes', *The Royal Hunt of the Sun*, 1964, p 9)

Such a view was being pursued in a much more doctrinaire manner in other parts of the theatre; but here, as in *Equus* (1973), John Dexter's productions succeeded in realizing Shaffer's intentions.

The action of *Equus* originates in a young boy's blinding of six horses with a metal spike, and ends with the healing, by the psychiatrist Dysart, of the psychosis which led him to do it. The interplay in the stage action between the clinical world and the fantasy world of the horses succeeds in sustaining a disturbing tension about what is going to happen to Dysart and the boy. But, at the play's end, it is the psychiatrist who remains the more interesting character, in his knowledge that by returning Alan to normality he is also returning him to another form of darkness. 'What way is this?' he asks. 'What dark is this?' Here, as in *Amadeus*, Shaffer's dramatic imagination has been seized by an idea of considerable interest and scope. In the later play, Salieri's appalled recognition that he is not 'beloved of God' as Mozart is, and that compared to Mozart's his music is worthless, dramatizes the anguish of the artist capable of recognizing genius in a contemporary; it compels him to plot Mozart's death. As in all Shaffer's major plays, a drama of ideas is conceived in terms of an action concerned with a crime. Shaffer's strength lies in the largeness with which the play is conceived and in its theatrical realization; his weakness in the development of the ideas which give life to it. Once we have grasped them, we may continue to be held by his theatrical skills – as, for example, the mime in *The Royal Hunt of the Sun* which recreates the crossing of the Andes and, later, the slaughter of the Incas – but the dialogue lacks an implicit dimension. It is about what it says.

John Mortimer (b. 1923), like Peter Shaffer, has worked within a tradition which owes much to naturalism; but he has extended this tradition not so much by theatrical devices as by his feeling for the bizarreness of individual character. Mortimer's characters are often in the true sense eccentric, even a little bit touched – for example, his two most famous barristers, Morgenhall in *The Dock Brief* and Rumpole; and this also results in their humour. Mortimer writes of fantasies, sometimes fulfilled, sometimes not; he is also a realist aware of the more poignant and sombre stuff of which fantasies are made. 'The truth, as I have found it', Mortimer has written, 'is that you can only work within that narrow seam which penetrates the depth of your past' ('Introduction', *Five Plays*, 1970, p 8). He does this most effectively and poignantly in the autobiographical *A Voyage Round My Father* (1970). The narrator's father – a barrister who has gone blind as a result of an accident – continues to live as though nothing has changed, mastering his briefs with the help of his wife, and indulging his passion for the garden he never sees.

The action moves backwards and forwards in time, involving the son as adult and boy, so that we see his father through present action and through recollection. The drama portrays a man alone and despondent: 'All education's perfectly useless, all advice's perfectly useless, you're alone in the world, remember.' But the father has not lost his curiosity and wonder. At the end of Act I the son leads the blind father (and the dramatic resonances are apparent) to the top of a hill – but not for the purpose of suicide. From there three counties can be seen; and the father advises the son: 'See everything, everything in Nature . . . That's the instinct of the maybeetle, twenty-four hours to live, so spend it looking around . . .' Together they observe the 'monstrous persistence of Nature'. At the end of Act II, the death of the father – a man who had no message, and probably had no belief – leaves his son bereft: 'I'd been told of all the things you're meant to feel. Sudden freedom, growing up, the end of dependence, the step into the sunlight, when no one is taller than you, and you in no one's shadow. [*Pause.*] I know what I felt. Lonely.'

Mortimer achieves in this dramatic portrait a play which combines freedom of form with subtlety of characterization. The father and his relationships are conceived with a clarity, as in Chekhov, which is specific but also representative; and the effect is poignant and memorable. For these reasons – and unlike some successful plays of the period – it survives the test of revival and reinterpretation.

The plays of Simon Gray (b. 1936) (who is thirteen years younger than John Mortimer) reflect a more caustic, introspective and self-regarding generation. Mortimer once described his plays as concerned with the middle classes in decline; the plays of Simon Gray depict the members of the middle class tearing themselves and each other apart. His characters are usually drawn from a limited social milieu: professional people, with literary or academic inclinations, educated at Oxford or Cambridge, and now living in London. This restricts the dramatic scope, but not the versatility of the dramatic style. What Simon Gray writes about, he knows very well; and his ear for inconsistency or inaccuracy in speech is as sharp as a piranha's teeth. He often uses as his central character – for example, Butley, Simon, Melon – a man who through his articulateness can manipulate, needle, control and dominate (or thinks he can) those with whom he comes into contact. Sharpness of wit – a major source of dramatic energy and pleasure in these plays – serves his characters as a means of analysing the ground at their feet (and trying to avoid its pitfalls); but it also serves as a means of self-analysis. In spite of their command of words, Gray's characters remain solipsists who relate only to themselves.

An act in a play by Simon Gray begins coolly – but as the feeling intensifies, so the layers of concealment and emotional self-deception are torn away, like a snake being skinned. This action of unmasking through laceration and self-laceration leaves little room for Gray's characters to be sympathetic – which is perhaps the more problematic for the comfortable circumstances in which they live. Here, *Quartermaine's Terms* (1981) gains by comparison with Gray's other plays. The central character, Quartermaine, is neither articulate nor competent. Like many Englishmen of his class and type – and unlike Gray's more self-conscious characters – Quartermaine is lost, and does not know it; or if he does, conceals it under exclamations of baffled surprise.

Simple dramatic devices are also indicative of Gray's increasing control of form. For example, in Act I, scene i, Quartermaine's colleagues in the common-room (we are in a not very successful School of English in Cambridge) cry off his invitation to the theatre, one by one, leaving him alone; in Act II, scene ii, they all invite him out on the same evening so that he does not know whom to accept. In each case, the action (which also has its humour) deepens Quartermaine's loneliness and isolation, until the new head dismisses him from the non-world of his non-common room.

Melon (1987), a recent play by Simon Gray, returns to comedy of a more analytic and sardonic kind. In its stylishness, it has been aptly compared to Restoration comedy, with which it also shares an awareness of the dangers in the sexual games people play with each other. In incisiveness of dialogue, and fluency of stage-action, Simon Gray has never written a more skilful play. But the accomplishment involved in using mental breakdown as the theme of a comedy of very black manners means restricting the action to that area where laughter can mollify, and the horror is kept at bay. 'One day – quite suddenly without the slightest warning – the ground opens at your feet', Melon says at the start. What happens after that, and what causes it (which seems to be the theme of this play) would require a dramatist of different powers, working in a very different mode.

Christopher Hampton (b. 1946) – a generation younger again than Simon Gray – is also a stylist of considerable skill and versatility. But Hampton uses style to distance the compulsive emotions with which he is concerned, while Simon Gray uses it as a means of investigation. Hampton's most recent work – an adaptation of

Laclos's *Les Liaisons dangereuses* – is especially well-suited to his gifts. The destructive element in sexual passion provides the dramatic tension; but the eighteenth-century style and setting makes it possible to dramatize a rational and objective interest in the way such passion works. Hampton's first play, *When Did You Last See My Mother?* (1966), concerned the seduction of a mother by her son's boyfriend. The mother's compulsive inability to stop coming back to the shabby flat where they live prefigures the much more complex relationship between Verlaine and Rimbaud which Hampton dramatized in *Total Eclipse* (1968). The play's most effective scenes concern Verlaine's ambivalence and indecision towards his wife Mathilde, and his inability to come to terms with how he is, as opposed to how society says he should be. Here, as elsewhere, Hampton uses a fluent episodic structure; but his individual scenes are shaped and crafted with precision and point.

In 1983 Hampton, after successfully translating two of von Horváth's plays, turned his attention to the lives of the German writers in exile in Hollywood during the Second World War: Thomas Mann, Heinrich Mann and Bertolt Brecht. The resulting play, *Tales from Hollywood*, uses Horváth as the narrator in an action which in real life he did not live to witness. A chronicle play of twenty-two scenes, *Tales from Hollywood* succeeds in being about the problems of the writer exiled from his own culture and also, in the contrast between Thomas and Heinrich Mann, about the American dream of success and failure. Heinrich, increasingly forgotten and impoverished, is married to the much younger and still attractive Nelly who, struggling with despair and drink, takes an overdose of sleeping pills. It is characteristic of Hampton's objectivity that the narrator tells the audience – drily and effectively – what ensues:

> He bundled her into a taxi, and got her to the nearest hospital, but they were very busy, as it was just before Christmas, and they didn't like the look of this shabby old foreigner, who didn't have enough on him, and they refused to take his cheque . . . At hospital number three they were far more helpful and were able to tell him right away that Nelly had just died . . .
>
> (Act II)

Through most of the play, Horváth is inspired by an ironic affection for Hollywood: the writer in him responds to what happens to his friends there, the poignancy of their lives and all that is involved in being in exile; and his spirit permeates the action. Among Hampton's many qualities is his ability to write plays which, while being about individuals, are not confined to the problems of contemporary

Britain, and which succeed in confronting his audiences with wider problems of culture and history. Unlike the work of many dramatists in the period, Hampton's is not parochial.

The plays so far considered all extend the boundaries of naturalism. I now turn to three dramatists – Joe Orton, Tom Stoppard and Alan Ayckbourn – whose most representative work has all been – in content or form, or both – even more radical.

Joe Orton's (1933–67) three best plays – *Entertaining Mr Sloane* (1964), *Loot* (1967) and *What the Butler Saw* (1969) – all employ a similar kind of humour, and depend for their success on performances of a particular kind. They need to be acted, as Orton himself pointed out, 'perfectly seriously', and with 'absolute realism'. The characters in Orton's plays say outrageous, bizarre and ferociously funny things with a polished sense of propriety. While they are treating sacred things as a lark, they are doing so as though butter would not melt in their mouths. Orton's characters are never surprised by their own improprieties; they take them entirely for granted; and when they object to other people's, the grounds are not moral but pragmatic. While everyone speaks as though they are irreproachable, their words and their actions have no foundation in any morality except that of the play.

In *Entertaining Mr Sloane* Sloane, a murderer on the run, takes a room with Kath, is seduced by her, makes her pregnant, murders her father-in-law who has discovered the truth about his criminal past, and becomes the lover of Kath's brother who employs Sloane as a chauffeur. His delay in doing so has nothing to do with scruple, only with knowing his trump card. At the end of the play, Kath agrees to Ed having Sloane for the next six months, and thereafter on a half-yearly basis – with provision for occasional visits so that Kath does not get too lonely:

ED: I'd bring him over myself in the car. Now you'll be more or less out of action for the next three months. So shall we say till next August? Agreed?

KATH: Perfect, Eddie.

(Act III)

As in the vulgar humour of the seaside postcard, moral positions do not apply; and nor do human feelings. *Loot* and *What the Butler Saw* extend the scope of the comedy beyond the sexual. In *Loot* a mother's funeral rites provide the opportunity for the son to stash the body in a cupboard and fill the coffin with banknotes, which he and his accomplice Dave have acquired in a robbery, in an attempt to evade the investigations of Inspector Truscott who poses as a man from the water board. Throughout the play, coffin, cupboard, corpse and banknotes are used as the instruments of farce, while the dialogue is composed of *non sequiturs* and bizarre logic, as, for example, when Truscott discovers the stolen banknotes in the casket:

TRUSCOTT: How dare you involve me in a situation for which no memo has been issued. In all my experience I've never come across a case like it. Every one of these fivers bears a portrait of the Queen. It's dreadful to contemplate the issues raised. Twenty thousand tiaras and twenty thousand smiles buried alive! She's a constitutional monarch, you know. She can't answer back.

(Act II)

This kind of dialogue, relentlessly unexpected in its twists, demands a particular kind of concentration from the audience. One laugh succeeds another, hectically; and, unlike *The Importance of Being Earnest*, the play does not relate to a social world in which the comedy of manners acts as ballast to the verbal invention. In *What the Butler Saw* the pace becomes even faster. Set in a private psychiatric clinic, the play exchanges one farcical situation for another, until a '*deus ex machina*' saves everyone from coming to a more or less bloody end. We do not laugh at character as we do in Feydeau's farces; we laugh at situations which enable cartoon-figures to jest – often tellingly, truly, cruelly – but always coldly. Orton's play is a feast of jesting, in which madness and sanity are not distinguishable; and a straight answer is always crooked. It is sustained by a dashing inventiveness of plot and repartee, and a smashing disdain for authority. But when the curtain falls, and laughter turns to silence, what remains is contempt.

Tom Stoppard (b. 1937) is as in love with ideas as other men are in love with ninepins. He likes to bowl them down as they occur to him: 'I write plays because writing dialogue is the only respectable way of contradicting yourself. I'm the kind of person who embarks on an endless leapfrog down the great moral issues, I put a position, rebut it, refute the rebuttal, and rebut the refutation . . .' (in Malcolm Page, *File on Stoppard*, 1986, p 87). This comment indicates how individual plays work, and also one of the similarities between them. *Rosencrantz and Guildenstern are Dead* (1967), Stoppard's first success, opens with the attendant lords spinning coins to pass the time. Heads have come up seventy times. Ros expresses no surprise at his impossible run of luck because he feels none. Whatever loads the odds against Guil remains as inscrutable as the role they have to play in Elsinore. As attendant lords they have been compared to Vladimir and Estragon in *Waiting for Godot* who also appear to have no choice in the roles they play. But the reference of Beckett's play is always at one level outwards – to questions of existence and being – while Stoppard's play is concerned with itself: with the relevance and irrelevance of the attendant lords to the tragedy of *Hamlet*.

The brilliance of the play is to be found in its language, which avoids pastiche. Stoppard invents in the stylized modern idiom of Ros and Guil a natural foil for the excerpts from Shakespeare's play. The placing of unimportant and unheroic figures at the centre of the tragic action may be thought to have a metaphorical relevance to modern times; but the play is sustained more by its cleverness and ingenuity, its pleasure in theatricality, and allusiveness than for anything it is about. (In this respect Stoppard's playing with the theatre seems a long journey from Pirandello's.)

Stoppard's next two major plays, *Jumpers* (1972) and *Travesties* (1974), also share this same quality of acrobatics in a void. In *Jumpers*, a moral philosopher wrestles with the problem of his lecture on God on one half of the stage, while his wife, an ex-musical comedy queen, has a breakdown on the other. When Dotty mentions God, she does so reflexively, and not as an invocation, while George's attempt to communicate with her exists at the level of 'have you been shaving your legs?' The humour and originality of the play consist more in the way they undercut each other's roles than in the relationship between them, even though the first implies the second. In *Travesties*, the reminiscences of Henry Carr about his time in Zurich during the First World War, his part in James Joyce's production of *The Importance of Being Earnest* (as a result of which he sued Joyce for a pair of trousers), and the coincidental presence in Zurich of Lenin and Tristan Tzara are interwoven in a 'dazzling pyrotechnical feat that combines Wildean pastiche, political history, artistic debate, spoof, reminiscence and song-and-dance in marvellously judicious proportions' (Michael Billington, in Malcolm Page, *File on Stoppard*, 1986, p 48). This is so; and the result is exhilarating, but also on reflection (and unlike Shaw) disheartening. Here is a mind able to master the great debates of our time – politics, art, life – so well that he can play with them, like a child with his toys. And he does. We may wonder if the relentless play is not better suited to the parody of detective fiction (and the role of dramatic critics) in *The Real Inspector Hound* (1968), where it does not matter who or what gets murdered for sport's sake. In *The Real Inspector Hound*, Stoppard's style is flawlessly related to his matter;

and the mirth he makes from them both results in a small dramatic masterpiece. Stoppard's more naturalistic plays, *Night and Day* (1978) and *The Real Thing* (1982), do not provide the same opportunities for his intellectual and theatrical nimbleness. But *The Real Thing* contains one memorable scene when Henry explains the relationship between writing and cricket; it also says a great deal about Stoppard's art. 'The cricket-bat is sprung like a dance floor,' he says. 'It's for hitting cricket balls with ... What we are trying to do is to write cricket-bats, so that when we throw up an idea and give it a little knock, it might ... travel' (Act II). As in cricket, the question is, how far?

Alan Ayckbourn (b. 1939) has written more than thirty successful plays. His skill as an entertainer who lightened the gloom for large audiences on rainy days at Scarborough (not to mention the West End) ensured for a long time that he was not considered worthy of critical attention. In 1983, Michael Billington's book on Ayckbourn began to redress the balance. Ayckbourn's plays since then have confirmed his reputation for technical audacity and an ability to write farces which recognize the pain and corruption of the modern world. *Absurd Person Singular* (1972) was a turning-point for Ayckbourn, as Billington pointed out. In the second act, Eva is determined to commit suicide: first by jumping from the window-ledge, then by impaling herself on the kitchen knife, and so on. At each turn she is frustrated by friends who do not realize what she is up to, and think they have come for a Christmas Eve party. The action is funny, and very sad: an image of human misunderstanding and incomprehension; and finally of isolation in the midst of what is intended for a festive celebration.

Ayckbourn is also a dramatist inspired by what can be done on the stage, in spite of the stage's limitations. In *Bedroom Farce* (1975) Ayckbourn's set reveals three bedrooms; in these three bedrooms – each visually defined as a particular and different social environment – we shall see the relationships and activities of four couples, all of whom have their problems. As in Feydeau, the multiple set is used for unexpected encounters at night which are comic, but also reveal the flaws and the strain in apparently stable relationships. In *Woman in Mind* (1985), Ayckbourn returns to this theme in a more extreme form. The action opens with Susan lying on the grass in her suburban garden, burbling incoherently. A lonely marriage to a vicar, in which communication has long since failed, has driven her to create a fantasy existence in which she is loved by a husband and family with whom she can, and does, converse. The return of her real son Rick without his wife, whom he has recently married, solely for the purpose of collecting some furniture to raise cash for his journey to Thailand is explained like this: Tess 'knows all about the theory of life. Don't worry. But she's still a bit short on the practical. And she needs to be introduced to certain elements of it gradually. Elements like you and Dad' (Act II). Not surprisingly, the play ends where it began with Susan lapsing into incoherence.

Ayckbourn's gift for writing humorous dialogue – like his inventiveness in relation to farcical situation – does not always mix easily with his growing responsiveness to despair and darkness. His recent play, *A Small Family Business* (1987), in which his use of the stage once again illustrates a master of farce at work, ends none the less with the daughter of the family, drugged in the darkened bathroom, staring ahead of her blankly. If Stoppard plays with words so that no proposition is to be taken seriously, Ayckbourn plays with stage-situation at the cost of any lasting empathy with his character's feelings.

POLITICAL DRAMA

Look Back in Anger by John Osborne (b. 1929) opened on 8 May 1956; and the date is often quoted as a watershed in modern dramatic history. It marks the beginning of a period when plays would no longer be concerned with middle-class heroes, or set in country-houses. Osborne's play gave voice to violent discontent in the character of a young man who was aware that he could find no place in the society around him. As Osborne's later work has proved, he was not really a political dramatist; and his work bears little relation to those who followed after him, and were. But *Look Back in Anger* prepared the way for them by making managements and directors aware of a new direction in contemporary writing, and by compelling audiences to perceive contemporary society from a lower-middle-class or working-class perspective.

With the exception of Osborne, the first wave of new dramatists produced single plays of interest rather than a developing *oeuvre*: N. F. Simpson's *A Resounding Tinkle* (1957), Ann Jellicoe's *The Sport of My Mad Mother* (1958), Willis Hall's *The Long and the Short and the Tall* (1959), Shelagh Delaney's *A Taste of Honey* (1958), and David Rudkin's *Afore Night Come* (1962). Arnold Wesker (b. 1932) produced a considerable body of work between 1959 and 1962, including his Jerusalem trilogy (1960) and *Chips with Everything* (1962). Although moments in Wesker's plays were memorable

– for example, Beatie's visionary monologue at the end of *Roots* (1969), and the 'silent, breath-taking and very funny raid' on the Naafi in *Chips with Everything* – he did not succeed in finding a style of greater scope than his personal voice.

John Arden (b. 1930) also looked in the 1960s as though he might develop into a dramatist of innovative power. But *Sergeant Musgrave's Dance* (1960) remains his most interesting work – the opening of Act III, when the skeleton of a dead soldier is displayed on the public scaffold and Musgrave performs his demonic dance around it, is memorable – but the play as a whole is confused in effect. Subtitled an 'unhistorical parable', the play is set in a mining town in the North of England eighty years ago. The audience is expected to respond to the characters as figures in a parable representing some general truth, and as characters in a play which has naturalistic roots, although the language of the play does not belong anywhere in particular. In addition, the message of the parable does not come across clearly. The play is opposed to violence, war and imperialism; but it also exemplifies the truth, that, when individuals go berserk as Musgrave does in believing himself the avenging instrument of God, the state must intervene and restore order with whatever force is necessary.

With Jimmy Porter, Osborne established a new voice in the theatre; but he also found his own voice, and this, although he has found many different dramatic disguises for it, has remained consistent. His central characters are driven by furious energy directed towards a void. In a world where there are no new brave causes left, they try to discover a role, or to endure the one they have been born to play. But they do so passionately and turbulently: 'One of us is mean and stupid and crazy. Which is it? Is it me? Is it me, standing here like an hysterical girl, hardly able to get my words out? Or is it her?' (*Look Back in Anger*, Act I). In *The Entertainer* (1957) Archie Rice (especially as he was created by Laurence Olivier), with his tatty jokes and determination to play his audience for all they are worth, remains a poignant image of a man trying to shore up something against his ruin. But the wider metaphorical identification of England and its Empire with the fading music-hall has not survived as well.

In *Luther* (1961), as in *The Entertainer* and *Inadmissible Evidence* (1965), Osborne attempted to extend the bounds of his basically naturalistic style. Bill Maitland, the solicitor in *Inadmissible Evidence*, cannot distinguish between fantasy and reality, and is the prisoner of his own dream – a dream which is a vision of his own helplessness:

'I am not equal to any of it. But I can't escape it. I can't forget it. And I can't begin again. You see?' (Act I).

In *A Patriot for Me* (1966) Osborne is again concerned with a man who is the prisoner of his own personality: in this case a homosexual chief of intelligence in the Imperial Army of Austria who is blackmailed into passing information to the Russians. As the countess remarks, 'The army provides a context of expression for people who would not otherwise have it.' Osborne combines a powerful sense of theatricality (for example, the transvestites' ball in this play) with the individual's need to find a context of expression in a world where it is increasingly hard to do so. The anger released by the contradictions of this struggle gives force to Osborne's drama; but, unlike later dramatists, his anger does not make him a propagandist for social reform. What his characters wish to preserve most is the illusion of central position.

Of the political dramatists of the period, Edward Bond (b. 1934) is the most demanding and rigorous. His plays originate in his Marxist analysis of society and his desire to create what he sees as a rational theatre. 'The playwright "should dramatize not the story but the analysis" and it is the analysis which dictates the structure of the story' (David L. Hirst, *Edward Bond*, 1985, p 145). In his note on violence which prefaces *Saved* (1965), Bond states that 'violence is not a function of human nature, but of human societies' (*Plays: One*, 1977, p 17). The action of *Saved* is certainly concerned with an environment where life is impoverished by social and educational deprivation. But the sixth scene of the play which holds the action together and which offers the spectacle of a father helping to stone his own baby to death, after rubbing its face in its excrement, does nothing to allay the obvious objections to the analysis – or indeed to illustrate it. Bond comments: 'Clearly the stoning to death of a baby in a London park is a typical understatement. Compared to the "strategic" bombing of German towns it is a negligible atrocity, compared to the cultural and emotional deprivation of most of our children its consequences are insignificant' (*Plays: One*, 1977, pp 310–11). Bond owes a considerable debt to Shaw, and shares with him a belief in the possibility of man becoming more moral and society more rational. But Shaw's drama exemplifies an enlightened – if not always convincing – reason, which Bond's persistently lacks.

Bond is primarily a visual dramatist. He thinks and feels in theatrical images whose impact is physical, as in the sixth scene of *Saved*. In *Lear*, the image of the wall which Lear has ordered to be built as a defence, and because it will make his kingdom free, dominates the play. In his blind old age he will come to recognize the wall as a form of violence; and he will be shot attempting to start its destruction. Bond identifies the wall with capitalism, although it has other more obvious associations, and may be interpreted in different ways. Bond explains in the preface that he sees the 'socialized morality' of contemporary society as a form of violence, which must result inevitably in aggression. In the last act of the play, Lear will repeat the charge to Cordelia that 'your law always does more harm than your crime, and your morality is a form of violence.' Bond's intention is to make his audience of 'honest, upright, lawful men who believe in order' feel that they are none of these things. Lear says in the final act: 'I have lived with murderers and thugs, there are limits to their greed and violence, but you decent, honest men devour the earth.' Tolstoy preached a similar gospel in his last novel, *Resurrection* (1899), but he also believed that the change had to come from within the individual; Bond believes that it will come about with the destruction of capitalism by violent means if necessary: 'left-wing political violence is justified when it helps to create a more rational society, and when that help cannot be given a pacific form' (*Plays: One*, 1977, p 17).

Bond's imagination, like his reason, is often drawn to violence in a way which finds no justification in his analysis; an example is the stage-direction in *Lear* which reads: 'Soldier bayonets her three times. Slight pause. She writhes. He bayonets her once again. She gives a spasm and dies.' The theatrical relish here is as obvious as it is questionable. When Bond writes comedy as in *The Sea* (1973) he at times achieves scenes of less doubtful effectiveness: Mrs Rafi's lament for the inadequacy of her life as a result of her social position ('that's a terrible state in which to move towards the end of your life: to have no love'), and the hermit's vision of a technologically dehumanized future are both memorable. On the other hand the view expressed in the later play, *Summer* (1982) that kindness and consideration are meaningless in a crooked world; and that kindness can have no meaning until social relationships are just seems obviously false. Bond intends his plays to dramatize the analysis: here, they are often at their weakest, while their strength lies in their visual power.

Among the other political dramatists of the 1970s and 1980s the most significant are Howard Brenton, David Hare, David Edgar, Howard Barker, Trevor Griffiths, Caryl Churchill and Stephen Poliakoff. (Of the plays not discussed in this chapter, Poliakoff's *Breaking the Silence* (1984) is among the best.) Howard Brenton (b. 1942) intended *Weapons of Happiness* (1976) to be a '"petrol bomb through the proscenium arch", blowing up bourgeois self-satisfaction and lighting the fire of change' (Roger Cornish and Violet Ketels, eds, *Landmarks of Modern British Drama: The Plays of the Seventies*, 1986, p 85). To achieve this would require writing of a high order and subtlety, while much of the work inspired by similar intentions is weakened by predictability of viewpoint and banality of characterization, as in *Weapons of Happiness*, where the factory-owner Ralph Makepeace is depicted as being an incompetent weakling, propped up by an unscrupulous police-force: 'You carry on running the country then, sir. Just let us heavies know when it really gets out of hand, eh?' As in the later play *Pravda* (1985) which Brenton wrote with Hare – and which took a legitimate stab at Fleet Street – the concern for veracity is not substantial enough. Dramatic characters become like cut-outs on a shooting-range; and they serve the same purpose.

Trevor Griffiths's (b. 1935) *Comedians*, which also appeared in 1976, is political drama of a quite different order. It succeeds in relating political feelings to more basic human emotions, which in turn determine the quality of life in any community. Eddie Waters is coaching a group of would-be comedians for an audition at a local club in front of Challenor, a talent-spotter. Challenor is only interested in success, which means giving an audience what it wants. Waters, whom we discover in Act III has visited Buchenwald shortly after the end of the Second World War, sees the true comedian's art as being therapeutic: 'A real comedian – that's a daring man. He *dares* to see what his listeners shy away from, fear to express. And what he sees is a sort of truth, about people, about their situation, about what hurts or terrifies them, about what's hard, above all, about what they want' (Act I). The comedian works through laughter, to release tension and say the unsayable. In Act II, the comedians do their turns, making us aware of the very different kinds of joke at which the audience on the stage laugh. The one true comedian, Gethin Price, ends his act with a monologue to the stuffed dummies of a lady and gentleman in evening dress. The brilliant comedian is capable only of hate: 'National Unity? Up yours, sunshine.' Challenged by his teacher, Waters, in the third act, to find something deeper than hate, he can only reply: 'I stand in no line. I refuse my consent.' Gethin Price belongs to the post-war generation for whom Waters's experience in the concentration camp and his recognition that we have got to get further than hate means little. What he sees is a society where nothing has changed, and truth is a fist you hit with. Griffiths successfully uses the comedians' turns

400 THE TWENTIETH CENTURY

of Act II to balance the discursive and static action of Acts I and III. Without being overtly didactic, *Comedians* confronts the audience with what it is appropriate or even possible to laugh at, while at the same time entertaining them with the old and effective device of watching good actors playing bad comedians well. Nevertheless, the final confrontation between Gethin Price and Waters clarifies little except the gap between their experience of living. The originality of the play consists in its exploitation of the comedians' art for ends which are political as well as theatrical.

David Hare's (b. 1947) *Plenty* (1978) and David Edgar's *Maydays* (1983) attempt more direct political comment by using the form of chronicle play. 'I planned a play in twelve scenes', Hare wrote, 'in which there would be twelve dramatic actions. Each of these actions is intended to be ambiguous, and it is up to the audience to decide what they feel about each event ... In the act of judging the audience learns something about its own values' (*Plenty*, with a note on performance by the author, 1978, p 87). Hare's twelve scenes span the years 1943–62, with the coming of peace, and later of plenty. The lack of brave new causes, lamented by Jimmy Porter, results in lives devoted to self-interested gain, and its attendant ills. In the character of Susan Traherne, whose post-war decline the play follows, Hare created a star part, as he and Brenton were later to do with Gaston le Roux in *Pravda*. But Hare's deliberate ambiguity in *Plenty* does not altogether come off. He deprives his audience of the evidence which would enable them to make up their minds whether the ills of his characters are due to some vicious mole of nature in them, or some degeneration in society which might have been avoided by political means. *The Bay at Nice* and *Wrecked Eggs* (both 1986), offer the same difficulty: the first play set in Russia in 1956 is sourly disillusioned, while the second play set in contemporary America is savagely disparaging. His recent trilogy of plays, *Racing Demon*, *Murmuring Judges* and *The Absence of War*, dramatizes the ills of contemporary society in Britain in the manner of the investigative journalist, leaving the audience to come to its own conclusions.

David Edgar's (b. 1948) *Maydays* lacks Hare's caustic levity, and is inspired by a moral earnestness characteristic of much of the political drama of the period. It begins with a communist rally in 1945, and ends at Greenham Common in the 1980s, its numerous scenes being concerned with crucial events in the history of socialism during that period. Character is expressed through political ideas, attitudes and actions; the stage is kept busy with the community of politics and the politics of the commune. The Soviet State and

Thatcher's Britain are alike in that they are both gaolers of the people. Unlike *Comedians*, *Maydays* attempts to convince its audience of its political viewpoint by direct confrontation, and, in spite of the occasional moment of joy implied in the title, assumes an interest in political history which restricts its appeal. His recent *Entertaining Strangers* (1987) is built on Ann Jellicoe's work in community theatre, and uses life in nineteenth-century Dorchester during an outbreak of cholera as a means of confronting the audience with the problem of social and moral responsibility. But here the central characters – Mrs Eldridge and the Reverend Henry Moule – are vividly and powerfully conceived.

The title of Caryl Churchill's (b. 1938) *Serious Money* (1987) indicates its opposition to the ideology of contemporary Britain. As she proved in her earlier plays, *Cloud Nine* (1979) and *Top Girls* (1982), Churchill can combine theatrical inventiveness with dialogue of crude energy. Her interest in dramatic characters as individuals is slight; her plays expose with ferocity and coarse humour all that is locked into people by what they are compelled to be, whether because they are women or because of the role society imposes upon them. In *Serious Money* the worship of money in the City is seen as a cult isolating those possessed by it from other human activities, and inspiring them with a frenzied enjoyment at its acquisition. The play's major success consists in conveying this enjoyment while at same time representing it as a manic obsession which one day will have to end. In this play about the religion of money Churchill indicates as it happens one way in which our 'general view of reality' has changed since the start of this period, and how deeply drama has been transformed since the work of Eliot and Fry with whom this chapter began.

From the eighties, two plays stand out as works which in their originality and theatrical effectiveness combine elements of the three forms of drama considered in this chapter. Brian Friel's *Translations* (1980) was the first production of the 'Field Day Theatre Company', formed to examine attitudes to Ireland as a whole. Set in 1833 in a hedge-school in County Donegal, where Irish is spoken, together with some Greek and Latin, but no English, the play succeeds in dramatizing the linguistic, political, and human confusion which has existed, and continues to exist in Ireland. 'Confusion is not an ignoble condition,' as the schoolmaster remarks; but it can lead to misunderstanding, oppression, violence and murder between different communities. Translations are necessary because of the lack of a common language. The play presents this fracture in personal relationships (the young lovers Yolland and Maire can only communicate through a few half-understood words, which none the less create one of the most poignant and memorable scenes in contemporary drama); and in the relationship between the British officers who come to rename the Irish villages for the purpose of creating a map, and the inhabitants of Baile Beag. 'A civilization can be imprisoned in a linguistic contour which no longer matches the landscape of fact'; but a translation 'will not necessarily enable people to interpret between privacies'. The play conjures with such perceptions about languages as the dialect of a tribe without distancing the audience from the humour and tragedy of their personal embodiment.

Timberlake Wertenbaker's *Our Country's Good* (1988), based on Thomas Keneally's novel *The Playmaker*, also uses the historical past to confront the audience with an image of the conflicts in contemporary culture. The setting is a convict ship and the convict colony at Sydney Cove in Australia in 1788. The action is concerned with the restoration of dignity and humanity to the convicts and some of their guardians by their participation in a production of *The Recruiting Officer*. As the enlightened Governor remarks, 'A play is a world in itself, a tiny colony we could almost say'; and each is seen to demand a respect for other people's parts, and the relationship between them. But the play opens with the merciless flogging of one of the convicts; and the play's rehearsal is interrupted by some of the cast being put back into chains, and Liz Morden threatened with hanging for stealing food from the stores. Humanity, civilization and truth need constantly to be defended against brutality, barbarism and lies; but in the end the performance of *The Recruiting Officer* becomes a jubilant celebration of the power of theatre to create a community in which, temporarily at least, man's inhumanity to man is overcome. As in Friel's *Translations*, the sustained power of the dramatic writing enables the action to be about the personal, *and* to transcend it. What the performers in *The Recruiting Officer* aim to do for their audience, and what the actors in *Our Country's Good* do for theirs, is paralleled in the best work being done by companies like Théâtre de Complicité which, in tours around Britain, are developing new styles of acting, physical and visual, upon which the life of drama depends.

BIBLIOGRAPHY

The place of publication of books mentioned in the text
or bibliographies is London, unless otherwise stated.

1. *Drama to 1950*

1 *General*

Clarke, Ian, *Edwardian Drama: A Critical Study*, 1989.

Davies, Andrew, *Other Theatres: The Development of Alternative and Experimental Theatre in Britain*, 1987.

Donoghue, Denis, *The Third Voice: Modern British and American Verse Drama*, Princeton, 1959.

Ellis-Fermor, Una, *The Irish Dramatic Movement*, rev. edn, 1954.

Hinchliffe, Arnold P., *Modern Verse Drama*, 1977.

Holledge, Julie, *Innocent Flowers: Women in the Edwardian Theatre*, 1981.

Hunt, Hugh, *The Abbey: Ireland's National Theatre 1904–1978*, Dublin, 1979.

MacCarthy, Desmond, *The Court Theatre 1904–1907: A Commentary and Criticism*, 1907.

McDonald, Jan, *The 'New Drama' 1900–1914*, 1986.

Marshall, Norman, *The Other Theatre*, 1947.

Maxwell, D. E. S., *A Critical History of Modern Irish Drama 1891–1980*, 1984.

Nicoll, Allardyce, *English Drama 1900–1930: The Beginnings of the Modern Period*, 1973.

O hAodha, Micheal, *Theatre in Ireland*, 1974.

Pick, John, *The West End: Mismanagement and Snobbery*, Eastbourne, 1983.

Pogson, Rex, *Miss Horniman and the Gaiety Theatre, Manchester*, 1952.

Reynolds, Ernest, *Modern English Drama: A Survey of the Theatre from 1900*, 1949.

Robinson, Lennox, *Ireland's Abbey Theatre: A History 1899–1951*, 1951.

Rowell, George, and Jackson, Anthony, *The Repertory Movement: A History of Regional Theatre in Britain*, 1984.

Sidnell, Michael J., *Dances of Death: The Group Theatre of London in the Thirties*, 1984.

Taylor, John Russell, *The Rise and Fall of the Well-Made Play*, 1967.

Trewin, J. C., *The Theatre since 1900*, 1951.

——*Dramatists of Today*, 1953.

Williamson, Audrey, *Theatre of Two Decades*, 1951.

Woodfield, James, *English Theatre in Transition 1881–1914*, 1984.

Worth, Katharine, *The Irish Drama of Europe from Yeats to Beckett*, 1970.

2 *Authors*

W. H. Auden and Christopher Isherwood
Plays, and Other Dramatic Writings by W. H. Auden 1928–1938, ed. Edward Mendelson, 1989.

Harley Granville Barker
Dymkowski, Christine, *Harley Granville Barker*, 1986.

Kennedy, Dennis, *Granville Barker and the Dream of Theatre*, 1985.

Morgan, Margery M., *A Drama of Political Man: A Study in the Plays of Harley Granville Barker*, 1961.

T. S. Eliot
Browne, E. Martin, *The Making of T. S. Eliot's Plays*, 1969.

Harding, D. W., *Experience into Words*, 1963.

Jones, D. E., *The Plays of T. S. Eliot*, 1963.

See also the bibliography to Chapter 6.

Sean O'Casey
The Letters of Sean O'Casey, vol 1 (1910–1941), ed. David Krause, 1975.

Armstrong, W. A., *Sean O'Casey*, 1967.

Ayling, Ronald, ed., *Sean O'Casey: Modern Judgements*, 1970.

Frayne, John P., *Sean O'Casey*, New York, 1975.

Kosok, Heinz, *Sean O'Casey: The Dramatist*, 1985.

Krause, David, *Sean O'Casey: The Man and his Work*, 1960.

O'Connor, Garry, *Sean O'Casey: A Life*, 1988.

Simmons, James, *Sean O'Casey*, 1983.

George Bernard Shaw
'Standard' edition, 34 vols, 1931–51. The most complete collection of Shaw's writing.
Bernard Shaw: Collected Plays with Their Prefaces, ed. Dan H. Laurence, 7 vols, 1970–4. The best edition.
Bernard Shaw: Collected Letters, ed. Dan H. Laurence, 4 vols, 1965–88.

Bentley, Eric, *Bernard Shaw*, Norfolk, Conn., 1947, rev. 1957, rev. British edn, 1967.
Berst, Charles A., *Bernard Shaw and the Art of Drama*, Urbana, Ill., 1973.
Ganz, Arthur, *George Bernard Shaw*, 1983.
Grene, Nicholas, *Bernard Shaw: A Critical View*, 1984.
Holroyd, Michael, *Bernard Shaw*, 4 vols, 1988–92. The best biography.
——, ed., *The Genius of Shaw*, 1979.
Meisel, Martin, *Shaw and the Nineteenth-Century Theatre*, Princeton, 1963.
Morgan, Margery M., *The Shavian Playground: An Exploration of the Art of George Bernard Shaw*, 1972.
Ohmann, Richard, *Shaw: The Style and the Man*, Middletown, Conn., 1962.
Purdom, C. B., *A Guide to the Plays of Bernard Shaw*, 1963.
Williams, Raymond, *Drama from Ibsen to Brecht*, 1968.

J. M. Synge
The Collected Letters of J. M. Synge, ed. Ann Saddlemyer, 2 vols, 1983–4.
J. M. Synge: Collected Works, ed. Robin Skelton, 4 vols, 1962–8.

Corkery, Daniel, *Synge and Anglo-Irish Literature*, Cork, 1966.
Greene, D. H., and Stephens, E. M., *J. M. Synge 1871–1909*, New York, 1959. The authorized biography.
Grene, Nicholas, *Synge: A Critical Study of the Plays*, 1975.
Kiberd, Declan, *Synge and the Irish Language*, New York, 1979.
Price, Alan, *Synge and Anglo-Irish Drama*, 1961.
Saddlemyer, Ann, *Synge and Modern Comedy*, Dublin, 1968.
Skelton, Robin, *The Writings of J. M. Synge*, 1971.

Oscar Wilde
The Importance of Being Earnest, ed. Russell Jackson, 1980.
Lady Windermere's Fan, ed. Ian Small, 1980.

Two Society Comedies: A Woman of No Importance *and* An Ideal Husband, ed. Ian Small and Russell Jackson, 1983.

The Artist as Critic: Critical Writings of Oscar Wilde, ed. Richard Ellmann, 1970.

The Letters of Oscar Wilde, ed. Rupert Hart-Davis, 1963.

More Letters of Oscar Wilde, ed. Rupert Hart-Davis, 1985.

Ellmann, Richard, *Oscar Wilde*, 1987. The best biography.

Powell, Kerry, *Oscar Wilde and the Theatre of the 1890s*, 1990.

Stone, Geoffrey, 'Serious Bunburyism: The Logic of *The Importance of Being Earnest*', *Essays in Criticism*, 26 (1976).

Worth, Katharine, *Oscar Wilde*, 1983.

W. B. Yeats

Flannery, James, *W. B. Yeats and the Idea of a Theatre: The Early Abbey Theatre in Theory and Practice*, 1976.

Miller, Liam, *The Noble Drama of W. B. Yeats*, Dublin, 1977.

O'Driscoll, Robert, and Reynolds, Lorna, eds, *Yeats and the Theatre*, Toronto, 1975.

Ure, Peter, *Yeats the Playwright*, 1963.

See also the bibliography to Chapter 6.

2. *Poetry to 1914*

1 *General*

Hynes, Samuel, *Edwardian Occasions*, 1972. Mainly on prose and ideas, but includes essays on Brooke and Thomas.

Leavis, F. R., *New Bearings in English Poetry*, 1932.

Lucas, John, *Modern English Poetry from Hardy to Hughes: A Critical Survey*, 1986. Includes discussion of de la Mare, Hardy and Kipling as poets.

Marsh, Edward, *Georgian Poetry 1911–1912*, 1912. Four further volumes were published, the last in 1922.

Millard, Kenneth, *Edwardian Poetry*, 1991. A straightforward introduction with an excellent bibliography.

Reeves, James, ed., *Georgian Poetry*, 1962.

Ross, Robert H., *The Georgian Revolt: Rise and Fall of a Poetic Ideal 1910–1922*, 1967.

Sisson, C. H., *English Poetry 1900–1950: An Assessment*, 1971. Simple, direct, sometimes shrewd.

Stead, C. K., *The New Poetic*, 1964.

Swinnerton, Frank, *The Georgian Literary Scene*, 1935. Revised three times, the last in 1969.

2 *Authors*

Rupert Brooke
Hassall, Christopher, *Brooke: A Biography*, 1964.
——, ed., *The Prose of Rupert Brooke*, 1956.
Keynes, Geoffrey, ed., *The Letters of Christopher Brooke*, 1968.
Rogers, Timothy, ed., *Christopher Brooke: A Reappraisal and Selection*, 1971.

W. H. Davies
Collected Poems, 1940.
Stonesifer, Richard J., *W. H. Davies: A Critical Biography*, 1963.

Walter de la Mare
The Complete Poems, 1969. De la Mare was also an accomplished anthologist (*Come Hither*, 1923, *Behold, This Dreamer*, 1939, etc.) and writer of fiction (see sp. *The Collected Tales*, ed. Edward Wagenknecht, 1950).

Thomas Hardy

Bayley, John, *An Essay on Hardy*, 1978.

Clements, Patricia, and Grindle, Julia, eds., *The Poetry of Thomas Hardy*, 1980.

Davie, Donald, *Thomas Hardy and British Poetry*, 1973.

Hynes, Samuel, *The Pattern of Hardy's Poetry*, 1961.

Paulin, Tom, *Thomas Hardy: The Poetry of Perception*, 1975.

Richardson, James, *Thomas Hardy: The Poetry of Necessity*, Chicago, 1977.

A. E. Housman

Carter, John, ed., *A. E. Housman: Selected Prose*, corrected edn., 1962.

Maas, Henry, ed., *The Letters of A. E. Housman*, 1971.

Page, Norman, *A. E. Housman: A Critical Biography*, 1983.

Ricks, C. B., ed., *A. E. Housman: A Collection of Critical Essays*, Englewood Cliffs, N. J., 1968. Includes essays by F. W. Bateson and Randall Jarrell, as well as by Ricks himself.

—— *A. E. Housman: Collected Poems and Selected Prose*, 1988.

Rudyard Kipling

Carrington, C. E., *Kipling: His Life and Work*, 1955.

Eliot, T. S., ed., *A Choice of Kipling's Verse*, 1941.

Gross, John, ed., *Rudyard Kipling: The Man, His Work and His World*, 1972. A very varied, intelligent and readable collection of essays, including Robert Conquest on the verse.

Henn, T. R., *Kipling*, 1967. One chapter on the poetry.

Mason, Philip, *Kipling: The Glass, the Shadow and the Fire*, 1975. A critical biography, dealing with both verse and prose.

Pinney, Thomas, ed., *The Letters of Rudyard Kipling*, vols 1 and 2 (1872–1899), 1990. To be continued, it is hoped.

Rutherford, Andrew, ed., *Kipling's Mind and Art*, 1964. Largely on the prose, but includes George Orwell's essay, from his *Critical Essays*, 1946.

——*Early Verse by Rudyard Kipling 1874–1889*, 1986. Poems not included in *Rudyard Kipling's Verse: Definitive Edition*, 1940.

Edward Thomas

The Collected Poems of Edward Thomas, ed. R. George Thomas, 1978.

Letters from Edward Thomas to Gordon Bottomley, ed. R. George Thomas, 1968.

Coombes, H., *Edward Thomas*, 1956.

Davie, Donald, 'The Edward Thomas Centenary', *Under Briggflatts: A History of Poetry in Great Britain 1960–1988*, 1989, pp. 167–76.

Longley, Edna, *Poetry in the Wars*, 1986. Includes two good essays on Thomas.

——, ed., '*A Language Not to be Betrayed*': *Selected Prose of Edward Thomas*, 1981.

Motion, Andrew, *The Poetry of Edward Thomas*, 1980.

Smith, Stan, *Edward Thomas*, 1986. Uses Thomas's prose well, good on his contradictory 'Englishness'.

Thomas, Helen, and Thomas, Myfanwy, *Under Storm's Wing*, 1988. Includes the two memoirs of her husband by H. T., *As It Was*, 1926, and *World without End*, 1931, with other relevant material.

Thomas, R. George, *Edward Thomas: A Portrait*, 1985.

W. B. Yeats
See the bibliography to Chapter 8.

3. *The Novel to 1914*

1 *General*

Batchelor, John, *The Edwardian Novelists*, 1982.
Bayley, John, *The Short Story: Henry James to Elizabeth Bowen*, 1988.
Bradbury, Malcolm, *The Social Context of Modern English Literature*, 1972.
Delbanco, Nicholas, *Group Portrait: Joseph Conrad, Stephen Crane, Ford Madox Ford, Henry James and H. G. Wells*, 1982.
Feuchtwanger, E. J., *Democracy and Empire: Britain 1865–1914*, 1985. A general history of the period.
Ford, Ford Madox, *The English Novel from the Earliest Days to the Death of Joseph Conrad*, 1930.
Friedman, Alan, *The Turn of the Novel*, 1966.
Hynes, Samuel, *The Edwardian Turn of Mind*, 1968.
Jefferson, George, *Edward Garnett: A Life in Literature*, 1982.
Kermode, Frank, *Essays on Fiction*, 1983. The American title was *The Art of Telling: Essays on Fiction*.
McDonald, Edward D., ed., *Phoenix: The Posthumous Papers of D. H. Lawrence*, 1936.
Read, Donald, ed., *Edwardian England*, 1982.
Rose, Jonathan, *The Edwardian Temperament 1895–1919*, Athens, Ohio, 1986.
Thompson, Paul, *The Edwardians: The Remaking of British Society*, 1975.
Thwaite, Ann, *Edmund Gosse: A Literary Landscape 1849–1928*, 1984.
Trotter, David, *The English Novel in History 1895–1920*, 1993.
Woolf, Virginia, *Collected Essays*, ed. Leonard Woolf, 4 vols, 1966. A new and more complete edition of the essays is now in progress, edited by Andrew McNeillie.

2 *Authors*

Arnold Bennett
Books and Persons: Being Comments on a Past Epoch 1908–1911, 1917.
The Journals of Arnold Bennett, 2 vols, 1933.
The Letters of Arnold Bennett, ed. James Hepburn, 4 vols, 1966–86.

Drabble, Margaret, *Arnold Bennett*, 1974. Biography.
Hepburn, James, ed., *Arnold Bennett: The Critical Heritage*, 1981.
Lucas, John, *Arnold Bennett: A Study of His Fiction*, 1974.
Wilson, Harris, ed., *Arnold Bennett and H. G. Wells: A Record of a Personal and a Literary Friendship*, 1960.

Joseph Conrad
Notes on Life and Letters, 1921.

Berthoud, Jacques, *Joseph Conrad: The Major Phase*, 1978.
Fleishman, A., *Conrad's Politics*, 1967.
Green, Martin, *Dreams of Adventure, Deeds of Empire*, 1980.
Guerard, Albert J., *Conrad the Novelist*, 1958.
Hawthorn, Jeremy, *Joseph Conrad: Language and Fictional Self-Consciousness*, 1979.
Karl, F. R., *Joseph Conrad, The Three Lives: A Biography*, 1979. Comprehensive rather than readable.
Sandison, Alan, *The Wheel of Empire*, 1967.
Sherry, Norman, *Conrad's Eastern World*, 1966.
—— *Conrad's Western World*, 1971. On the relation of the fictions to life, often Conrad's life.
Watt, Ian, *Conrad in the Nineteenth Century*, 1980.

Ford Madox Ford
The English Novel from the Earliest Days to the Death of Joseph Conrad, 1930.
There is no standard edition of the works of Ford Madox Ford.

Cassell, Richard A., ed., *Ford Madox Ford*, 1972. A good collection of earlier views of Ford.
Green, Robert, *Ford Madox Ford: Prose and Politics*, 1981.
Judd, Alan, *Ford Madox Ford*, 1990. Large biography.
Lid, R. W., *Ford Madox Ford: The Essence of His Art*, Berkeley, Calif., 1964.
Meixner, Jerome, *Ford Madox Ford's Novels: A Critical Study*, Minneapolis, Minn., 1962.

E. M. Forster
The Works of E. M. Forster, ed. Elizabeth Heine (Abinger edn), 14 vols, 1975–83. An excellent edition containing much supplementary material from manuscript.

Selected Letters, eds Mary Lago and P. N. Furbank, 1983–5.
Aspects of the Novel, 1927.

Furbank, P. N., *E. M. Forster: A Life*. One of the best modern biographies.

Johnstone, J. K., *The Bloomsbury Group*, 1954.
Leavis, F. R., 'E. M. Forster', *The Common Pursuit*, 1952.
Levine, June Perry, *Creation and Criticism: 'A Passage to India'*, 1971.
Stone, Wilfred, *The Cave and the Mountain: A Study of E. M. Forster*, Stanford, Calif., 1966.
Trilling, Lionel, *E. M. Forster*, 1944.

Henry James
Henry James and H. G. Wells: A Record of Their Friendship, Their Debate on the Art of Fiction and Their Quarrel, edited with an introduction by Leon Edel and Gordon N. Ray, 1958.
Literary Criticism, 2 vols, ed. by Leon Edel and Mark Wilson, New York, 1984.

Rudyard Kipling
Bodelson, C. A., *Aspects of Kipling's Art*, 1964.
Green, Roger Lancelyn, ed., *Kipling: The Critical Heritage*, 1971.
McClure, John A., *Kipling and Conrad: The Colonial Fiction*, Cambridge, Mass., 1981.
Tompkins, J. M. S., *The Art of Rudyard Kipling*, 1959.
Wilson, Angus, *The Strange Ride of Rudyard Kipling: His Life and Works*, 1977.

H. G. Wells
Experiment in Autobiography, 2 vols, 1934.

Batchelor, John, *H. G. Wells*, 1985. Introductory.
Bergonzi, Bernard, *The Early H. G. Wells*, 1961.
Brome, Vincent, *H. G. Wells: A Biography*, 1952.
Edel, Leon N., and Ray, Gordon N., eds, *Henry James and H. G. Wells: A Record of Their Friendship, Their Debate on the Art of Fiction, and their Quarrel*, 1958.
Hillegas, Mark R., *The Future as Nightmare: H. G. Wells and the Anti-Utopians*, New York, 1967.
Kemp, Peter, *H. G. Wells and the Culminating Ape*, 1982.
Parrinder, Patrick, ed., *H. G. Wells: The Critical Heritage*, 1972.

—— and Philmus, Robert M., eds., *H. G. Wells's Literary Criticism*, Sussex and New Jersey, 1980.
Ray, Gordon N., *H. G. Wells and Rebecca West*, 1974.

4. *Poetry of the First World War*

1 *General*

Bergonzi, Bernard, *Heroes' Twilight: A Study of the Literature of the Great War*, 1965.

Crawford, Fred D., *British Poets of the Great War*, Selinsgrove, Pa., 1988. With a good bibliography.

Fussell, Paul, *The Great War and Modern Memory*, New York, 1975.

Graham, Desmond, *The Truth of War: Owen, Blunden and Rosenberg*, 1984.

Hibberd, Dominic, *Poetry of the First World War*, 1981. An anthology of criticism with a good chronological range.

—— and Onions, J., eds, *Poetry of the Great War: An Anthology*, 1986. Contains much unfamiliar and representative material.

Hynes, Samuel, *A War Imagined: The First World War and English Culture*, 1990.

Johnston, John H., *English Poetry of the First World War: A Study in the Evolution of Lyric and Narrative Form*, Princeton, 1964.

Parfitt, George, *English Fiction of the First World War: A Study*, 1988.

—— *English Poetry of the First World War*, 1990.

Reilly, Catherine W., ed., *Scars upon My Heart: Women's Poetry and Verse of the First World War*, 1981.

——, ed., *Poetry of the First World War*, 1978. A bibliography.

Silkin, Jon, *Out of Battle: The Poetry of the First World War*, 1972.

2 *Authors*

Richard Aldington
The Complete Poems, 1948.
Death of a Hero, 1929; unexpurgated edn, introduced by Christopher Ridgway, 1984.

Gates, Norman T., *The Poetry of Richard Aldington: A Critical Evaluation and an Anthology of Uncollected Poems*, University Park, Pa., 1974.

Edmund Blunden
Poems of Many Years, 1957. A substantial and wide-ranging selection.
Undertones of War, 1928. Memoir.

Thorpe, Michael, *The Poetry of Edmund Blunden*, Bridge Books: Kent Editions, n.p., 1971.

Rupert Brooke
See the bibliography to Chapter 2.

Wilfrid Gibson
Collected Poems 1905–1925, 1925.

Robert Graves
Collected Poems 1975, 1975. Not a complete collection.
Poems about War, ed. William Graves, 1988. Includes rare and previously unpublished work from the early years.
Goodbye to All That, 1929; rev. 1957. Memoir.
In Broken Images: Selected Letters 1914–1946, ed. Paul O'Prey, 1982.

Day, Douglas, *Swifter than Reason: The Poetry and Criticism of Robert Graves*, 1963.
Kirkham, Michael, *The Poetry of Robert Graves*, 1969.

Ivor Gurney
Collected Poems, ed. P. J. Kavanagh, 1982. Text carefully prepared, but a selection only.
'*Severn and Somme*' and '*War's Embers*', ed. R. K. R. Thornton, 1987. The two books Gurney himself published, with good annotations.
Collected Letters, ed. R. K. R. Thornton, 1991.
Hill, Geoffrey, 'Gurney's "Hobby"', *Essays in Criticism*, 34 (1984), pp. 97–128.

David Jones
See the bibliography to Chapter 6.

D. H. Lawrence
See the bibliography to Chapter 5.

Frederic Manning
Eidola, 1917. His war poetry, not reprinted.
The Middle Parts of Fortune: Somme and Ancre 1916, privately printed 1929; reissued 1977. The expurgated trade edition was called *Her Privates We*. Fiction close to memoir.

Marwil, Jonathan, *Frederic Manning: An Unfinished Life*, Durham, N. C., 1988. The life is oddly elusive.

Wilfred Owen
The Poems of Wilfred Owen, ed. Jon Stallworthy, 2 vols, 1985. A careful and scholarly edition.
Collected Letters, ed. Harold Owen and John Bell, 1967.
Hibberd, Dominic, *Owen the Poet*, 1986.
Owen, Harold, *Journey from Obscurity*, 3 vols, 1963–5. The memoirs of Owen's brother.
Stallworthy, Jon, *Wilfred Owen*, 1974. A very good biography.
Welland, Dennis, *Wilfred Owen: A Critical Study*, 1960; rev. edn, 1978.

Herbert Read
In Retreat, 1925. Memoir.
Collected Poems, 1966.

Skelton, Robin, ed., *Herbert Read: A Memorial Symposium*, 1970.

Edgell Rickword
Behind the Eyes: Collected Poems and Translations, 1986.

Hobday, Charles, *Edgell Rickword: A Poet at War*, 1989.

Isaac Rosenberg
The Collected Works, ed. Ian Parsons, 1979.

Cohen, Joseph, *Journey to the Trenches: The Life of Isaac Rosenberg 1890–1918*, 1975.
Harding, D. W., 'Isaac Rosenberg', *Experience into Words*, 1963.
Liddiard, Jean, *Isaac Rosenberg: The Half-Used Life*, 1975.

Siegfried Sassoon
Collected Poems 1908–1956, 1961.
The War Poems, ed. Rupert Hart-Davis, 1983.
Diaries, ed. Rupert Hart-Davis, 3 vols, 1983–5. Excellent, covering the years 1915–25.
The Complete Memoirs of George Sherston, 1937. Comprises the semi-autobiographical *Memoirs of a Fox-Hunting Man*, 1928, *Memoirs of an Infantry Officer*, 1930, and *Sherston's Progress*, 1936. There is a parallel series of autobiographical volumes, of which see sp. *Siegfried's Journey, 1916–1920*, 1945.

Thorpe, Michael, *Siegfried Sassoon: A Critical Study*, 1966.

Charles Sorley
Marlborough and Other Poems, 1916.
The Letters, 1919.
The Poems and Selected Letters, ed. Hilda D. Spear, Dundee, 1978.

Edward Thomas
See the bibliography to Chapter 2.

Arthur Graeme West
The Diary of a Dead Officer, 1918.

Higonnet, M. R., Jensen, J., Michel, S. and Weitz, M. C., eds.,
    Behind the Lines: Gender and the Two World Wars, 1987.

5. *The Novel in the 1920s*

1 *General*

Cavaliero, Glen, *The Rural Tradition in the English Novel 1900–1939*, 1977. Informative on popular fiction among other things.

Coveney, Peter, *The Image of Childhood*, 1967.

Friedman, M. J., *Stream of Consciousness: A Study in Literary Method*, 1955.

Hewitt, Douglas, *English Fiction of the Early Modern Period 1890–1940*, 1988.

Kiely, Robert, *Beyond Egotism: Joyce, Woolf, Lawrence*, 1980.

Mendilow, A. A., *Time and the Novel*, 1952.

Shaw, Valerie, *The Short Story: A Critical Introduction*, 1983.

2 *Authors*

Ivy Compton-Burnett

Baldanza, Frank, *Ivy Compton-Burnett*, 1955.

Burkhart, Charles, *I. Compton-Burnett*, 1965.

——, ed., *The Art of I. Compton-Burnett*, 1972.

Liddell, Robert, *The Novels of I. Compton-Burnett*, 1955.

Spurling, Hilary, *Ivy When Young: The Early Life of Ivy Compton-Burnett 1884–1919*, 1974.

——*Secrets of a Woman's Heart: The Later Life of Ivy Compton-Burnett 1920–1969*, 1984.

Aldous Huxley

Letters, ed. Grover Smith, 1969.

Bedford, Sybille, *Aldous Huxley: A Biography*, 2 vols, 1973–4.

Bowering, Peter, *Aldous Huxley: A Study of the Major Novels*, 1968.

Ferns, C. S., *Aldous Huxley: Novelist*, 1980.

Meckier, Jerome, *Aldous Huxley: Satire and Structure*, 1969.

James Joyce

The Critical Writings, ed. Ellsworth Mason and Richard Ellmann, 1959.

Poems and Shorter Writings, ed. Richard Ellmann, A. Walton Litz and John Whittier-Ferguson, 1991.

Stephen Hero, ed. T. Spencer, 1944; rev. John J. Slocum and Herbert Cahoon, 1956.

Ulysses: A Critical and Synoptic Edition, ed. H. W. Gabler, 3 vols,
     1984. A controversial text. Philip Gaskell and Clive Hart,
     '*Ulysses': A Review of Three Texts*, 1989, should be referred to.
The Letters, ed. Richard Ellmann, 1957–66.

Attridge, Derek, ed., *The Cambridge Companion to James Joyce*,
     1990.
——and Ferrer, Daniel, eds, *Poststructuralist Joyce: Essays from the
     French*, 1984.
Benstock, Bernard, ed., *The Augmented Ninth*, Syracuse, N. Y.,
     1988. Proceedings of an important international conference.
Ellmann, Richard, *James Joyce*, 1959; rev. edn, 1982. Rightly admired
     biography.
——*Ulysses on the Liffey*, 1972.
Gifford, Don H., '*Ulysses' Annotated*, Berkeley, Calif., 1988.
Goldberg, S. L., *The Classical Temper*, 1961.
Groden, Michael, '*Ulysses' in Progress*, 1977.
Kenner, Hugh, *Joyce's Voices*, 1975.
——'*Ulysses*', 1980.
Lawrence, Karen, *The Odyssey of Style in 'Ulysses'*, Princeton, 1981.
Litz, A. Walton, *The Art of James Joyce*, 1961.
Peake, C. H., *James Joyce: The Citizen and the Artist*, 1977.
Schwarz, Daniel, *Reading Joyce's 'Ulysses'*, 1987.

D. H. Lawrence
The Letters of D. H. Lawrence, general editor, James T. Boulton,
     1979–92. Seven volumes.
The Cambridge edition of the Works and Letters has been in
     progress since 1979 and contains some material from drafts and
     much textual annotation.

Aldritt, Keith, *The Visual Imagination of D. H. Lawrence*, 1971.
Banerjee, A., ed., *D. H. Lawrence's Poetry: Demon Liberated – A
     Collection of Primary and Secondary Material*, 1990.
Black, Michael, *D. H. Lawrence: The Early Fiction*, 1986.
Clarke, Colin, *River of Dissolution: D. H. Lawrence and English
     Romanticism*, 1969.
Cushman, Keith, *D. H. Lawrence at Work*, 1979.
Delany, Paul, *D. H. Lawrence's Nightmare: The Writer and His
     Circle in the Years of the Great War*, 1979.
Delaveney, Emile, *D. H. Lawrence and Edward Carpenter: A Study
     in Edwardian Transition*, 1971.

'E. T.' (Jessie Chambers), *Lawrence: A Personal Record*, enlarged, 1965.

Ford, George, *Double Measure: A Study of the Novels and Stories of D. H. Lawrence*, New York, 1965.

Leavis, F. R., *D. H. Lawrence, Novelist*, 1955.

Miko, Stephen J., *Toward 'Women in Love': The Emergence of a Lawrentian Aesthetic*, 1971.

Moore, Harry T., *The Priest of Love: A Life of D. H. Lawrence*, 1974. Revised version of his *The Intelligent Heart*, 1954.

Nehls, Edward, ed., *D. H. Lawrence: A Composite Biography*, 3 vols, Madison, Wis., 1957–9.

Sagar, Keith, *D. H. Lawrence: A Calendar of His Works, with a Checklist of His Manuscripts by Lindeth Vasey*, 1979. A very helpful volume.

——*D. H. Lawrence: Life into Art*, 1985.

Worthen, John, *D. H. Lawrence: The Early Years 1885–1912*, 1991. There will be two further volumes of this biography, by David Ellis and Mark Kinkead-Weekes.

——*D. H. Lawrence and the Idea of the Novel*, 1979.

Percy Wyndham Lewis
Blasting and Bombardiering, 1937.
Rude Assignment: An Intellectual Autobiography, 1950.
The Letters, ed. W. J. Rose, 1963.

Jameson, Fredric, *Fables of Aggression: Wyndham Lewis: The Modernist as Fascist*, 1979.

Meyers, Jeffrey, *The Enemy: A Biography of Wyndham Lewis*, 1980.

John Cowper Powys
Cavaliero, Glen, *John Cowper Powys: Novelist*, 1973.
Graves, Richard Percival, *The Powys Brothers*, 1983.
Knight, G. Wilson, *The Saturnian Quest*, 1964.

Dorothy Richardson
Journey to Paradise: Short Stories and Autobiographical Sketches, ed. Trudi Tate, 1989. An interesting supplement to *Pilgrimage*.

Rosenberg, John, *Dorothy Richardson: The Genius They Forgot*, 1973. A critical biography.

Virginia Woolf
The Diary, ed. Anne Olivier Bell, 5 vols, 1977–84.
The Essays, ed. Andrew McNeillie, 6 vols, 1986– .

The Letters, ed. Nigel Nicolson, 6 vols, 1975–80.

Moments of Being, ed. Jeanne Schulkind, 1976; rev. and enlarged edn, 1985.

Bell, Quentin, *Virginia Woolf: A Biography*, 2 vols, 1972.

Clements, Patricia, and Grundy, Isobel, eds, *Virginia Woolf: New Critical Essays*, 1983.

Gordon, Lyndall, *Virginia Woolf: A Writer's Life*, 1984.

Hafley, James, *The Glass Roof: Virginia Woolf as Novelist*, 1954.

Lee, Hermione, *The Novels of Virginia Woolf*, 1977.

McLaurin, Allen, *Virginia Woolf: The Echoes Enslaved*, 1973.

Meisel, Perry, *The Absent Father: Virginia Woolf and Walter Pater*, New Haven, Conn., 1980.

Warner, Eric, ed., *Virginia Woolf: A Centenary Perspective*, 1984.

Zwerdling, Alex, *Virginia Woolf and the Real World*, 1986.

6. *Poetry in the 1920s*

1 *General*

Kenner, Hugh, *The Pound Era*, 1971. An ambitious and readable account of the Modernist movement.

Kermode, Frank, *Romantic Image*, 1957.

Leavis, F. R., *New Bearings in English Poetry*, 1932.

McDiarmid, Lucy, *Saving Civilization: Yeats, Eliot and Auden Between the Wars*, 1984.

Stead, C. K., *The New Poetic*, 1964.

2 *Authors*

T. S. Eliot

The Waste Land: A Facsimile and Transcript of the Original Drafts, ed. Valerie Eliot, 1971.

The Letters of T. S. Eliot, vol. 1 (1898–1922), ed. Valerie Eliot, 1988.

Ackroyd, Peter, *T. S. Eliot: A Life*, 1984.

Gallup, D. C., *T. S. Eliot: A Bibliography*, 1962; rev. edn, 1969.

Gordon, Lyndall, *Eliot's Early Years*, 1977.

——*Eliot's New Life*, 1988.

Howarth, Herbert, *Notes on Some Figures Behind T. S. Eliot*, 1964.

Criticism

Browne, E. Martin, *The Making of T. S. Eliot's Plays*, 1969. Eliot worked with the author in production of his plays.

Bush, Ronald, *T. S. Eliot: A Study in Character and Style*, New York, 1984.

Clarke, Graham, *T. S. Eliot: Critical Assessments*, 4 vols, 1990. A very large and well-devised collection of early reviews and general studies of the poet.

Ellmann, Maud, *The Poetics of Impersonality: T. S. Eliot and Ezra Pound*, 1987.

Everett, Barbara, 'Eliot's *Four Quartets* and French Symbolism', *English*, 29 (1980), pp 1–38.

Freed, Lewis, *T. S. Eliot: The Critic as Philosopher*, West Lafayette, Ind., 1979.

Gardner, Helen, *The Art of T. S. Eliot*, 1949; enlarged edn, 1968. A simple introductory account with emphasis on the religious poetry.

——*The Composition of Four Quartets*, 1978. The drafts are not as interesting as those for *The Waste Land*, but they are worth having, here.

Kearns, Cleo McNelly, *T. S. Eliot and Indic Traditions: A Study in Poetry and Belief*, 1987.

Kenner, Hugh, *The Invisible Poet: T. S. Eliot*, 1960. A sophisticated but entertaining account of Eliot's career as a writer. Not very good on his relations with Englishness.

Kermode, Frank, *The Classic*, 1975. The first chapter is an insufficiently known study of Eliot's notion of Empire and his relations to Virgil and Dante.

Kojecky, Roger, *T. S. Eliot's Social Criticism*, 1971.

Leavis, F. R., '*Four Quartets*', *The Living Principle*, 1975, pp 155–264. Penetrating, excessively long.

——'T. S. Eliot as Critic', '*Anna Karenina' and Other Essays*, 1967, pp 177–96. Hostile. Leavis wrote extensively and well on Eliot. See his *New Bearings in English Poetry*, 1932, and reviews by him and others in the journal *Scrutiny*.

Litz, A. Walton, ed., *Eliot in His Time: Essays on the Occasion of the Fiftieth Anniversary of The Waste Land*, Princeton, 1973.

Martin, Graham, *Eliot in Perspective: A Symposium*, 1970. Essays by Gabriel Pearson (early poetry) and Katharine Worth (plays) particularly memorable.

Mason, H. A., 'Eliot's "Ode" – A Neglected Poem?', *Cambridge Quarterly*, 19 (1990), pp 304–35. Oblique, informed account of an important, previously inaccessible poem, here reprinted.

Menand, Louis, *Discovering Modernism: T. S. Eliot and His Context*, New York, 1987.

Miller, J. Hillis, *Poets of Reality; Six Twentieth-Century Writers*, Cambridge, Mass., 1974. Good chapter on Eliot.

Moody, A. D., *Thomas Stearns Eliot: Poet*, 1979.

Ricks, Christopher, *T. S. Eliot and Prejudice*, 1988. Particularly good on the charge of anti-Semitism, but also a persuasive account of the whole poetic work.

Smith, Grover, *T. S. Eliot's Poetry and Plays: A Study in Sources and Meaning*, Chicago, 1956. A very thorough account of sources.

Tate, Allen, ed., *T. S. Eliot: The Man and His Work*, 1967. Strong on reminiscences.

W. B. Yeats

The Letters of W. B. Yeats, ed. Allen Wade, 1954. A generous selection.

The Collected Letters of W. B. Yeats, vol. I (1865–1895), eds John Kelly and E. Domville, 1986.

Ellmann, Richard, *Yeats: The Man and the Masks*, 1949; enlarged edn, 1979. The best biography.

Criticism

Bloom, Harold, *Yeats*, New York, 1971.

Cullingford, Elizabeth, *Yeats, Ireland and Fascism*, 1981.

Donoghue, Denis, *Yeats*, 1971. Straighforward but rhetorical introductory account.

Ellmann, Richard, *The Identity of Yeats*, 1954. Not very powerful critically, but informed and informative.

Fletcher, Ian, Gordon, Donald, and Kermode, Frank, *W. B. Yeats: Images of a Poet*, 1961. The succinctly learned catalogue of an exhibition at the Whitworth Art Gallery, University of Manchester.

Henn, T. R., *The Lonely Tower: Studies in the Poetry of W. B. Yeats*, 1950.

Jeffares, A. N., ed., *W. B. Yeats: The Critical Heritage*, 1977.

——*A New Commentary on the Poems of W. B. Yeats*, 1975.

——and Cross, K. G. W., eds, *In Excited Reverie: A Centenary Tribute to W. B. Yeats 1865–1939*, 1965.

——and Knowland, A. S., *A Commentary on the Collected Plays of W. B. Yeats*, 1975.

Kermode, Frank, *Romantic Image*, 1957.

Leavis, F. R., 'Yeats: The Problem and the Challenge', in Leavis, F. R. and Q. D., *Lectures in America*, 1969.

Longenbach, James, *Stone Cottage: Pound, Yeats and Modernism*, New York, 1988.

MacNeice, Louis, *The Poetry of W. B. Yeats*, 1941.

Parkinson, Thomas, *W. B. Yeats, Self-Critic*, Berkeley, Calif., 1951.

——*W. B. Yeats, The Later Poetry*, Berkeley, Calif., 1964.

Stallworthy, Jon, *Between the Lines: Yeats's Poetry in the Making*, 1965.

Whitaker, T. R., *Swan and Shadow: Yeats's Dialogue with History*, Chapel Hill, N. C., 1964.

3 *Other Authors*

Fitzgerald, Penelope, *Charlotte Mew and Her Friends*, 1984.

Forde, Victoria, *The Poetry of Basil Bunting*, 1991.

Hague, René, *A Commentary on 'The Anathemata'*, Wellingborough, 1977.

——, ed., *Dai Greatcoat: A Self-Portrait of David Jones in his Letters*, 1980.

Mathias, John, ed., *David Jones: Man and Poet*, Orono, Maine, 1988.

Middleton, Christopher, ed., 'Documents on Imagism from the Papers of F. S. Flint', *The Review*, Oxford, No 15 (1965).

Moody, A. D., 'H. D. Imagiste', *Agenda*, 25 (1987–8).

7. *The Novel in the 1930s and 1940s*

1 *General*

Allen, Walter, *Tradition and Dream: The English and American Novel from the Twenties to Our Time*, 1964.

Atkins, John, *Six Novelists Look at Society*, 1977. Includes Bowen and Isherwood.

Cunningham, Valentine, *British Writers of the Thirties*, 1988. With an extensive bibliography.

Hynes, Samuel, *The Auden Generation*, 1976.

Karl, Frederick R., *A Reader's Guide to the Contemporary English Novel*, 1963.

Manlove, C. A., *Modern Fantasy*, 1975. Deals at length with C. S. Lewis, J. R. R. Tolkien and Mervyn Peake.

O'Faolain, Sean, *The Vanishing Hero: Studies in Novelists of the Twenties*, 1956.

Stevenson, Randall, *The British Novel since the Thirties*, 1986.

2 *Authors*

Samuel Beckett
Proust, 1931. Together with *Three Dialogues with Georges Duthuit*, 1965, fundamental to discussion of Beckett's fiction.

Bair, Deirdre, *Beckett: A Biography*, 1978.

Federman, Raymond, *Journey to Chaos: Samuel Beckett's Early Fiction*, Berkeley, Calif., 1965.

Fletcher, John, *The Novels of Beckett*, 1964.

Kenner, Hugh, *Beckett: A Critical Study*, 1961; rev. edn, 1968.

——*A Reader's Guide to Samuel Beckett*, 1973.

Knowlson, James and Pilling, John, *Frescoes of the Skull: The Later Prose and Drama of Samuel Beckett*, 1980.

Pilling, John, *Samuel Beckett*, 1976.

Worth, Katharine, ed., *Beckett the Shapemaker*, 1976.

Elizabeth Bowen
Pictures and Conversations: Chapters of an Autobiography, 1975.

Glendinning, Victoria, *Bowen: Portrait of a Writer*, 1977. Biography.

Lee, Hermione, *Elizabeth Bowen: An Estimation*, 1981.

Joyce Cary

Adams, Hazard, *Joyce Cary's Trilogies: Pursuit of the Particular Real*, Tallahassee, Fla., 1983.

Bishop, Alan, *Gentleman Rider: A Biography of Joyce Cary*, 1988.

——, ed., *Joyce Cary: Selected Essays*, 1976.

Cook, Cornelia, *Joyce Cary: Liberal Principles*, 1981.

Hardy, Barbara, 'Form in Joyce Cary's Novels', *Essays in Criticism*, 4 (1954), pp 180–90.

Mahood, M. M., *Cary's Africa*, 1964.

Wright, Andrew, *Cary: A Preface to His Novels*, 1958.

Lewis Grassic Gibbon

Munro, I. S., *Leslie Mitchell: Lewis Grassic Gibbon*, 1966.

Young, Douglas S., *Beyond the Sunset: A Study of Lewis Grassic Gibbon*, 1973.

Henry Green

Pack My Bag: A Self-Portrait, 1940.

Mengham, Rod, *The Idiom of the Time: The Writings of Henry Green*, 1982.

Stokes, Edward, *The Novels of Henry Green*, 1959.

Graham Greene

A Sort of Life, 1971. Memoir, with sequel, *Ways of Escape*, 1980.

Allain, Marie-Françoise, *The Other Man: Conversations with Graham Greene*, 1983.

Allott, Kenneth, and Farris, Miriam, *The Art of Graham Greene*, 1951.

Kermode, Frank, 'Mr Greene's Eggs and Crosses', *Puzzles and Epiphanies*, 1962, pp 176–87.

O'Donnell, Donat, *Maria Cross*, 1953. Includes an important essay on Greene. Reprinted under the author's real name, Conor Cruise O'Brien.

Spurling, John, *Graham Greene*, 1983.

Stratford, Philip, *Faith and Fiction: Creative Process in Greene and Mauriac*, Notre Dame, Ind., 1964.

Christopher Isherwood

Lions and Shadows: An Education in the Twenties, 1938.

Finney, Brian, *Christopher Isherwood: A Critical Biography*, 1979.

Piazza, Paul, *Christopher Isherwood: Myth and Anti-Myth*, New York, 1977.

George Orwell
Collected Journalism, Essays and Letters, ed. Sonia Orwell and Ian Angus, 4 vols, 1968.

Crick, Bernard, *George Orwell: A Life*, 1980.
Gross, Miriam, ed., *The World of Orwell*, 1971.
Rodden, John, *The Politics of Literary Reputation: The Making and Claiming of 'St George' Orwell*, 1989.
Sandison, Alan, *The Last Man in Europe: An Essay on George Orwell*, 1974.
Williams, Raymond, *Orwell*, 1971; enlarged edn, 1984.
Zwerdling, Alex, *Orwell and the Left*, New Haven, Conn., 1974.

Jean Rhys
Smile Please, 1979. Her early life on Dominica.
Letters 1931–1966, ed. Francis Wyndham and Diana Melly, 1984.

Angier, Carole, *Jean Rhys: Life and Work*, 1990. Biography.
Harrison, Nancy R., *Jean Rhys and the Novel as Women's Text*, Chapel Hill, N. C., 1988.

Rex Warner
McLeod, A. L., ed., *The Achievement of Rex Warner*, Sydney, 1965.

Evelyn Waugh
A Little Learning, 1964. The first volume of a projected autobiography.
The Diaries of Evelyn Waugh, ed. M. Davie, 1976.
The Letters of Evelyn Waugh, ed. Mark Amory, 1980.
The Essays, Articles and Reviews of Evelyn Waugh, ed. Donat Gallagher, 1983.
Mr Wu and Mrs Stitch: The Letters of Evelyn Waugh and Diana Cooper, ed. Artemis Cooper, 1991.

Bradbury, Malcolm, *Evelyn Waugh*, 1964.
Carens, James F., *The Satiric Art of Waugh*, 1966.
Myers, William, *Evelyn Waugh and the Problem of Evil*, 1991.
Stannard, Martin, *Evelyn Waugh: The Early Years 1903–1939*, 1986. The second volume of this life was published in 1990.

8. *Poetry in the 1930s and 1940s*

1 *General*

Bergonzi, Bernard, *Reading the Thirties*, 1978.

Cunningham, Valentine, *British Writers of the Thirties*, 1989.

Ford, Hugh D., *A Poet's War: British Poets and the Spanish Civil War*, Philadelphia, 1965.

Fraser, G. S., *Essays on Twentieth-Century Poetry*, Leicester, 1977.

Hynes, Samuel, *The Auden Generation*, 1976.

MacNeice, Louis, *Modern Poetry: A Personal Essay*, 1938.

Maxwell, D. E. S., *Poets of the Thirties*, 1969.

Symons, Julian, *The Thirties*, 1960; revised as *The Thirties: A Dream Revolved*, 1975; and *The Thirties and the Nineties*, 1990.

Tolley, A. T., *The Poetry of the Thirties*, 1975.

—— *Poetry of the Forties*, 1985.

2 *Authors*

W. H. Auden

The English Auden: Poems, Essays and Dramatic Writings, 1927–1939, ed. Edward Mendelson, 1977. The interest of this collection lies in its use of early versions of the poems, as well as in its gathering of fugitive pieces.

The Enchafed Flood, or The Romantic Iconography of the Sea, New York, 1950. Auden's most idiosyncratic book of literary criticism.

The Dyer's Hand and Other Essays, 1962.

Forewords and Afterwords, ed. Edward Mendelson, 1973.

Secondary Worlds, 1968.

Callan, Norman, *Auden: A Carnival of Intellect*, New York, 1983.

Carpenter, Humphrey, *W. H. Auden: A Biography*, 1981.

Everett, Barbara, *Auden*, 1964.

Fuller, John, *A Reader's Guide to W. H. Auden*, 1970. An exceptionally helpful book.

Jarrell, Randall, *The Third Book of Criticism*, 1975. Includes two important essays on Auden.

McDiarmid, Lucy, *Saving Civilization: Yeats, Eliot and Auden Between the Wars*, 1984.

Mendelson, Edward, *Early Auden*, 1981.

Replogle, Justin, *Auden's Poetry*, 1969.

Smith, Stan, *W. H. Auden*, 1985.
Spears, Monroe K., *The Poetry of W. H. Auden: The Disenchanted Island*, New York, 1963.

George Barker
Fraser, Robert, ed., 'George Barker at Seventy', *P. N. Review* 31, 1983.

Julian Bell
Stansky, Peter, and Abrahams, William, *Journey to the Frontier: Julian Bell and John Cornford: their lives and the 1930s*, 1966.

John Cornford
See under Julian Bell, above.

C. Day-Lewis
Day-Lewis, Sean, *C. Day-Lewis: An English Literary Life*, 1980.

Keith Douglas
The Complete Poems, ed. Desmond Graham, 1978.
Alamein to Zem-Zem, 1946.
A Prose Miscellany, ed. Desmond Graham, 1985.

Graham, Desmond, *Keith Douglas: 1920–1944*, 1974.
Longley, Edna, '"Shit or Bust": The Importance of Keith Douglas', *Poetry in the Wars*, 1986.
Scammell, William, *Keith Douglas: A Study*, 1988.

William Empson
Gardiner, Philip and Averil, *The God Approached: A Commentary on the Poems of William Empson*, 1978.
Gill, Roma, ed., *William Empson: The Man and his Work*, 1974.
The Review, 6–7, 1983. A special Empson number of this little magazine.

David Gascoyne
Paris Journal 1937–1939, 1978.
Journal 1936–1937, 1980.
A Short Survey of Surrealism, 1935.

Patrick Kavanagh
The Complete Poems, ed. Peter Kavanagh, New York, 1972.

Sidney Keyes
Guenther, John, *Sidney Keyes: A Biographical Enquiry*, 1967.

Alun Lewis
Letters to my Wife, ed. Gweno Lewis, Bridgend, Mid Glamorgan, 1989.

Pikoulis, John, *Alun Lewis: A Life*, Bridgend, Mid Glamorgan, 1984.

Louis MacNeice
The Strings Are False: An Unfinished Autobiography, 1965.
The Poetry of W. B. Yeats, 1941.
Varieties of Parable, 1965. His last extended essay in criticism.
Selected Literary Criticism, ed. Alan Heuser, 1987.
Selected Prose, ed. Alan Heuser, 1990.

Brown, Terence, *Louis MacNeice: Sceptical Vision*, Dublin, 1975.
Longley, Edna, *Louis MacNeice: A Study*, 1988.
McKinnon, William T., *Apollo's Blended Dream: A Study of the Poetry of Louis MacNeice*, 1971.
Marsack, Robin, *The Cave of Making: The Poetry of Louis MacNeice*, 1982.

Kathleen Raine
Farewell Happy Fields: Memories of Childhood, 1973.
The Land Unknown, 1975. Sequel to the above.
Blake and Tradition, 1969. Her major scholarly work.
Defending Ancient Springs, 1967. Critical essays defining her position as a poet.

Stevie Smith
Me Again: Uncollected Writings, ed. Jack Barbera and William McBrien, 1981.
Novel on Yellow Paper, 1936.
Over the Frontier, 1938.
The Holiday, 1949. Last of her three ventures into fiction.

Spalding, Frances, *Stevie Smith: A Critical Biography*, 1988.

Stephen Spender
World Within World: The Autobiography of Stephen Spender, 1951.

——*The Thirties and After*, 1978. An interesting collection of miscellaneous pieces.

——*Journals 1939–83*, ed. John Goldsmith, 1985.

Dylan Thomas

——*Collected Poems 1934–1953*, eds. Walford Davies and Ralph Maud, 1988. Text carefully prepared and annotated, with excellent commentary.

——*The Collected Letters*, ed. Paul Ferris, 1985.

——*Early Prose Writings*, ed. Walford Davies, 1971.

——*Poet in the Making: The Notebooks of Dylan Thomas*, 1968; revised as *The Notebook Poems*, 1989.

Davies, Walford, ed. *Dylan Thomas: New Critical Essays*, 1972.

Ferris, Paul, *Dylan Thomas: A Biography*, 1977.

Holbrook, David, *Dylan Thomas: The Code of Night*, 1972. A rather hostile account, but with much psychological insight.

Maud, Ralph N., *Entrances to Dylan Thomas's Poetry*, 1963.

Tindall, William York, *A Reader's Guide to Dylan Thomas*, 1962.

Vernon Watkins

Norris, Leslie, ed., *Vernon Watkins 1906–1967*, 1970.

Charles Williams

Hadfield, Alice Mary, *Charles Williams: An Exploration of His Life and Work*, 1983.

Cavaliero, Glen, *Charles Williams: Poet of Theology*, 1983.

9. *The Novel since 1950*

1 *General*

Allen, Walter, *Tradition and Dream: The English and American Novel from the Twenties to Our Time*, 1964.

Bergonzi, Bernard, *The Situation of the Novel*, 1970; rev. edn, 1979.

Bradbury, Malcolm, *Possibilities: Essays on the State of the Novel*, 1973. Includes essays on Fowles, Murdoch and Spark.

——, and Palmer, David, eds, *The Contemporary English Novel*, (Stratford-upon-Avon Studies 18), 1979. Eight essays on aspects of fiction in this period.

Haffenden, John, *Novelists in Interview*, 1985. The novelists interviewed include Martin Amis, Malcolm Bradbury, Anita Brookner, Angela Carter, William Golding, David Lodge, Ian McEwan, Iris Murdoch and Salman Rushdie.

Kermode, Frank, 'The House of Fiction', *Partisan Review*, XXX.1, Spring 1963, pp 61–82. Interviews with seven English novelists, including Iris Murdoch and Muriel Spark.

Rabinovitz, Rubin, *The Reaction against Experiment in the English Novel 1950–1960*, New York, 1967.

Stevenson, Randall, *The British Novel since the Thirties: An Introduction*, 1986.

2 *Authors*

Kingsley Amis

Everett, Barbara, 'Philistines', *London Review of Books*, 9.7, 2 April 1987. On Amis and Larkin.

Green, Martin, 'Kingsley Amis: The Protest against Protest', *The English Novel in the Twentieth Century: The Doom of Empire*, 1984.

Lodge, David, 'The Modern, The Contemporary, and the Importance of Being Amis', *Language of Fiction*, 1966, pp 243–67.

McDermott, John, *Kingsley Amis: An English Novelist*, 1988.

Lawrence Durrell

Kermode, Frank, 'Durrell and Others', *Puzzles and Epiphanies*, 1962, pp 214–27.

Moore, Harry T., ed., *The World of Lawrence Durrell*, Carbondale, Ill., 1962.

John Fowles
Conradi, Peter, *John Fowles*, 1982.

William Golding
The Hot Gates, 1965.
A Moving Target, 1982. Both these collections of essays include pertinent reflections on his own work.

Carey, John, ed., *William Golding: The Man and His Books*, 1986. Biographical as well as critical essays.
Crompton, Don, *A View from the Spire*, 1985. On the later novels.
Kinkead-Weekes, Mark, and Ian Gregor, *William Golding: A Critical Study*, 1967; rev. and enlarged edn, 1984.
Kermode, Frank, 'William Golding', *Modern Essays*, 1971, pp 238–60.

Brian Moore
McSweeney, Kerry, *Four Contemporary Novelists: Angus Wilson, Brian Moore, John Fowles, V. S. Naipaul*, Montreal, 1983.

Iris Murdoch
'Against Dryness', *Encounter*, XVI, 1, January 1961, pp 16–20.

Byatt, A. S., *Degrees of Freedom: The Novels of Iris Murdoch*, 1965.
Todd, Richard, *Iris Murdoch*, 1984.

Anthony Powell
Kermode, Frank, 'The Interpretation of the Times', *Puzzles and Epiphanies*, 1962, pp 214–27.

Muriel Spark
Harrison, Bernard, *Inconvenient Fictions: Literature and the Limits of Theory*, New Haven, Conn., 1991. Two thoughtful essays.
Kemp, Peter, *Muriel Spark*, 1974.
Kermode, Frank, 'Muriel Spark', *Modern Essays*, 1971, pp 267–83.
Page, Norman, *Muriel Spark*, 1990.
Parrinder, Patrick, 'Muriel Spark and Her Critics', *Critical Quarterly*, 25 (1983), pp 23–32.

10. *Poetry since 1950*

1 *General*

Conquest, Robert, *New Lines*, 1956. Defining anthology of 'The Movement'.

Dodsworth, Martin, ed., *The Survival of Poetry*, 1970. Includes essays on Gunn, Hughes and Larkin.

Dunn, Douglas, ed., *Two Decades of Irish Writing*, 1975.

Enright, D. J., ed., *Poets of the 1950s*, Tokyo, 1955. Important predecessor of Conquest's *New Lines*.

Fraser, G. S., *Essays on Twentieth-Century Poets*, Leicester, 1977.

Fulton, Robin, *Contemporary Scottish Poetry*, Edinburgh, 1974. See also Fulton's 'Ishmael among the Phenomena', *Scottish International Review*, 5.8, 1972.

Haffenden, John, ed., *Viewpoints: Poets in Conversation*, 1981. Among those interviewed are Dunn, Heaney, Hill and Raine.

Hobsbaum, Philip, 'The Present State of British Poetry', *Lines Review*, 45, June 1973.

Jones, Peter, and Schmidt, Michael, eds., *British Poetry since 1970: A Critical Survey*, 1980.

Kersnowski, F., *The Outsiders: The Poets of Contemporary Ireland*, Grand Rapids, Mich., 1979.

Martin, Graham, and Furbank, P. N., eds., *Twentieth-Century Poetry: Critical Essays and Documents*, 1975. Covers the whole period.

Morrison, Blake, *The Movement: English Poetry and Fiction of the 1950s*, 1980.

Perkins, David, *A History of Modern Poetry*, 2 vols, Cambridge, Mass., 1976–87.

Press, John, *A Map of Modern English Verse*, 1969.

Rosenthal, M. L., and Gall, Sally M., *The Modern Poetic Sequence*, 1983. British and American.

Scott, Alexander *et al.*, 'Scottish Poetry 1920–1975', *Akros* 10.28, 1975.

Thwaite, Anthony, *Twentieth-Century English Poetry*, 1978.

Tomlinson, Charles, 'Some Aspects of Poetry since the War', *The New Pelican Guide to English Literature*, vol 8, *The Present*, ed. Boris Ford, 1983.

—— *The Sense of the Past* (Kenneth Allott Lecture), Liverpool, 1983.

2 *Authors*

Ian Hamilton Finlay
Bann, Stephen, *Ian Hamilton Finlay: An Illustrated Essay*, Scottish National Gallery: Edinburgh, 1972.

Seamus Heaney
Preoccupations: Selected Prose 1968–1978, 1980.
The Government of the Tongue: The 1986 T. S. Eliot Lectures and other Critical Writings, 1988.

Corcoran, Neil, *Seamus Heaney*, 1986.
Morrison, Blake, *Seamus Heaney*, 1982.

Geoffrey Hill
The Lords of Limit: Essays on Literature and Ideas, 1984.
The Enemy's Country: Words, Contexture and Other Circumstances of Language, 1991.

Hart, Henry, *The Poetry of Geoffrey Hill*, Carbondale, Ill., 1986.
Robinson, Peter, ed., *Geoffrey Hill: Essays on his Work*, 1985.
Sherry, Vincent, *The Uncommon Tongue; The Poetry and Criticism of Geoffrey Hill*, Ann Arbor, Mich., 1987.

Ted Hughes
Dodsworth, Martin, 'Ted Hughes and Geoffrey Hill: An Antithesis', *The New Pelican Guide to English Literature Vol. 8, The Present*, ed. Boris Ford, 1983.
Gifford, Terry, and Roberts, Neil, *Ted Hughes: A Critical Study*, 1981.
Sagar, Keith, *The Art of Ted Hughes*, 1975.
——, ed., *The Achievement of Ted Hughes*, 1983. With an important section of 'uncollected and unpublished poems'.

Philip Larkin
Brownjohn, Alan, *Philip Larkin*, 1975.
Everett, Barbara, *Poets in Their Time: Essays on English Poetry from Donne to Larkin*, 1986.
Hartley, George, ed., *Philip Larkin, 1922–1985: A Tribute*, 1988.
Motion, Andrew, *Philip Larkin*, 1982.
Thwaite, Anthony, ed., *Larkin at Sixty*, 1982.

Norman MacCaig
Frykman, Erik, '*Unemphatic Marvels': A Study of Norman MacCaig's Poetry*, Gothenburg, 1977.

Hugh MacDiarmid
——, *The Letters of Hugh MacDiarmid*, ed. Alan Bold, 1984.

Buthlay, Kenneth, *Hugh MacDiarmid*, 1964.
Morgan, Edwin, *Hugh MacDiarmid*, 1977.
Oxenhorn, Harvey, *Elemental Things: The Poetry of Hugh MacDiarmid*, Edinburgh, 1983. Substantial.
Watson, Roderick, *Hugh MacDiarmid*, 1976.

Peter Porter
Morrison, Blake, 'A Philosopher of Captions, *Times Literary Supplement*, 11 April 1983.

Charles Tomlinson
Some Americans: A Personal Record, Berkeley, Cal., 1981.
Poetry and Metamorphosis, 1983.
ed., *The Oxford Book of Verse in English Translation*, 1980.

Betjeman, John, *et al*., 'Fifteen Ways of Looking at a Tomlinson', *PNReview* 5.1 (1977). A special issue of the journal with 'Charles Tomlinson at Fifty: A Celebration'.

11. *Drama Since 1950*

1 *General*

Bigsby, C. W., ed., *Contemporary English Drama* (Stratford-upon-Avon Studies 19), 1981.

Brown, John Russell, *Theatre Language: A Study of Arden, Osborne, Pinter and Wesker*, 1972.

Bull, John, *New British Political Dramatists*, 1984. Concentrates on Howard Brenton, David Edgar, Trevor Griffiths and David Hare.

Cave, Richard Allen, *New British Drama in Performance on the London Stage, 1970–1985*, 1987.

Cornish, Roger, and Ketels, Violet, eds., *Landmarks of Modern British Drama*, 2 vols, 1985–6. The two volumes deal with *The Plays of the Sixties* and *The Plays of the Seventies*, and each consists of a general introduction and prefaces to chosen plays of selected dramatists.

Dutton, Richard, *Modern Tragicomedy and the British Tradition: Beckett, Pinter, Stoppard, Albee and Storey*, 1986.

Elsom, John, *Post-War British Theatre*, 1976.

Gascoigne, Bamber, *Twentieth-Century Drama*, 1962.

Harrington, J. P., ed., *Modern Irish Drama*, 1991.

Hayman, Ronald, *British Theatre since 1955*, 1979.

Innes, C., *Modern British Drama, 1890–1990*, 1992.

Itzin, Catherine, *Stages in the Revolution: Political Theatre in Britain since 1968*, 1980.

Kennedy, Andrew, *Six Dramatists in Search of a Language: Studies in Dramatic Language*, 1975. Deals with Shaw, Eliot, Beckett, Pinter, Osborne and Arden.

King, Kimball, *Twenty Modern British Playwrights: A Bibliography 1956–1976*, New York, 1977. An indispensable aid to research.

Peter, John, *Vladimir's Carrot: Modern Drama and the Modern Imagination*, 1987. Relations between modern drama and European culture in the last hundred years.

Taylor, John Russell, *Anger and After*, 1962.

—— *The Second Wave: British Drama of the Sixties*, 1971.

Trussler, Simon, ed., *New Theatre Voices of the Seventies*, 1981.

Tynan, Kenneth, *A View of the English Stage, 1944–65*, 1975.

Worth, Katharine, *Revolutions in Modern English Drama*, 1972.

2 *Authors*

John Arden
Gray, Frances, *John Arden*, 1982.
Hayman, Ronald, *John Arden*, 1968; revised, 1969.
Hunt, Albert, *Arden: A Study of his Plays*, 1974.
Page, Malcolm, ed., *File on Arden*, 1985. One of a useful series presenting a comprehensive selection of reviews, interviews, etc., of the author concerned.

Alan Ayckbourn
Billington, Michael, *Alan Ayckbourn*, 1983.
Page, Malcolm, ed., *File on Ayckbourn*, 1989.
Watson, Ian, *Conversations with Ayckbourn*, 1981; revised, 1988.

Samuel Beckett
See the reading list for Chapter 7.

Edward Bond
Theatre Poems and Songs, ed. Malcolm Hay and Philip Roberts, 1978.
Hay, Malcolm, and Roberts, Philip, *Bond: A Study of his Plays*, 1980.
Hirst, David, *Edward Bond*, 1985.
Roberts, Philip, ed., *File on Bond*, 1985.

Howard Brenton
Boon, Richard, *Brenton the Playwright*, 1991.
Mitchell, Tony, ed., *File on Brenton*, 1988.

Caryl Churchill
Kritzer, Amelia Howe, *The Plays of Caryl Churchill: Theatre of Empowerment*, 1991.

Brian Friel
Dantanus, Ulf, *Brian Friel: A Study*, 1988.
Pine, Richard, *Brian Friel and Ireland's Drama*, 1990.

Trevor Griffiths
Poole, Mike, and Wyver, John, *Powerplays: Trevor Griffiths in Television*, 1984.

David Hare
Page, Malcolm, ed., *File on Hare*, 1990.

Joe Orton
Bigsby, C. W. E., *Joe Orton*, 1982.
Charney, Maurice, *Joe Orton*, 1984.
Lahr, John, *Prick Up Your Ears: The Biography of Joe Orton*, 1978.

John Osborne
A Better Class of Person: An Autobiography 1929–1956, 1981.
Almost A Gentleman: An Autobiography 1955–1966, 1991.
Carter, Alan, *John Osborne*, Edinburgh, 1969.
Hayman, Ronald, *John Osborne*, 1968; revised, 1969.

Harold Pinter
——, *Poems and Prose 1949–1977*, 1978.

Almansi, Guido, and Henderson, Simon, *Harold Pinter*, 1983.
Dukore, Bernard F., *Harold Pinter*, 1982; revised, 1988.
Esslin, Martin, *The Peopled Wound: The Plays of Harold Pinter*, 1970; revised as *Pinter: A Study of his Plays*, 1973.
Gale, Steven, ed., *Critical Essays on Harold Pinter*, 1990.
Lahr, John and Anthea, eds., *A Casebook on Harold Pinter's "The Homecoming"*, 1974.
Thompson, David T., *Pinter: The Player's Playwright*, 1985.

Tom Stoppard
Billington, Michael, *Stoppard the Playwright*, 1987.
Hunter, Jim, *Tom Stoppard's Plays*, 1982.
Jenkins, Antony, *The Theatre of Tom Stoppard*, 1987.
Page, Malcolm, ed., *File on Stoppard*, 1986.
Sammels, Neil, *Tom Stoppard: The Artist as Critic*, 1988.

TABLE OF DATES

The following table provides a conspectus of the period, relating literature to other events of the time. It does not contain the dates of all the works of all the authors dealt with in the preceding pages.

Dramatic works usually appear under the year of performance.

1901　Death of Queen Victoria. Accession of Edward VII. First wireless communication between Europe and North America.

　　　Kipling, *Kim*.

1902　End of Boer War.

　　　Bennett, *Anna of the Five Towns*; Hardy, *Poems of the Past and the Present*; James, *The Wings of the Dove*.

1903　First successful flight in aeroplane.

　　　Butler, *The Way of All Flesh*; Conrad, *Youth*; James, *The Ambassadors*; Shaw, *Man and Superman*.

1904　Russo–Japanese War.

　　　Entente cordiale between Britain and France.

　　　Barrie, *Peter Pan*; Chesterton, *The Napoleon of Notting Hill*; Conrad, *Nostromo*; James, *The Golden Bowl*; Shaw, *Candida*; Synge, *Riders to the Sea*.

1905　Failed revolution in Russia.

　　　Einstein's Special Theory of Relativity.

　　　Barker, *The Voysey Inheritance*; Forster, *Where Angels Fear to Tread*; Wells, *Kipps*.

1906　Liberal government, Campbell-Bannerman P. M.

　　　Galsworthy, *The Man of Property*; Kipling, *Puck of Pook's Hill*.

1907　Barker, *Waste*; Conrad, *The Secret Agent*; Forster, *The Longest Journey*; Joyce, *Chamber Music*; Synge, *The Playboy of the Western World*.

1908　Asquith P. M. Old-age pensions introduced.

Bennett, *The Old Wives' Tale*; Forster, *A Room with a View*.

1909   First flight over English Channel.
Davidson d. Swinburne d. Synge d.
Hardy, *Time's Laughingstocks*; Kipling, *Actions and Reactions*; Pound, *Personae*; Wells, *Tono-Bungay*.

1910   Death of Edward VII. Accession of George V.
First post-impressionist exhibition in London.
Barker, *The Madras House*; Bennett, *Clayhanger*; Forster, *Howards End*; Synge, *Deirdre of the Sorrows*; Wells, *The History of Mr Polly*; Yeats, *The Green Helmet and other Poems*.
Stravinsky, *The Firebird* (ballet).

1911   National Health Insurance Act.
Conrad, *Under Western Eyes*; Lawrence, *The White Peacock*.

1912   Agitation for women's vote.
Sinking of the *Titanic*.
De la Mare, *The Listeners*; Lawrence, *The Trespasser*; Marsh, ed., *Georgian Anthology*.

1913   Conrad, *Chance*; Lawrence, *Sons and Lovers*.

1914   First World War.
Hardy, *Satires of Circumstance*; Joyce, *Dubliners*; Pound, ed., *Des Imagistes*; Shaw, *Pygmalion*; Yeats, *Responsibilities*.

1915   Coalition government, Asquith P. M.
Brooke d. Grenfell d.
Brooke, *1914 and Other Poems*; Ford, *The Good Soldier*; Lawrence, *The Rainbow*; Richardson, *Pointed Roofs* (Vol 1 of *Pilgrimage*); Woolf, *The Voyage Out*.

1916   Lloyd George P. M.
Allied troops withdraw from Gallipoli.
Easter Rising, Dublin.
James d.
Joyce, *A Portrait of the Artist as a Young Man*.

1917   Russian Revolution. Bolsheviks seize power.
Hulme d. E. Thomas d.
United States enters the war against Germany.
Eliot, *Prufrock and Other Observations*.

1918   Peace treaty between Germany and Russia.
Armistice ends First World War, November.
Coalition government after election, Lloyd George P. M.

1929   Labour government, MacDonald P. M.
        Wall Street Crash.
        Graves, *Goodbye to All That*; Green, *Living*; Rhys, *Postures*
            (later *Quartet*).
1930   Widespread unemployment.
        Lawrence d.
        Auden, *Poems*; Coward, *Private Lives*; Eliot, *Ash
            Wednesday*; Lewis, *The Apes of God*; Sassoon, *Memoirs
            of an Infantry Officer*; Waugh, *Vile Bodies*.
1931   MacDonald forms a National Government.
        Japanese invade Manchuria.
        Bennett d.
        Rhys, *After Leaving Mr Mackenzie*; Woolf, *The Waves*.
1932   Hunger march of unemployed to London.
        Auden, *The Orators*; Gibbon, *Sunset Song* (Vol 1 of
            A Scots Quair); Huxley, *Brave New World*.
1933   Hitler chancellor of Germany.
        Orwell, *Down and Out in London and Paris*; J. C. Powys, *A
            Glastonbury Romance*; Yeats, *The Winding Stair*.
1934   Beckett, *More Pricks than Kicks*; Rhys, *Voyage in the Dark*;
            D. Thomas, *Eighteen Poems*; Waugh, *A Handful of Dust*.
1935   Baldwin P. M.
        Italian invasion of Abyssinia.
        Auden and Isherwood, *The Dog Beneath the Skin*; Eliot,
            Murder in the Cathedral; Empson, *Poems*; Greene,
            England Made Me; Isherwood, *Mr Norris Changes
            Trains*.
1936   Death of George V. Accession and abdication of Edward
            VIII, accession of George VI.
        Outbreak of Spanish Civil War.
        Chesterton d. Housman d. Kipling d.
        Auden, *Look Stranger!*; Eliot, *Collected Poems 1909–1935*;
            Orwell, *Keep the Aspidistra Flying*.
1937   Chamberlain P. M.
        Japanese occupy Peking and Shanghai.
        Auden and Isherwood, *The Ascent of F6*; Jones, *In
            Parenthesis*; Lewis, *The Revenge for Love*; Tolkien, *The
            Hobbit*; Woolf, *The Years*.
1938   Hitler annexes Austria; Munich agreement.
        Beckett, *Murphy*; Bowen, *The Death of the Heart*; Durrell,
            The Black Book; Greene, *Brighton Rock*; Orwell, *Homage
            to Catalonia*.

1939   End of Spanish Civil War.
       Germany invades Poland; outbreak of Second World War.
       Ford d. Yeats d.
       Cary, *Mister Johnson*; Eliot, *The Family Reunion*; Green,
          Party Going; Greene, *The Confidential Agent*; Isherwood,
          Goodbye to Berlin; Joyce, *Finnegans Wake*; Orwell,
          Coming Up for Air; Rhys, *Good Morning Midnight*.
1940   Churchill P. M.
       Fall of France; British troops evacuated from Dunkirk.
       Italy joins Germany in war.
       Auden, *Another Time*; Eliot, *East Coker*; Greene, *The Power
          and the Glory*; Yeats, *Last Poems and Plays*.
1941   Germany invades Russia; Japanese raid Pearl Harbour.
       United States enters war.
       Joyce d. Woolf d.
       Auden, *New Year Letter*; Eliot, *The Dry Salvages*; Warner,
          The Aerodrome; Woolf, *Between the Acts*.
1942   Siege of Stalingrad ends in German defeat.
       Cary, *To Be a Pilgrim*.
1943   Invasion and surrender of Italy.
       Green, *Caught*.
1944   Invasion of France.
       Douglas d.
       Cary, *The Horse's Mouth*; Eliot, *Four Quartets*.
1945   War ends in Europe. Atomic bombs dropped on Japan
          bring end to war in east also.
       Labour government elected, Attlee P. M.
       Auden, *For the Time Being*; Green, *Loving*; Keyes, *Collected
          Poems*; Larkin, *The North Ship*; Orwell, *Animal Farm*;
          Waugh, *Brideshead Revisited*.
1946   First Assembly of United Nations.
       Nationalization of coal.
       Wells d.
       Green, *Back*; Larkin, *Jill*; Peake, *Titus Groan*; D. Thomas,
          Deaths and Entrances.
1947   Nationalization of transport.
       India and Pakistan become independent.
       Larkin, *A Girl in Winter*.
1948   Communists seize power in Czechoslovakia.
       Russian blockade of Berlin begins Cold War.
       Auden, *The Age of Anxiety*; Greene, *The Heart of the Matter*.
1949   Communist government in China.

North Atlantic Treaty Organization set up.

Bowen, *The Heat of the Day*; Eliot, *The Cocktail Party*; MacNeice, *Collected Poems 1925–1948*; Orwell, *Nineteen Eighty-Four*.

1950   Korean War.

Orwell d. Shaw d.

Auden, *Collected Shorter Poems 1930–1944*; Beckett, *Molloy* (in French).

1951   Conservative government, Churchill P. M.

Douglas, *Collected Poems*; Powell, *A Question of Upbringing* (Vol 1 of *A Dance to the Music of Time*).

1952   Death of George VI. Accession of Elizabeth II.

Auden, *Nones*; Jones, *The Anathemata*; D. Thomas, *Collected Poems*; Waugh, *Men at Arms* (Vol 1 of *Sword of Honour* trilogy).

1953   End of Korean War.

Stalin d.

D. Thomas d.

Beckett, *Watt*.

1954   K. Amis, *Lucky Jim*; Golding, *Lord of the Flies*; Gunn, *Fighting Terms*; Murdoch, *Under the Net*; D. Thomas, *Under Milk Wood*; Tolkien, *The Fellowship of the Ring* (Vol 1 of *The Lord of the Rings*).

1955   Eden P. M.

Auden, *The Shield of Achilles*; Beckett, *Waiting for Godot* (first English performance); Davie, *Brides of Reason*; Golding, *The Inheritors*; Greene, *The Quiet American*; Larkin, *The Less Deceived*; Moore, *The Lonely Passion of Judith Hearne*; Tomlinson, *The Necklace*.

1956   Attempted anti-Russian revolution in Hungary.

France and England unsuccessfully resist Egyptian nationalization of Suez Canal.

De la Mare d.

Behan, *The Quare Fellow*; Conquest, ed., *New Lines*; Golding, *Pincher Martin*; Osborne, *Look Back in Anger*.

1957   Macmillan P. M.

Russian sputnik in orbit.

Cary d. Lewis d.

Beckett, *Endgame*; Davie, *A Winter Talent*; Durrell, *Justine* (Vol 1 of *The Alexandria Quartet*); Hughes, *The Hawk in the Rain*; Osborne, *The Entertainer*; Spark, *The Comforters*; Taylor, *Angel*.

1958   Fall of Fourth French Republic; De Gaulle President of
       France.
       Behan, *The Hostage*; Betjeman, *Collected Poems*; Moore,
       The Feast of Lupercal; Murdoch, *The Bell*; Pinter, *The
       Birthday Party*.
1959   Castro takes power in Cuba.
       Golding, *Free Fall*; Hill, *For the Unfallen*; Sillitoe, *The
       Loneliness of the Long Distance Runner*; Spark, *Memento
       Mori*.
1960   United Nations intervene in Congo.
       Unexpurgated text of *Lady Chatterley's Lover* judged not
       obscene.
       K. Amis, *Take a Girl Like You*; Hughes, *Lupercal*; Larkin,
       The Whitsun Weddings; Pinter, *The Caretaker*; Tomlinson,
       Seeing is Believing (English edition; 1958 in US).
1961   Seven new British universities founded.
       H. D. d.
       Clarke, *Later Poems*; Greene, *A Burnt-Out Case*; Gunn,
       My Sad Captains; Osborne, *Luther*; Spark, *The Prime of
       Miss Jean Brodie*.
1962   Cuban missile crisis.
       Beckett, *Happy Days*.
1963   Douglas-Home P. M.
       Huxley d. MacNeice d. J. C. Powys d.
       K. Amis, *One Fat Englishman*; Spark, *The Girls of Slender
       Means*.
1964   Labour government, Wilson P. M.
       Fall of Khrushchev.
       Behan d. O'Casey d.
       Golding, *The Spire*; Isherwood, *A Single Man*; Orton,
       Entertaining Mr Sloane.
1965   Unilateral Declaration of Independence, Rhodesia.
       Large-scale American involvement in fighting in Vietnam.
       Eliot d.
       Bond, *Saved*; Bunting, *Briggflatts*; Pinter, *The Homecoming*;
       Spark, *The Mandelbaum Gate*.
1966   Chinese Cultural Revolution.
       Waugh d.
       Heaney, *Death of a Naturalist*; Morgan, *The Second Life*;
       Rhys, *Wide Sargasso Sea*; Stoppard, *Rosencrantz and
       Guildenstern are Dead*; Tomlinson, *American Scenes*.
1967   Legalization, within limits, of homosexuality and abortion.

Orton d. Sassoon d.

Golding, *The Pyramid*; Hughes, *Wodwo*; Orton, *Loot*.

1968   Renewal of conflict between Catholic and Protestant groups in Northern Ireland.

Russian force quells Czech uprising.

End of theatrical censorship by Lord Chamberlain.

Bunting, *Collected Poems*; Hill, *King Log*;

Stoppard, *The Real Inspector Hound*.

1969   Abolition of capital punishment.

American moon landings.

Dunn, *Terry Street*; Heaney, *Door into the Dark*; Fowles, *The French Lieutenant's Woman*; Orton, *What the Butler Saw*.

1970   Age of majority reduced from 21 to 18.

Conservative government, Heath P. M.

Forster d.

Hughes, *Crow*.

1971   Settlement of Rhodesian crisis.

Bond, *Lear*; Gunn, *Moly*; Hill, *Mercian Hymns*; Moore, *Fergus*; Spark, *Not to Disturb*.

1972   Introduction of direct rule in Northern Ireland.

Pound d.

Davie, *Collected Poems 1950–1970*; Montague, *The Rough Field*; Stoppard, *Jumpers*.

1973   Britain joins the European Economic Community.

Auden d. Bowen d. Green d. Tolkien d.

Shaffer, *Equus*.

1974   Labour government, Wilson P. M.

Blunden d. Clarke d. Jones d.

K. Amis, *Ending Up*; Larkin, *High Windows*; Sisson, *In the Trojan Ditch*; Stoppard, *Travesties*; Tomlinson, *The Way In*.

1975   Fighting ends in Vietnam.

Bradbury, *The History Man*; Heaney, *North*; Powell, *Hearing Secret Harmonies* (completing *A Dance to the Music of Time*).

1976   Callaghan P. M.

K. Amis, *The Alteration*; Griffiths, *Comedians*.

1977   Pact between Liberal and Labour parties.

Charter 77 human rights group formed in Czechoslovakia.

Chatwin, *In Patagonia*; Pym, *Quartet in Autumn*; Redgrove, *From Every Chink of the Ark*.

1978   US–Chinese diplomatic relations established.

Hare, *Plenty*; Hill, *Tenebrae*; McEwan, *The Cement Garden*.

1979   Conservative Government, Thatcher P. M.
Rhys d.
Golding, *Darkness Visible*; Heaney, *Field Work*; Hughes,
    Moortown.

1980   Russia invades Afghanistan.
Pym d.
Golding, *Rites of Passage*.

1981   Martial law in Poland.
M. Amis, *Other People*; Gray, *Quartermaine's Terms*;
    McEwan, *The Comfort of Strangers*; Moore, *The
    Temptation of Eileen Hughes*; Rushdie, *Midnight's Children*.

1982   Falkland Islands War.
Chatwin, *On the Black Hill*; Greene, *Monsignor Quixote*;
    Gunn, *The Passages of Joy*; Ishiguro, *A Pale View of the
    Hills*; Mo, *Sour Sweet*.

1983   Breakdown of civil order in Lebanon.
Hill, *The Mystery of the Charity of Charles Péguy*; Moore,
    Cold Heaven; Pinter, *Betrayal*; Spark, *Loitering with
    Intent*; Swift, *Waterland*; Trevor, *Fools of Fortune*.

1984   Miners' strike leads to violent confrontations with police.
Empson d.
K. Amis, *Stanley and the Women*; M. Amis, *Money*; Barnes,
    Flaubert's Parrot; Brookner, *Hotel du Lac*; Carter, *Nights
    at the Circus*; Golding, *The Paper Men*.

1985   Miners' strike collapses.
Anglo-Irish agreement.
Bunting d. Graves d. Larkin d.
Dunn, *Elegies*; Moore, *Black Robe*.

1986   Treaty paves way for Channel Tunnel.
Isherwood d.
K. Amis, *The Old Devils*; Barnes, *Staring at the Sun*.

1987   Intense Palestinian opposition in Israel.
Golding, *Close Quarters*; McEwan, *The Child in Time*.

1988   Russian withdrawal from Afghanistan.
Chatwin, *Utz*; Larkin, *Collected Poems*; Rushdie, *The
    Satanic Verses*.

1989   Beckett d. Chatwin d.
M. Amis, *London Fields*; Barnes, *A History of the World in
    $10\frac{1}{2}$ Chapters*; Golding, *Fire Down Below*.

1990   Major P. M.
Byatt, *Possession*; McEwan, *The Innocent*.

INDEX